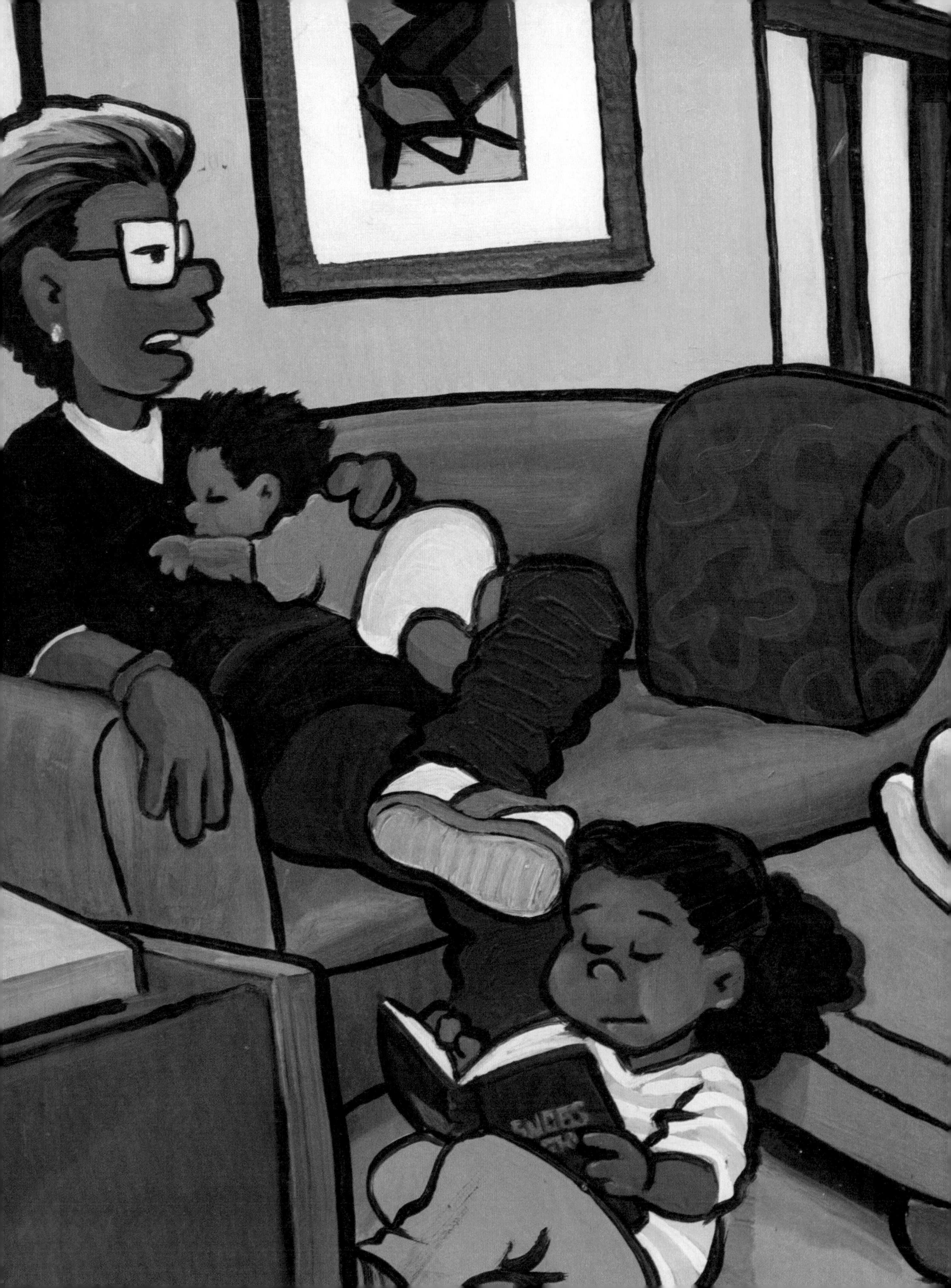

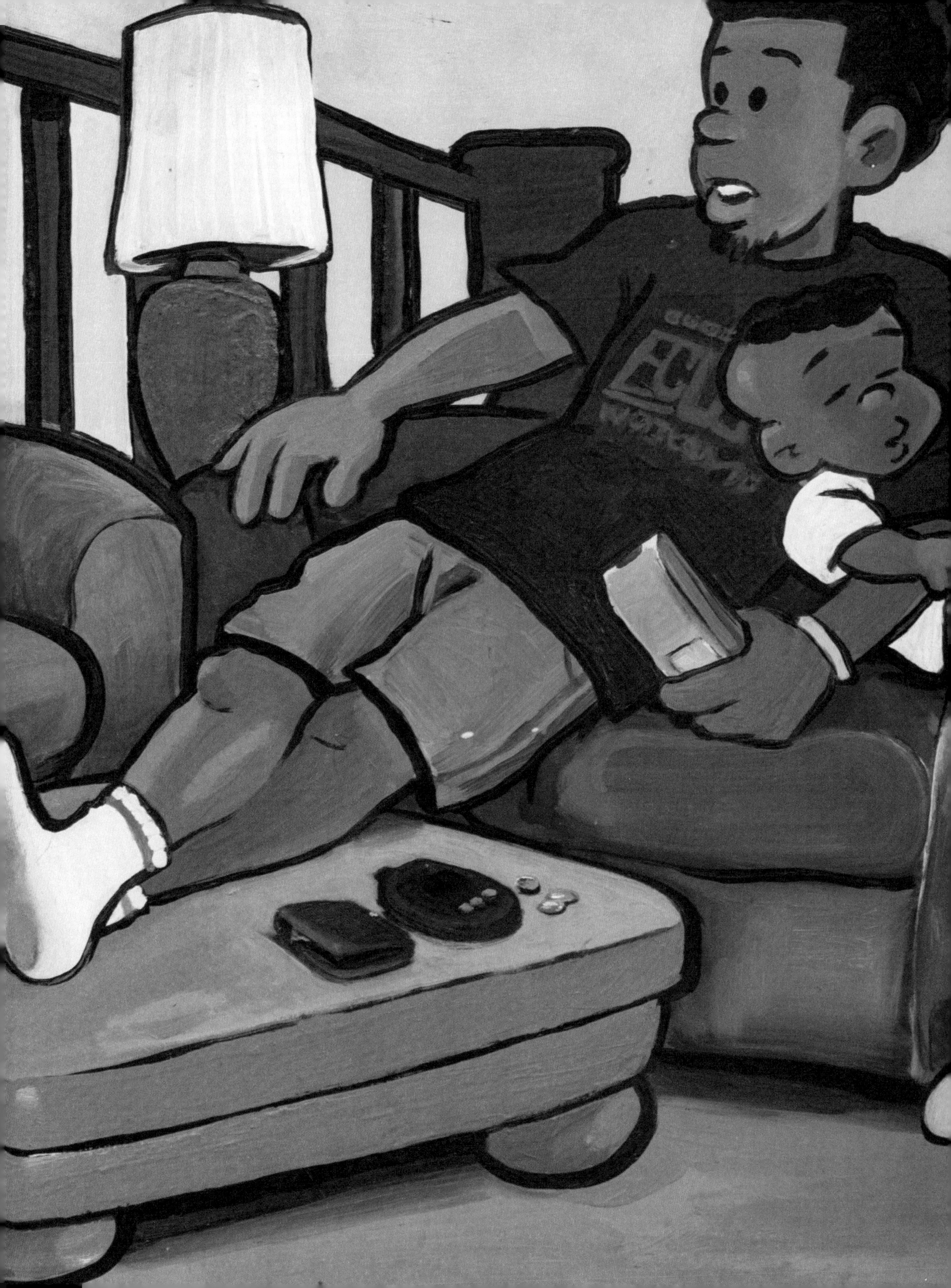

Previous page:
Marcy's working late
2'x4' acrylic on wood
by Robb Armstrong
Photographed by Johnny Dycus

Andrews McMeel Publishing
a division of Andrews McMeel Universal
1130 Walnut Street, Kansas City, Missouri 64106
www.andrewsmcmeel.com

20 21 22 23 24 SDB 10 9 8 7 6 5 4 3 2 1

ISBN: 978-1-5248-6162-9

Library of Congress Control Number: 2020936867

On a Roll!

BOOYAH!
Yay Sunny!
KAPOW!
Distributed by Andrews McMeel Syndication www.gocomics.com
FEARLESS a cartoonist's guide to life
robbarmstrong.com
©2017 Ruff Sketch, Inc.
THANKS FOR STAYING OPEN UNTIL SHE GOT THAT STRIKE.
NO PROBLEM.
YOU OWE $463.00, AND I NEED A RIDE HOME.
5-13-17

JUMP START

Starring
JOE & MARCY

BY ROBB ARMSTRONG

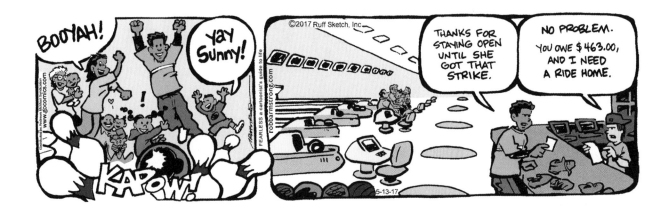

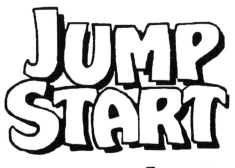

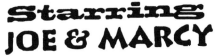

Andrews McMeel
PUBLISHING®

"JumpStart doesn't mean anything."

That was the answer given to me by my editor after I asked, "What does the title, 'JumpStart,' mean, exactly?"

It was 1989, and the strip was to be launched within days. Unfortunately, we had not decided on a title for my new strip. My syndicate faxed me a short list of titles to consider, but only one was circled: "JumpStart."

"It's upbeat, and the sales team will have an easier time selling it," explained Sarah Gillespie at United Feature Syndicate.

"But what does it have to do with 'Joe,' the cop, and his new wife, 'Marcy,' the nurse?"

Sarah then shut down this interrogation by saying, "We're the syndicate who came up with the title, 'PEANUTS.' To this day, Charles Schulz has no idea what it means."

"Sounds good to me," I said. "Got a nice ring to it!"

Roll Call

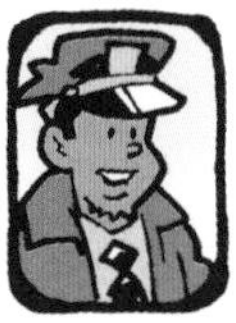

Joe Cobb
Philly cop. Husband. Father of 4. Eagles superfan.

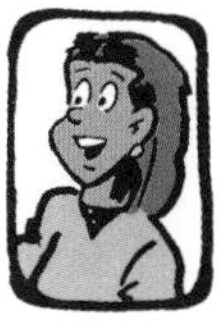

Marcy Cobb
Nurse. Wife. Director of Health Sciences Pavilion. Mother of 4.

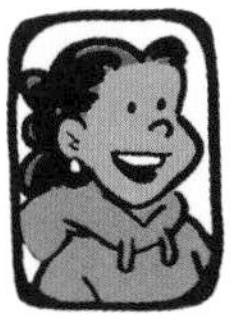

Sunny
Daughter of Joe and Marcy. Nature lover.

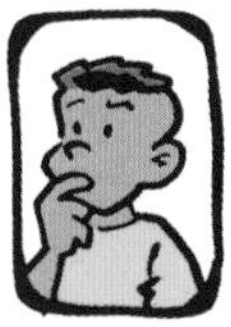

Jojo
Son of Joe and Marcy. Future president.

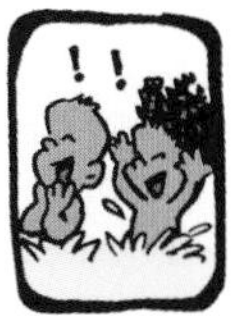

! !

Teddy and Tommi Cobb
Twins living in an alternate universe.

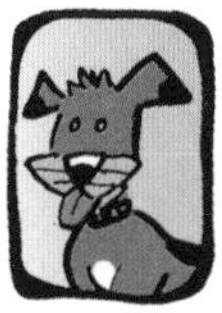

Mortimer
Heroic K9. Cobb family pet. Killer of The Sockness Monster.

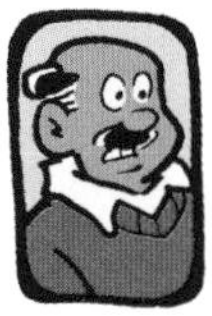

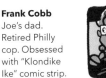

Frank Cobb
Joe's dad. Retired Philly cop. Obsessed with "Klondike Ike" comic strip.

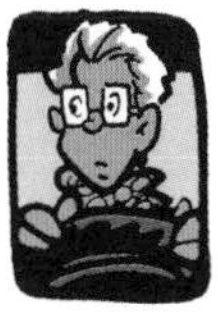

Dot Cobb
Joe's mother. Grammar cop. World's scariest driver.

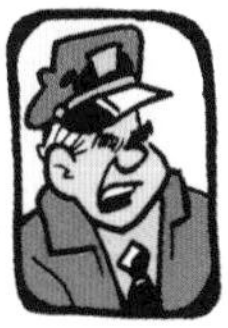

Edmund Crunchy
Joe's partner. Formerly Frank's partner.

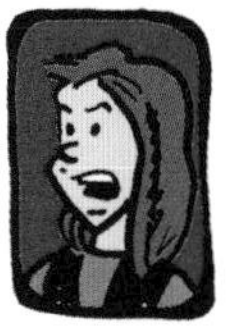

Captain Yolanda Ruiz
Precinct boss. Married to Edmund Crunchy.

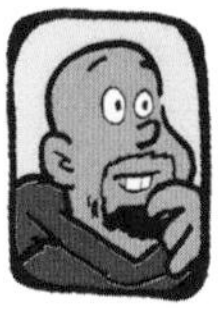

Clarence Glover
Joe's BFF. Orthodontist. Loudmouth. Married to Charlene.

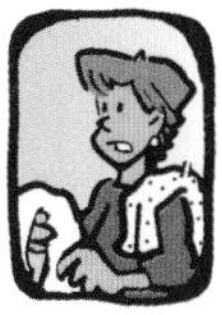

Charlene Glover
Mother of CJ, Jasmine, and Olivet. Sculptor and mechanic.

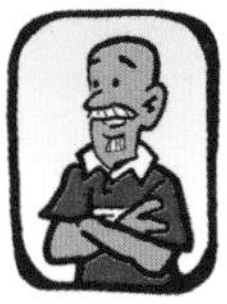

Clayton Glover
Father of 12 huge sons. Stepdad to Marcy. Husband of Maureen.

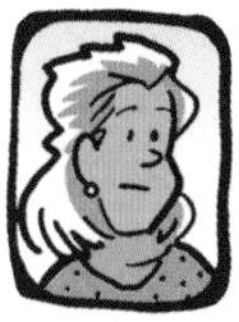

Maureen Glover
Marcy's mother.

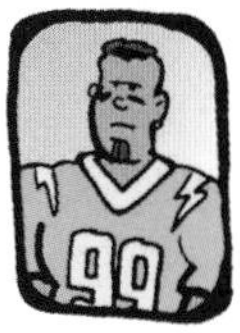

99

Marcus Glover
Superstar athlete. Cheapskate.

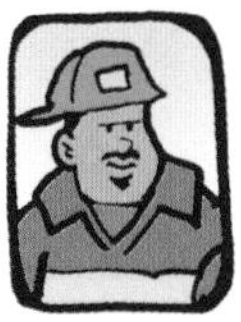

Sam Glover
Engine 53 battalion chief. Softball rival of Joe and Crunchy.

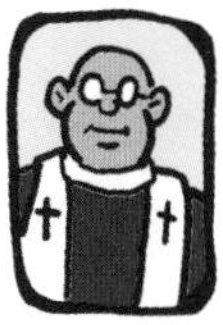

Pastor Chuck Glover
Inherited the church from his retired father.

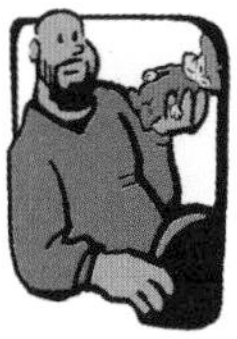

Otis Glover
Eight-foot-tall kindergarten teacher. Olivet won't let him out of her sight.

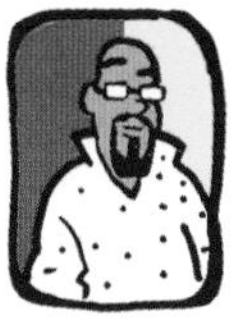

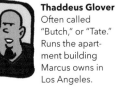

Vance Glover
Orthodontist, like Clarence. He lives in Miami.

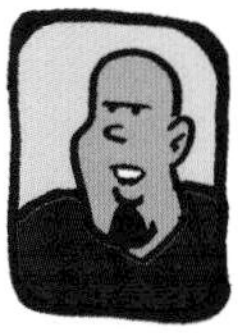

Thaddeus Glover
Often called "Butch," or "Tate." Runs the apartment building Marcus owns in Los Angeles.

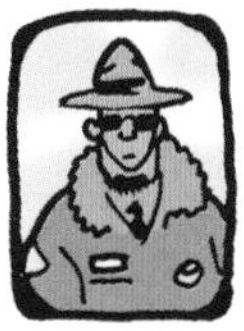

"Moose" Glover
Pennsylvania State Trooper. Real name is Maurice.

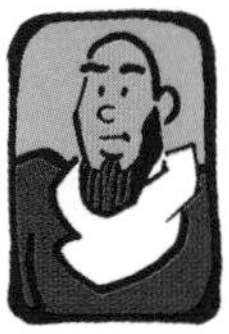

Bernard Glover
Owns a luxury car dealership.

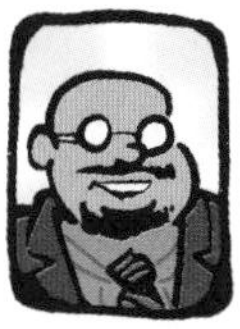

Roland Glover
Sportscaster. Twin brother of Raymond.

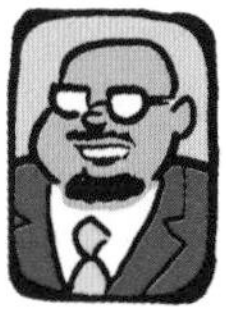

Raymond Glover
Philly weatherman. Not to be confused with Roland.

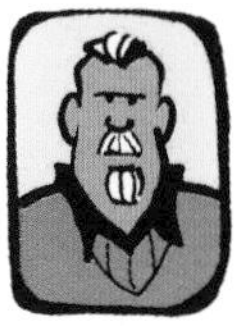

Clayton Glover Jr.
The eldest of the 12. Dentist.

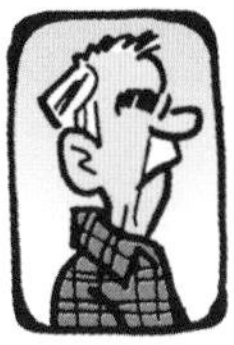

George Crunchy
Retired parole officer. Married to Sarah, Delray's mother.

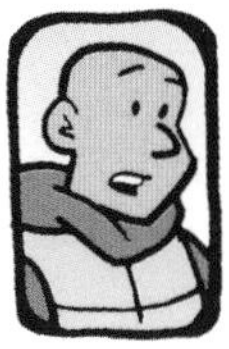

Delray Crunchy
Ex-con and former owner of Mortimer. Married to Dana, Marcy's boss.

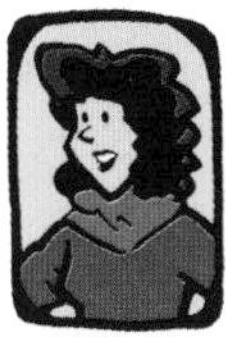

Dana Worthington
Heiress. Philanthropist. New wife to Delray. New mom to Kenny Sharcane.

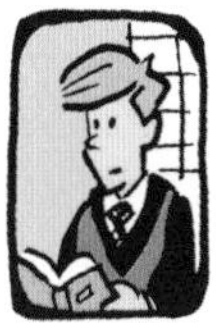

Kenny (Sharcane) Crunchy
Newly adopted by Delray and Dana. Son of the convicted Antonio Sharcane.

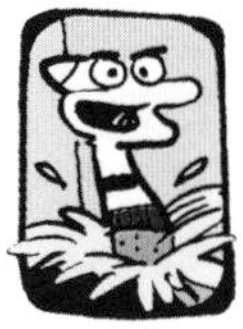

The Sockness Monster
Joe's sock puppet. Often attacked by Mortimer.

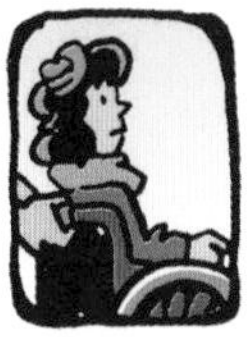

Sarah Crunchy
Saved by Mortimer, but now confined to a wheelchair.

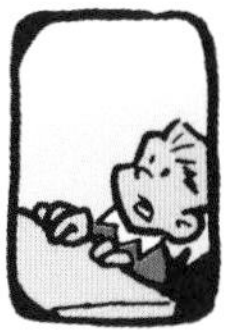

Dexter Wright
Classmate of Sunny's. In competition with Kenny for Sunny's attention.

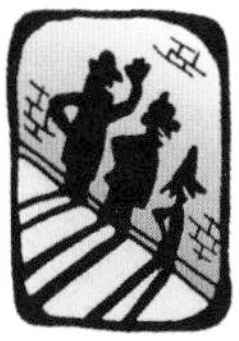

Willarbee, Percival, and Cross
Looming schoolyard bullies who torment Jojo and Benny.

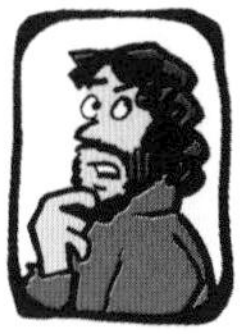

Antonio Sharcane
"The Shark." Dumped a stolen car with a baby inside, rescued by Mortimer.

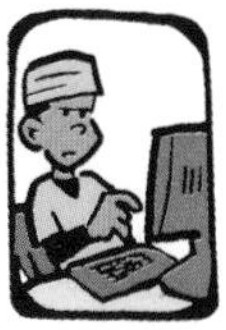

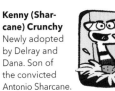

Doctor Appleby
His mother named him, "DOCTOR APPLEBY."

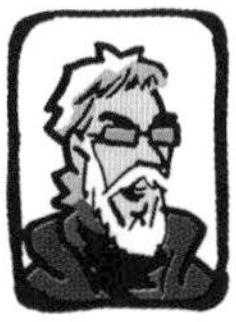

Vic Van Streck
Cartoonist. Creator of "Klondike Ike," the best comic strip in the world.

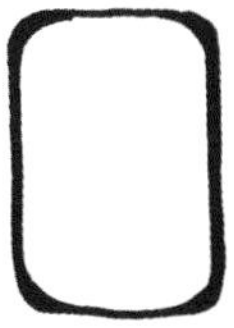

Snoog-A-Boo
Crunchy and Yolanda's dog. He's so smart he can–HEY! Where did he GO?

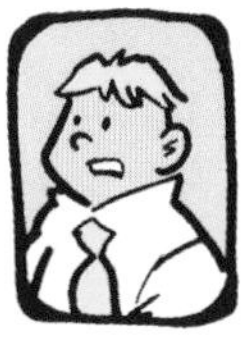

Benny
Jojo's best friend.

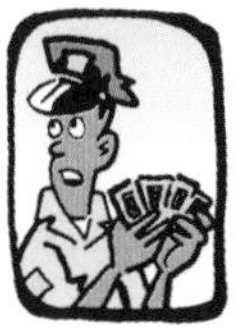

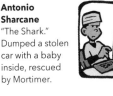

Officer Darryl Peterson
Joe's annoying young rival at work.

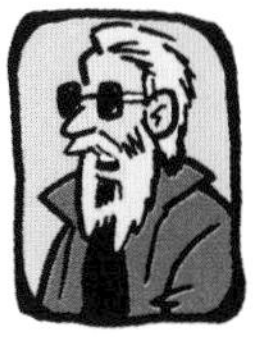

Ray Ramsey
Delray's deceased father. Or is this Tom Lazarus, a doppelganger?

Frank Cobb reading "Klondike Ike"
22"x28" acrylic on canvas
by Robb Armstrong
Photographed by Johnny Dycus

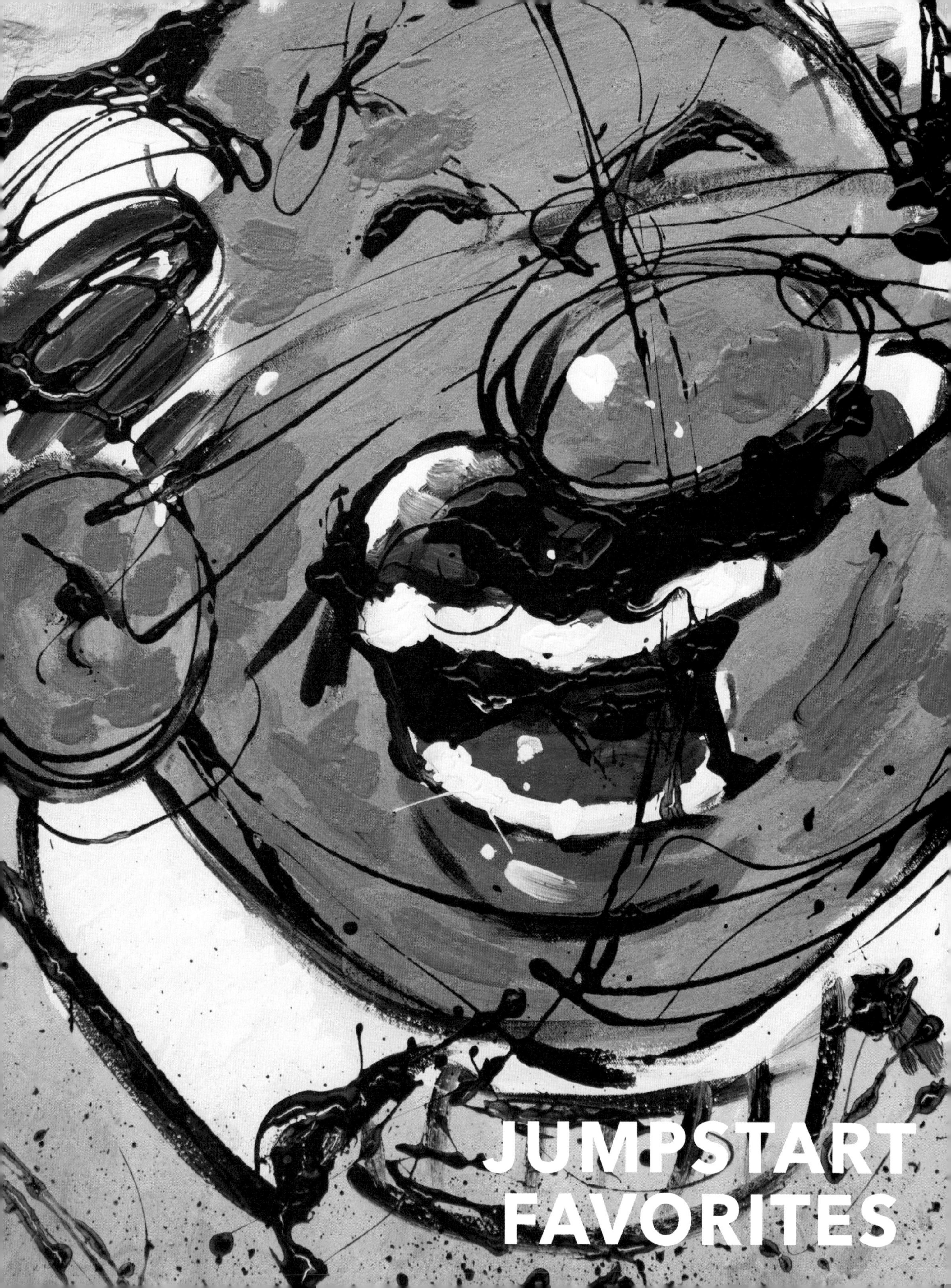

JUMPSTART FAVORITES

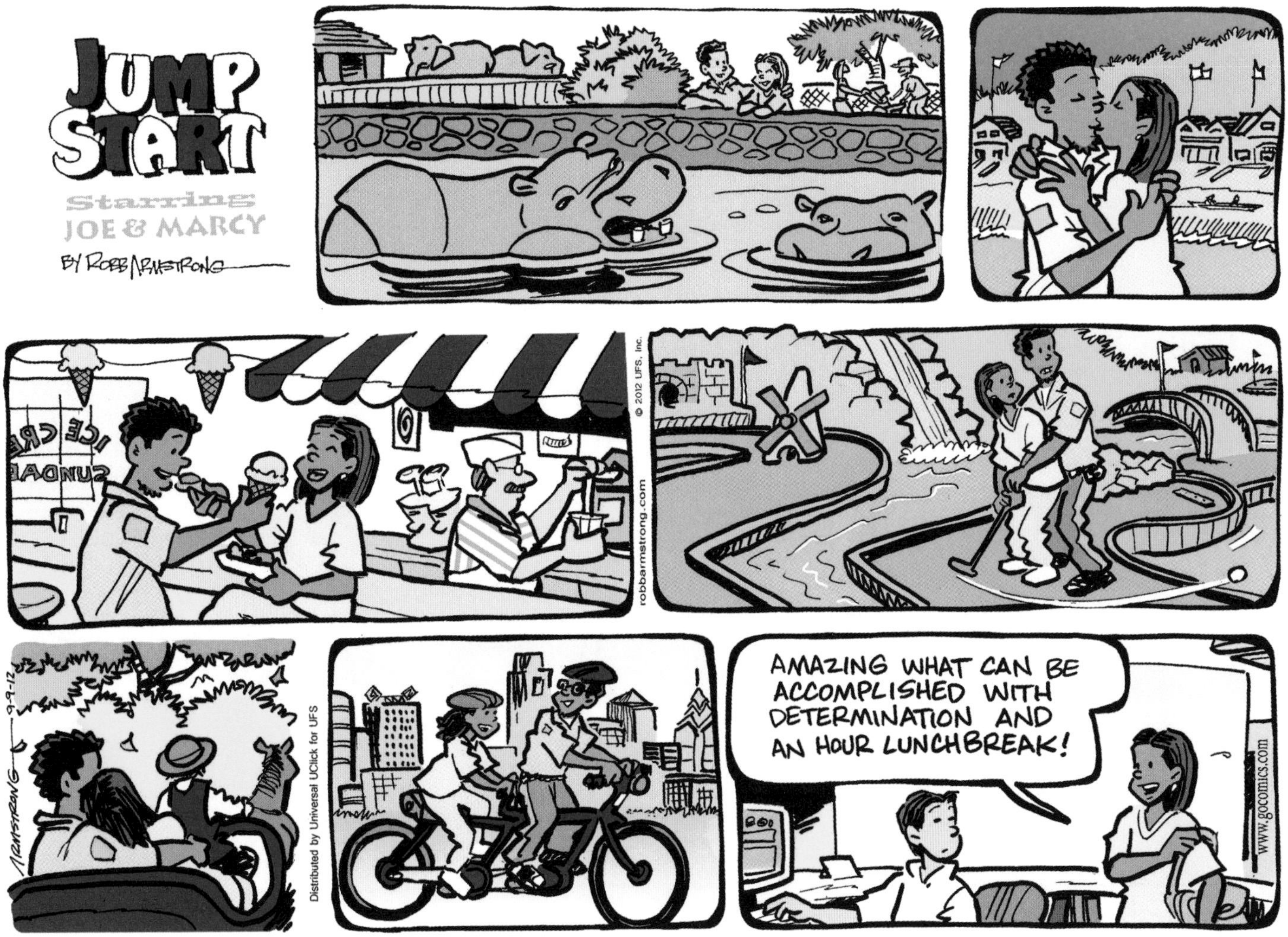
JUMP START
Starring JOE & MARCY
BY ROBB ARMSTRONG
© 2012 UFS, Inc.
robbarmstrong.com
Distributed by Universal UClick for UFS
AMAZING WHAT CAN BE ACCOMPLISHED WITH DETERMINATION AND AN HOUR LUNCHBREAK!
www.gocomics.com

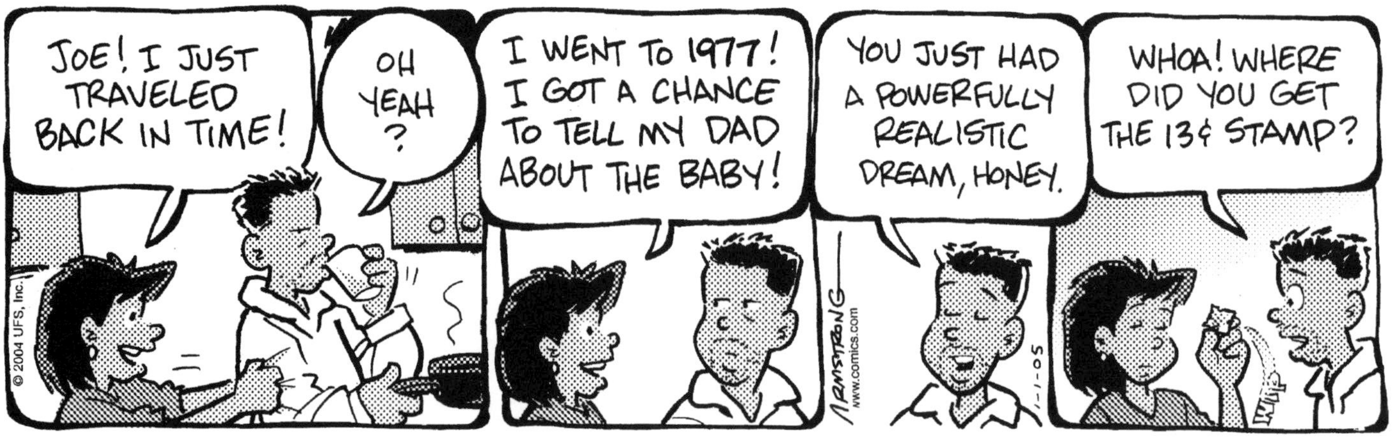
JOE! I JUST TRAVELED BACK IN TIME!
OH YEAH?
I WENT TO 1977! I GOT A CHANCE TO TELL MY DAD ABOUT THE BABY!
YOU JUST HAD A POWERFULLY REALISTIC DREAM, HONEY.
WHOA! WHERE DID YOU GET THE 13¢ STAMP?
© 2004 UFS, Inc.
ARMSTRONG
www.comics.com
1-1-05

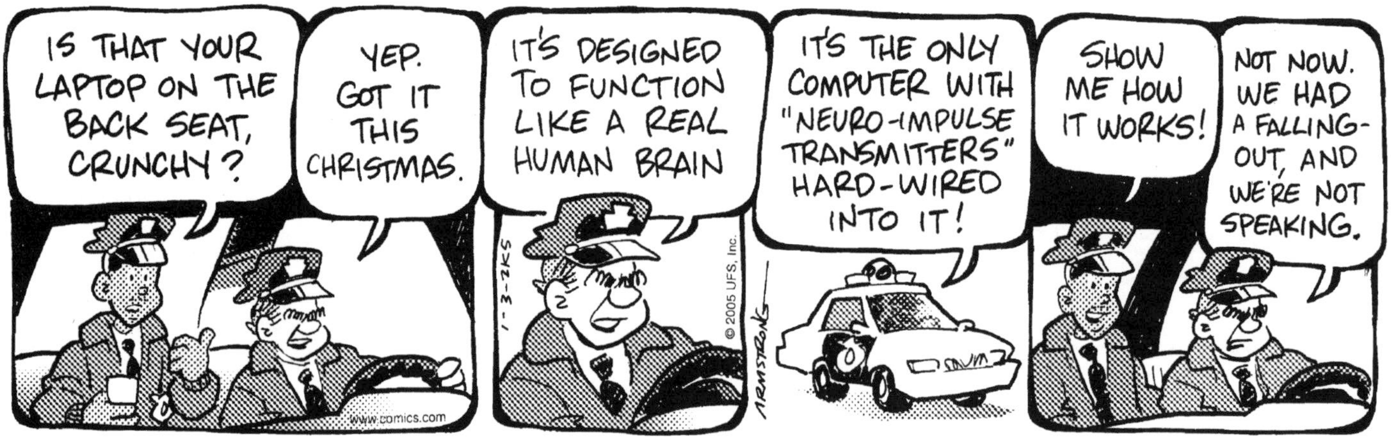
IS THAT YOUR LAPTOP ON THE BACK SEAT, CRUNCHY?
YEP. GOT IT THIS CHRISTMAS.
IT'S DESIGNED TO FUNCTION LIKE A REAL HUMAN BRAIN
IT'S THE ONLY COMPUTER WITH "NEURO-IMPULSE TRANSMITTERS" HARD-WIRED INTO IT!
SHOW ME HOW IT WORKS!
NOT NOW. WE HAD A FALLING-OUT, AND WE'RE NOT SPEAKING.
www.comics.com
© 2005 UFS, Inc.
ARMSTRONG

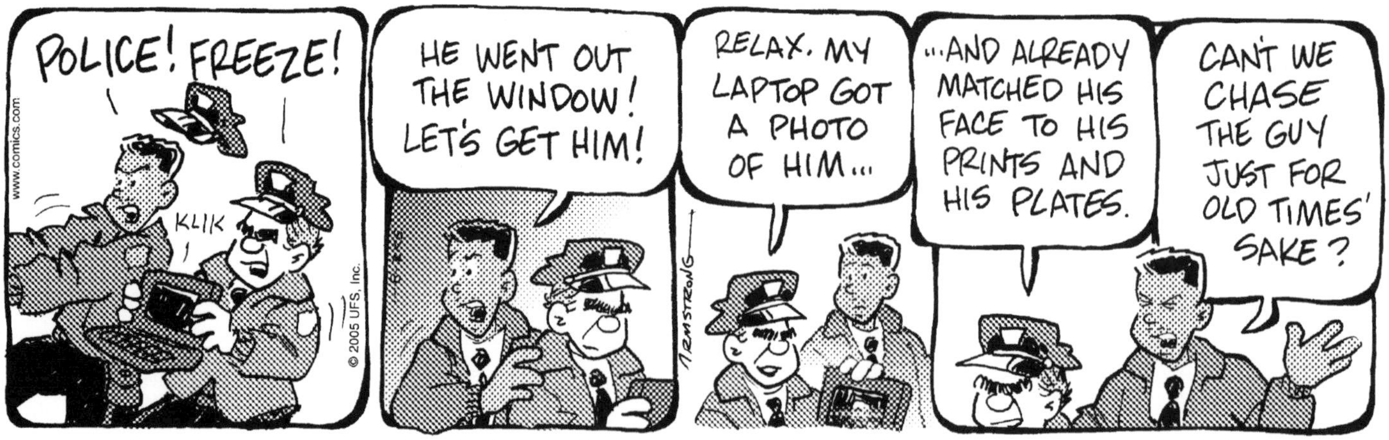
POLICE! FREEZE!
KLIK
HE WENT OUT THE WINDOW! LET'S GET HIM!
RELAX. MY LAPTOP GOT A PHOTO OF HIM...
...AND ALREADY MATCHED HIS FACE TO HIS PRINTS AND HIS PLATES.
CAN'T WE CHASE THE GUY JUST FOR OLD TIMES' SAKE?
www.comics.com
© 2005 UFS, Inc.
ARMSTRONG

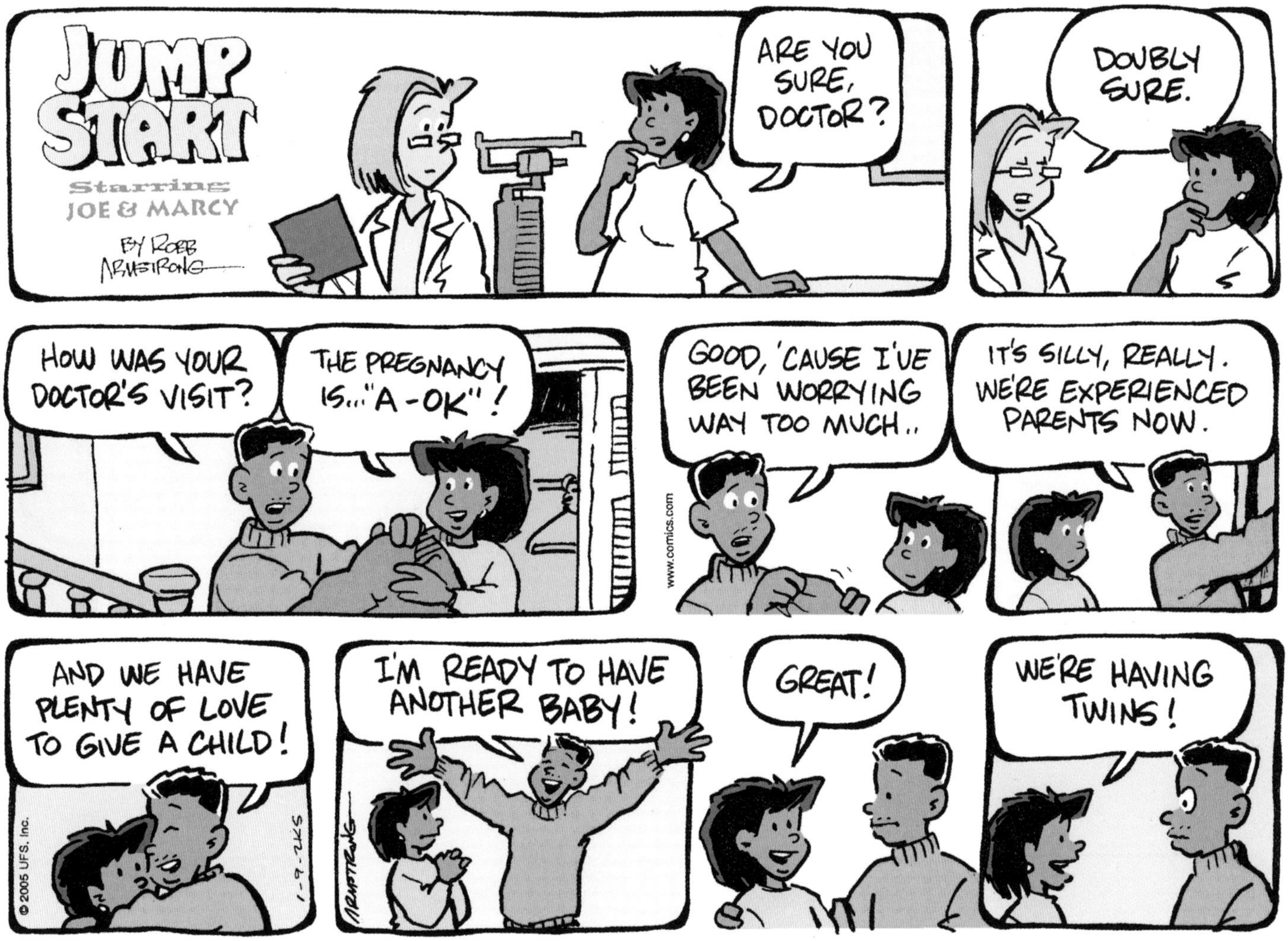
JUMP START
Starring JOE & MARCY
BY ROBB ARMSTRONG
ARE YOU SURE, DOCTOR?
DOUBLY SURE.
HOW WAS YOUR DOCTOR'S VISIT?
THE PREGNANCY IS..."A-OK"!
GOOD, 'CAUSE I'VE BEEN WORRYING WAY TOO MUCH..
IT'S SILLY, REALLY. WE'RE EXPERIENCED PARENTS NOW.
AND WE HAVE PLENTY OF LOVE TO GIVE A CHILD!
I'M READY TO HAVE ANOTHER BABY!
GREAT!
WE'RE HAVING TWINS!
www.comics.com
© 2005 UFS, Inc.
1-9-2K5

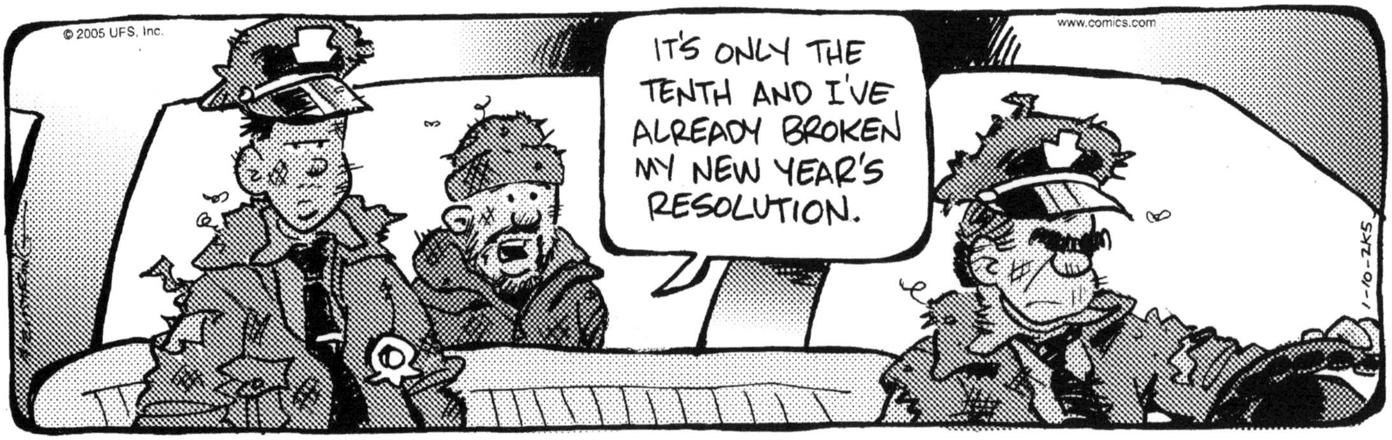
© 2005 UFS, Inc.
www.comics.com
IT'S ONLY THE TENTH AND I'VE ALREADY BROKEN MY NEW YEAR'S RESOLUTION.
1-10-2KS

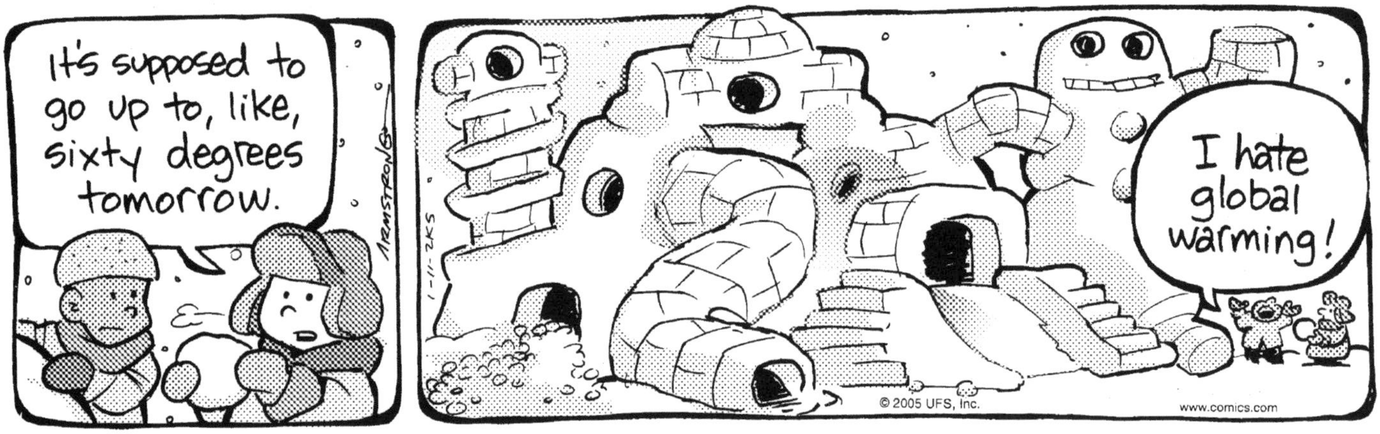
It's supposed to go up to, like, sixty degrees tomorrow.
ARMSTRONG
1-11-2KS
I hate global warming!
© 2005 UFS, Inc.
www.comics.com

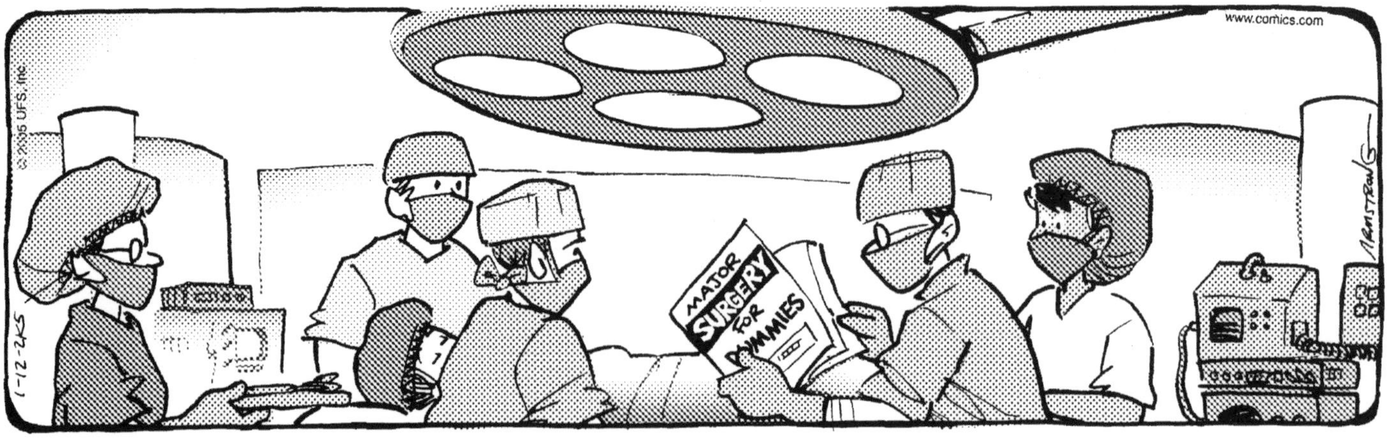
www.comics.com
© 2005 UFS, Inc.
1-12-2KS
MAJOR SURGERY FOR DUMMIES
ARMSTRONG

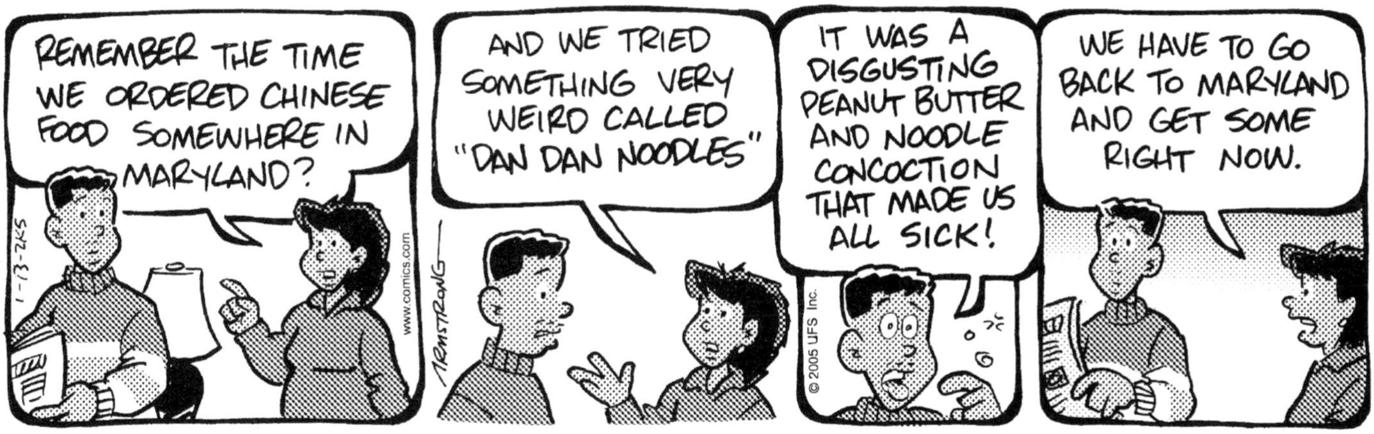
REMEMBER THE TIME WE ORDERED CHINESE FOOD SOMEWHERE IN MARYLAND?
AND WE TRIED SOMETHING VERY WEIRD CALLED "DAN DAN NOODLES"
IT WAS A DISGUSTING PEANUT BUTTER AND NOODLE CONCOCTION THAT MADE US ALL SICK!
WE HAVE TO GO BACK TO MARYLAND AND GET SOME RIGHT NOW.
© 2005 UFS Inc.
www.comics.com

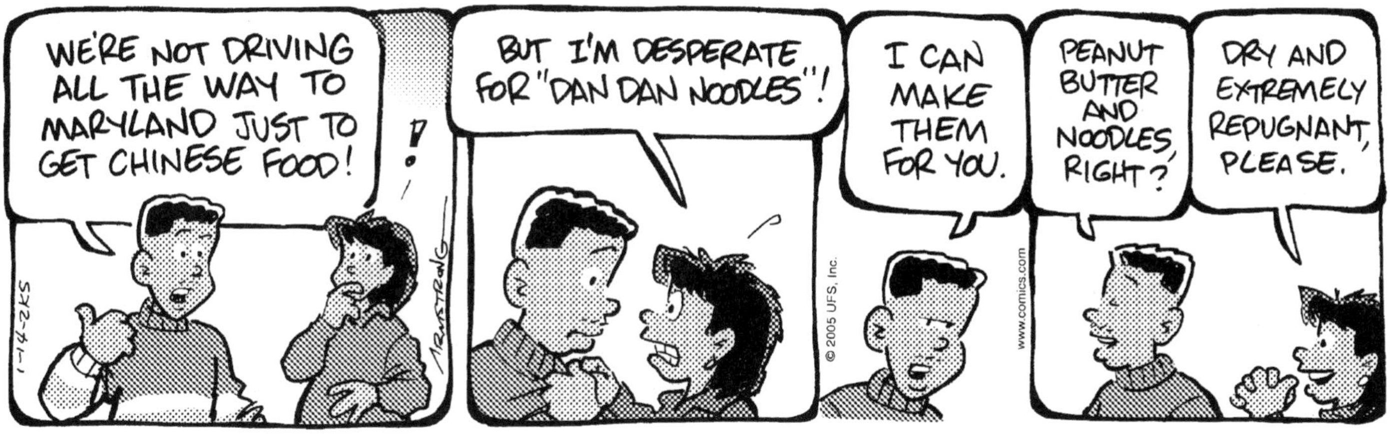
WE'RE NOT DRIVING ALL THE WAY TO MARYLAND JUST TO GET CHINESE FOOD!
BUT I'M DESPERATE FOR "DAN DAN NOODLES"!
I CAN MAKE THEM FOR YOU.
PEANUT BUTTER AND NOODLES, RIGHT?
DRY AND EXTREMELY REPUGNANT, PLEASE.
© 2005 UFS, Inc.
www.comics.com

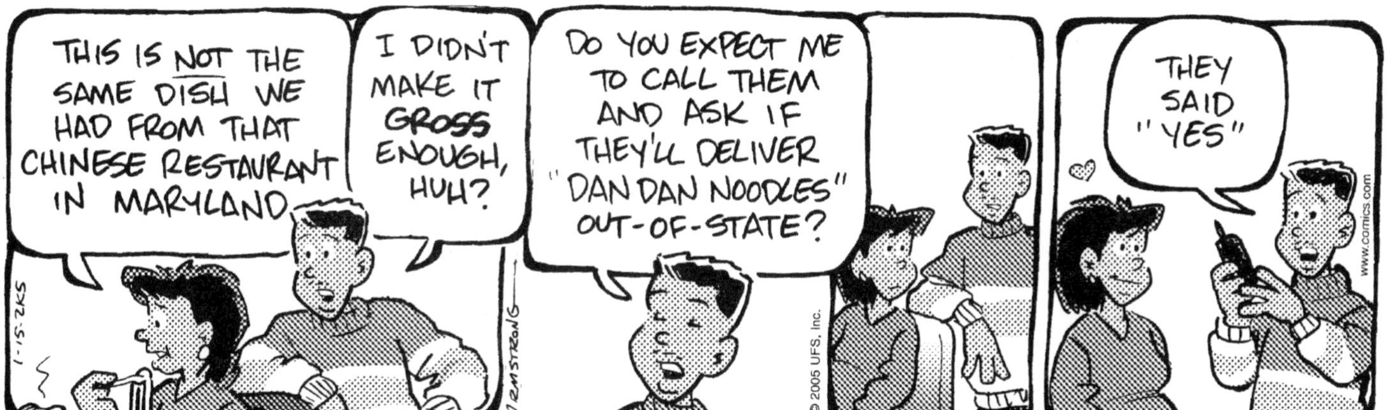
THIS IS NOT THE SAME DISH WE HAD FROM THAT CHINESE RESTAURANT IN MARYLAND.
I DIDN'T MAKE IT GROSS ENOUGH, HUH?
DO YOU EXPECT ME TO CALL THEM AND ASK IF THEY'LL DELIVER "DAN DAN NOODLES" OUT-OF-STATE?
THEY SAID "YES"
© 2005 UFS, Inc.
www.comics.com

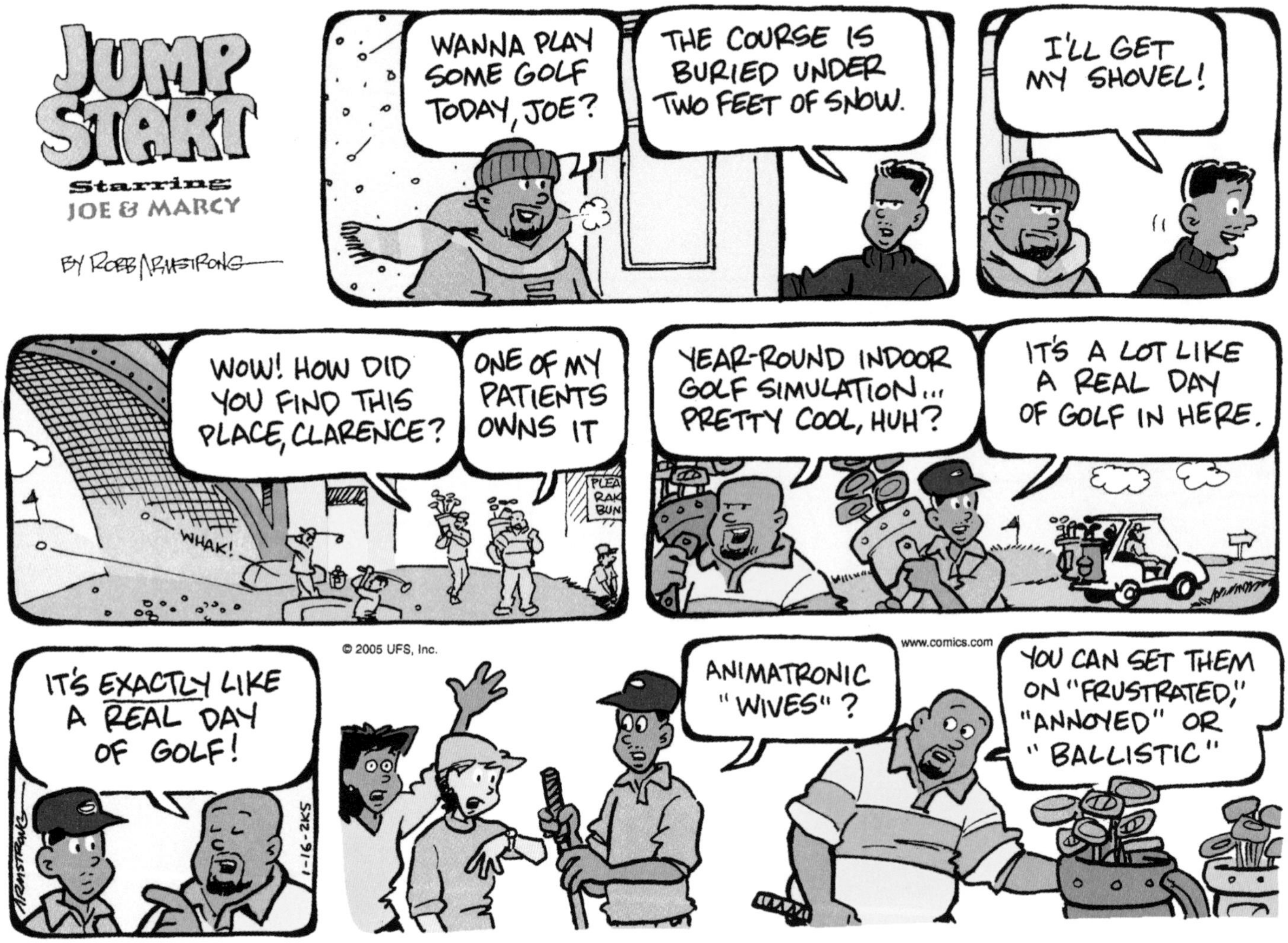
JUMP START
Starring
JOE & MARCY
BY ROBB ARMSTRONG
WANNA PLAY SOME GOLF TODAY, JOE?
THE COURSE IS BURIED UNDER TWO FEET OF SNOW.
I'LL GET MY SHOVEL!
WOW! HOW DID YOU FIND THIS PLACE, CLARENCE?
ONE OF MY PATIENTS OWNS IT
WHAK!
YEAR-ROUND INDOOR GOLF SIMULATION... PRETTY COOL, HUH?
IT'S A LOT LIKE A REAL DAY OF GOLF IN HERE.
IT'S EXACTLY LIKE A REAL DAY OF GOLF!
ARMSTRONG
1-16-2K5
© 2005 UFS, Inc.
ANIMATRONIC "WIVES"?
www.comics.com
YOU CAN SET THEM ON "FRUSTRATED," "ANNOYED" OR "BALLISTIC"

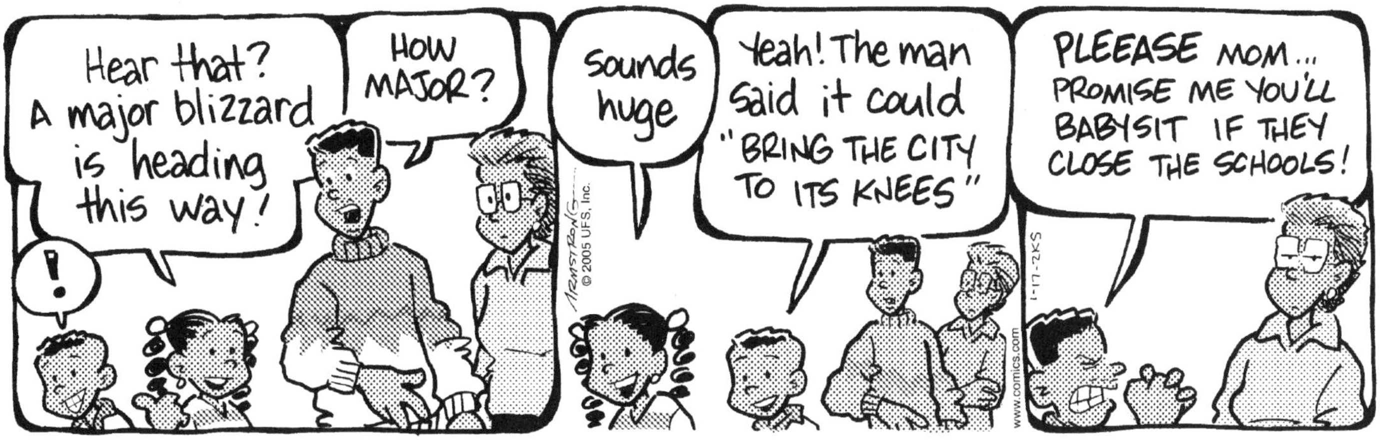
Hear that? A major blizzard is heading this way!
!
HOW MAJOR?
ARMSTRONG
© 2005 UFS, Inc.
Sounds huge
Yeah! The man said it could "BRING THE CITY TO ITS KNEES"
www.comics.com
1-17-2KS
PLEEASE MOM... PROMISE ME YOU'LL BABYSIT IF THEY CLOSE THE SCHOOLS!

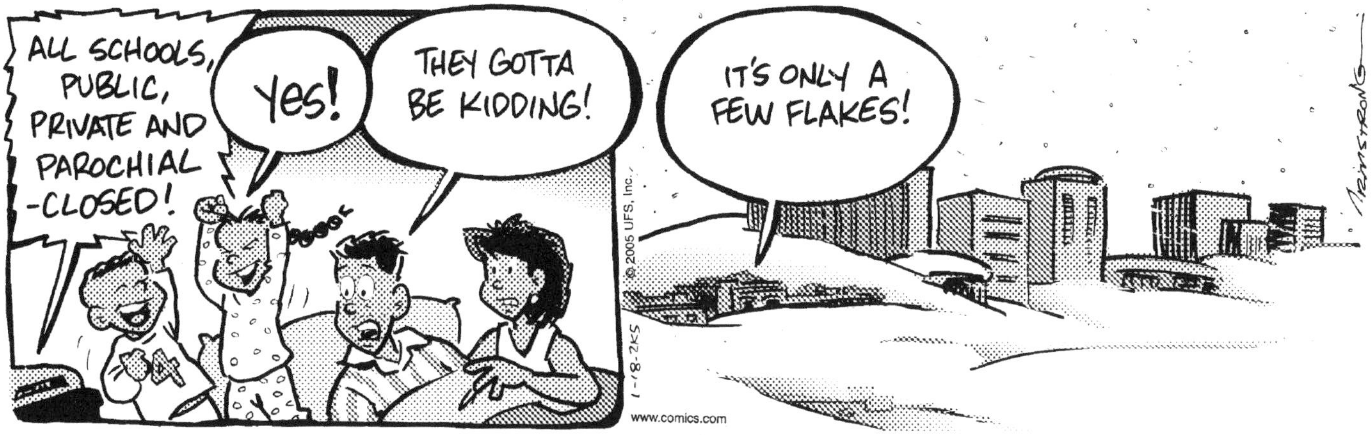
ALL SCHOOLS, PUBLIC, PRIVATE AND PAROCHIAL -CLOSED!
Yes!
THEY GOTTA BE KIDDING!
© 2005 UFS, Inc.
1-18-2KS
www.comics.com
IT'S ONLY A FEW FLAKES!
ARMSTRONG

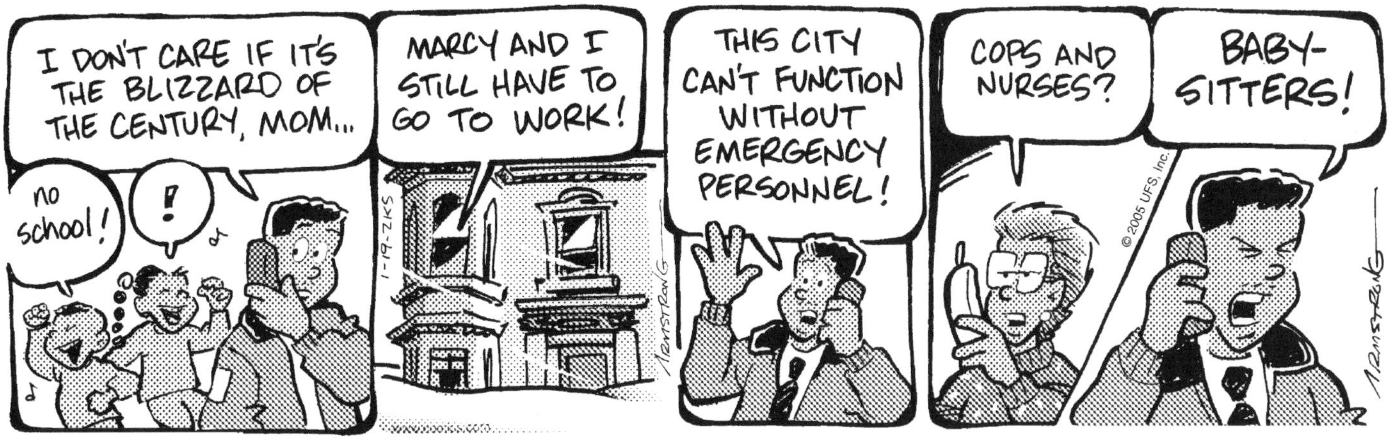
I DON'T CARE IF IT'S THE BLIZZARD OF THE CENTURY, MOM...
no school!
!
MARCY AND I STILL HAVE TO GO TO WORK!
1-19-2KS
ARMSTRONG
THIS CITY CAN'T FUNCTION WITHOUT EMERGENCY PERSONNEL!
COPS AND NURSES?
© 2005 UFS, Inc.
BABY-SITTERS!
ARMSTRONG

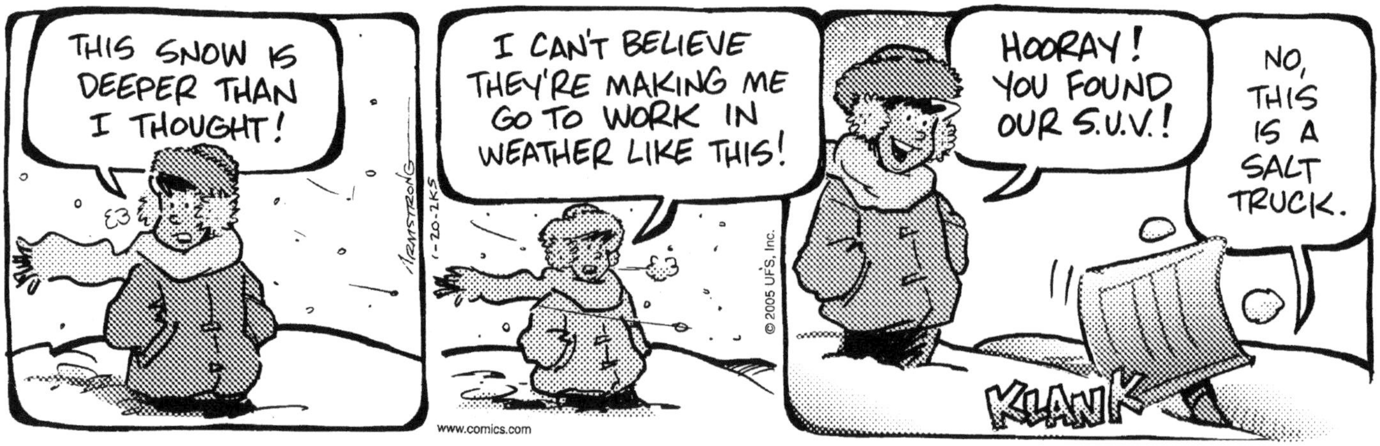
THIS SNOW IS DEEPER THAN I THOUGHT!
I CAN'T BELIEVE THEY'RE MAKING ME GO TO WORK IN WEATHER LIKE THIS!
HOORAY! YOU FOUND OUR S.U.V.!
NO, THIS IS A SALT TRUCK.
KLANK
www.comics.com

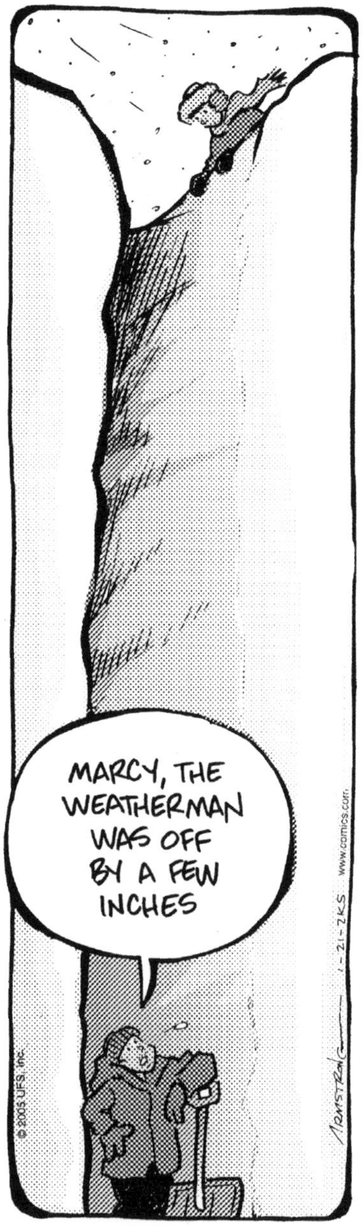
MARCY, THE WEATHERMAN WAS OFF BY A FEW INCHES
www.comics.com

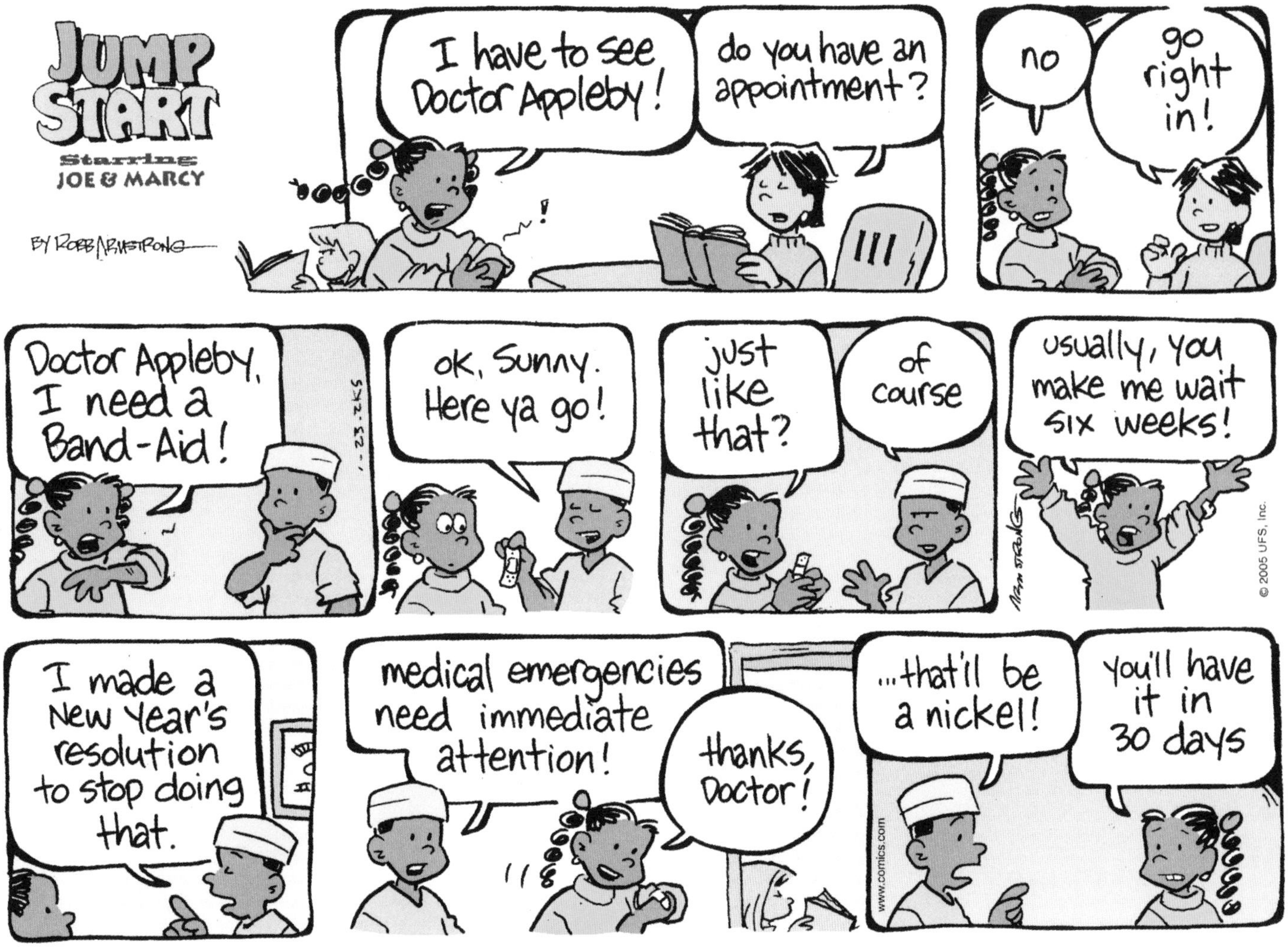
JUMP START
Starring JOE & MARCY
BY ROBB ARMSTRONG
I have to see Doctor Appleby!
do you have an appointment?
no
go right in!
Doctor Appleby, I need a Band-Aid!
ok, Sunny. Here ya go!
just like that?
of course
usually, you make me wait six weeks!
© 2005 UFS, Inc.
I made a New Year's resolution to stop doing that.
medical emergencies need immediate attention!
thanks, Doctor!
...that'll be a nickel!
You'll have it in 30 days
www.comics.com

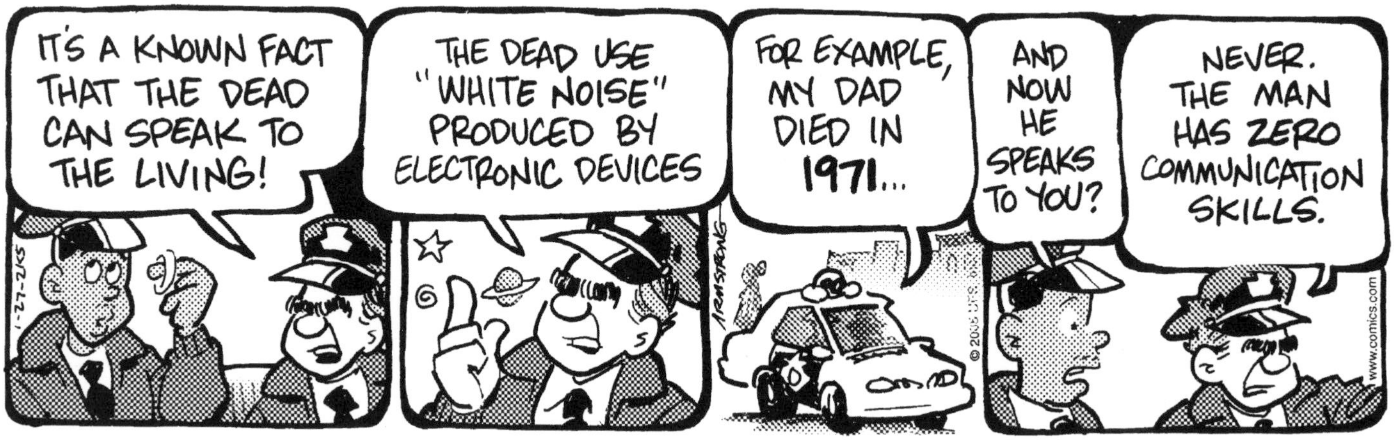

IT'S A KNOWN FACT THAT THE DEAD CAN SPEAK TO THE LIVING!
THE DEAD USE "WHITE NOISE" PRODUCED BY ELECTRONIC DEVICES
FOR EXAMPLE, MY DAD DIED IN 1971...
AND NOW HE SPEAKS TO YOU?
NEVER. THE MAN HAS ZERO COMMUNICATION SKILLS.
© 2005 UFS
www.comics.com

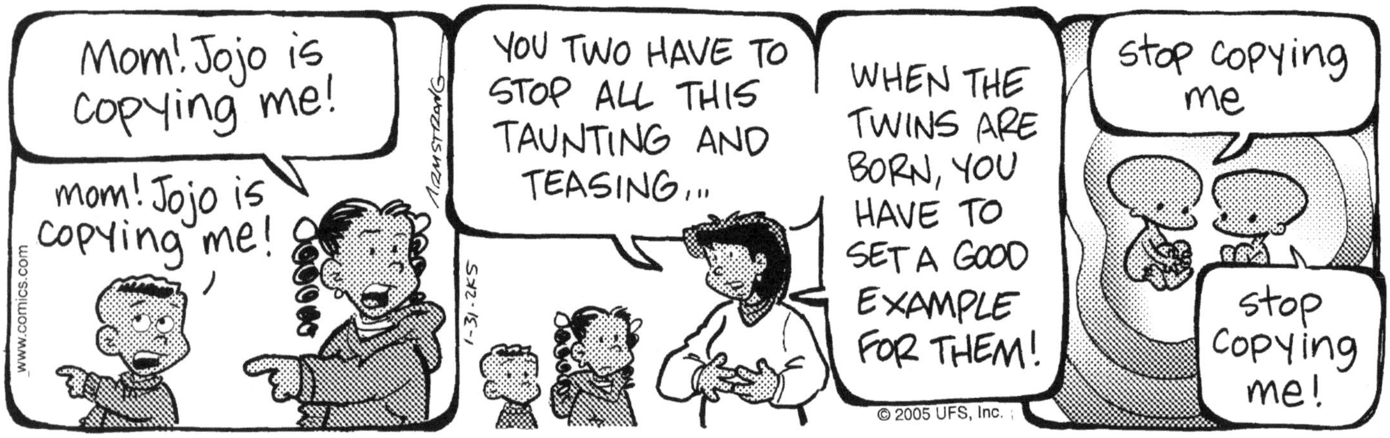

Mom! Jojo is copying me!
mom! Jojo is copying me!
YOU TWO HAVE TO STOP ALL THIS TAUNTING AND TEASING...
WHEN THE TWINS ARE BORN, YOU HAVE TO SET A GOOD EXAMPLE FOR THEM!
stop copying me
stop copying me!
© 2005 UFS, Inc.
www.comics.com

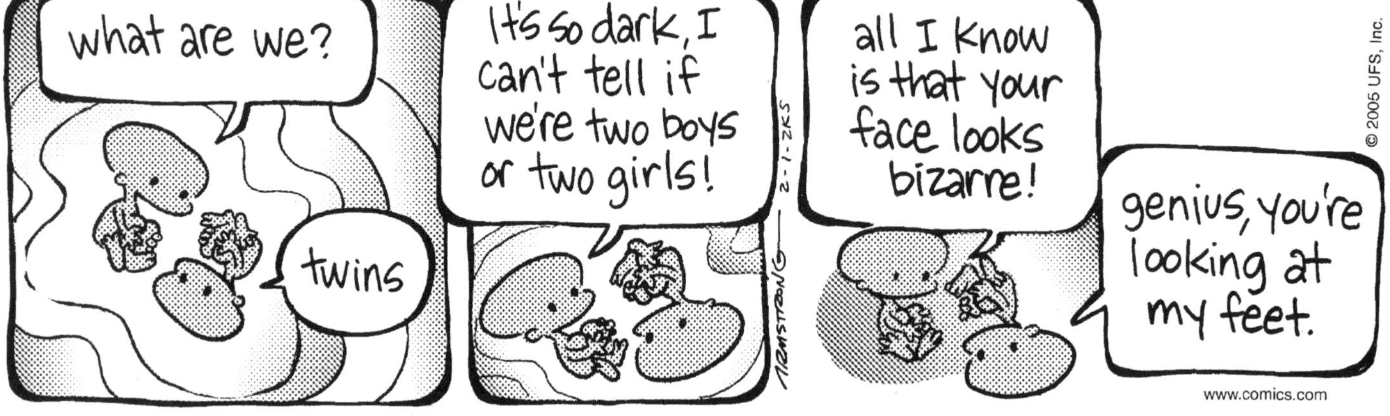

what are we?
twins
It's so dark, I can't tell if we're two boys or two girls!
all I know is that your face looks bizarre!
genius, you're looking at my feet.
© 2005 UFS, Inc.
www.comics.com

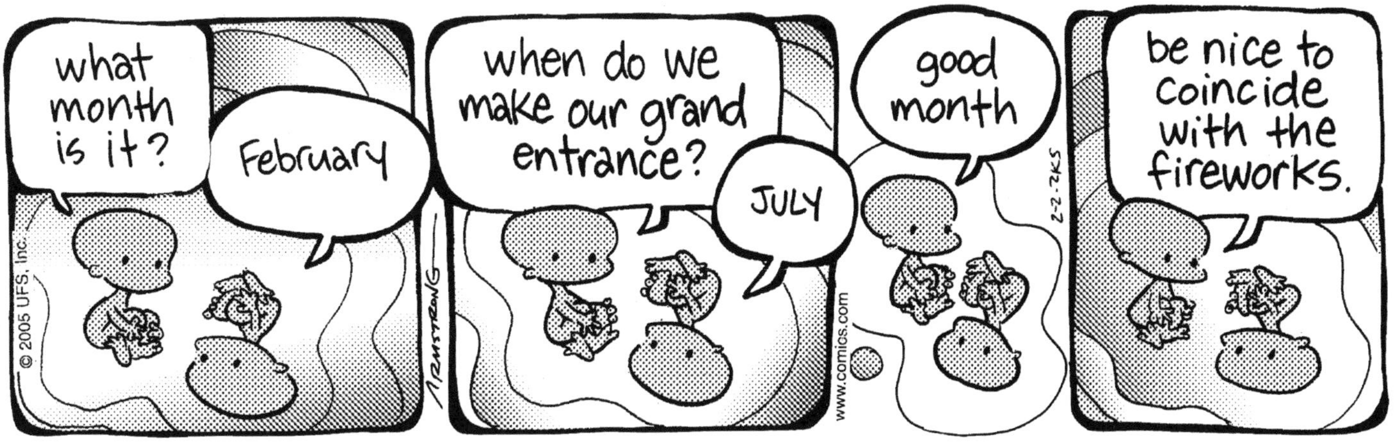
what month is it?
February
when do we make our grand entrance?
JULY
good month
be nice to coincide with the fireworks.
© 2005 UFS, Inc.
ARMSTRONG
www.comics.com
2-2-2KS

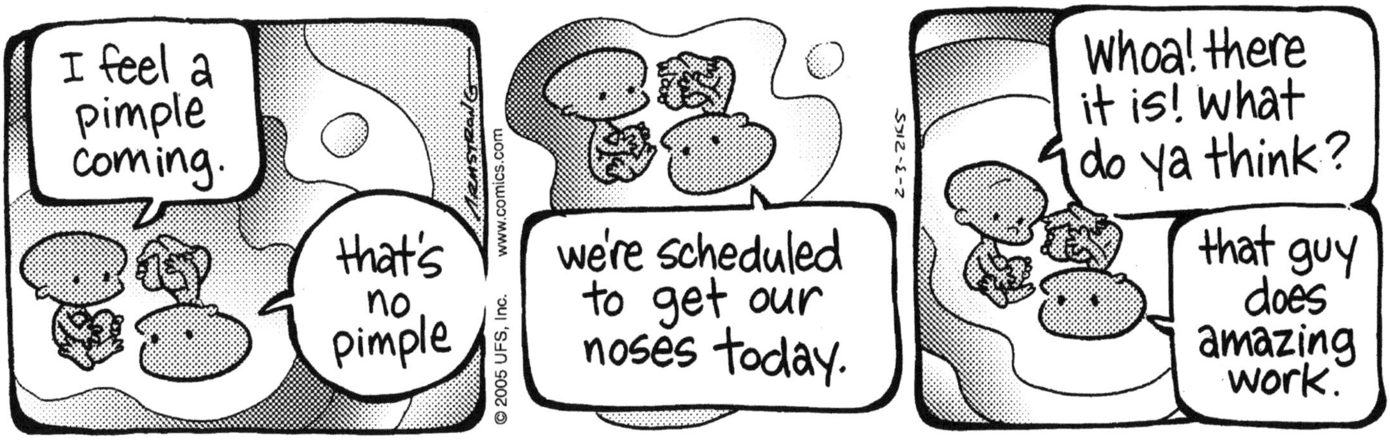
I feel a pimple coming.
that's no pimple
ARMSTRONG
www.comics.com
© 2005 UFS, Inc.
we're scheduled to get our noses today.
2-3-2KS
Whoa! there it is! what do ya think?
that guy does amazing work.

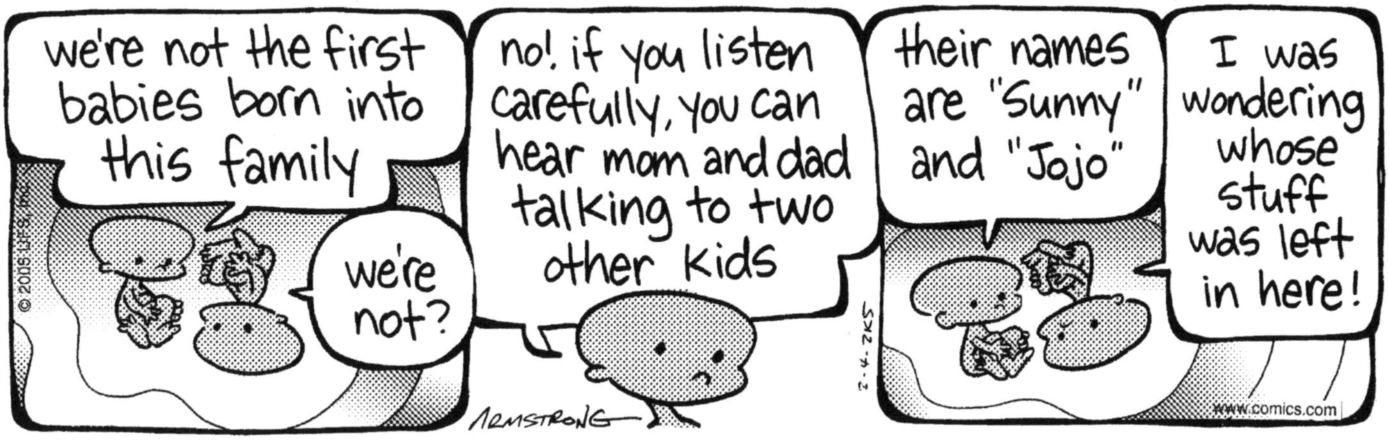
we're not the first babies born into this family
we're not?
no! if you listen carefully, you can hear mom and dad talking to two other kids
ARMSTRONG
their names are "Sunny" and "Jojo"
I was wondering whose stuff was left in here!
2-4-2KS
www.comics.com

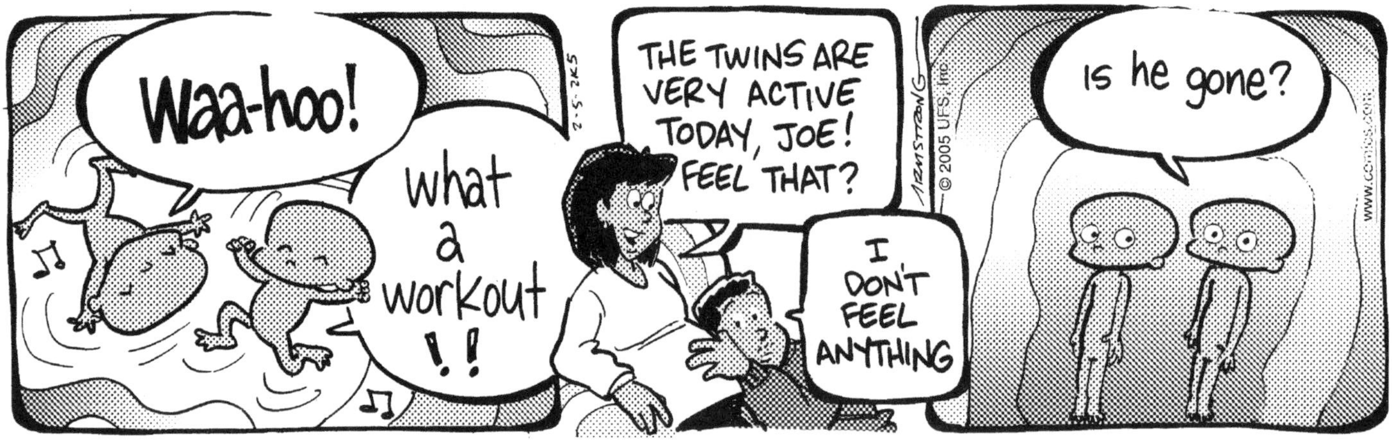
Waa-hoo!
what a workout !!
THE TWINS ARE VERY ACTIVE TODAY, JOE! FEEL THAT?
I DON'T FEEL ANYTHING
is he gone?
© 2005 UFS, Inc.
www.comics.com

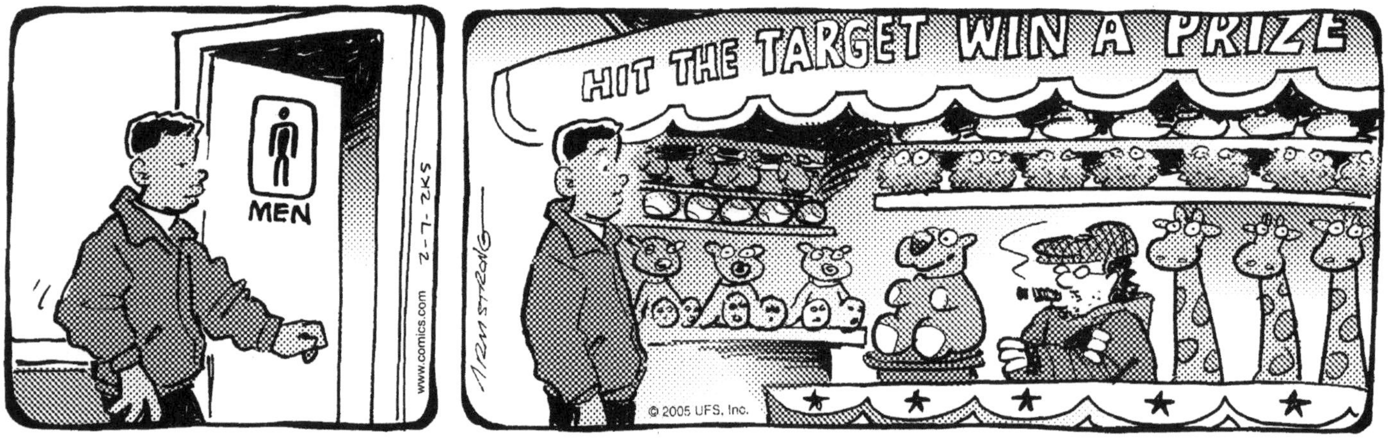
MEN
HIT THE TARGET WIN A PRIZE
www.comics.com
© 2005 UFS, Inc.

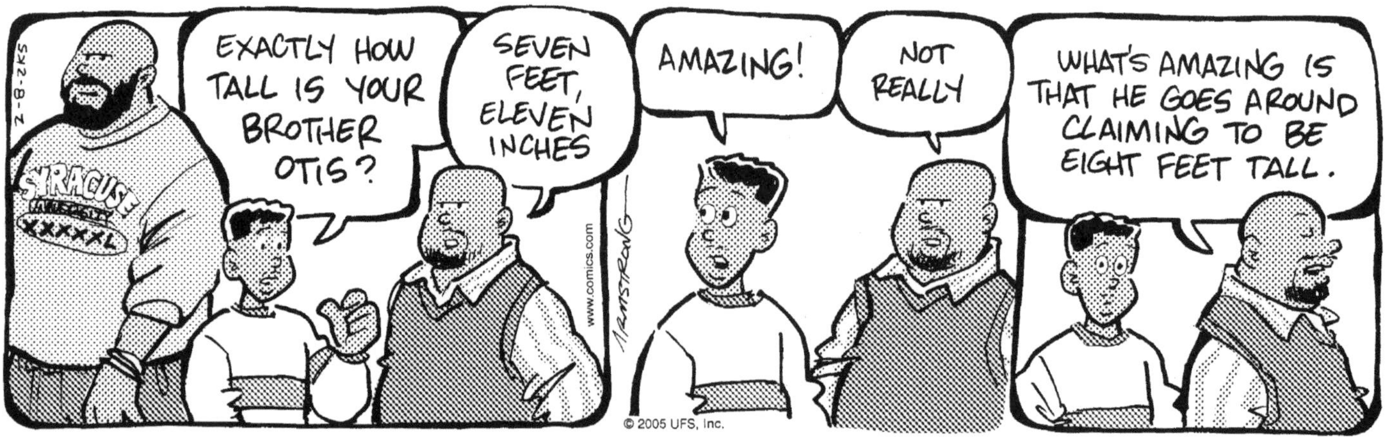
SYRACUSE
XXXXXL
EXACTLY HOW TALL IS YOUR BROTHER OTIS?
SEVEN FEET, ELEVEN INCHES
AMAZING!
NOT REALLY
WHAT'S AMAZING IS THAT HE GOES AROUND CLAIMING TO BE EIGHT FEET TALL.
www.comics.com
© 2005 UFS, Inc.

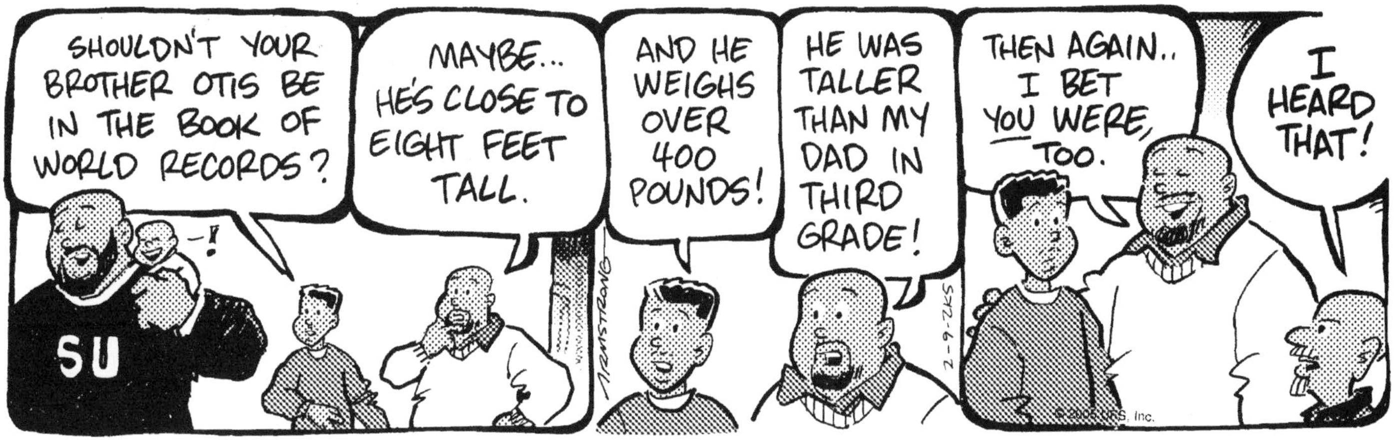
SHOULDN'T YOUR BROTHER OTIS BE IN THE BOOK OF WORLD RECORDS?
MAYBE... HE'S CLOSE TO EIGHT FEET TALL.
AND HE WEIGHS OVER 400 POUNDS!
HE WAS TALLER THAN MY DAD IN THIRD GRADE!
THEN AGAIN.. I BET YOU WERE, TOO.
I HEARD THAT!

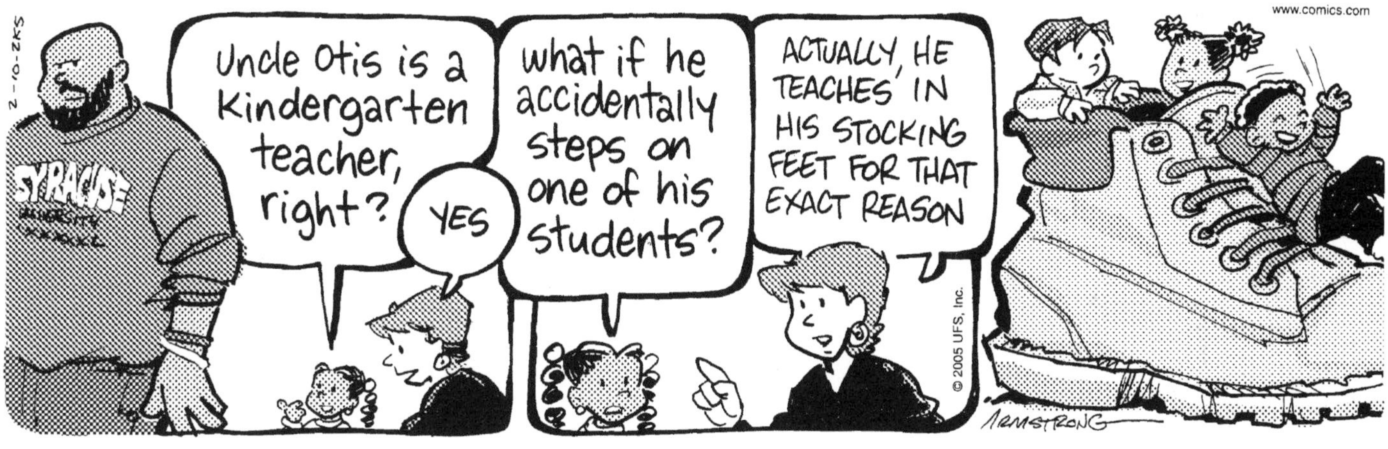
www.comics.com
Uncle Otis is a Kindergarten teacher, right?
YES
what if he accidentally steps on one of his students?
ACTUALLY, HE TEACHES IN HIS STOCKING FEET FOR THAT EXACT REASON
© 2005 UFS, Inc.

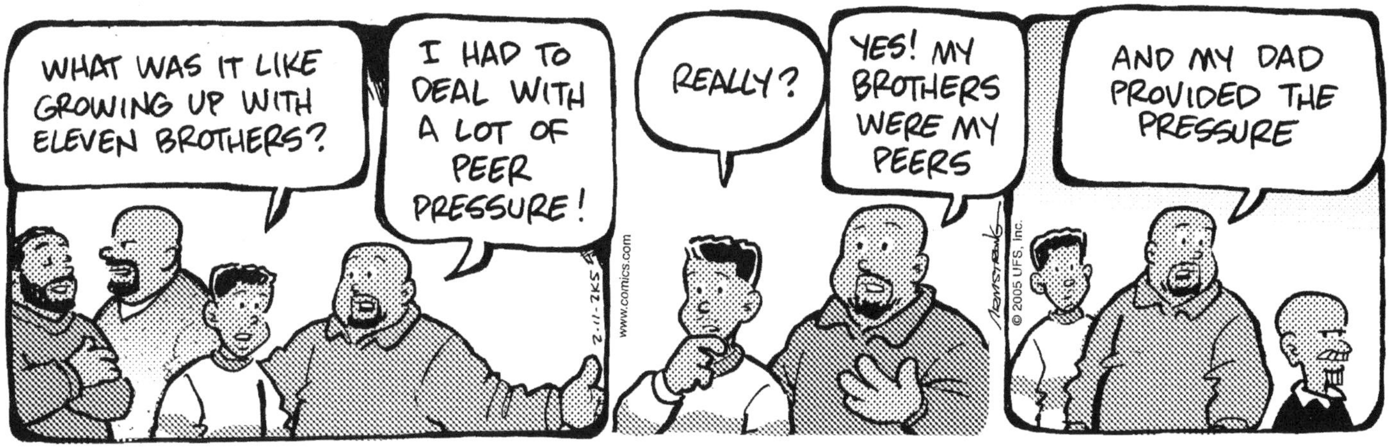
WHAT WAS IT LIKE GROWING UP WITH ELEVEN BROTHERS?
I HAD TO DEAL WITH A LOT OF PEER PRESSURE!
www.comics.com
REALLY?
YES! MY BROTHERS WERE MY PEERS
© 2005 UFS, Inc.
AND MY DAD PROVIDED THE PRESSURE

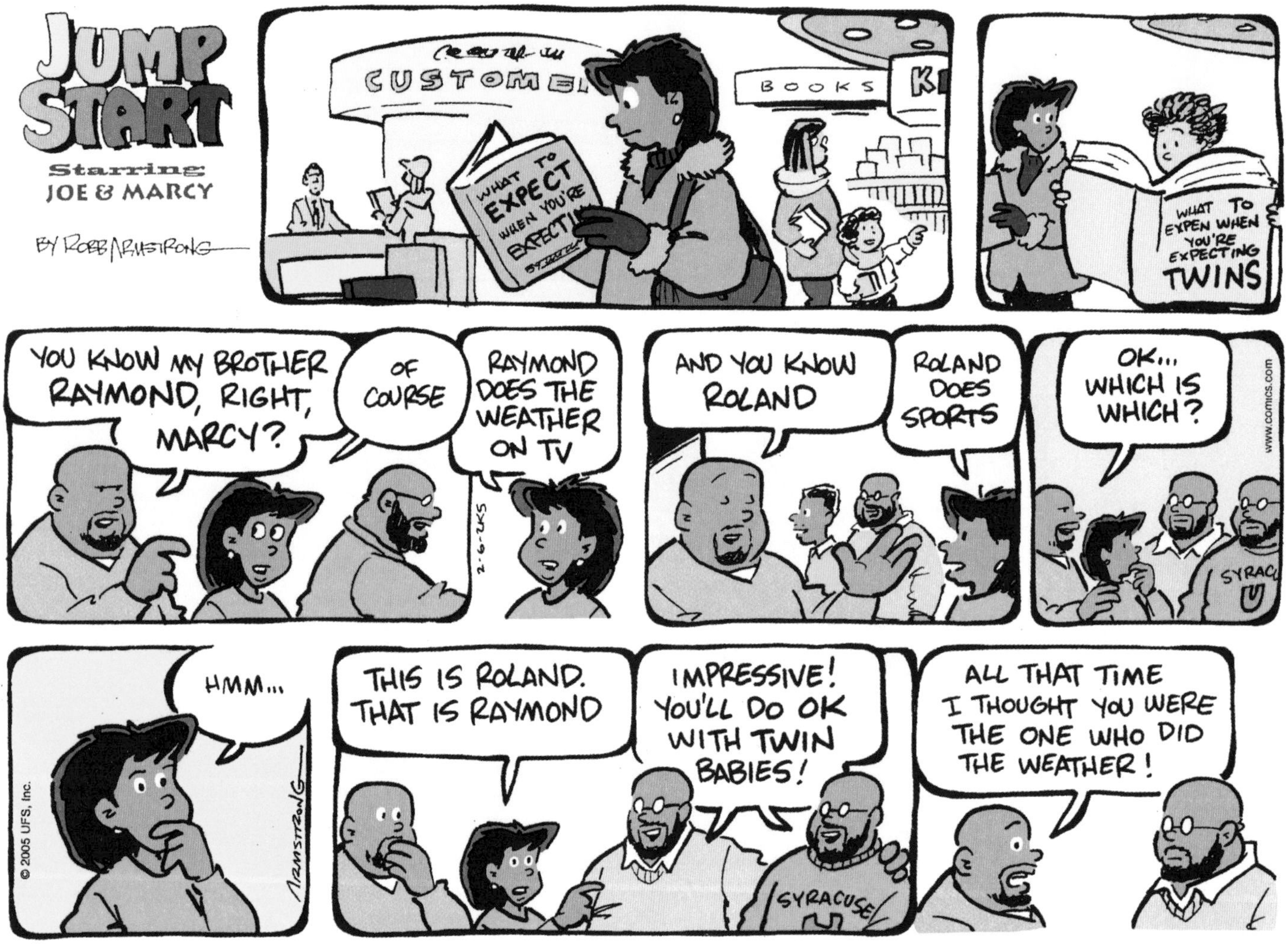
JUMP START
Starring: JOE & MARCY
BY ROBB ARMSTRONG
CUSTOME
BOOKS
WHAT TO EXPECT WHEN YOU'RE EXPECTIN
WHAT TO EXPEN WHEN YOU'RE EXPECTING TWINS
YOU KNOW MY BROTHER RAYMOND, RIGHT, MARCY?
OF COURSE
RAYMOND DOES THE WEATHER ON TV
AND YOU KNOW ROLAND
ROLAND DOES SPORTS
OK... WHICH IS WHICH?
www.comics.com
HMM...
© 2005 UFS, Inc.
THIS IS ROLAND. THAT IS RAYMOND
IMPRESSIVE! YOU'LL DO OK WITH TWIN BABIES!
SYRACUSE
ALL THAT TIME I THOUGHT YOU WERE THE ONE WHO DID THE WEATHER!

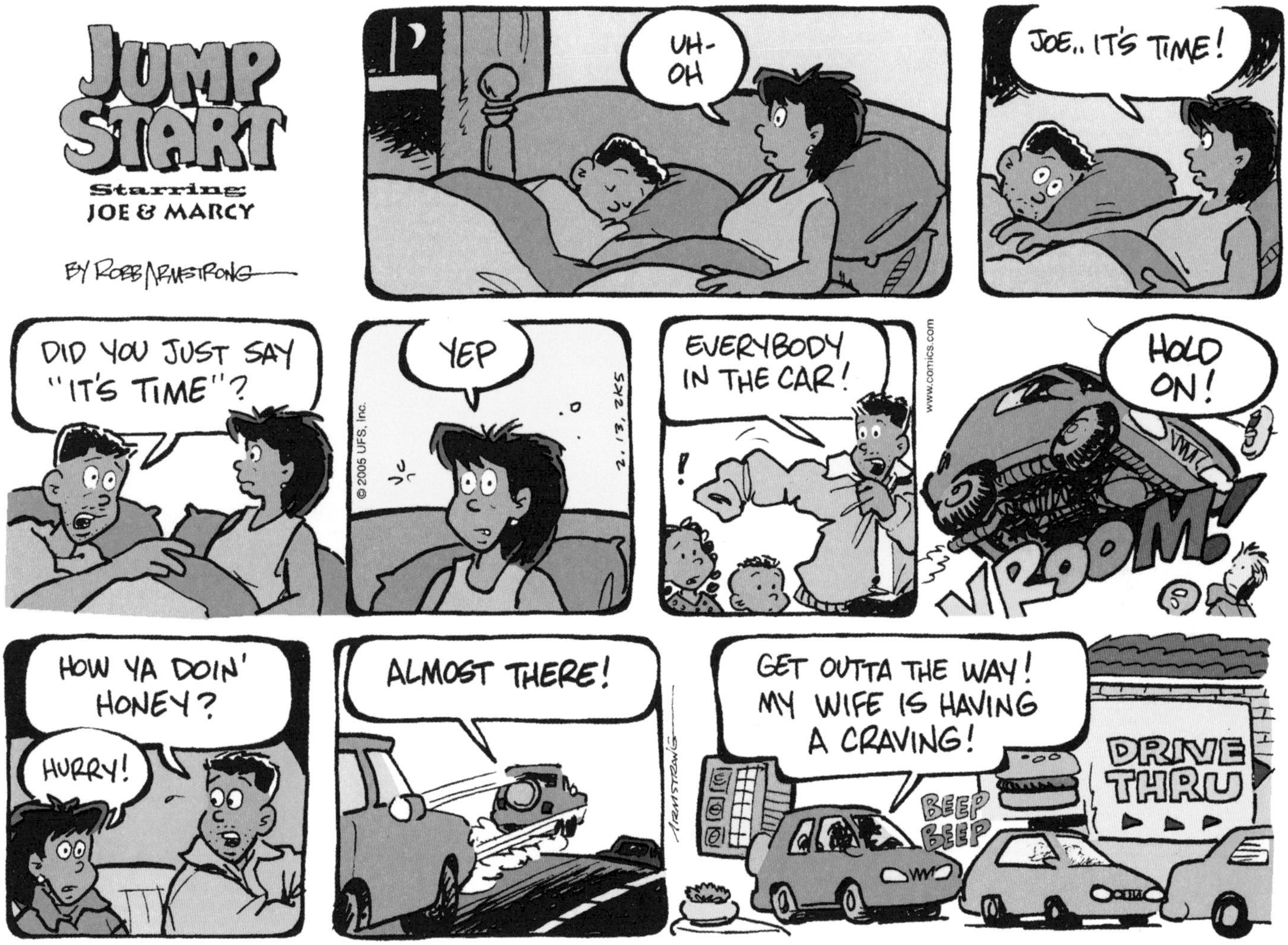
JUMP START
Starring JOE & MARCY
BY ROBB ARMSTRONG
UH-OH
JOE.. IT'S TIME!
DID YOU JUST SAY "IT'S TIME"?
YEP
© 2005 UFS, Inc.
2.13.2K5
EVERYBODY IN THE CAR!
www.comics.com
HOLD ON!
VROOM!
HOW YA DOIN' HONEY?
HURRY!
ALMOST THERE!
ARMSTRONG
GET OUTTA THE WAY! MY WIFE IS HAVING A CRAVING!
BEEP BEEP
DRIVE THRU

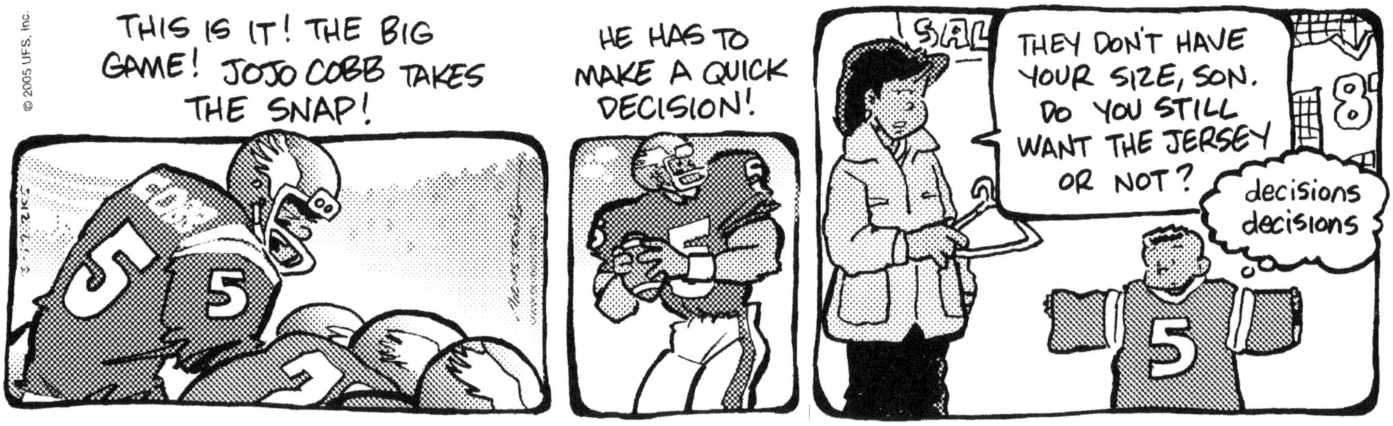
© 2005 UFS, Inc.
THIS IS IT! THE BIG GAME! JOJO COBB TAKES THE SNAP!
HE HAS TO MAKE A QUICK DECISION!
THEY DON'T HAVE YOUR SIZE, SON. DO YOU STILL WANT THE JERSEY OR NOT?
decisions decisions

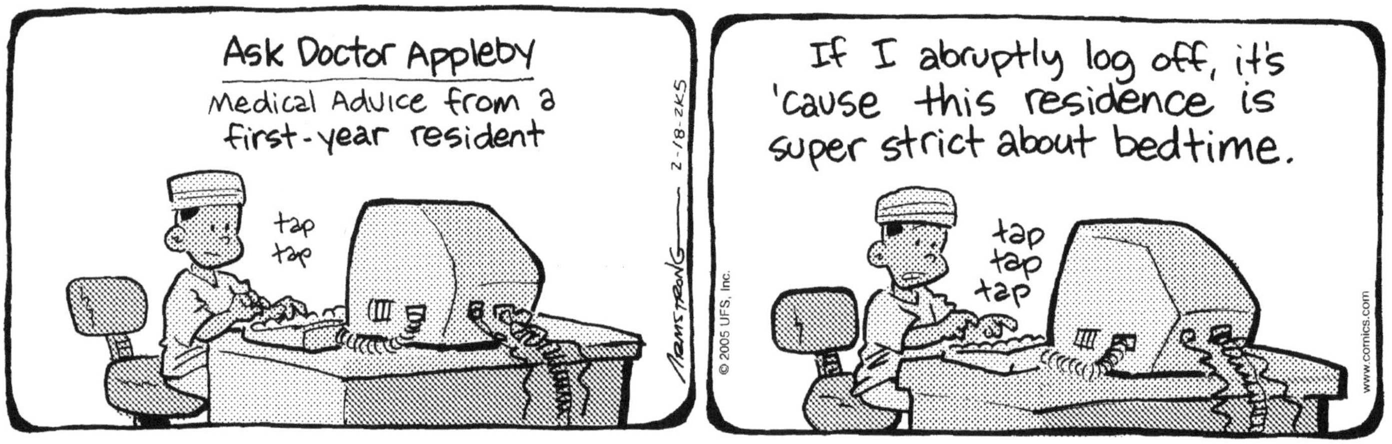
Ask Doctor Appleby
Medical Advice from a first-year resident
tap tap
2-18-2K5
ARMSTRONG
© 2005 UFS, Inc.
If I abruptly log off, it's 'cause this residence is super strict about bedtime.
tap tap tap
www.comics.com

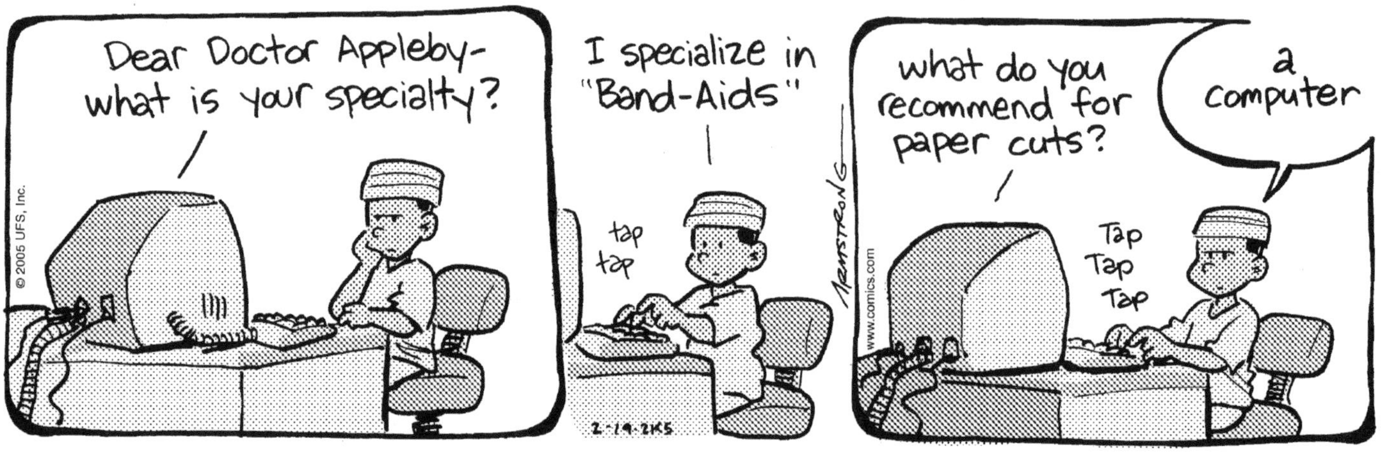
© 2005 UFS, Inc.
Dear Doctor Appleby- what is your specialty?
I specialize in "Band-Aids"
tap tap
2-19-2K5
ARMSTRONG
www.comics.com
what do you recommend for paper cuts?
a computer
Tap Tap Tap

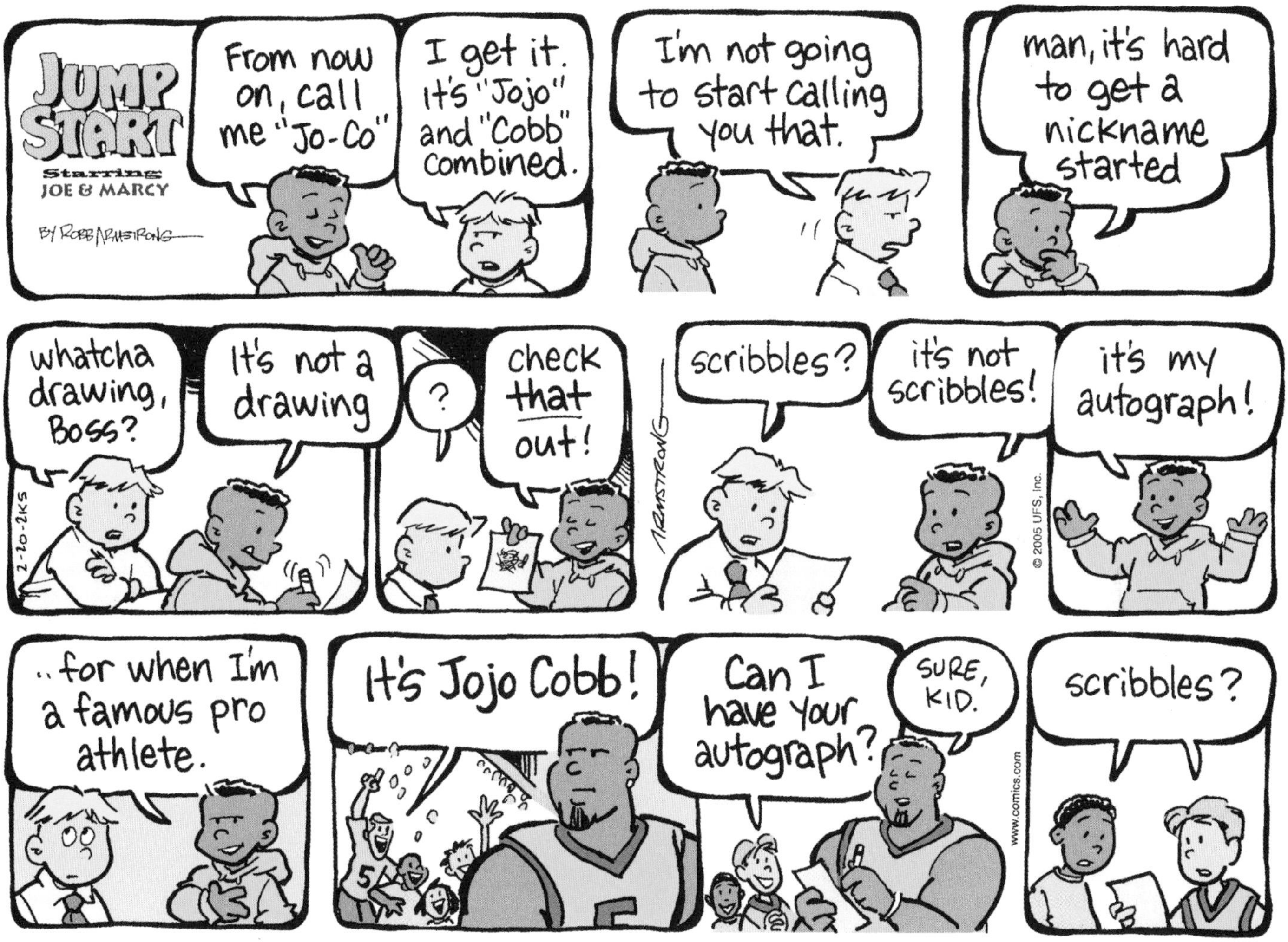
JUMP START
Starring JOE & MARCY
BY ROBB ARMSTRONG
From now on, call me "Jo-Co"
I get it. It's "Jojo" and "Cobb" combined.
I'm not going to start calling you that.
man, it's hard to get a nickname started
whatcha drawing, Boss?
It's not a drawing
?
check that out!
ARMSTRONG
2-20-2K5
scribbles?
it's not scribbles!
it's my autograph!
© 2005 UFS, Inc.
..for when I'm a famous pro athlete.
It's Jojo Cobb!
Can I have your autograph?
SURE, KID.
www.comics.com
scribbles?

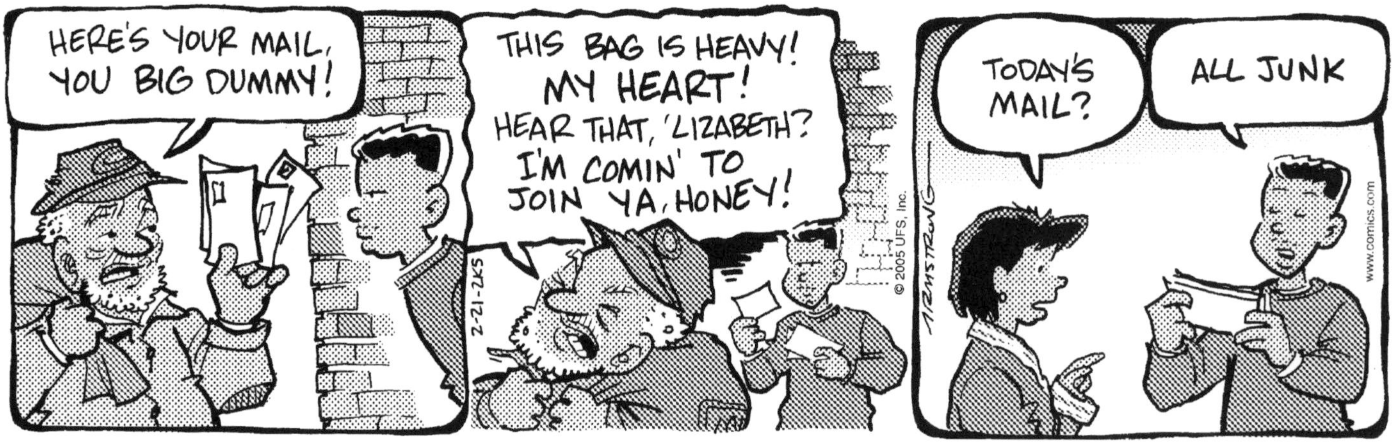
HERE'S YOUR MAIL, YOU BIG DUMMY!
THIS BAG IS HEAVY! MY HEART! HEAR THAT, 'LIZABETH? I'M COMIN' TO JOIN YA, HONEY!
2-21-2K5
© 2005 UFS, Inc.
ARMSTRONG
TODAY'S MAIL?
ALL JUNK
www.comics.com

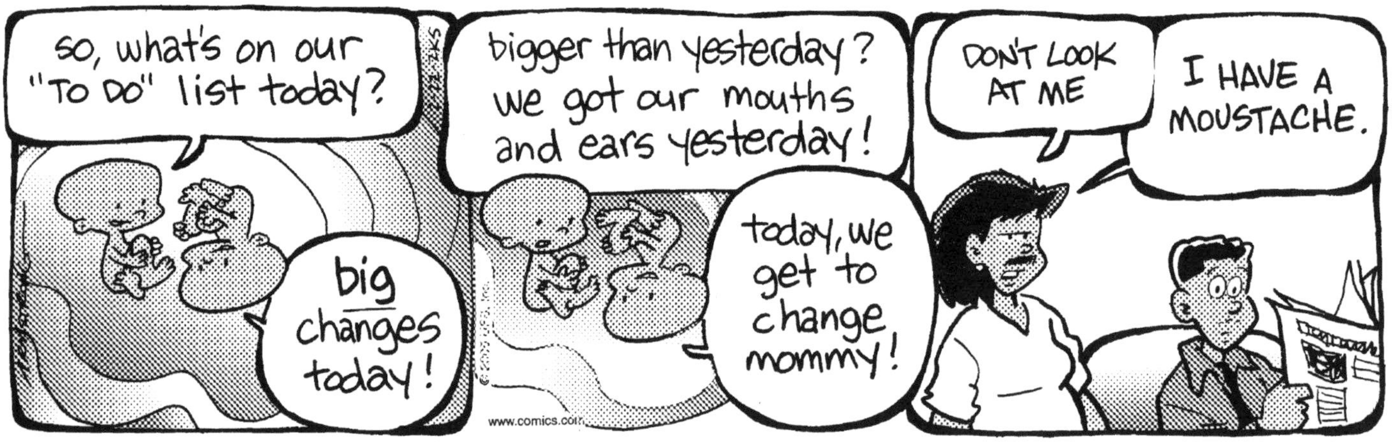
so, what's on our "TO DO" list today?
big changes today!
bigger than yesterday? we got our mouths and ears yesterday!
today, we get to change mommy!
www.comics.com
DON'T LOOK AT ME
I HAVE A MOUSTACHE.

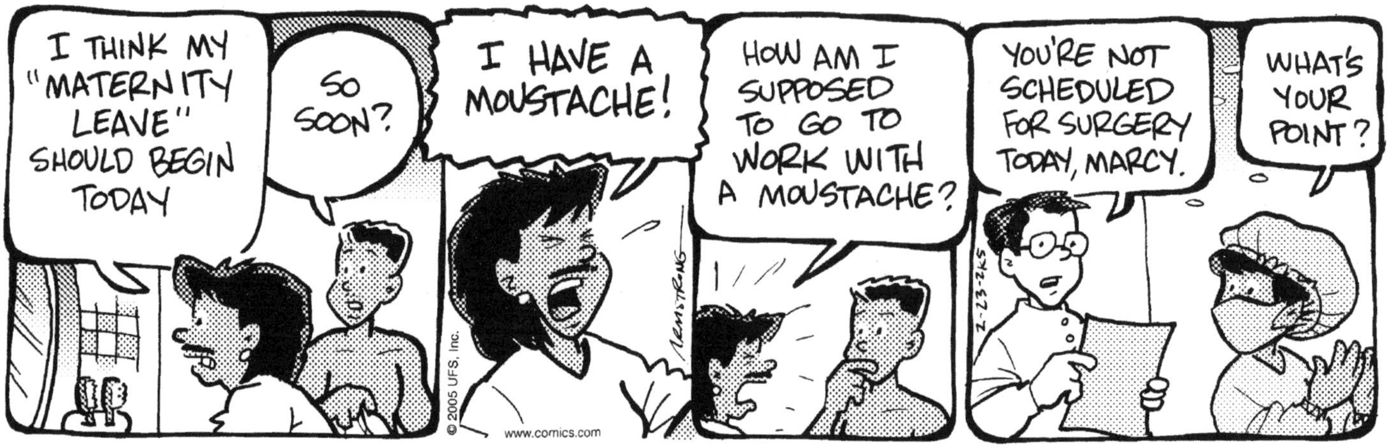
I THINK MY "MATERNITY LEAVE" SHOULD BEGIN TODAY
SO SOON?
I HAVE A MOUSTACHE!
© 2005 UFS, Inc.
www.comics.com
ARMSTRONG
HOW AM I SUPPOSED TO GO TO WORK WITH A MOUSTACHE?
YOU'RE NOT SCHEDULED FOR SURGERY TODAY, MARCY.
2-23-2K5
WHAT'S YOUR POINT?

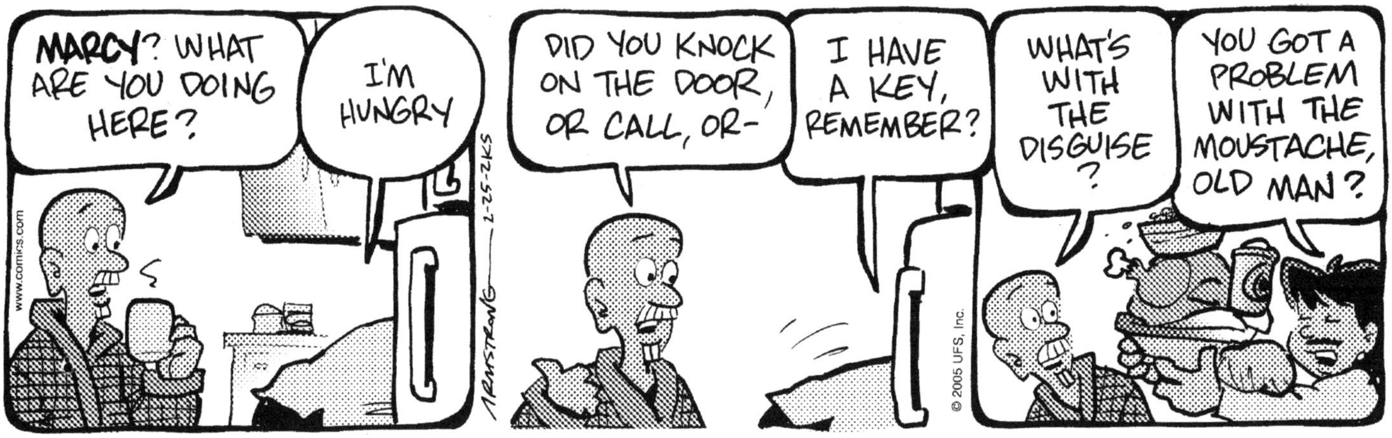
MARCY? WHAT ARE YOU DOING HERE?
I'M HUNGRY
DID YOU KNOCK ON THE DOOR, OR CALL, OR-
I HAVE A KEY, REMEMBER?
WHAT'S WITH THE DISGUISE?
YOU GOT A PROBLEM WITH THE MOUSTACHE, OLD MAN?
www.comics.com
ARMSTRONG
2-25-2KS
© 2005 UFS, Inc.

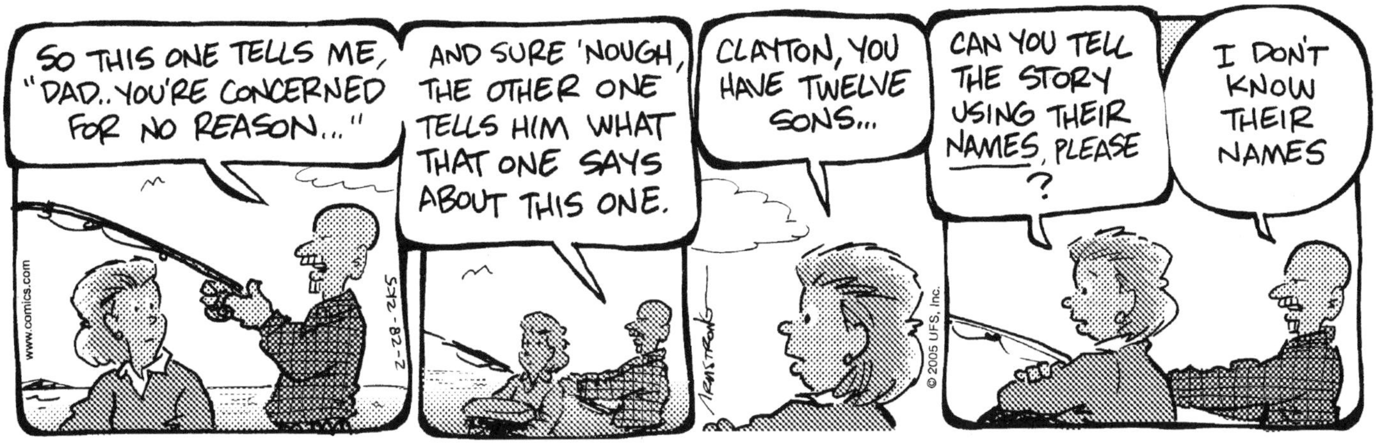
SO THIS ONE TELLS ME, "DAD.. YOU'RE CONCERNED FOR NO REASON..."
AND SURE 'NOUGH, THE OTHER ONE TELLS HIM WHAT THAT ONE SAYS ABOUT THIS ONE.
CLAYTON, YOU HAVE TWELVE SONS...
CAN YOU TELL THE STORY USING THEIR NAMES, PLEASE?
I DON'T KNOW THEIR NAMES
www.comics.com
2-28-2KS
ARMSTRONG
© 2005 UFS, Inc.

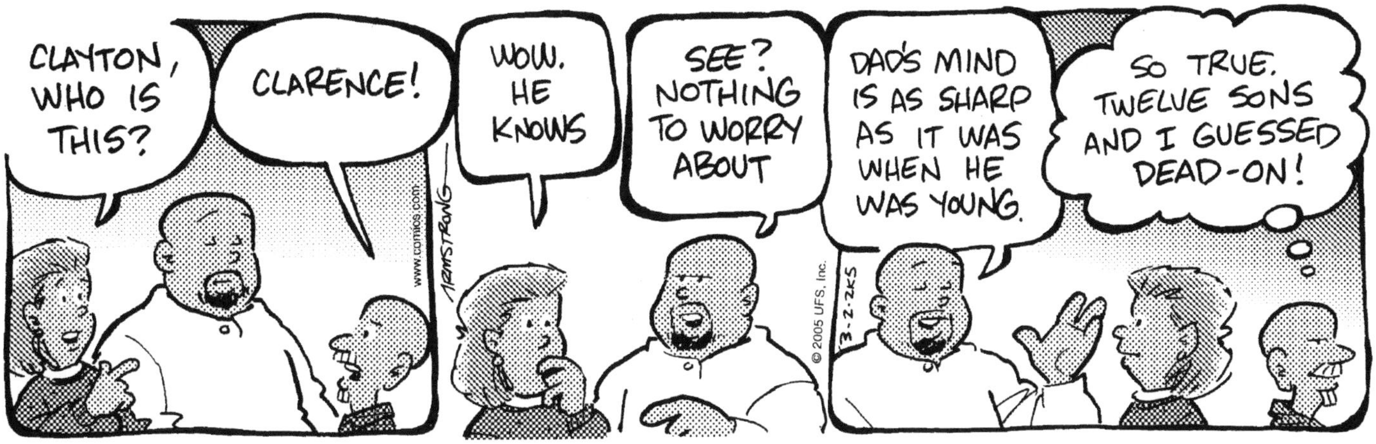
CLAYTON, WHO IS THIS?
CLARENCE!
WOW. HE KNOWS
SEE? NOTHING TO WORRY ABOUT
DAD'S MIND IS AS SHARP AS IT WAS WHEN HE WAS YOUNG.
SO TRUE. TWELVE SONS AND I GUESSED DEAD-ON!
www.comics.com
ARMSTRONG
© 2005 UFS, Inc.
3-2-2KS

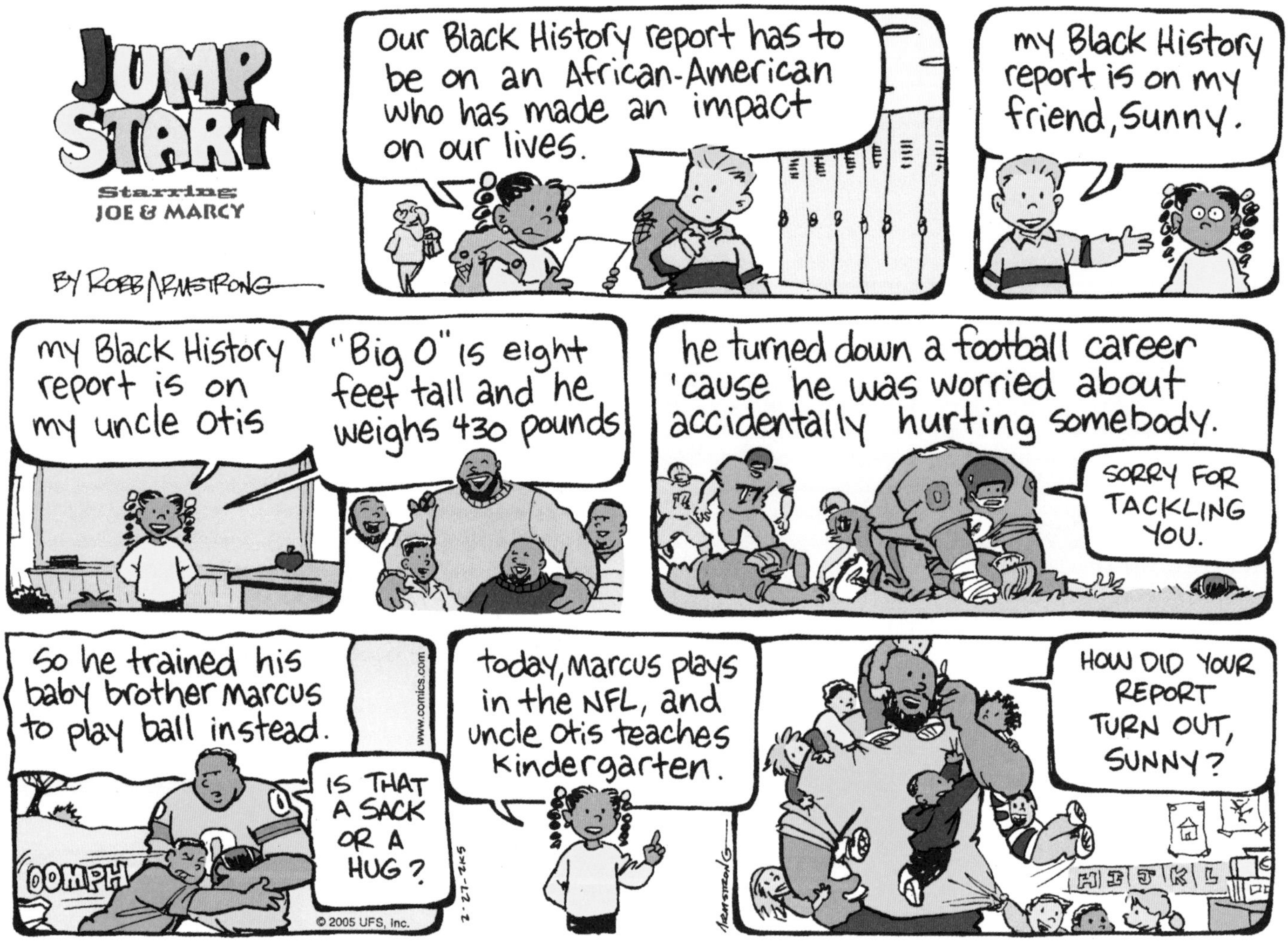
JUMP START
Starring JOE & MARCY
BY ROBB ARMSTRONG
Our Black History report has to be on an African-American who has made an impact on our lives.
my Black History report is on my friend, Sunny.
my Black History report is on my uncle Otis
"Big O" is eight feet tall and he weighs 430 pounds
he turned down a football career 'cause he was worried about accidentally hurting somebody.
SORRY FOR TACKLING YOU.
So he trained his baby brother Marcus to play ball instead.
OOMPH
IS THAT A SACK OR A HUG?
www.comics.com
© 2005 UFS, Inc.
today, Marcus plays in the NFL, and uncle Otis teaches Kindergarten.
HOW DID YOUR REPORT TURN OUT, SUNNY?

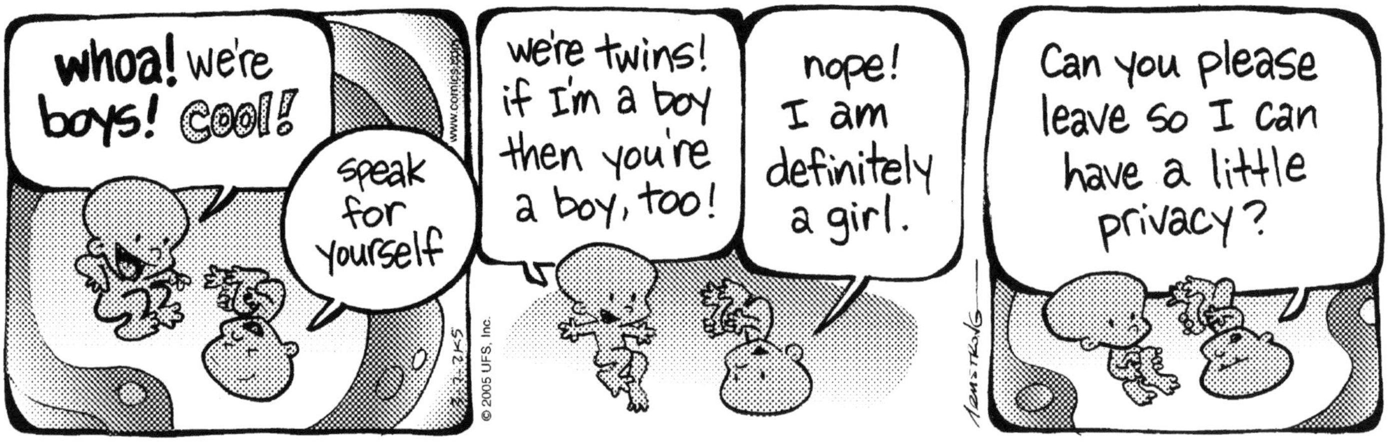
whoa! we're boys! COOL!
speak for yourself
www.comics.com
3-7-2K5
© 2005 UFS, Inc.
we're twins! if I'm a boy then you're a boy, too!
nope! I am definitely a girl.
ARMSTRONG
Can you please leave so I can have a little privacy?

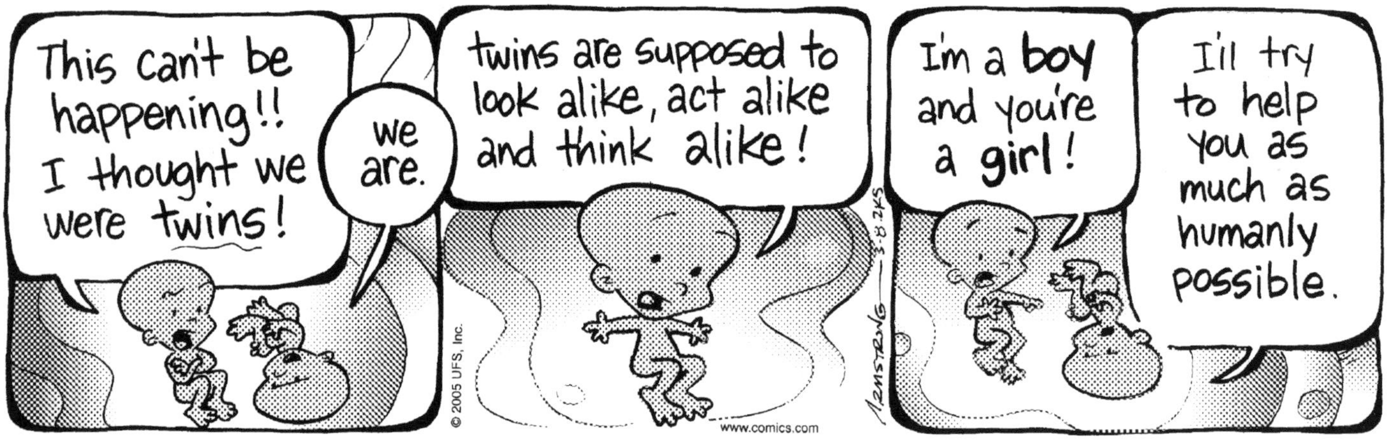
This can't be happening!! I thought we were twins!
we are.
© 2005 UFS, Inc.
twins are supposed to look alike, act alike and think alike!
www.comics.com
3-8-2K5
ARMSTRONG
I'm a boy and you're a girl!
I'll try to help you as much as humanly possible.

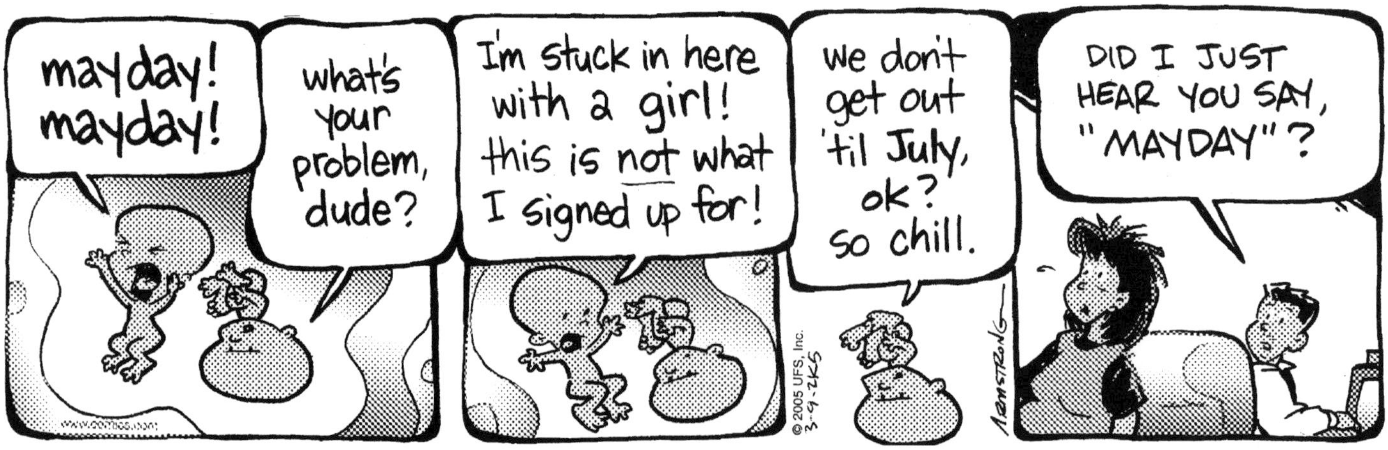
mayday! mayday!
what's your problem, dude?
I'm stuck in here with a girl! this is not what I signed up for!
© 2005 UFS, Inc.
3-9-2K5
we don't get out 'til July, ok? so chill.
ARMSTRONG
DID I JUST HEAR YOU SAY, "MAYDAY"?

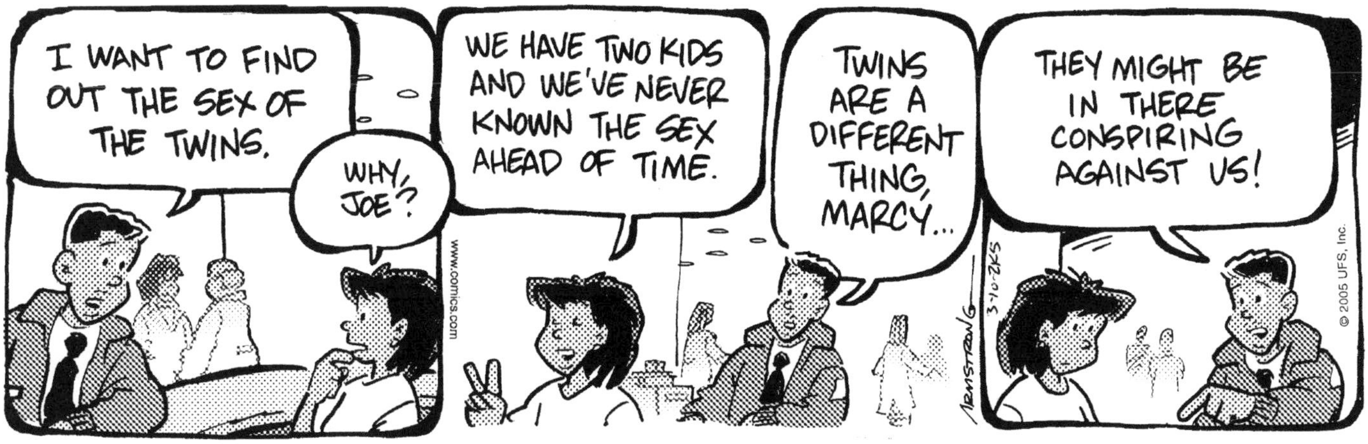
I WANT TO FIND OUT THE SEX OF THE TWINS.
WHY, JOE?
WE HAVE TWO KIDS AND WE'VE NEVER KNOWN THE SEX AHEAD OF TIME.
TWINS ARE A DIFFERENT THING, MARCY...
THEY MIGHT BE IN THERE CONSPIRING AGAINST US!
www.comics.com
© 2005 UFS, Inc.

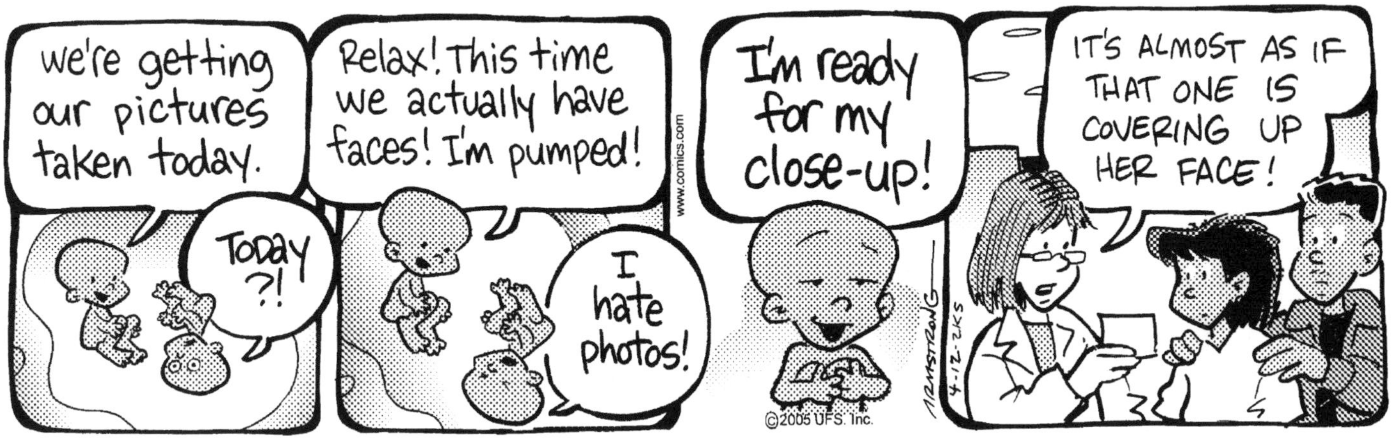
we're getting our pictures taken today.
TODAY?!
Relax! This time we actually have faces! I'm pumped!
I hate photos!
www.comics.com
I'm ready for my close-up!
©2005 UFS, Inc.
IT'S ALMOST AS IF THAT ONE IS COVERING UP HER FACE!

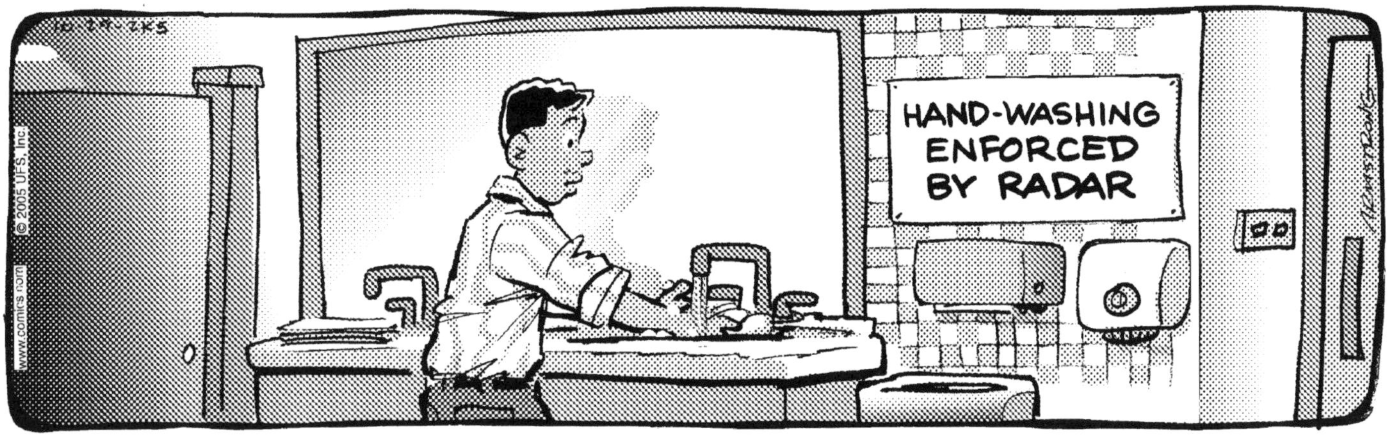
HAND-WASHING ENFORCED BY RADAR
www.comics.com
© 2005 UFS, Inc.

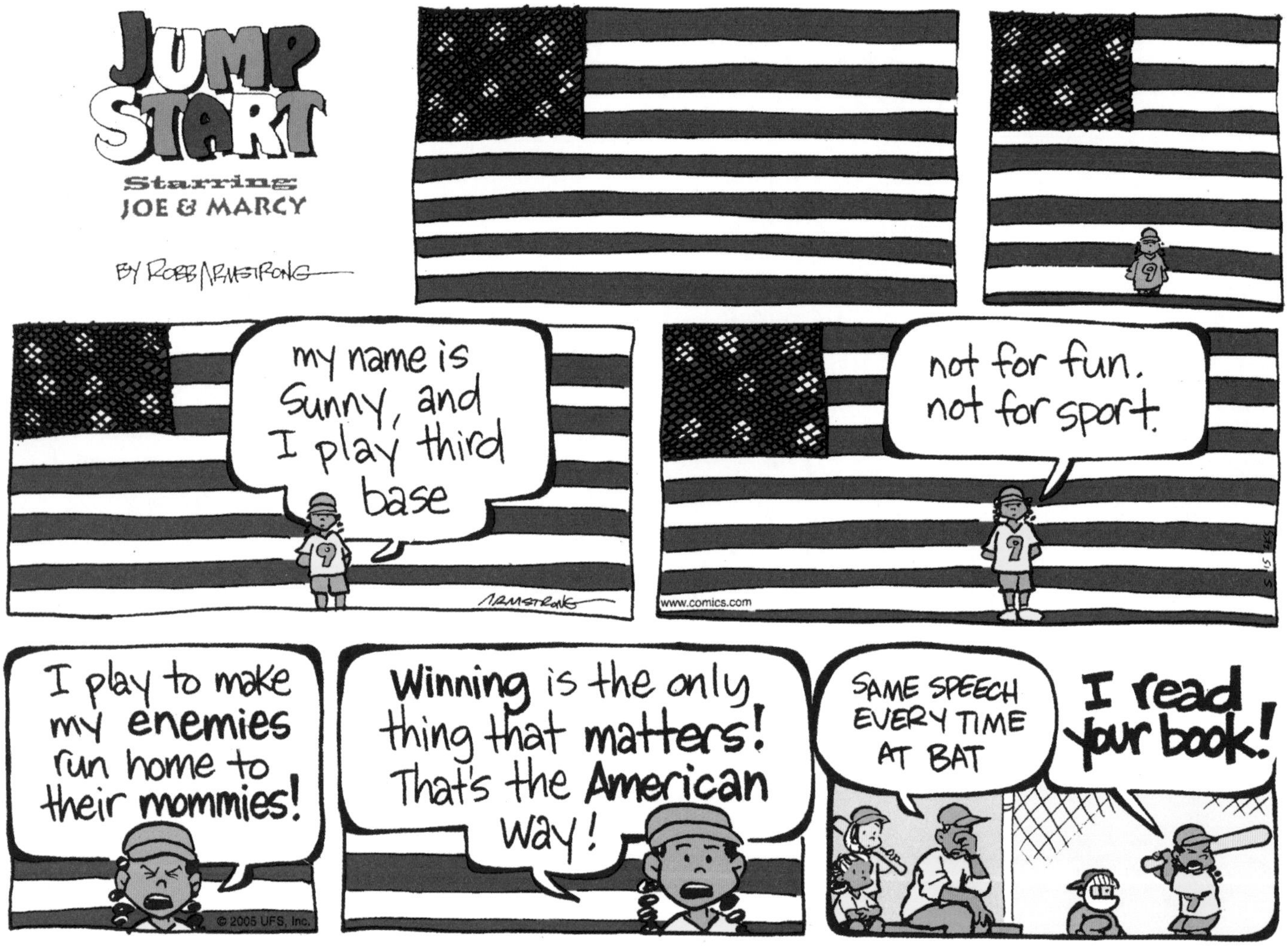
JUMP START
Starring JOE & MARCY
BY ROBB ARMSTRONG
my name is Sunny, and I play third base
ARMSTRONG
not for fun. not for sport.
www.comics.com
I play to make my enemies run home to their mommies!
© 2005 UFS, Inc.
Winning is the only thing that matters! That's the American way!
SAME SPEECH EVERY TIME AT BAT
I read your book!

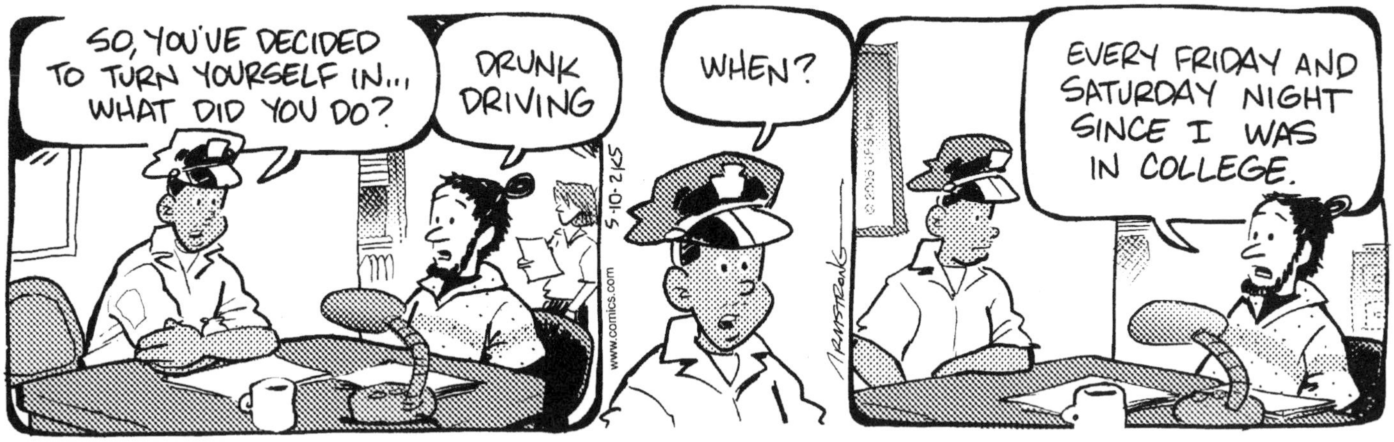
SO, YOU'VE DECIDED TO TURN YOURSELF IN... WHAT DID YOU DO?
DRUNK DRIVING
5-10-2K5
www.comics.com
WHEN?
ARMSTRONG
EVERY FRIDAY AND SATURDAY NIGHT SINCE I WAS IN COLLEGE.

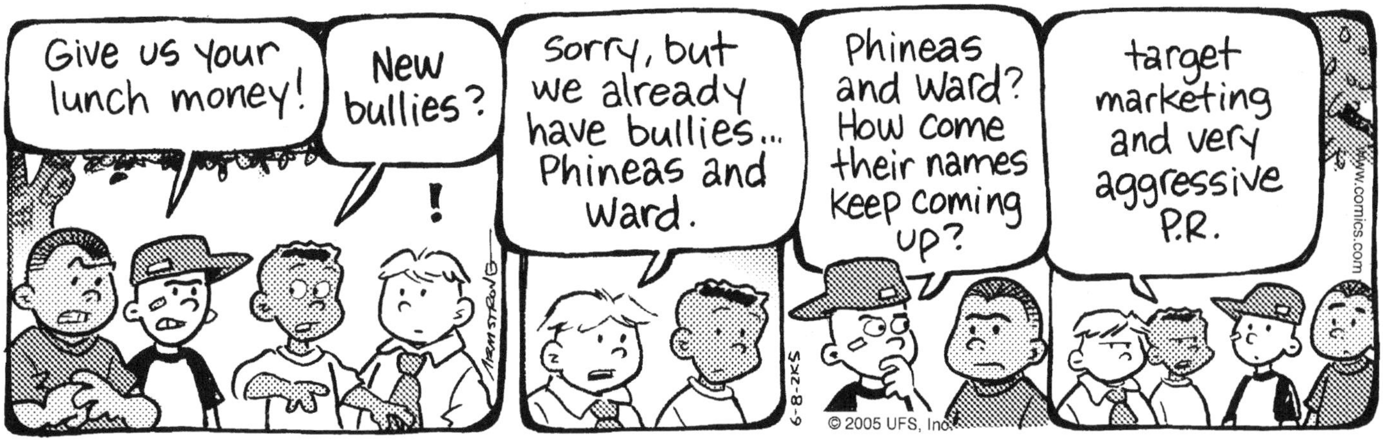
Give us your lunch money!
New bullies?
!
ARMSTRONG
Sorry, but we already have bullies... Phineas and Ward.
6-8-2K5
Phineas and Ward? How come their names keep coming up?
© 2005 UFS, Inc.
target marketing and very aggressive P.R.
www.comics.com

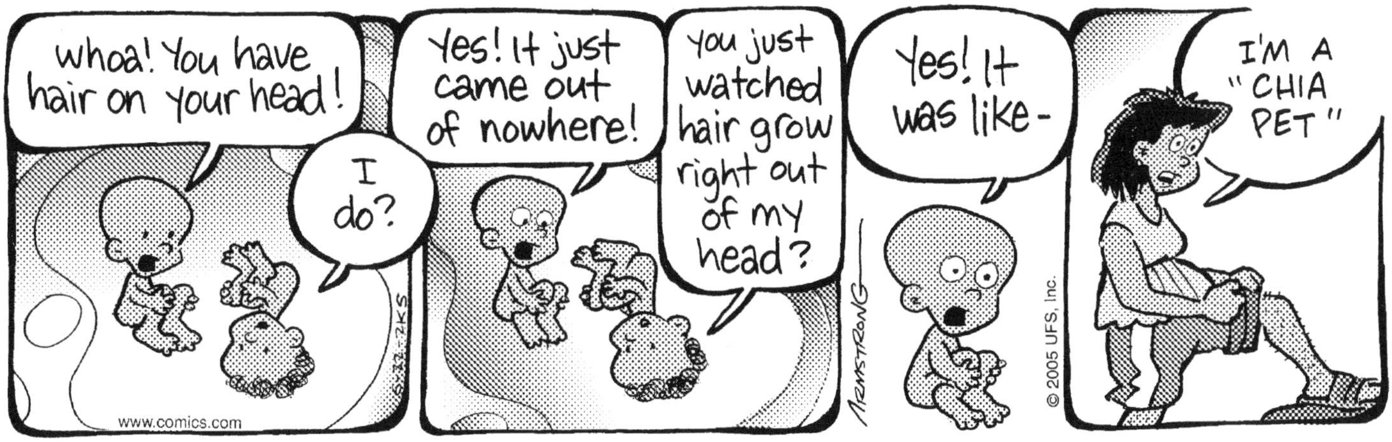
whoa! You have hair on your head!
I do?
www.comics.com
Yes! It just came out of nowhere!
You just watched hair grow right out of my head?
ARMSTRONG
Yes! It was like-
© 2005 UFS, Inc.
I'M A "CHIA PET"

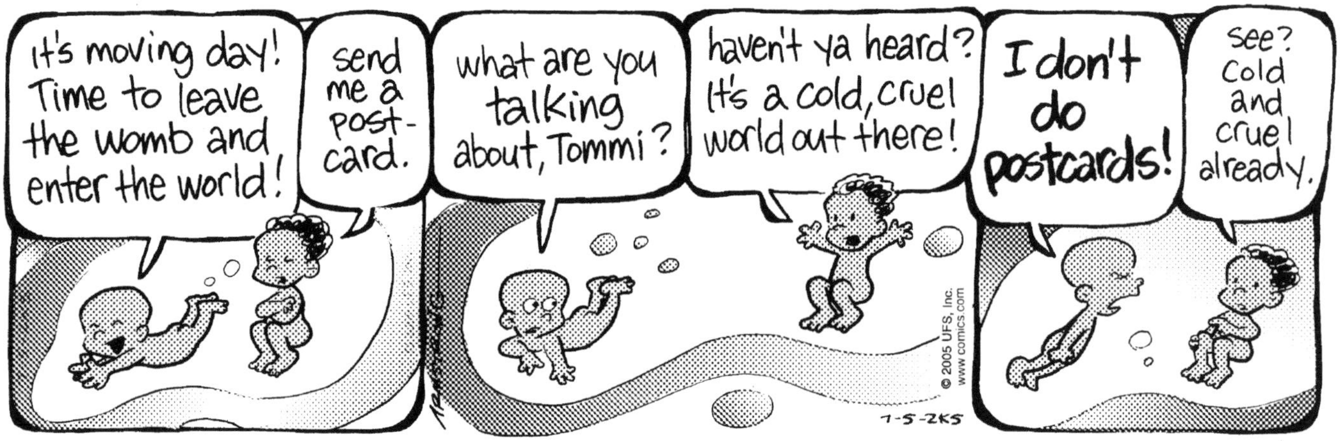
it's moving day! Time to leave the womb and enter the world!
send me a post-card.
what are you talking about, Tommi?
haven't ya heard? It's a cold, cruel world out there!
© 2005 UFS, Inc. www.comics.com
I don't do postcards!
see? Cold and cruel already.
7-5-2K5

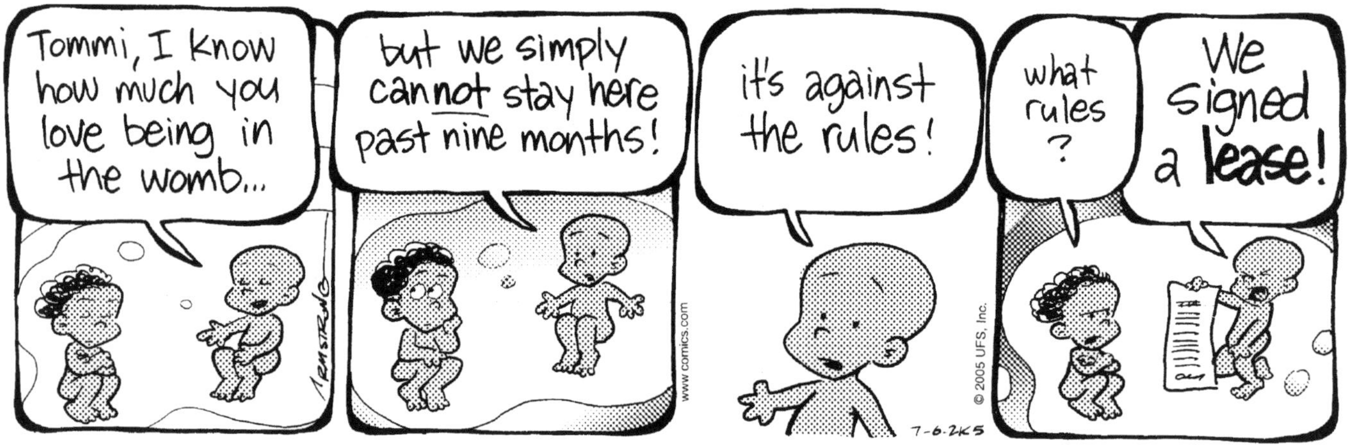
Tommi, I know how much you love being in the womb...
but we simply cannot stay here past nine months!
www.comics.com
it's against the rules!
© 2005 UFS, Inc.
what rules?
We signed a lease!
7-6-2K5

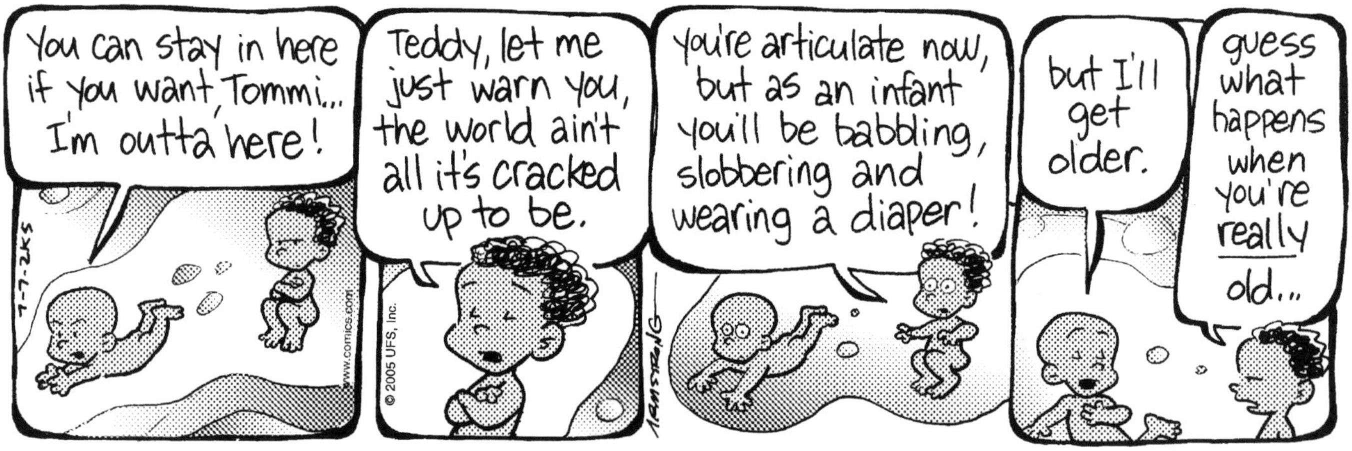
You can stay in here if you want, Tommi... I'm outta here!
7-7-2K5
www.comics.com
Teddy, let me just warn you, the world ain't all it's cracked up to be.
© 2005 UFS, Inc.
you're articulate now, but as an infant you'll be babbling, slobbering and wearing a diaper!
but I'll get older.
guess what happens when you're really old...

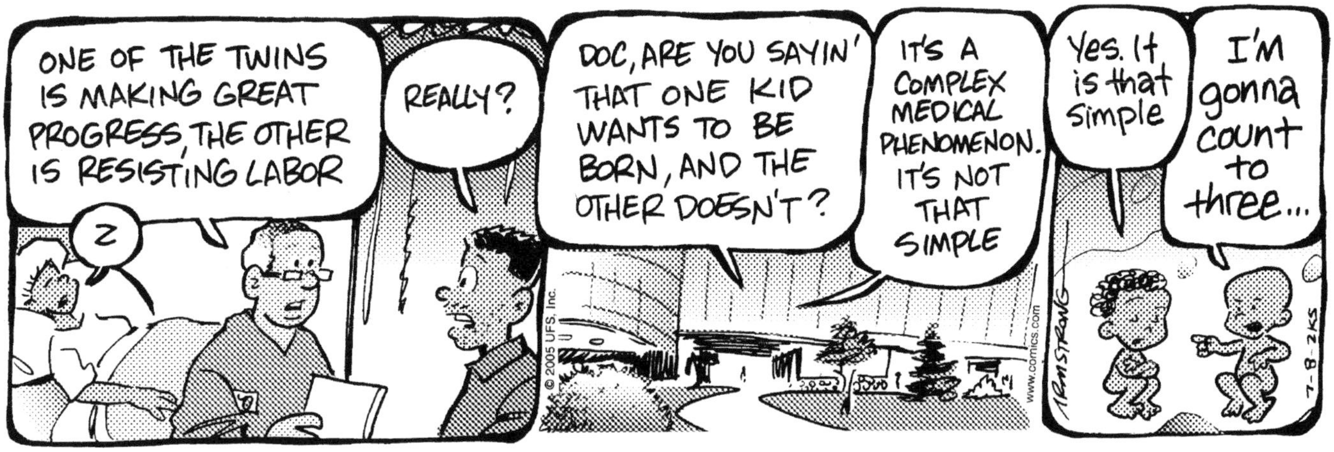
ONE OF THE TWINS IS MAKING GREAT PROGRESS, THE OTHER IS RESISTING LABOR
Z
REALLY?
DOC, ARE YOU SAYIN' THAT ONE KID WANTS TO BE BORN, AND THE OTHER DOESN'T?
IT'S A COMPLEX MEDICAL PHENOMENON. IT'S NOT THAT SIMPLE
Yes. It is that simple
I'M gonna count to three...
© 2005 UFS, Inc.
www.comics.com
ARMSTRONG
7-8-2KS

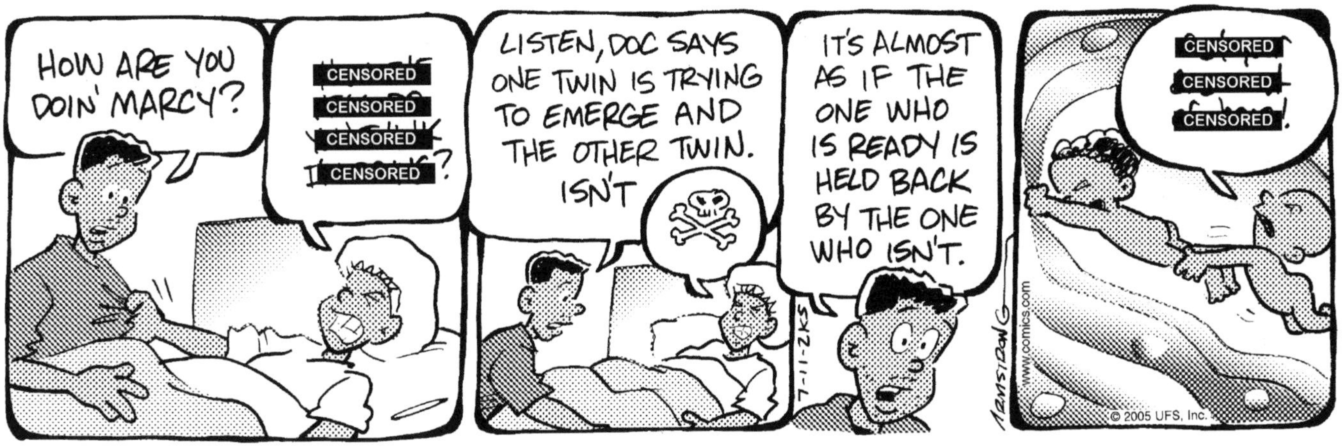
HOW ARE YOU DOIN' MARCY?
CENSORED
CENSORED
CENSORED
CENSORED?
LISTEN, DOC SAYS ONE TWIN IS TRYING TO EMERGE AND THE OTHER TWIN. ISN'T
IT'S ALMOST AS IF THE ONE WHO IS READY IS HELD BACK BY THE ONE WHO ISN'T.
7-11-2KS
ARMSTRONG
www.comics.com
CENSORED
CENSORED
CENSORED.
© 2005 UFS, Inc.

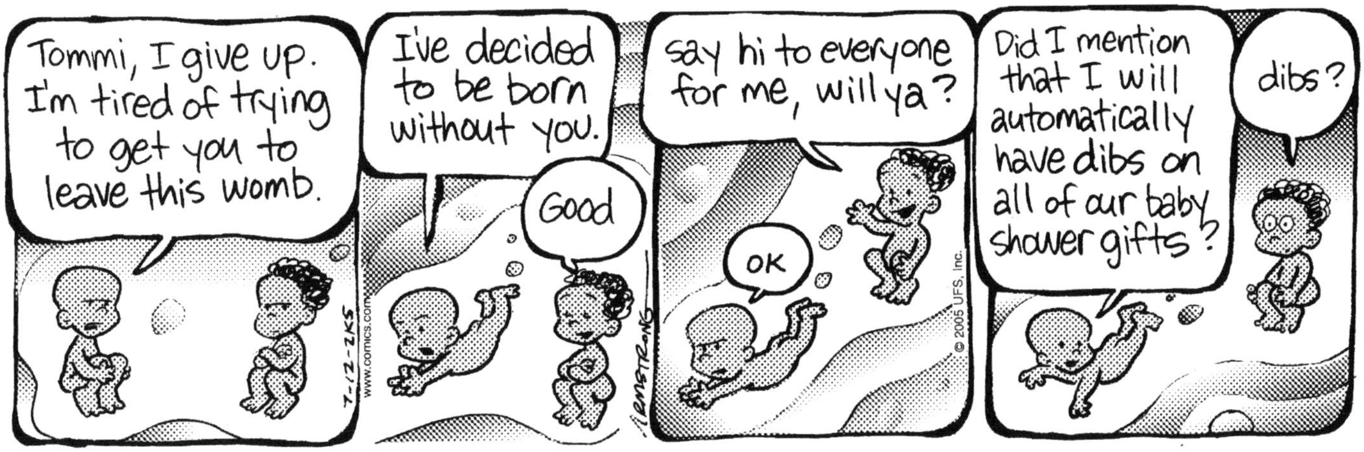
Tommi, I give up. I'm tired of trying to get you to leave this womb.
7-12-2KS
www.comics.com
I've decided to be born without you.
Good
ARMSTRONG
say hi to everyone for me, will ya?
OK
© 2005 UFS, Inc.
Did I mention that I will automatically have dibs on all of our baby shower gifts?
dibs?

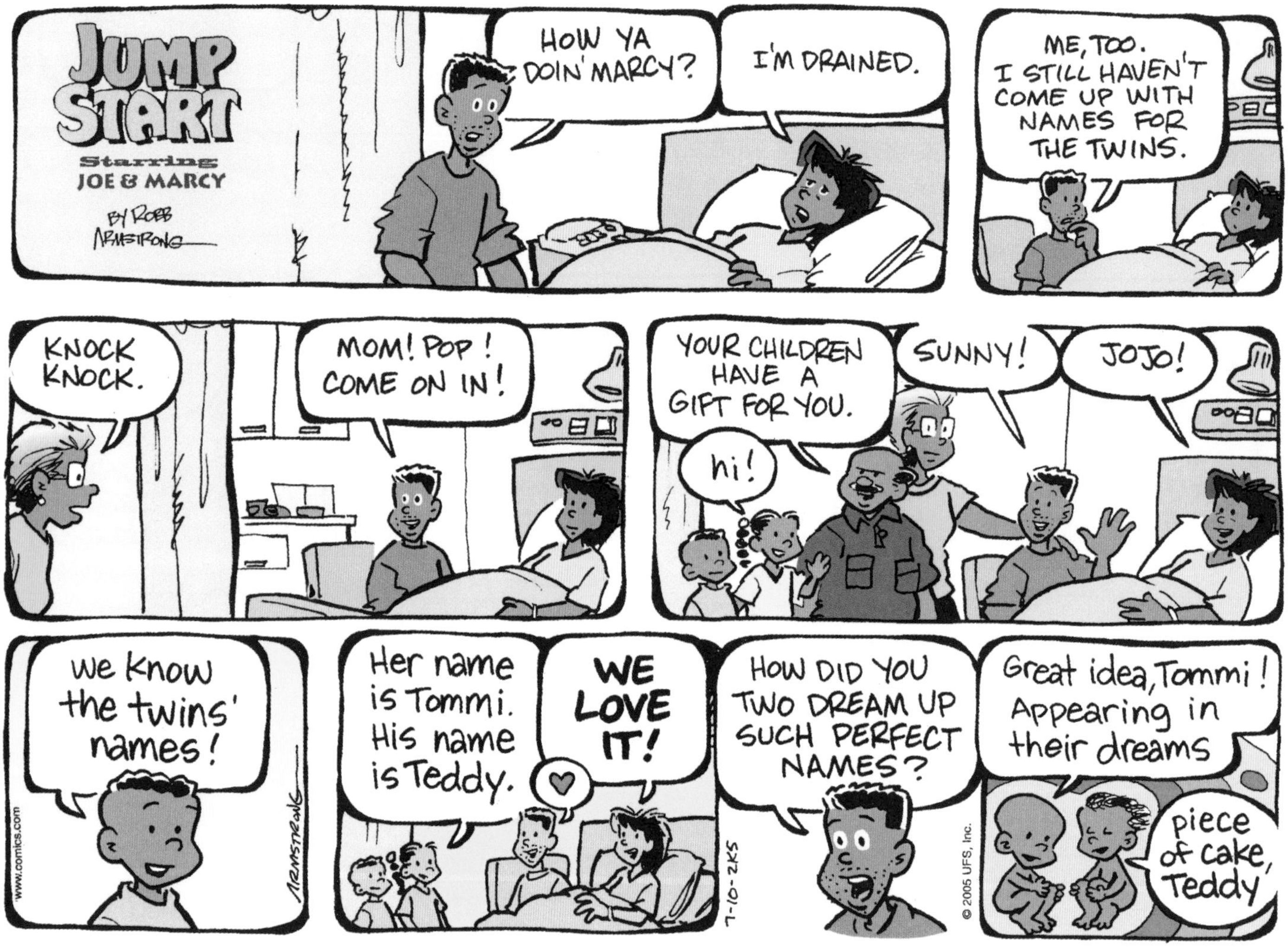
JUMP START
Starring
JOE & MARCY
BY ROBB ARMSTRONG
HOW YA DOIN' MARCY?
I'M DRAINED.
ME, TOO. I STILL HAVEN'T COME UP WITH NAMES FOR THE TWINS.
KNOCK KNOCK.
MOM! POP! COME ON IN!
YOUR CHILDREN HAVE A GIFT FOR YOU.
SUNNY!
JOJO!
hi!
we know the twins' names!
Her name is Tommi. His name is Teddy.
WE LOVE IT!
HOW DID YOU TWO DREAM UP SUCH PERFECT NAMES?
Great idea, Tommi! Appearing in their dreams
piece of cake, Teddy
www.comics.com
ARMSTRONG
7-10-2K5
© 2005 UFS, Inc.

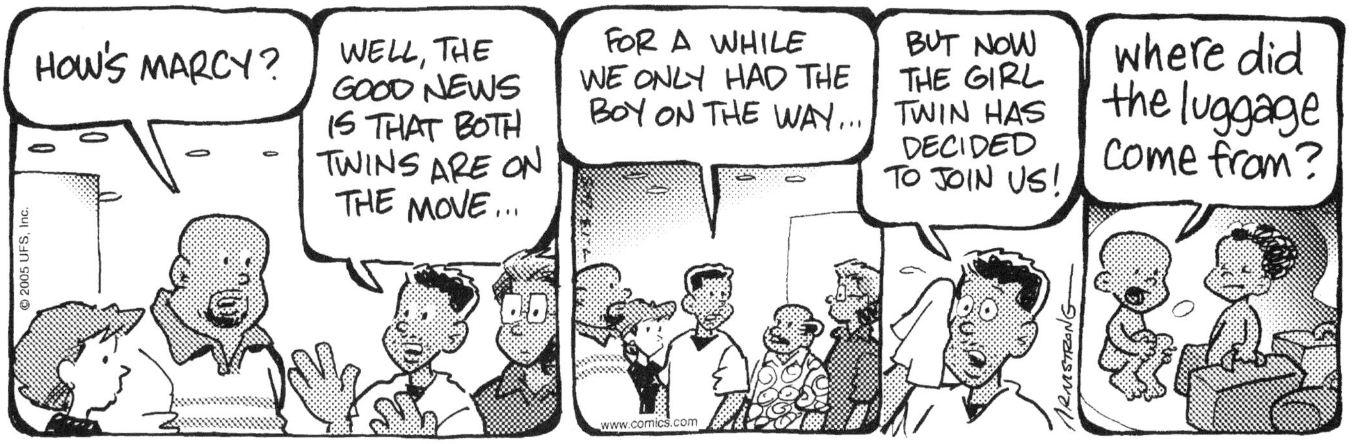
HOW'S MARCY?
WELL, THE GOOD NEWS IS THAT BOTH TWINS ARE ON THE MOVE...
FOR A WHILE WE ONLY HAD THE BOY ON THE WAY...
BUT NOW THE GIRL TWIN HAS DECIDED TO JOIN US!
where did the luggage come from?
© 2005 UFS, Inc.
www.comics.com

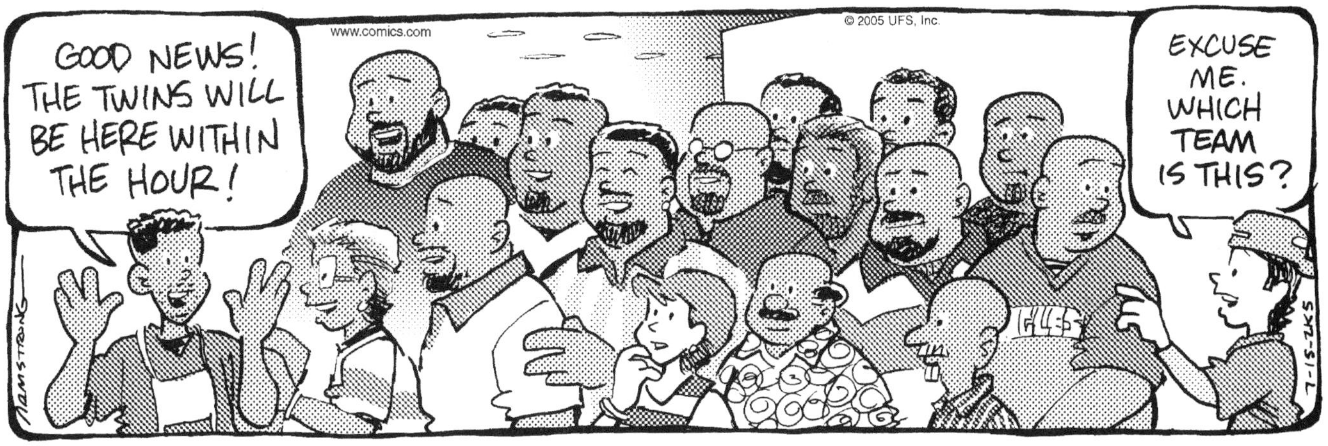
GOOD NEWS! THE TWINS WILL BE HERE WITHIN THE HOUR!
EXCUSE ME. WHICH TEAM IS THIS?
www.comics.com
© 2005 UFS, Inc.
7-15-2K5

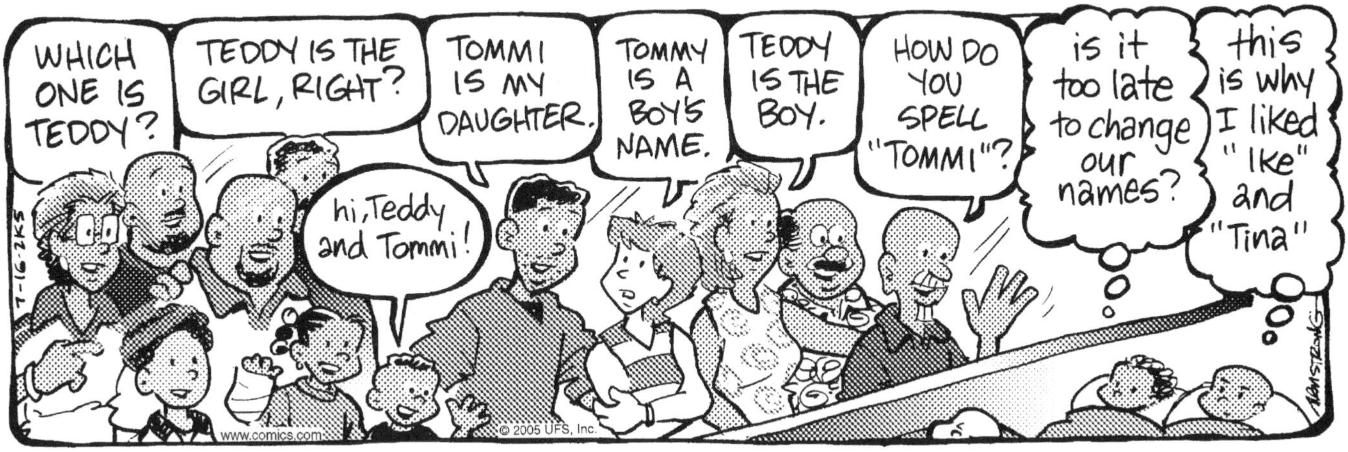
WHICH ONE IS TEDDY?
TEDDY IS THE GIRL, RIGHT?
TOMMI IS MY DAUGHTER.
TOMMY IS A BOY'S NAME.
TEDDY IS THE BOY.
HOW DO YOU SPELL "TOMMI"?
hi, Teddy and Tommi!
is it too late to change our names?
this is why I liked "Ike" and "Tina"
7-16-2K5
www.comics.com
© 2005 UFS, Inc.

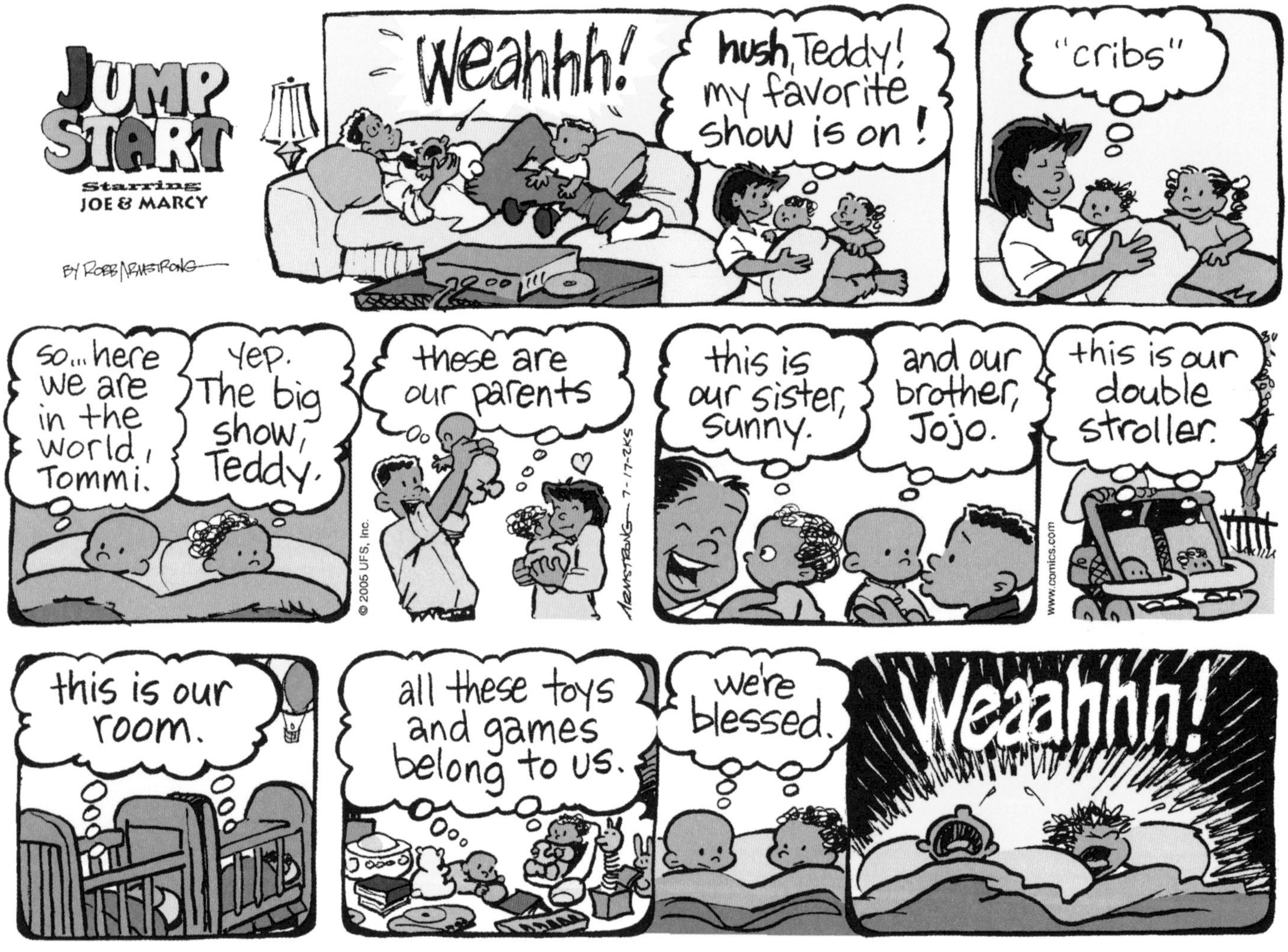
JUMP START
Starring JOE & MARCY
BY ROBB ARMSTRONG
Weahhh!
hush, Teddy! my favorite show is on!
"cribs"
so... here we are in the world, Tommi.
yep. The big show, Teddy.
these are our parents
© 2005 UFS, Inc.
this is our sister, Sunny.
and our brother, Jojo.
this is our double stroller.
www.comics.com
this is our room.
all these toys and games belong to us.
we're blessed.
Weaahhh!

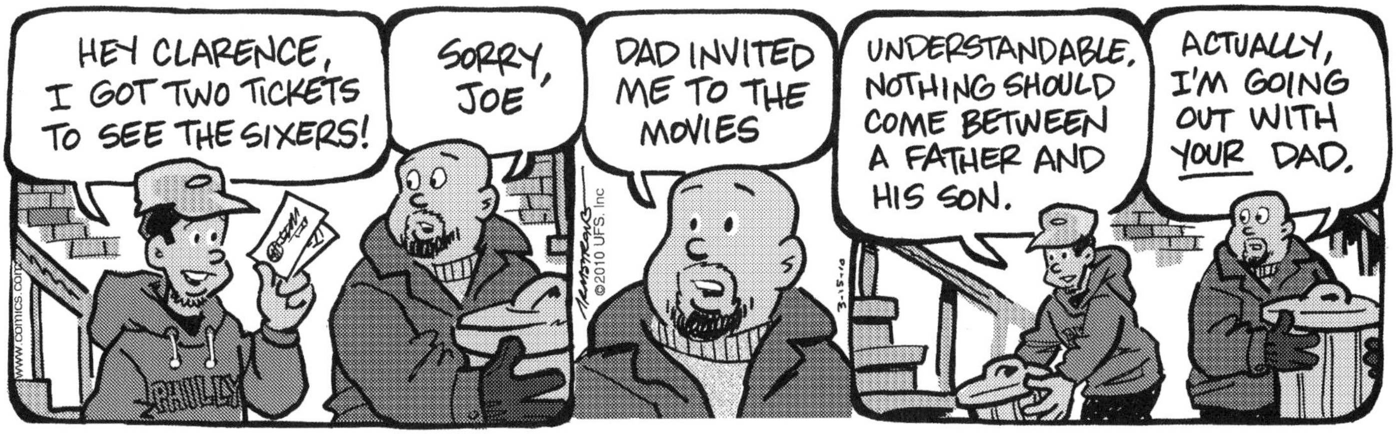
HEY CLARENCE, I GOT TWO TICKETS TO SEE THE SIXERS!
SORRY, JOE
DAD INVITED ME TO THE MOVIES
UNDERSTANDABLE. NOTHING SHOULD COME BETWEEN A FATHER AND HIS SON.
ACTUALLY, I'M GOING OUT WITH YOUR DAD.
PHILLY
www.comics.com
©2010 UFS, Inc
3-15-10

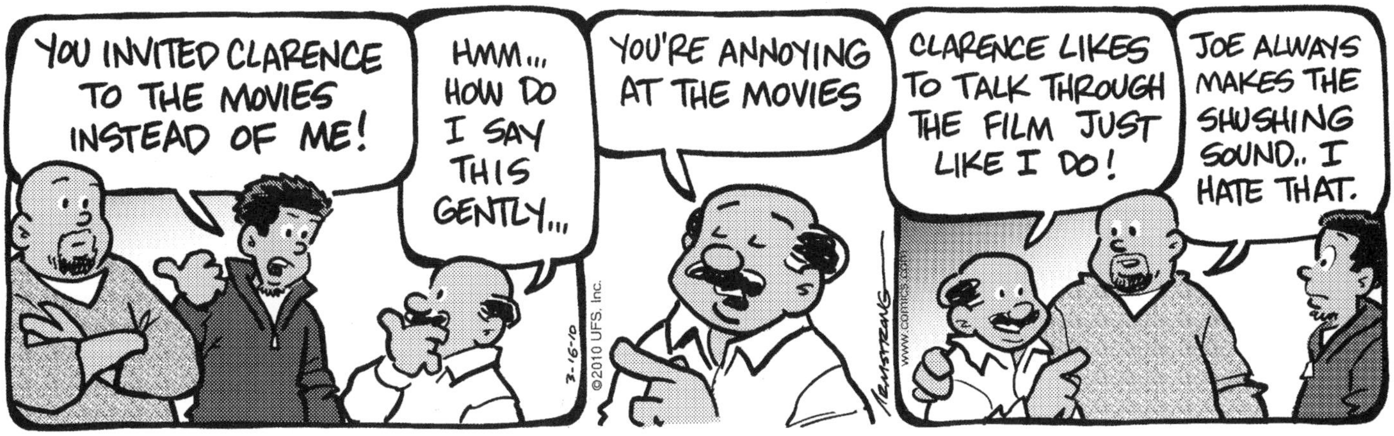
YOU INVITED CLARENCE TO THE MOVIES INSTEAD OF ME!
HMM... HOW DO I SAY THIS GENTLY...
YOU'RE ANNOYING AT THE MOVIES
CLARENCE LIKES TO TALK THROUGH THE FILM JUST LIKE I DO!
JOE ALWAYS MAKES THE SHUSHING SOUND.. I HATE THAT.
3-16-10
©2010 UFS, Inc.
www.comics.com

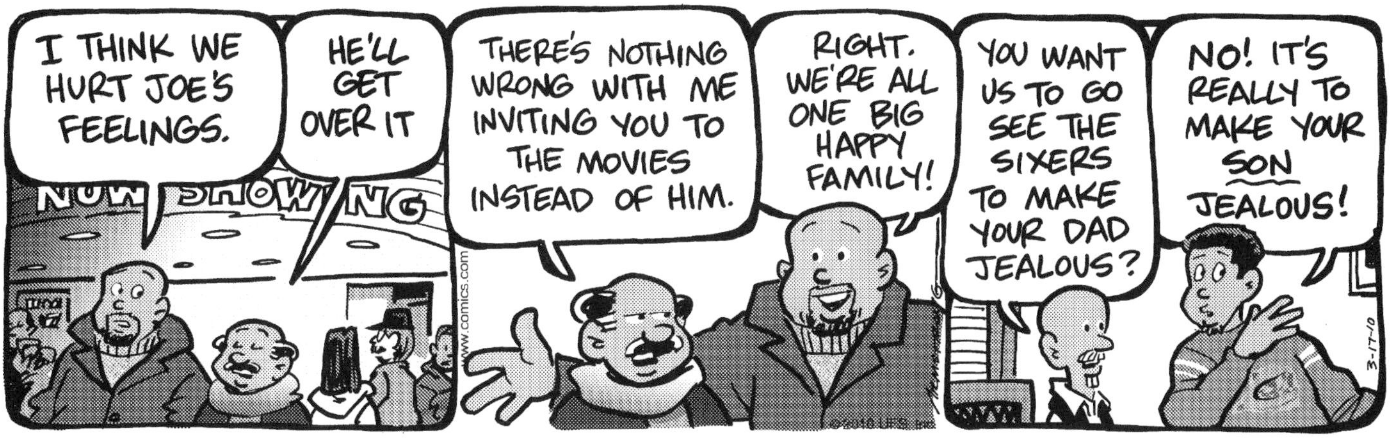
I THINK WE HURT JOE'S FEELINGS.
HE'LL GET OVER IT
NOW SHOWING
THERE'S NOTHING WRONG WITH ME INVITING YOU TO THE MOVIES INSTEAD OF HIM.
RIGHT. WE'RE ALL ONE BIG HAPPY FAMILY!
YOU WANT US TO GO SEE THE SIXERS TO MAKE YOUR DAD JEALOUS?
NO! IT'S REALLY TO MAKE YOUR SON JEALOUS!
www.comics.com
3-17-10

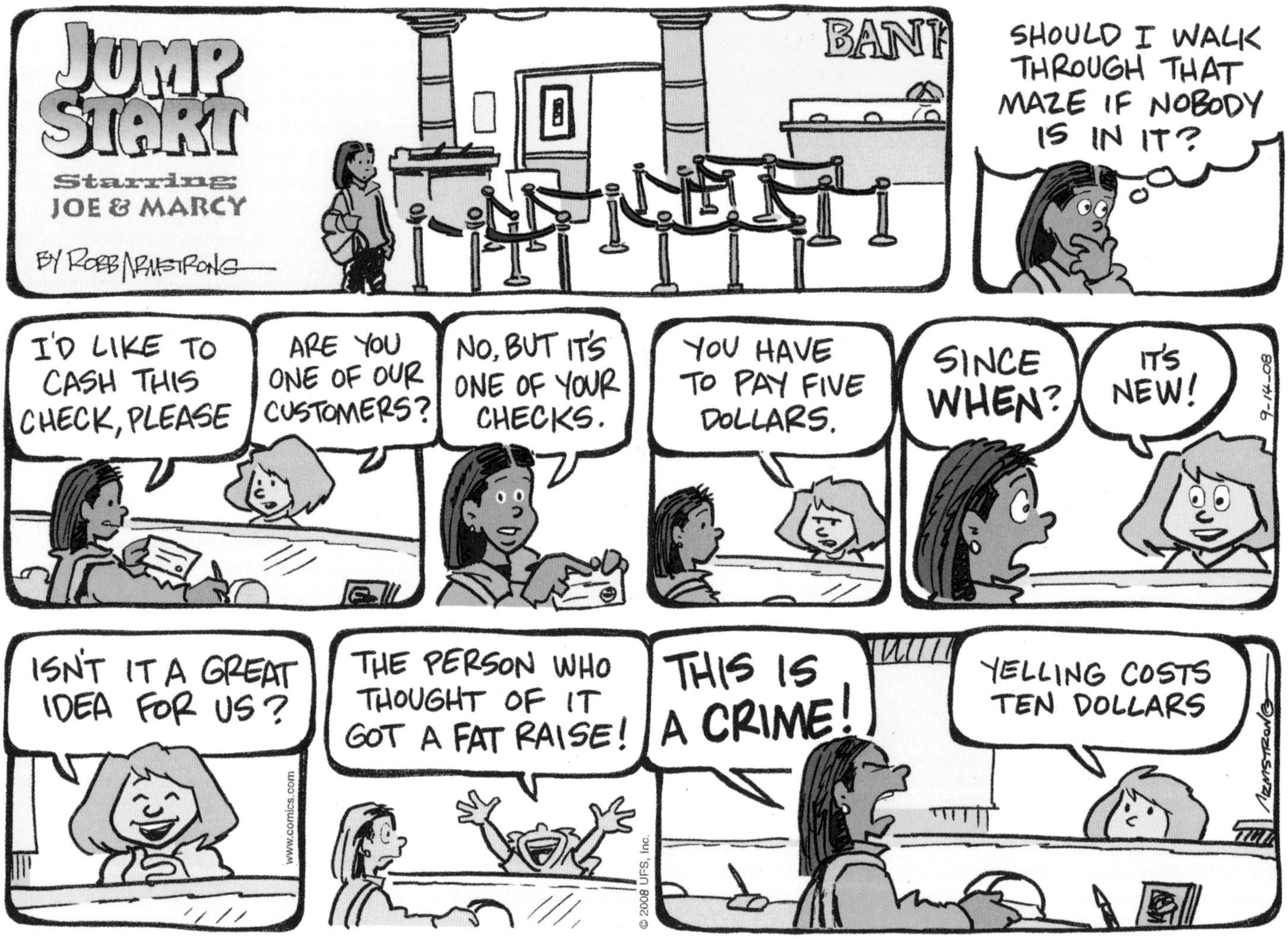
JUMP START
Starring: JOE & MARCY
BY ROBB ARMSTRONG
BANK
SHOULD I WALK THROUGH THAT MAZE IF NOBODY IS IN IT?
I'D LIKE TO CASH THIS CHECK, PLEASE
ARE YOU ONE OF OUR CUSTOMERS?
NO, BUT IT'S ONE OF YOUR CHECKS.
YOU HAVE TO PAY FIVE DOLLARS.
SINCE WHEN?
IT'S NEW!
9-14-08
ISN'T IT A GREAT IDEA FOR US?
www.comics.com
THE PERSON WHO THOUGHT OF IT GOT A FAT RAISE!
© 2008 UFS, Inc.
THIS IS A CRIME!
YELLING COSTS TEN DOLLARS
ARMSTRONG

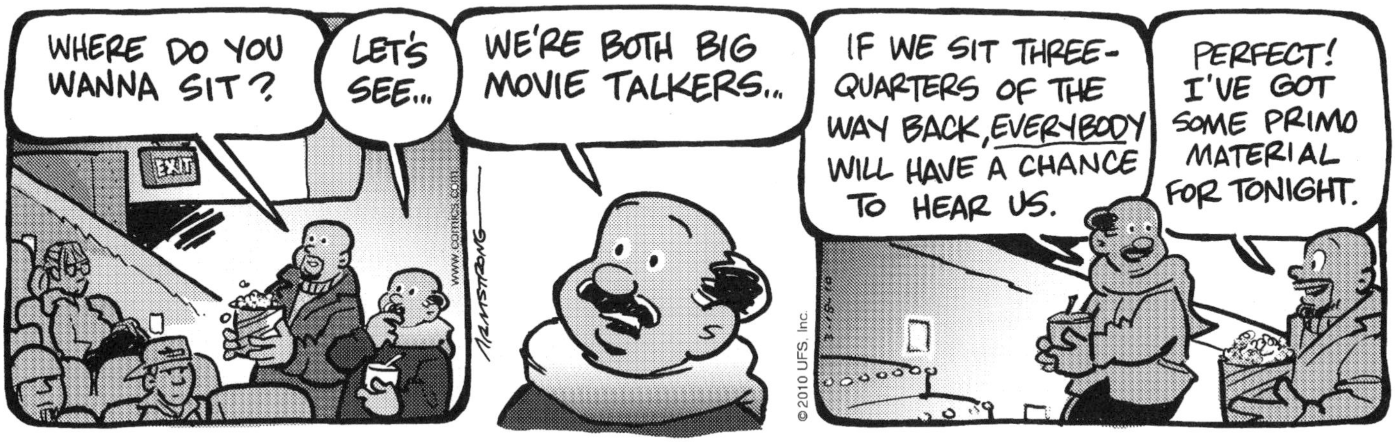
WHERE DO YOU WANNA SIT?
LET'S SEE...
WE'RE BOTH BIG MOVIE TALKERS...
IF WE SIT THREE-QUARTERS OF THE WAY BACK, EVERYBODY WILL HAVE A CHANCE TO HEAR US.
PERFECT! I'VE GOT SOME PRIMO MATERIAL FOR TONIGHT.
EXIT
www.comics.com
© 2010 UFS, Inc.

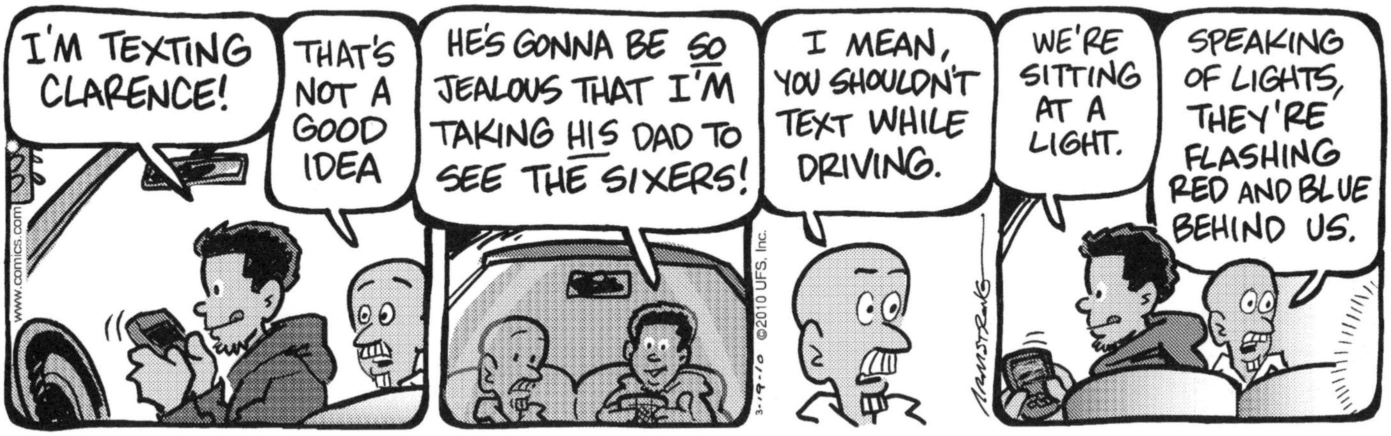
I'M TEXTING CLARENCE!
THAT'S NOT A GOOD IDEA
HE'S GONNA BE SO JEALOUS THAT I'M TAKING HIS DAD TO SEE THE SIXERS!
I MEAN, YOU SHOULDN'T TEXT WHILE DRIVING.
WE'RE SITTING AT A LIGHT.
SPEAKING OF LIGHTS, THEY'RE FLASHING RED AND BLUE BEHIND US.
www.comics.com
©2010 UFS, Inc.
3-19-10

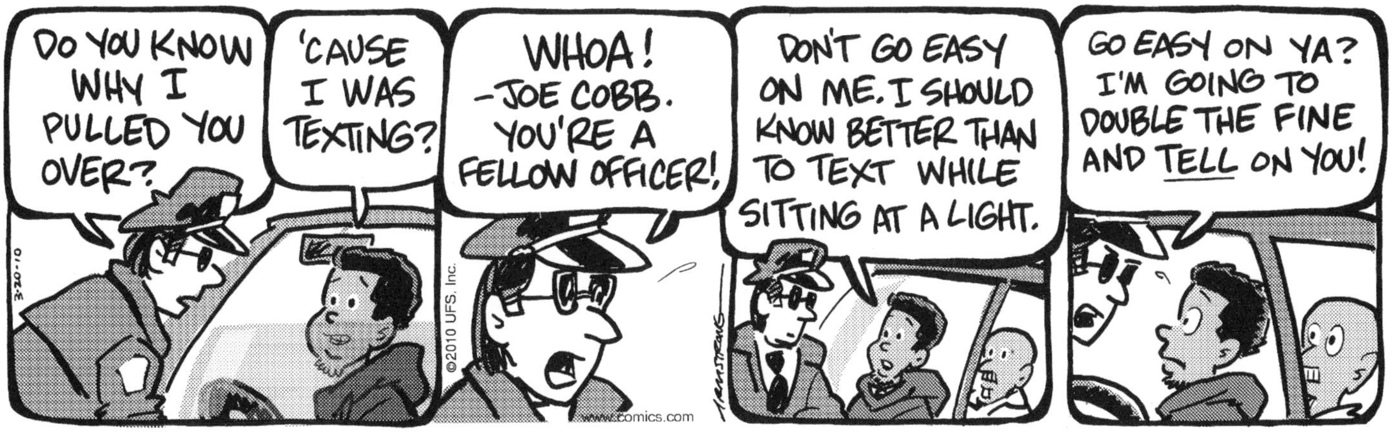
DO YOU KNOW WHY I PULLED YOU OVER?
'CAUSE I WAS TEXTING?
WHOA! -JOE COBB. YOU'RE A FELLOW OFFICER!
DON'T GO EASY ON ME. I SHOULD KNOW BETTER THAN TO TEXT WHILE SITTING AT A LIGHT.
GO EASY ON YA? I'M GOING TO DOUBLE THE FINE AND TELL ON YOU!
3-20-10
©2010 UFS, Inc.
www.comics.com

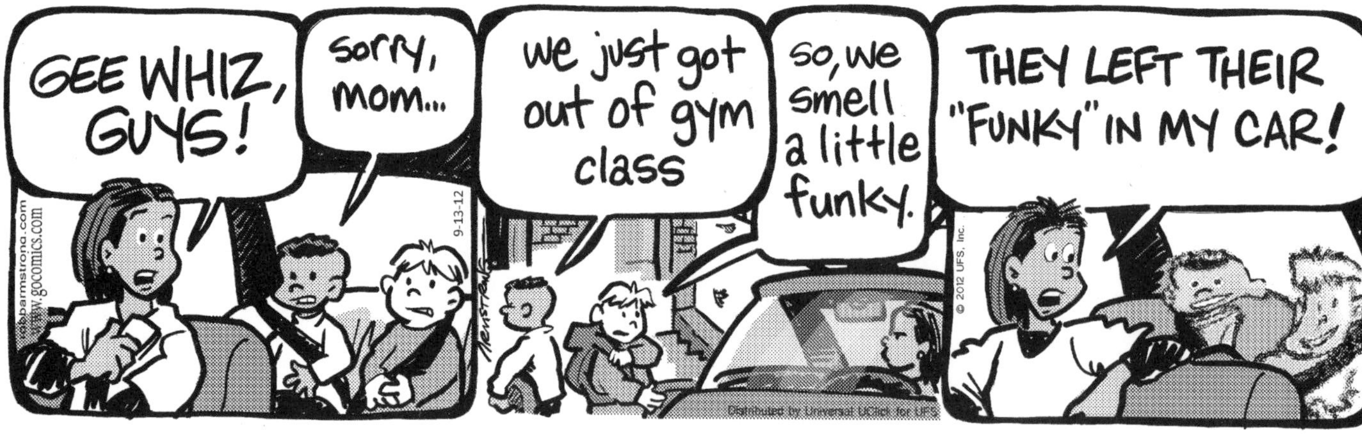
GEE WHIZ, GUYS!
sorry, mom...
we just got out of gym class
so, we smell a little funky.
THEY LEFT THEIR "FUNKY" IN MY CAR!
9-13-12
robbarmstrong.com
www.gocomics.com
© 2012 UFS, Inc.
Distributed by Universal UClick for UFS

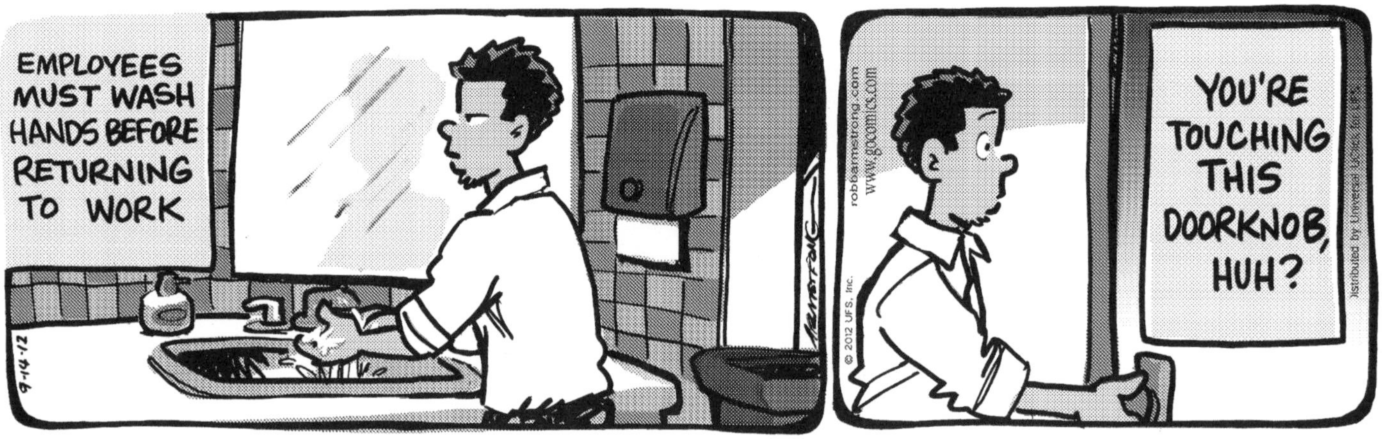
EMPLOYEES MUST WASH HANDS BEFORE RETURNING TO WORK
YOU'RE TOUCHING THIS DOORKNOB, HUH?
9-14-12
robbarmstrong.com
www.gocomics.com
© 2012 UFS, Inc.

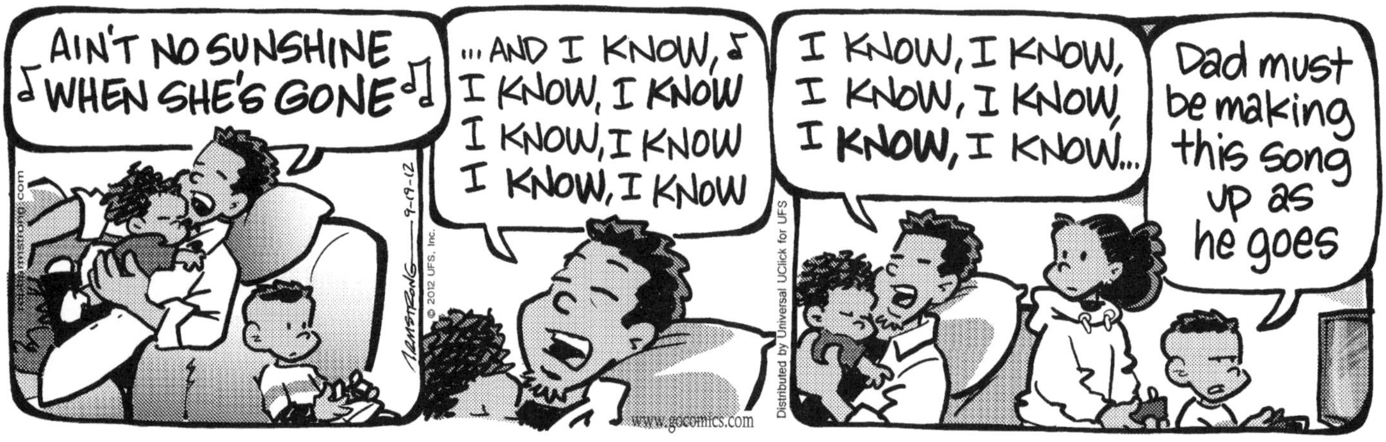
AIN'T NO SUNSHINE WHEN SHE'S GONE
...AND I KNOW, I KNOW, I KNOW I KNOW, I KNOW I KNOW, I KNOW
I KNOW, I KNOW, I KNOW, I KNOW, I KNOW, I KNOW...
Dad must be making this song up as he goes
9-19-12
© 2012 UFS, Inc.
www.gocomics.com
Distributed by Universal UClick for UFS

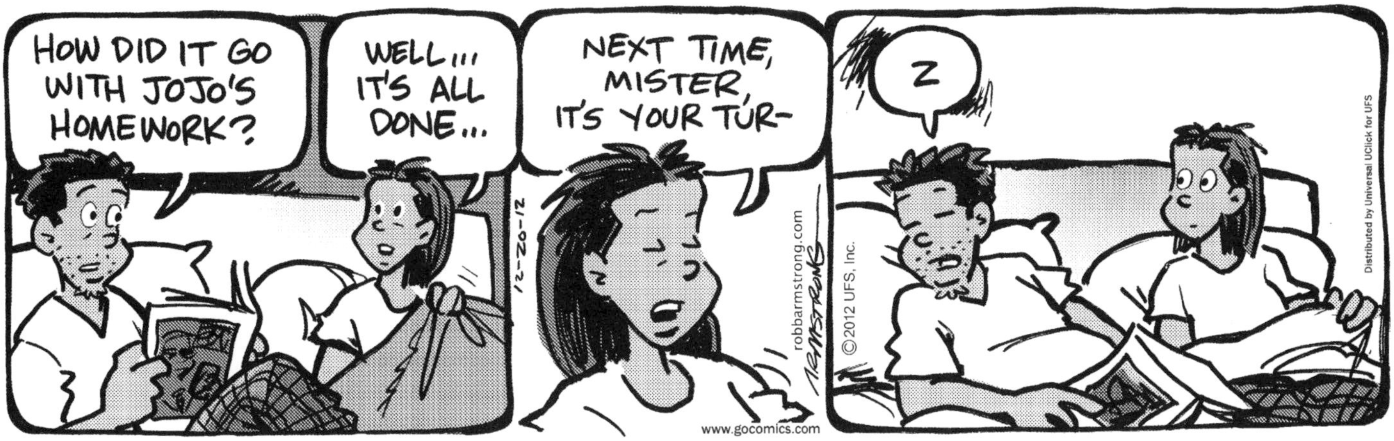
HOW DID IT GO WITH JOJO'S HOMEWORK?
WELL... IT'S ALL DONE...
NEXT TIME, MISTER, IT'S YOUR TUR-
Z
12-20-12
ARMSTRONG
robbarmstrong.com
www.gocomics.com
©2012 UFS, Inc.
Distributed by Universal UClick for UFS

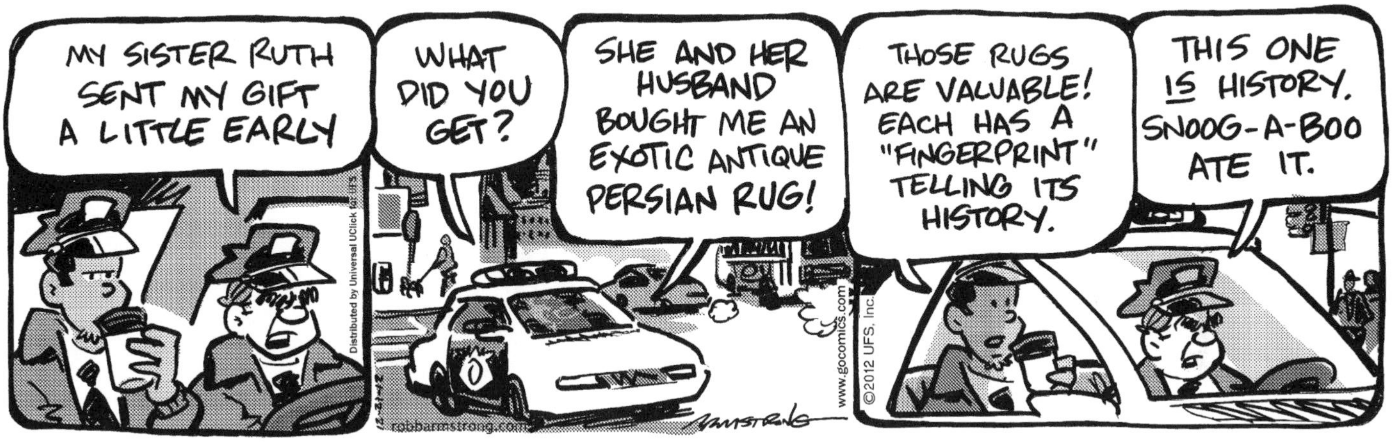
MY SISTER RUTH SENT MY GIFT A LITTLE EARLY
WHAT DID YOU GET?
SHE AND HER HUSBAND BOUGHT ME AN EXOTIC ANTIQUE PERSIAN RUG!
THOSE RUGS ARE VALUABLE! EACH HAS A "FINGERPRINT" TELLING ITS HISTORY.
THIS ONE IS HISTORY. SNOOG-A-BOO ATE IT.
Distributed by Universal UClick for UFS
robbarmstrong.com
ARMSTRONG
www.gocomics.com
©2012 UFS, Inc.

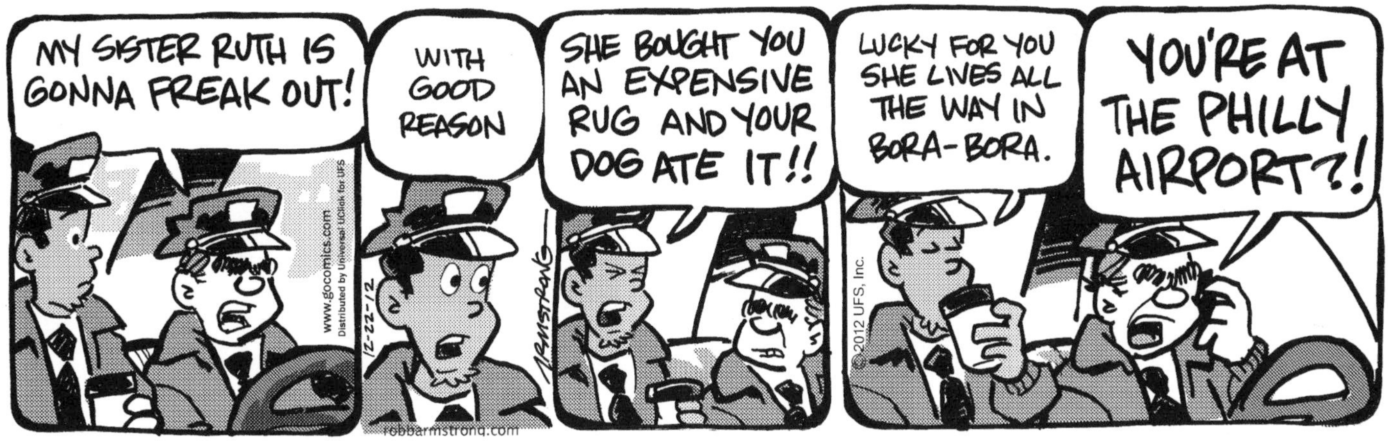
MY SISTER RUTH IS GONNA FREAK OUT!
WITH GOOD REASON
SHE BOUGHT YOU AN EXPENSIVE RUG AND YOUR DOG ATE IT!!
LUCKY FOR YOU SHE LIVES ALL THE WAY IN BORA-BORA.
YOU'RE AT THE PHILLY AIRPORT?!
www.gocomics.com
Distributed by Universal UClick for UFS
12-22-12
ARMSTRONG
robbarmstrong.com
©2012 UFS, Inc.

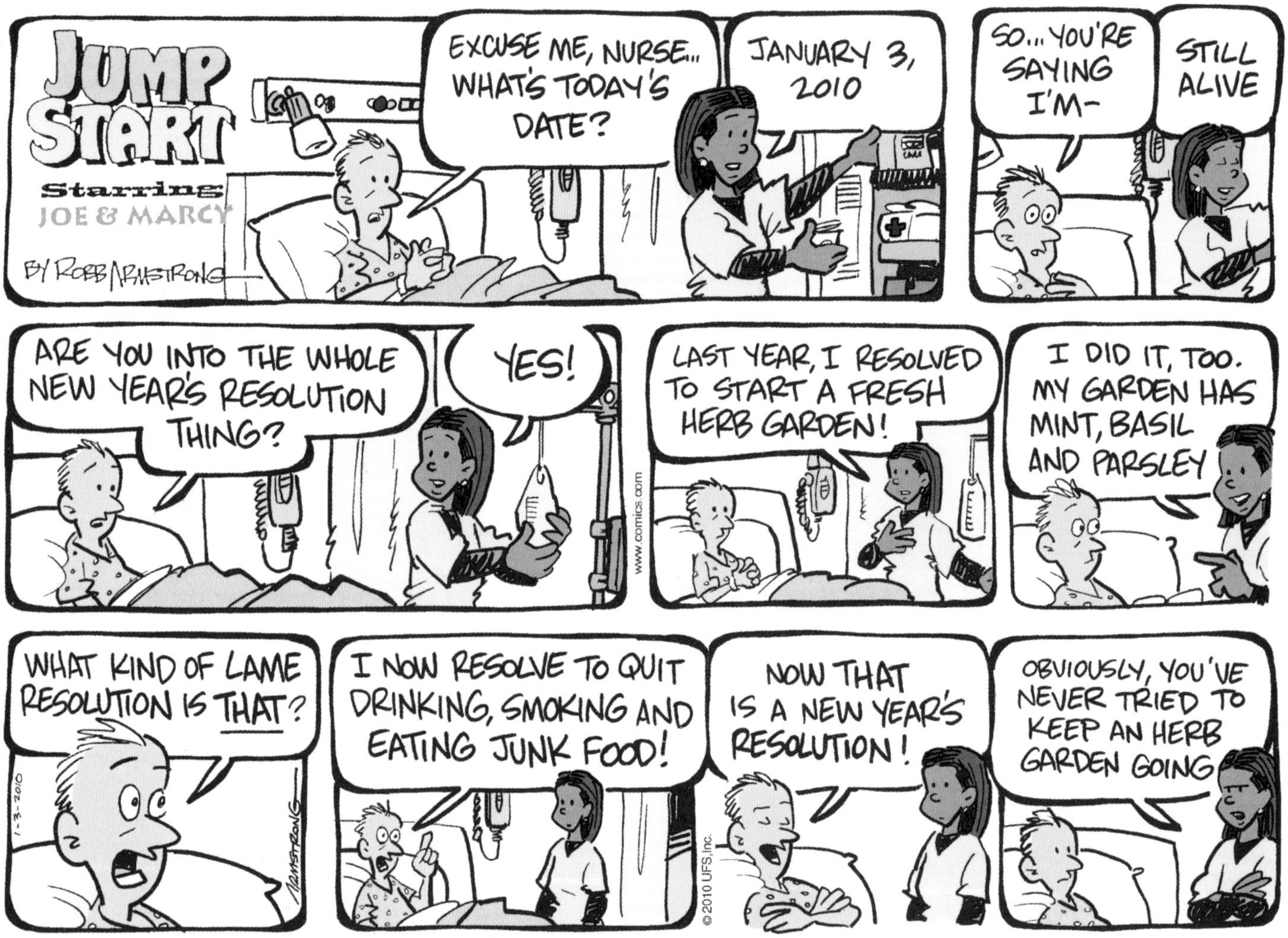
JUMP START
Starring
JOE & MARCY
BY ROBB ARMSTRONG
EXCUSE ME, NURSE... WHAT'S TODAY'S DATE?
JANUARY 3, 2010
SO... YOU'RE SAYING I'M-
STILL ALIVE
ARE YOU INTO THE WHOLE NEW YEAR'S RESOLUTION THING?
YES!
LAST YEAR, I RESOLVED TO START A FRESH HERB GARDEN!
I DID IT, TOO. MY GARDEN HAS MINT, BASIL AND PARSLEY
WHAT KIND OF LAME RESOLUTION IS THAT?
I NOW RESOLVE TO QUIT DRINKING, SMOKING AND EATING JUNK FOOD!
NOW THAT IS A NEW YEAR'S RESOLUTION!
OBVIOUSLY, YOU'VE NEVER TRIED TO KEEP AN HERB GARDEN GOING
www.comics.com
1-3-2010
ARMSTRONG
© 2010 UFS, Inc.

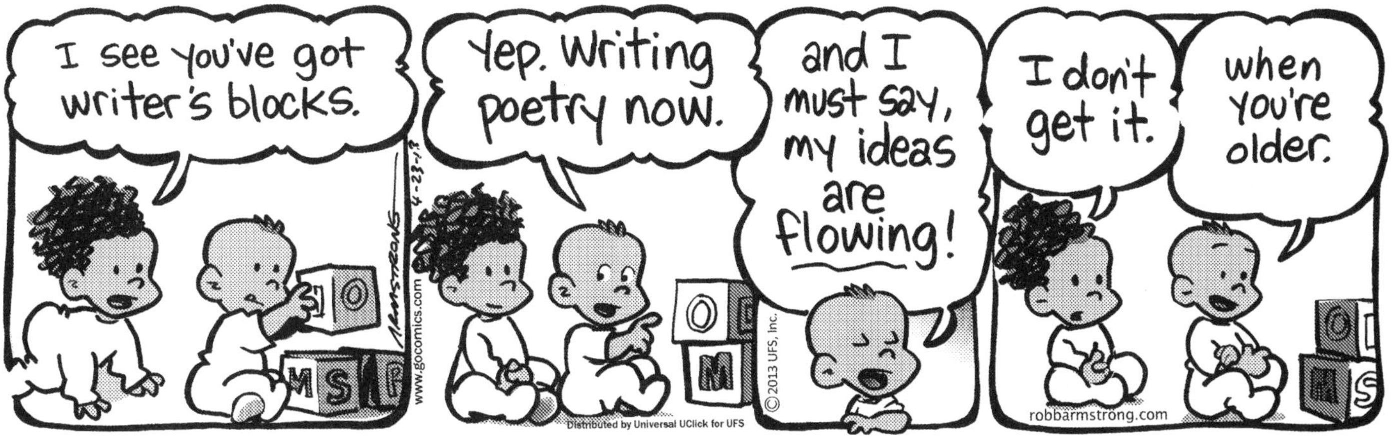
I see you've got writer's blocks.
Yep. Writing poetry now.
and I must say, my ideas are flowing!
I don't get it.
when you're older.
ARMSTRONG 4-23-13
www.gocomics.com
Distributed by Universal UClick for UFS
© 2013 UFS, Inc.
robbarmstrong.com

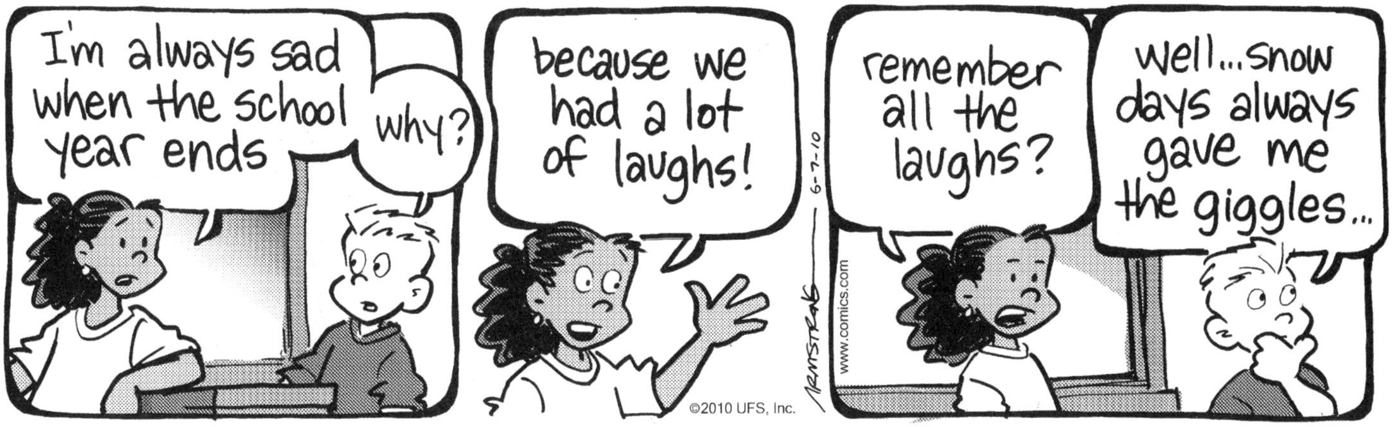
I'm always sad when the school year ends
why?
because we had a lot of laughs!
remember all the laughs?
well...snow days always gave me the giggles...
6-7-10
ARMSTRONG
www.comics.com
©2010 UFS, Inc.

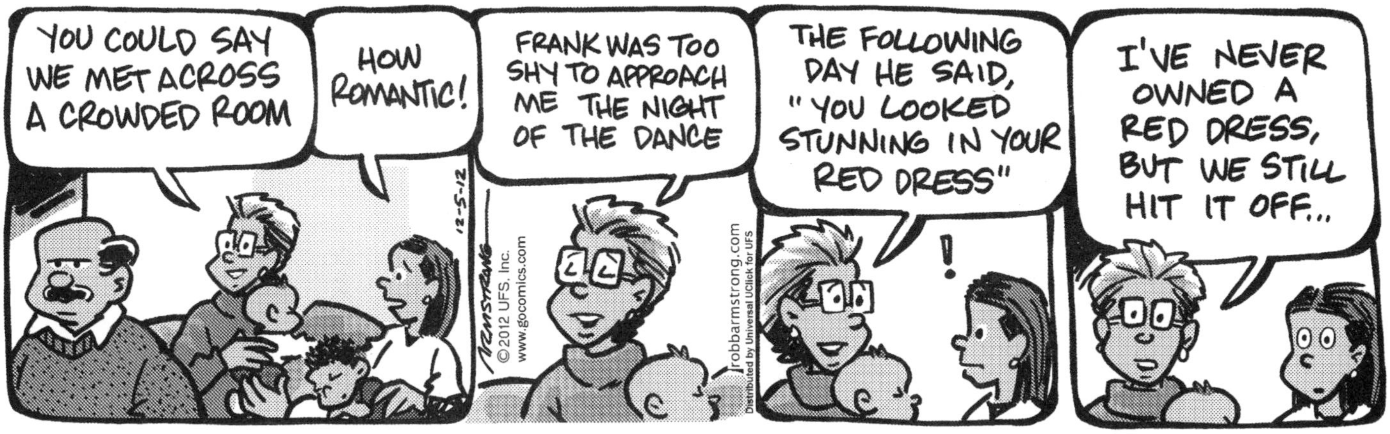
YOU COULD SAY WE MET ACROSS A CROWDED ROOM
HOW ROMANTIC!
FRANK WAS TOO SHY TO APPROACH ME THE NIGHT OF THE DANCE
THE FOLLOWING DAY HE SAID, "YOU LOOKED STUNNING IN YOUR RED DRESS"
!
I'VE NEVER OWNED A RED DRESS, BUT WE STILL HIT IT OFF...
12-5-12
ARMSTRONG
© 2012 UFS, Inc.
www.gocomics.com
robbarmstrong.com
Distributed by Universal UClick for UFS

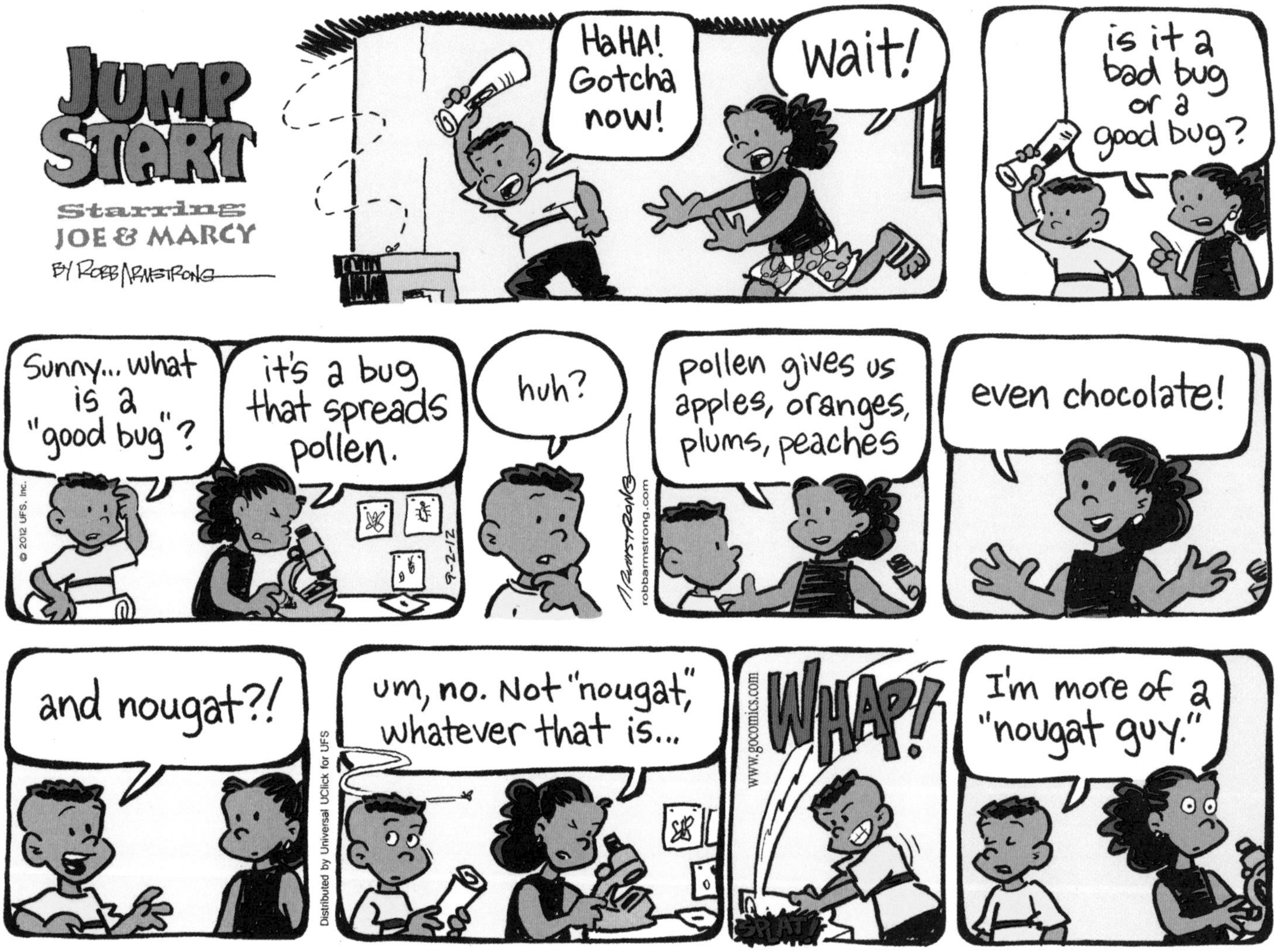
JUMP START
Starring JOE & MARCY
BY ROBB ARMSTRONG
HaHA! Gotcha now!
Wait!
is it a bad bug or a good bug?
Sunny... what is a "good bug"?
it's a bug that spreads pollen.
© 2012 UFS, Inc.
9-2-12
huh?
robbarmstrong.com
pollen gives us apples, oranges, plums, peaches
even chocolate!
and nougat?!
Distributed by Universal UClick for UFS
um, no. Not "nougat," whatever that is...
www.gocomics.com
WHAP!
SPLAT!
I'm more of a "nougat guy."

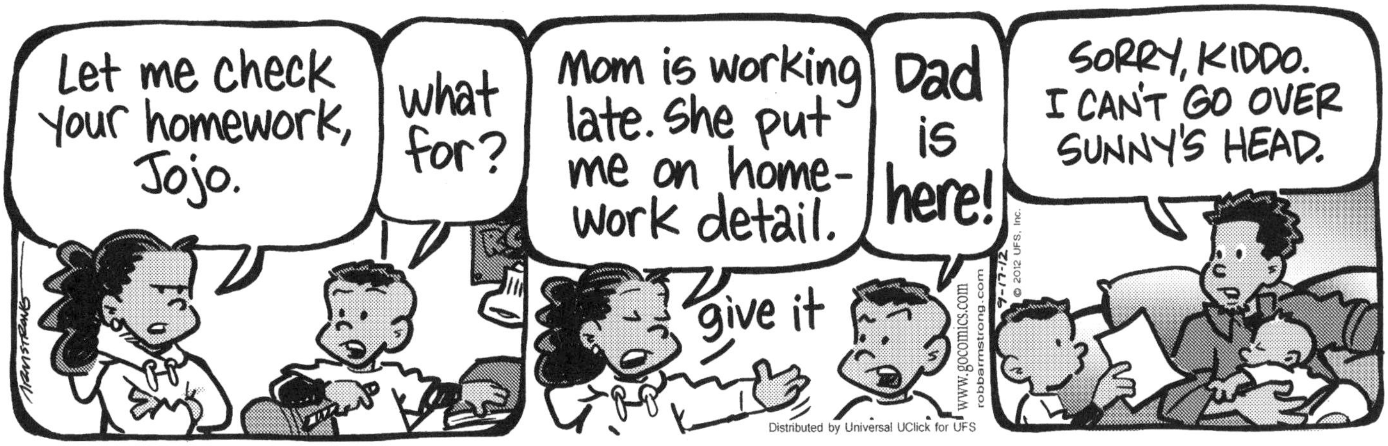
Let me check your homework, Jojo.
what for?
Mom is working late. She put me on homework detail.
give it
Dad is here!
SORRY, KIDDO. I CAN'T GO OVER SUNNY'S HEAD.
ARMSTRONG
www.gocomics.com
robbarmstrong.com
9-17-12
© 2012 UFS, Inc.
Distributed by Universal UClick for UFS

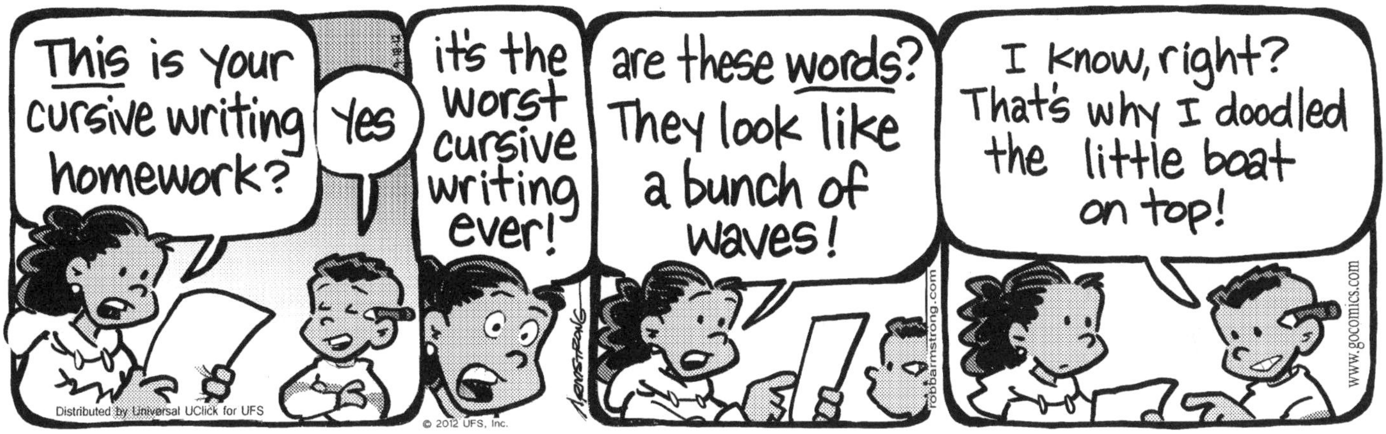
This is your cursive writing homework?
Yes
it's the worst cursive writing ever!
are these words? They look like a bunch of waves!
I know, right? That's why I doodled the little boat on top!
ARMSTRONG
Distributed by Universal UClick for UFS
© 2012 UFS, Inc.
robbarmstrong.com
www.gocomics.com

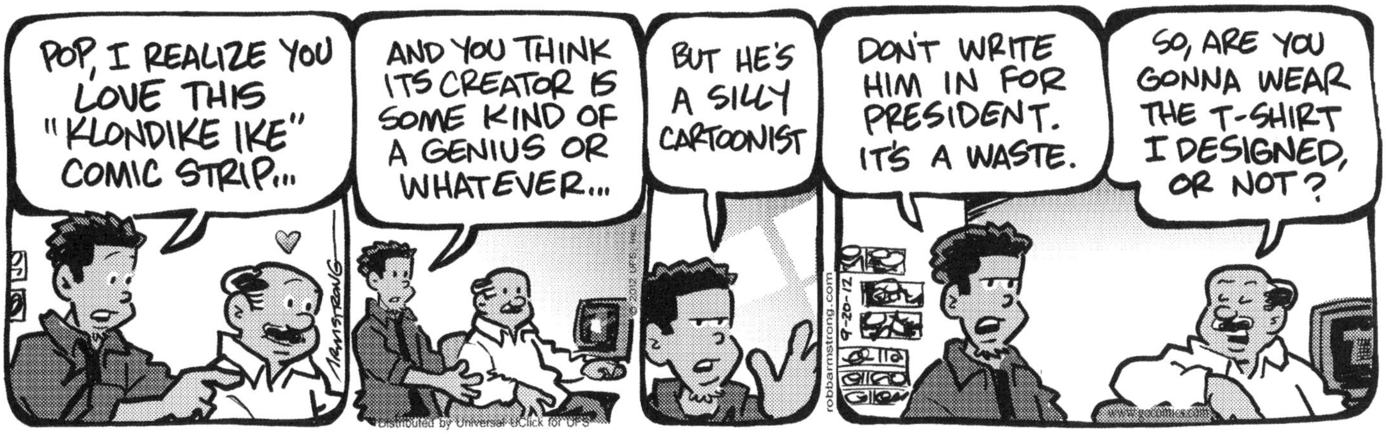
POP, I REALIZE YOU LOVE THIS "KLONDIKE IKE" COMIC STRIP...
AND YOU THINK ITS CREATOR IS SOME KIND OF A GENIUS OR WHATEVER...
BUT HE'S A SILLY CARTOONIST
DON'T WRITE HIM IN FOR PRESIDENT. IT'S A WASTE.
SO, ARE YOU GONNA WEAR THE T-SHIRT I DESIGNED, OR NOT?
ARMSTRONG
© 2012 UFS, Inc.
Distributed by Universal UClick for UFS
robbarmstrong.com
9-20-12

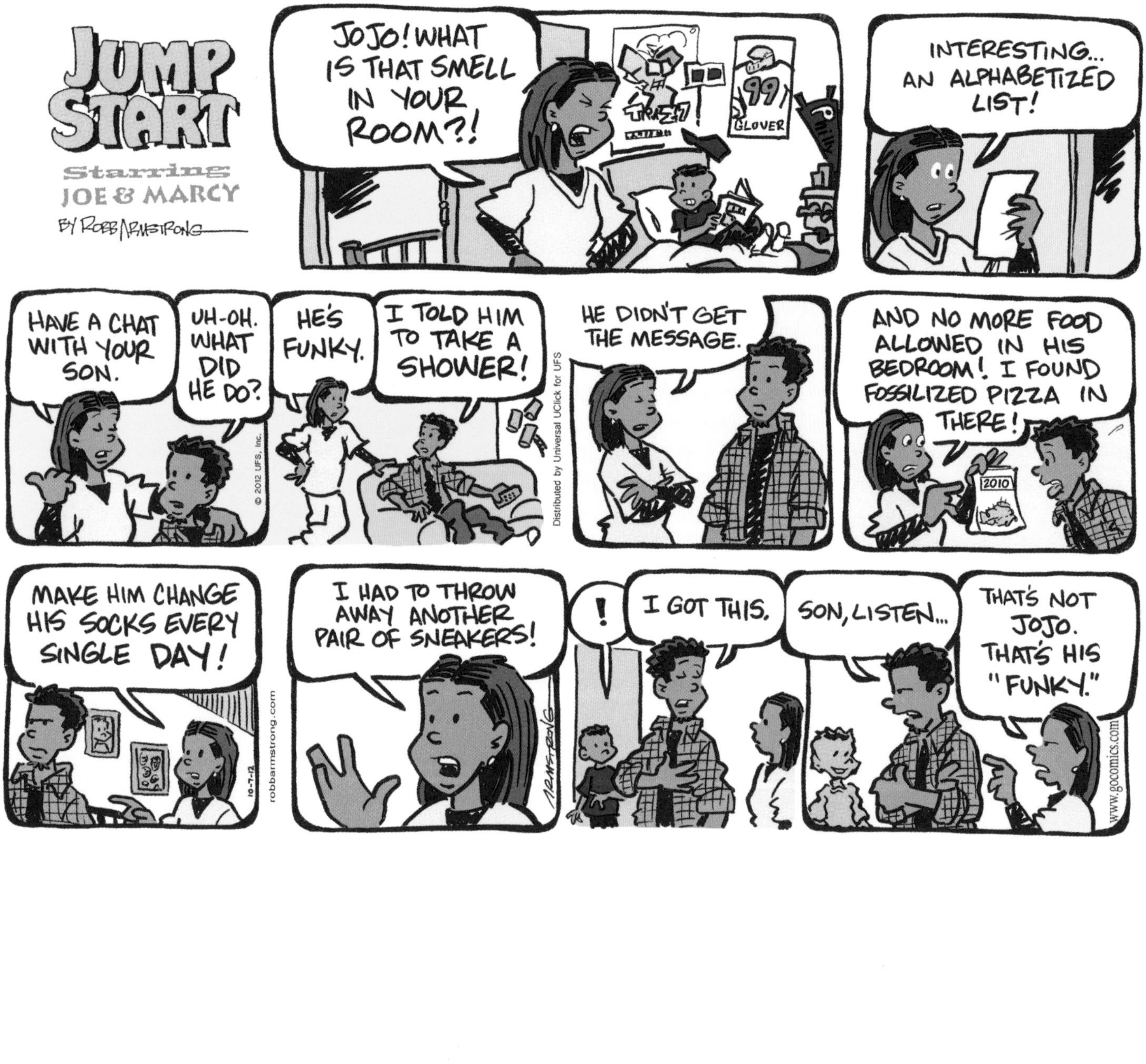
JUMP START
Starring
JOE & MARCY
BY ROBB ARMSTRONG
JOJO! WHAT IS THAT SMELL IN YOUR ROOM?!
99
GLOVER
INTERESTING... AN ALPHABETIZED LIST!
HAVE A CHAT WITH YOUR SON.
UH-OH. WHAT DID HE DO?
© 2012 UFS, Inc.
HE'S FUNKY.
I TOLD HIM TO TAKE A SHOWER!
Distributed by Universal UClick for UFS
HE DIDN'T GET THE MESSAGE.
AND NO MORE FOOD ALLOWED IN HIS BEDROOM! I FOUND FOSSILIZED PIZZA IN THERE!
2010
MAKE HIM CHANGE HIS SOCKS EVERY SINGLE DAY!
10-7-12
robbarmstrong.com
I HAD TO THROW AWAY ANOTHER PAIR OF SNEAKERS!
ARMSTRONG
!
I GOT THIS.
SON, LISTEN...
THAT'S NOT JOJO. THAT'S HIS "FUNKY."
www.gocomics.com

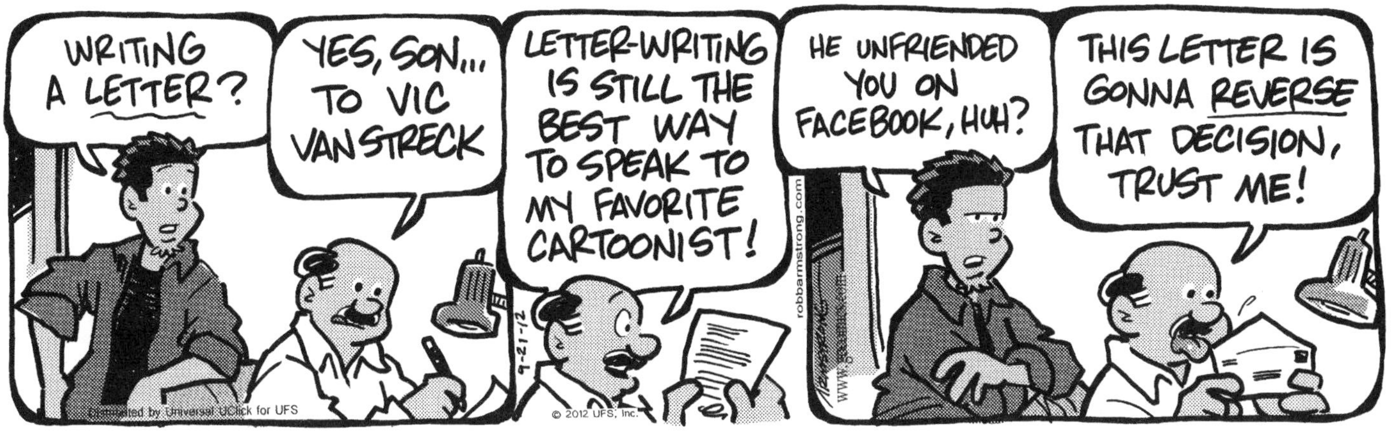
WRITING A LETTER?
YES, SON... TO VIC VAN STRECK
LETTER-WRITING IS STILL THE BEST WAY TO SPEAK TO MY FAVORITE CARTOONIST!
HE UNFRIENDED YOU ON FACEBOOK, HUH?
THIS LETTER IS GONNA REVERSE THAT DECISION, TRUST ME!
Distributed by Universal UClick for UFS
© 2012 UFS, Inc.
9-21-12
robbarmstrong.com
www.gocomics.com

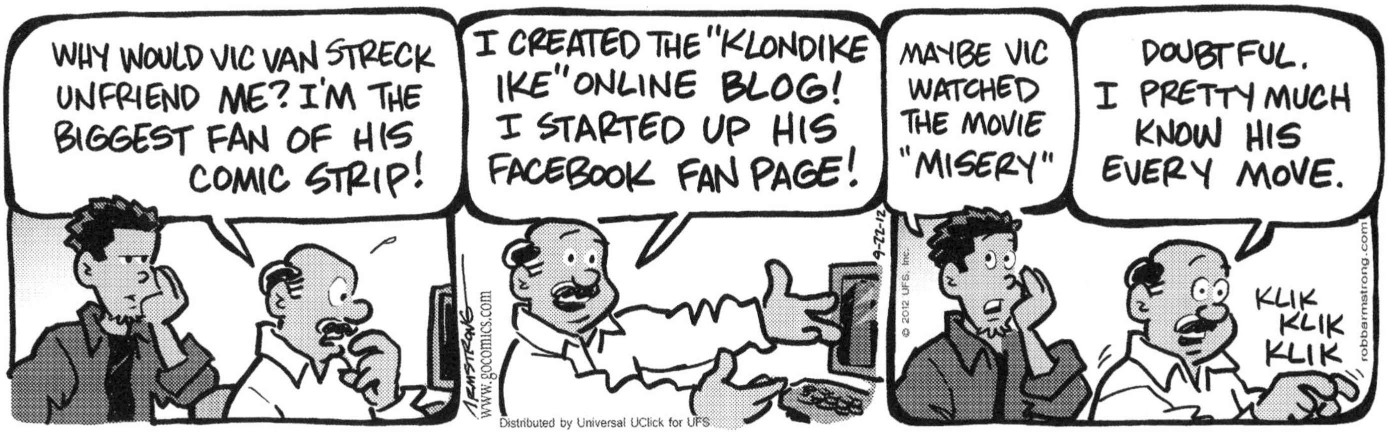
WHY WOULD VIC VAN STRECK UNFRIEND ME? I'M THE BIGGEST FAN OF HIS COMIC STRIP!
I CREATED THE "KLONDIKE IKE" ONLINE BLOG! I STARTED UP HIS FACEBOOK FAN PAGE!
MAYBE VIC WATCHED THE MOVIE "MISERY"
DOUBTFUL. I PRETTY MUCH KNOW HIS EVERY MOVE.
KLIK KLIK KLIK
ARMSTRONG
www.gocomics.com
Distributed by Universal UClick for UFS
© 2012 UFS, Inc.
9-22-12
robbarmstrong.com

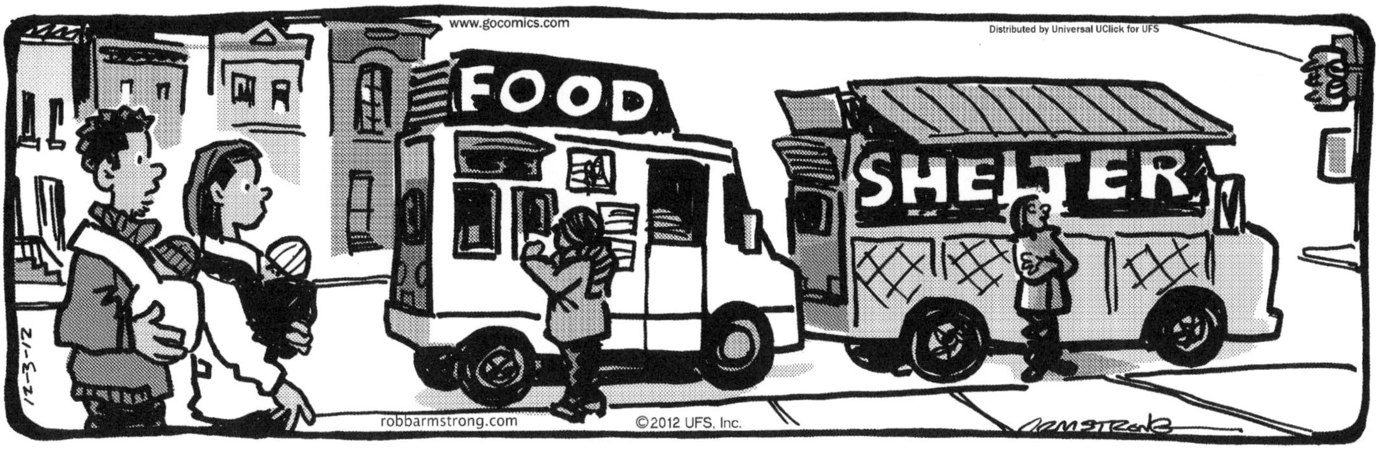
www.gocomics.com
Distributed by Universal UClick for UFS
FOOD
SHELTER
12-3-12
robbarmstrong.com
©2012 UFS, Inc.
ARMSTRONG

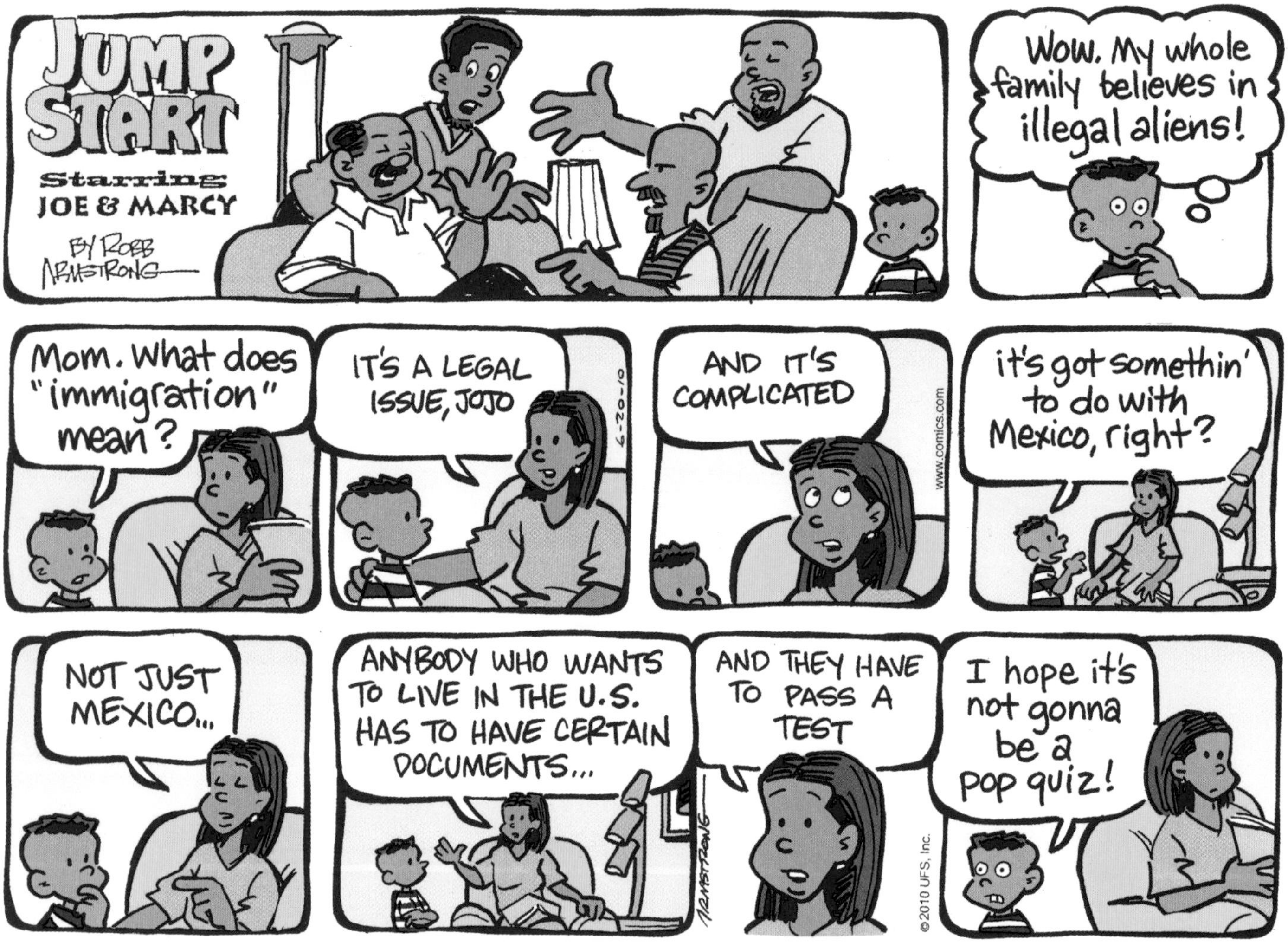
JUMP START
Starring JOE & MARCY
BY ROBB ARMSTRONG
Wow. My whole family believes in illegal aliens!
Mom. What does "immigration" mean?
IT'S A LEGAL ISSUE, JOJO
6-20-10
AND IT'S COMPLICATED
www.comics.com
it's got somethin' to do with Mexico, right?
NOT JUST MEXICO...
ANYBODY WHO WANTS TO LIVE IN THE U.S. HAS TO HAVE CERTAIN DOCUMENTS...
ARMSTRONG
AND THEY HAVE TO PASS A TEST
© 2010 UFS, Inc.
I hope it's not gonna be a pop quiz!

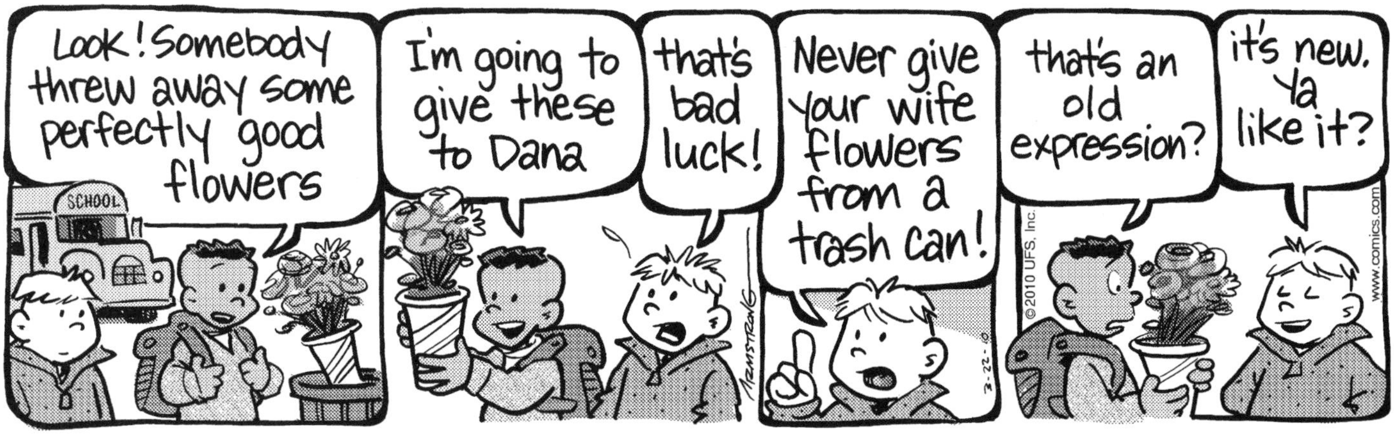
Look! Somebody threw away some perfectly good flowers
SCHOOL
I'm going to give these to Dana
that's bad luck!
Never give your wife flowers from a trash can!
that's an old expression?
it's new. Ya like it?
©2010 UFS, Inc.
www.comics.com

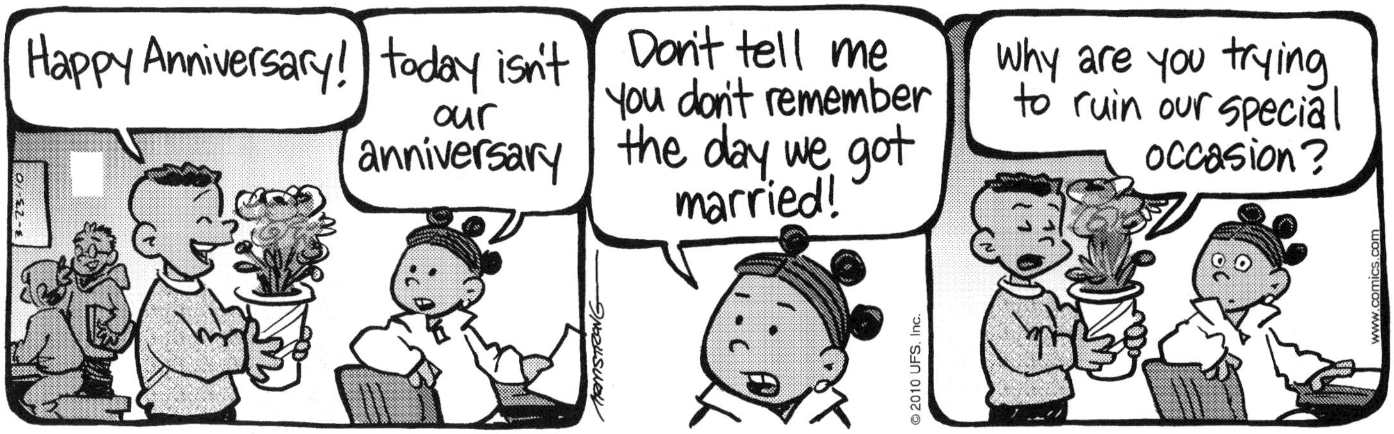
Happy Anniversary!
today isn't our anniversary
Don't tell me you don't remember the day we got married!
Why are you trying to ruin our special occasion?
© 2010 UFS, Inc.
www.comics.com

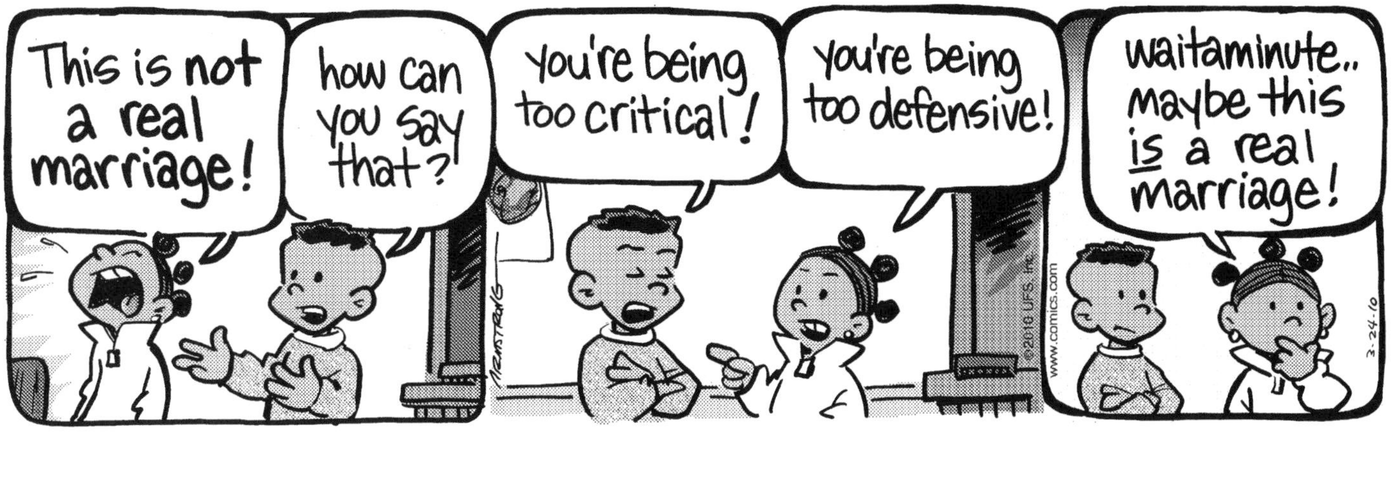
This is not a real marriage!
how can you say that?
You're being too critical!
You're being too defensive!
waitaminute.. maybe this is a real marriage!
©2010 UFS, Inc.
www.comics.com

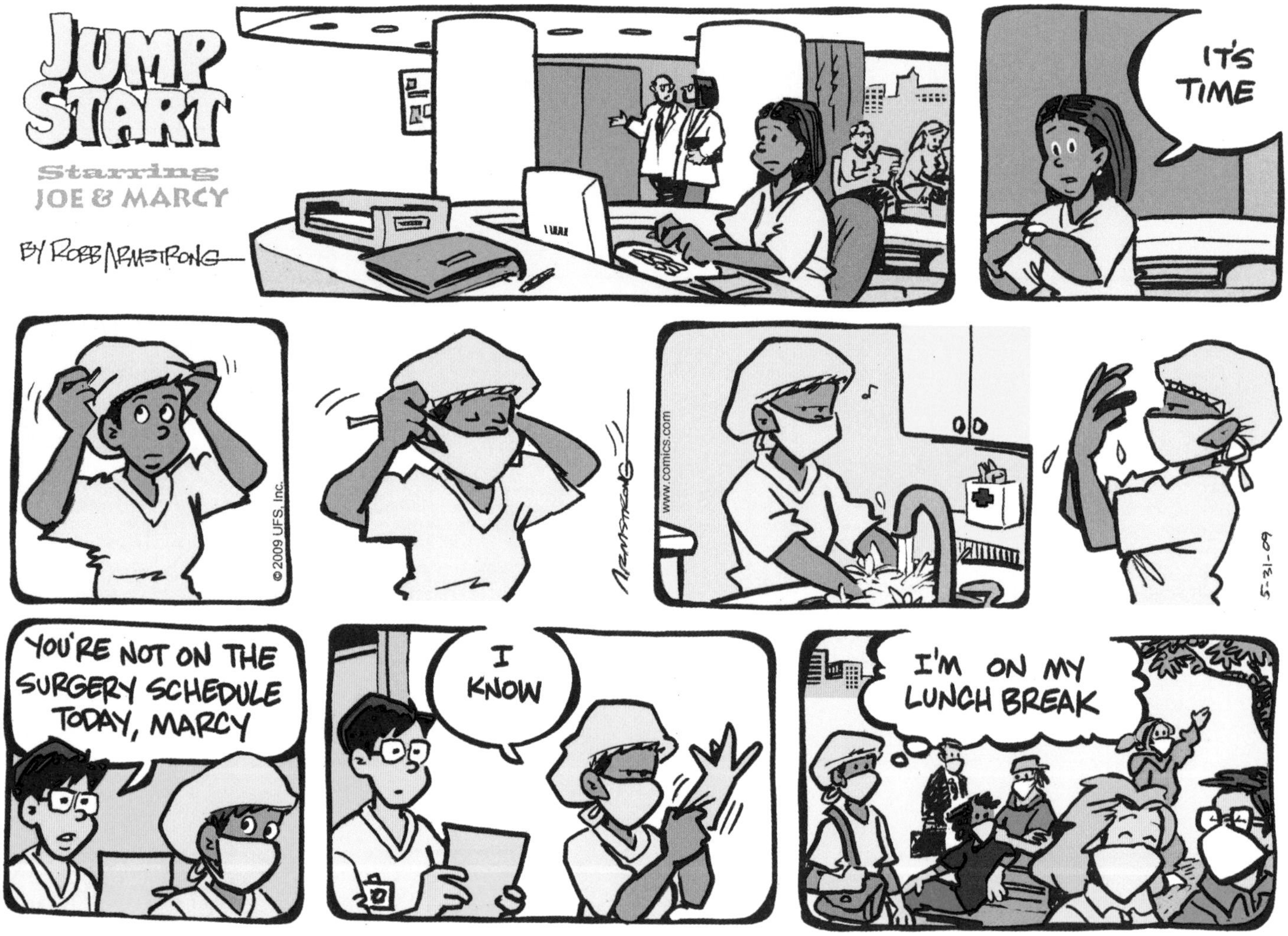
JUMP START
Starring
JOE & MARCY
BY ROBB ARMSTRONG
IT'S TIME
© 2009 UFS, Inc.
www.comics.com
5-31-09
YOU'RE NOT ON THE SURGERY SCHEDULE TODAY, MARCY
I KNOW
I'M ON MY LUNCH BREAK

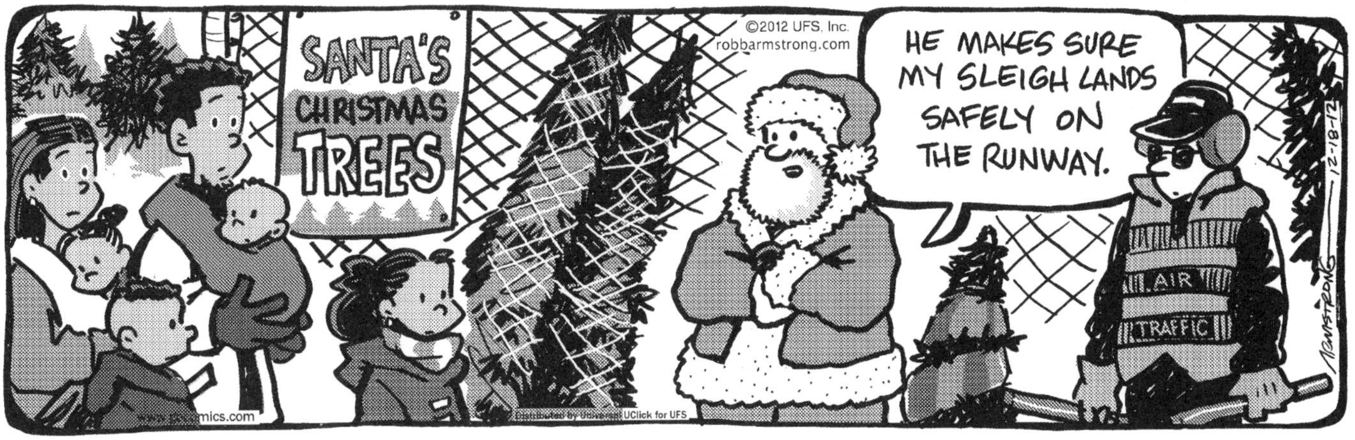
SANTA'S CHRISTMAS TREES
©2012 UFS, Inc.
robbarmstrong.com
HE MAKES SURE MY SLEIGH LANDS SAFELY ON THE RUNWAY.
12-18-12
AIR
TRAFFIC
ARMSTRONG
www.gocomics.com
Distributed by Universal UClick for UFS

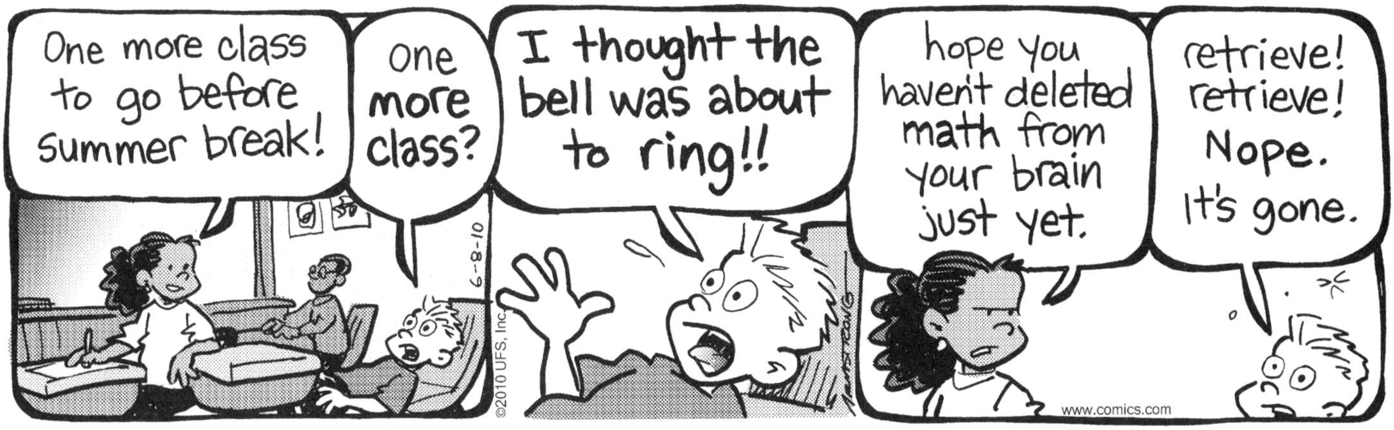
One more class to go before summer break!
One more class?
6-8-10
©2010 UFS, Inc.
I thought the bell was about to ring!!
ARMSTRONG
hope you haven't deleted math from your brain just yet.
retrieve! retrieve! Nope. It's gone.
www.comics.com

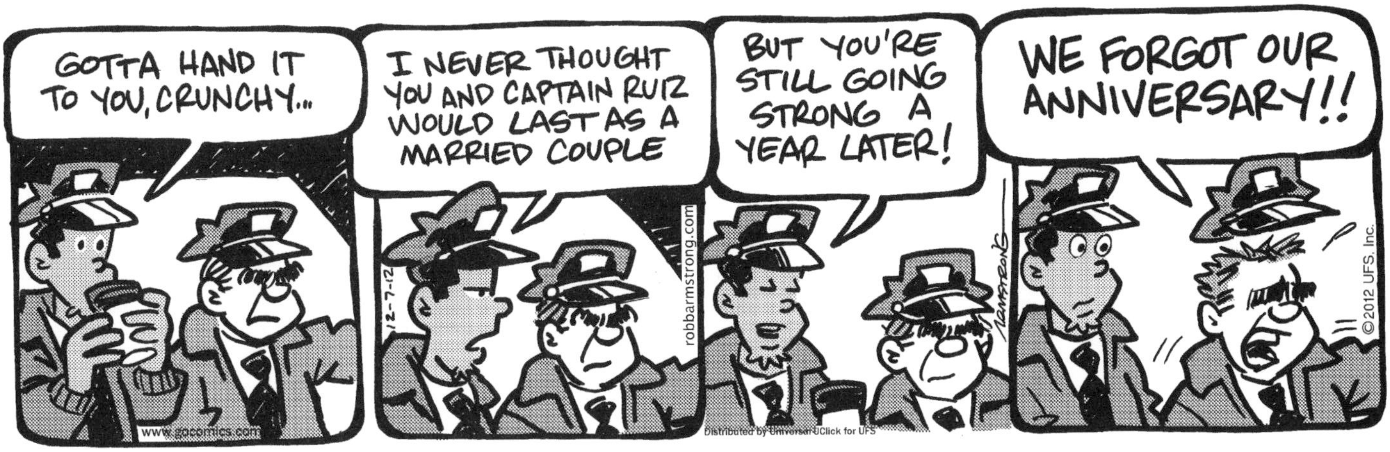
GOTTA HAND IT TO YOU, CRUNCHY...
www.gocomics.com
I NEVER THOUGHT YOU AND CAPTAIN RUIZ WOULD LAST AS A MARRIED COUPLE
12-7-12
robbarmstrong.com
BUT YOU'RE STILL GOING STRONG A YEAR LATER!
ARMSTRONG
Distributed by Universal UClick for UFS
WE FORGOT OUR ANNIVERSARY!!
©2012 UFS, Inc.

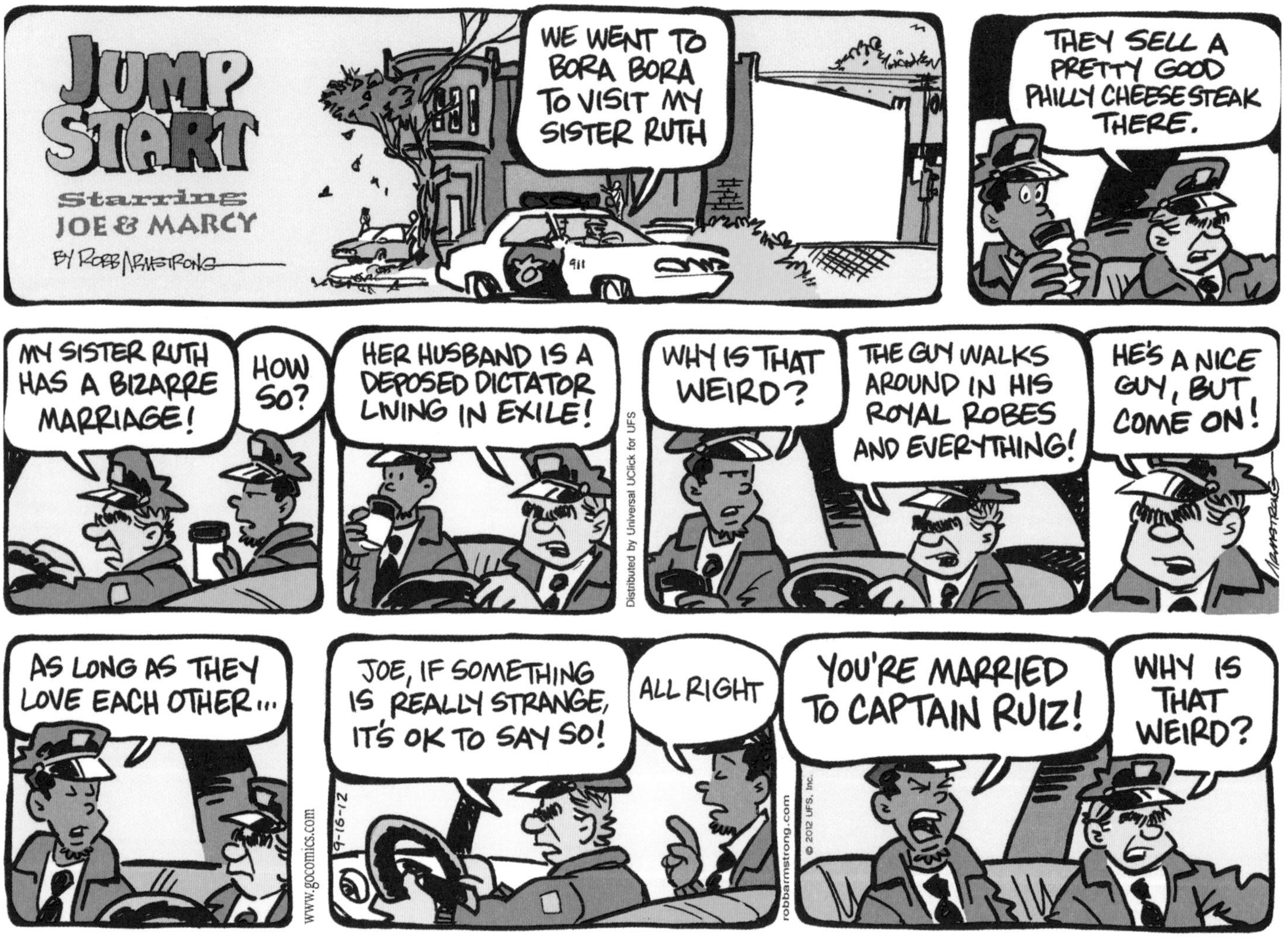
JUMP START
Starring JOE & MARCY
BY ROBB ARMSTRONG
WE WENT TO BORA BORA TO VISIT MY SISTER RUTH
THEY SELL A PRETTY GOOD PHILLY CHEESESTEAK THERE.
MY SISTER RUTH HAS A BIZARRE MARRIAGE!
HOW SO?
HER HUSBAND IS A DEPOSED DICTATOR LIVING IN EXILE!
Distributed by Universal UClick for UFS
WHY IS THAT WEIRD?
THE GUY WALKS AROUND IN HIS ROYAL ROBES AND EVERYTHING!
HE'S A NICE GUY, BUT COME ON!
AS LONG AS THEY LOVE EACH OTHER...
www.gocomics.com
9-16-12
JOE, IF SOMETHING IS REALLY STRANGE, IT'S OK TO SAY SO!
ALL RIGHT
robbarmstrong.com
© 2012 UFS, Inc.
YOU'RE MARRIED TO CAPTAIN RUIZ!
WHY IS THAT WEIRD?

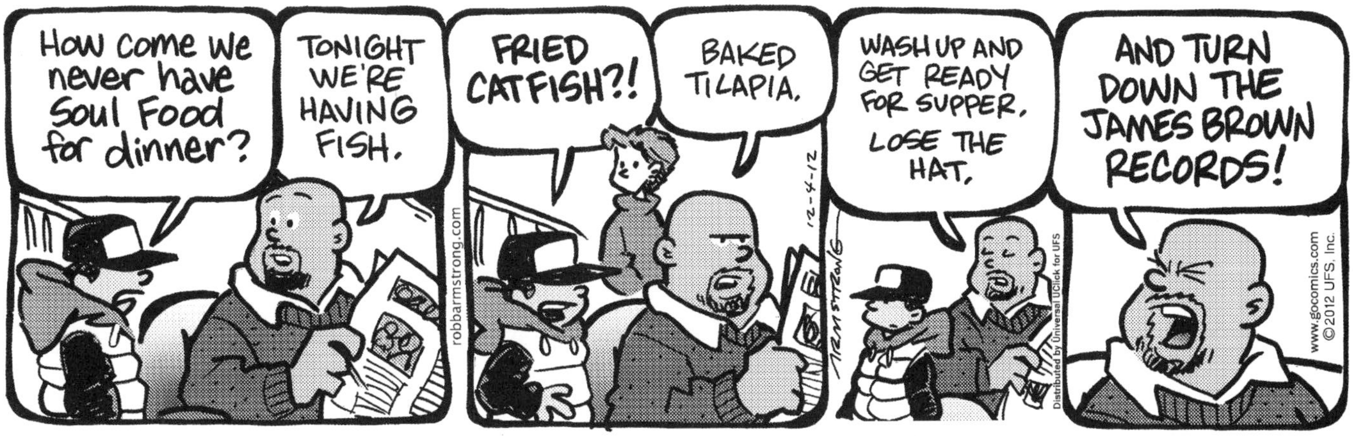
How come we never have Soul Food for dinner?
TONIGHT WE'RE HAVING FISH.
FRIED CATFISH?!
BAKED TILAPIA.
WASH UP AND GET READY FOR SUPPER.
LOSE THE HAT.
AND TURN DOWN THE JAMES BROWN RECORDS!

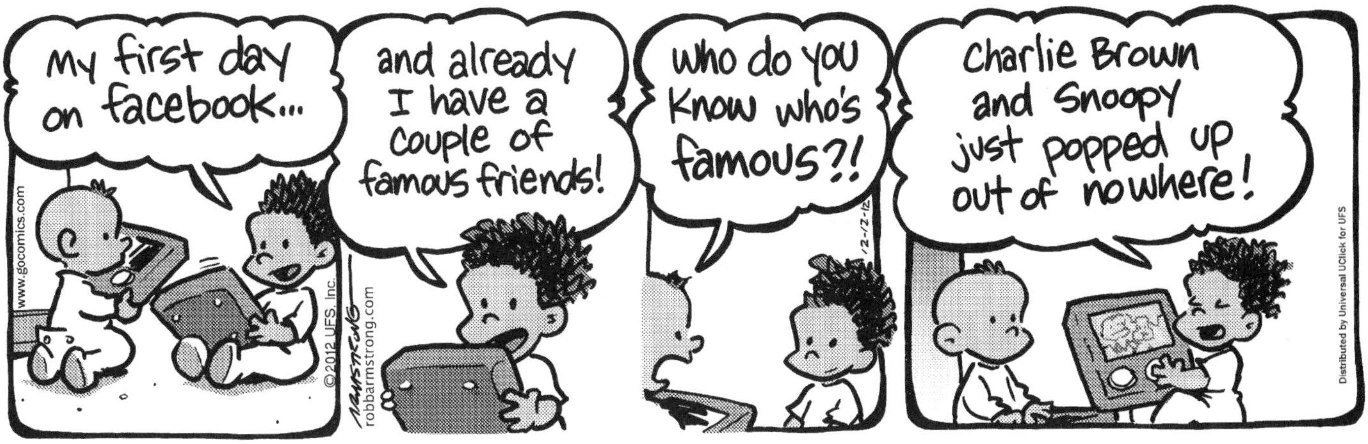
My first day on facebook...
and already I have a couple of famous friends!
who do you know who's famous?!
Charlie Brown and Snoopy just popped up out of nowhere!

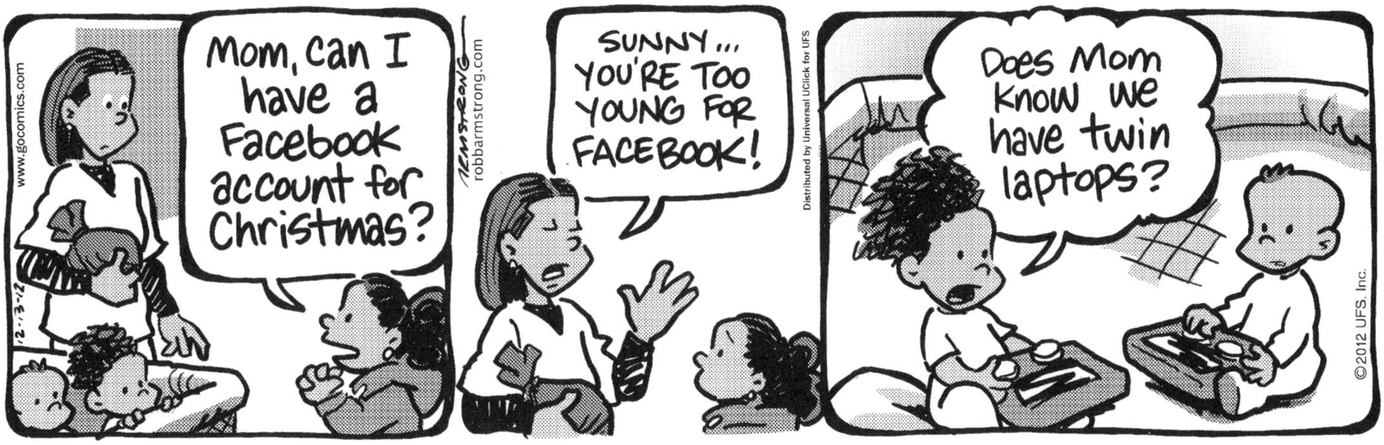
Mom, can I have a Facebook account for Christmas?
SUNNY... YOU'RE TOO YOUNG FOR FACEBOOK!
Does Mom know we have twin laptops?

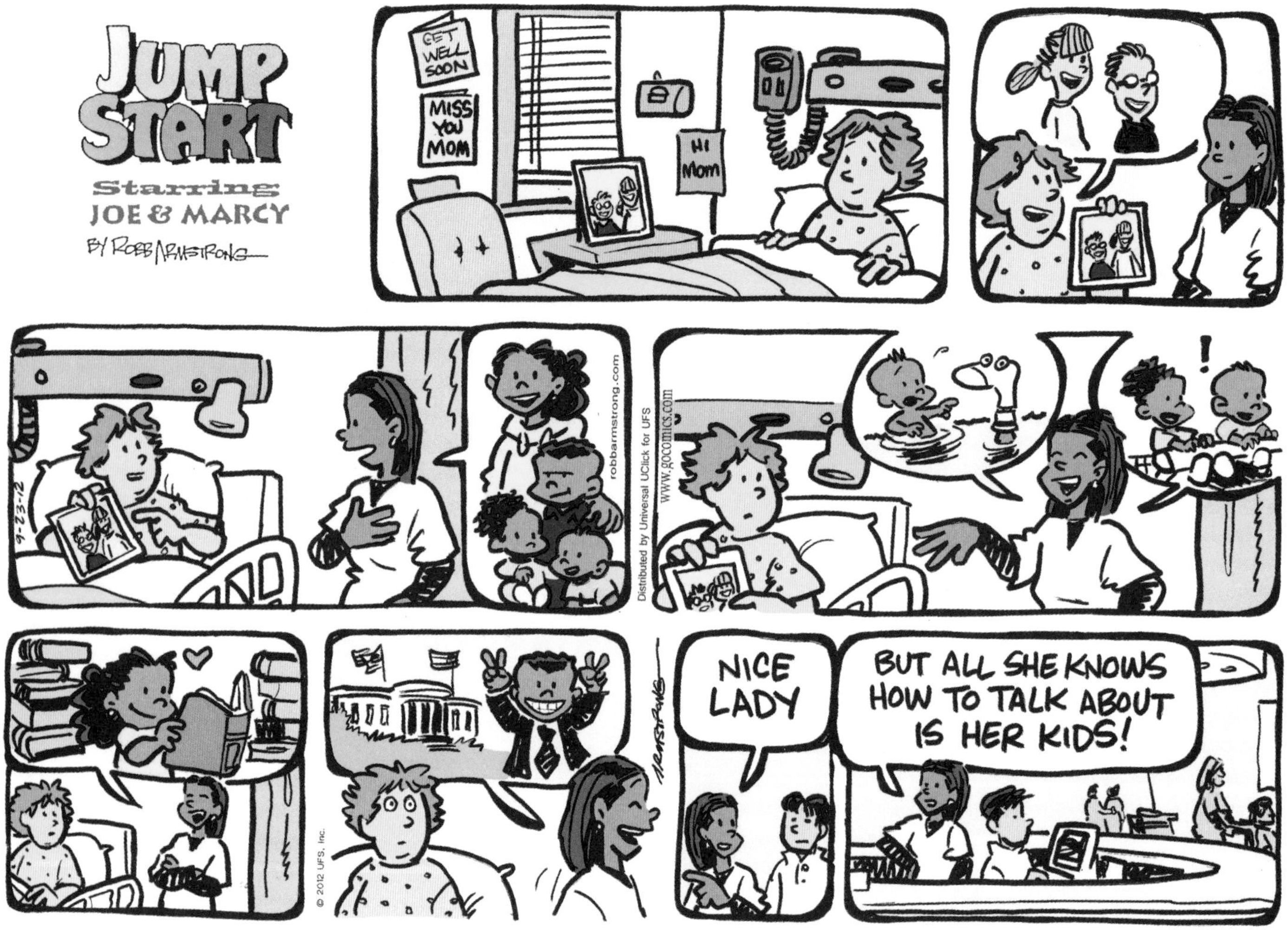

JUMP START
Starring JOE & MARCY
BY ROBB ARMSTRONG
GET WELL SOON
MISS YOU MOM
HI MOM
9-23-12
robbarmstrong.com
Distributed by Universal UClick for UFS
www.gocomics.com
!
© 2012 UFS, Inc.
NICE LADY
BUT ALL SHE KNOWS HOW TO TALK ABOUT IS HER KIDS!

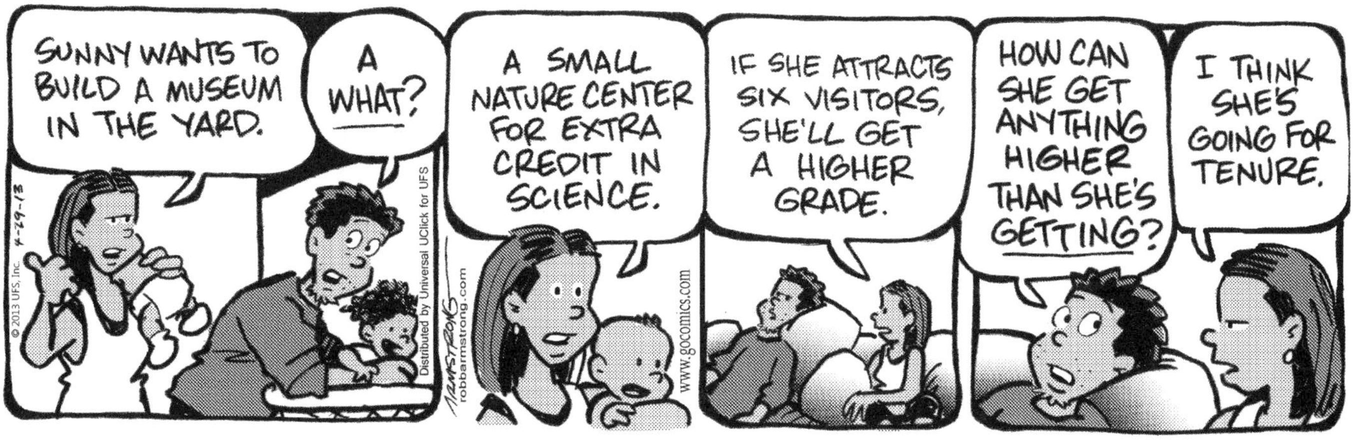
SUNNY WANTS TO BUILD A MUSEUM IN THE YARD.
A WHAT?
A SMALL NATURE CENTER FOR EXTRA CREDIT IN SCIENCE.
IF SHE ATTRACTS SIX VISITORS, SHE'LL GET A HIGHER GRADE.
HOW CAN SHE GET ANYTHING HIGHER THAN SHE'S GETTING?
I THINK SHE'S GOING FOR TENURE.
© 2013 UFS, Inc.
Distributed by Universal UClick for UFS
robbarmstrong.com
www.gocomics.com

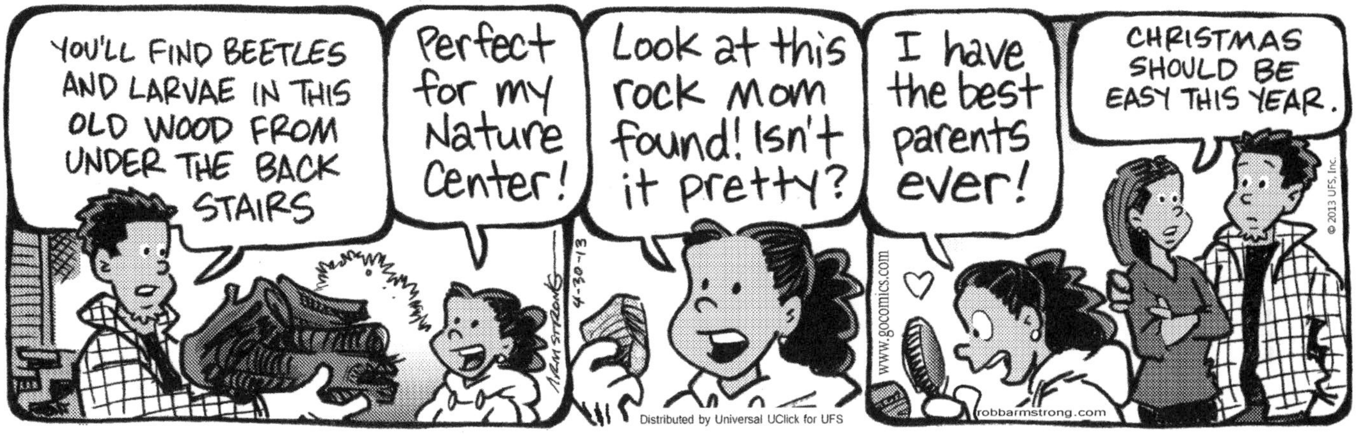
YOU'LL FIND BEETLES AND LARVAE IN THIS OLD WOOD FROM UNDER THE BACK STAIRS
Perfect for my Nature Center!
Look at this rock Mom found! Isn't it pretty?
I have the best parents ever!
CHRISTMAS SHOULD BE EASY THIS YEAR.
Distributed by Universal UClick for UFS
www.gocomics.com
robbarmstrong.com
© 2013 UFS, Inc.

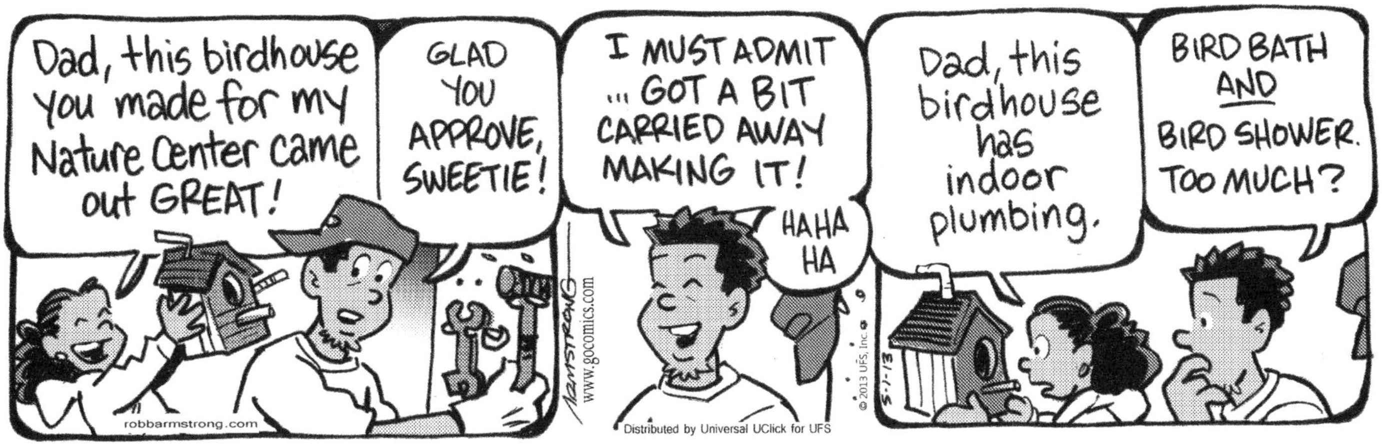
Dad, this birdhouse you made for my Nature Center came out GREAT!
GLAD YOU APPROVE, SWEETIE!
I MUST ADMIT ... GOT A BIT CARRIED AWAY MAKING IT!
HAHA HA
Dad, this birdhouse has indoor plumbing.
BIRD BATH AND BIRD SHOWER. TOO MUCH?
robbarmstrong.com
www.gocomics.com
Distributed by Universal UClick for UFS
© 2013 UFS, Inc.

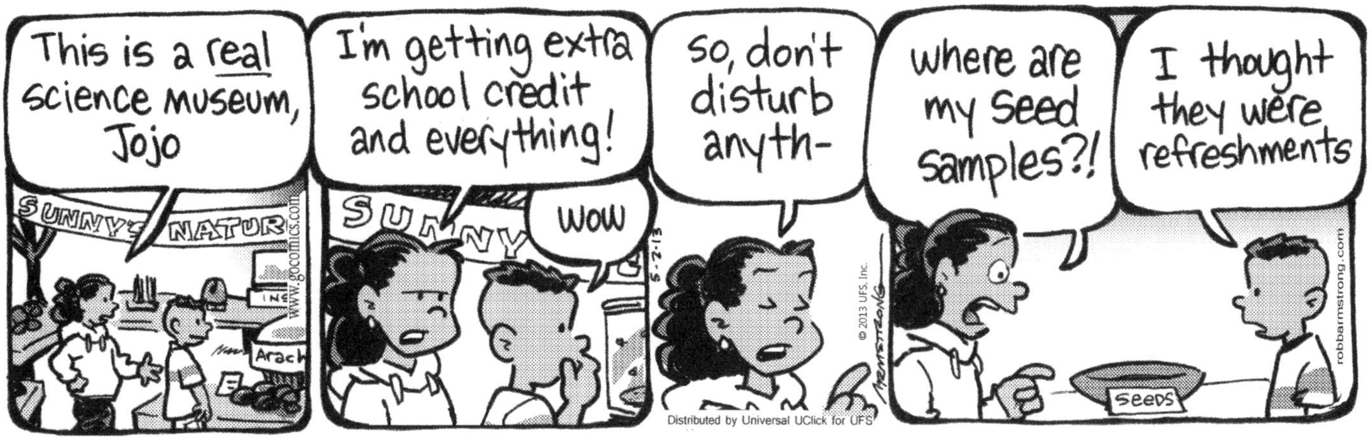
This is a real science museum, Jojo
SUNNY'S NATUR
www.gocomics.com
Arach
I'm getting extra school credit and everything!
SUNNY
Wow
5-2-13
So, don't disturb anyth-
© 2013 UFS, Inc.
ARMSTRONG
Distributed by Universal UClick for UFS
Where are my seed samples?!
I thought they were refreshments
SEEDS
robbarmstrong.com

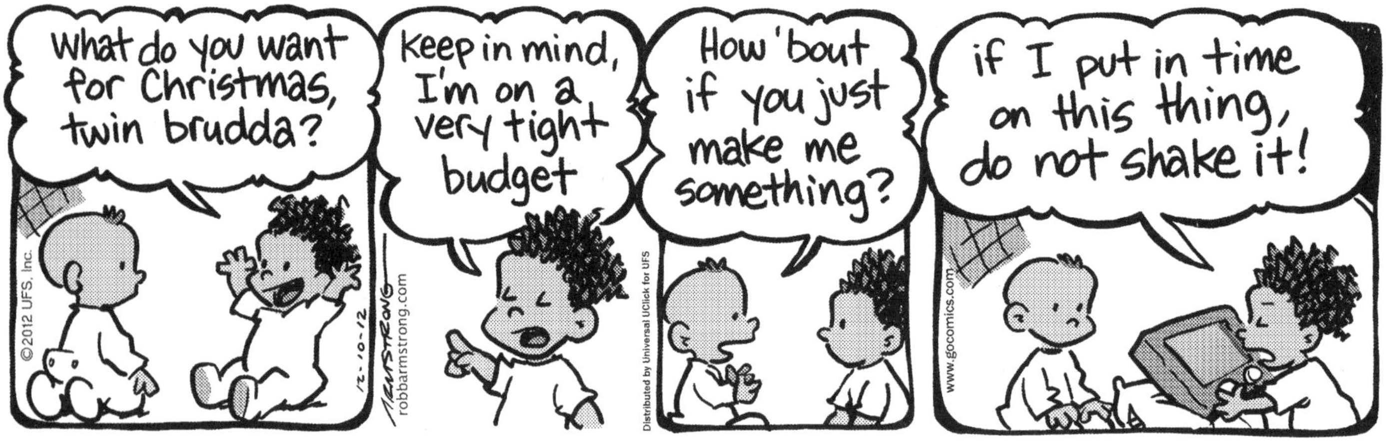
What do you want for Christmas, twin brudda?
©2012 UFS, Inc.
12-10-12
ARMSTRONG
robbarmstrong.com
Keep in mind, I'm on a very tight budget
Distributed by Universal UClick for UFS
How 'bout if you just make me something?
www.gocomics.com
if I put in time on this thing, do not shake it!

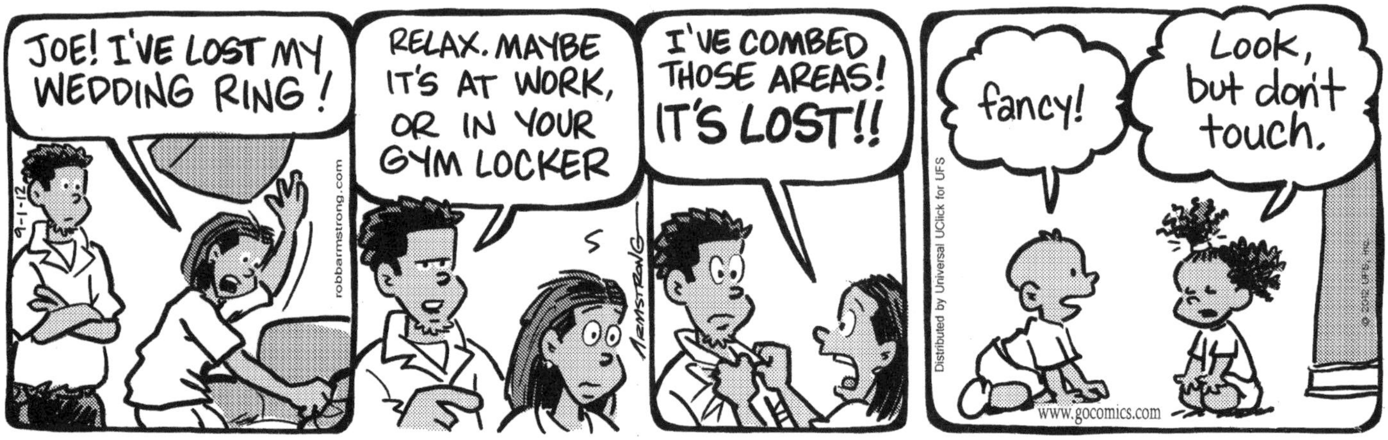
9-1-12
JOE! I'VE LOST MY WEDDING RING!
robbarmstrong.com
RELAX. MAYBE IT'S AT WORK, OR IN YOUR GYM LOCKER
ARMSTRONG
I'VE COMBED THOSE AREAS! IT'S LOST!!
Distributed by Universal UClick for UFS
fancy!
Look, but don't touch.
www.gocomics.com

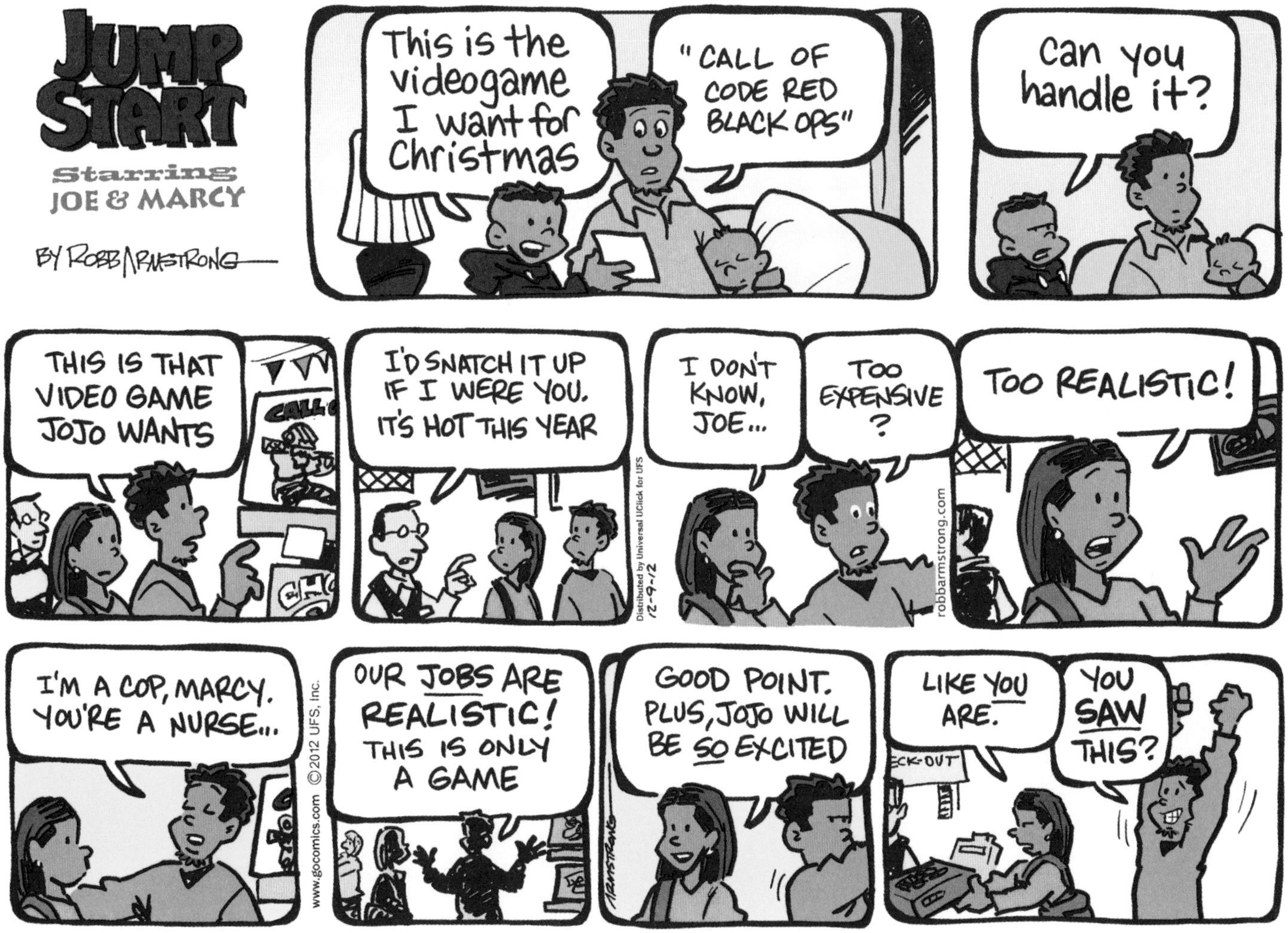
JUMP START
Starring JOE & MARCY
BY ROBB ARMSTRONG
This is the videogame I want for Christmas
"CALL OF CODE RED BLACK OPS"
Can you handle it?
THIS IS THAT VIDEO GAME JOJO WANTS
I'D SNATCH IT UP IF I WERE YOU. IT'S HOT THIS YEAR
Distributed by Universal UClick for UFS
12-9-12
I DON'T KNOW, JOE...
TOO EXPENSIVE ?
robbarmstrong.com
TOO REALISTIC!
I'M A COP, MARCY. YOU'RE A NURSE...
www.gocomics.com ©2012 UFS, Inc.
OUR JOBS ARE REALISTIC! THIS IS ONLY A GAME
GOOD POINT. PLUS, JOJO WILL BE SO EXCITED
LIKE YOU ARE.
YOU SAW THIS?

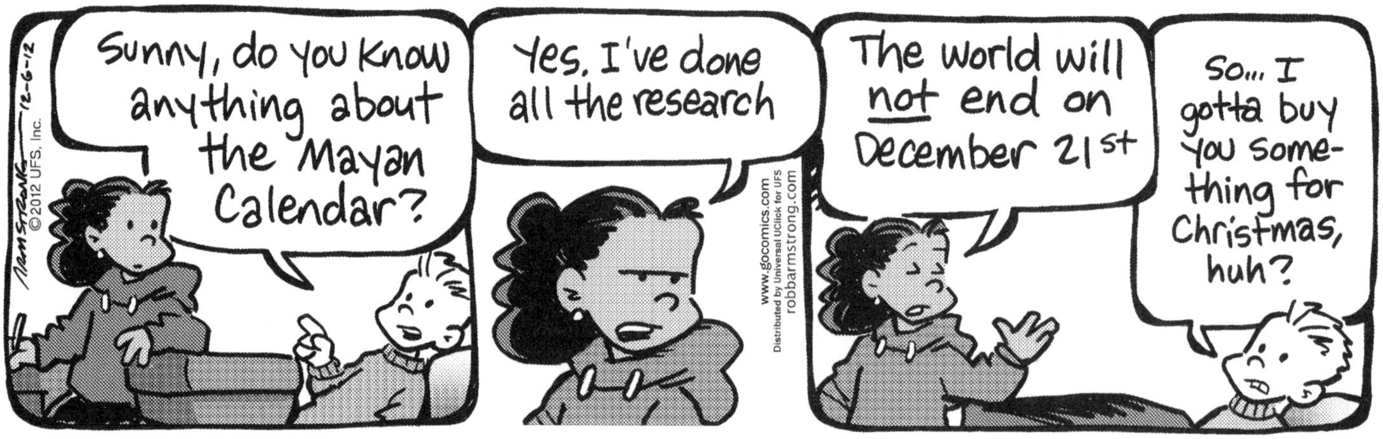
Sunny, do you know anything about the Mayan Calendar?
Yes. I've done all the research
The world will not end on December 21st
So... I gotta buy you some-thing for Christmas, huh?
©2012 UFS, Inc.
www.gocomics.com
robbarmstrong.com
Distributed by Universal UClick for UFS

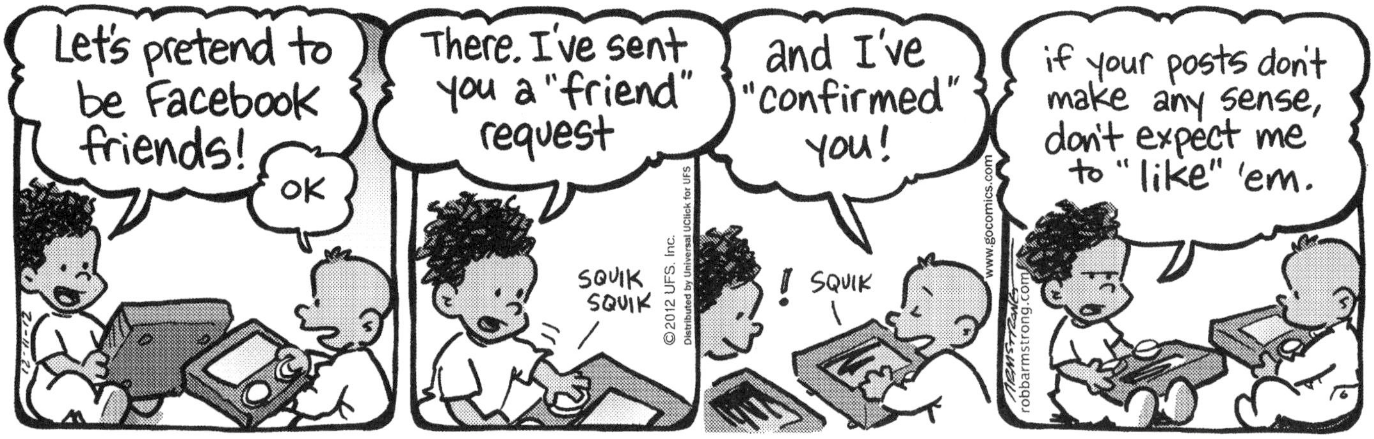
Let's pretend to be Facebook friends!
OK
There. I've sent you a "friend" request
SQUIK SQUIK
and I've "confirmed" you!
!
SQUIK
if your posts don't make any sense, don't expect me to "like" 'em.
©2012 UFS, Inc.
Distributed by Universal UClick for UFS
www.gocomics.com
robbarmstrong.com

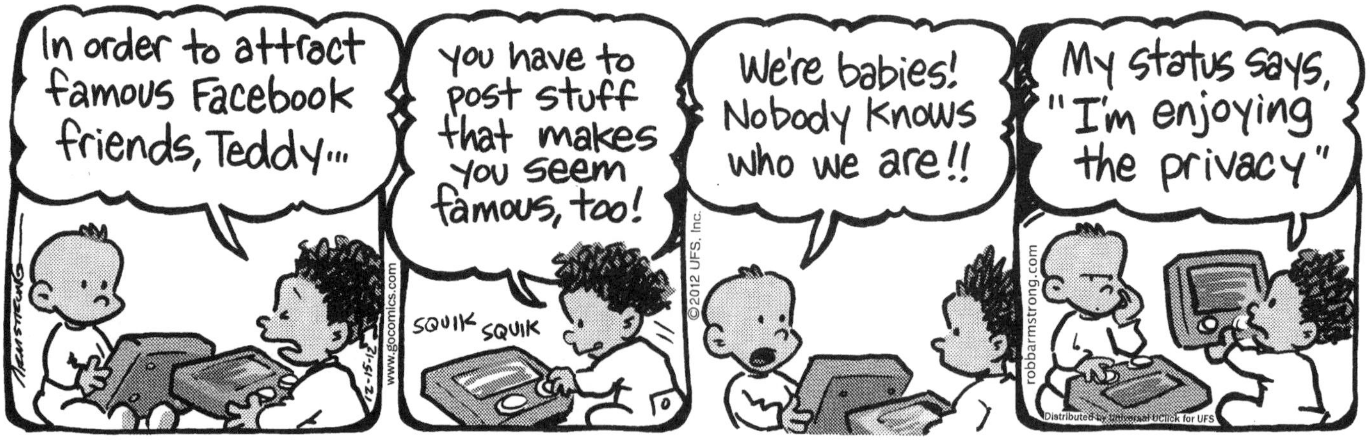
In order to attract famous Facebook friends, Teddy...
You have to post stuff that makes you seem famous, too!
SQUIK SQUIK
We're babies! Nobody knows who we are!!
My status says, "I'm enjoying the privacy"
www.gocomics.com
©2012 UFS, Inc.
robbarmstrong.com
Distributed by Universal UClick for UFS

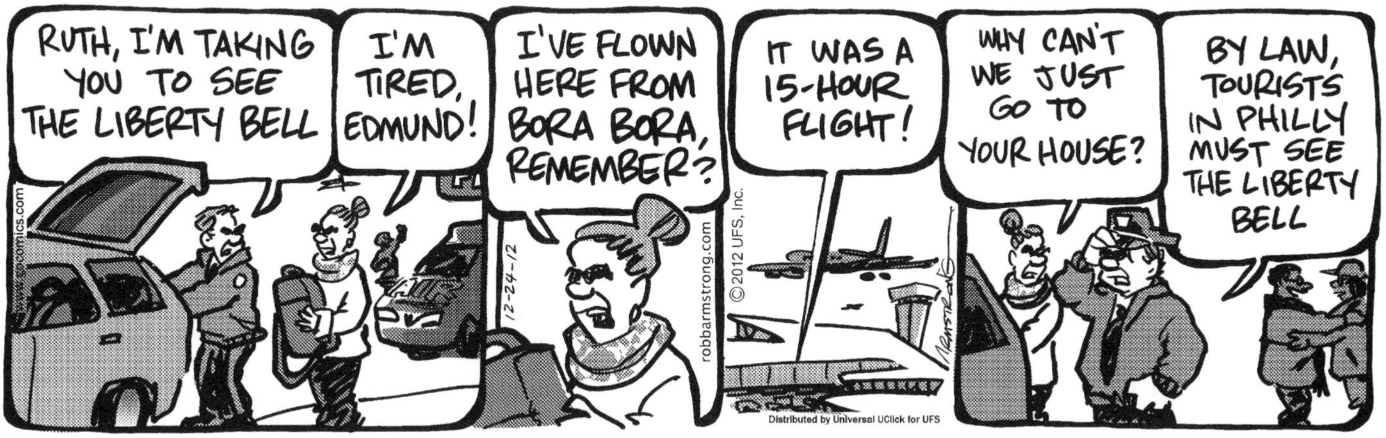
RUTH, I'M TAKING YOU TO SEE THE LIBERTY BELL
I'M TIRED, EDMUND!
I'VE FLOWN HERE FROM BORA BORA, REMEMBER?
IT WAS A 15-HOUR FLIGHT!
WHY CAN'T WE JUST GO TO YOUR HOUSE?
BY LAW, TOURISTS IN PHILLY MUST SEE THE LIBERTY BELL
12-24-12
©2012 UFS, Inc.
robbarmstrong.com
www.gocomics.com
Distributed by Universal UClick for UFS

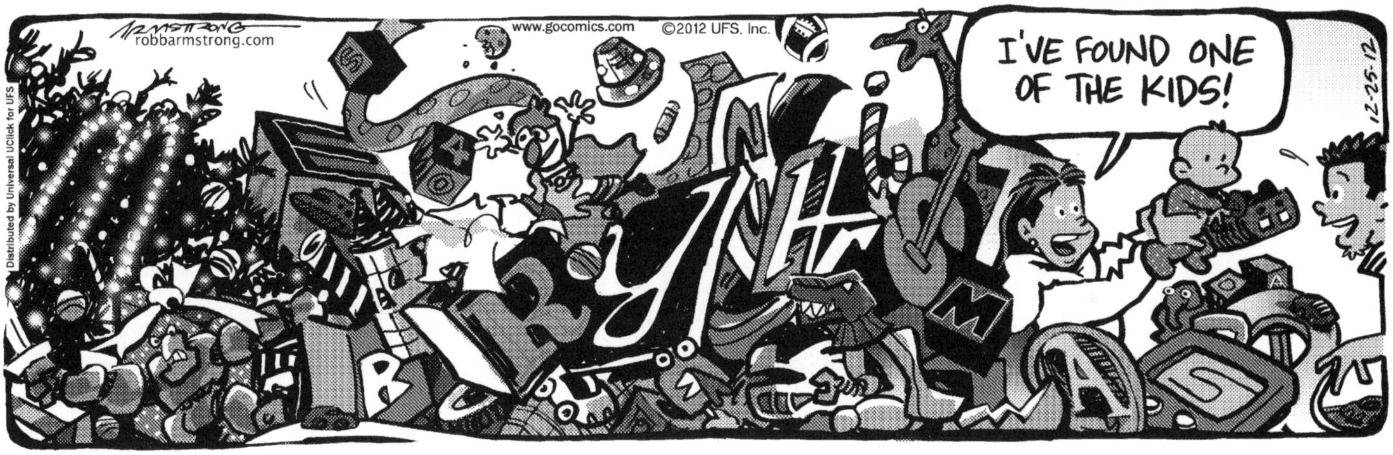
ARMSTRONG
robbarmstrong.com
www.gocomics.com
©2012 UFS, Inc.
I'VE FOUND ONE OF THE KIDS!
12-25-12
Distributed by Universal UClick for UFS

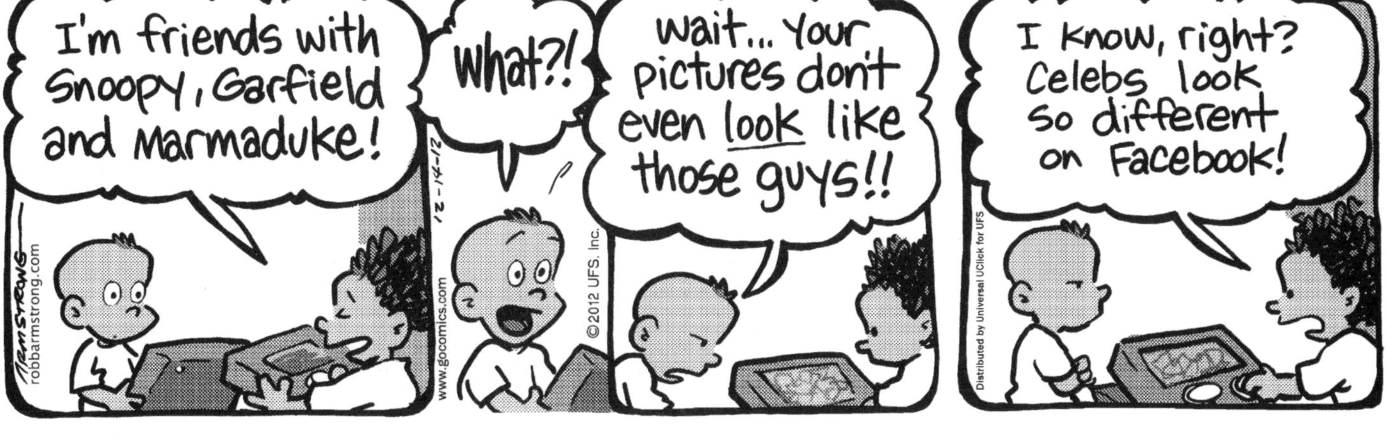
I'm friends with Snoopy, Garfield and Marmaduke!
What?!
Wait... Your pictures don't even look like those guys!!
I know, right? Celebs look so different on Facebook!
ARMSTRONG
robbarmstrong.com
12-14-12
www.gocomics.com
©2012 UFS, Inc.
Distributed by Universal UClick for UFS

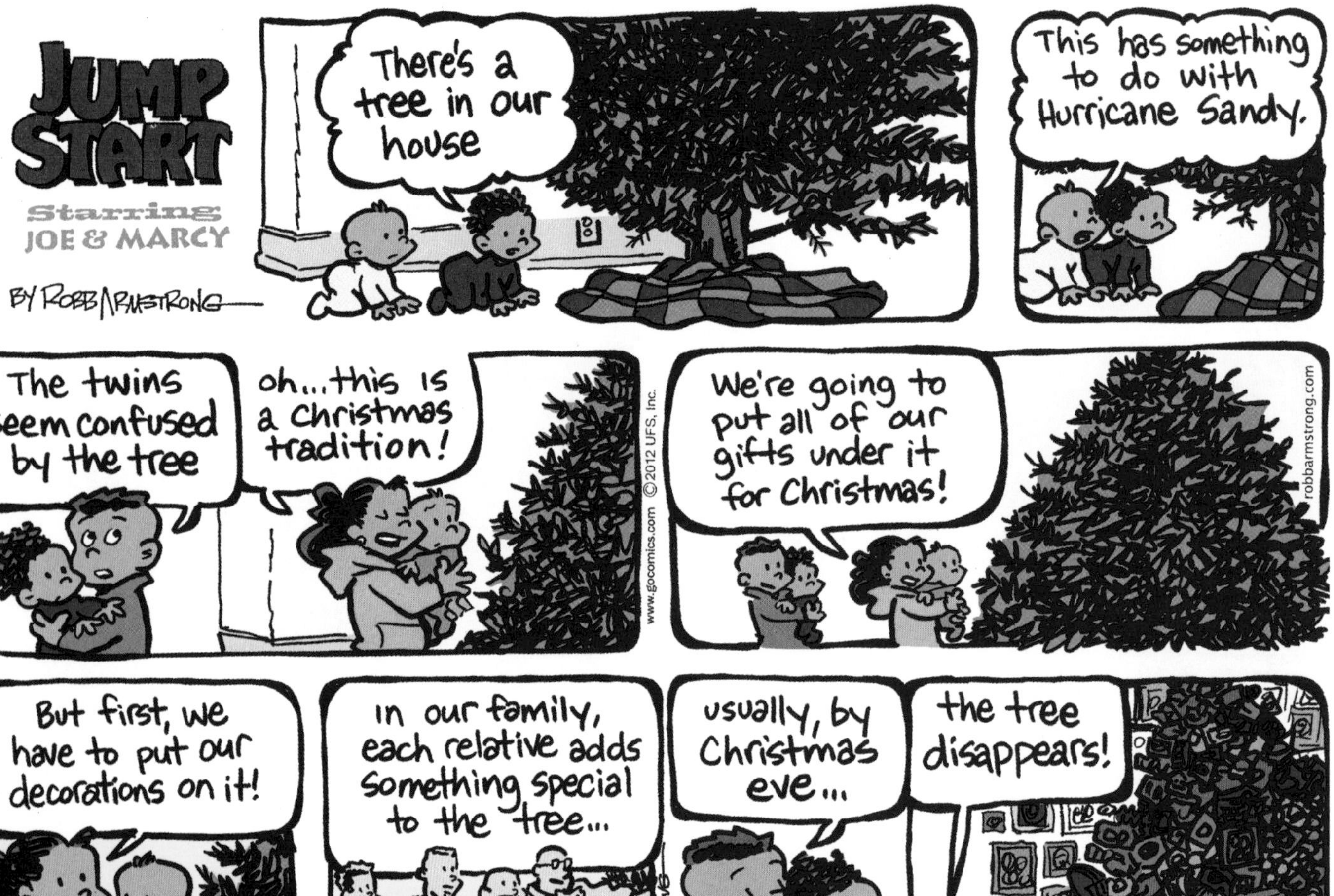
JUMP START
Starring JOE & MARCY
BY ROBB ARMSTRONG
There's a tree in our house
This has something to do with Hurricane Sandy.
The twins seem confused by the tree
oh... this is a christmas tradition!
www.gocomics.com © 2012 UFS, Inc.
We're going to put all of our gifts under it for Christmas!
robbarmstrong.com
But first, we have to put our decorations on it!
in our family, each relative adds something special to the tree...
usually, by Christmas eve...
Distributed by Universal UClick for UFS
12-16-12
the tree disappears!

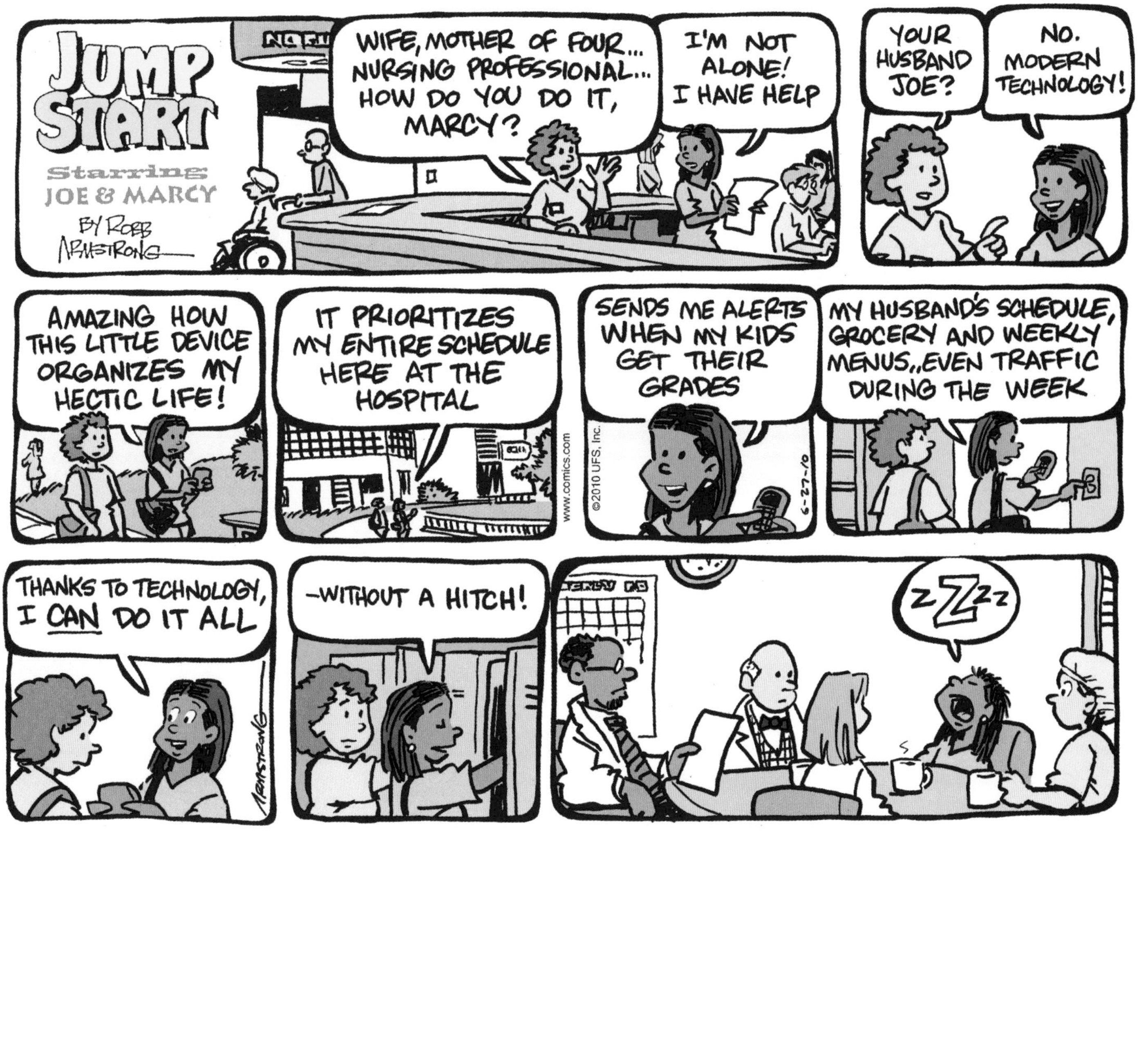
JUMP START
Starring JOE & MARCY
BY ROBB ARMSTRONG
WIFE, MOTHER OF FOUR... NURSING PROFESSIONAL... HOW DO YOU DO IT, MARCY?
I'M NOT ALONE! I HAVE HELP
YOUR HUSBAND JOE?
NO. MODERN TECHNOLOGY!
AMAZING HOW THIS LITTLE DEVICE ORGANIZES MY HECTIC LIFE!
IT PRIORITIZES MY ENTIRE SCHEDULE HERE AT THE HOSPITAL
www.comics.com
©2010 UFS, Inc.
SENDS ME ALERTS WHEN MY KIDS GET THEIR GRADES
6-27-10
MY HUSBAND'S SCHEDULE, GROCERY AND WEEKLY MENUS,,EVEN TRAFFIC DURING THE WEEK
THANKS TO TECHNOLOGY, I CAN DO IT ALL
ARMSTRONG
-WITHOUT A HITCH!
Z Z Z z z

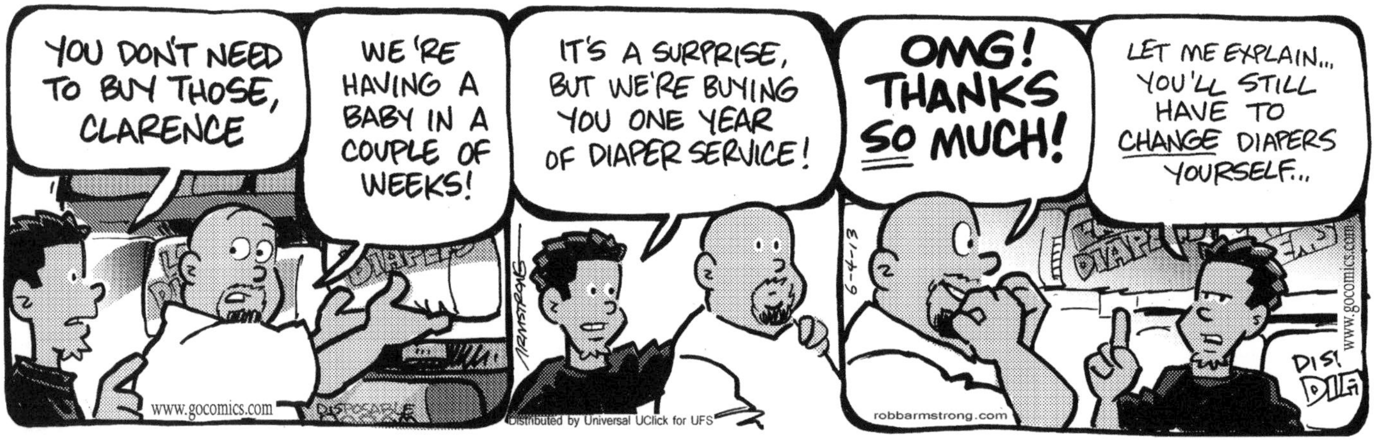
YOU DON'T NEED TO BUY THOSE, CLARENCE
WE'RE HAVING A BABY IN A COUPLE OF WEEKS!
IT'S A SURPRISE, BUT WE'RE BUYING YOU ONE YEAR OF DIAPER SERVICE!
OMG! THANKS SO MUCH!
LET ME EXPLAIN... YOU'LL STILL HAVE TO CHANGE DIAPERS YOURSELF...
6-4-13
ARMSTRONG
www.gocomics.com
Distributed by Universal UClick for UFS
robbarmstrong.com

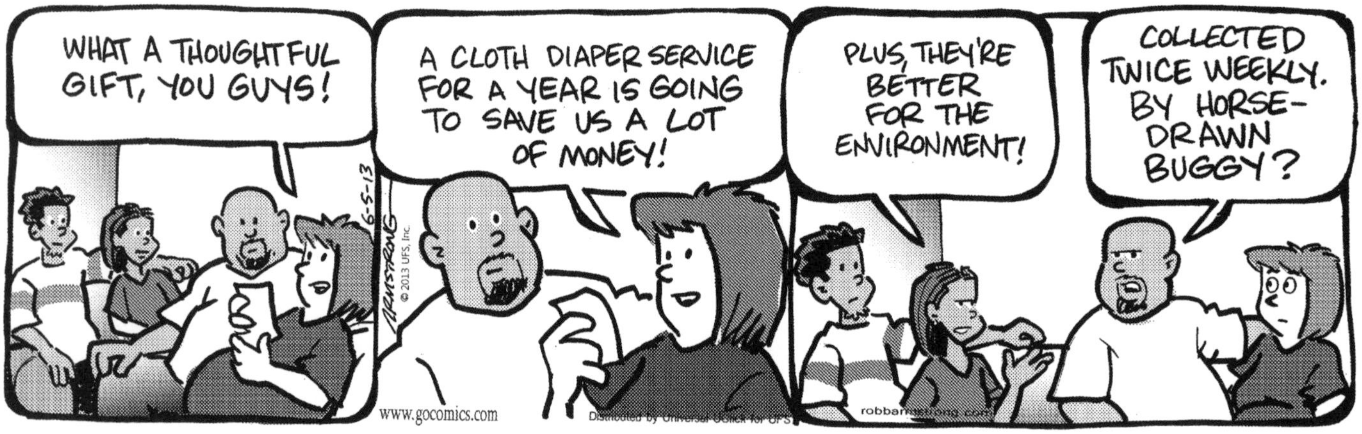
WHAT A THOUGHTFUL GIFT, YOU GUYS!
A CLOTH DIAPER SERVICE FOR A YEAR IS GOING TO SAVE US A LOT OF MONEY!
PLUS, THEY'RE BETTER FOR THE ENVIRONMENT!
COLLECTED TWICE WEEKLY. BY HORSE-DRAWN BUGGY?
6-5-13
ARMSTRONG
© 2013 UFS, Inc.
www.gocomics.com

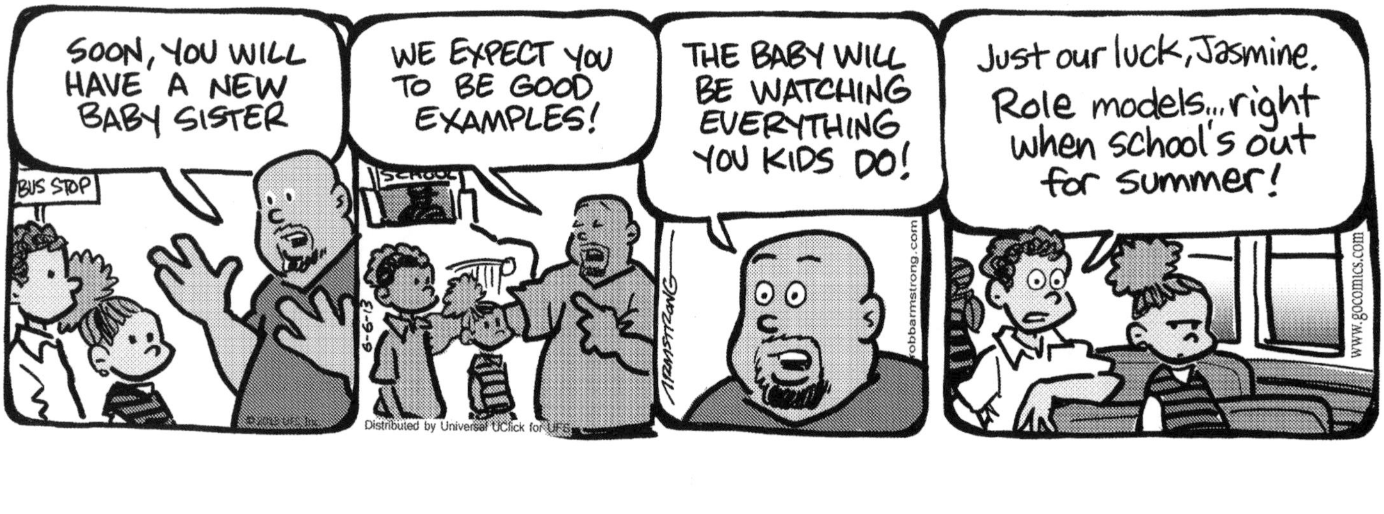
SOON, YOU WILL HAVE A NEW BABY SISTER
BUS STOP
WE EXPECT YOU TO BE GOOD EXAMPLES!
THE BABY WILL BE WATCHING EVERYTHING YOU KIDS DO!
Just our luck, Jasmine. Role models... right when school's out for summer!
6-6-13
ARMSTRONG
Distributed by Universal UClick for UFS
robbarmstrong.com
www.gocomics.com

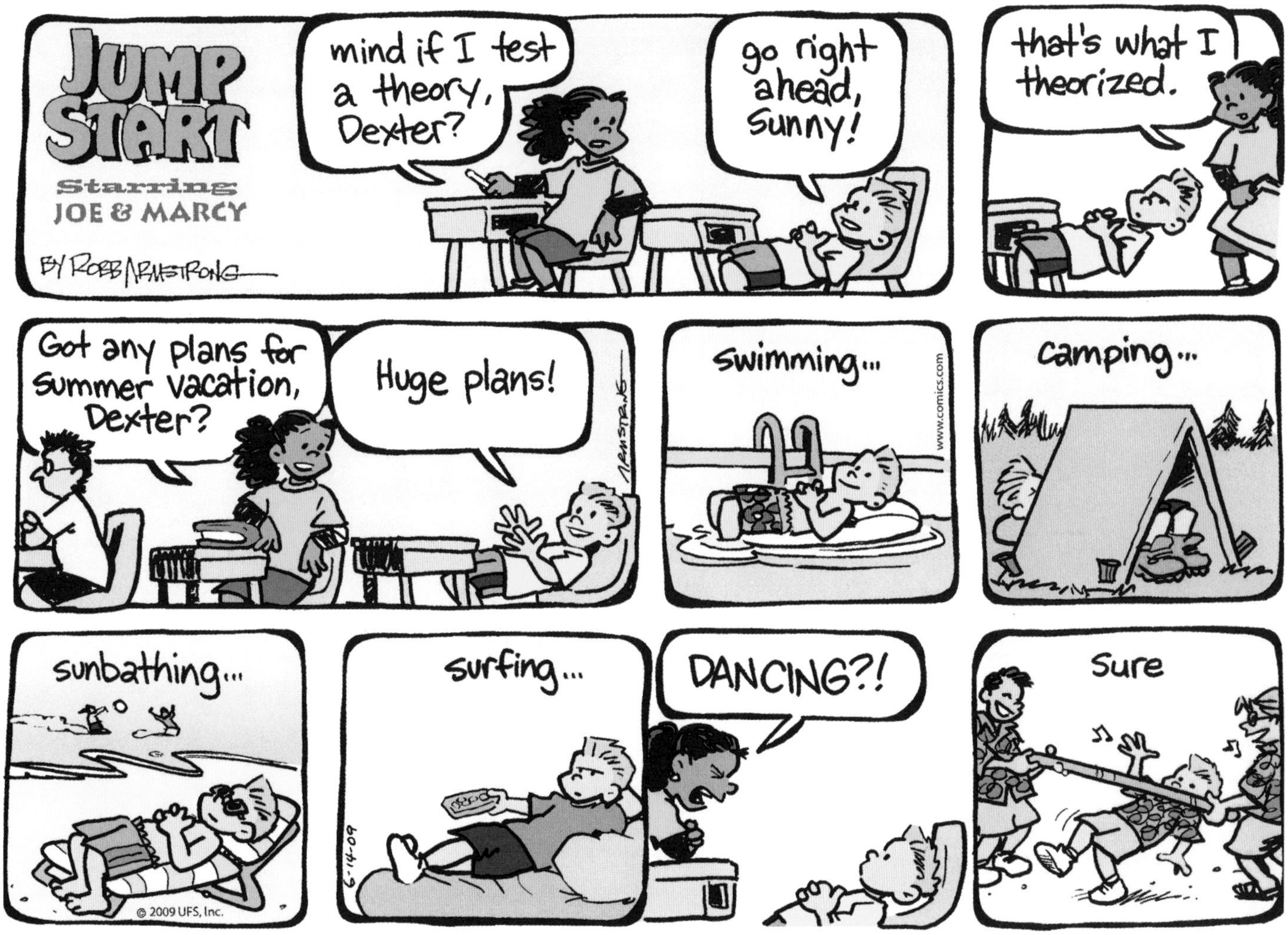
JUMP START
Starring
JOE & MARCY
BY ROBB ARMSTRONG
mind if I test a theory, Dexter?
go right ahead, Sunny!
that's what I theorized.
Got any plans for summer vacation, Dexter?
Huge plans!
swimming...
www.comics.com
camping...
sunbathing...
© 2009 UFS, Inc.
surfing...
6-14-09
DANCING?!
Sure

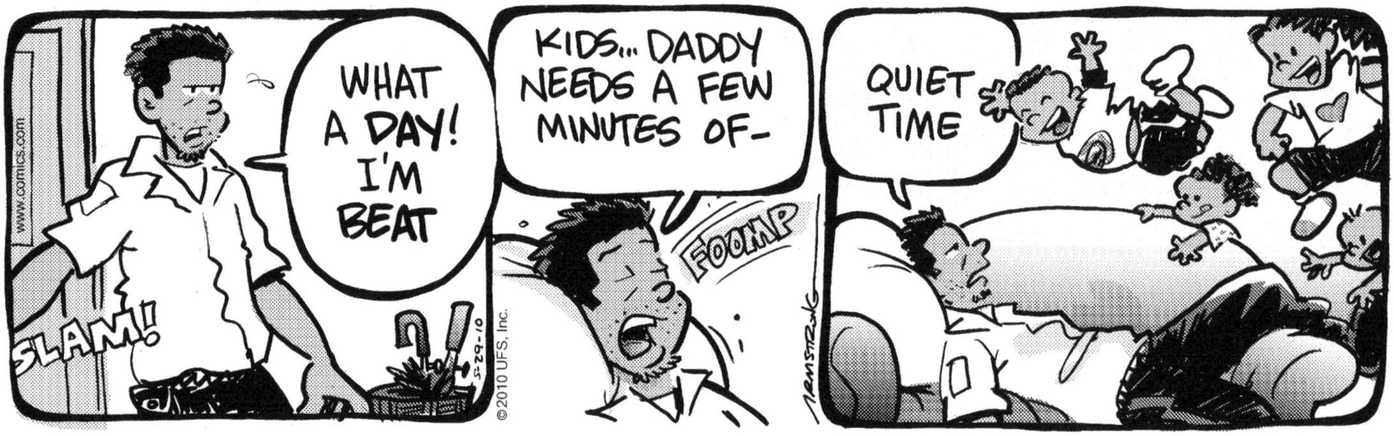
WHAT A DAY! I'M BEAT
SLAM!
KIDS... DADDY NEEDS A FEW MINUTES OF-
FOOMP
QUIET TIME
www.comics.com
© 2010 UFS, Inc.
5-29-10
ARMSTRONG

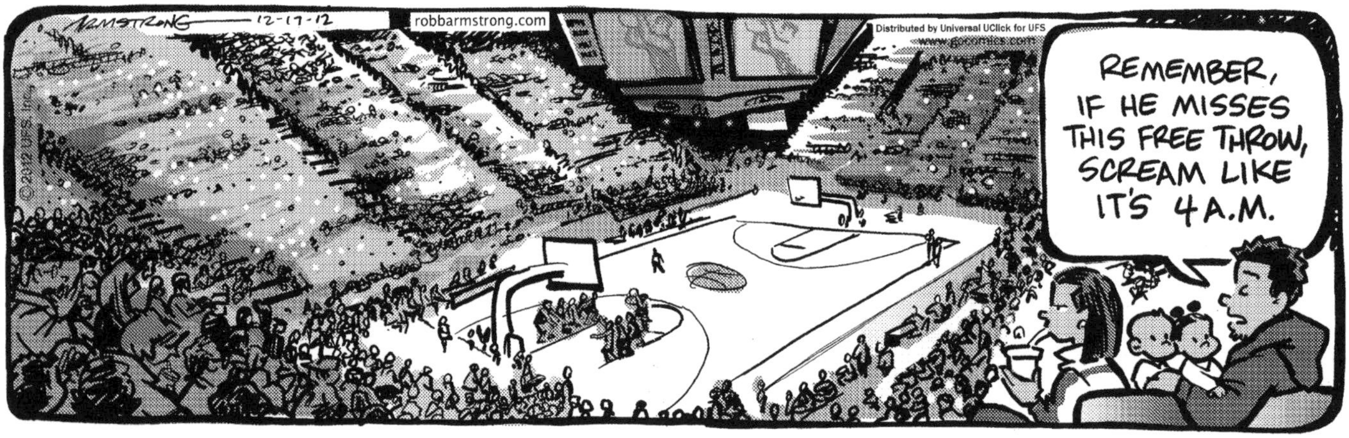
ARMSTRONG 12-17-12
robbarmstrong.com
Distributed by Universal UClick for UFS
REMEMBER, IF HE MISSES THIS FREE THROW, SCREAM LIKE IT'S 4 A.M.

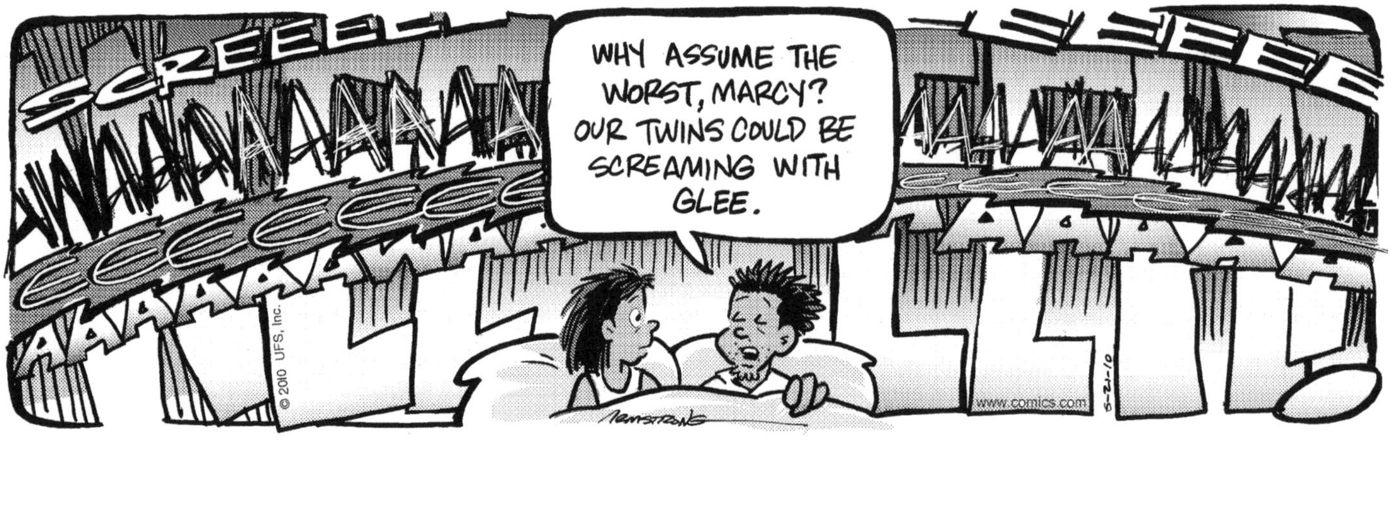
SCREEE--EEEE
WAAAAAAAA
EEEEEEEE
AAAAAA
WHY ASSUME THE WORST, MARCY? OUR TWINS COULD BE SCREAMING WITH GLEE.
© 2010 UFS, Inc.
www.comics.com
5-21-10
ARMSTRONG

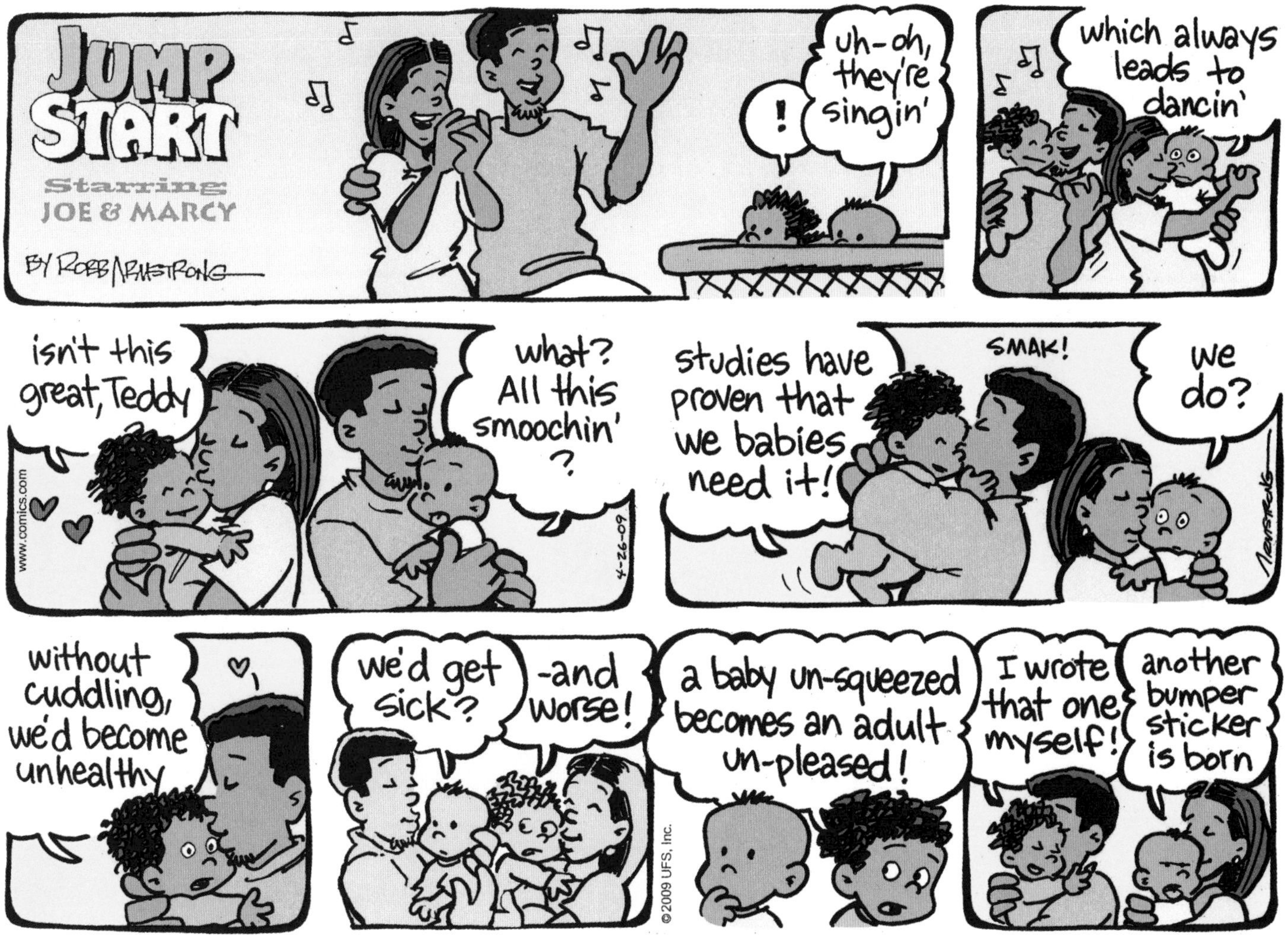
JUMP START
Starring
JOE & MARCY
BY ROBB ARMSTRONG
!
uh-oh, they're singin'
which always leads to dancin'
isn't this great, Teddy
what? All this smoochin' ?
www.comics.com
4-26-09
studies have proven that we babies need it!
SMAK!
we do?
ARMSTRONG
without cuddling, we'd become unhealthy
we'd get sick?
-and worse!
©2009 UFS, Inc.
a baby un-squeezed becomes an adult un-pleased!
I wrote that one myself!
another bumper sticker is born

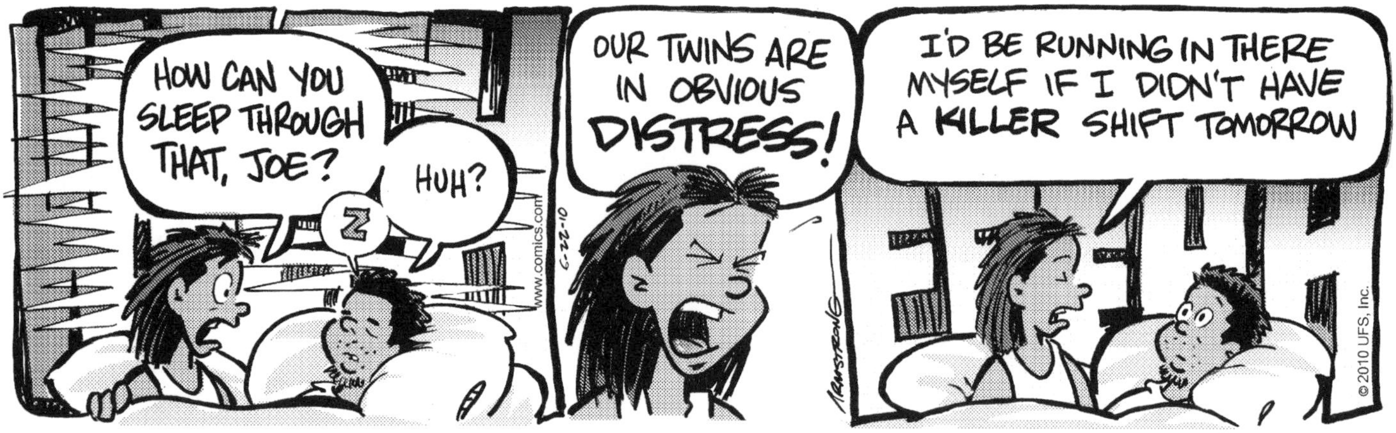
HOW CAN YOU SLEEP THROUGH THAT, JOE?
HUH?
Z
www.comics.com
6-22-10
OUR TWINS ARE IN OBVIOUS DISTRESS!
ARMSTRONG
I'D BE RUNNING IN THERE MYSELF IF I DIDN'T HAVE A KILLER SHIFT TOMORROW
© 2010 UFS, Inc.

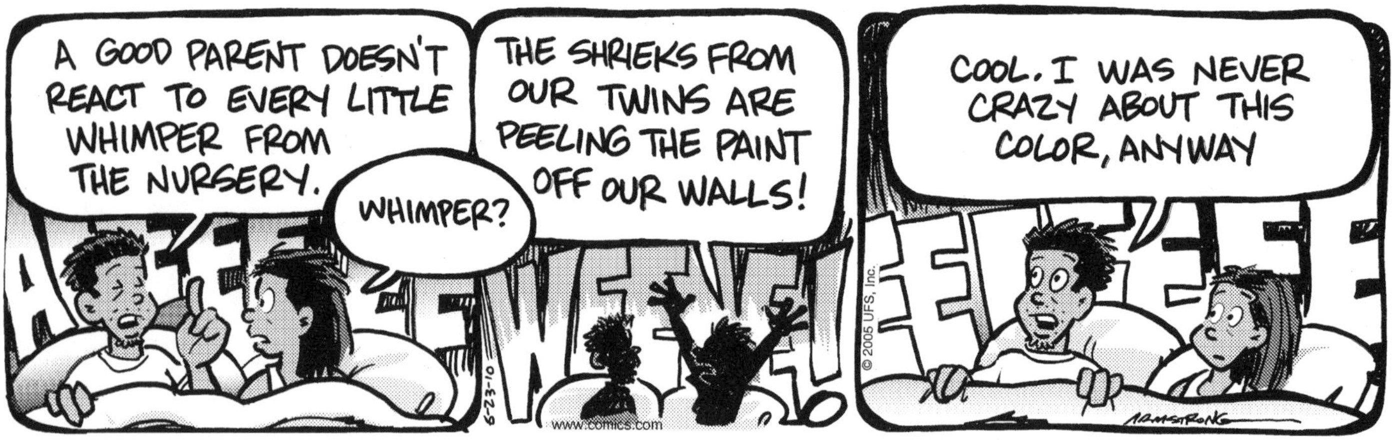
A GOOD PARENT DOESN'T REACT TO EVERY LITTLE WHIMPER FROM THE NURSERY.
WHIMPER?
6-23-10
THE SHRIEKS FROM OUR TWINS ARE PEELING THE PAINT OFF OUR WALLS!
www.comics.com
© 2005 UFS, Inc.
COOL. I WAS NEVER CRAZY ABOUT THIS COLOR, ANYWAY
ARMSTRONG

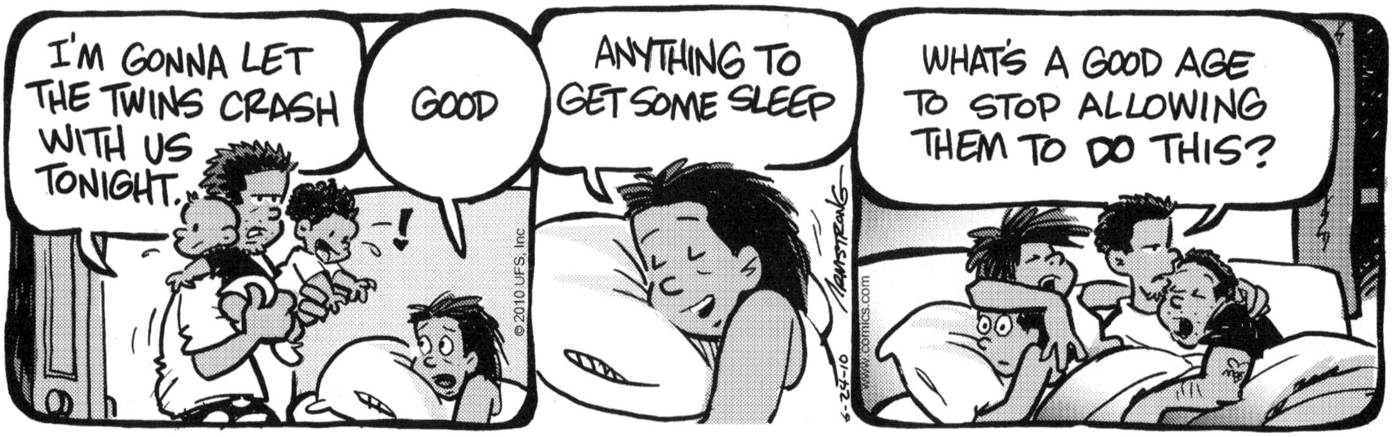
I'M GONNA LET THE TWINS CRASH WITH US TONIGHT.
GOOD
© 2010 UFS, Inc.
ANYTHING TO GET SOME SLEEP
ARMSTRONG
www.comics.com
6-24-10
WHAT'S A GOOD AGE TO STOP ALLOWING THEM TO DO THIS?

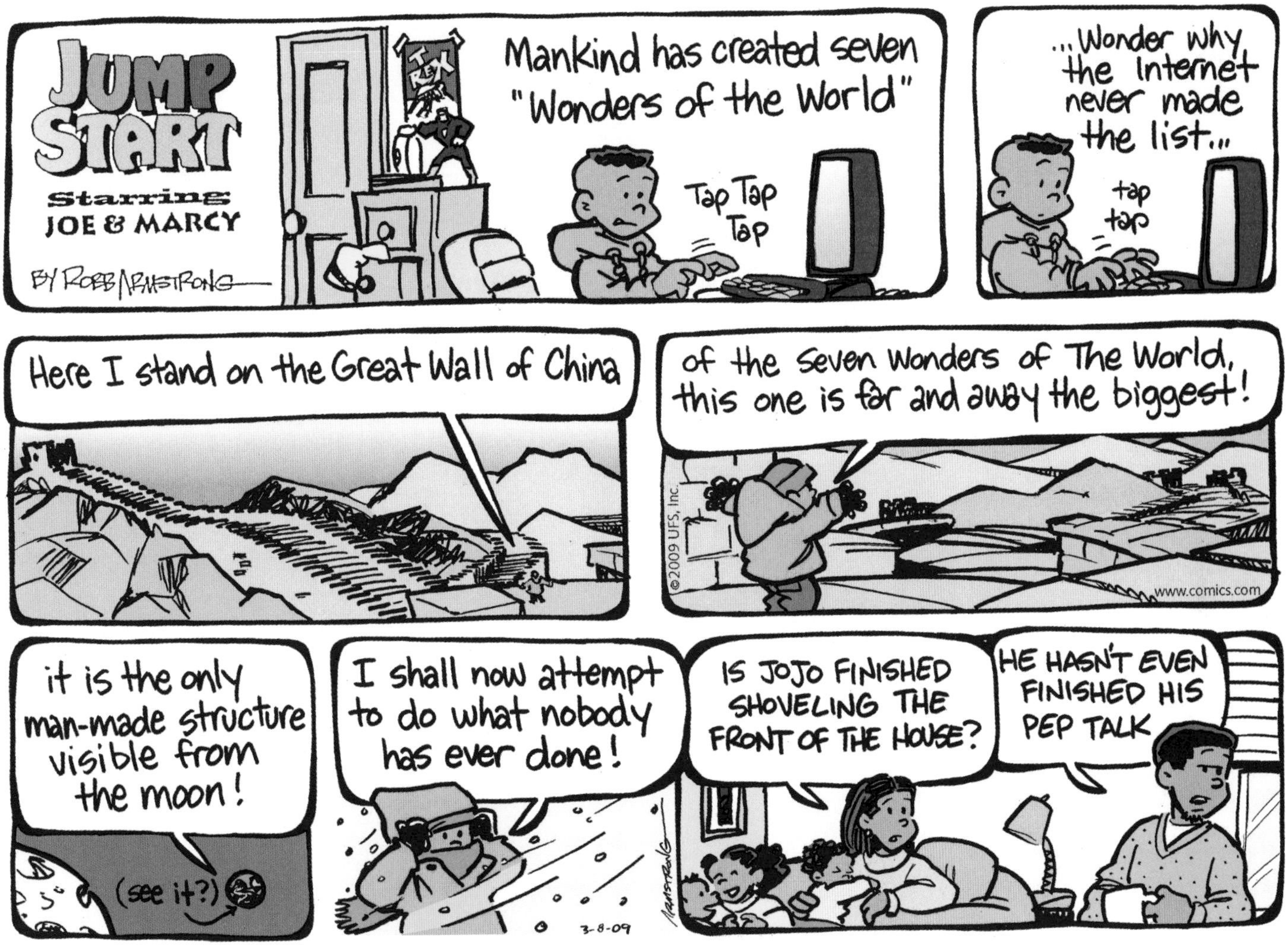
JUMP START
Starring JOE & MARCY
BY ROBB ARMSTRONG
Mankind has created seven "Wonders of the World"
Tap Tap Tap
...Wonder why the Internet never made the list...
tap tap
Here I stand on the Great Wall of China
of the seven wonders of The World, this one is far and away the biggest!
©2009 UFS, Inc.
www.comics.com
it is the only man-made structure visible from the moon!
(see it?)
I shall now attempt to do what nobody has ever done!
3-8-09
IS JOJO FINISHED SHOVELING THE FRONT OF THE HOUSE?
HE HASN'T EVEN FINISHED HIS PEP TALK

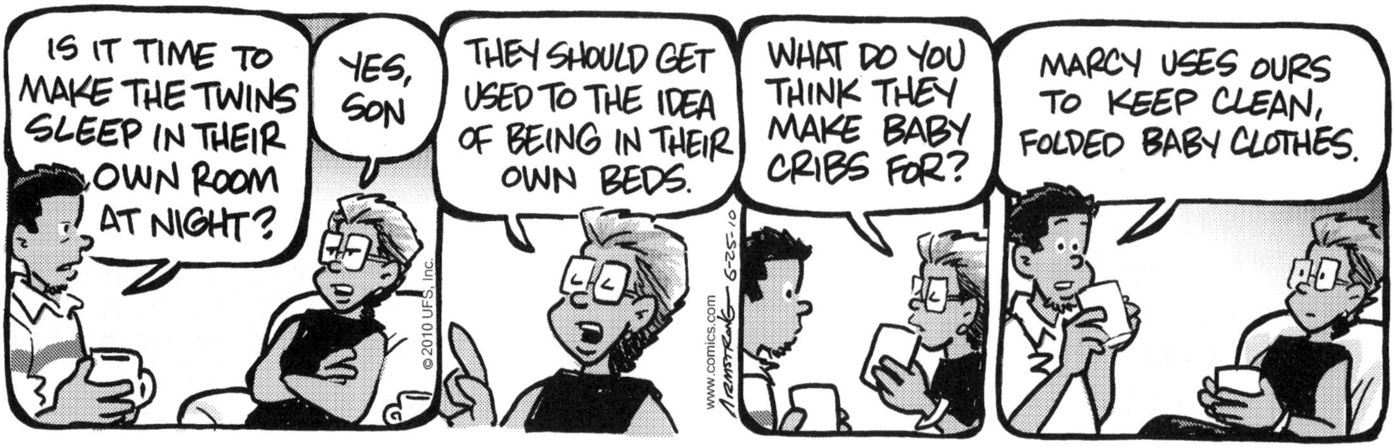
IS IT TIME TO MAKE THE TWINS SLEEP IN THEIR OWN ROOM AT NIGHT?
YES, SON
THEY SHOULD GET USED TO THE IDEA OF BEING IN THEIR OWN BEDS.
WHAT DO YOU THINK THEY MAKE BABY CRIBS FOR?
MARCY USES OURS TO KEEP CLEAN, FOLDED BABY CLOTHES.
© 2010 UFS, Inc.
www.comics.com
ARMSTRONG
6-25-10

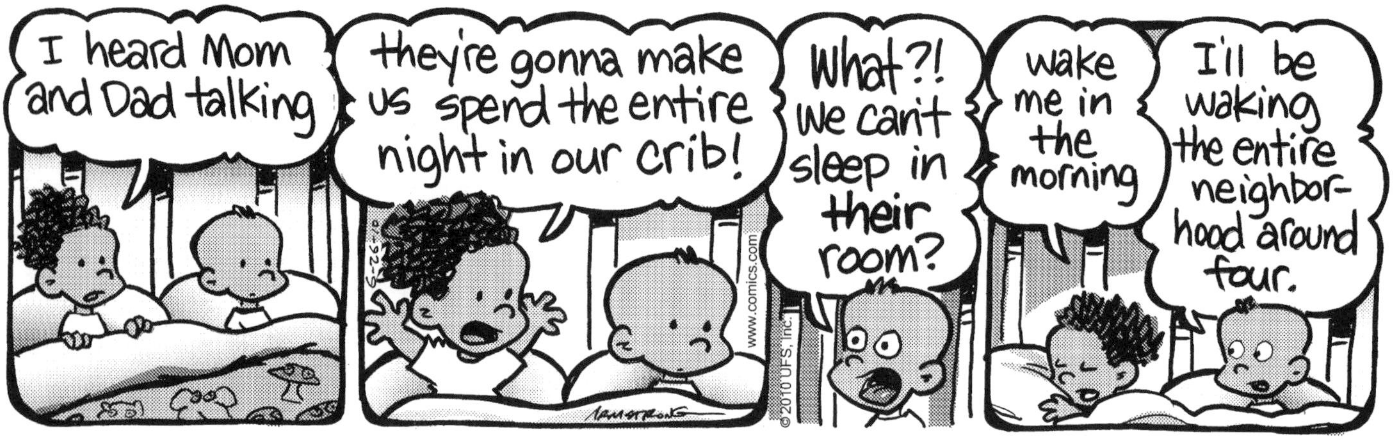
I heard Mom and Dad talking
they're gonna make us spend the entire night in our crib!
What?! We can't sleep in their room?
wake me in the morning
I'll be waking the entire neighbor-hood around four.
6-26-10
www.comics.com
© 2010 UFS, Inc.
ARMSTRONG

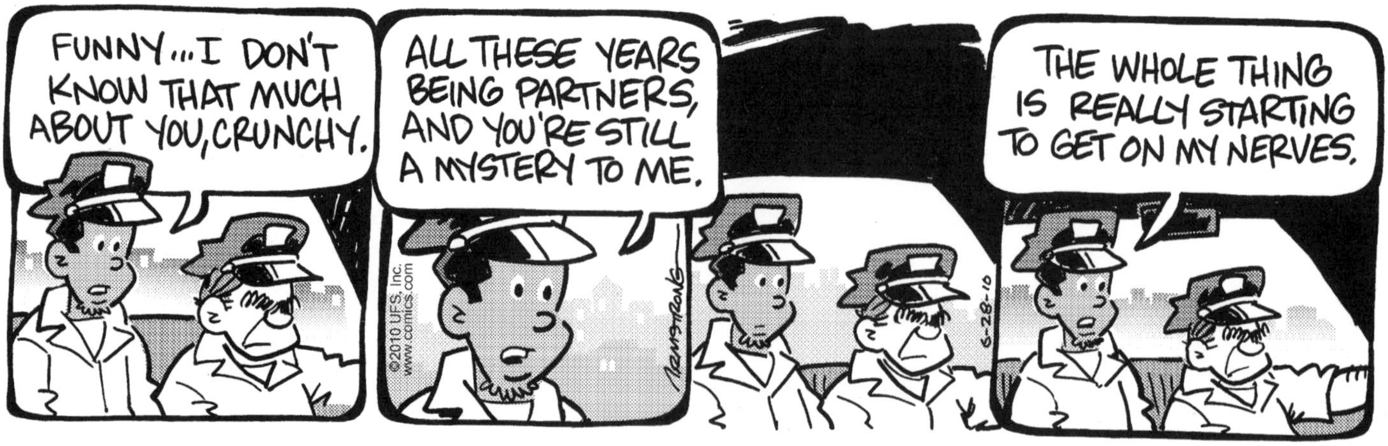
FUNNY...I DON'T KNOW THAT MUCH ABOUT YOU, CRUNCHY.
ALL THESE YEARS BEING PARTNERS, AND YOU'RE STILL A MYSTERY TO ME.
THE WHOLE THING IS REALLY STARTING TO GET ON MY NERVES.
© 2010 UFS, Inc.
www.comics.com
ARMSTRONG
6-28-10

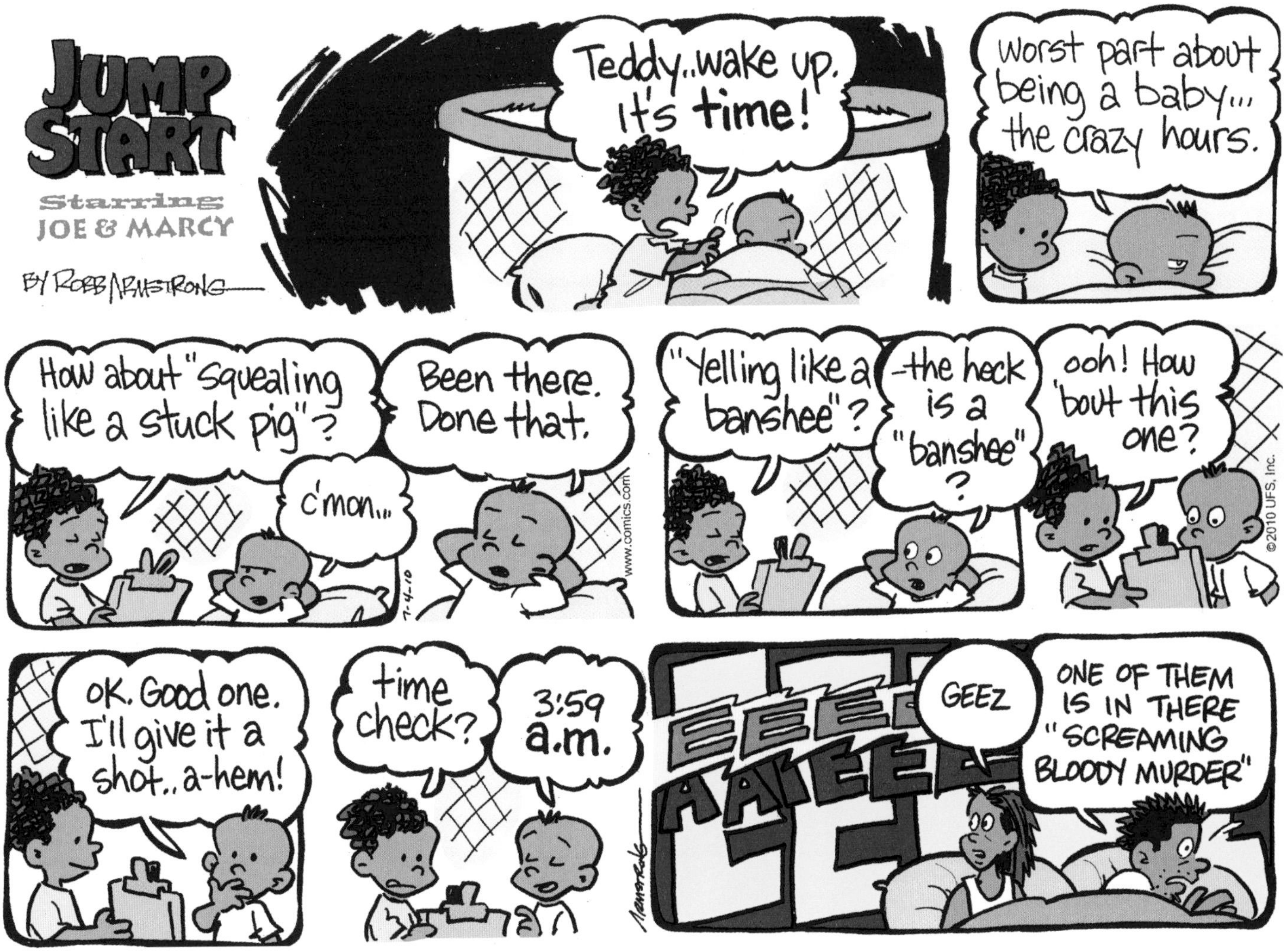
JUMP START
Starring
JOE & MARCY
BY ROBB ARMSTRONG
Teddy..wake up. It's time!
worst part about being a baby... the crazy hours.
How about "squealing like a stuck pig"?
c'mon...
Been there. Done that.
7-4-10
www.comics.com
"Yelling like a banshee"?
-the heck is a "banshee"?
ooh! How 'bout this one?
©2010 UFS, Inc.
OK. Good one. I'll give it a shot.. a-hem!
time check?
3:59 a.m.
EEEE AAEEE
GEEZ
ONE OF THEM IS IN THERE "SCREAMING BLOODY MURDER"

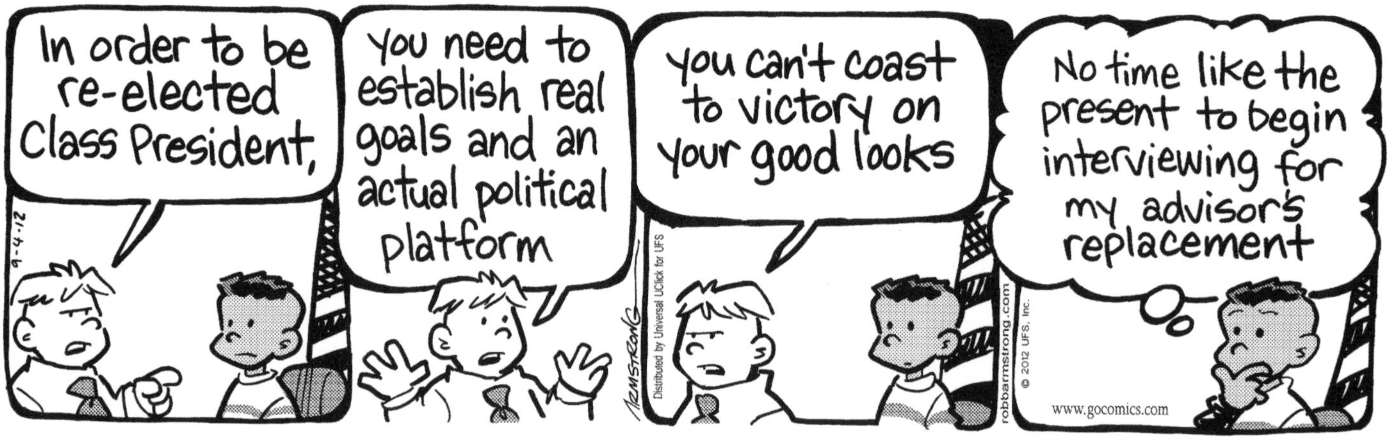
In order to be re-elected Class President,
You need to establish real goals and an actual political platform
You can't coast to victory on your good looks
No time like the present to begin interviewing for my advisor's replacement
www.gocomics.com

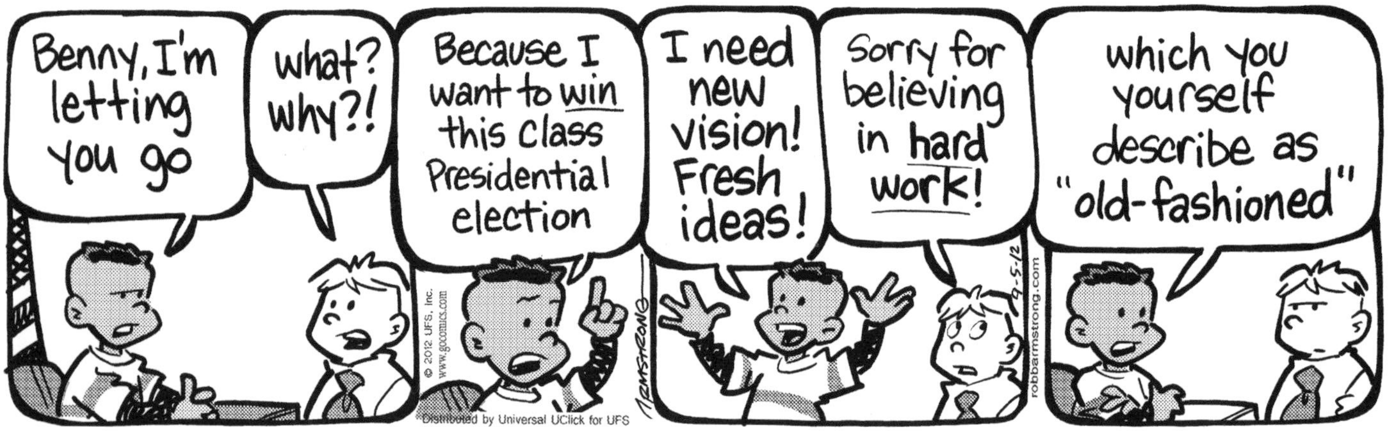
Benny, I'm letting you go
what? why?!
Because I want to win this Class Presidential election
I need new vision! Fresh ideas!
Sorry for believing in hard work!
which you yourself describe as "old-fashioned"
Distributed by Universal UClick for UFS

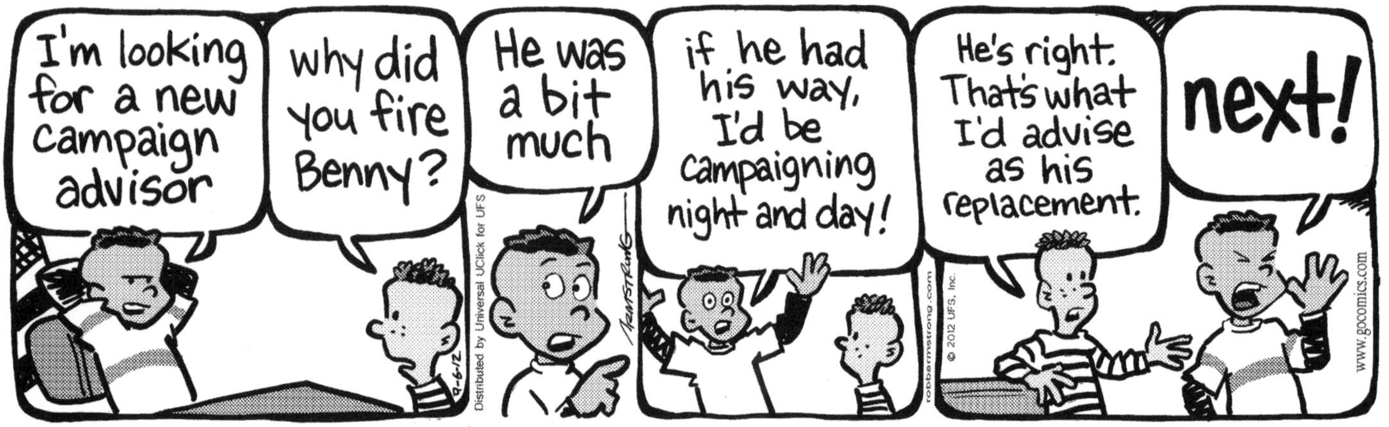
I'm looking for a new campaign advisor
why did you fire Benny?
He was a bit much
if he had his way, I'd be campaigning night and day!
He's right. That's what I'd advise as his replacement.
next!
www.gocomics.com

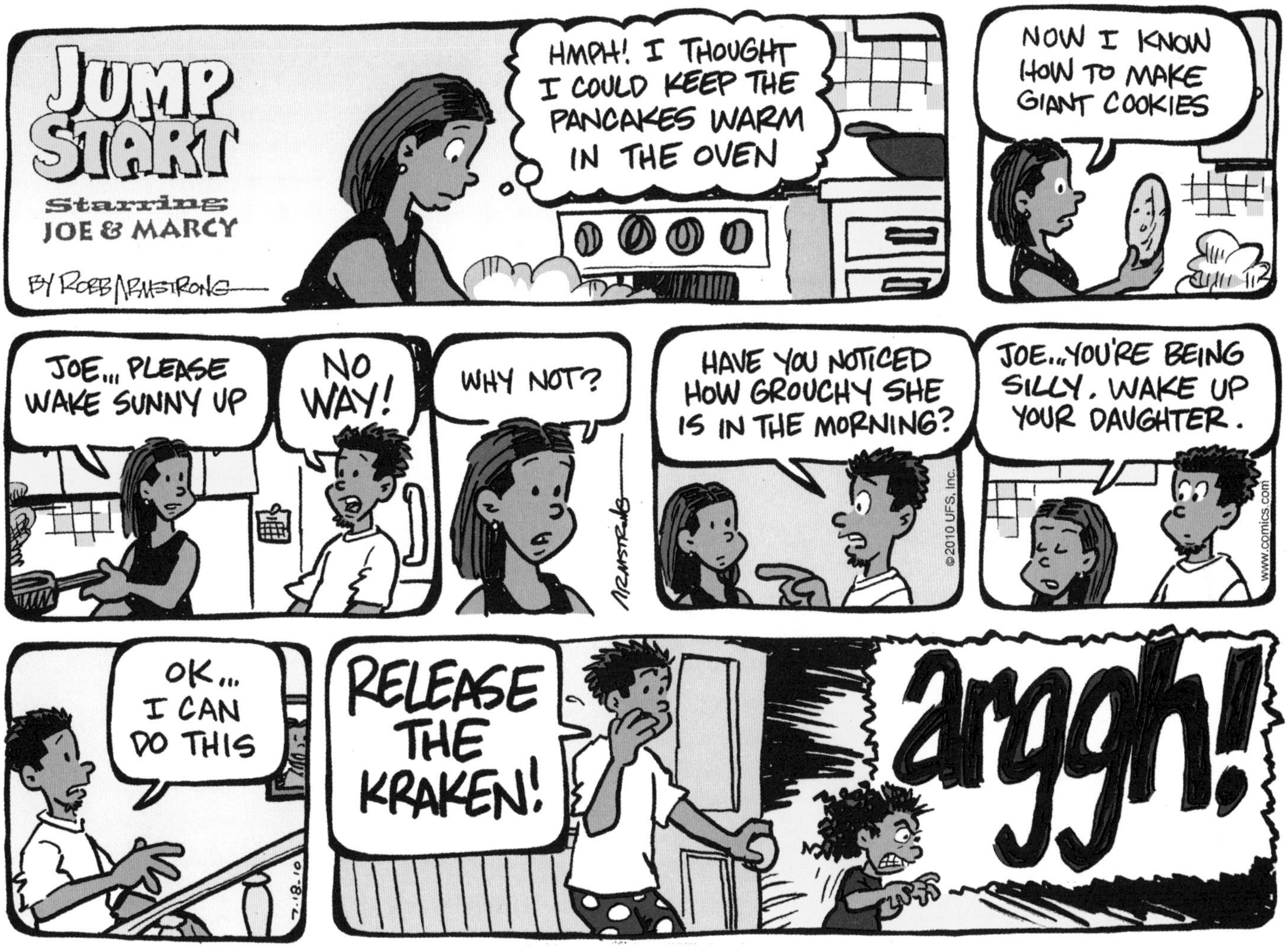
JUMP START
Starring JOE & MARCY
BY ROBB ARMSTRONG
HMPH! I THOUGHT I COULD KEEP THE PANCAKES WARM IN THE OVEN
NOW I KNOW HOW TO MAKE GIANT COOKIES
JOE... PLEASE WAKE SUNNY UP
NO WAY!
WHY NOT?
HAVE YOU NOTICED HOW GROUCHY SHE IS IN THE MORNING?
©2010 UFS, Inc.
JOE... YOU'RE BEING SILLY. WAKE UP YOUR DAUGHTER.
www.comics.com
OK... I CAN DO THIS
7.18.10
RELEASE THE KRAKEN!
arggh!

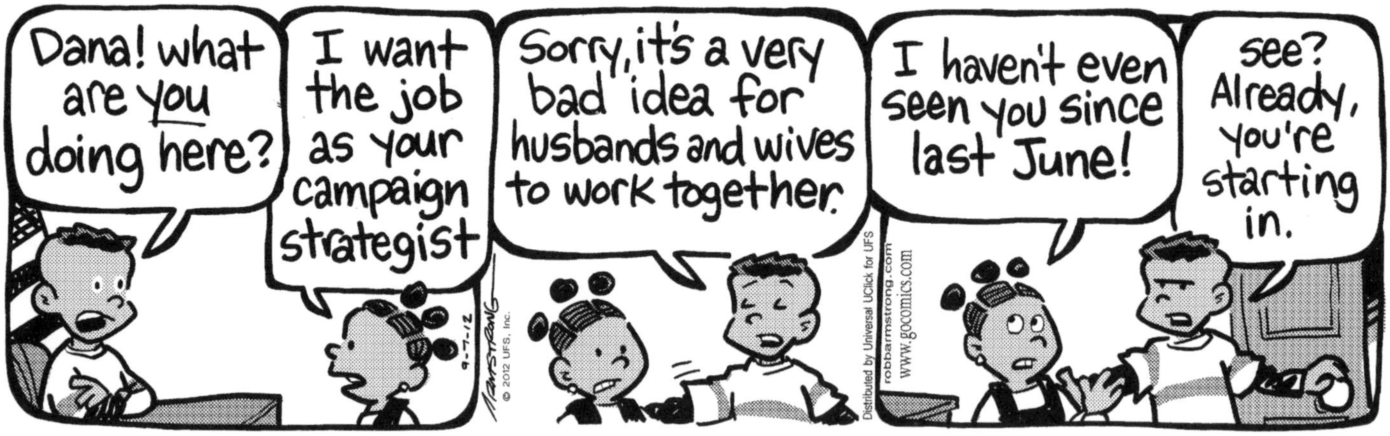
Dana! what are you doing here?
I want the job as your campaign strategist
Sorry, it's a very bad idea for husbands and wives to work together.
I haven't even seen you since last June!
see? Already, you're starting in.
9-7-12
© 2012 UFS, Inc.
Distributed by Universal UClick for UFS
robbarmstrong.com
www.gocomics.com

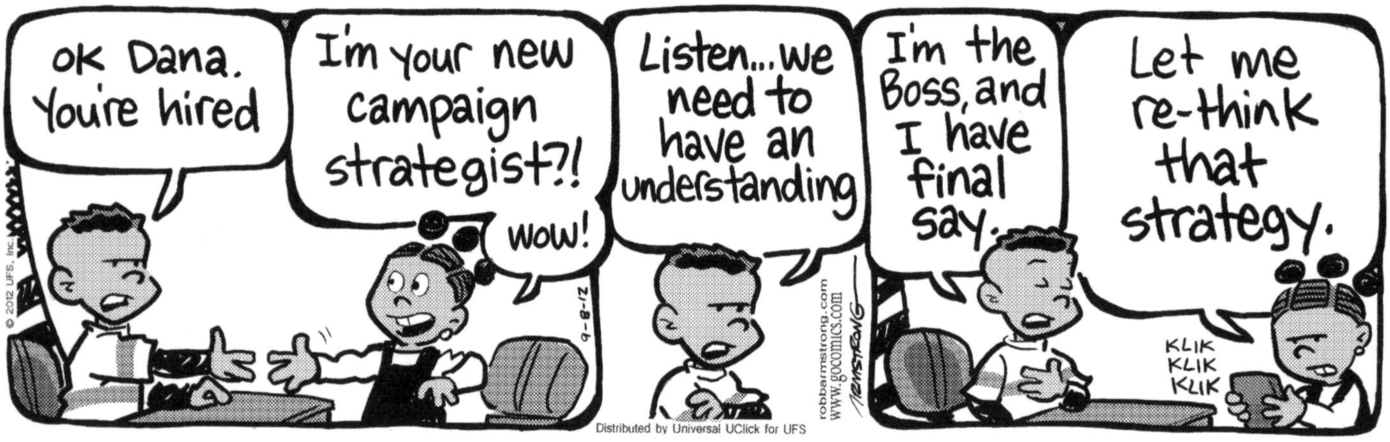
ok Dana. You're hired
I'm your new campaign strategist?!
wow!
Listen...we need to have an understanding
I'm the Boss, and I have final say.
Let me re-think that strategy.
KLIK KLIK KLIK
9-8-12
© 2012 UFS, Inc.
Distributed by Universal UClick for UFS
robbarmstrong.com
www.gocomics.com

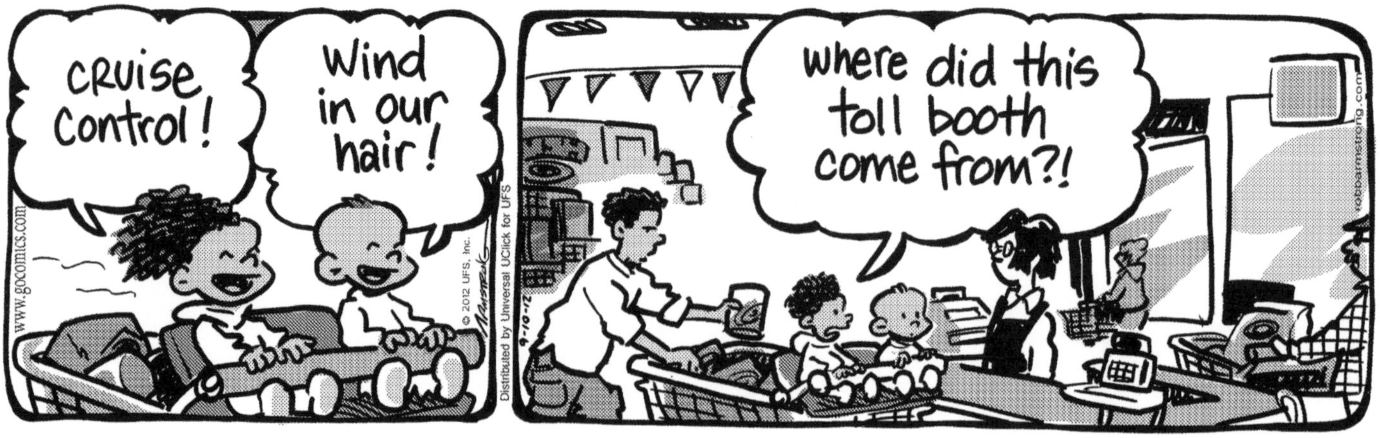
CRuise Control!
Wind in our hair!
where did this toll booth come from?!
9-10-12
© 2012 UFS, Inc.
Distributed by Universal UClick for UFS
www.gocomics.com
robbarmstrong.com

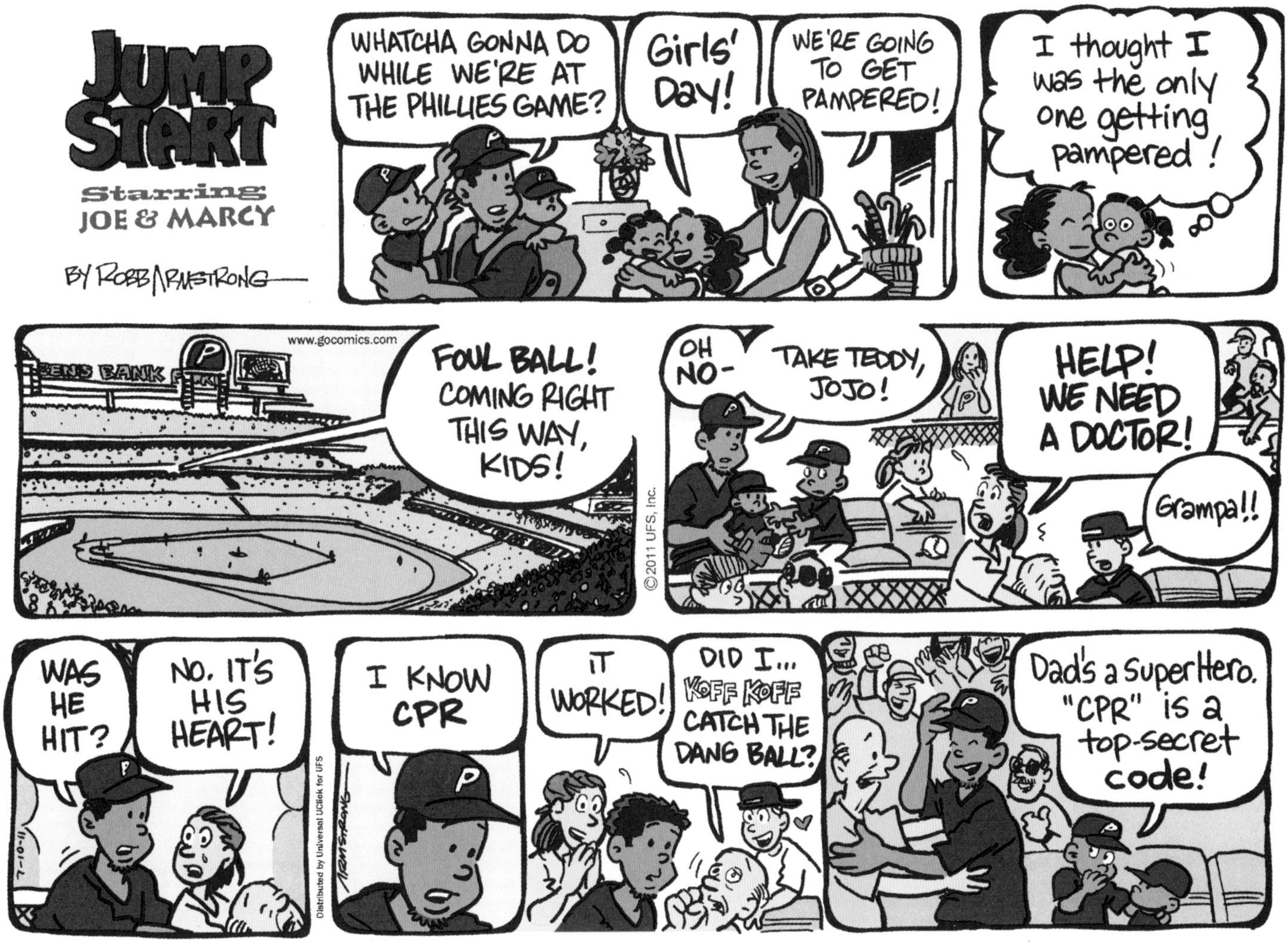
JUMP START
Starring
JOE & MARCY
BY ROBB ARMSTRONG
WHATCHA GONNA DO WHILE WE'RE AT THE PHILLIES GAME?
Girls' Day!
WE'RE GOING TO GET PAMPERED!
I thought I was the only one getting pampered!
www.gocomics.com
FOUL BALL! COMING RIGHT THIS WAY, KIDS!
©2011 UFS, Inc.
OH NO-
TAKE TEDDY, JOJO!
HELP! WE NEED A DOCTOR!
Grampa!!
WAS HE HIT?
NO. IT'S HIS HEART!
7-10-11
Distributed by Universal Uclick for UFS
I KNOW CPR
IT WORKED!
DID I... KOFF KOFF CATCH THE DANG BALL?
Dad's a SuperHero. "CPR" is a top-secret code!

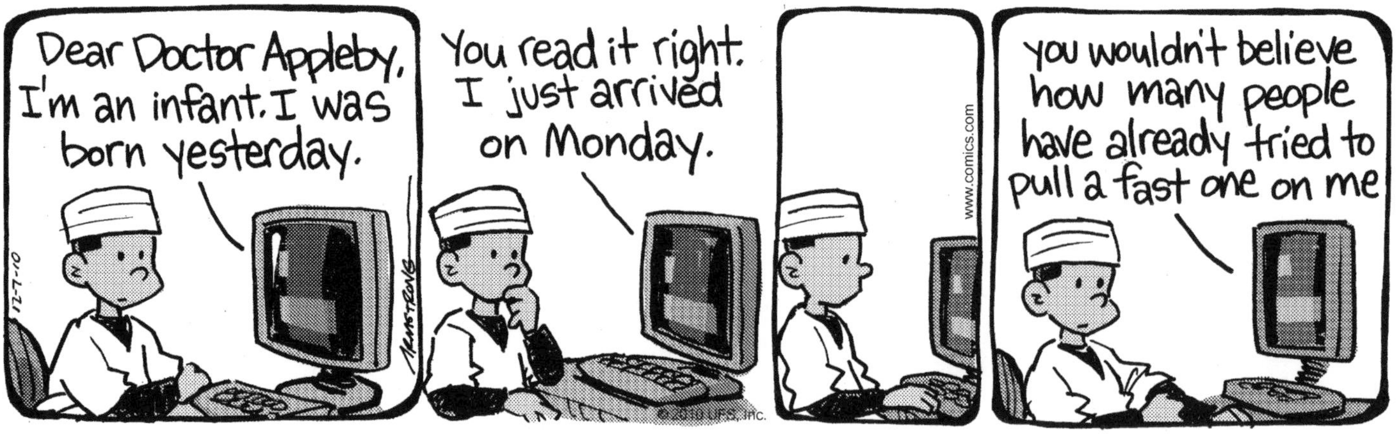
Dear Doctor Appleby, I'm an infant. I was born yesterday.
You read it right. I just arrived on Monday.
you wouldn't believe how many people have already tried to pull a fast one on me
12-7-10
www.comics.com
© 2010 UFS, Inc.

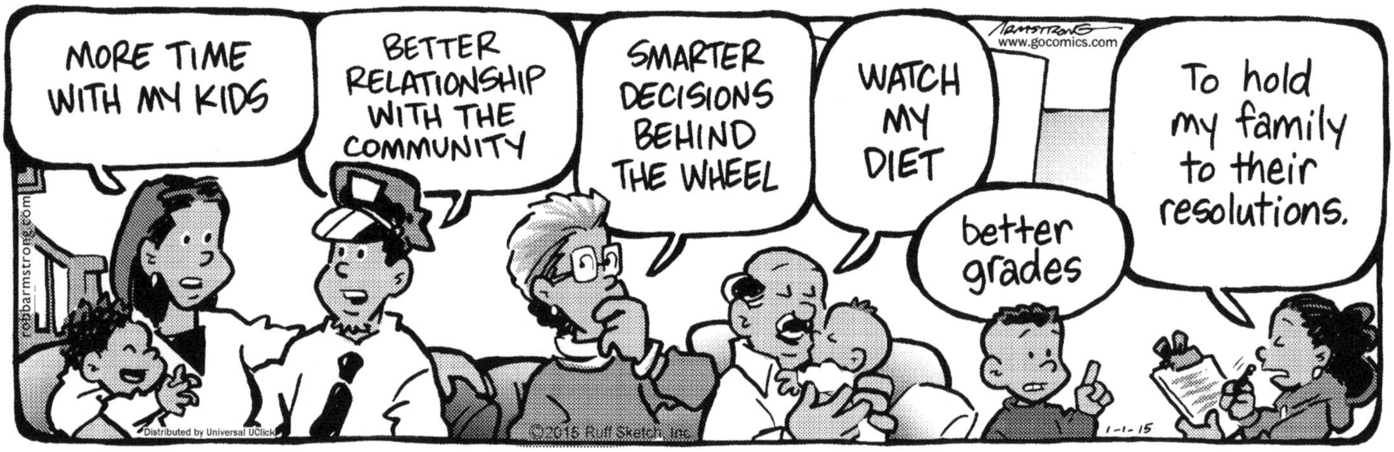
MORE TIME WITH MY KIDS
BETTER RELATIONSHIP WITH THE COMMUNITY
SMARTER DECISIONS BEHIND THE WHEEL
WATCH MY DIET
better grades
To hold my family to their resolutions.
www.gocomics.com
robbarmstrong.com
Distributed by Universal UClick
©2015 Ruff Sketch, Inc.
1-1-15

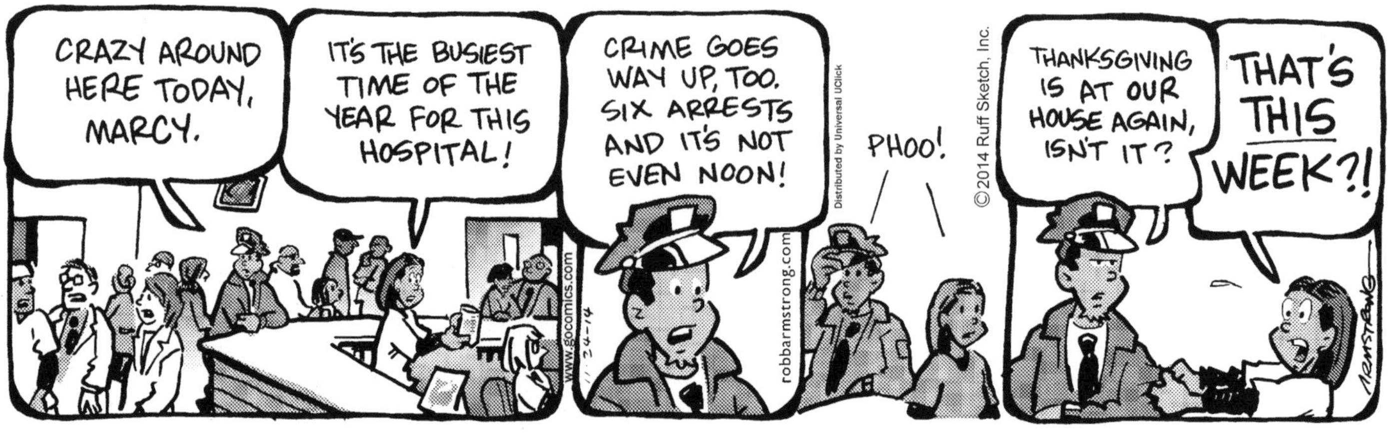
CRAZY AROUND HERE TODAY, MARCY.
IT'S THE BUSIEST TIME OF THE YEAR FOR THIS HOSPITAL!
CRIME GOES WAY UP, TOO. SIX ARRESTS AND IT'S NOT EVEN NOON!
PHOO!
THANKSGIVING IS AT OUR HOUSE AGAIN, ISN'T IT?
THAT'S THIS WEEK?!
www.gocomics.com
robbarmstrong.com
Distributed by Universal UClick
©2014 Ruff Sketch, Inc.

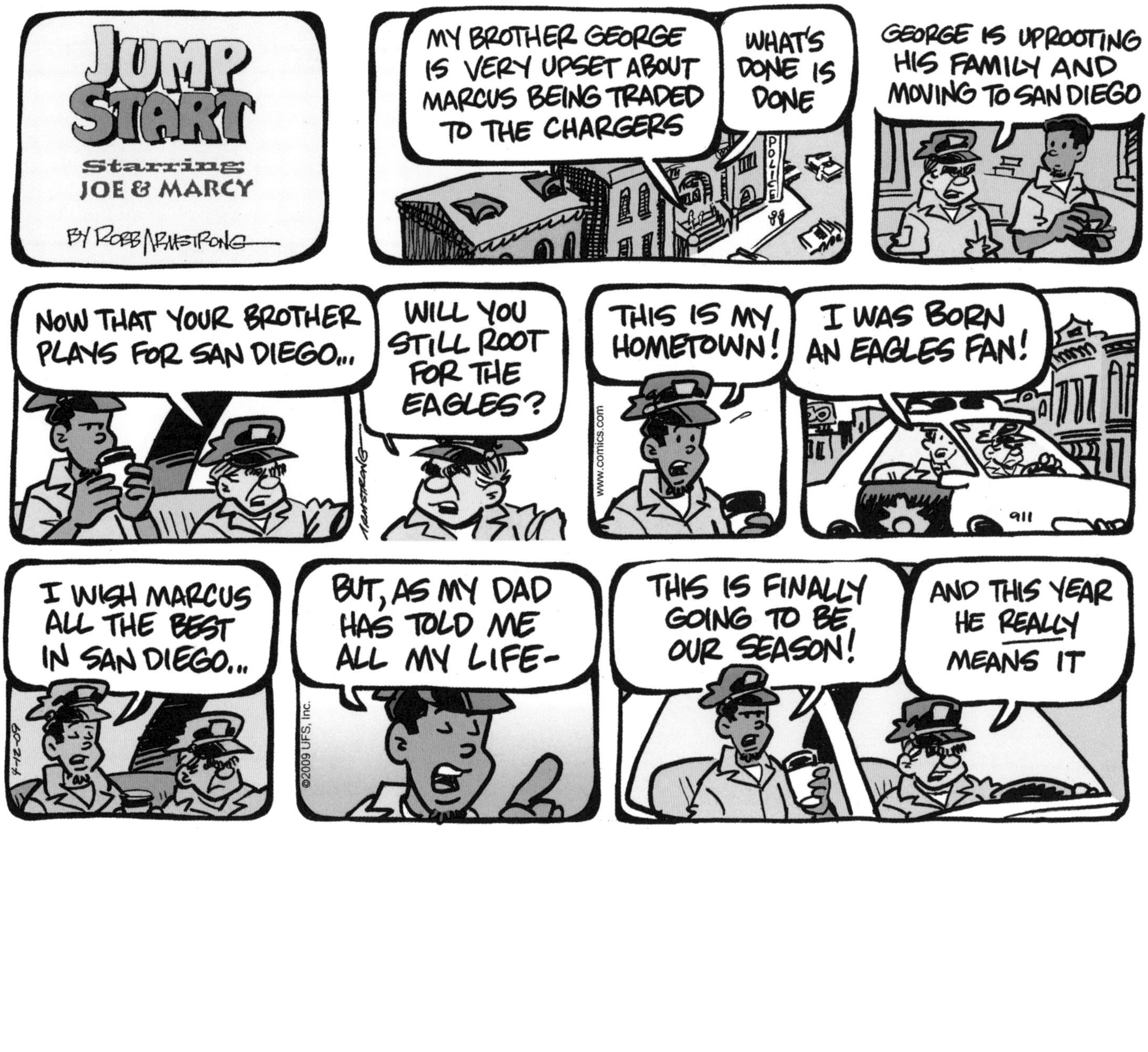
JUMP START
Starring
JOE & MARCY
BY ROBB ARMSTRONG
MY BROTHER GEORGE IS VERY UPSET ABOUT MARCUS BEING TRADED TO THE CHARGERS
WHAT'S DONE IS DONE
POLICE
GEORGE IS UPROOTING HIS FAMILY AND MOVING TO SAN DIEGO
NOW THAT YOUR BROTHER PLAYS FOR SAN DIEGO...
WILL YOU STILL ROOT FOR THE EAGLES?
THIS IS MY HOMETOWN!
www.comics.com
I WAS BORN AN EAGLES FAN!
911
I WISH MARCUS ALL THE BEST IN SAN DIEGO...
4-12-09
BUT, AS MY DAD HAS TOLD ME ALL MY LIFE-
©2009 UFS, Inc.
THIS IS FINALLY GOING TO BE OUR SEASON!
AND THIS YEAR HE REALLY MEANS IT

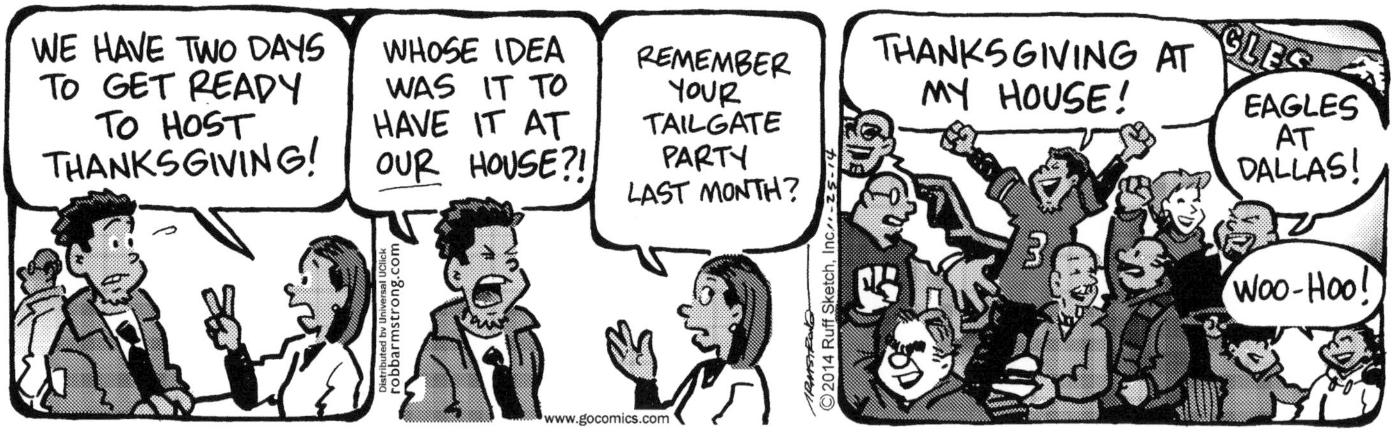
WE HAVE TWO DAYS TO GET READY TO HOST THANKSGIVING!
WHOSE IDEA WAS IT TO HAVE IT AT OUR HOUSE?!
REMEMBER YOUR TAILGATE PARTY LAST MONTH?
THANKSGIVING AT MY HOUSE!
EAGLES AT DALLAS!
WOO-HOO!
Distributed by Universal UClick
robbarmstrong.com
www.gocomics.com
© 2014 Ruff Sketch, Inc.

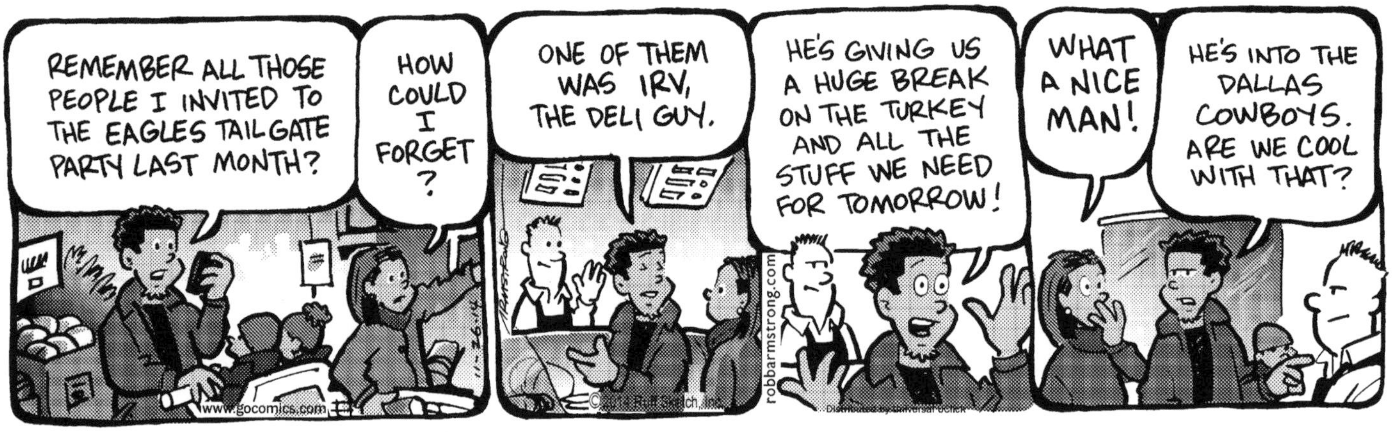
REMEMBER ALL THOSE PEOPLE I INVITED TO THE EAGLES TAILGATE PARTY LAST MONTH?
HOW COULD I FORGET?
ONE OF THEM WAS IRV, THE DELI GUY.
HE'S GIVING US A HUGE BREAK ON THE TURKEY AND ALL THE STUFF WE NEED FOR TOMORROW!
WHAT A NICE MAN!
HE'S INTO THE DALLAS COWBOYS. ARE WE COOL WITH THAT?
www.gocomics.com
©2014 Ruff Sketch, Inc.
robbarmstrong.com

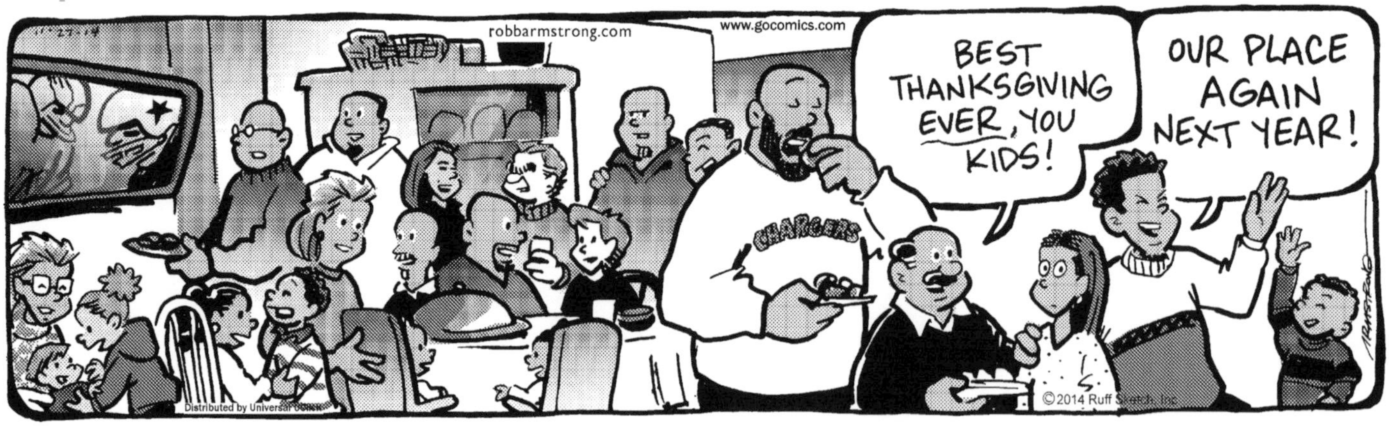
robbarmstrong.com
www.gocomics.com
BEST THANKSGIVING EVER, YOU KIDS!
OUR PLACE AGAIN NEXT YEAR!
CHARGERS
Distributed by Universal Uclick
©2014 Ruff Sketch, Inc.

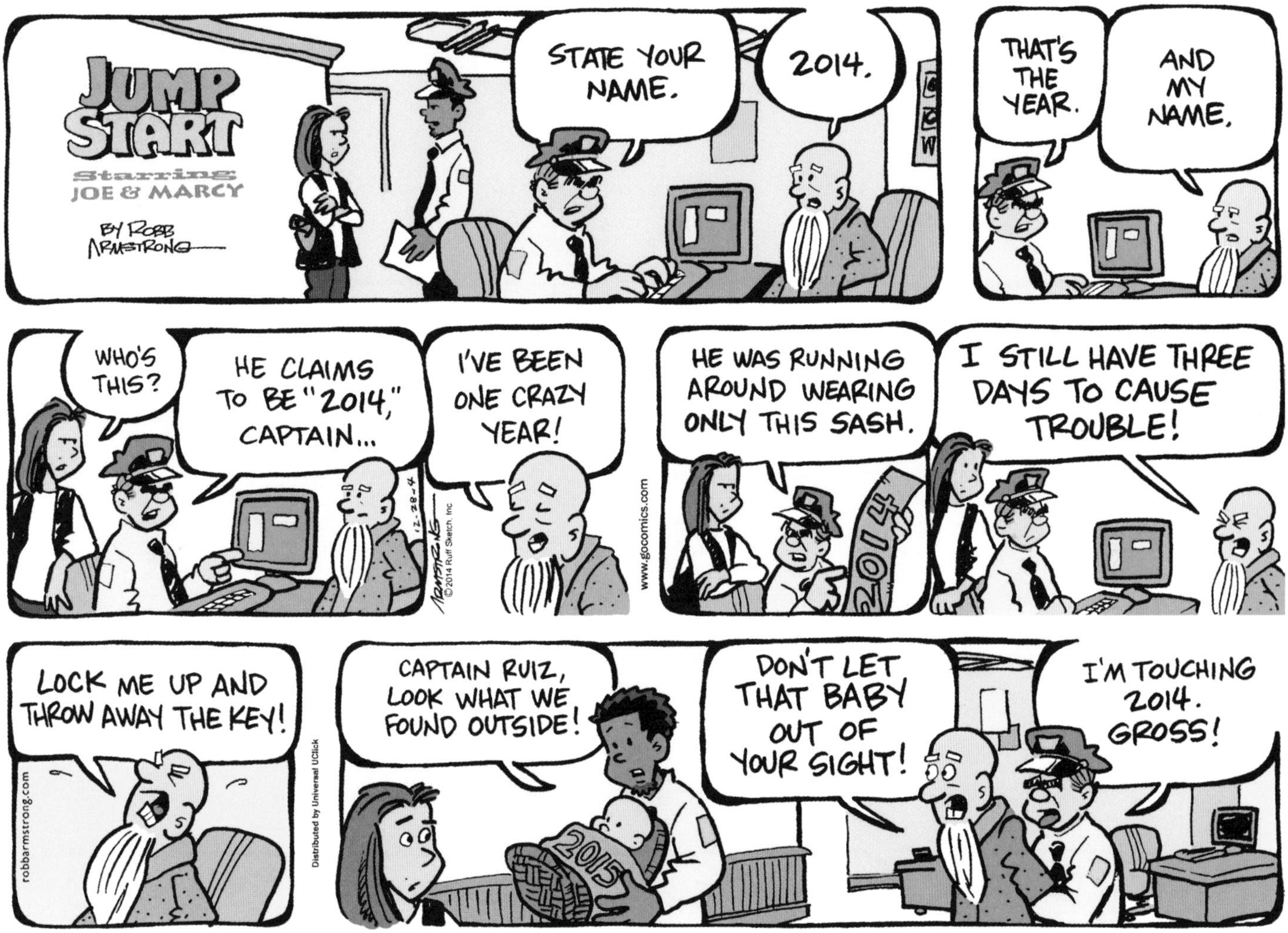
JUMP START
Starring JOE & MARCY
BY ROBB ARMSTRONG
STATE YOUR NAME.
2014.
THAT'S THE YEAR.
AND MY NAME.
WHO'S THIS?
HE CLAIMS TO BE "2014," CAPTAIN...
I'VE BEEN ONE CRAZY YEAR!
ARMSTRONG 12-28-14
©2014 Ruff Sketch, Inc.
www.gocomics.com
HE WAS RUNNING AROUND WEARING ONLY THIS SASH.
2014
I STILL HAVE THREE DAYS TO CAUSE TROUBLE!
LOCK ME UP AND THROW AWAY THE KEY!
robbarmstrong.com
Distributed by Universal UClick
CAPTAIN RUIZ, LOOK WHAT WE FOUND OUTSIDE!
2015
DON'T LET THAT BABY OUT OF YOUR SIGHT!
I'M TOUCHING 2014. GROSS!

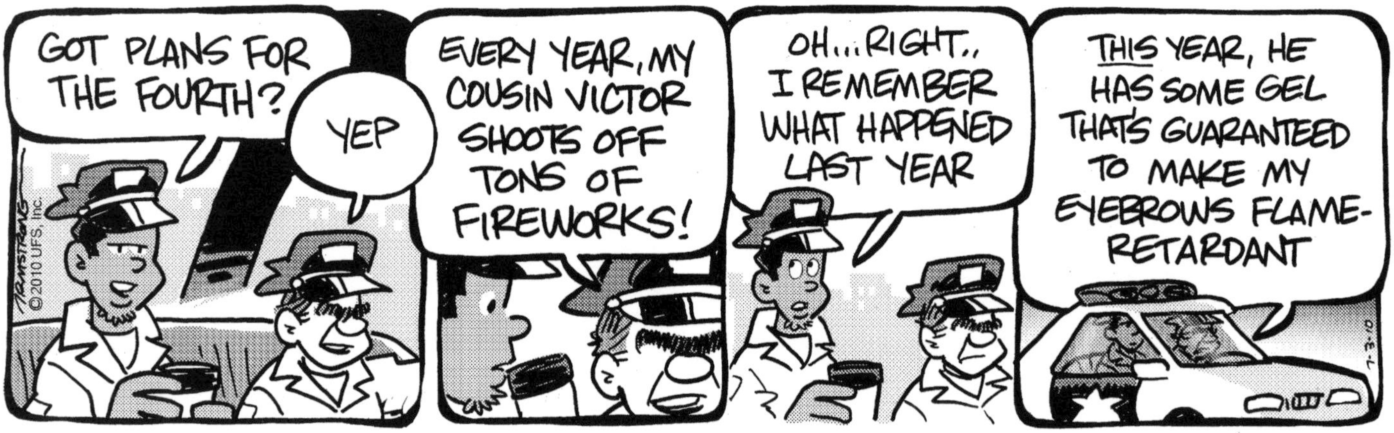
GOT PLANS FOR THE FOURTH?
YEP
EVERY YEAR, MY COUSIN VICTOR SHOOTS OFF TONS OF FIREWORKS!
OH... RIGHT.. I REMEMBER WHAT HAPPENED LAST YEAR
THIS YEAR, HE HAS SOME GEL THAT'S GUARANTEED TO MAKE MY EYEBROWS FLAME-RETARDANT
© 2010 UFS, Inc.

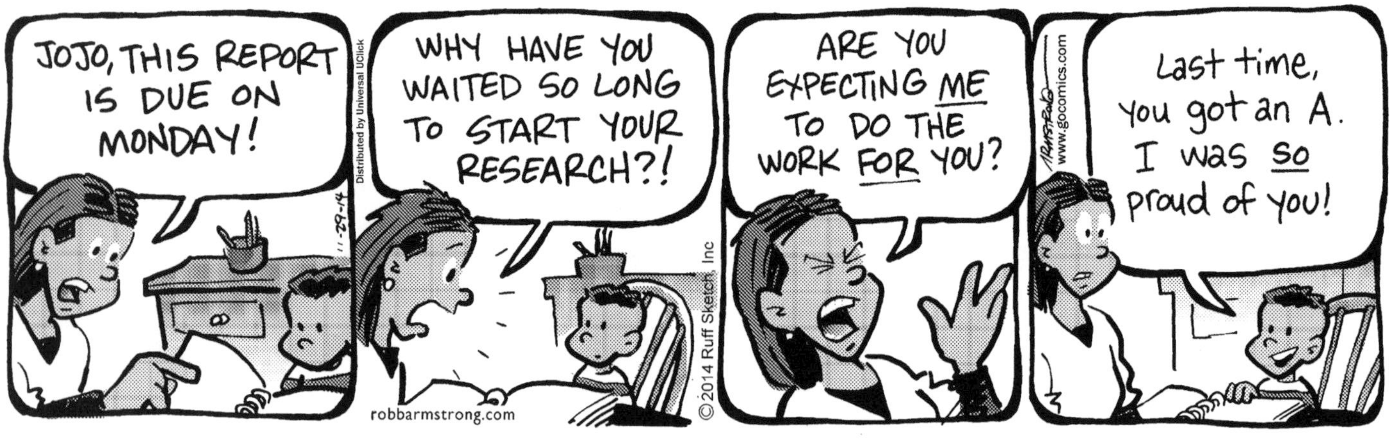
JOJO, THIS REPORT IS DUE ON MONDAY!
Distributed by Universal UClick
WHY HAVE YOU WAITED SO LONG TO START YOUR RESEARCH?!
robbarmstrong.com
© 2014 Ruff Sketch, Inc
ARE YOU EXPECTING ME TO DO THE WORK FOR YOU?
www.gocomics.com
Last time, you got an A. I was so proud of you!

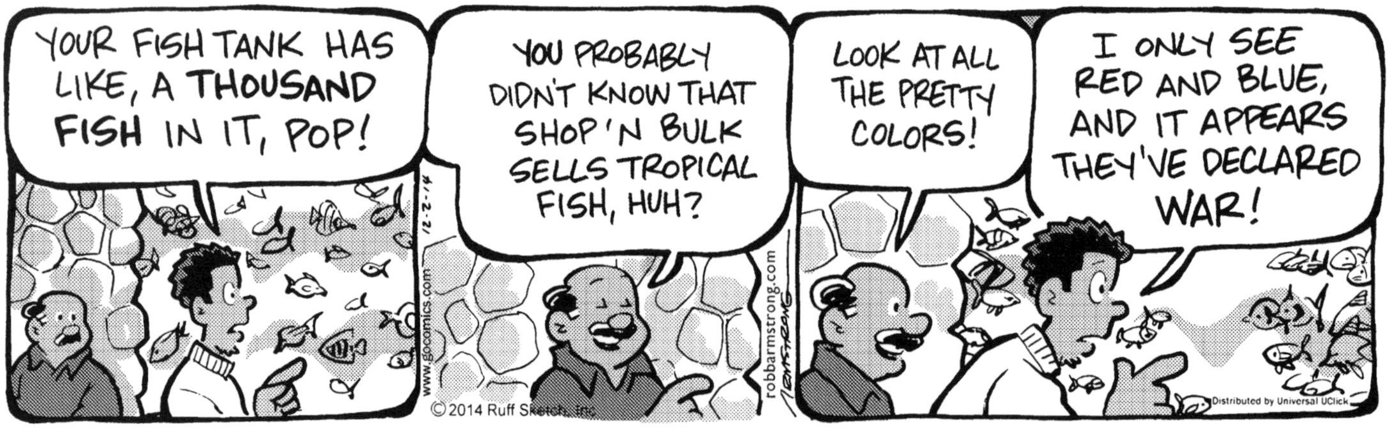
YOUR FISH TANK HAS LIKE, A THOUSAND FISH IN IT, POP!
www.gocomics.com
YOU PROBABLY DIDN'T KNOW THAT SHOP'N BULK SELLS TROPICAL FISH, HUH?
© 2014 Ruff Sketch, Inc
robbarmstrong.com
LOOK AT ALL THE PRETTY COLORS!
I ONLY SEE RED AND BLUE, AND IT APPEARS THEY'VE DECLARED WAR!
Distributed by Universal UClick

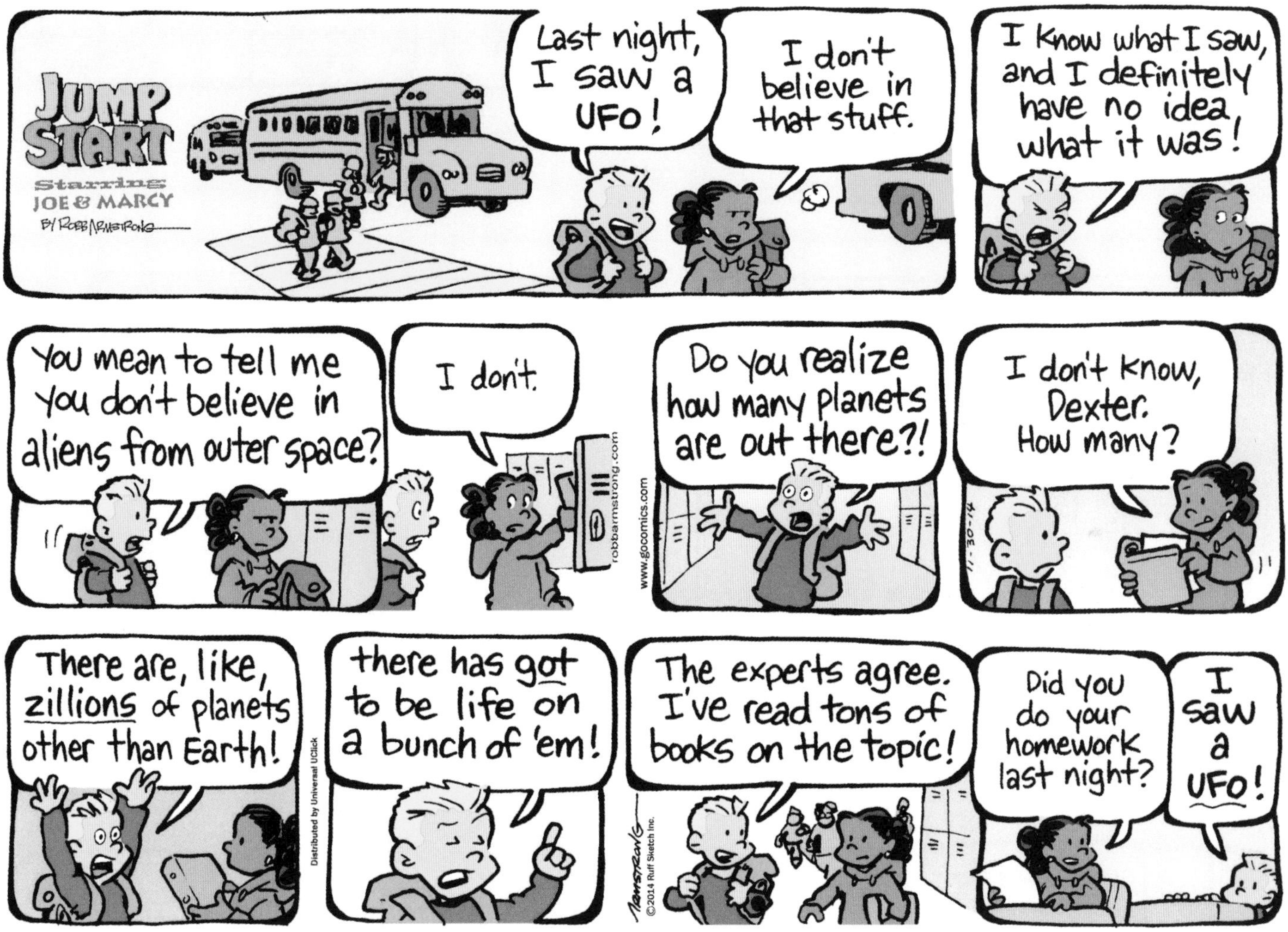
JUMP START
Starring JOE & MARCY
BY ROBB ARMSTRONG
Last night, I saw a UFO!
I don't believe in that stuff.
I know what I saw, and I definitely have no idea what it was!
You mean to tell me you don't believe in aliens from outer space?
I don't.
robbarmstrong.com
www.gocomics.com
Do you realize how many planets are out there?!
11-30-14
I don't know, Dexter. How many?
There are, like, zillions of planets other than Earth!
Distributed by Universal UClick
there has got to be life on a bunch of 'em!
ARMSTRONG
©2014 Ruff Sketch Inc.
The experts agree. I've read tons of books on the topic!
Did you do your homework last night?
I saw a UFO!

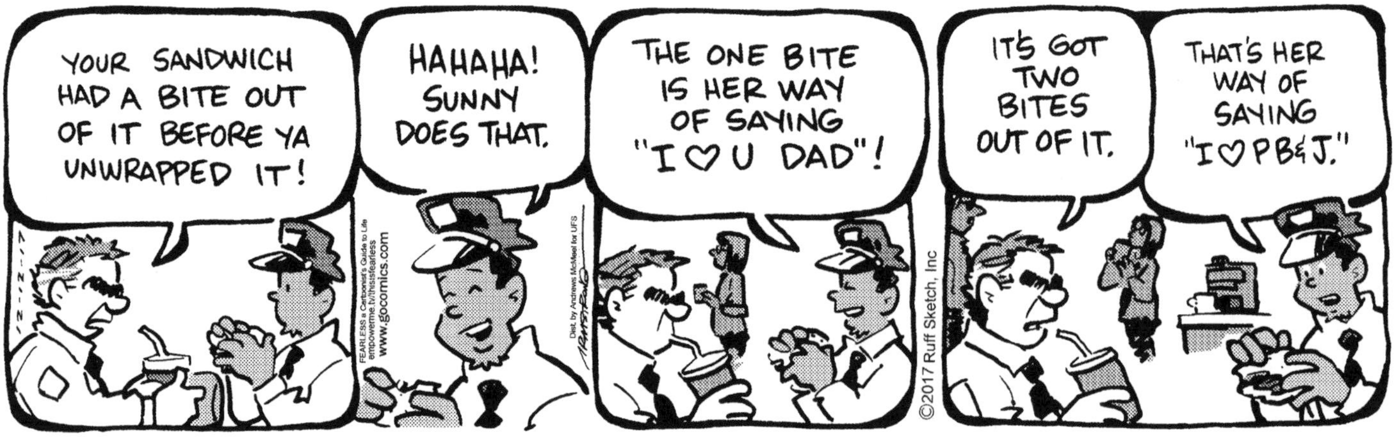
YOUR SANDWICH HAD A BITE OUT OF IT BEFORE YA UNWRAPPED IT!
HAHAHA! SUNNY DOES THAT.
THE ONE BITE IS HER WAY OF SAYING "I ♡ U DAD"!
IT'S GOT TWO BITES OUT OF IT.
THAT'S HER WAY OF SAYING "I ♡ PB&J."
www.gocomics.com
©2017 Ruff Sketch, Inc

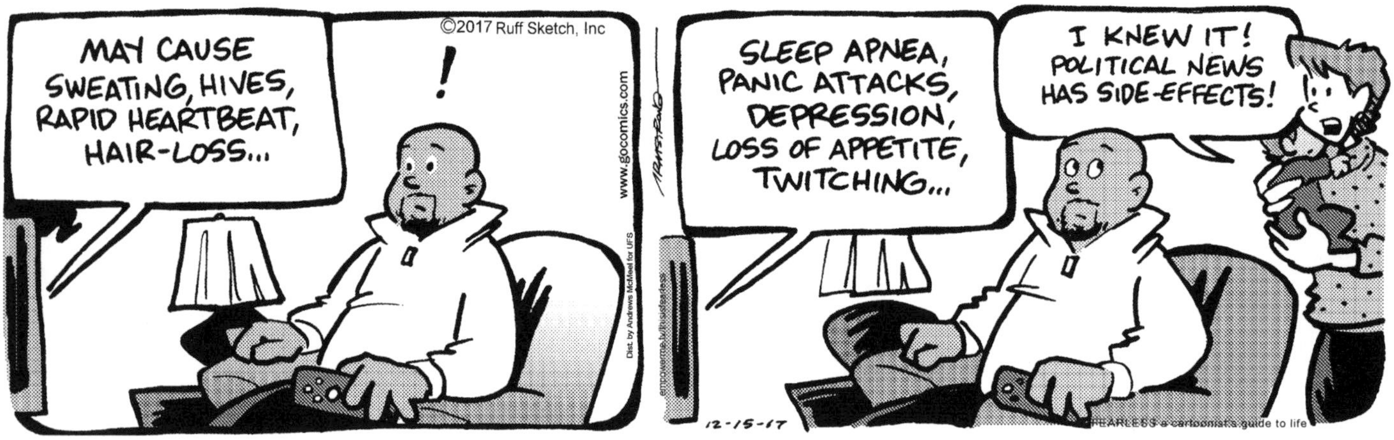
MAY CAUSE SWEATING, HIVES, RAPID HEARTBEAT, HAIR-LOSS...
!
©2017 Ruff Sketch, Inc
www.gocomics.com
SLEEP APNEA, PANIC ATTACKS, DEPRESSION, LOSS OF APPETITE, TWITCHING...
I KNEW IT! POLITICAL NEWS HAS SIDE-EFFECTS!
12-15-17
FEARLESS a cartoonist's guide to life

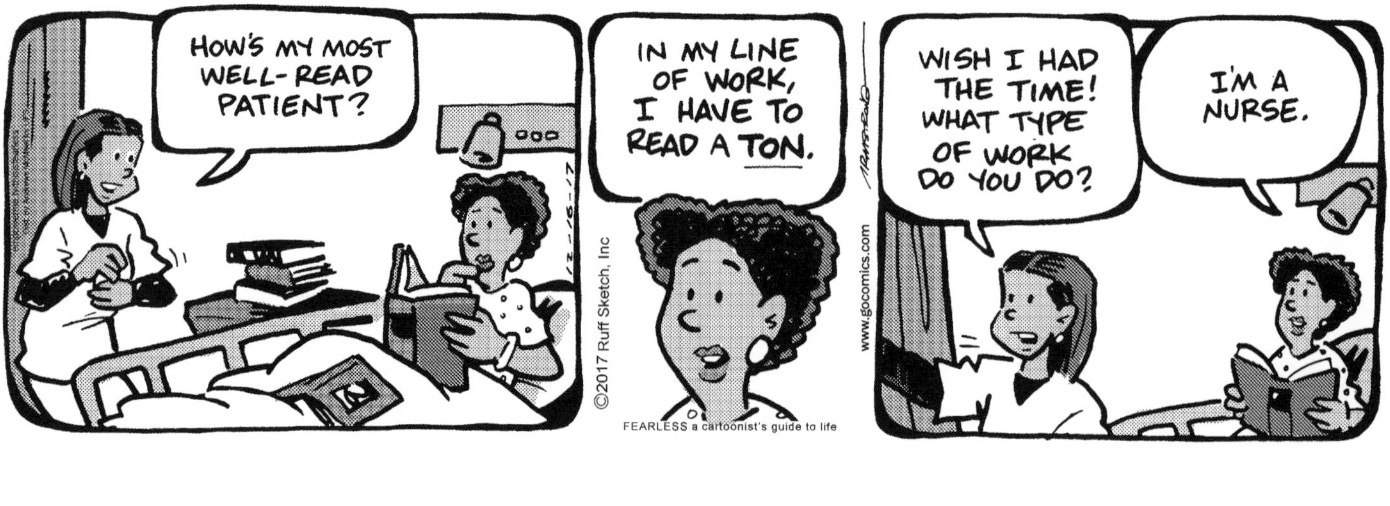
HOW'S MY MOST WELL-READ PATIENT?
IN MY LINE OF WORK, I HAVE TO READ A TON.
WISH I HAD THE TIME! WHAT TYPE OF WORK DO YOU DO?
I'M A NURSE.
©2017 Ruff Sketch, Inc
www.gocomics.com
FEARLESS a cartoonist's guide to life

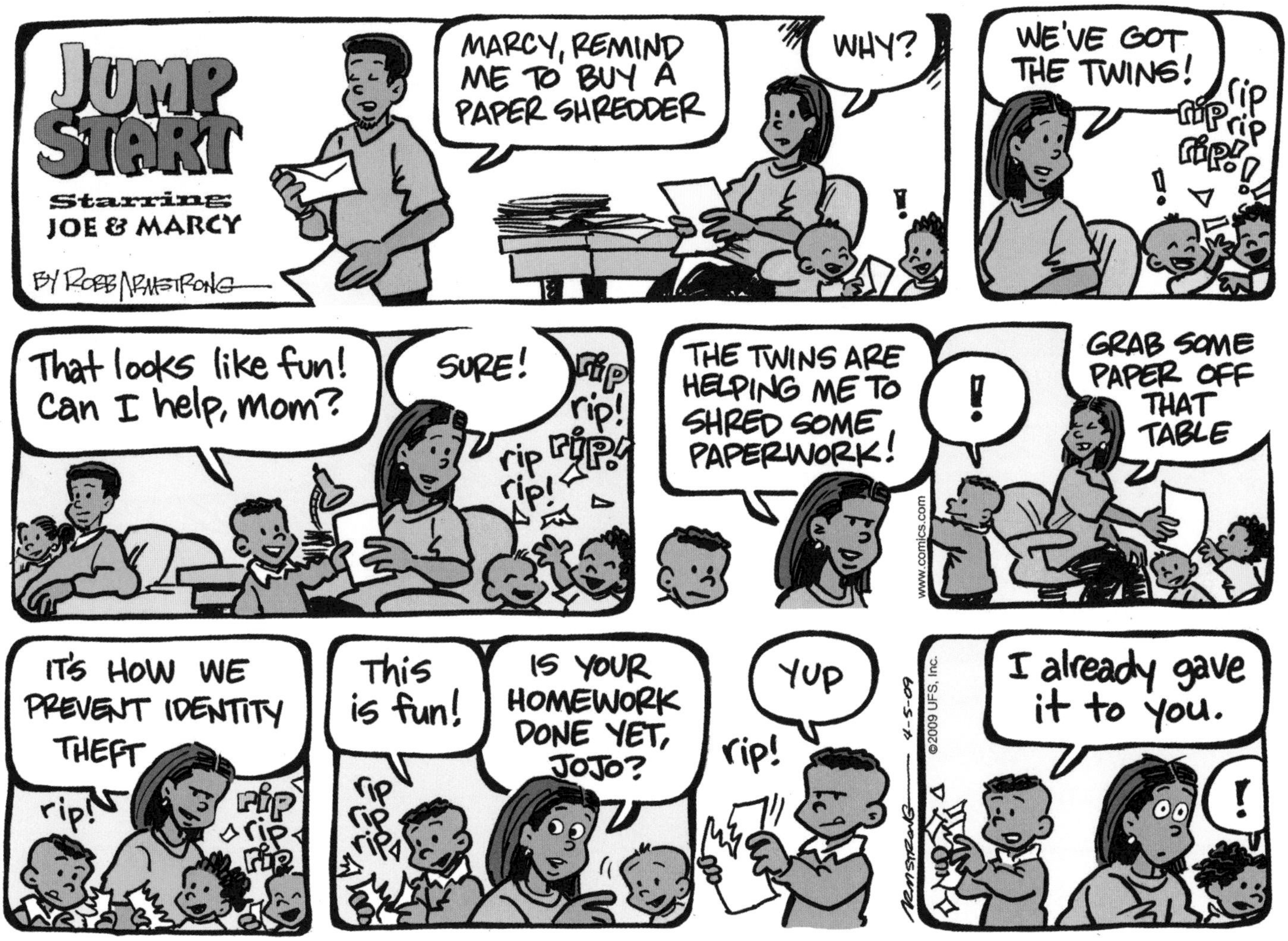
JUMP START
Starring JOE & MARCY
BY ROBB ARMSTRONG
MARCY, REMIND ME TO BUY A PAPER SHREDDER
WHY?
!
WE'VE GOT THE TWINS!
rip rip rip rip!
!
That looks like fun! Can I help, mom?
SURE!
rip rip! rip!
rip rip!
THE TWINS ARE HELPING ME TO SHRED SOME PAPERWORK!
!
GRAB SOME PAPER OFF THAT TABLE
www.comics.com
IT'S HOW WE PREVENT IDENTITY THEFT
rip!
rip rip rip
This is fun!
IS YOUR HOMEWORK DONE YET, JOJO?
rip rip rip
YUP
rip!
4-5-09
©2009 UFS, Inc.
ARMSTRONG
I already gave it to you.
!

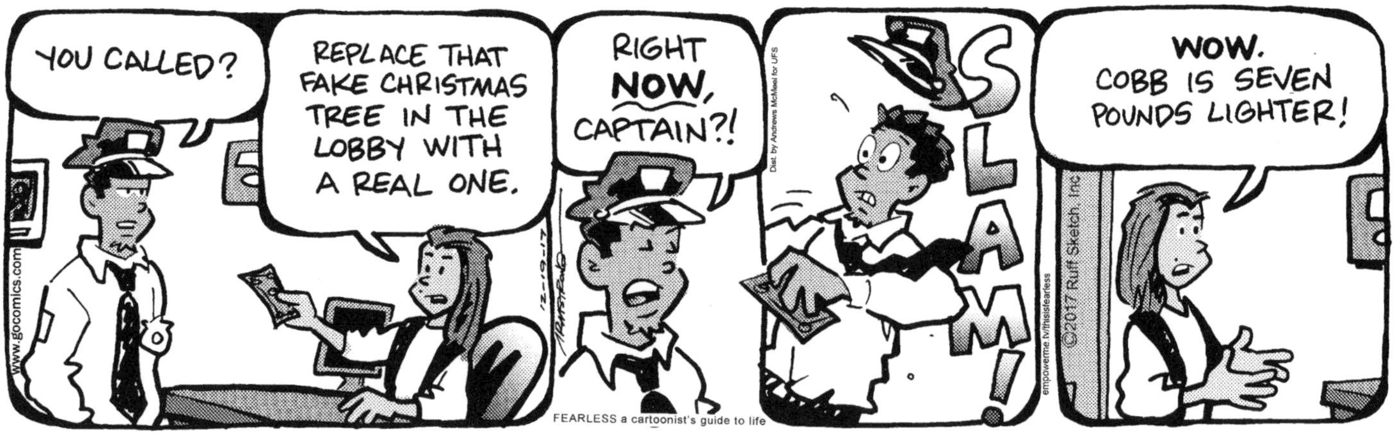
YOU CALLED?
REPLACE THAT FAKE CHRISTMAS TREE IN THE LOBBY WITH A REAL ONE.
RIGHT NOW, CAPTAIN?!
SLAM!
WOW. COBB IS SEVEN POUNDS LIGHTER!
FEARLESS a cartoonist's guide to life
©2017 Ruff Sketch, Inc

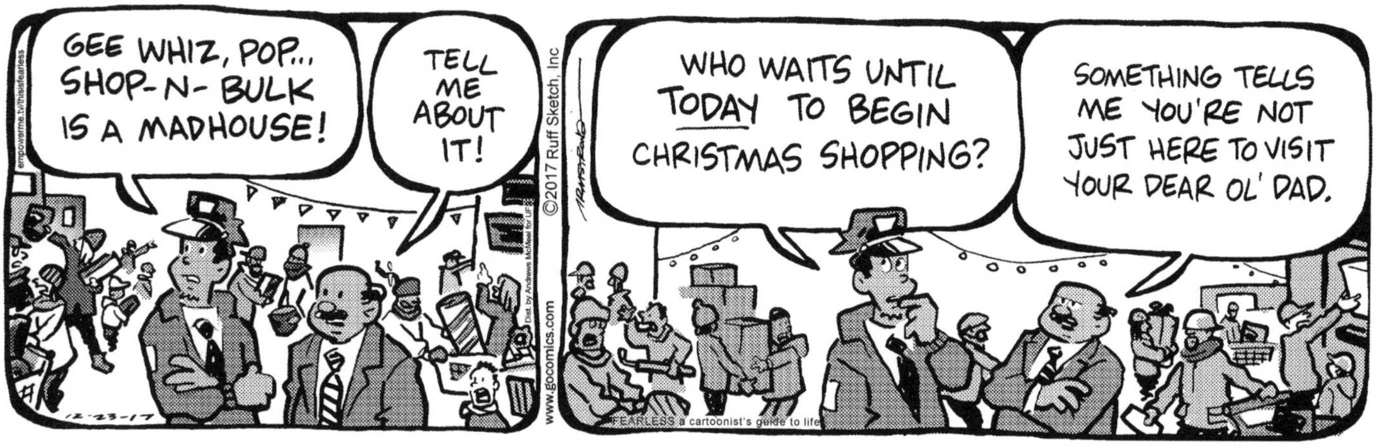
GEE WHIZ, POP.. SHOP-N-BULK IS A MADHOUSE!
TELL ME ABOUT IT!
WHO WAITS UNTIL TODAY TO BEGIN CHRISTMAS SHOPPING?
SOMETHING TELLS ME YOU'RE NOT JUST HERE TO VISIT YOUR DEAR OL' DAD.
FEARLESS a cartoonist's guide to life
©2017 Ruff Sketch, Inc

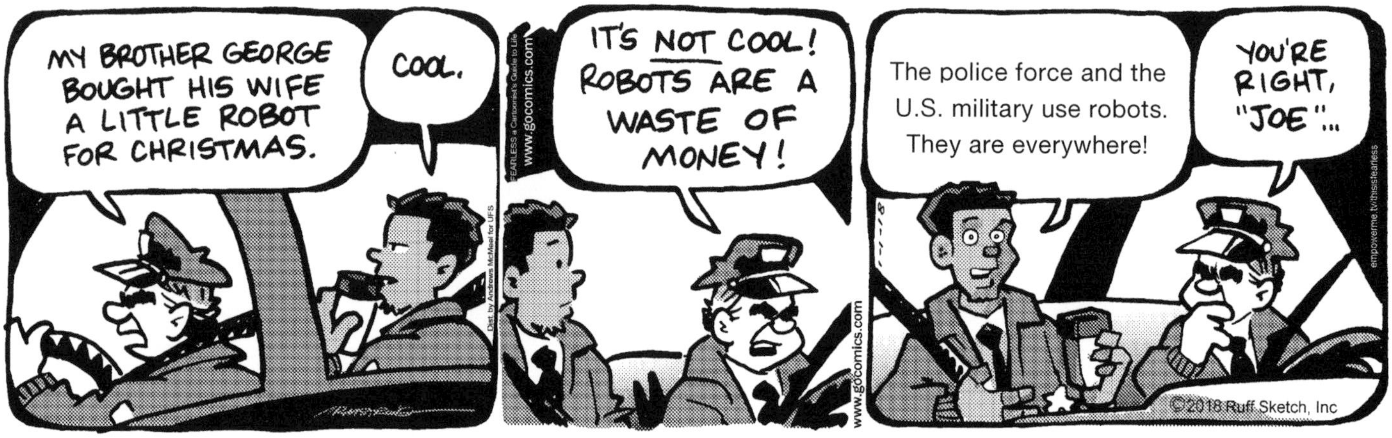
MY BROTHER GEORGE BOUGHT HIS WIFE A LITTLE ROBOT FOR CHRISTMAS.
COOL.
IT'S NOT COOL! ROBOTS ARE A WASTE OF MONEY!
The police force and the U.S. military use robots. They are everywhere!
YOU'RE RIGHT, "JOE"...
©2018 Ruff Sketch, Inc

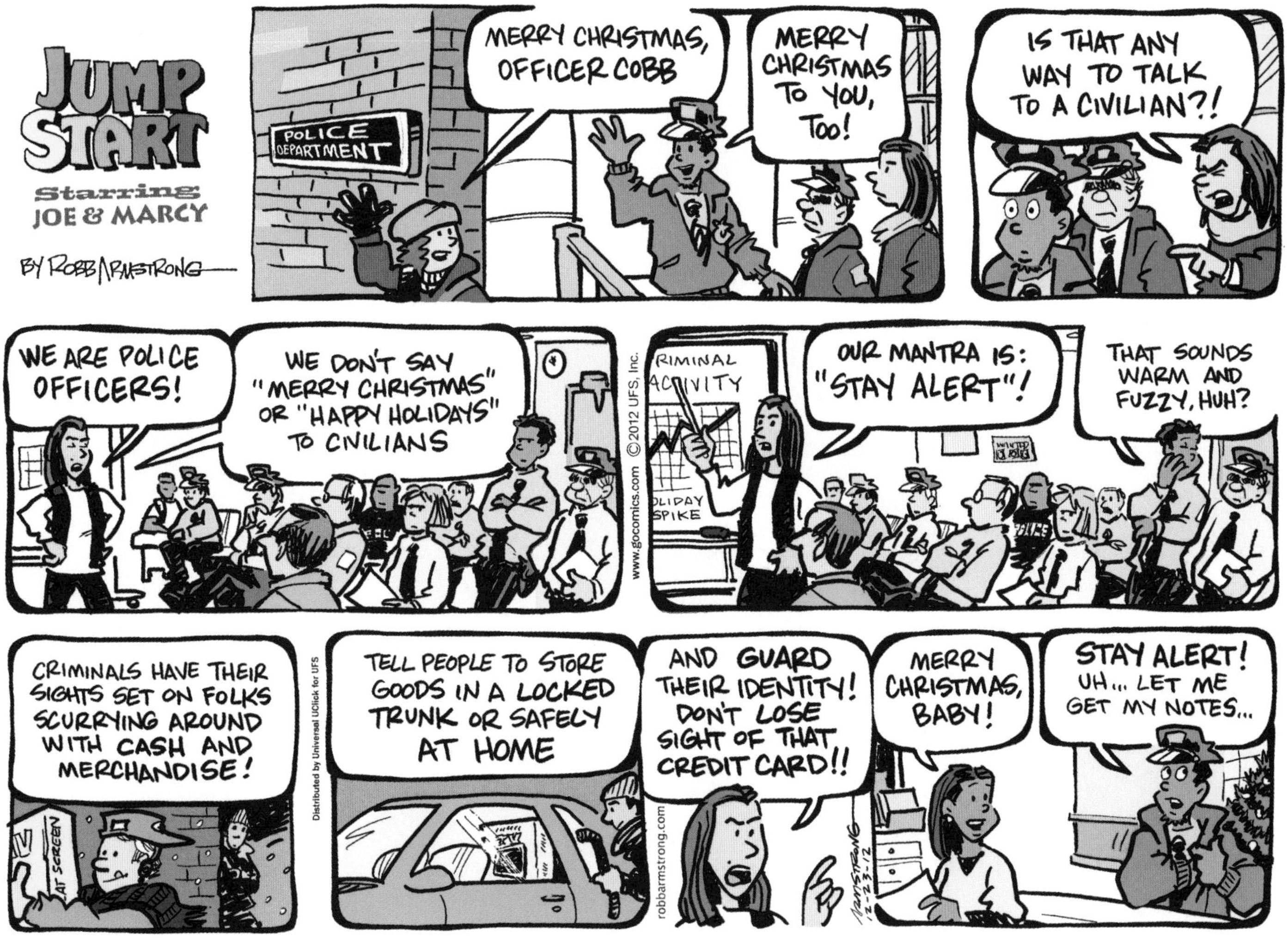
JUMP START
Starring JOE & MARCY
BY ROBB ARMSTRONG
POLICE DEPARTMENT
MERRY CHRISTMAS, OFFICER COBB
MERRY CHRISTMAS TO YOU, TOO!
IS THAT ANY WAY TO TALK TO A CIVILIAN?!
WE ARE POLICE OFFICERS!
WE DON'T SAY "MERRY CHRISTMAS" OR "HAPPY HOLIDAYS" TO CIVILIANS
CRIMINAL ACTIVITY
HOLIDAY SPIKE
OUR MANTRA IS: "STAY ALERT"!
THAT SOUNDS WARM AND FUZZY, HUH?
www.gocomics.com ©2012 UFS, Inc.
CRIMINALS HAVE THEIR SIGHTS SET ON FOLKS SCURRYING AROUND WITH CASH AND MERCHANDISE!
Distributed by Universal UClick for UFS
TELL PEOPLE TO STORE GOODS IN A LOCKED TRUNK OR SAFELY AT HOME
AND GUARD THEIR IDENTITY! DON'T LOSE SIGHT OF THAT CREDIT CARD!!
robbarmstrong.com
MERRY CHRISTMAS, BABY!
STAY ALERT! UH... LET ME GET MY NOTES...

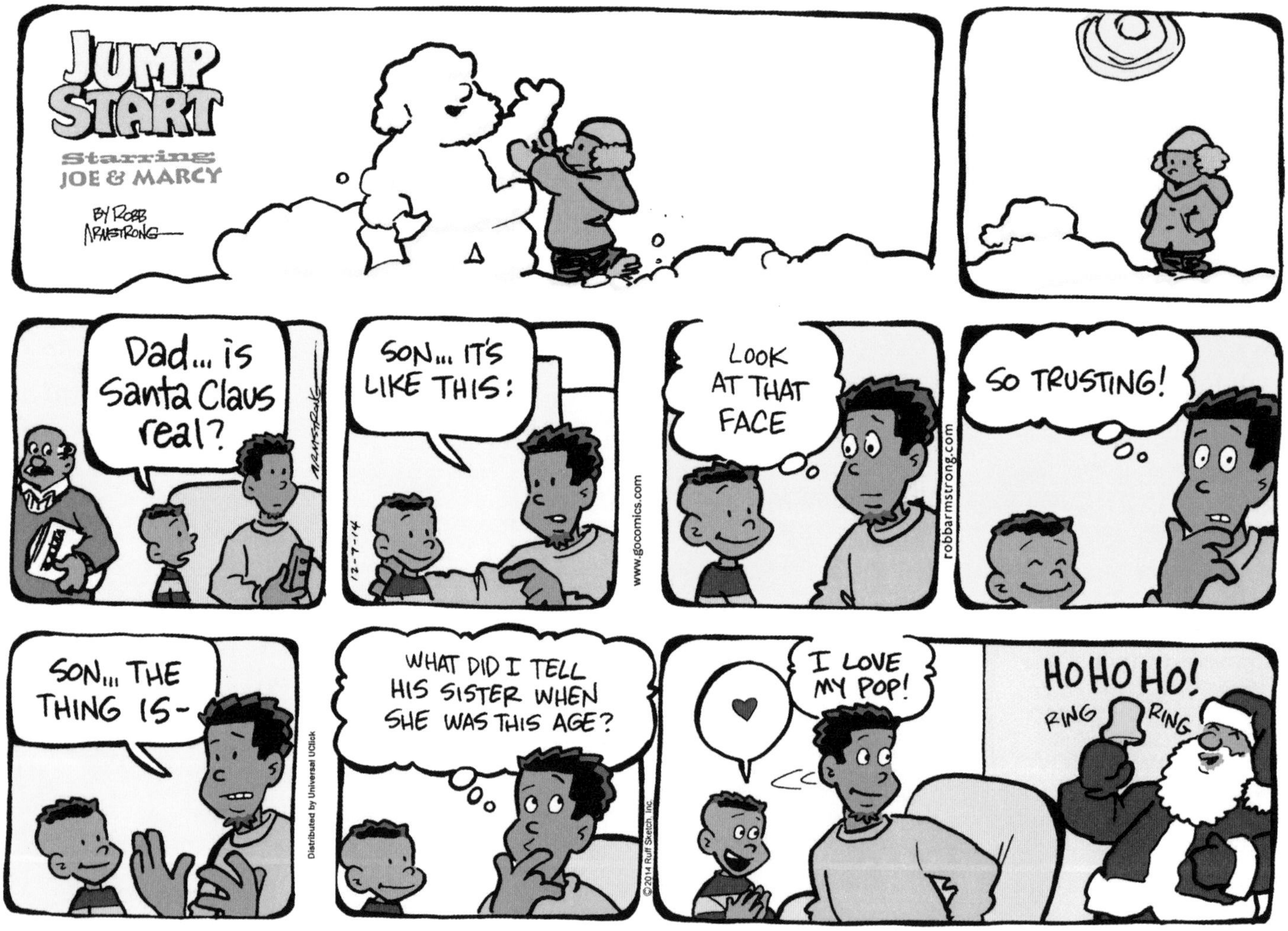
JUMP START
Starring JOE & MARCY
BY ROBB ARMSTRONG
Dad... is Santa Claus real?
ARMSTRONG
SON... IT'S LIKE THIS:
12-7-14
www.gocomics.com
LOOK AT THAT FACE
robbarmstrong.com
SO TRUSTING!
SON... THE THING IS-
Distributed by Universal UClick
WHAT DID I TELL HIS SISTER WHEN SHE WAS THIS AGE?
©2014 Ruff Sketch, Inc.
I LOVE MY POP!
HO HO HO!
RING RING

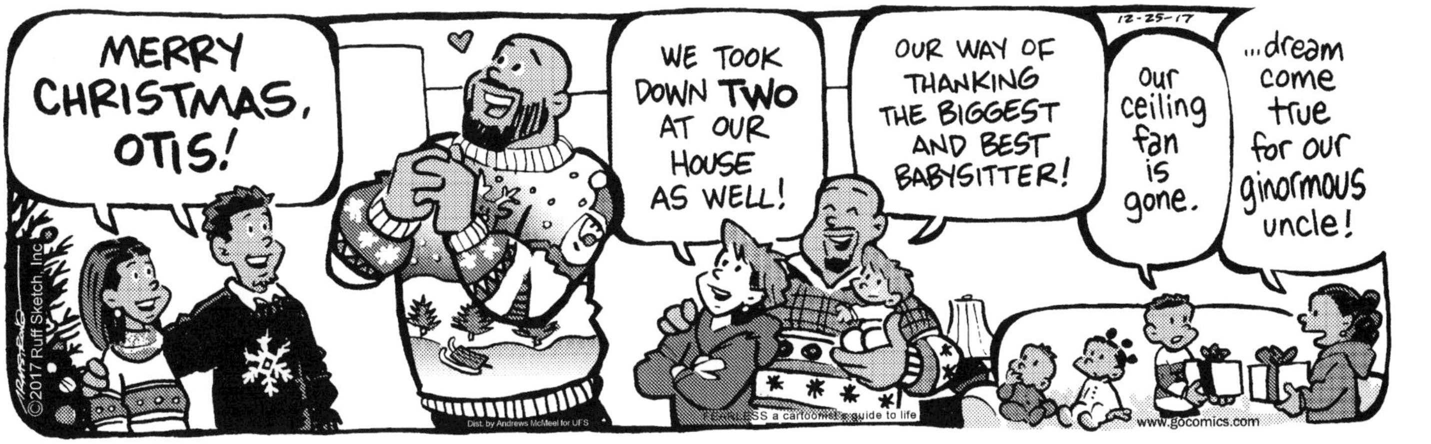
MERRY CHRISTMAS, OTIS!
WE TOOK DOWN TWO AT OUR HOUSE AS WELL!
OUR WAY OF THANKING THE BIGGEST AND BEST BABYSITTER!
12-25-17
Our ceiling fan is gone.
...dream come true for our ginormous uncle!
©2017 Ruff Sketch, Inc
Dist. by Andrews McMeel for UFS
FEARLESS a cartoonist's guide to life
www.gocomics.com

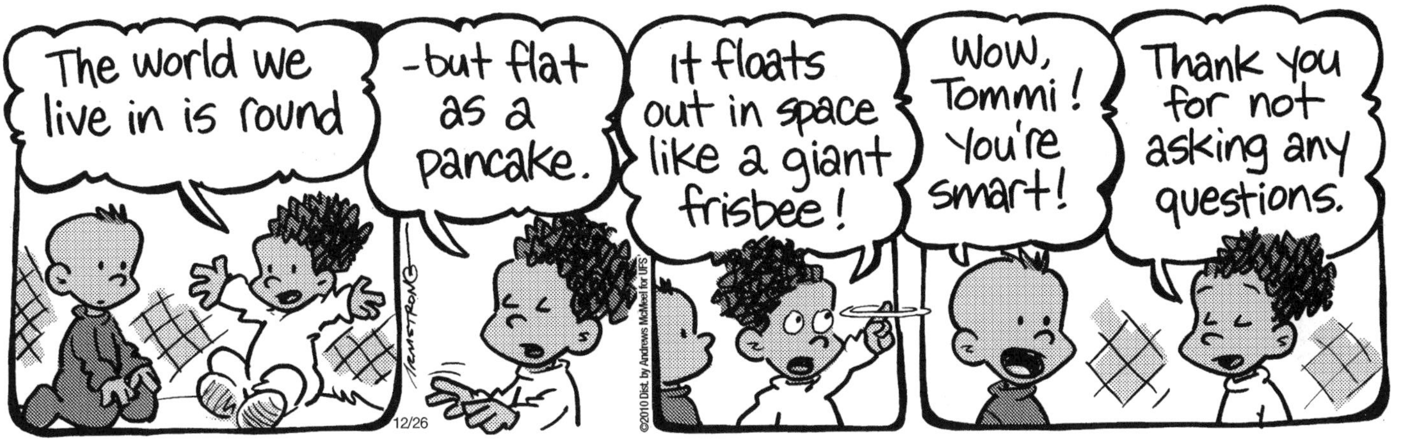
The world we live in is round
12/26
-but flat as a pancake.
©2010 Dist. by Andrews McMeel for UFS
It floats out in space like a giant frisbee!
WOW, Tommi! You're smart!
Thank you for not asking any questions.

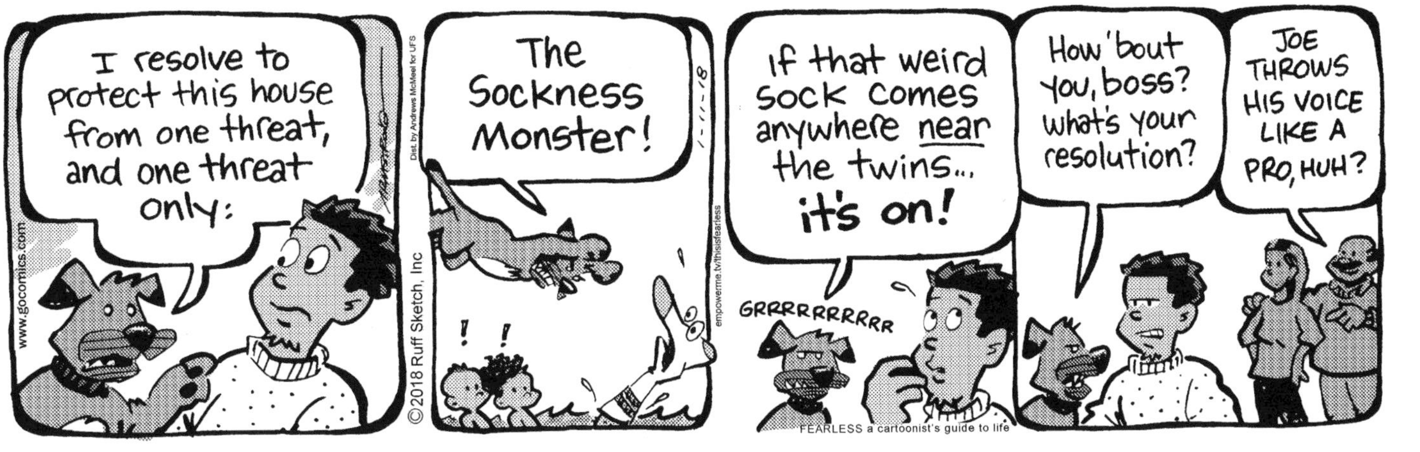
I resolve to protect this house from one threat, and one threat only:
www.gocomics.com
Dist. by Andrews McMeel for UFS
©2018 Ruff Sketch, Inc
The Sockness Monster!
1-11-18
empowerme.tv/thisisfearless
If that weird sock comes anywhere near the twins... it's on!
GRRRRRRRRRR
How 'bout you, boss? What's your resolution?
JOE THROWS HIS VOICE LIKE A PRO, HUH?
FEARLESS a cartoonist's guide to life

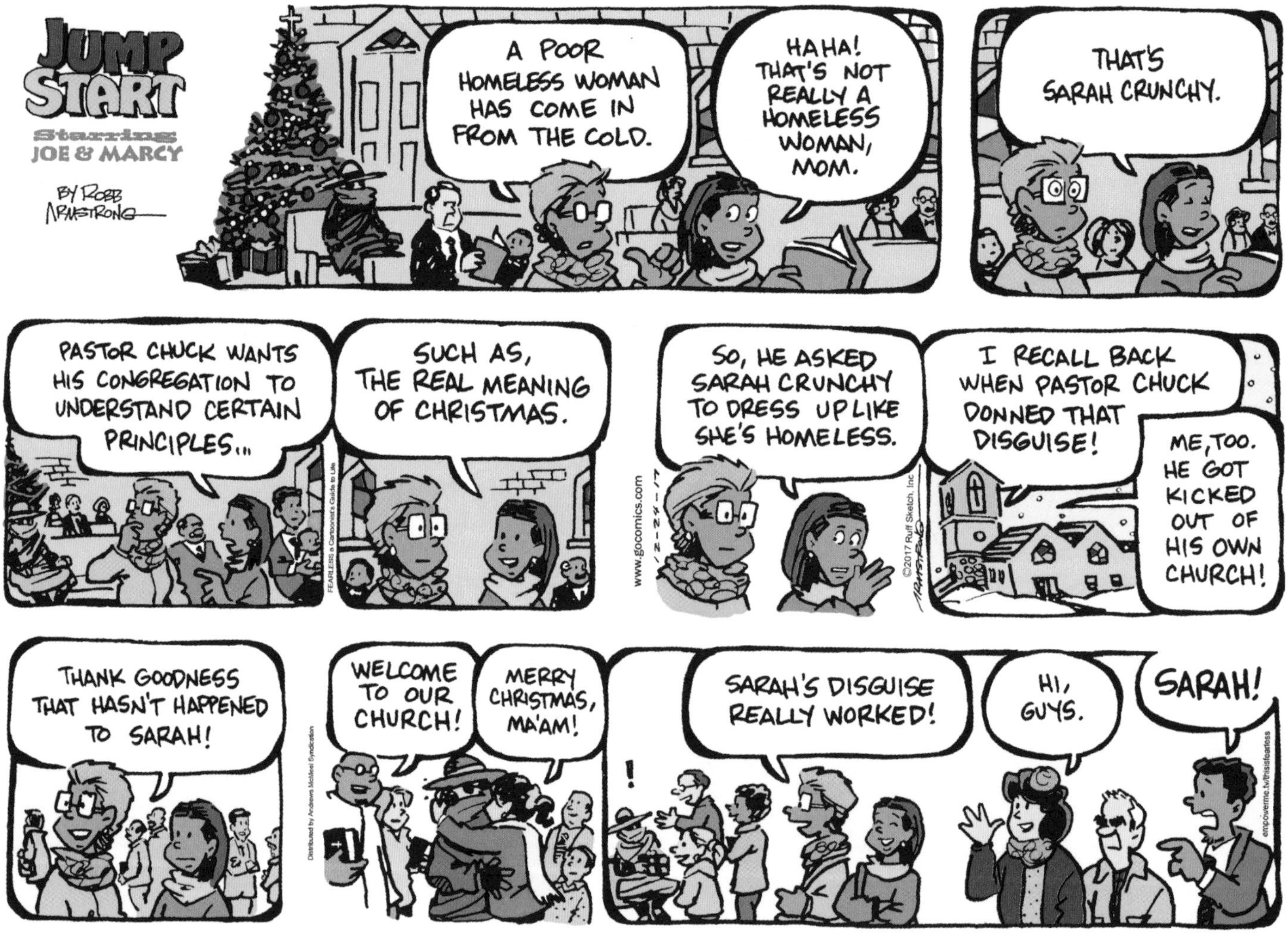
JUMP START
Starring JOE & MARCY
BY ROBB ARMSTRONG
A POOR HOMELESS WOMAN HAS COME IN FROM THE COLD.
HAHA! THAT'S NOT REALLY A HOMELESS WOMAN, MOM.
THAT'S SARAH CRUNCHY.
PASTOR CHUCK WANTS HIS CONGREGATION TO UNDERSTAND CERTAIN PRINCIPLES...
SUCH AS, THE REAL MEANING OF CHRISTMAS.
SO, HE ASKED SARAH CRUNCHY TO DRESS UP LIKE SHE'S HOMELESS.
I RECALL BACK WHEN PASTOR CHUCK DONNED THAT DISGUISE!
ME, TOO. HE GOT KICKED OUT OF HIS OWN CHURCH!
THANK GOODNESS THAT HASN'T HAPPENED TO SARAH!
WELCOME TO OUR CHURCH!
MERRY CHRISTMAS, MA'AM!
!
SARAH'S DISGUISE REALLY WORKED!
HI, GUYS.
SARAH!
FEARLESS a Cartoonist's Guide to Life
www.gocomics.com
©2017 Ruff Sketch, Inc
Distributed by Andrews McMeel Syndication
empowerme.tv/thisisfearless

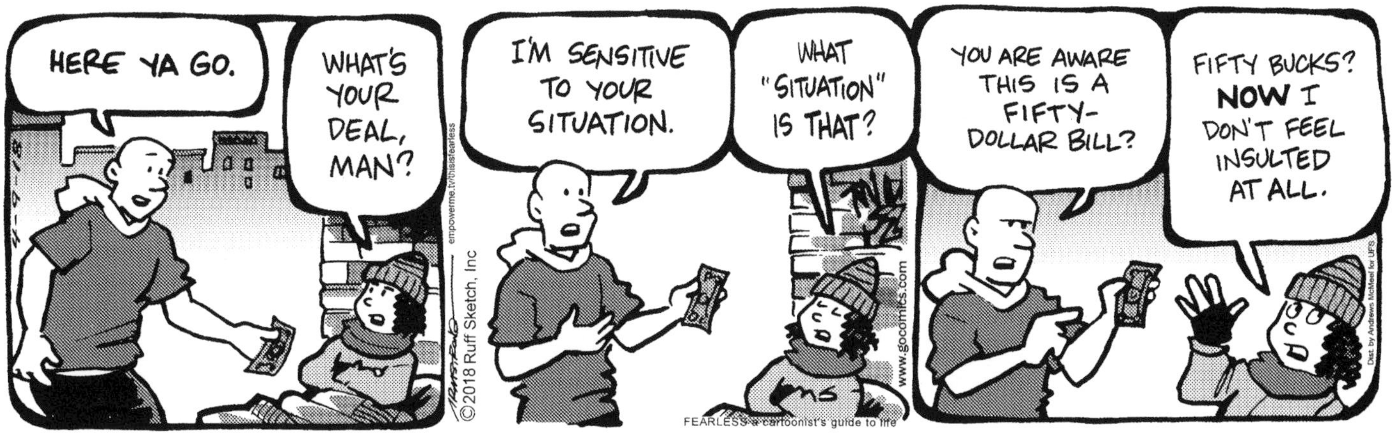
HERE YA GO.
WHAT'S YOUR DEAL, MAN?
I'M SENSITIVE TO YOUR SITUATION.
WHAT "SITUATION" IS THAT?
YOU ARE AWARE THIS IS A FIFTY-DOLLAR BILL?
FIFTY BUCKS? NOW I DON'T FEEL INSULTED AT ALL.
©2018 Ruff Sketch, Inc
empowerme.tv/thisisfearless
www.gocomics.com
FEARLESS a cartoonist's guide to life
Dist. by Andrews McMeel for UFS

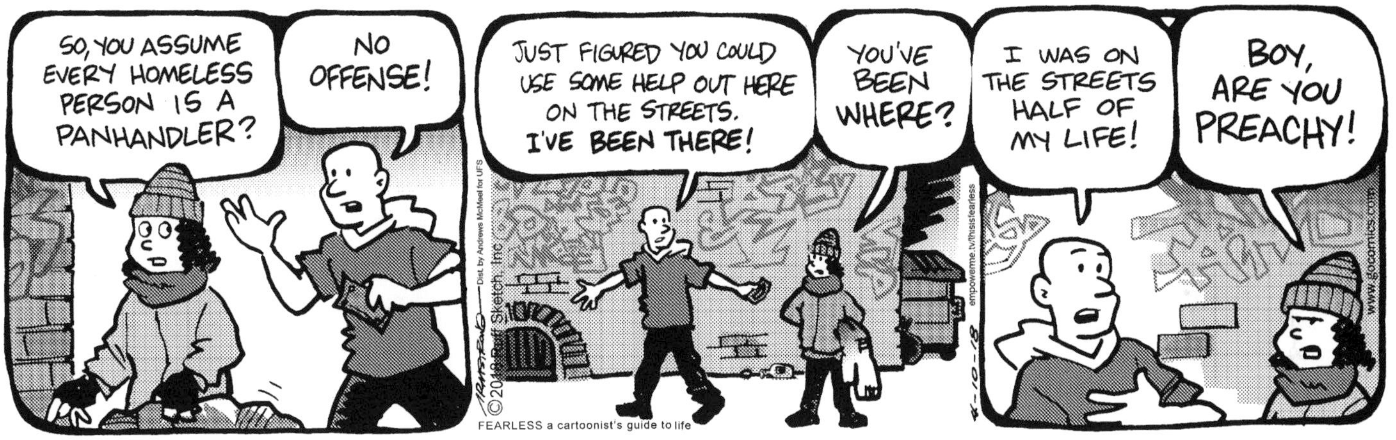
SO, YOU ASSUME EVERY HOMELESS PERSON IS A PANHANDLER?
NO OFFENSE!
JUST FIGURED YOU COULD USE SOME HELP OUT HERE ON THE STREETS. I'VE BEEN THERE!
YOU'VE BEEN WHERE?
I WAS ON THE STREETS HALF OF MY LIFE!
BOY, ARE YOU PREACHY!
©2018 Ruff Sketch, Inc
Dist. by Andrews McMeel for UFS
empowerme.tv/thisisfearless
www.gocomics.com
FEARLESS a cartoonist's guide to life

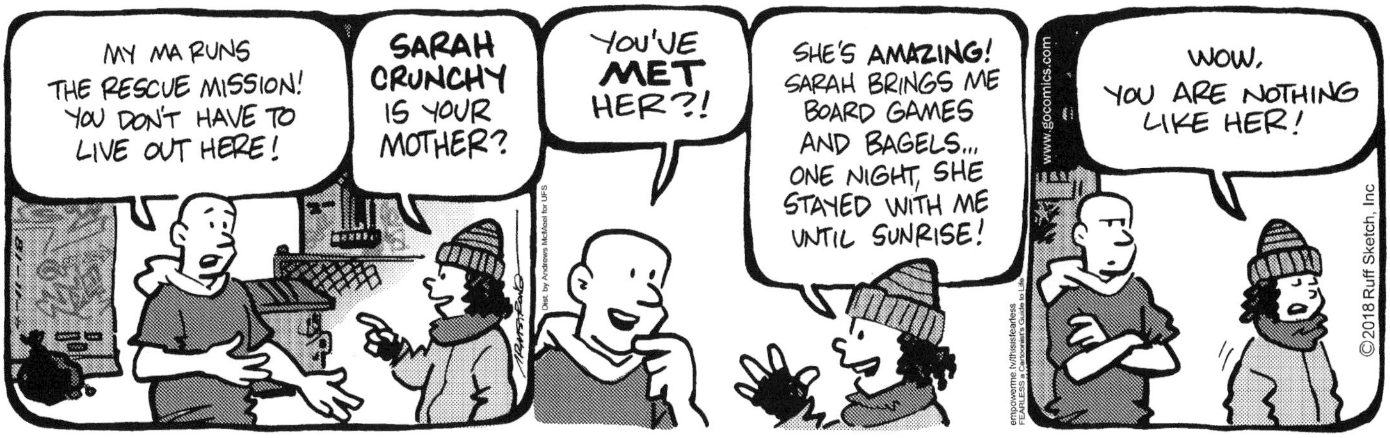
MY MA RUNS THE RESCUE MISSION! YOU DON'T HAVE TO LIVE OUT HERE!
SARAH CRUNCHY IS YOUR MOTHER?
YOU'VE MET HER?!
SHE'S AMAZING! SARAH BRINGS ME BOARD GAMES AND BAGELS... ONE NIGHT, SHE STAYED WITH ME UNTIL SUNRISE!
WOW. YOU ARE NOTHING LIKE HER!
Dist. by Andrews McMeel for UFS
www.gocomics.com
empowerme.tv/thisisfearless
FEARLESS a Cartoonist's Guide to Life
©2018 Ruff Sketch, Inc

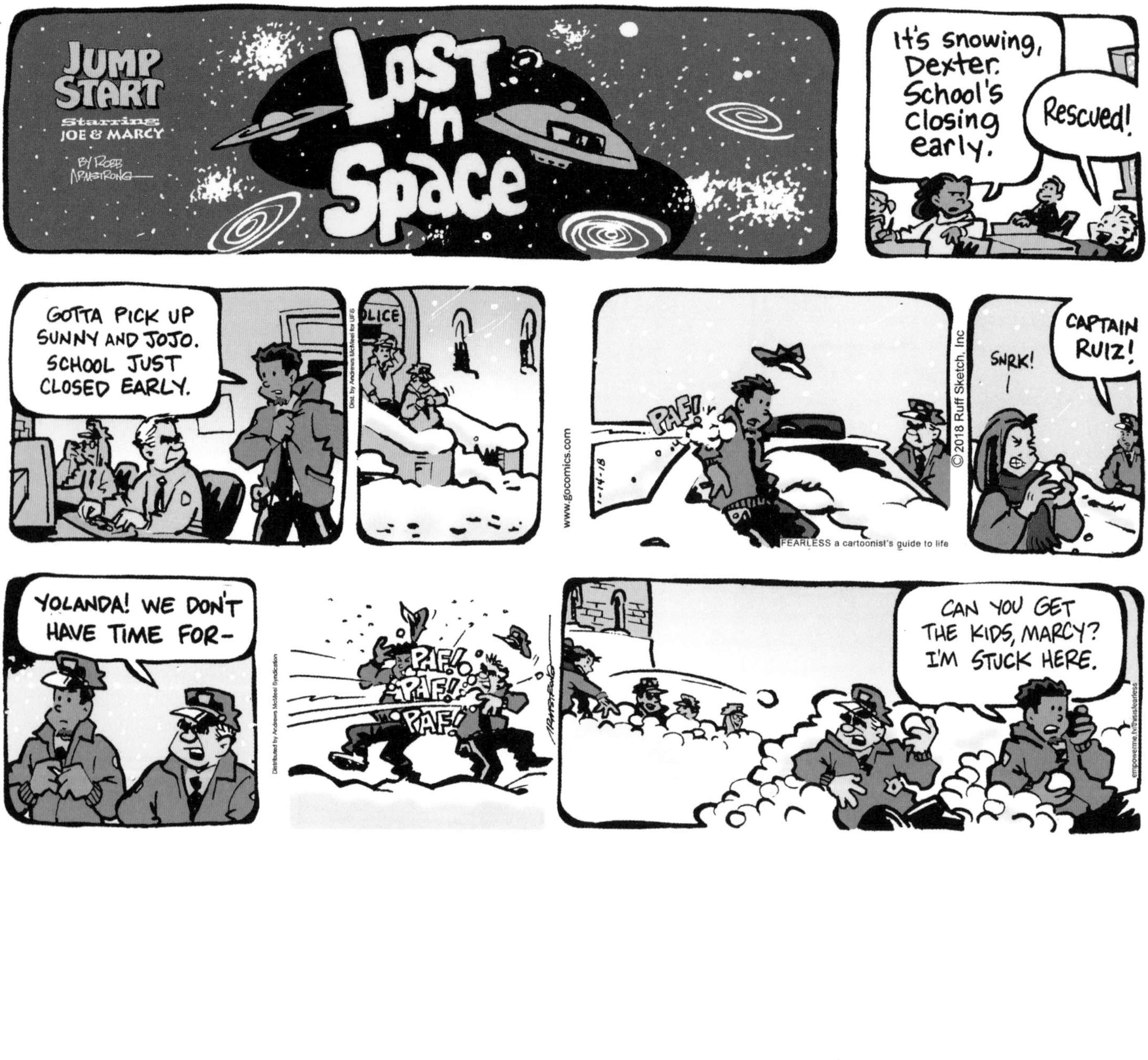

JUMP START
Starring JOE & MARCY
BY ROBB ARMSTRONG
Lost 'n Space
It's snowing, Dexter. School's closing early.
Rescued!
GOTTA PICK UP SUNNY AND JOJO. SCHOOL JUST CLOSED EARLY.
Dist. by Andrews McMeel for UFS
OLICE
www.gocomics.com
1-14-18
PAF!
©2018 Ruff Sketch, Inc
FEARLESS a cartoonist's guide to life
SNRK!
CAPTAIN RUIZ!
YOLANDA! WE DON'T HAVE TIME FOR-
Distributed by Andrews McMeel Syndication
PAF!
PAF!
PAF!
CAN YOU GET THE KIDS, MARCY? I'M STUCK HERE.

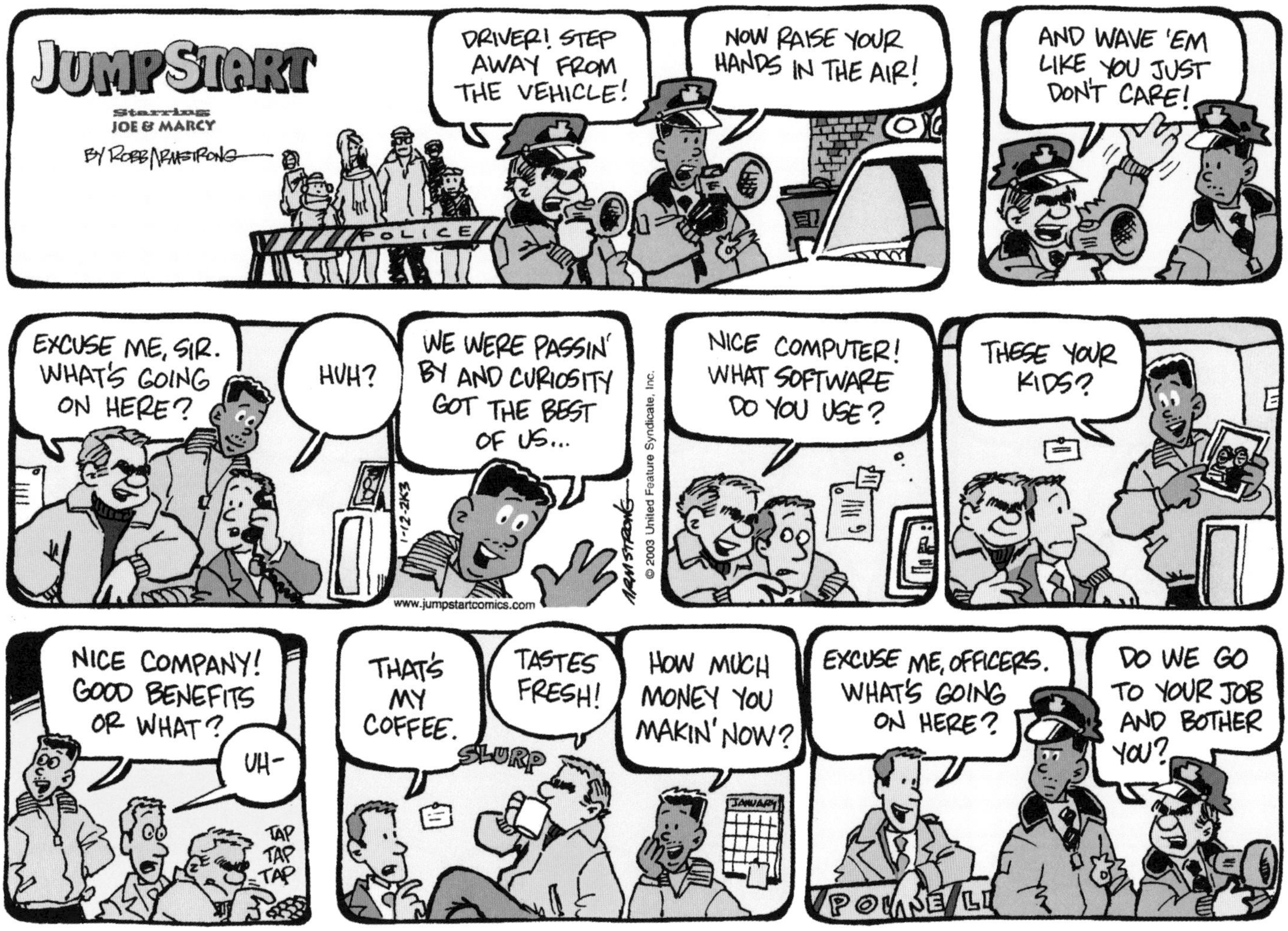
JUMPSTART
Starring JOE & MARCY
BY ROBB ARMSTRONG
DRIVER! STEP AWAY FROM THE VEHICLE!
NOW RAISE YOUR HANDS IN THE AIR!
POLICE
AND WAVE 'EM LIKE YOU JUST DON'T CARE!
EXCUSE ME, SIR. WHAT'S GOING ON HERE?
HUH?
WE WERE PASSIN' BY AND CURIOSITY GOT THE BEST OF US...
1-12-2K3
www.jumpstartcomics.com
ARMSTRONG
© 2003 United Feature Syndicate, Inc.
NICE COMPUTER! WHAT SOFTWARE DO YOU USE?
THESE YOUR KIDS?
NICE COMPANY! GOOD BENEFITS OR WHAT?
UH-
TAP TAP TAP
THAT'S MY COFFEE.
TASTES FRESH!
SLURP
HOW MUCH MONEY YOU MAKIN' NOW?
JANUARY
EXCUSE ME, OFFICERS. WHAT'S GOING ON HERE?
DO WE GO TO YOUR JOB AND BOTHER YOU?

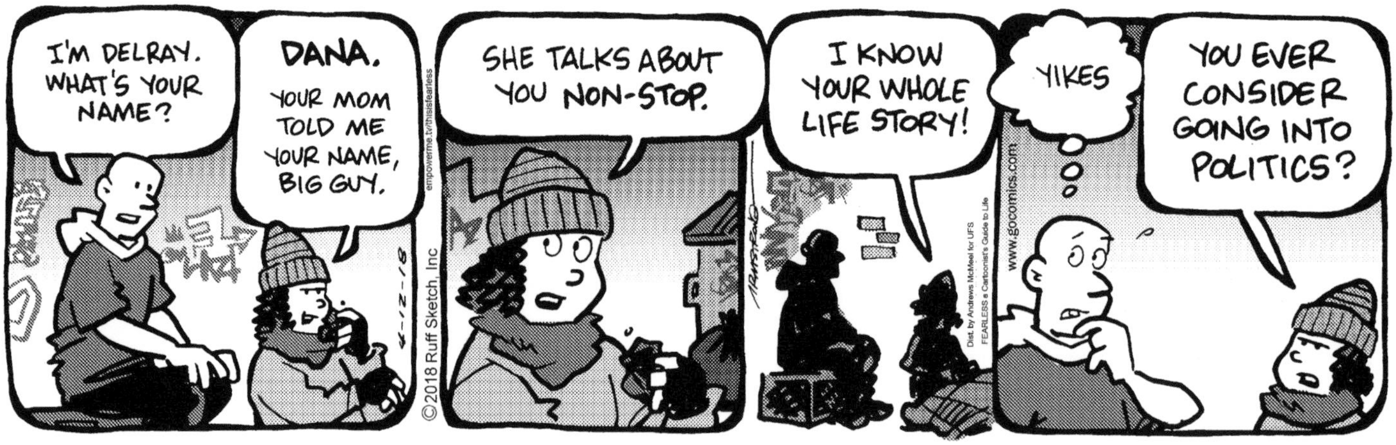
I'M DELRAY. WHAT'S YOUR NAME?
DANA.
YOUR MOM TOLD ME YOUR NAME, BIG GUY.
©2018 Ruff Sketch, Inc
empowerme.tv/thisisfearless
SHE TALKS ABOUT YOU NON-STOP.
I KNOW YOUR WHOLE LIFE STORY!
Dist. by Andrews McMeel for UFS
FEARLESS a Cartoonist's Guide to Life
www.gocomics.com
YIKES
YOU EVER CONSIDER GOING INTO POLITICS?

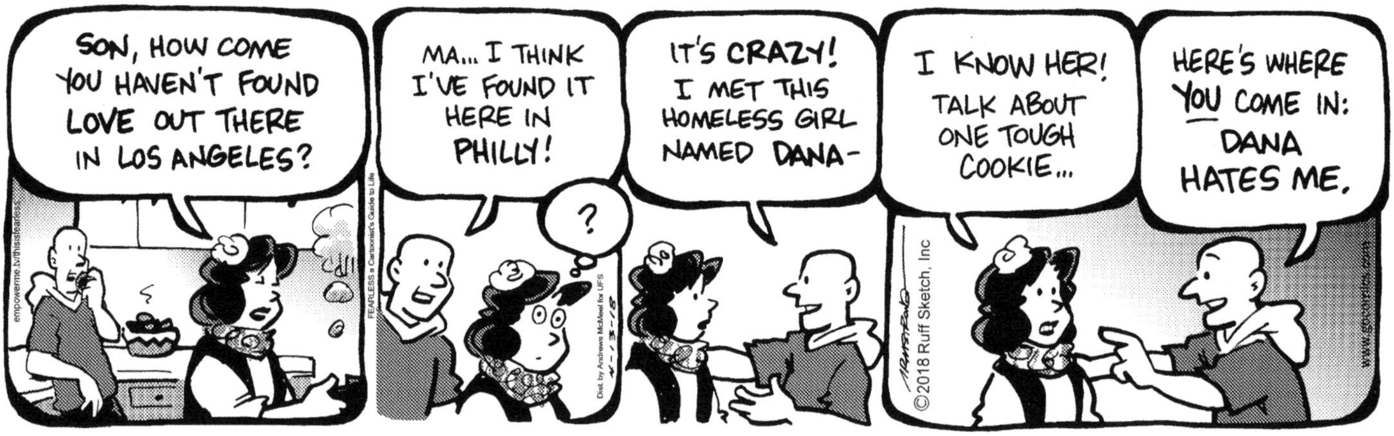
SON, HOW COME YOU HAVEN'T FOUND LOVE OUT THERE IN LOS ANGELES?
empowerme.tv/thisisfearless
FEARLESS a Cartoonist's Guide to Life
MA... I THINK I'VE FOUND IT HERE IN PHILLY!
?
Dist. by Andrews McMeel for UFS
IT'S CRAZY! I MET THIS HOMELESS GIRL NAMED DANA-
I KNOW HER! TALK ABOUT ONE TOUGH COOKIE...
©2018 Ruff Sketch, Inc
HERE'S WHERE YOU COME IN: DANA HATES ME.
www.gocomics.com

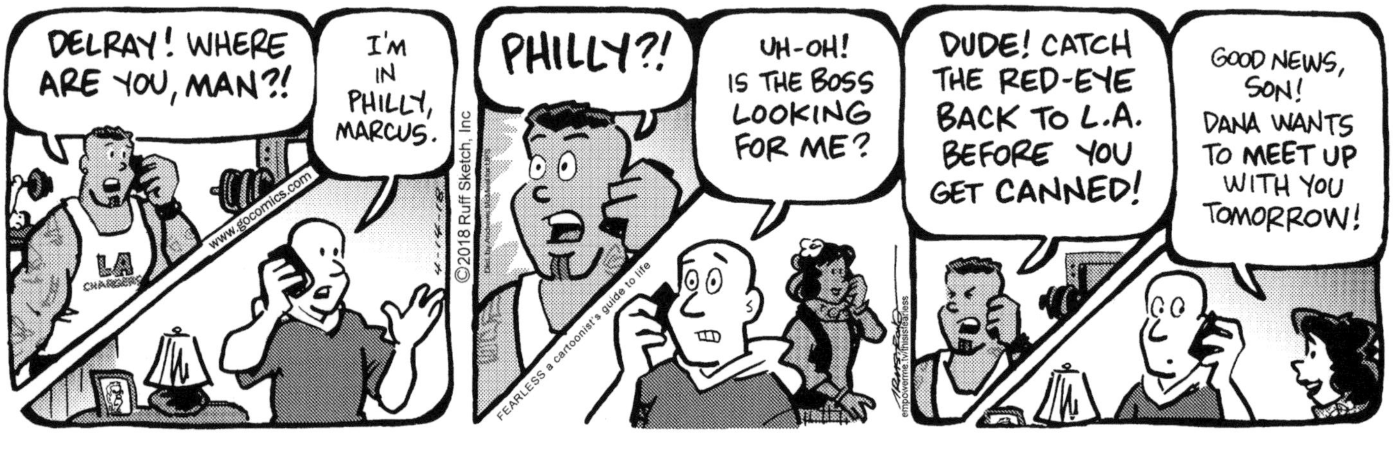
DELRAY! WHERE ARE YOU, MAN?!
I'M IN PHILLY, MARCUS.
LA
www.gocomics.com
©2018 Ruff Sketch, Inc
PHILLY?!
UH-OH! IS THE BOSS LOOKING FOR ME?
FEARLESS a cartoonist's guide to life
DUDE! CATCH THE RED-EYE BACK TO L.A. BEFORE YOU GET CANNED!
empowerme.tv/thisisfearless
GOOD NEWS, SON! DANA WANTS TO MEET UP WITH YOU TOMORROW!

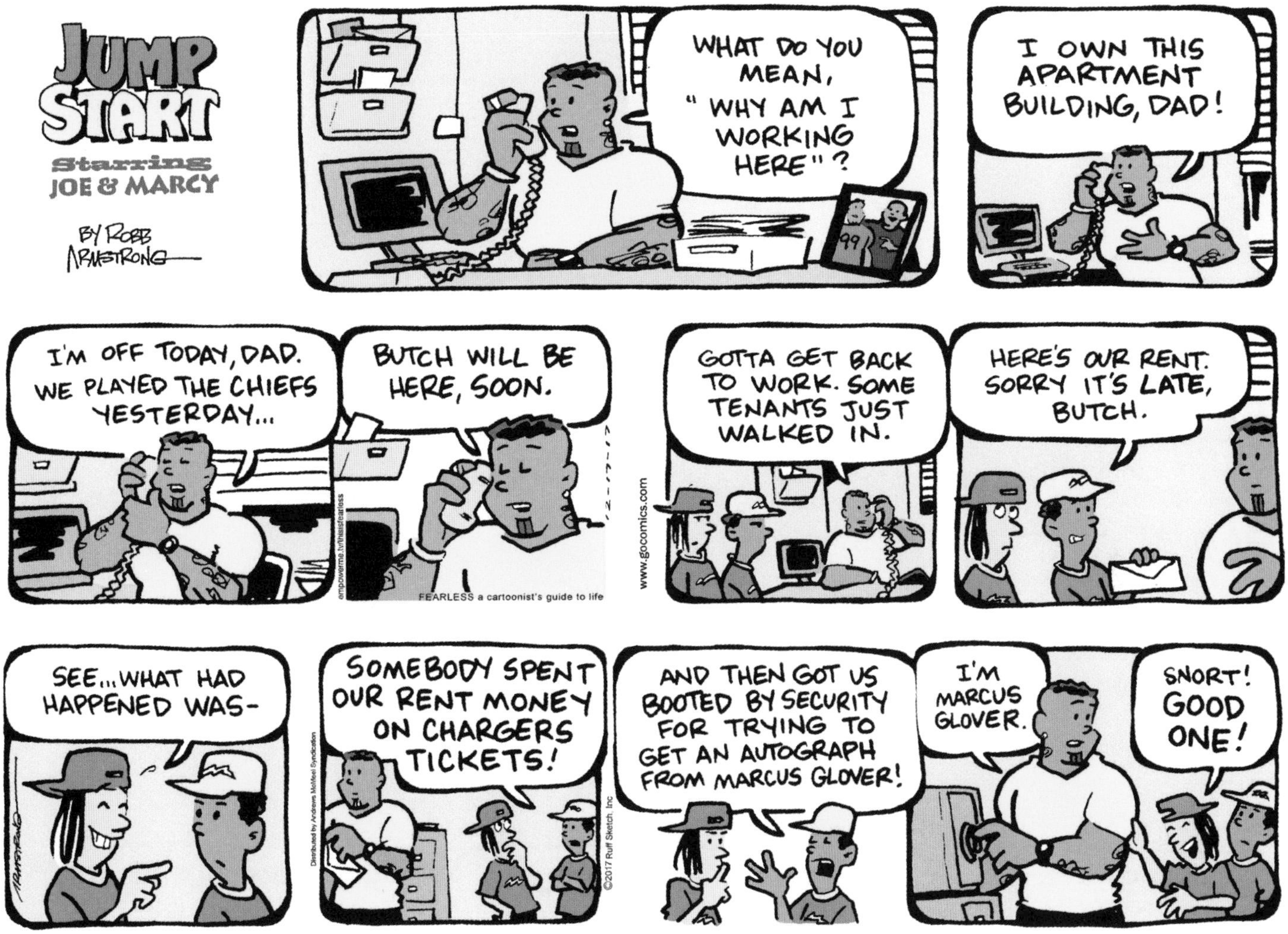
JUMP START
Starring JOE & MARCY
BY ROBB ARMSTRONG
WHAT DO YOU MEAN, "WHY AM I WORKING HERE"?
I OWN THIS APARTMENT BUILDING, DAD!
I'M OFF TODAY, DAD. WE PLAYED THE CHIEFS YESTERDAY...
BUTCH WILL BE HERE, SOON.
empowerme.tv/thisisfearless
FEARLESS a cartoonist's guide to life
www.gocomics.com
GOTTA GET BACK TO WORK. SOME TENANTS JUST WALKED IN.
HERE'S OUR RENT. SORRY IT'S LATE, BUTCH.
SEE... WHAT HAD HAPPENED WAS-
Distributed by Andrews McMeel Syndication
SOMEBODY SPENT OUR RENT MONEY ON CHARGERS TICKETS!
©2017 Ruff Sketch, Inc
AND THEN GOT US BOOTED BY SECURITY FOR TRYING TO GET AN AUTOGRAPH FROM MARCUS GLOVER!
I'M MARCUS GLOVER.
SNORT! GOOD ONE!

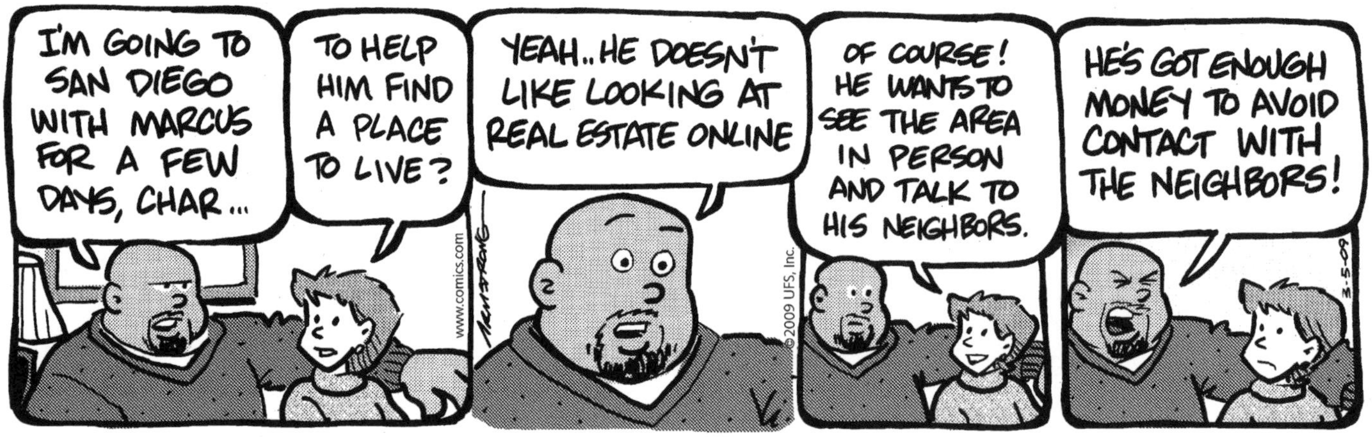
I'M GOING TO SAN DIEGO WITH MARCUS FOR A FEW DAYS, CHAR...
TO HELP HIM FIND A PLACE TO LIVE?
YEAH.. HE DOESN'T LIKE LOOKING AT REAL ESTATE ONLINE
OF COURSE! HE WANTS TO SEE THE AREA IN PERSON AND TALK TO HIS NEIGHBORS.
HE'S GOT ENOUGH MONEY TO AVOID CONTACT WITH THE NEIGHBORS!
www.comics.com
©2009 UFS, Inc.
3-5-09

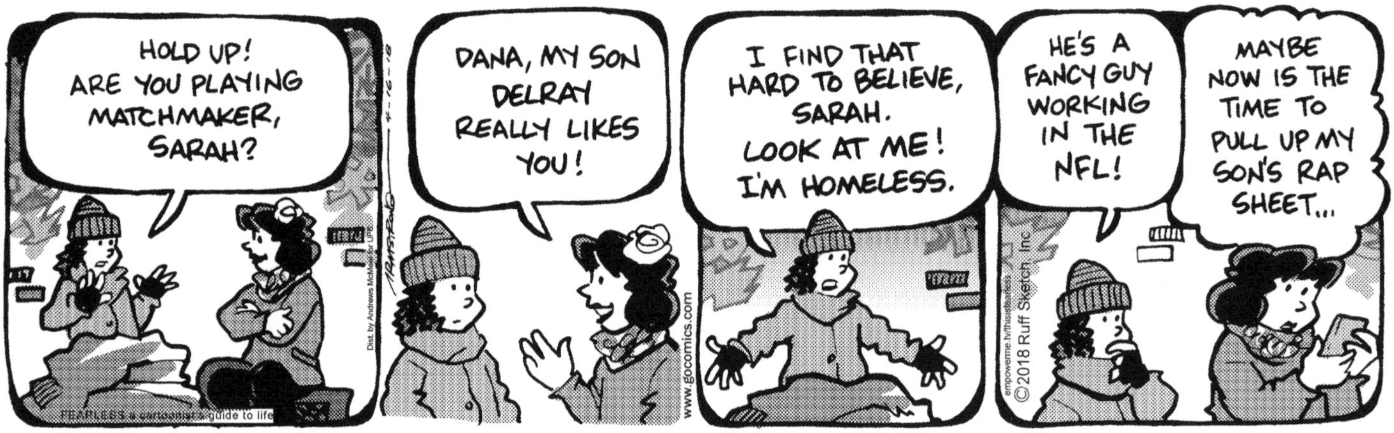
HOLD UP! ARE YOU PLAYING MATCHMAKER, SARAH?
DANA, MY SON DELRAY REALLY LIKES YOU!
I FIND THAT HARD TO BELIEVE, SARAH. LOOK AT ME! I'M HOMELESS.
HE'S A FANCY GUY WORKING IN THE NFL!
MAYBE NOW IS THE TIME TO PULL UP MY SON'S RAP SHEET...
4-16-18
FEARLESS a cartoonist's guide to life
www.gocomics.com
©2018 Ruff Sketch, Inc.

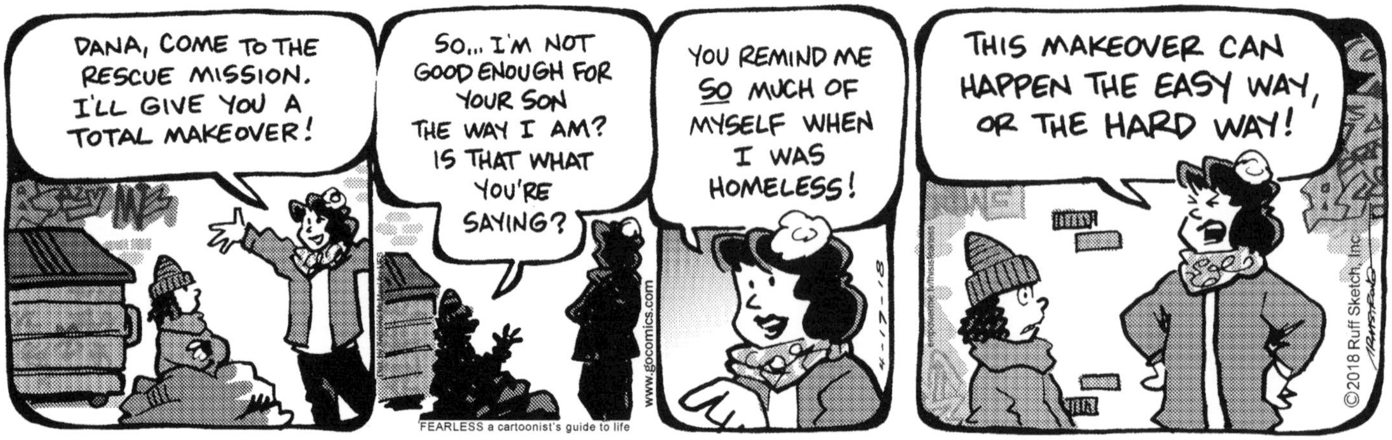
DANA, COME TO THE RESCUE MISSION. I'LL GIVE YOU A TOTAL MAKEOVER!
SO... I'M NOT GOOD ENOUGH FOR YOUR SON THE WAY I AM? IS THAT WHAT YOU'RE SAYING?
YOU REMIND ME SO MUCH OF MYSELF WHEN I WAS HOMELESS!
THIS MAKEOVER CAN HAPPEN THE EASY WAY, OR THE HARD WAY!
FEARLESS a cartoonist's guide to life
www.gocomics.com
4-17-18
©2018 Ruff Sketch, Inc.

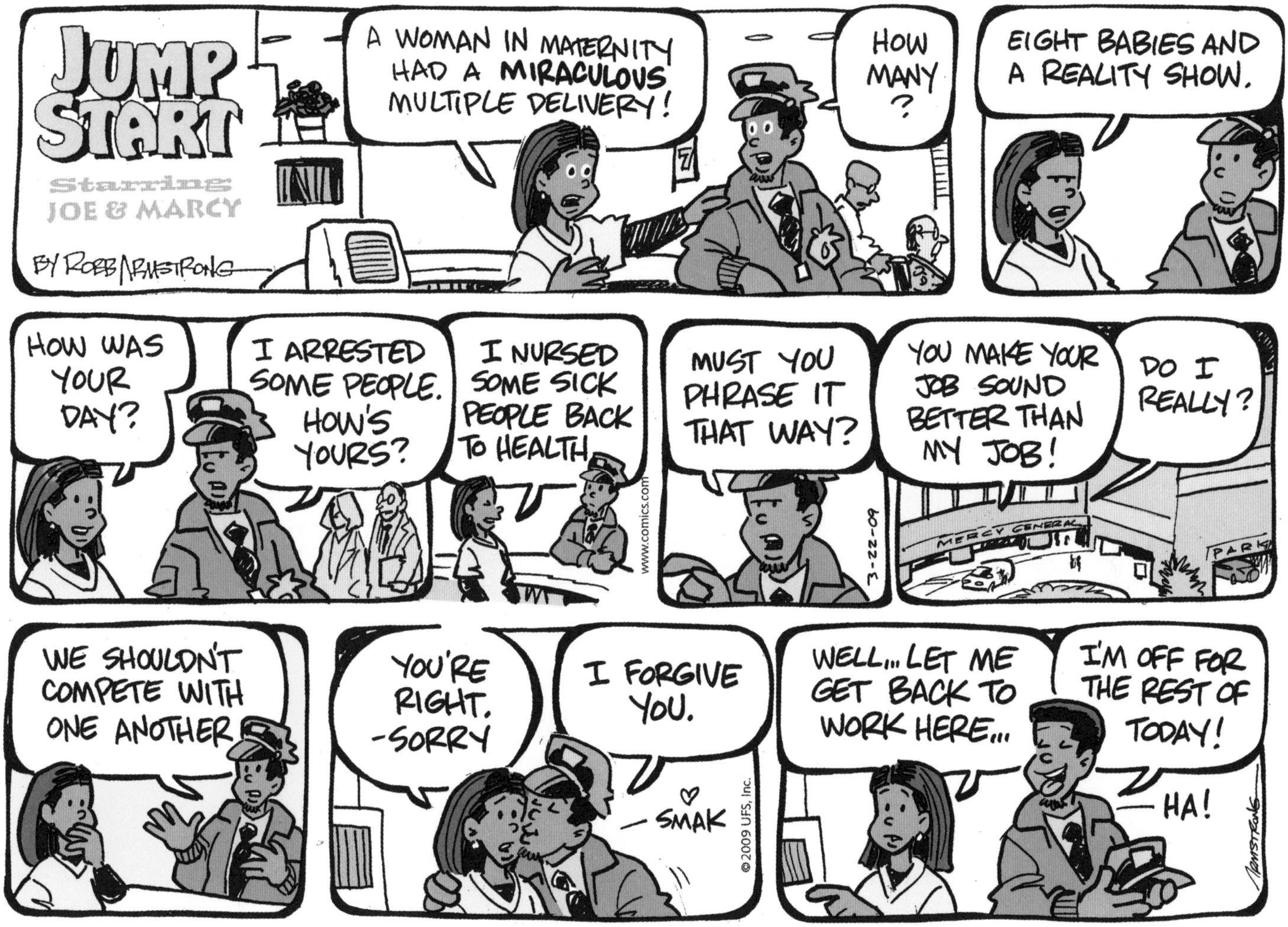
JUMP START
Starring JOE & MARCY
BY ROBB ARMSTRONG
A WOMAN IN MATERNITY HAD A **MIRACULOUS** MULTIPLE DELIVERY!
HOW MANY ?
EIGHT BABIES AND A REALITY SHOW.
HOW WAS YOUR DAY?
I ARRESTED SOME PEOPLE. HOW'S YOURS?
I NURSED SOME SICK PEOPLE BACK TO HEALTH.
www.comics.com
MUST YOU PHRASE IT THAT WAY?
3-22-09
YOU MAKE YOUR JOB SOUND BETTER THAN MY JOB!
DO I REALLY?
MERCY GENERAL
PARK
WE SHOULDN'T COMPETE WITH ONE ANOTHER.
YOU'RE RIGHT. -SORRY
I FORGIVE YOU.
SMAK
© 2009 UFS, Inc.
WELL... LET ME GET BACK TO WORK HERE...
I'M OFF FOR THE REST OF TODAY!
HA!
ARMSTRONG

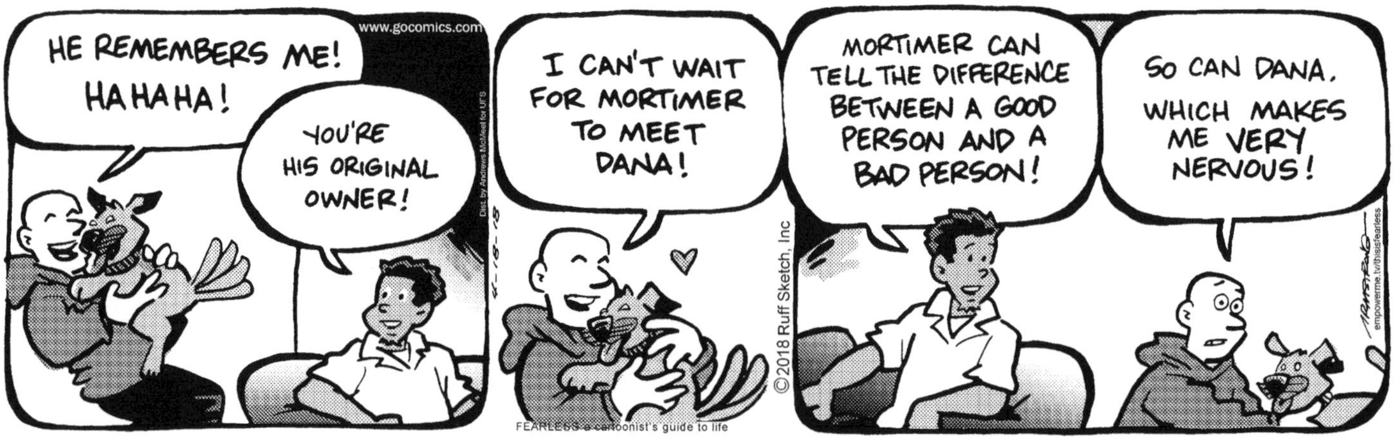
www.gocomics.com
HE REMEMBERS ME! HAHAHA!
YOU'RE HIS ORIGINAL OWNER!
Dist. by Andrews McMeel for UFS
I CAN'T WAIT FOR MORTIMER TO MEET DANA!
FEARLESS a cartoonist's guide to life
©2018 Ruff Sketch, Inc
MORTIMER CAN TELL THE DIFFERENCE BETWEEN A GOOD PERSON AND A BAD PERSON!
SO CAN DANA. WHICH MAKES ME VERY NERVOUS!
empowerme.tv/thisisfearless

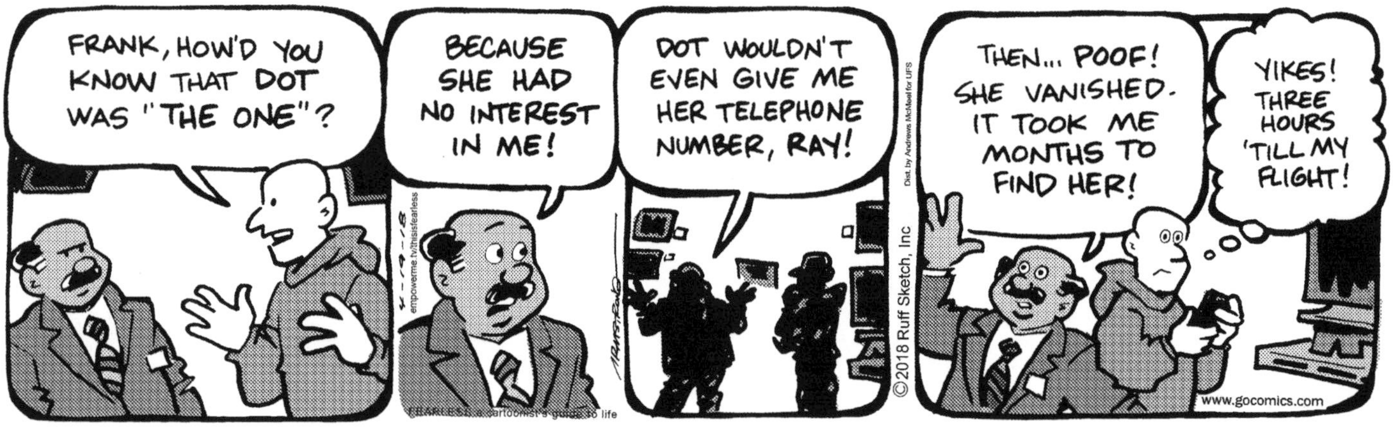
FRANK, HOW'D YOU KNOW THAT DOT WAS "THE ONE"?
BECAUSE SHE HAD NO INTEREST IN ME!
empowerme.tv/thisisfearless
DOT WOULDN'T EVEN GIVE ME HER TELEPHONE NUMBER, RAY!
©2018 Ruff Sketch, Inc
Dist. by Andrews McMeel for UFS
THEN... POOF! SHE VANISHED. IT TOOK ME MONTHS TO FIND HER!
YIKES! THREE HOURS 'TILL MY FLIGHT!
www.gocomics.com

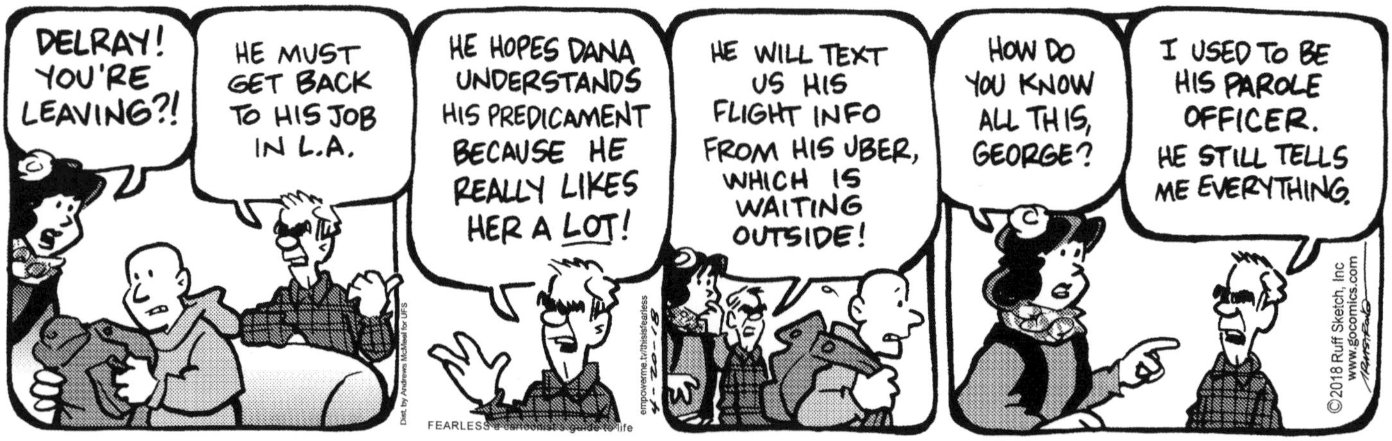
DELRAY! YOU'RE LEAVING?!
HE MUST GET BACK TO HIS JOB IN L.A.
Dist. by Andrews McMeel for UFS
HE HOPES DANA UNDERSTANDS HIS PREDICAMENT BECAUSE HE REALLY LIKES HER A LOT!
FEARLESS a cartoonist's guide to life
empowerme.tv/thisisfearless
HE WILL TEXT US HIS FLIGHT INFO FROM HIS UBER, WHICH IS WAITING OUTSIDE!
HOW DO YOU KNOW ALL THIS, GEORGE?
I USED TO BE HIS PAROLE OFFICER. HE STILL TELLS ME EVERYTHING.
©2018 Ruff Sketch, Inc
www.gocomics.com

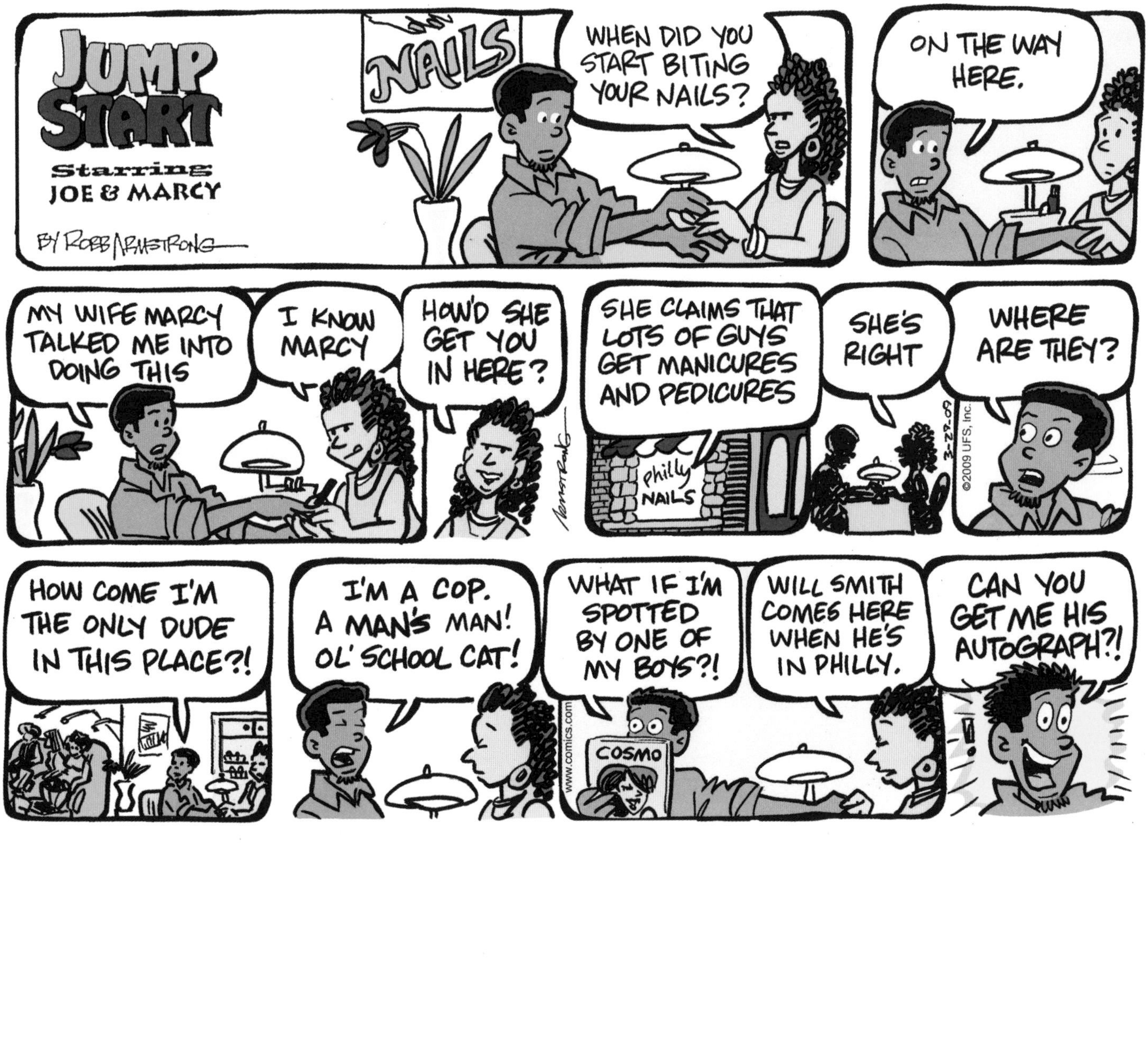
JUMP START
Starring JOE & MARCY
BY ROBB ARMSTRONG
NAILS
WHEN DID YOU START BITING YOUR NAILS?
ON THE WAY HERE.
MY WIFE MARCY TALKED ME INTO DOING THIS
I KNOW MARCY
HOW'D SHE GET YOU IN HERE?
SHE CLAIMS THAT LOTS OF GUYS GET MANICURES AND PEDICURES
Philly NAILS
SHE'S RIGHT
WHERE ARE THEY?
©2009 UFS, Inc.
HOW COME I'M THE ONLY DUDE IN THIS PLACE?!
I'M A COP. A MAN'S MAN! OL' SCHOOL CAT!
WHAT IF I'M SPOTTED BY ONE OF MY BOYS?!
www.comics.com
COSMO
WILL SMITH COMES HERE WHEN HE'S IN PHILLY.
CAN YOU GET ME HIS AUTOGRAPH?!

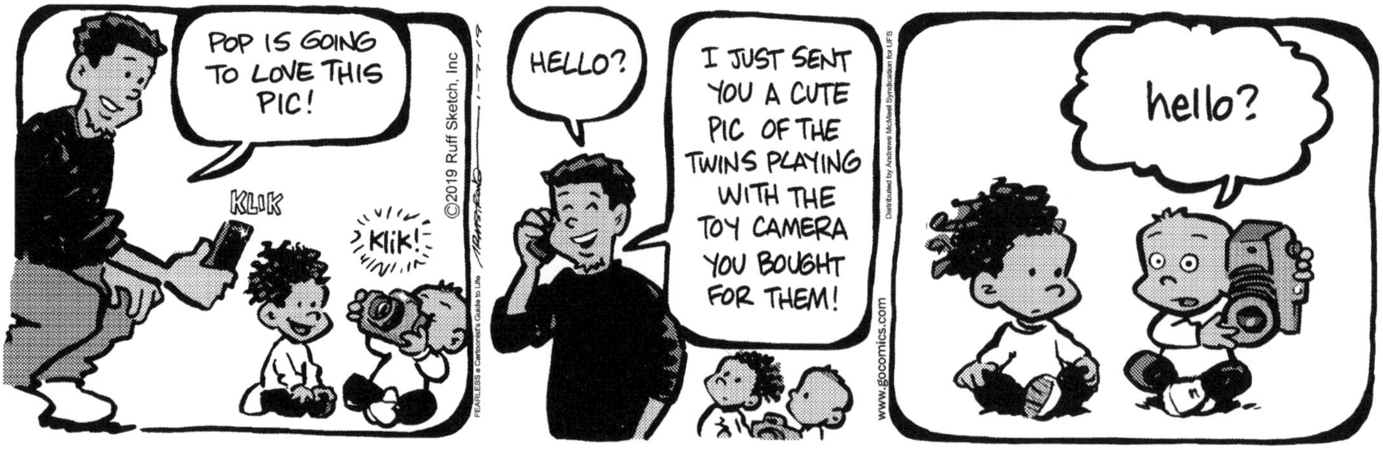
POP IS GOING TO LOVE THIS PIC!
KLIK
KliK!
©2019 Ruff Sketch, Inc
HELLO?
I JUST SENT YOU A CUTE PIC OF THE TWINS PLAYING WITH THE TOY CAMERA YOU BOUGHT FOR THEM!
www.gocomics.com
hello?

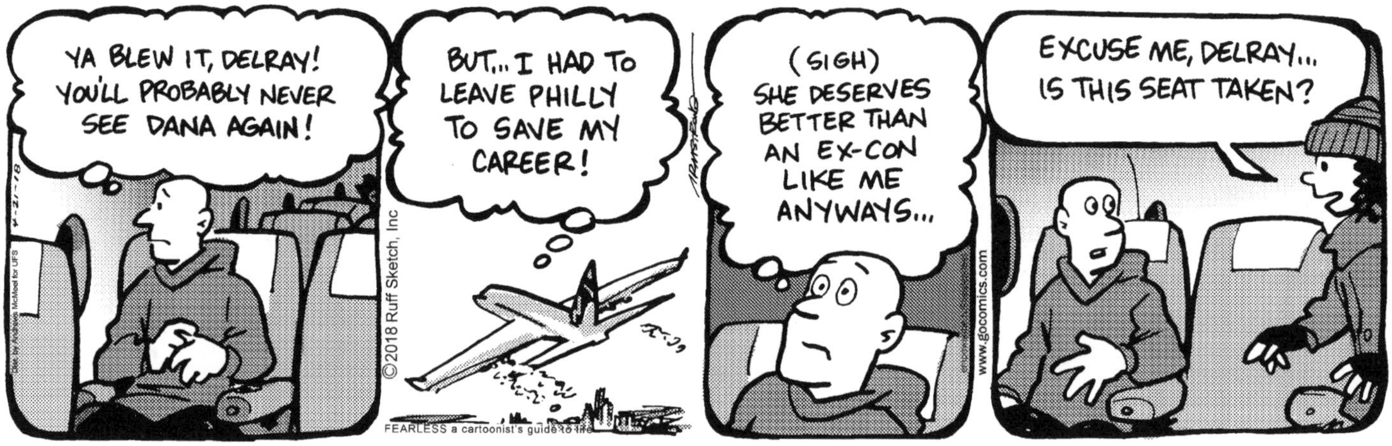
YA BLEW IT, DELRAY! YOU'LL PROBABLY NEVER SEE DANA AGAIN!
BUT... I HAD TO LEAVE PHILLY TO SAVE MY CAREER!
©2018 Ruff Sketch, Inc
FEARLESS a cartoonist's guide to life
(SIGH) SHE DESERVES BETTER THAN AN EX-CON LIKE ME ANYWAYS...
www.gocomics.com
EXCUSE ME, DELRAY... IS THIS SEAT TAKEN?

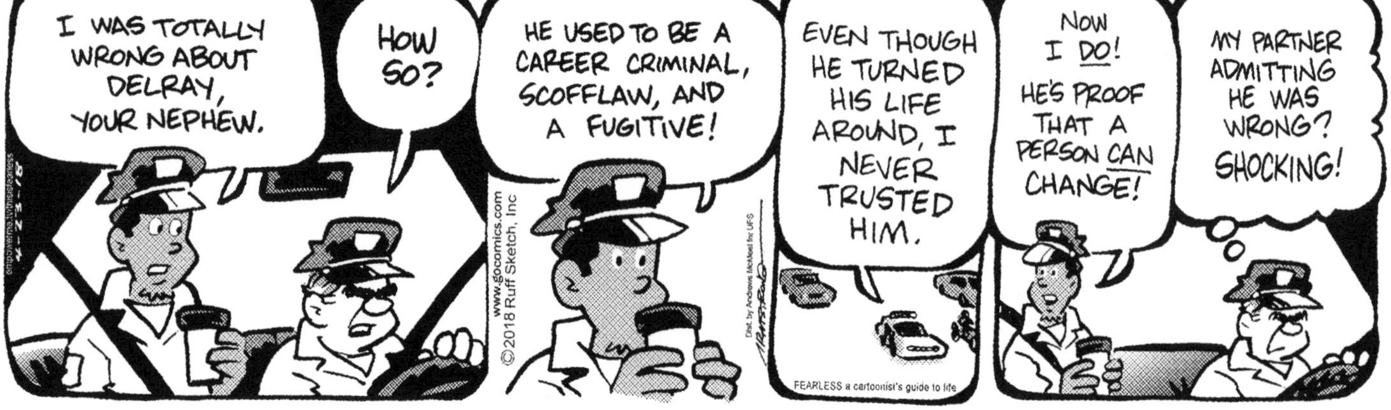
I WAS TOTALLY WRONG ABOUT DELRAY, YOUR NEPHEW.
HOW SO?
www.gocomics.com
©2018 Ruff Sketch, Inc
HE USED TO BE A CAREER CRIMINAL, SCOFFLAW, AND A FUGITIVE!
EVEN THOUGH HE TURNED HIS LIFE AROUND, I NEVER TRUSTED HIM.
FEARLESS a cartoonist's guide to life
NOW I DO! HE'S PROOF THAT A PERSON CAN CHANGE!
MY PARTNER ADMITTING HE WAS WRONG? SHOCKING!

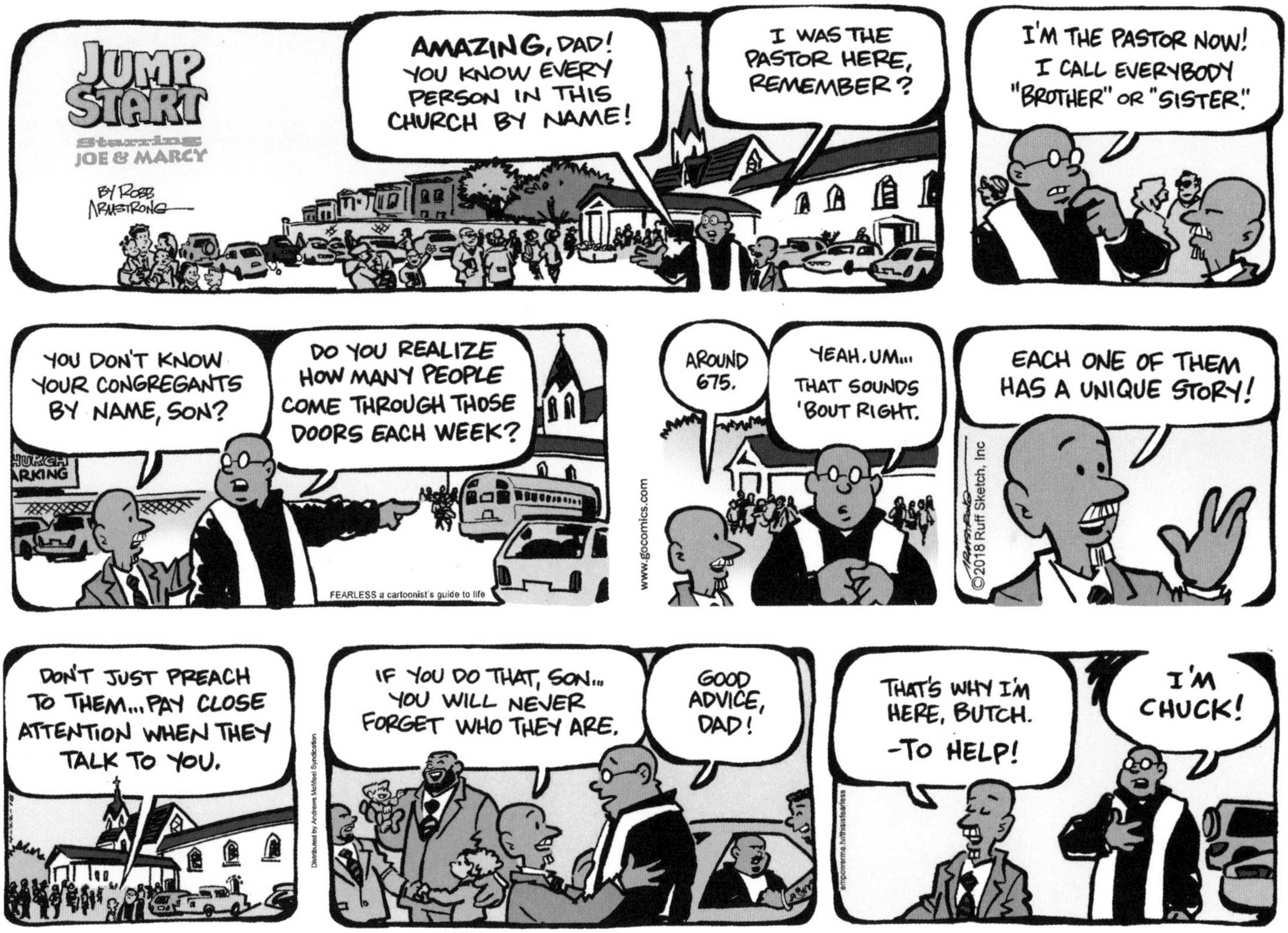
JUMP START
Starring JOE & MARCY
BY ROBB ARMSTRONG
AMAZING, DAD! YOU KNOW EVERY PERSON IN THIS CHURCH BY NAME!
I WAS THE PASTOR HERE, REMEMBER?
I'M THE PASTOR NOW! I CALL EVERYBODY "BROTHER" OR "SISTER."
YOU DON'T KNOW YOUR CONGREGANTS BY NAME, SON?
DO YOU REALIZE HOW MANY PEOPLE COME THROUGH THOSE DOORS EACH WEEK?
CHURCH PARKING
FEARLESS a cartoonist's guide to life
www.gocomics.com
AROUND 675.
YEAH, UM... THAT SOUNDS 'BOUT RIGHT.
EACH ONE OF THEM HAS A UNIQUE STORY!
©2018 Ruff Sketch, Inc
DON'T JUST PREACH TO THEM... PAY CLOSE ATTENTION WHEN THEY TALK TO YOU.
Distributed by Andrews McMeel Syndication
IF YOU DO THAT, SON... YOU WILL NEVER FORGET WHO THEY ARE.
GOOD ADVICE, DAD!
THAT'S WHY I'M HERE, BUTCH. -TO HELP!
I'M CHUCK!
empowerme.tv/thisisfearless

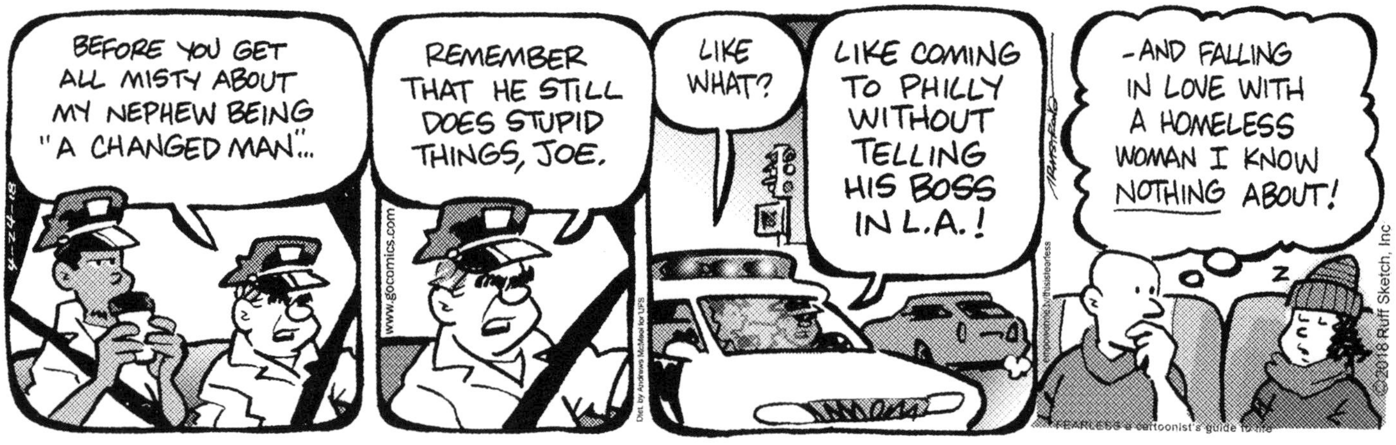
4-24-18
BEFORE YOU GET ALL MISTY ABOUT MY NEPHEW BEING "A CHANGED MAN"...
REMEMBER THAT HE STILL DOES STUPID THINGS, JOE.
www.gocomics.com
LIKE WHAT?
LIKE COMING TO PHILLY WITHOUT TELLING HIS BOSS IN L.A.!
-AND FALLING IN LOVE WITH A HOMELESS WOMAN I KNOW NOTHING ABOUT!
Z
©2018 Ruff Sketch, Inc

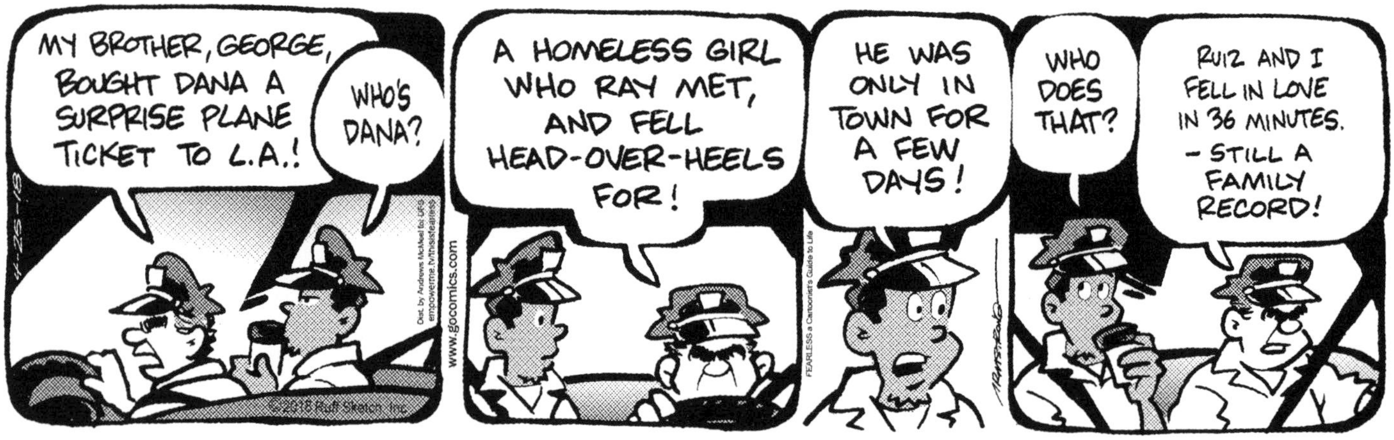
4-25-18
MY BROTHER, GEORGE, BOUGHT DANA A SURPRISE PLANE TICKET TO L.A.!
WHO'S DANA?
©2018 Ruff Sketch, Inc
www.gocomics.com
A HOMELESS GIRL WHO RAY MET, AND FELL HEAD-OVER-HEELS FOR!
HE WAS ONLY IN TOWN FOR A FEW DAYS!
WHO DOES THAT?
RUIZ AND I FELL IN LOVE IN 36 MINUTES.
- STILL A FAMILY RECORD!

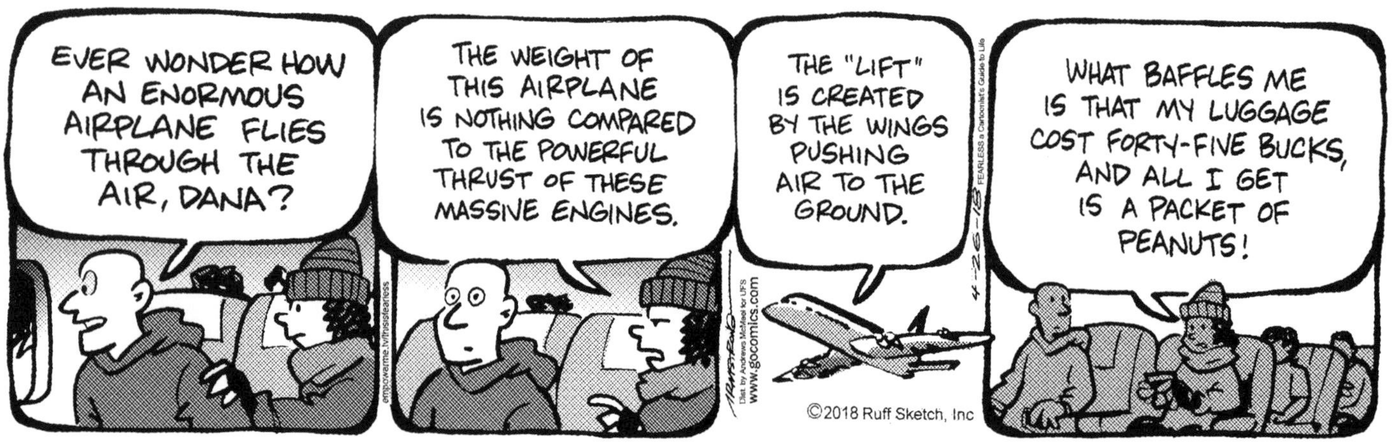
EVER WONDER HOW AN ENORMOUS AIRPLANE FLIES THROUGH THE AIR, DANA?
THE WEIGHT OF THIS AIRPLANE IS NOTHING COMPARED TO THE POWERFUL THRUST OF THESE MASSIVE ENGINES.
www.gocomics.com
THE "LIFT" IS CREATED BY THE WINGS PUSHING AIR TO THE GROUND.
4-26-18
©2018 Ruff Sketch, Inc
WHAT BAFFLES ME IS THAT MY LUGGAGE COST FORTY-FIVE BUCKS, AND ALL I GET IS A PACKET OF PEANUTS!

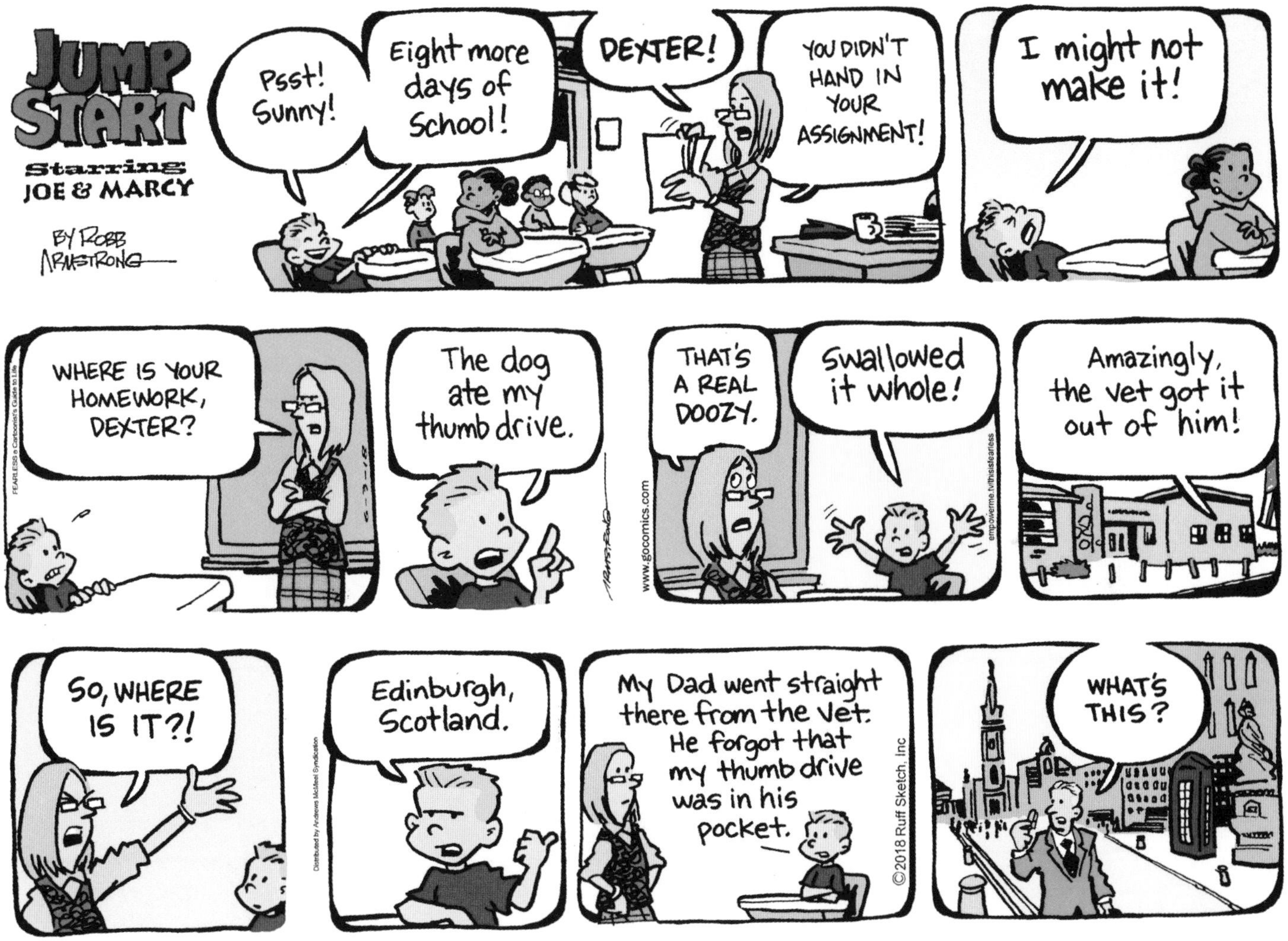
JUMP START
Starring JOE & MARCY
BY ROBB ARMSTRONG
Psst! Sunny!
Eight more days of School!
DEXTER!
YOU DIDN'T HAND IN YOUR ASSIGNMENT!
I might not make it!
WHERE IS YOUR HOMEWORK, DEXTER?
The dog ate my thumb drive.
THAT'S A REAL DOOZY.
Swallowed it whole!
Amazingly, the vet got it out of him!
SO, WHERE IS IT?!
Edinburgh, Scotland.
My Dad went straight there from the vet. He forgot that my thumb drive was in his pocket.
WHAT'S THIS?

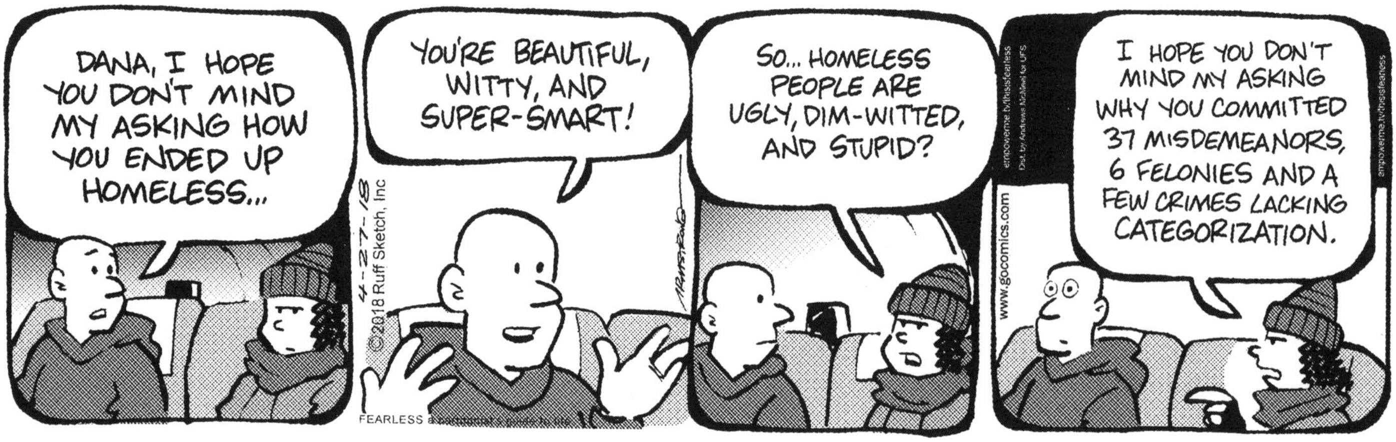
DANA, I HOPE YOU DON'T MIND MY ASKING HOW YOU ENDED UP HOMELESS...
YOU'RE BEAUTIFUL, WITTY, AND SUPER-SMART!
SO... HOMELESS PEOPLE ARE UGLY, DIM-WITTED, AND STUPID?
I HOPE YOU DON'T MIND MY ASKING WHY YOU COMMITTED 37 MISDEMEANORS, 6 FELONIES AND A FEW CRIMES LACKING CATEGORIZATION.
4-27-18
©2018 Ruff Sketch, Inc
www.gocomics.com
FEARLESS a cartoonist's guide to life

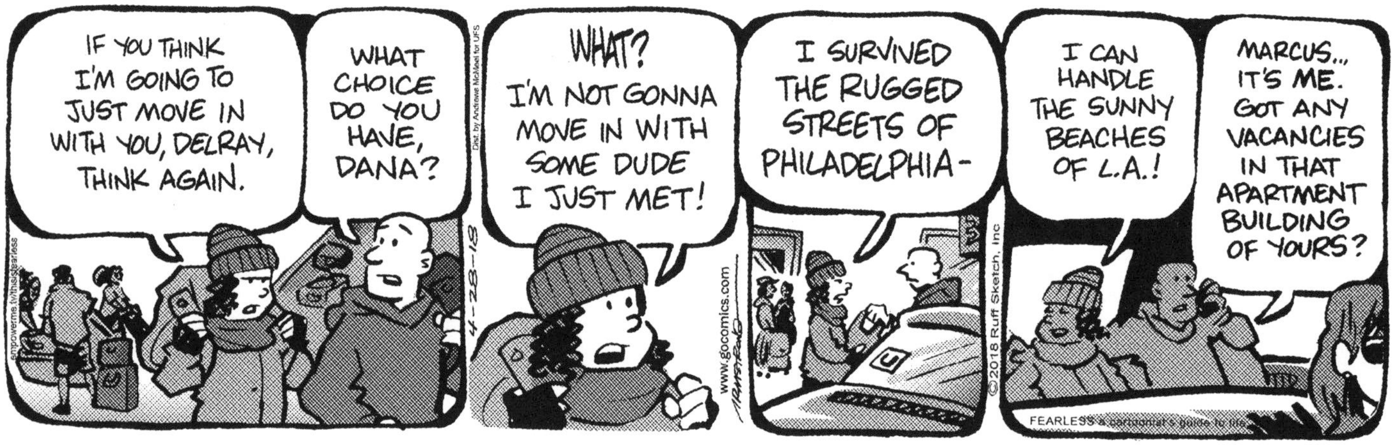
IF YOU THINK I'M GOING TO JUST MOVE IN WITH YOU, DELRAY, THINK AGAIN.
WHAT CHOICE DO YOU HAVE, DANA?
WHAT? I'M NOT GONNA MOVE IN WITH SOME DUDE I JUST MET!
I SURVIVED THE RUGGED STREETS OF PHILADELPHIA-
I CAN HANDLE THE SUNNY BEACHES OF L.A.!
MARCUS... IT'S ME. GOT ANY VACANCIES IN THAT APARTMENT BUILDING OF YOURS?
4-28-18
www.gocomics.com
©2018 Ruff Sketch, Inc
FEARLESS a cartoonist's guide to life

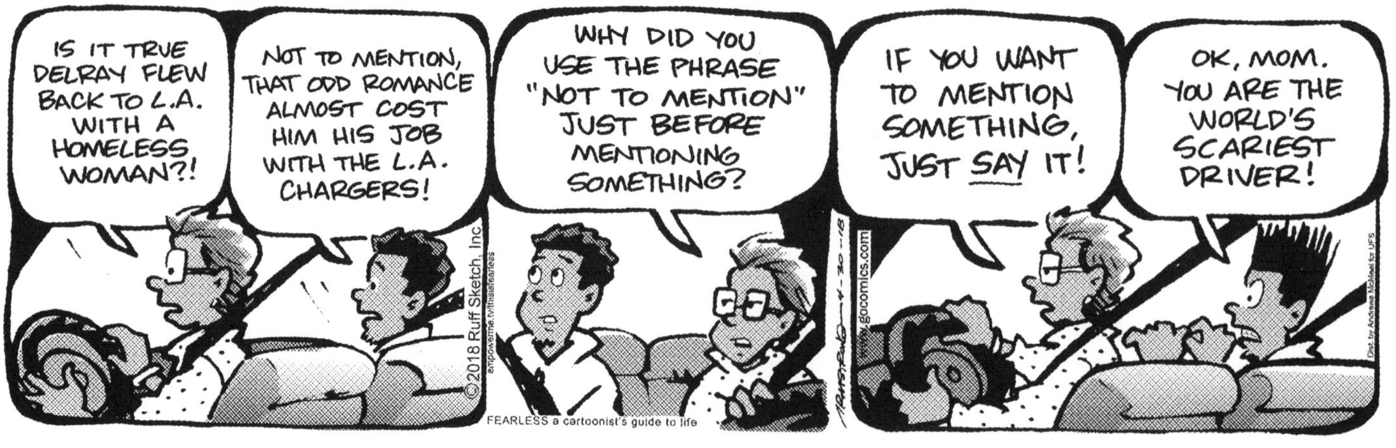
IS IT TRUE DELRAY FLEW BACK TO L.A. WITH A HOMELESS WOMAN?!
NOT TO MENTION, THAT ODD ROMANCE ALMOST COST HIM HIS JOB WITH THE L.A. CHARGERS!
WHY DID YOU USE THE PHRASE "NOT TO MENTION" JUST BEFORE MENTIONING SOMETHING?
IF YOU WANT TO MENTION SOMETHING, JUST SAY IT!
OK, MOM. YOU ARE THE WORLD'S SCARIEST DRIVER!
©2018 Ruff Sketch, Inc
4-30-18
www.gocomics.com
FEARLESS a cartoonist's guide to life

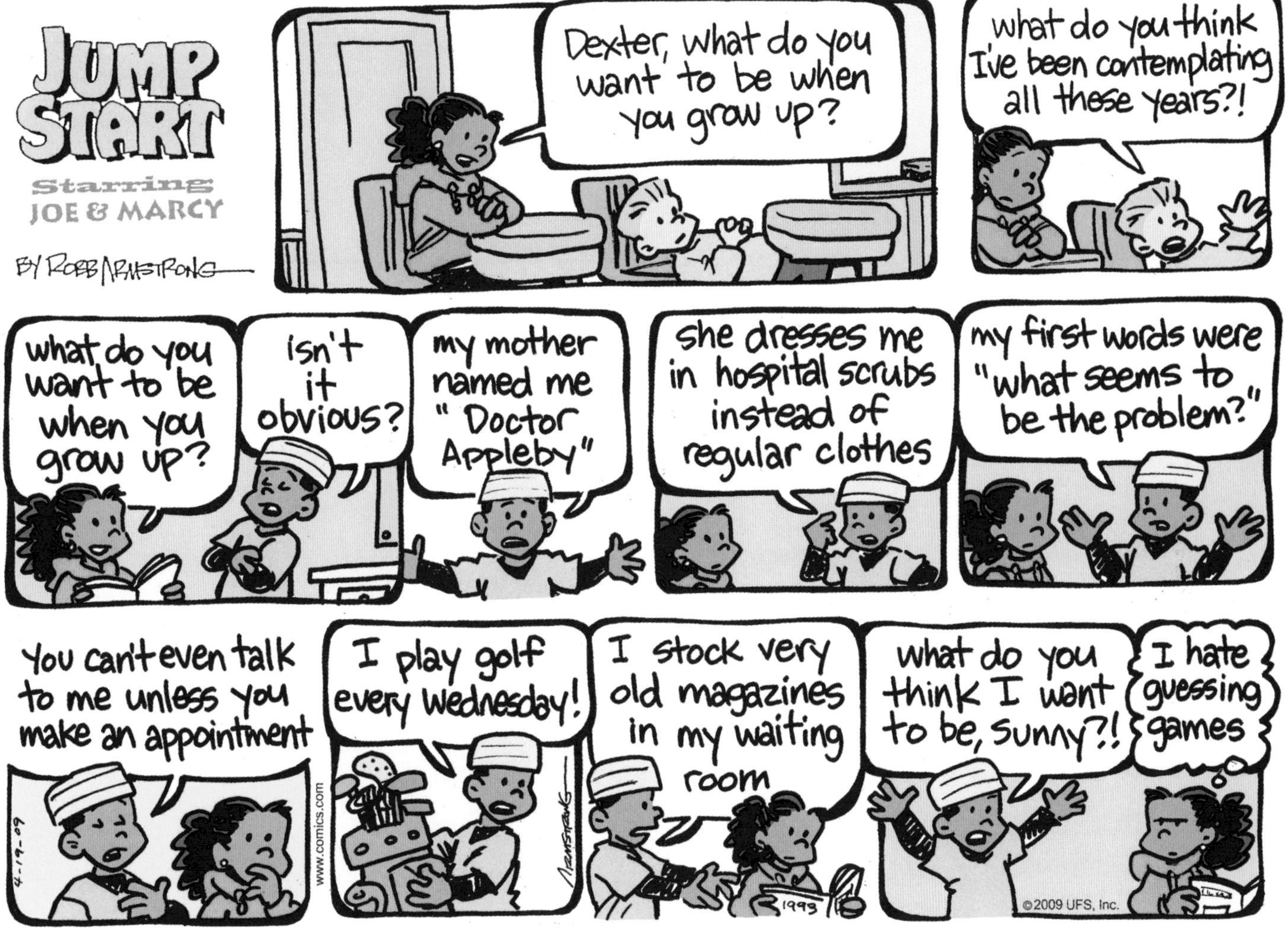
JUMP START
Starring JOE & MARCY
BY ROBB ARMSTRONG
Dexter, what do you want to be when you grow up?
what do you think I've been contemplating all these years?!
what do you want to be when you grow up?
isn't it obvious?
my mother named me "Doctor Appleby"
she dresses me in hospital scrubs instead of regular clothes
my first words were "what seems to be the problem?"
You can't even talk to me unless you make an appointment
4-19-09
www.comics.com
I play golf every Wednesday!
I stock very old magazines in my waiting room
1995
what do you think I want to be, Sunny?!
I hate guessing games
©2009 UFS, Inc.

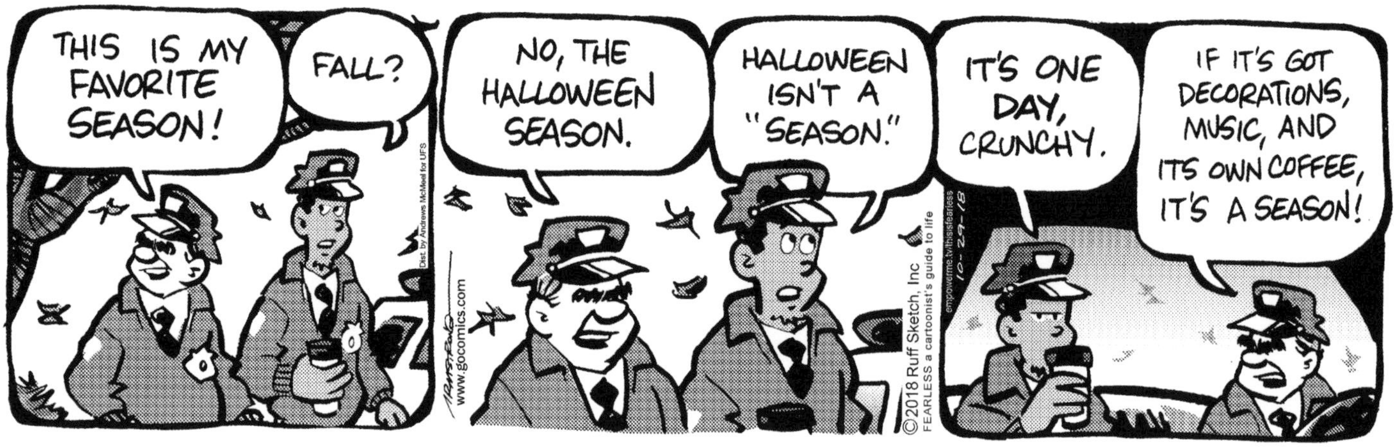
THIS IS MY FAVORITE SEASON!
FALL?
NO, THE HALLOWEEN SEASON.
HALLOWEEN ISN'T A "SEASON."
IT'S ONE DAY, CRUNCHY.
IF IT'S GOT DECORATIONS, MUSIC, AND ITS OWN COFFEE, IT'S A SEASON!
www.gocomics.com
©2018 Ruff Sketch, Inc
FEARLESS a cartoonist's guide to life
10-29-18

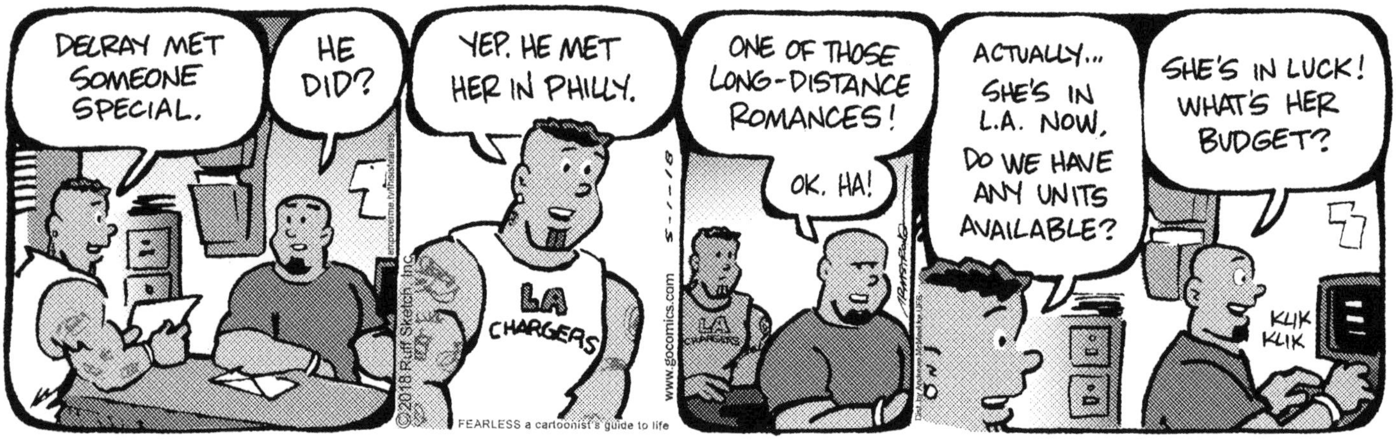
DELRAY MET SOMEONE SPECIAL.
HE DID?
YEP. HE MET HER IN PHILLY.
LA CHARGERS
ONE OF THOSE LONG-DISTANCE ROMANCES!
OK. HA!
ACTUALLY... SHE'S IN L.A. NOW. DO WE HAVE ANY UNITS AVAILABLE?
SHE'S IN LUCK! WHAT'S HER BUDGET?
KLIK KLIK
©2018 Ruff Sketch, Inc
www.gocomics.com
FEARLESS a cartoonist's guide to life
5-1-18

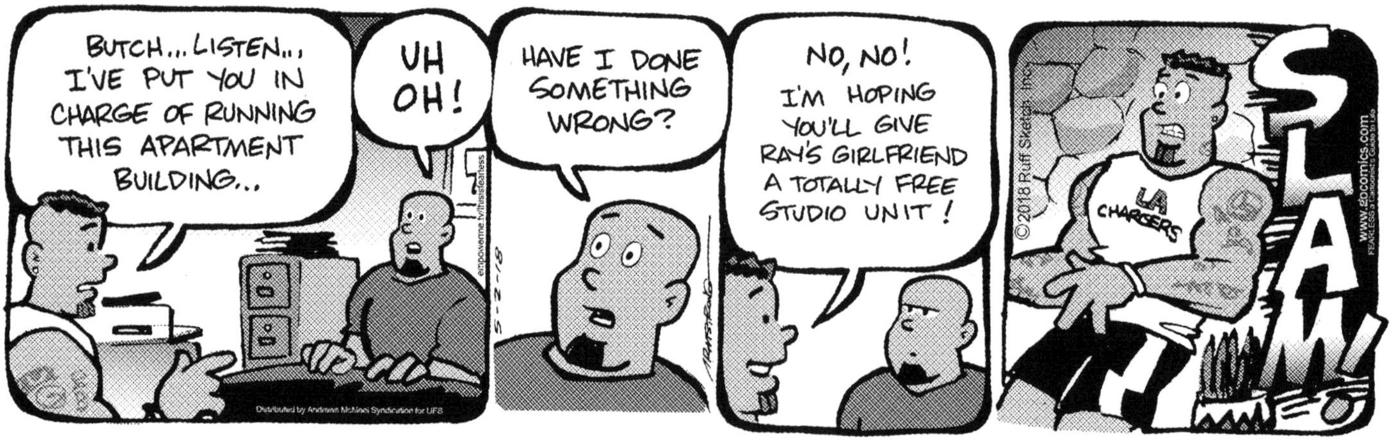
BUTCH... LISTEN... I'VE PUT YOU IN CHARGE OF RUNNING THIS APARTMENT BUILDING...
UH OH!
HAVE I DONE SOMETHING WRONG?
NO, NO! I'M HOPING YOU'LL GIVE RAY'S GIRLFRIEND A TOTALLY FREE STUDIO UNIT!
LA CHARGERS
SLAM!
©2018 Ruff Sketch, Inc
www.gocomics.com
5-2-18

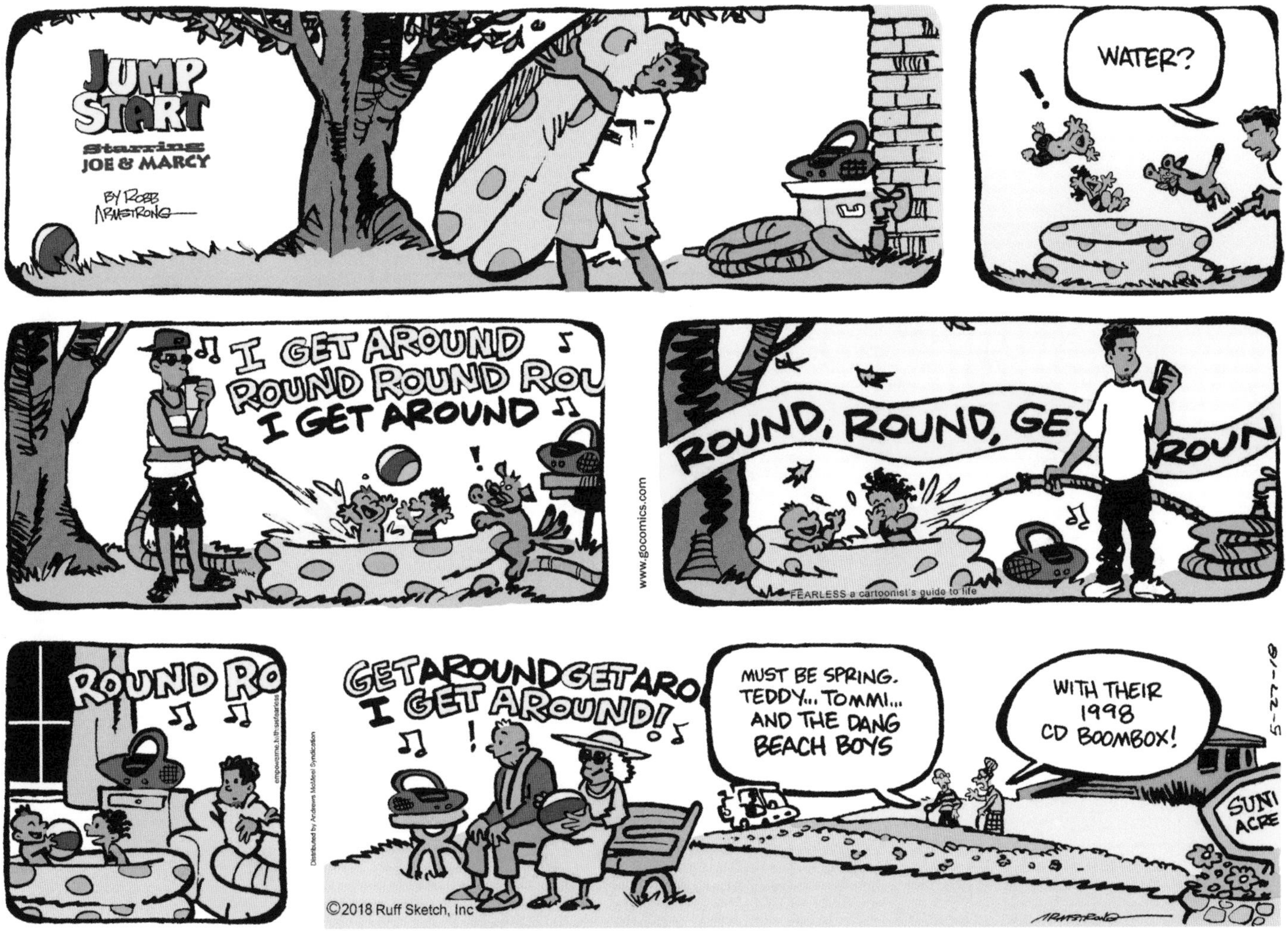
JUMP START
Starring JOE & MARCY
BY ROBB ARMSTRONG
WATER?
!
I GET AROUND ROUND ROUND ROU
I GET AROUND
!
ROUND, ROUND, GET AROUN
www.gocomics.com
FEARLESS a cartoonist's guide to life
ROUND RO
Distributed by Andrews McMeel Syndication
GETAROUNDGETARO I GET AROUND!
!
MUST BE SPRING. TEDDY... TOMMI... AND THE DANG BEACH BOYS
WITH THEIR 1998 CD BOOMBOX!
5-27-18
©2018 Ruff Sketch, Inc

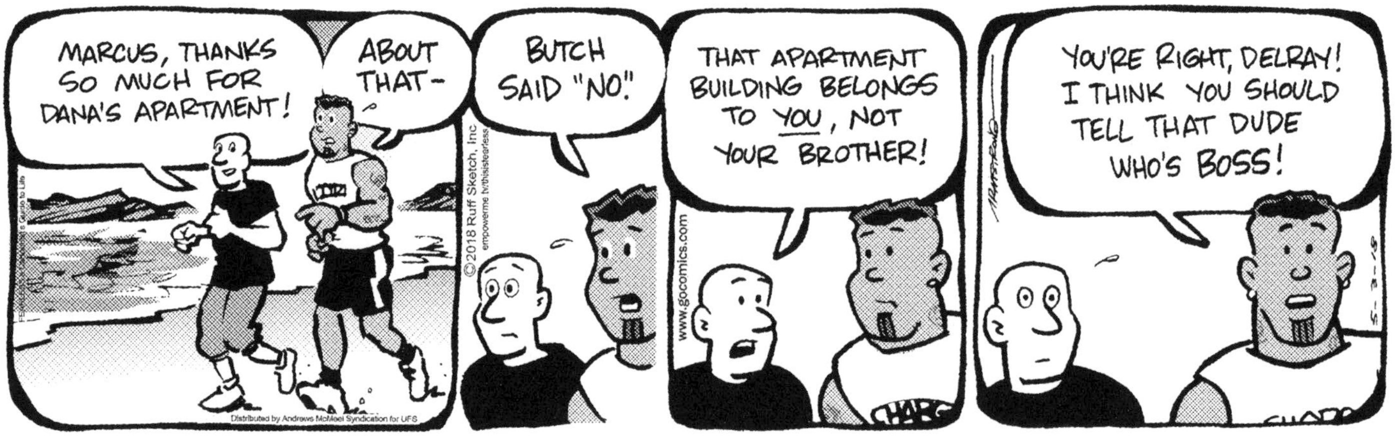
MARCUS, THANKS SO MUCH FOR DANA'S APARTMENT!
ABOUT THAT-
BUTCH SAID "NO."
THAT APARTMENT BUILDING BELONGS TO YOU, NOT YOUR BROTHER!
YOU'RE RIGHT, DELRAY! I THINK YOU SHOULD TELL THAT DUDE WHO'S BOSS!
©2018 Ruff Sketch, Inc
www.gocomics.com
Distributed by Andrews McMeel Syndication for UFS

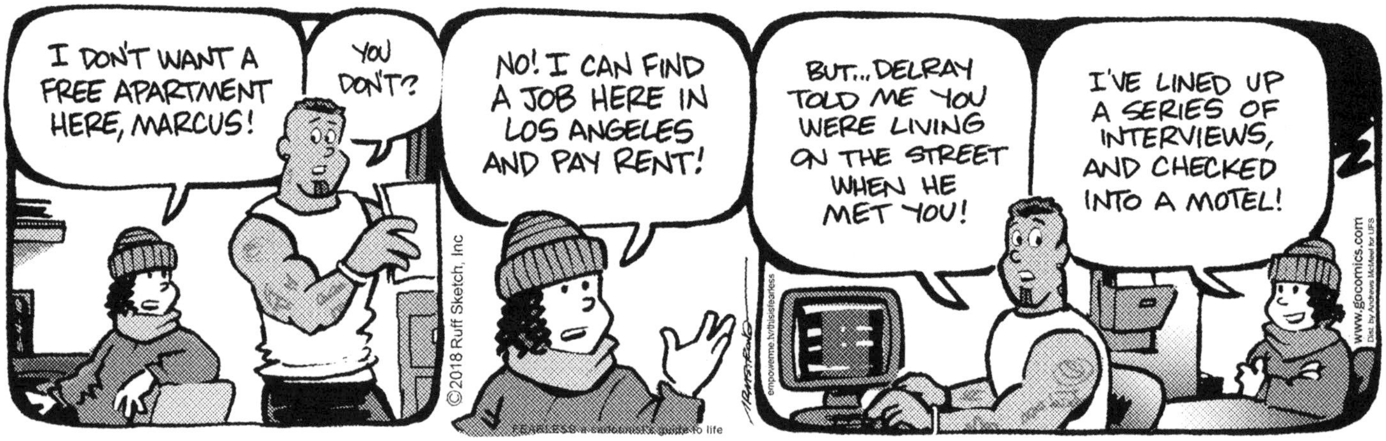
I DON'T WANT A FREE APARTMENT HERE, MARCUS!
YOU DON'T?
NO! I CAN FIND A JOB HERE IN LOS ANGELES AND PAY RENT!
BUT... DELRAY TOLD ME YOU WERE LIVING ON THE STREET WHEN HE MET YOU!
I'VE LINED UP A SERIES OF INTERVIEWS, AND CHECKED INTO A MOTEL!
©2018 Ruff Sketch, Inc
www.gocomics.com

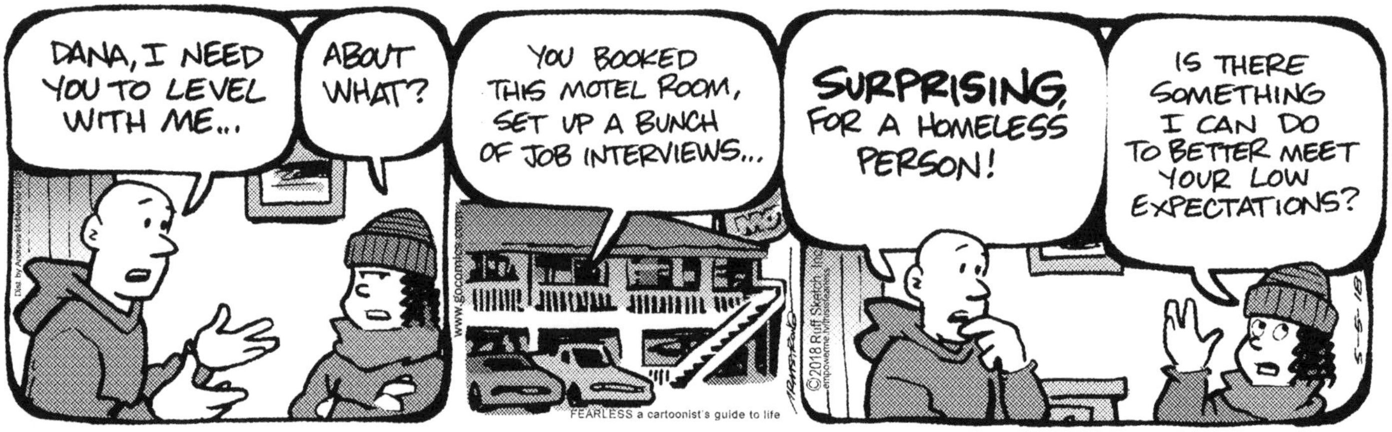
DANA, I NEED YOU TO LEVEL WITH ME...
ABOUT WHAT?
YOU BOOKED THIS MOTEL ROOM, SET UP A BUNCH OF JOB INTERVIEWS...
SURPRISING, FOR A HOMELESS PERSON!
IS THERE SOMETHING I CAN DO TO BETTER MEET YOUR LOW EXPECTATIONS?
www.gocomics.com
©2018 Ruff Sketch, Inc
FEARLESS a cartoonist's guide to life

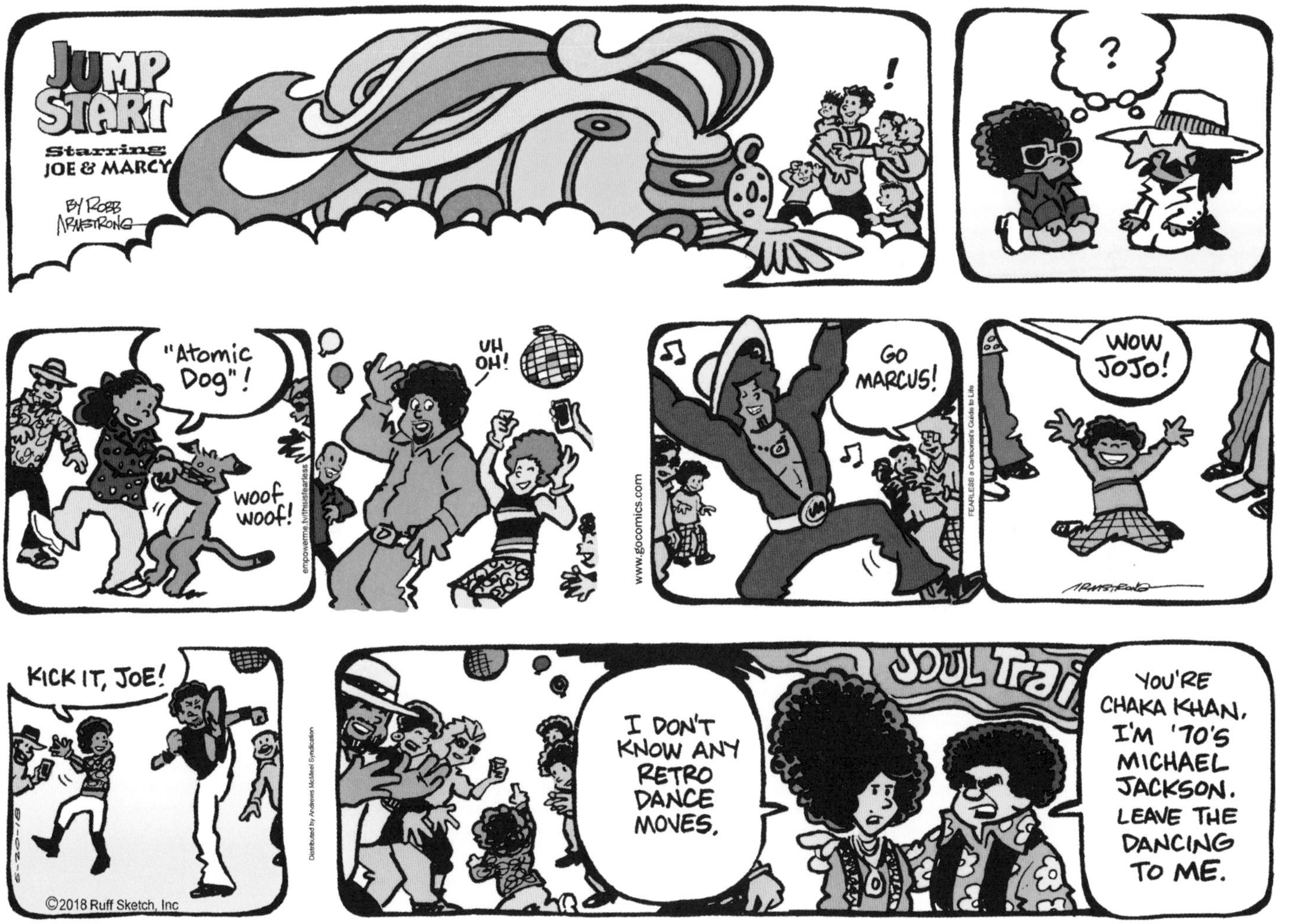
JUMP START
Starring JOE & MARCY
BY ROBB ARMSTRONG
!
?
"Atomic Dog"!
woof woof!
empowerme.tv/thisisfearless
UH OH!
www.gocomics.com
GO MARCUS!
FEARLESS a Cartoonist's Guide to Life
WOW JOJO!
ARMSTRONG
KICK IT, JOE!
6-20-18
©2018 Ruff Sketch, Inc
Distributed by Andrews McMeel Syndication
SOUL TRAI
I DON'T KNOW ANY RETRO DANCE MOVES.
YOU'RE CHAKA KHAN. I'M '70'S MICHAEL JACKSON. LEAVE THE DANCING TO ME.

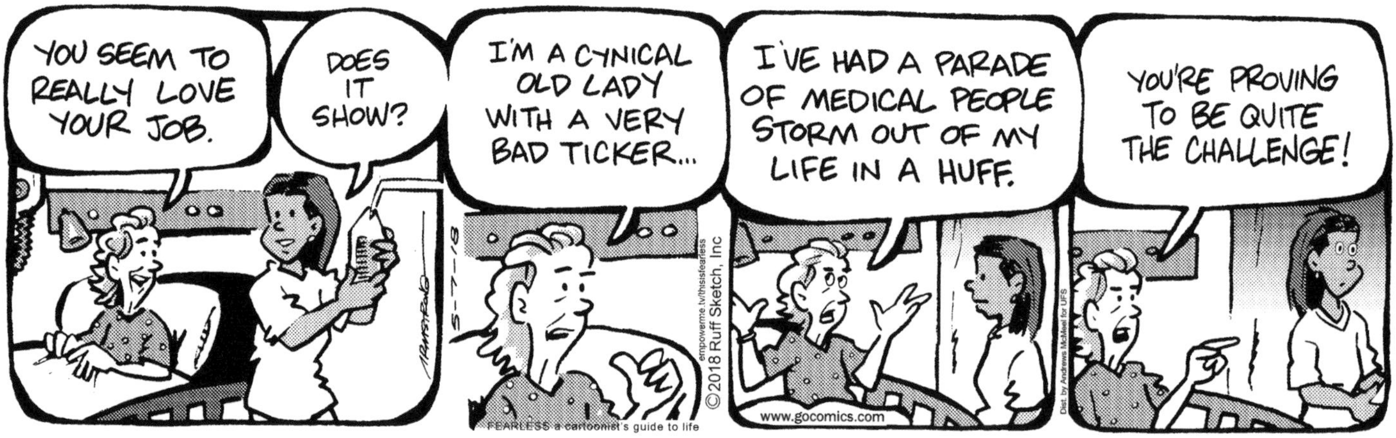
YOU SEEM TO REALLY LOVE YOUR JOB.
DOES IT SHOW?
I'M A CYNICAL OLD LADY WITH A VERY BAD TICKER...
I'VE HAD A PARADE OF MEDICAL PEOPLE STORM OUT OF MY LIFE IN A HUFF.
YOU'RE PROVING TO BE QUITE THE CHALLENGE!
5-7-18
empowerme.tv/thisisfearless
©2018 Ruff Sketch, Inc
FEARLESS a cartoonist's guide to life
www.gocomics.com
Dist. by Andrews McMeel for UFS

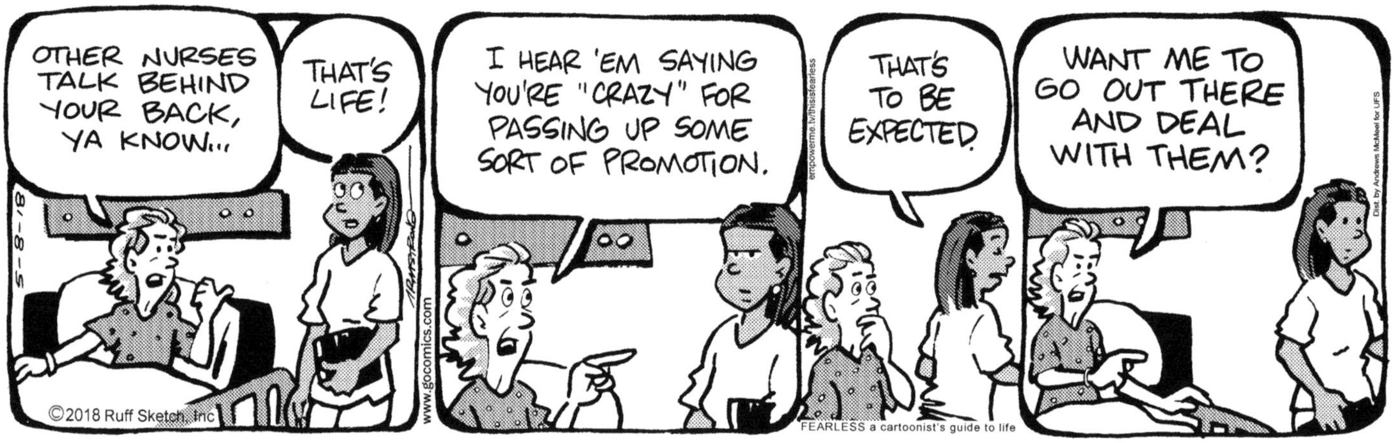
OTHER NURSES TALK BEHIND YOUR BACK, YA KNOW...
THAT'S LIFE!
I HEAR 'EM SAYING YOU'RE "CRAZY" FOR PASSING UP SOME SORT OF PROMOTION.
THAT'S TO BE EXPECTED.
WANT ME TO GO OUT THERE AND DEAL WITH THEM?
5-8-18
©2018 Ruff Sketch, Inc
www.gocomics.com
empowerme.tv/thisisfearless
FEARLESS a cartoonist's guide to life
Dist. by Andrews McMeel for UFS

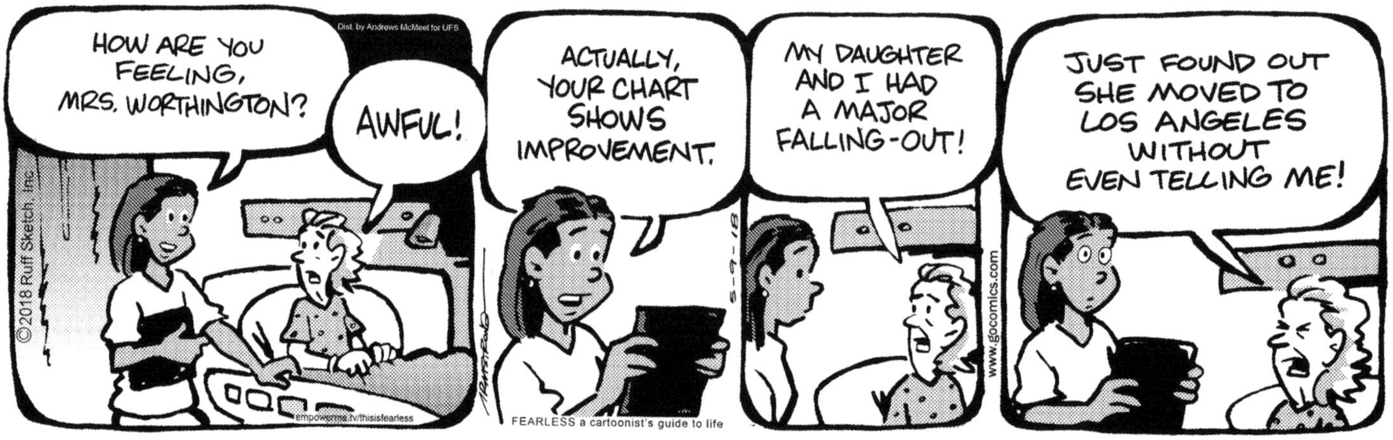
HOW ARE YOU FEELING, MRS. WORTHINGTON?
AWFUL!
ACTUALLY, YOUR CHART SHOWS IMPROVEMENT.
MY DAUGHTER AND I HAD A MAJOR FALLING-OUT!
JUST FOUND OUT SHE MOVED TO LOS ANGELES WITHOUT EVEN TELLING ME!
Dist. by Andrews McMeel for UFS
©2018 Ruff Sketch, Inc
empowerme.tv/thisisfearless
FEARLESS a cartoonist's guide to life
5-9-18
www.gocomics.com

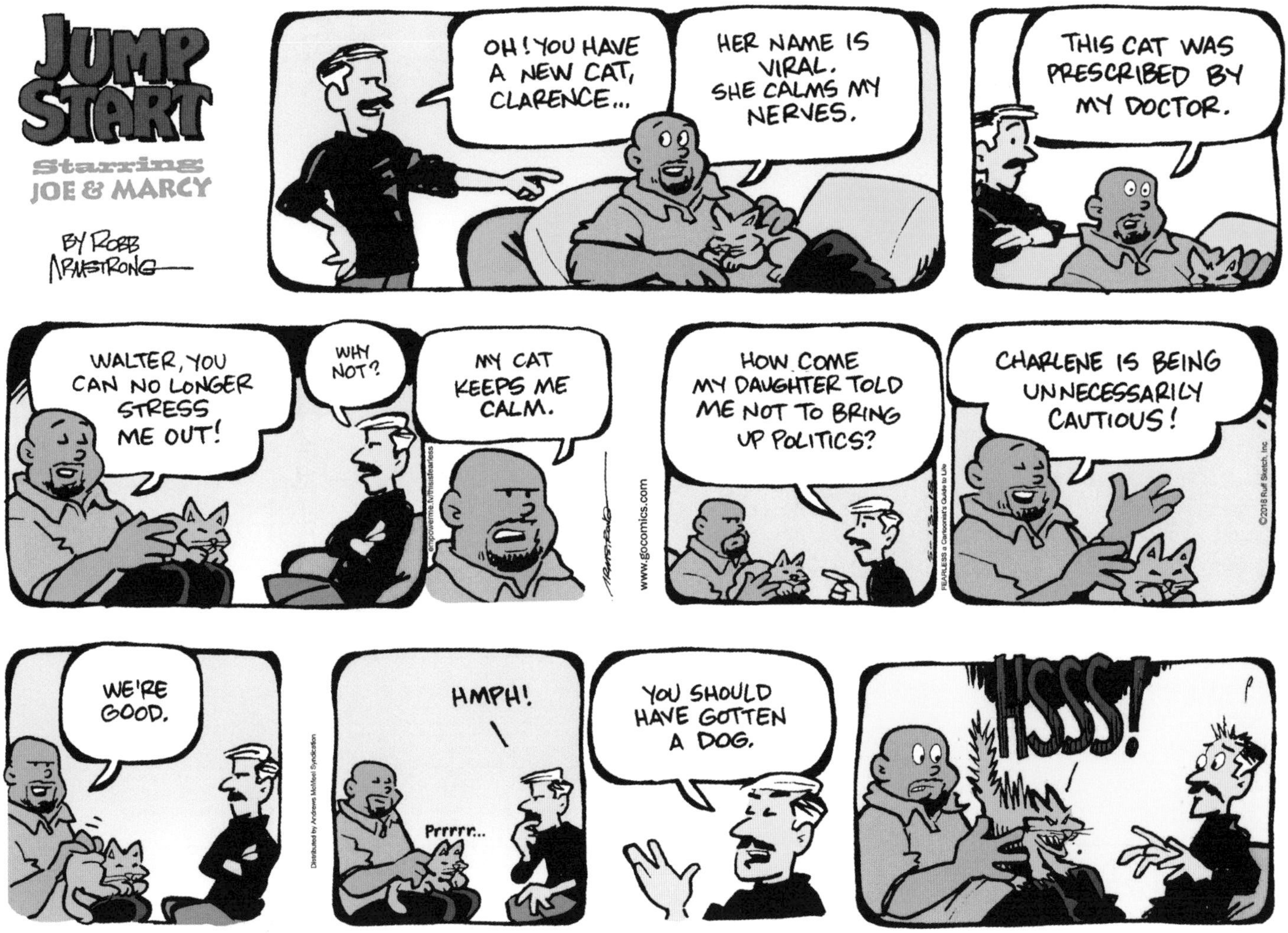
JUMP START
Starring JOE & MARCY
BY ROBB ARMSTRONG
OH! YOU HAVE A NEW CAT, CLARENCE...
HER NAME IS VIRAL. SHE CALMS MY NERVES.
THIS CAT WAS PRESCRIBED BY MY DOCTOR.
WALTER, YOU CAN NO LONGER STRESS ME OUT!
WHY NOT?
MY CAT KEEPS ME CALM.
HOW COME MY DAUGHTER TOLD ME NOT TO BRING UP POLITICS?
CHARLENE IS BEING UNNECESSARILY CAUTIOUS!
WE'RE GOOD.
HMPH!
Prrrrr...
YOU SHOULD HAVE GOTTEN A DOG.
HSSS!
www.gocomics.com
©2018 Ruff Sketch, Inc.
Distributed by Andrews McMeel Syndication

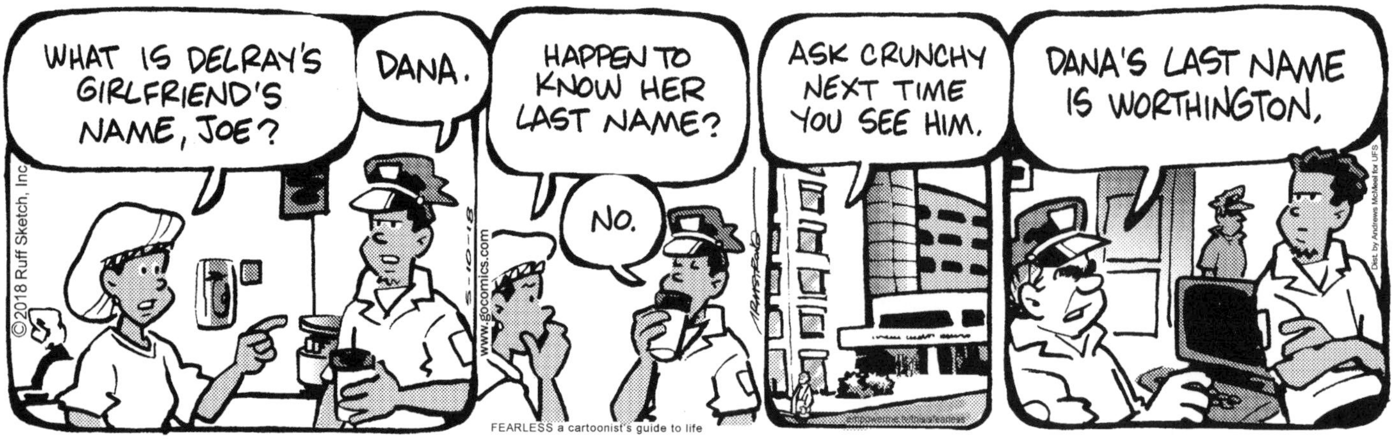
WHAT IS DELRAY'S GIRLFRIEND'S NAME, JOE?
DANA.
HAPPEN TO KNOW HER LAST NAME?
NO.
ASK CRUNCHY NEXT TIME YOU SEE HIM.
DANA'S LAST NAME IS WORTHINGTON.
©2018 Ruff Sketch, Inc
5-10-18
www.gocomics.com
FEARLESS a cartoonist's guide to life
Dist. by Andrews McMeel for UFS

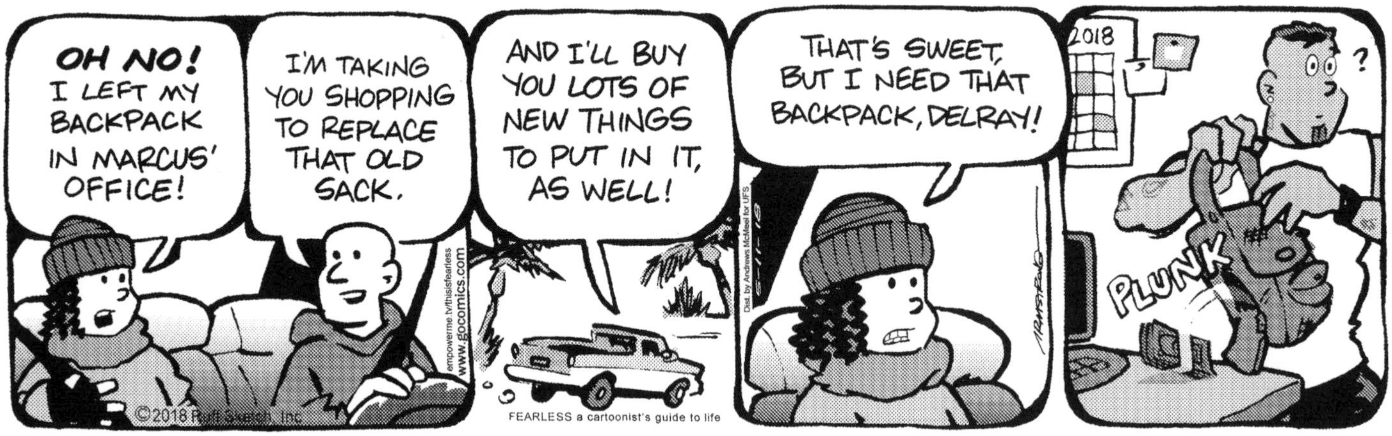
OH NO! I LEFT MY BACKPACK IN MARCUS' OFFICE!
I'M TAKING YOU SHOPPING TO REPLACE THAT OLD SACK.
AND I'LL BUY YOU LOTS OF NEW THINGS TO PUT IN IT, AS WELL!
THAT'S SWEET, BUT I NEED THAT BACKPACK, DELRAY!
2018
?
PLUNK
©2018 Ruff Sketch, Inc
www.gocomics.com
FEARLESS a cartoonist's guide to life
Dist. by Andrews McMeel for UFS

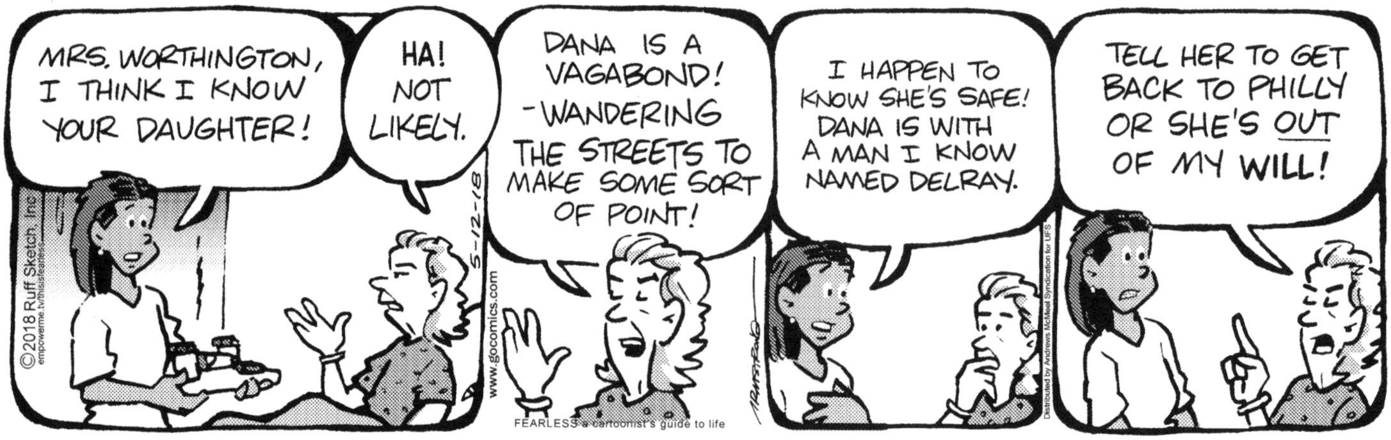
MRS. WORTHINGTON, I THINK I KNOW YOUR DAUGHTER!
HA! NOT LIKELY.
DANA IS A VAGABOND! -WANDERING THE STREETS TO MAKE SOME SORT OF POINT!
I HAPPEN TO KNOW SHE'S SAFE! DANA IS WITH A MAN I KNOW NAMED DELRAY.
TELL HER TO GET BACK TO PHILLY OR SHE'S OUT OF MY WILL!
©2018 Ruff Sketch, Inc
5-12-18
www.gocomics.com
FEARLESS a cartoonist's guide to life
Distributed by Andrews McMeel Syndication for UFS

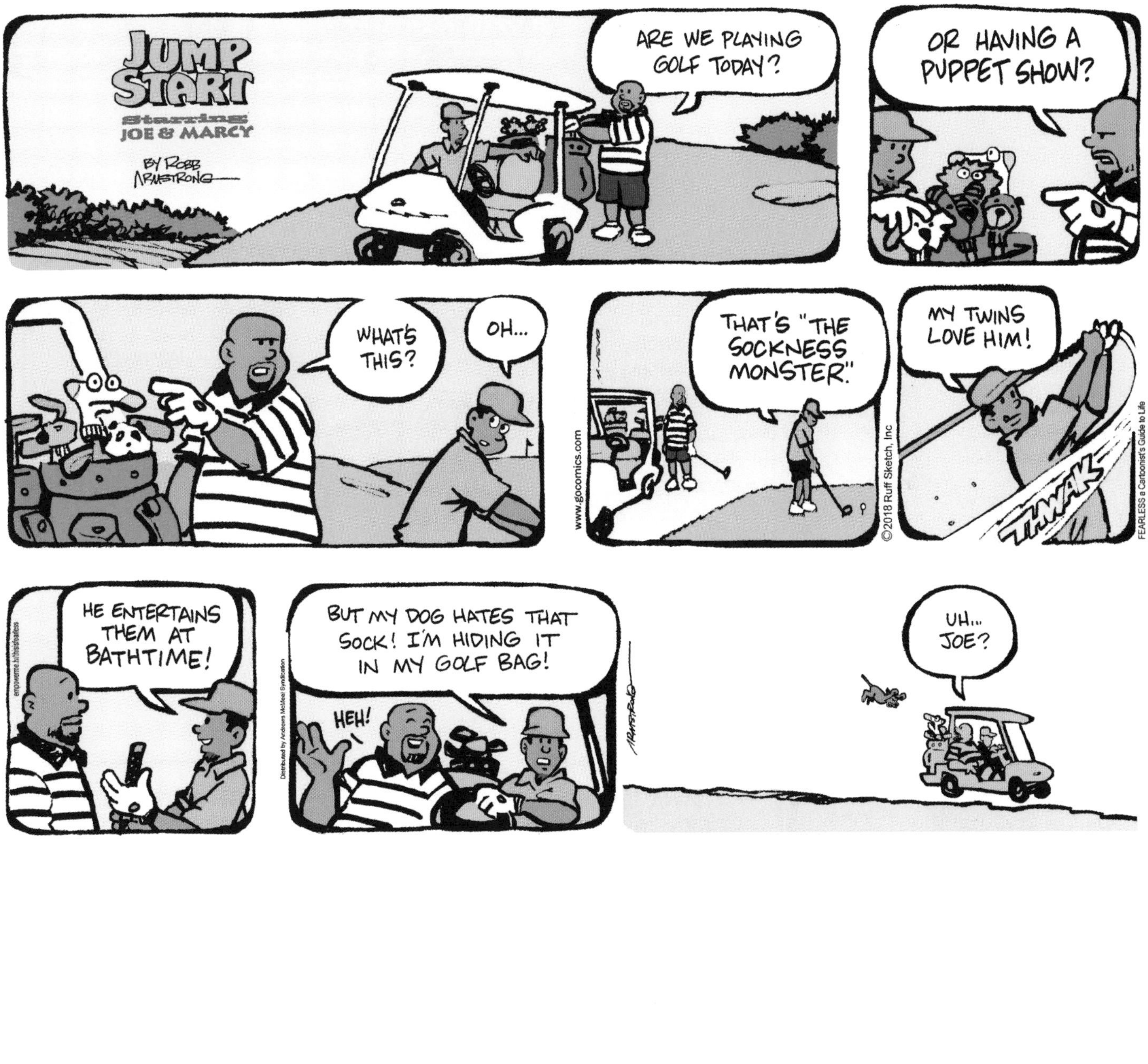
JUMP START
Starring JOE & MARCY
BY ROBB ARMSTRONG
ARE WE PLAYING GOLF TODAY?
OR HAVING A PUPPET SHOW?
WHAT'S THIS?
OH...
THAT'S "THE SOCKNESS MONSTER."
MY TWINS LOVE HIM!
THWAK
www.gocomics.com
©2018 Ruff Sketch, Inc
FEARLESS a Cartoonist's Guide to Life
HE ENTERTAINS THEM AT BATHTIME!
Distributed by Andrews McMeel Syndication
BUT MY DOG HATES THAT SOCK! I'M HIDING IT IN MY GOLF BAG!
HEH!
UH... JOE?

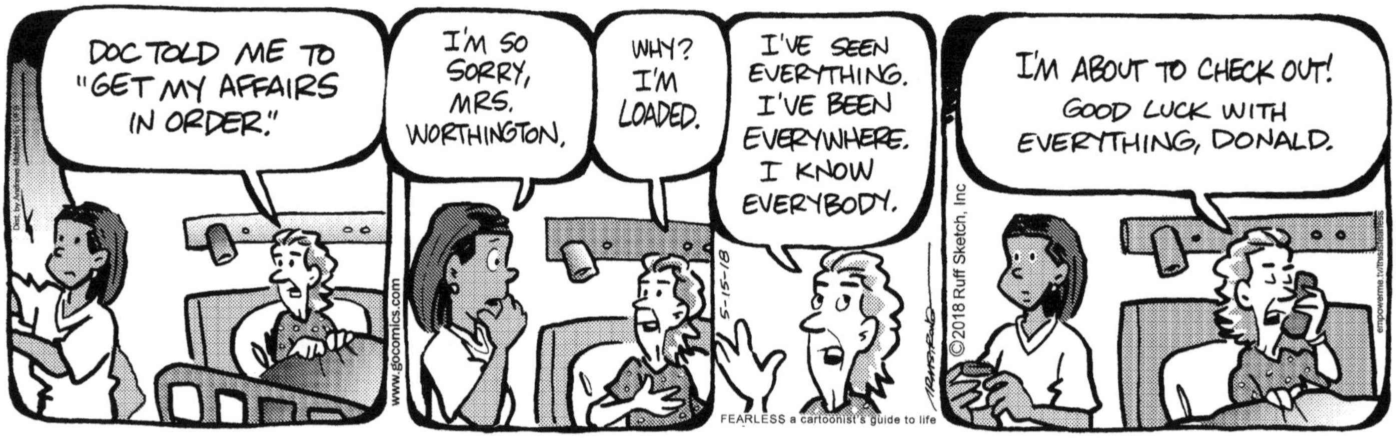
DOC TOLD ME TO "GET MY AFFAIRS IN ORDER."
I'M SO SORRY, MRS. WORTHINGTON.
WHY? I'M LOADED.
I'VE SEEN EVERYTHING. I'VE BEEN EVERYWHERE. I KNOW EVERYBODY.
I'M ABOUT TO CHECK OUT!
GOOD LUCK WITH EVERYTHING, DONALD.
www.gocomics.com
5-15-18
©2018 Ruff Sketch, Inc
FEARLESS a cartoonist's guide to life

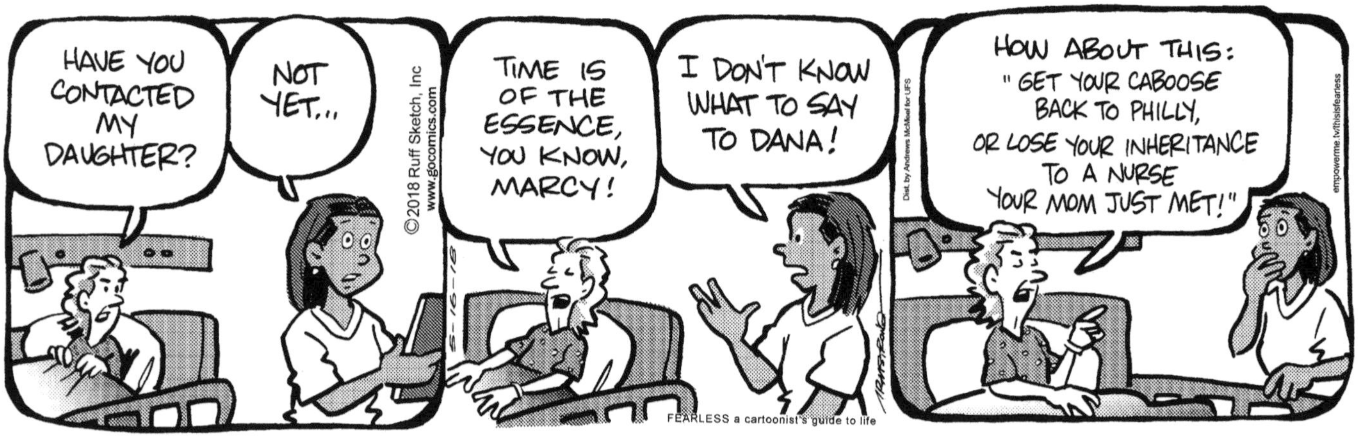
HAVE YOU CONTACTED MY DAUGHTER?
NOT YET...
©2018 Ruff Sketch, Inc
www.gocomics.com
5-16-18
TIME IS OF THE ESSENCE, YOU KNOW, MARCY!
I DON'T KNOW WHAT TO SAY TO DANA!
HOW ABOUT THIS:
"GET YOUR CABOOSE BACK TO PHILLY, OR LOSE YOUR INHERITANCE TO A NURSE YOUR MOM JUST MET!"
FEARLESS a cartoonist's guide to life

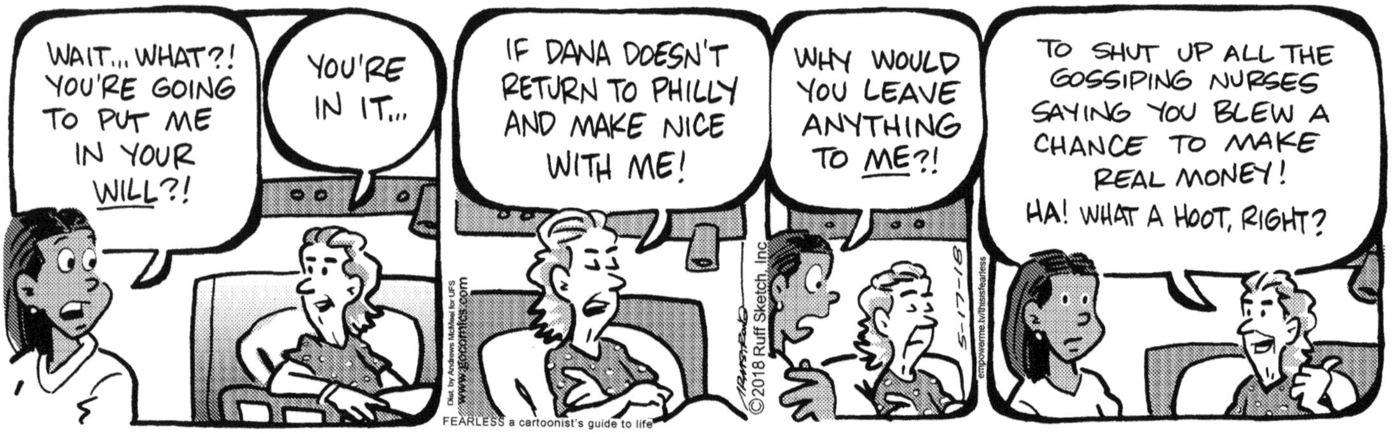
WAIT... WHAT?! YOU'RE GOING TO PUT ME IN YOUR WILL?!
YOU'RE IN IT...
IF DANA DOESN'T RETURN TO PHILLY AND MAKE NICE WITH ME!
WHY WOULD YOU LEAVE ANYTHING TO ME?!
TO SHUT UP ALL THE GOSSIPING NURSES SAYING YOU BLEW A CHANCE TO MAKE REAL MONEY!
HA! WHAT A HOOT, RIGHT?
©2018 Ruff Sketch, Inc
5-17-18
FEARLESS a cartoonist's guide to life

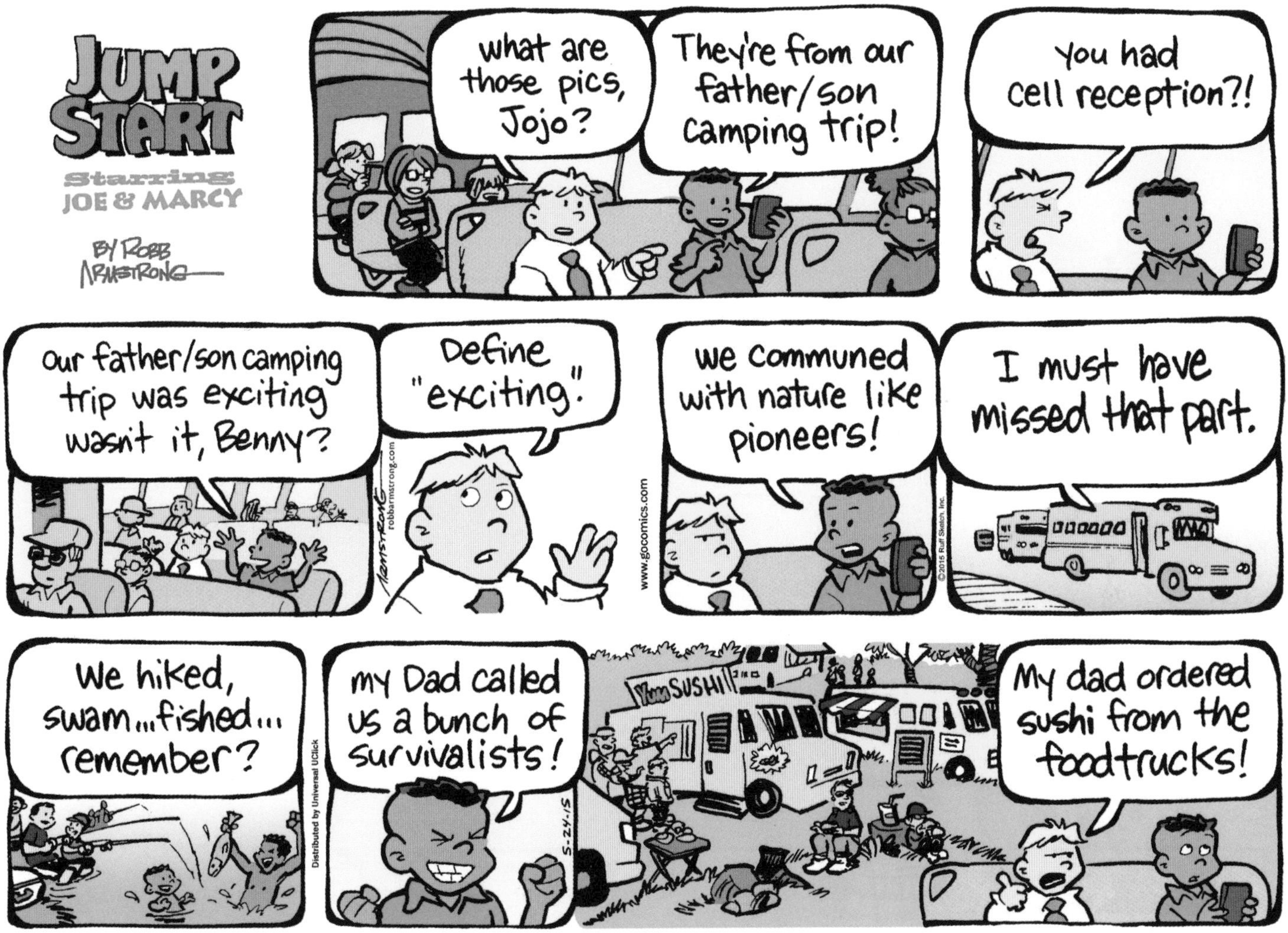
JUMP START
Starring JOE & MARCY
BY ROBB ARMSTRONG
what are those pics, Jojo?
They're from our father/son camping trip!
You had cell reception?!
our father/son camping trip was exciting wasn't it, Benny?
Define "exciting."
we communed with nature like pioneers!
I must have missed that part.
We hiked, swam...fished... remember?
my Dad called us a bunch of survivalists!
My dad ordered sushi from the foodtrucks!
YUM SUSHI
robbarmstrong.com
www.gocomics.com
©2015 Ruff Sketch, Inc.
Distributed by Universal UClick
5-24-15

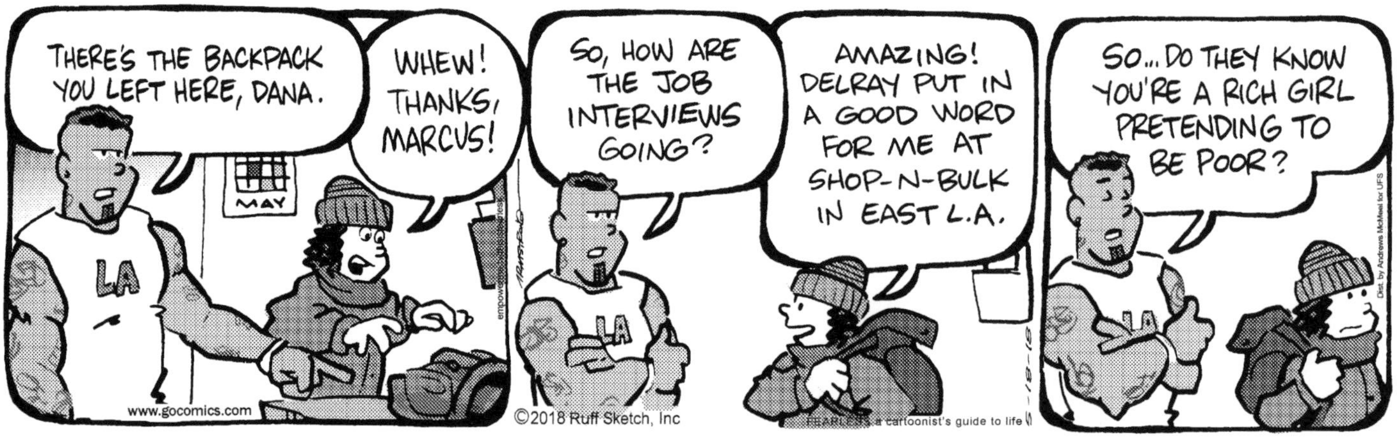
THERE'S THE BACKPACK YOU LEFT HERE, DANA.
WHEW! THANKS, MARCUS!
MAY
www.gocomics.com
SO, HOW ARE THE JOB INTERVIEWS GOING?
©2018 Ruff Sketch, Inc
AMAZING! DELRAY PUT IN A GOOD WORD FOR ME AT SHOP-N-BULK IN EAST L.A.
5-18-18
FEARLESS a cartoonist's guide to life
SO... DO THEY KNOW YOU'RE A RICH GIRL PRETENDING TO BE POOR?
Dist. by Andrews McMeel for UFS

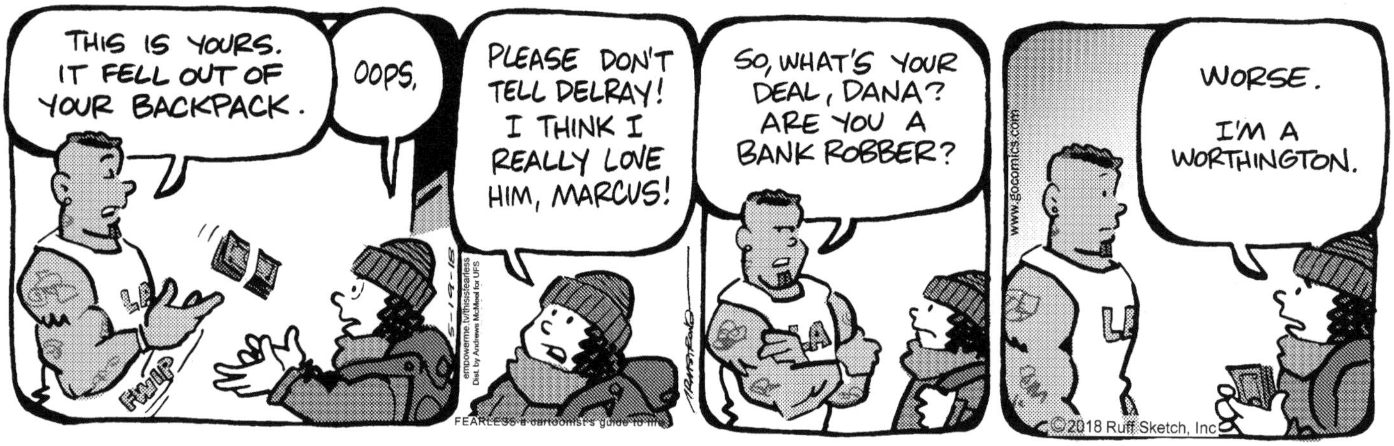
THIS IS YOURS. IT FELL OUT OF YOUR BACKPACK.
OOPS.
FWIP
5-19-18
empowerme.tv/thisisfearless
Dist. by Andrews McMeel for UFS
PLEASE DON'T TELL DELRAY! I THINK I REALLY LOVE HIM, MARCUS!
FEARLESS a cartoonist's guide to life
SO, WHAT'S YOUR DEAL, DANA? ARE YOU A BANK ROBBER?
www.gocomics.com
WORSE.
I'M A WORTHINGTON.
©2018 Ruff Sketch, Inc

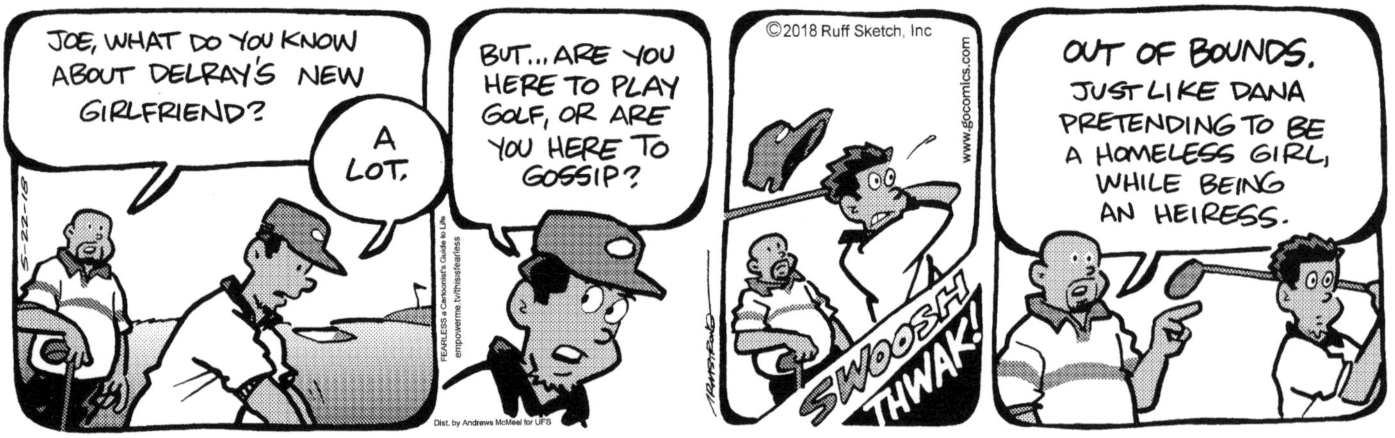
JOE, WHAT DO YOU KNOW ABOUT DELRAY'S NEW GIRLFRIEND?
A LOT.
5-22-18
FEARLESS a Cartoonist's Guide to Life
empowerme.tv/thisisfearless
BUT... ARE YOU HERE TO PLAY GOLF, OR ARE YOU HERE TO GOSSIP?
Dist. by Andrews McMeel for UFS
©2018 Ruff Sketch, Inc
www.gocomics.com
SWOOSH
THWAK!
OUT OF BOUNDS.
JUST LIKE DANA PRETENDING TO BE A HOMELESS GIRL, WHILE BEING AN HEIRESS.

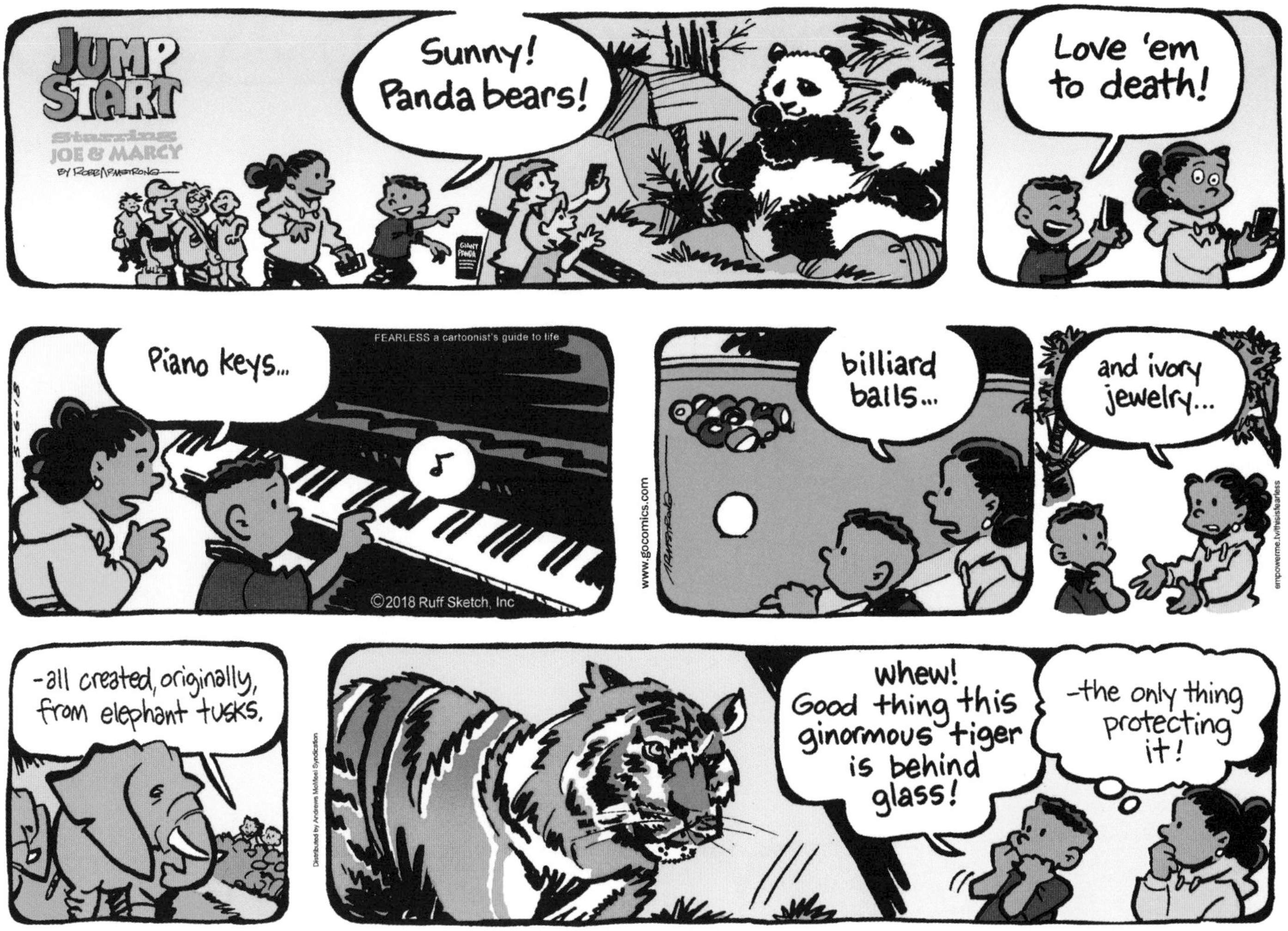

JUMP START
Starring JOE & MARCY
Sunny! Panda bears!
Love 'em to death!
FEARLESS a cartoonist's guide to life
Piano keys...
©2018 Ruff Sketch, Inc
www.gocomics.com
billiard balls...
and ivory jewelry...
-all created, originally, from elephant tusks.
Distributed by Andrews McMeel Syndication
whew! Good thing this ginormous tiger is behind glass!
-the only thing protecting it!

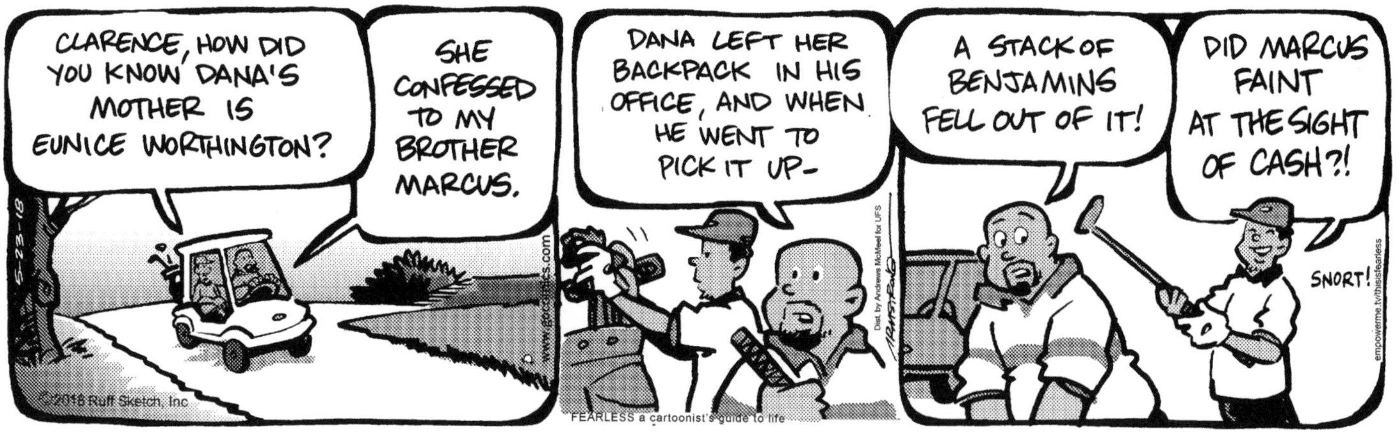
CLARENCE, HOW DID YOU KNOW DANA'S MOTHER IS EUNICE WORTHINGTON?
SHE CONFESSED TO MY BROTHER MARCUS.
DANA LEFT HER BACKPACK IN HIS OFFICE, AND WHEN HE WENT TO PICK IT UP-
A STACK OF BENJAMINS FELL OUT OF IT!
DID MARCUS FAINT AT THE SIGHT OF CASH?!
SNORT!
©2018 Ruff Sketch, Inc
www.gocomics.com
FEARLESS a cartoonist's guide to life

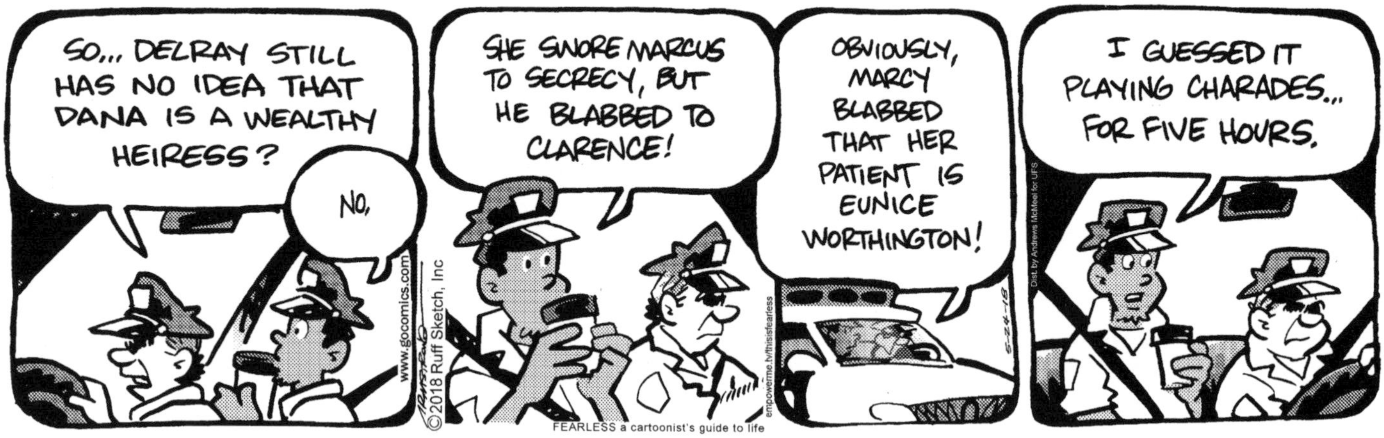
SO... DELRAY STILL HAS NO IDEA THAT DANA IS A WEALTHY HEIRESS?
NO.
SHE SWORE MARCUS TO SECRECY, BUT HE BLABBED TO CLARENCE!
OBVIOUSLY, MARCY BLABBED THAT HER PATIENT IS EUNICE WORTHINGTON!
I GUESSED IT PLAYING CHARADES... FOR FIVE HOURS.
www.gocomics.com
©2018 Ruff Sketch, Inc
FEARLESS a cartoonist's guide to life

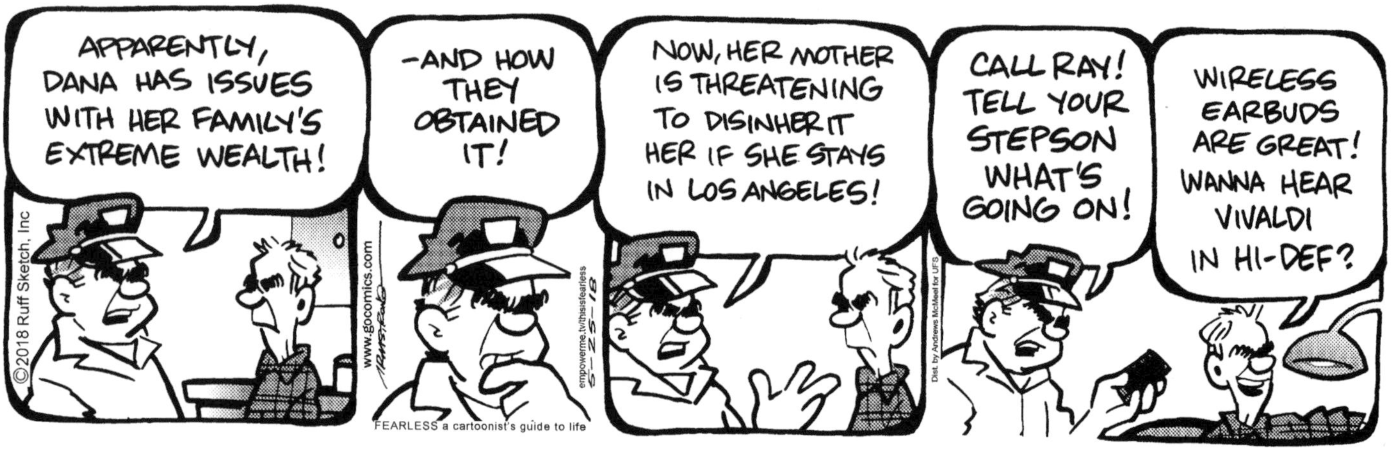
APPARENTLY, DANA HAS ISSUES WITH HER FAMILY'S EXTREME WEALTH!
-AND HOW THEY OBTAINED IT!
NOW, HER MOTHER IS THREATENING TO DISINHERIT HER IF SHE STAYS IN LOS ANGELES!
CALL RAY! TELL YOUR STEPSON WHAT'S GOING ON!
WIRELESS EARBUDS ARE GREAT! WANNA HEAR VIVALDI IN HI-DEF?
©2018 Ruff Sketch, Inc
www.gocomics.com
FEARLESS a cartoonist's guide to life

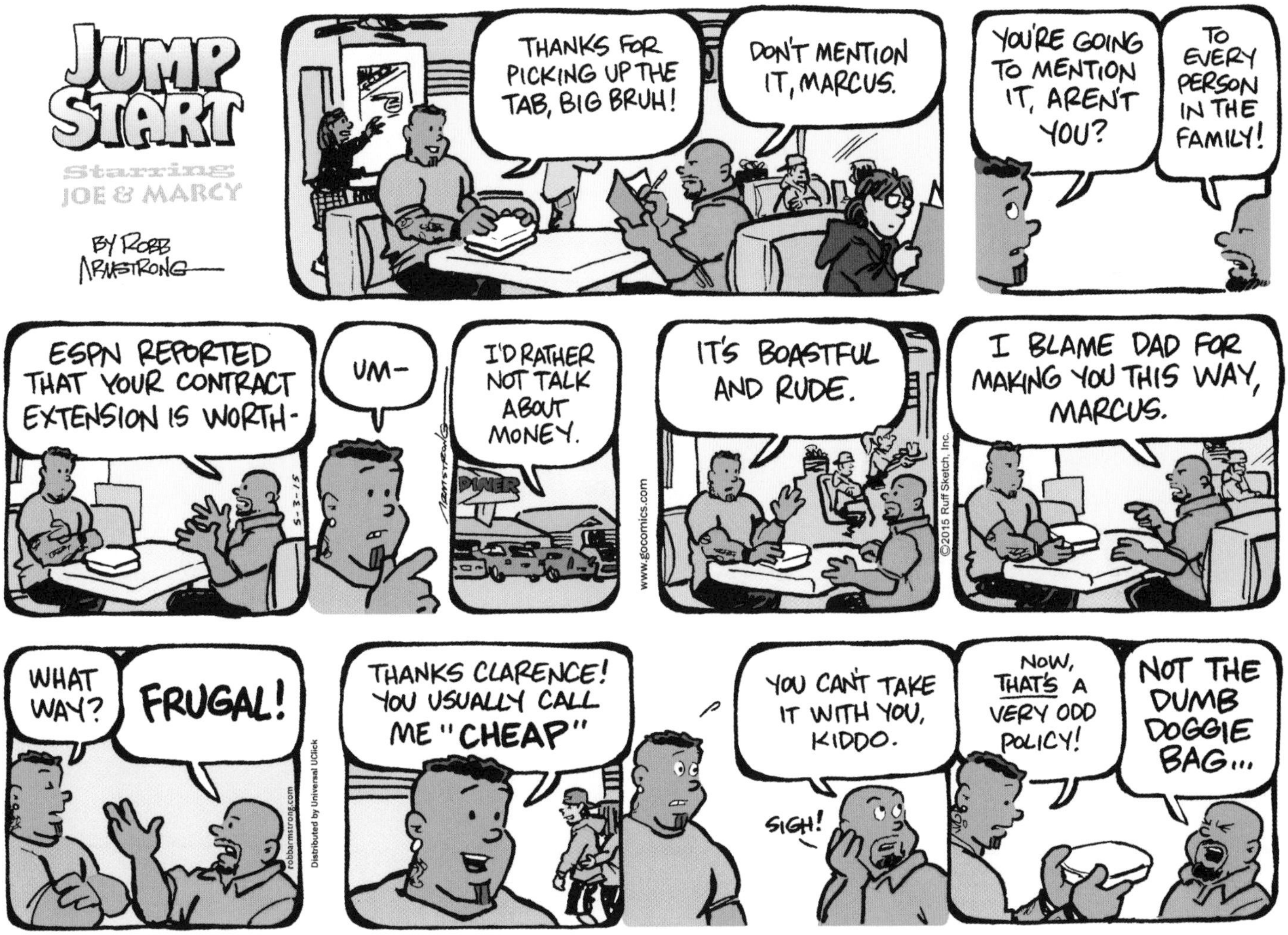
JUMP START
Starring JOE & MARCY
BY ROBB ARMSTRONG
THANKS FOR PICKING UP THE TAB, BIG BRUH!
DON'T MENTION IT, MARCUS.
YOU'RE GOING TO MENTION IT, AREN'T YOU?
TO EVERY PERSON IN THE FAMILY!
ESPN REPORTED THAT YOUR CONTRACT EXTENSION IS WORTH-
5-3-15
UM-
I'D RATHER NOT TALK ABOUT MONEY.
DINER
www.gocomics.com
IT'S BOASTFUL AND RUDE.
©2015 Ruff Sketch, Inc.
I BLAME DAD FOR MAKING YOU THIS WAY, MARCUS.
WHAT WAY?
FRUGAL!
robbarmstrong.com
Distributed by Universal UClick
THANKS CLARENCE! YOU USUALLY CALL ME "CHEAP"
YOU CAN'T TAKE IT WITH YOU, KIDDO.
SIGH!
NOW, THAT'S A VERY ODD POLICY!
NOT THE DUMB DOGGIE BAG...

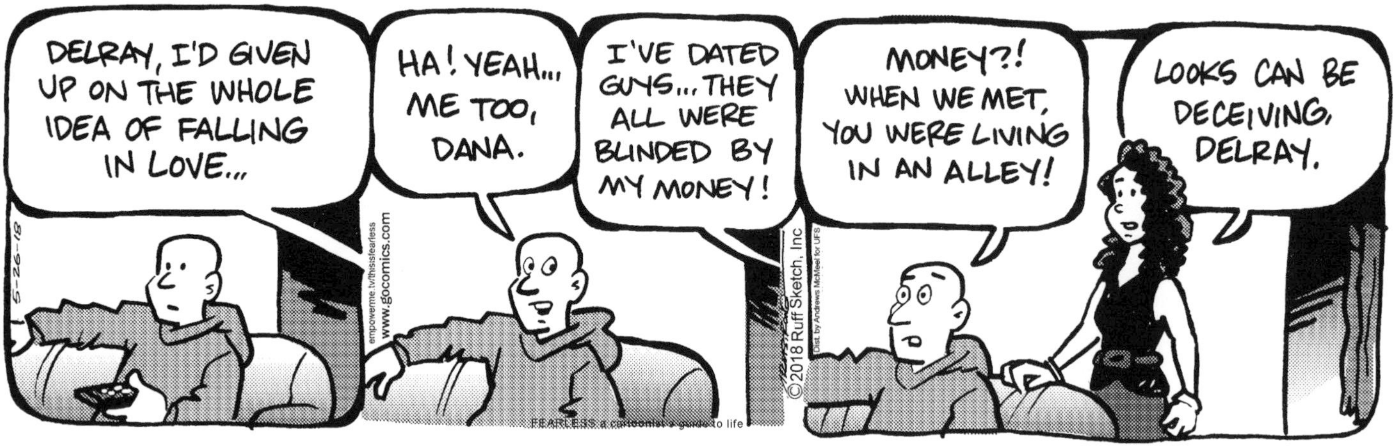
5-26-18
DELRAY, I'D GIVEN UP ON THE WHOLE IDEA OF FALLING IN LOVE...
HA! YEAH... ME TOO, DANA.
I'VE DATED GUYS... THEY ALL WERE BLINDED BY MY MONEY!
MONEY?! WHEN WE MET, YOU WERE LIVING IN AN ALLEY!
LOOKS CAN BE DECEIVING, DELRAY.
empowerme.tv/thisisfearless
www.gocomics.com
©2018 Ruff Sketch, Inc
Dist. by Andrews McMeel for UFS
FEARLESS a cartoonist's guide to life

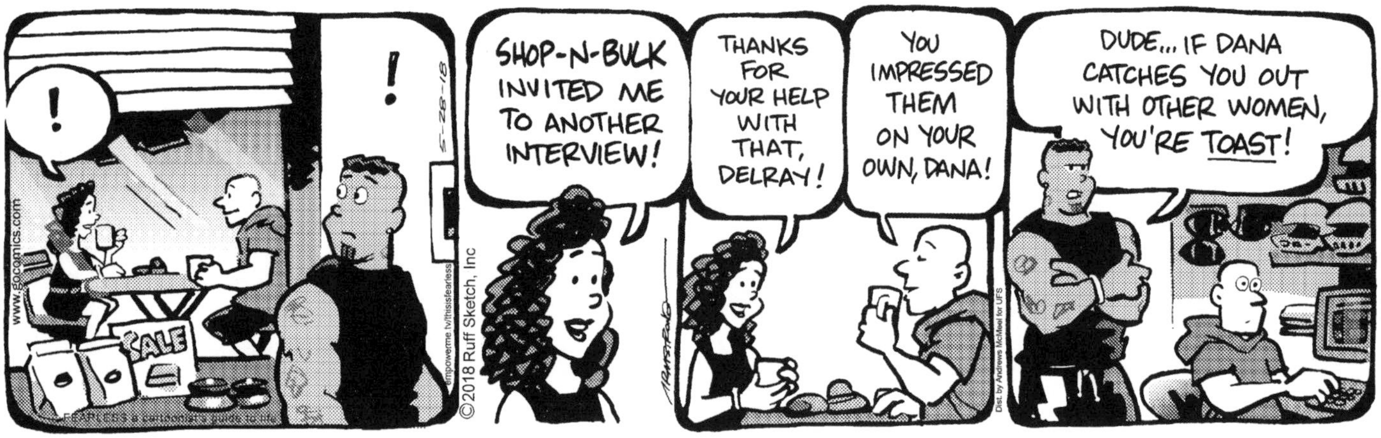
!
!
5-28-18
SALE
SHOP-N-BULK INVITED ME TO ANOTHER INTERVIEW!
THANKS FOR YOUR HELP WITH THAT, DELRAY!
YOU IMPRESSED THEM ON YOUR OWN, DANA!
DUDE... IF DANA CATCHES YOU OUT WITH OTHER WOMEN, YOU'RE TOAST!
www.gocomics.com
empowerme.tv/thisisfearless
©2018 Ruff Sketch, Inc
Dist. by Andrews McMeel for UFS
FEARLESS a cartoonist's guide to life

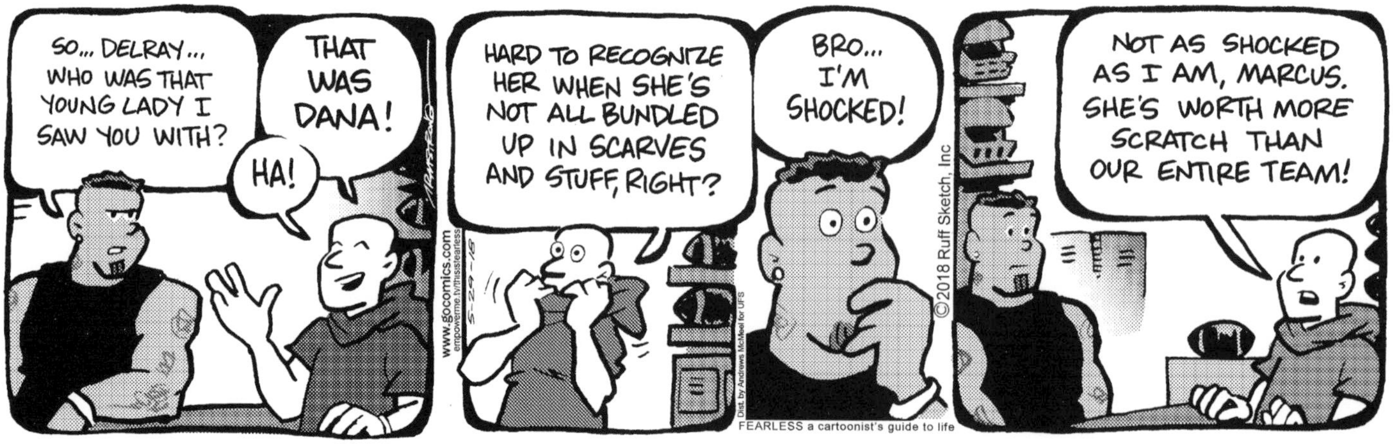
SO... DELRAY... WHO WAS THAT YOUNG LADY I SAW YOU WITH?
THAT WAS DANA!
HA!
HARD TO RECOGNIZE HER WHEN SHE'S NOT ALL BUNDLED UP IN SCARVES AND STUFF, RIGHT?
BRO... I'M SHOCKED!
NOT AS SHOCKED AS I AM, MARCUS. SHE'S WORTH MORE SCRATCH THAN OUR ENTIRE TEAM!
5-29-18
www.gocomics.com
empowerme.tv/thisisfearless
©2018 Ruff Sketch, Inc
Dist. by Andrews McMeel for UFS
FEARLESS a cartoonist's guide to life

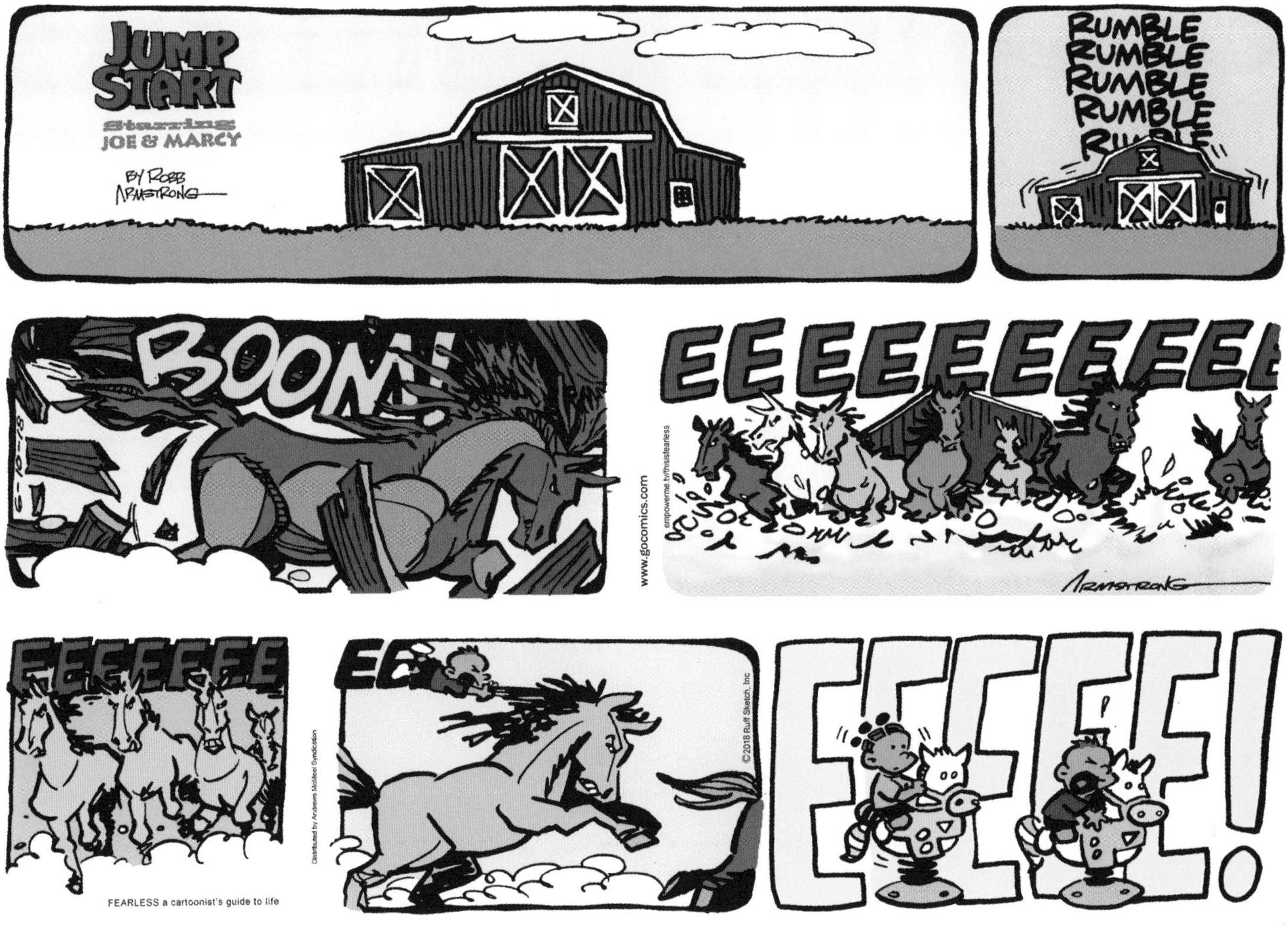
JUMP START
Starring JOE & MARCY
BY ROBB ARMSTRONG
RUMBLE
RUMBLE
RUMBLE
RUMBLE
BOOM!
6-10-18
EEEEEEEEEE
www.gocomics.com
empowerme.tv/thisisfearless
ARMSTRONG
EEEEEEE
FEARLESS a cartoonist's guide to life
Distributed by Andrews McMeel Syndication
EE
©2018 Ruff Sketch, Inc
EEEEE!

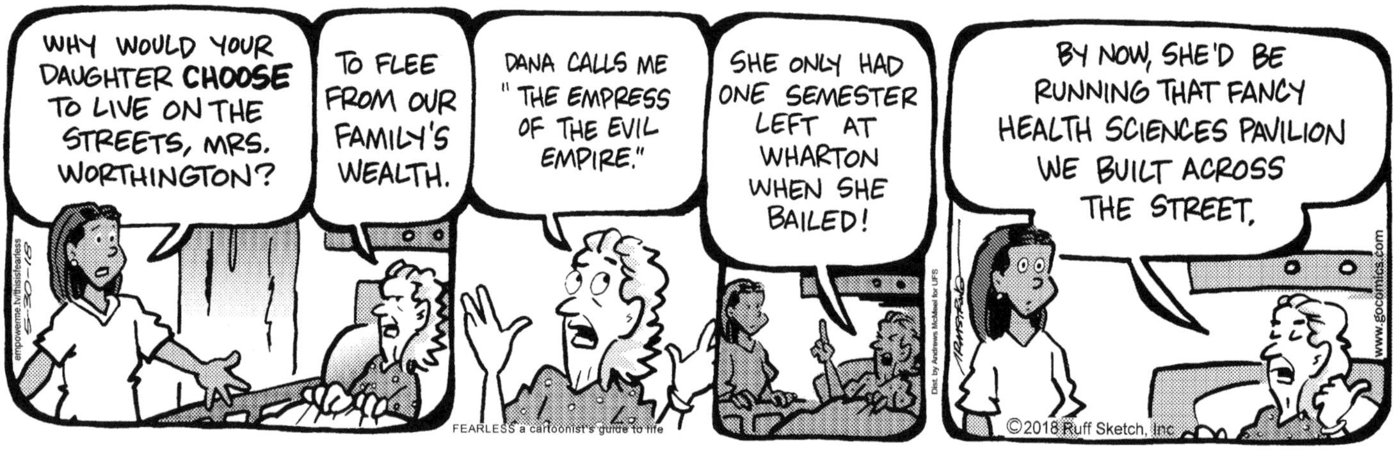
WHY WOULD YOUR DAUGHTER **CHOOSE** TO LIVE ON THE STREETS, MRS. WORTHINGTON?
TO FLEE FROM OUR FAMILY'S WEALTH.
DANA CALLS ME "THE EMPRESS OF THE EVIL EMPIRE."
SHE ONLY HAD ONE SEMESTER LEFT AT WHARTON WHEN SHE BAILED!
BY NOW, SHE'D BE RUNNING THAT FANCY HEALTH SCIENCES PAVILION WE BUILT ACROSS THE STREET.
5-30-18
empowerme.tv/thisisfearless
FEARLESS a cartoonist's guide to life
©2018 Ruff Sketch, Inc
www.gocomics.com

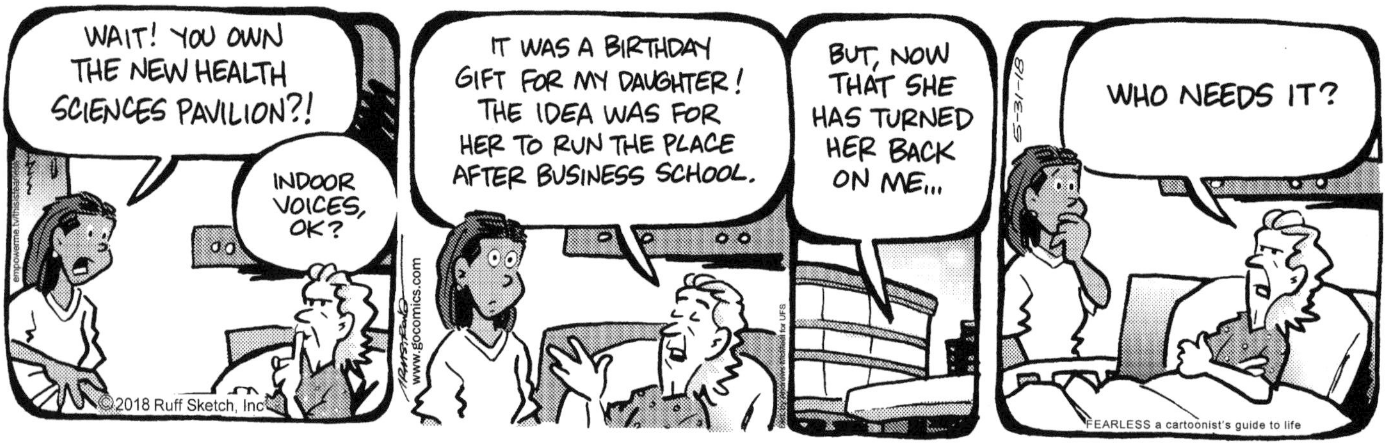
WAIT! YOU OWN THE NEW HEALTH SCIENCES PAVILION?!
INDOOR VOICES, OK?
IT WAS A BIRTHDAY GIFT FOR MY DAUGHTER! THE IDEA WAS FOR HER TO RUN THE PLACE AFTER BUSINESS SCHOOL.
BUT, NOW THAT SHE HAS TURNED HER BACK ON ME...
WHO NEEDS IT?
5-31-18
©2018 Ruff Sketch, Inc
www.gocomics.com
FEARLESS a cartoonist's guide to life

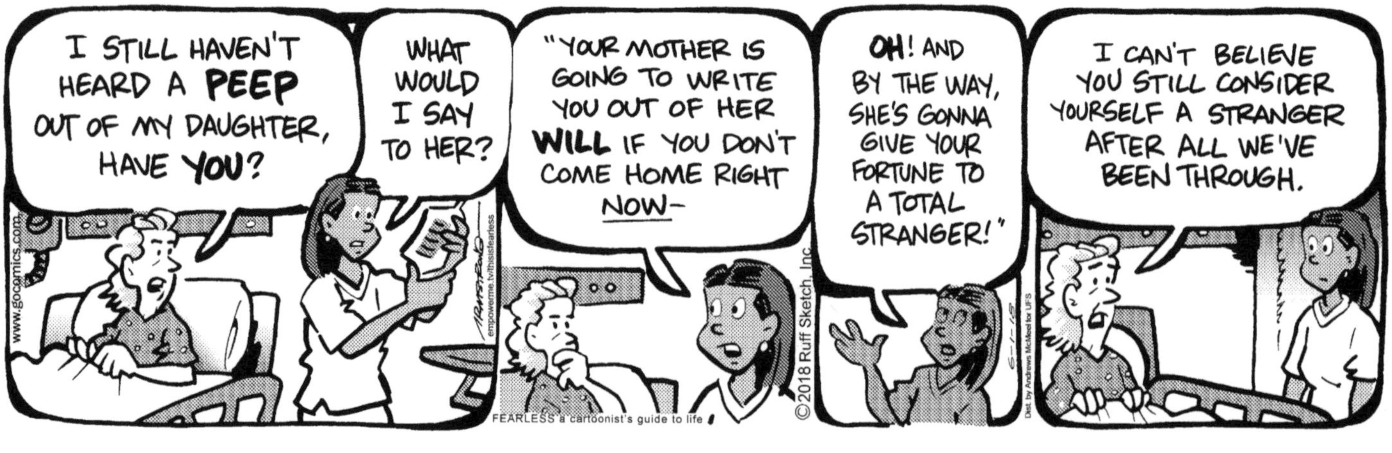
I STILL HAVEN'T HEARD A **PEEP** OUT OF MY DAUGHTER, HAVE **YOU**?
WHAT WOULD I SAY TO HER?
"YOUR MOTHER IS GOING TO WRITE YOU OUT OF HER **WILL** IF YOU DON'T COME HOME RIGHT NOW-
OH! AND BY THE WAY, SHE'S GONNA GIVE YOUR FORTUNE TO A TOTAL STRANGER!"
I CAN'T BELIEVE YOU STILL CONSIDER YOURSELF A STRANGER AFTER ALL WE'VE BEEN THROUGH.
www.gocomics.com
empowerme.tv/thisisfearless
FEARLESS a cartoonist's guide to life
©2018 Ruff Sketch, Inc
6-1-18

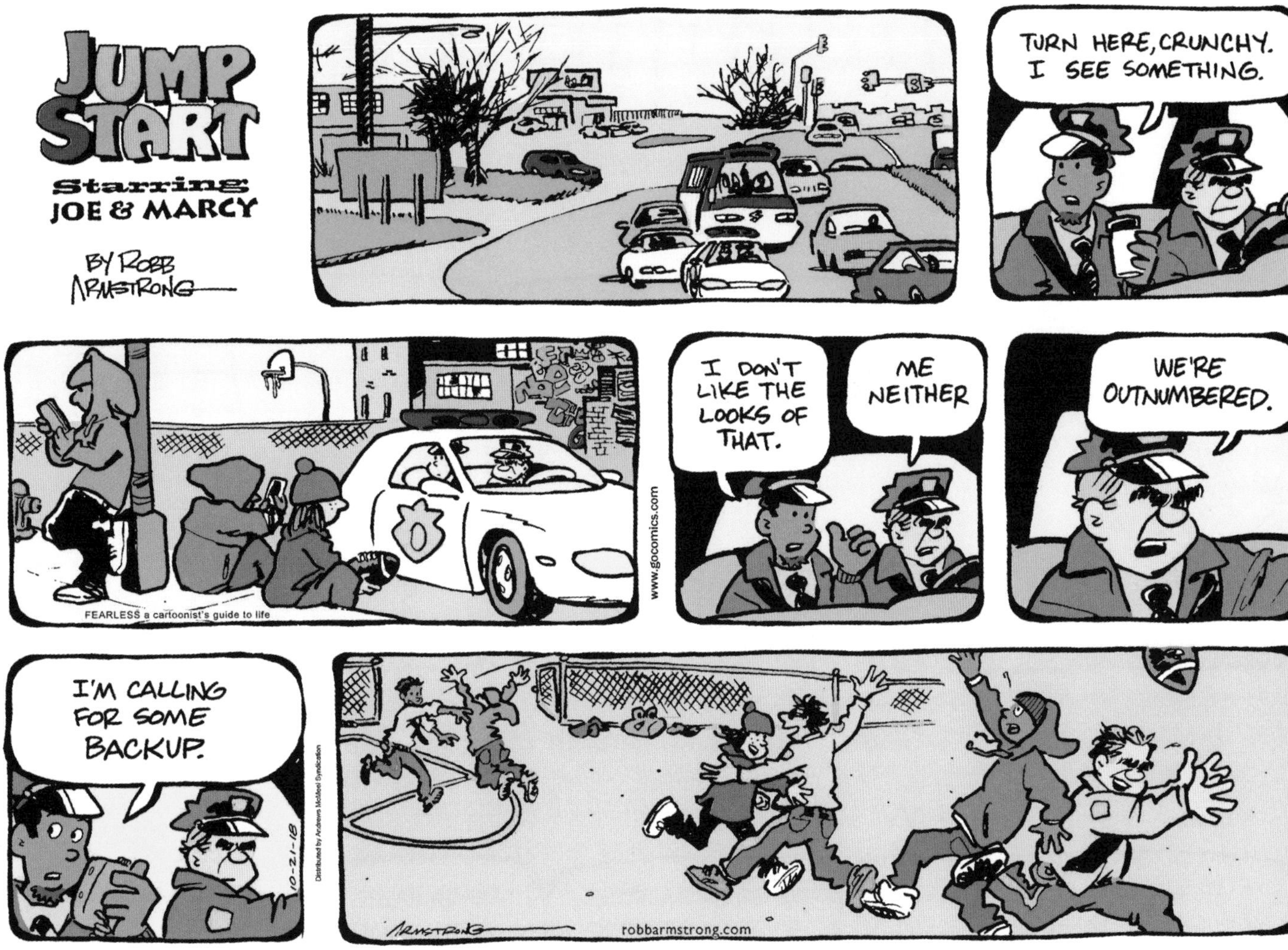

JUMP START
Starring
JOE & MARCY
BY ROBB ARMSTRONG
TURN HERE, CRUNCHY. I SEE SOMETHING.
FEARLESS a cartoonist's guide to life
www.gocomics.com
I DON'T LIKE THE LOOKS OF THAT.
ME NEITHER
WE'RE OUTNUMBERED.
I'M CALLING FOR SOME BACKUP.
10-21-18
Distributed by Andrews McMeel Syndication
ARMSTRONG
robbarmstrong.com

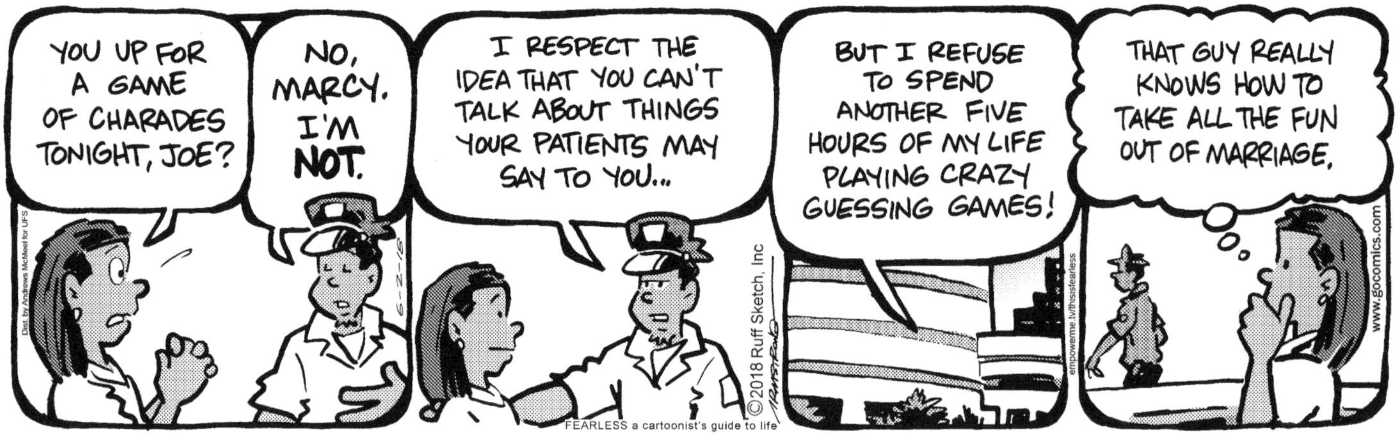
YOU UP FOR A GAME OF CHARADES TONIGHT, JOE?
NO, MARCY. I'M **NOT**.
I RESPECT THE IDEA THAT YOU CAN'T TALK ABOUT THINGS YOUR PATIENTS MAY SAY TO YOU...
BUT I REFUSE TO SPEND ANOTHER FIVE HOURS OF MY LIFE PLAYING CRAZY GUESSING GAMES!
THAT GUY REALLY KNOWS HOW TO TAKE ALL THE FUN OUT OF MARRIAGE.
Dist. by Andrews McMeel for UFS
6-2-18
©2018 Ruff Sketch, Inc
FEARLESS a cartoonist's guide to life
empowerme.tv/thisisfearless
www.gocomics.com

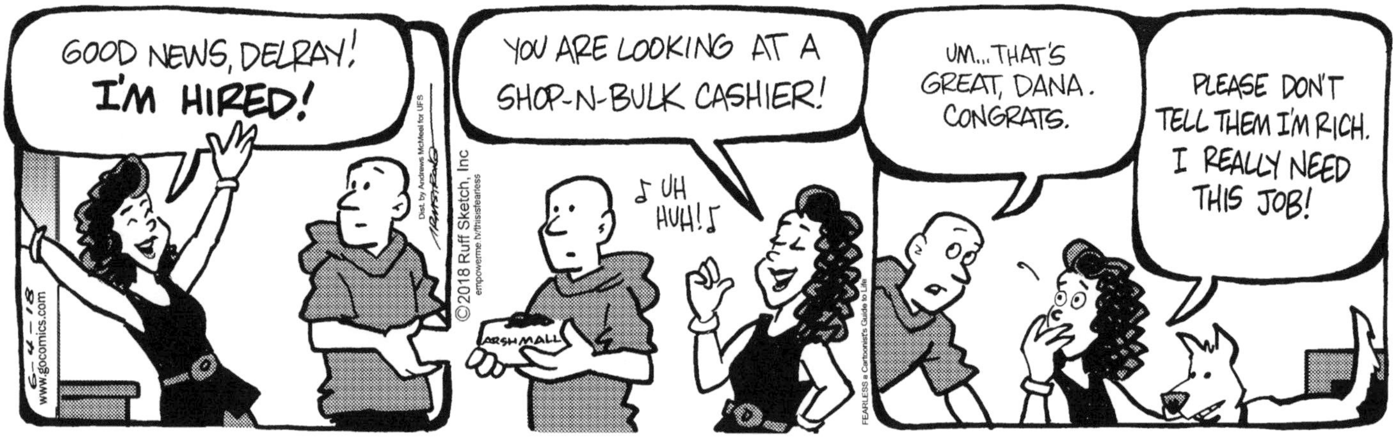
GOOD NEWS, DELRAY! **I'M HIRED!**
6-4-18
www.gocomics.com
Dist. by Andrews McMeel for UFS
YOU ARE LOOKING AT A SHOP-N-BULK CASHIER!
♪ UH HUH! ♪
©2018 Ruff Sketch, Inc
empowerme.tv/thisisfearless
UM...THAT'S GREAT, DANA. CONGRATS.
PLEASE DON'T TELL THEM I'M RICH. I REALLY NEED THIS JOB!
FEARLESS a Cartoonist's Guide to Life

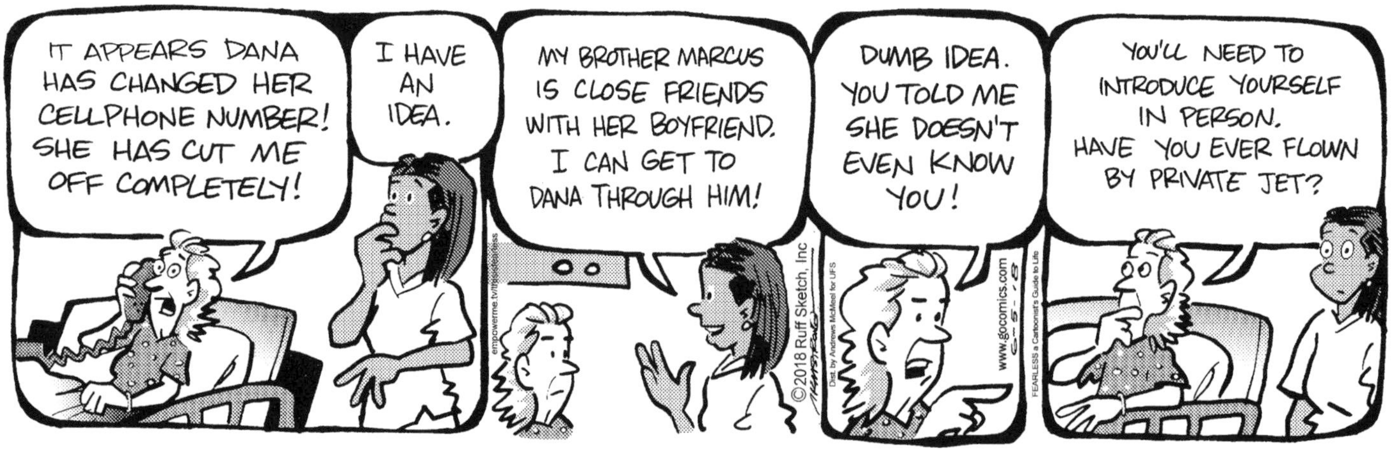
IT APPEARS DANA HAS CHANGED HER CELLPHONE NUMBER! SHE HAS CUT ME OFF COMPLETELY!
I HAVE AN IDEA.
MY BROTHER MARCUS IS CLOSE FRIENDS WITH HER BOYFRIEND. I CAN GET TO DANA THROUGH HIM!
empowerme.tv/thisisfearless
©2018 Ruff Sketch, Inc
DUMB IDEA. YOU TOLD ME SHE DOESN'T EVEN KNOW YOU!
Dist. by Andrews McMeel for UFS
www.gocomics.com
6-5-18
FEARLESS a Cartoonist's Guide to Life
YOU'LL NEED TO INTRODUCE YOURSELF IN PERSON. HAVE YOU EVER FLOWN BY PRIVATE JET?

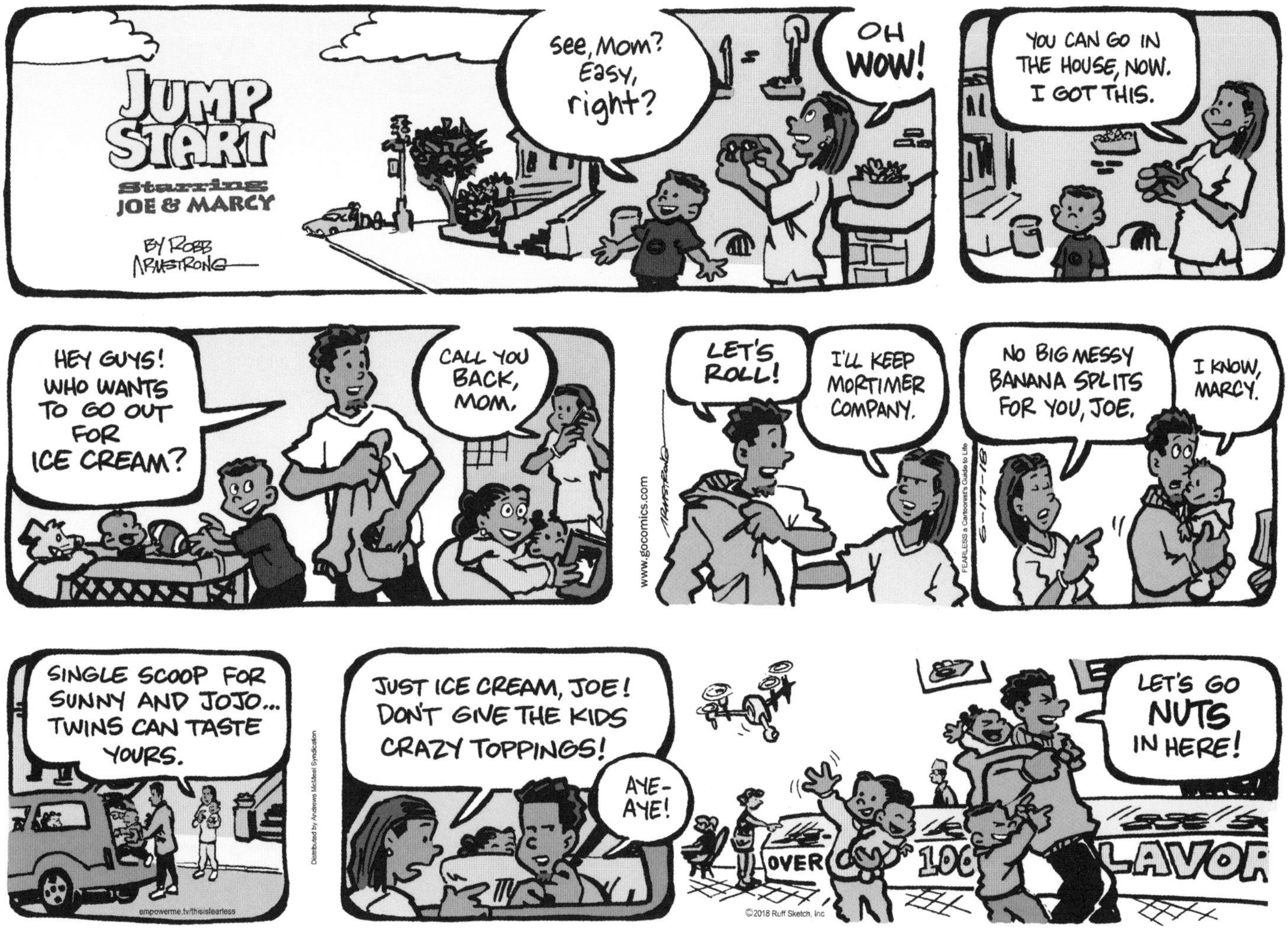
JUMP START
Starring JOE & MARCY
BY ROBB ARMSTRONG
See, Mom? Easy, right?
OH WOW!
YOU CAN GO IN THE HOUSE, NOW. I GOT THIS.
HEY GUYS! WHO WANTS TO GO OUT FOR ICE CREAM?
CALL YOU BACK, MOM.
www.gocomics.com
LET'S ROLL!
I'LL KEEP MORTIMER COMPANY.
6-17-18
FEARLESS: a Cartoonist's Guide to Life
NO BIG MESSY BANANA SPLITS FOR YOU, JOE.
I KNOW, MARCY.
SINGLE SCOOP FOR SUNNY AND JOJO... TWINS CAN TASTE YOURS.
empowerme.tv/thisisfearless
Distributed by Andrews McMeel Syndication
JUST ICE CREAM, JOE! DON'T GIVE THE KIDS CRAZY TOPPINGS!
AYE-AYE!
OVER
LAVOR
LET'S GO NUTS IN HERE!
©2018 Ruff Sketch, Inc

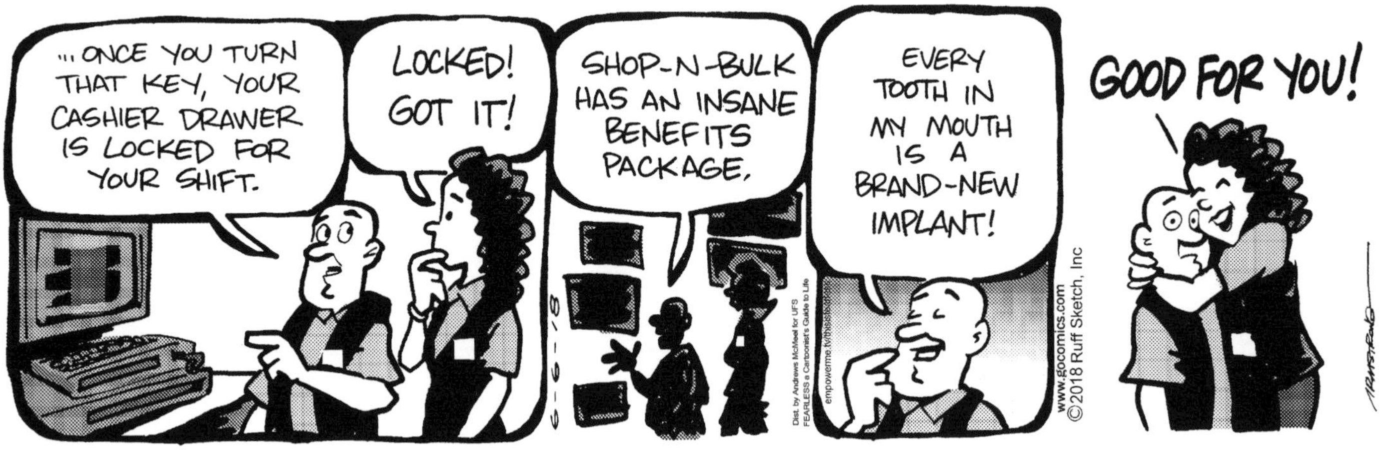
...ONCE YOU TURN THAT KEY, YOUR CASHIER DRAWER IS LOCKED FOR YOUR SHIFT.
LOCKED! GOT IT!
6-6-18
SHOP-N-BULK HAS AN INSANE BENEFITS PACKAGE.
Dist. by Andrews McMeel for UFS
FEARLESS a Cartoonist's Guide to Life
empowerme.tv/thisisfearless
EVERY TOOTH IN MY MOUTH IS A BRAND-NEW IMPLANT!
www.gocomics.com
©2018 Ruff Sketch, Inc
GOOD FOR YOU!

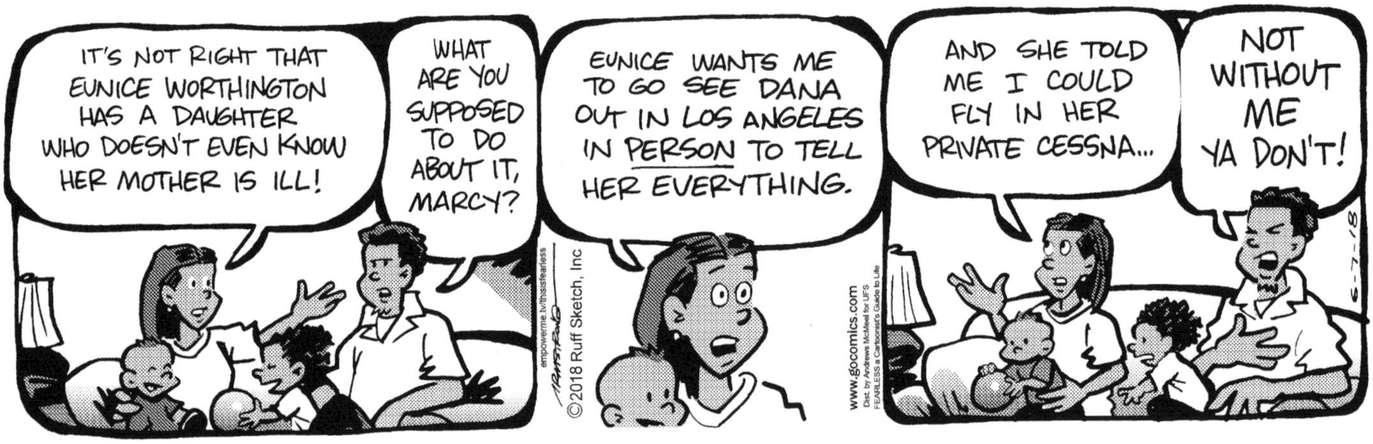
IT'S NOT RIGHT THAT EUNICE WORTHINGTON HAS A DAUGHTER WHO DOESN'T EVEN KNOW HER MOTHER IS ILL!
WHAT ARE YOU SUPPOSED TO DO ABOUT IT, MARCY?
empowerme.tv/thisisfearless
©2018 Ruff Sketch, Inc
EUNICE WANTS ME TO GO SEE DANA OUT IN LOS ANGELES IN PERSON TO TELL HER EVERYTHING.
www.gocomics.com
Dist. by Andrews McMeel for UFS
FEARLESS a Cartoonist's Guide to Life
AND SHE TOLD ME I COULD FLY IN HER PRIVATE CESSNA...
NOT WITHOUT ME YA DON'T!
6-7-18

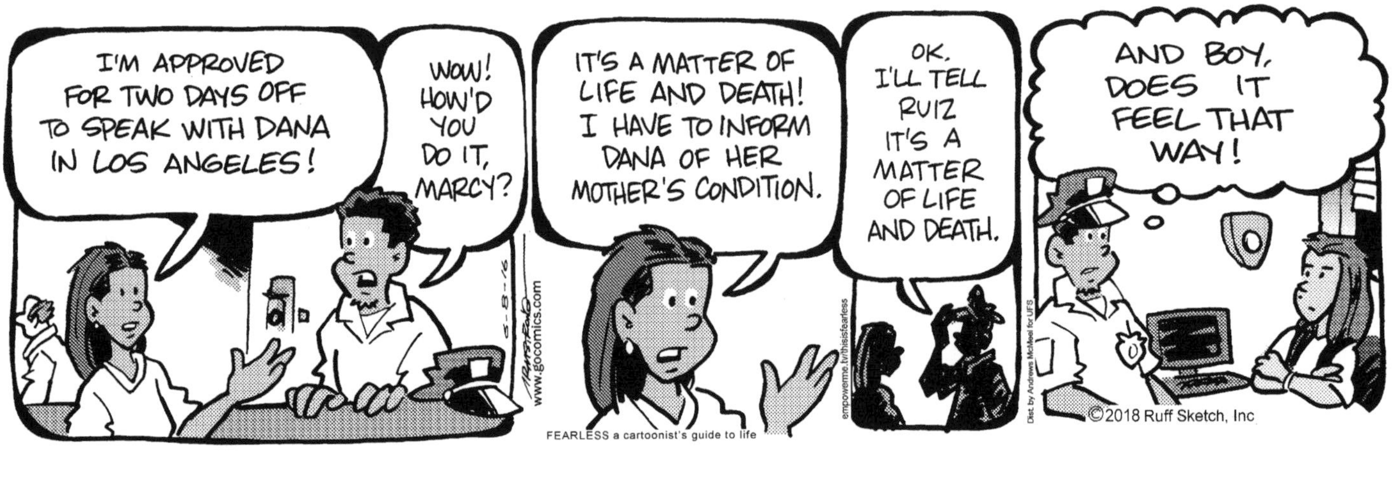
I'M APPROVED FOR TWO DAYS OFF TO SPEAK WITH DANA IN LOS ANGELES!
WOW! HOW'D YOU DO IT, MARCY?
6-8-18
www.gocomics.com
IT'S A MATTER OF LIFE AND DEATH! I HAVE TO INFORM DANA OF HER MOTHER'S CONDITION.
FEARLESS a cartoonist's guide to life
OK. I'LL TELL RUIZ IT'S A MATTER OF LIFE AND DEATH.
empowerme.tv/thisisfearless
AND BOY, DOES IT FEEL THAT WAY!
Dist. by Andrews McMeel for UFS
©2018 Ruff Sketch, Inc

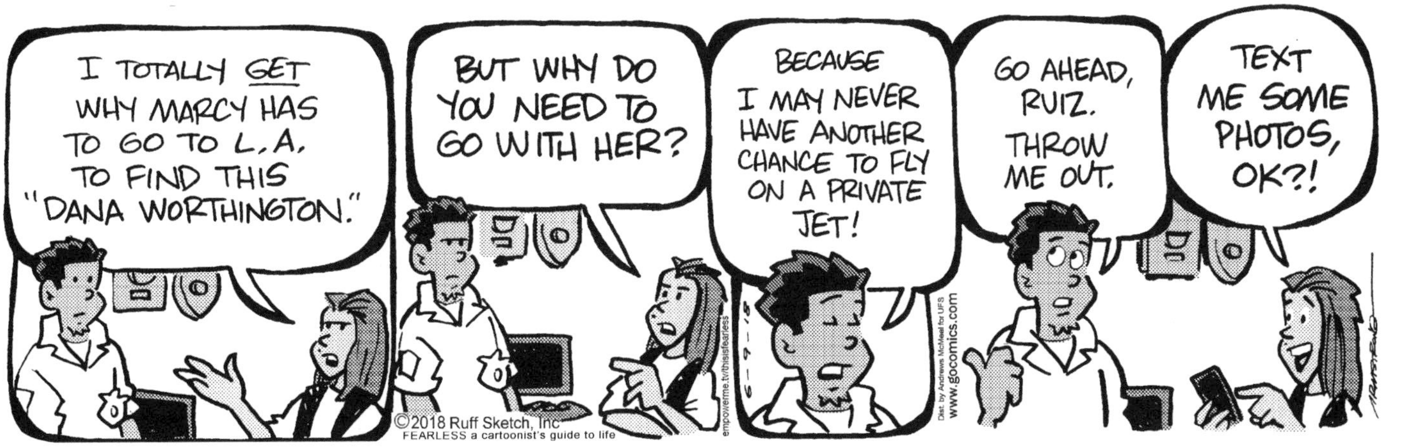
I TOTALLY GET WHY MARCY HAS TO GO TO L.A. TO FIND THIS "DANA WORTHINGTON."
BUT WHY DO YOU NEED TO GO WITH HER?
BECAUSE I MAY NEVER HAVE ANOTHER CHANCE TO FLY ON A PRIVATE JET!
GO AHEAD, RUIZ. THROW ME OUT.
TEXT ME SOME PHOTOS, OK?!
©2018 Ruff Sketch, Inc
FEARLESS a cartoonist's guide to life
empowerme.tv/thisisfearless
6-9-18
Dist. by Andrews McMeel for UFS
www.gocomics.com

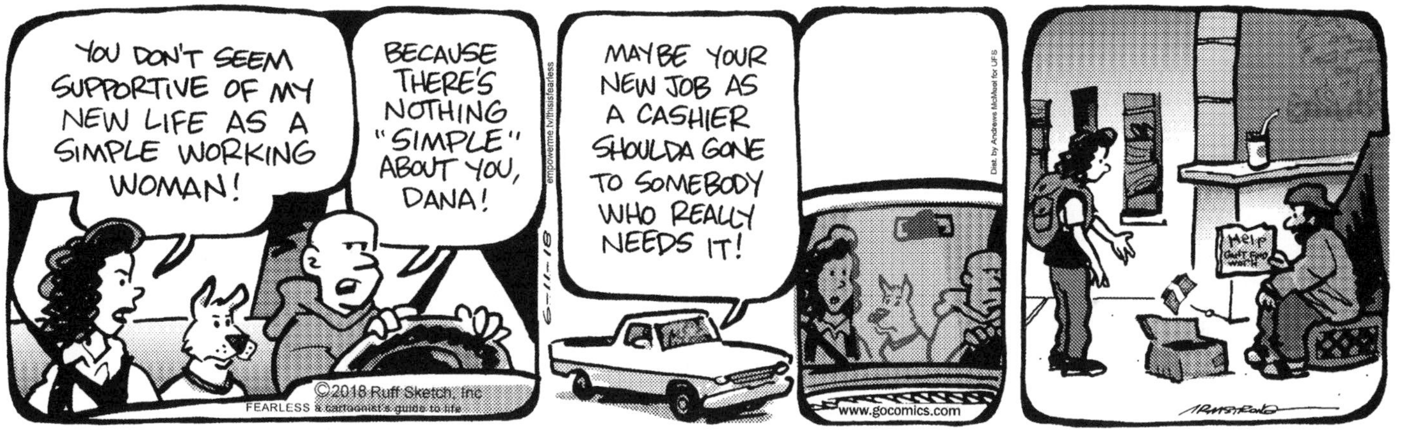
YOU DON'T SEEM SUPPORTIVE OF MY NEW LIFE AS A SIMPLE WORKING WOMAN!
BECAUSE THERE'S NOTHING "SIMPLE" ABOUT YOU, DANA!
MAYBE YOUR NEW JOB AS A CASHIER SHOULDA GONE TO SOMEBODY WHO REALLY NEEDS IT!
©2018 Ruff Sketch, Inc
FEARLESS a cartoonist's guide to life
empowerme.tv/thisisfearless
6-11-18
Dist. by Andrews McMeel for UFS
www.gocomics.com
Help

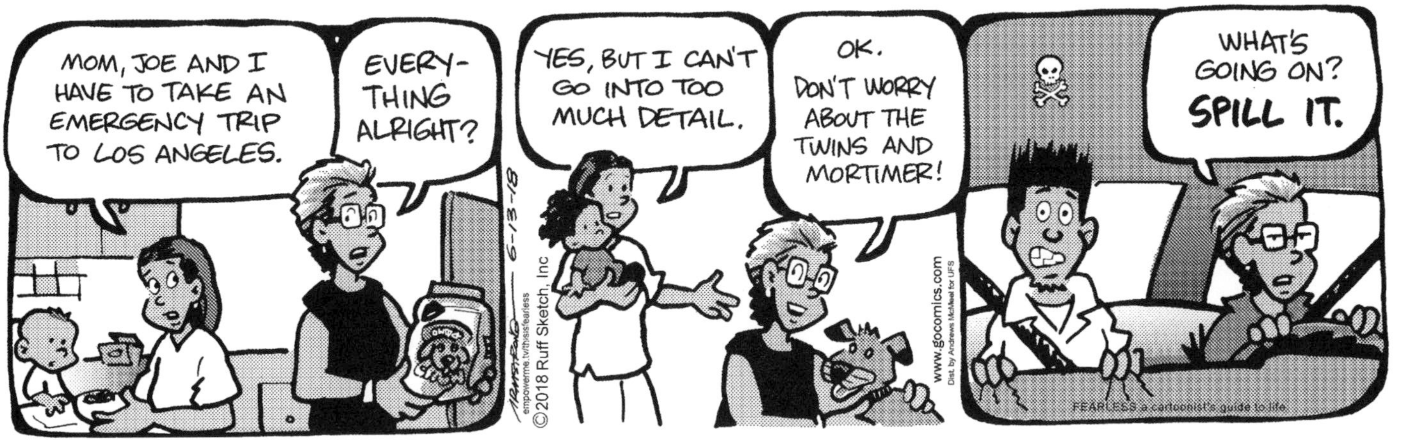
MOM, JOE AND I HAVE TO TAKE AN EMERGENCY TRIP TO LOS ANGELES.
EVERY-THING ALRIGHT?
YES, BUT I CAN'T GO INTO TOO MUCH DETAIL.
OK. DON'T WORRY ABOUT THE TWINS AND MORTIMER!
WHAT'S GOING ON? SPILL IT.
6-13-18
empowerme.tv/thisisfearless
©2018 Ruff Sketch, Inc
www.gocomics.com
Dist. by Andrews McMeel for UFS
FEARLESS a cartoonist's guide to life

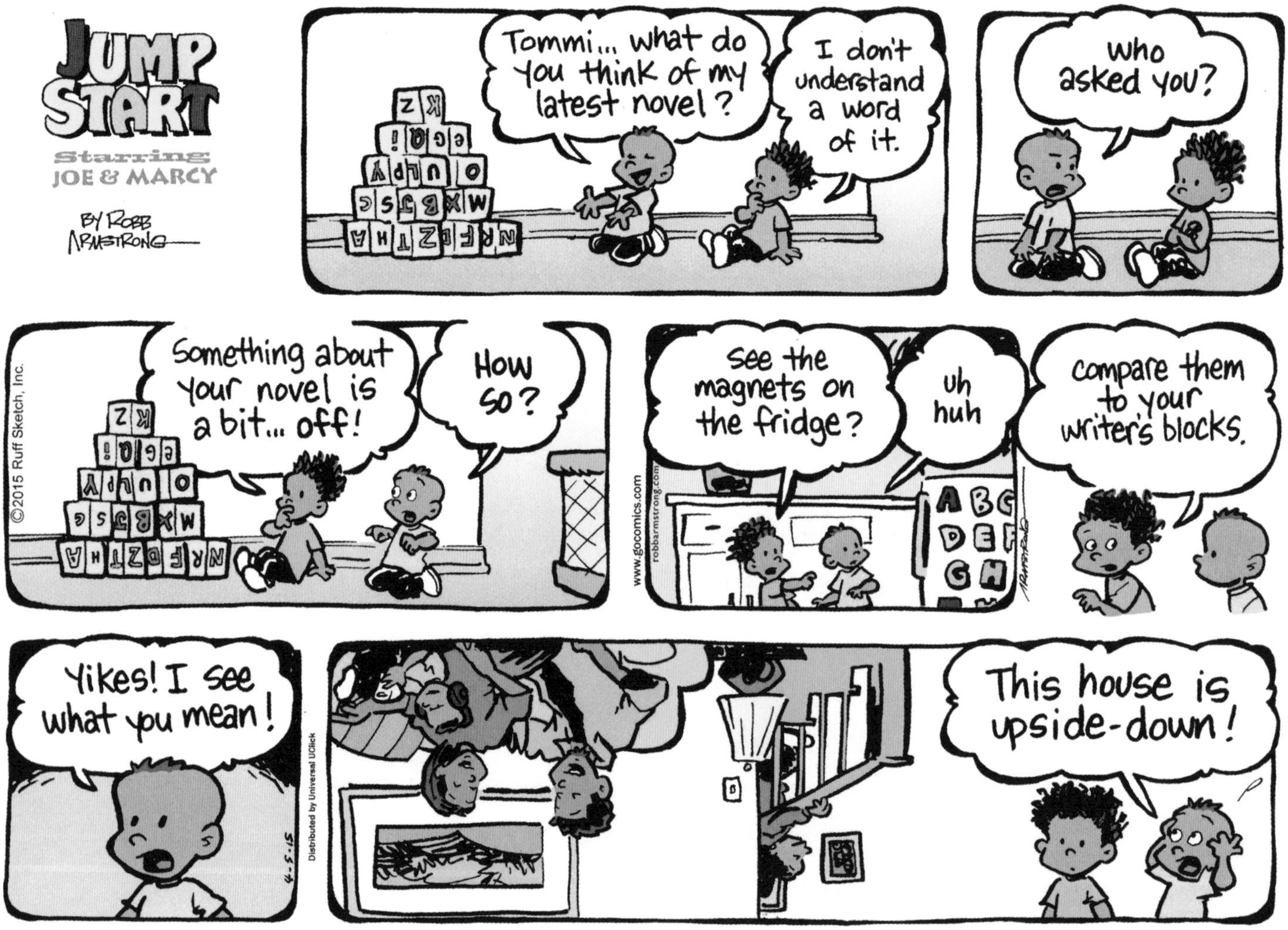
JUMP START
Starring JOE & MARCY
BY ROBB ARMSTRONG
Tommi... what do you think of my latest novel?
I don't understand a word of it.
Who asked you?
©2015 Ruff Sketch, Inc.
Something about your novel is a bit... off!
How so?
www.gocomics.com
robbarmstrong.com
See the magnets on the fridge?
uh huh
Compare them to your writer's blocks.
Yikes! I see what you mean!
4-5-15
Distributed by Universal UClick
This house is upside-down!

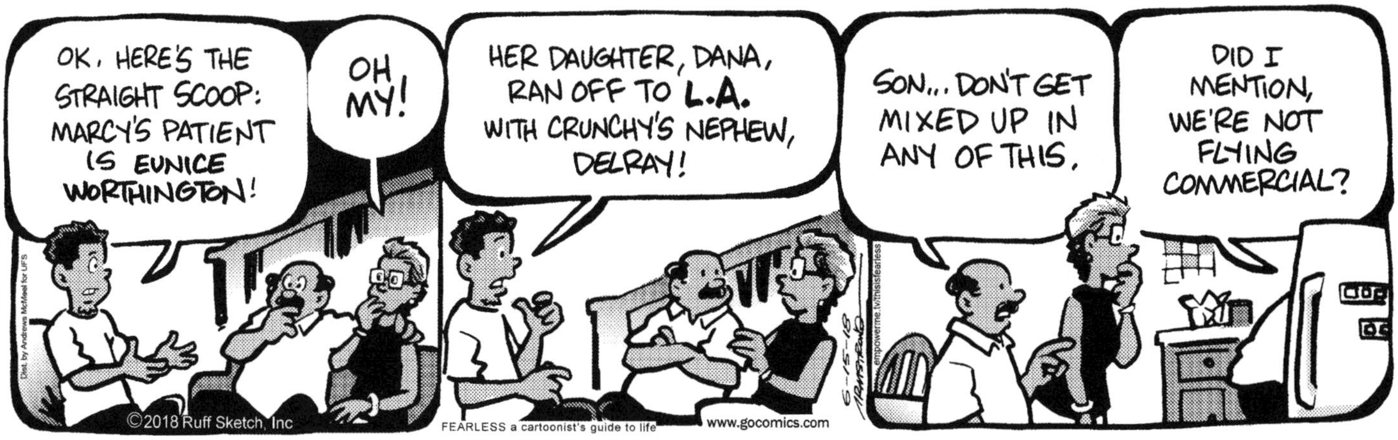
OK, HERE'S THE STRAIGHT SCOOP: MARCY'S PATIENT IS EUNICE WORTHINGTON!
OH MY!
HER DAUGHTER, DANA, RAN OFF TO L.A. WITH CRUNCHY'S NEPHEW, DELRAY!
SON... DON'T GET MIXED UP IN ANY OF THIS.
DID I MENTION, WE'RE NOT FLYING COMMERCIAL?
©2018 Ruff Sketch, Inc
FEARLESS a cartoonist's guide to life
www.gocomics.com
empowerme.tv/thisisfearless
Dist. by Andrews McMeel for UFS
6-15-18

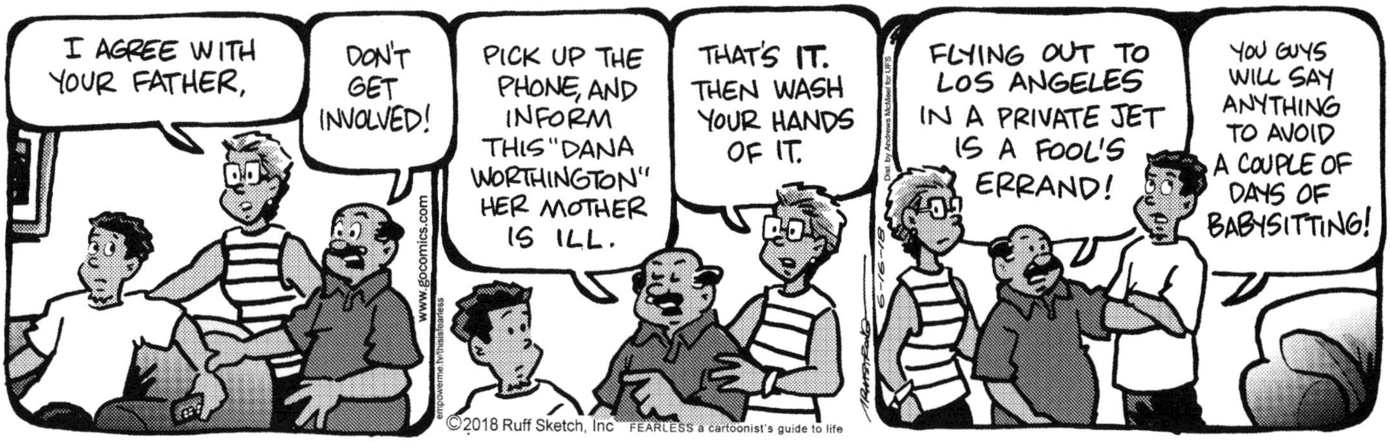
I AGREE WITH YOUR FATHER.
DON'T GET INVOLVED!
PICK UP THE PHONE, AND INFORM THIS "DANA WORTHINGTON" HER MOTHER IS ILL.
THAT'S IT. THEN WASH YOUR HANDS OF IT.
FLYING OUT TO LOS ANGELES IN A PRIVATE JET IS A FOOL'S ERRAND!
YOU GUYS WILL SAY ANYTHING TO AVOID A COUPLE OF DAYS OF BABYSITTING!
www.gocomics.com
empowerme.tv/thisisfearless
©2018 Ruff Sketch, Inc
FEARLESS a cartoonist's guide to life
Dist. by Andrews McMeel for UFS
6-16-18

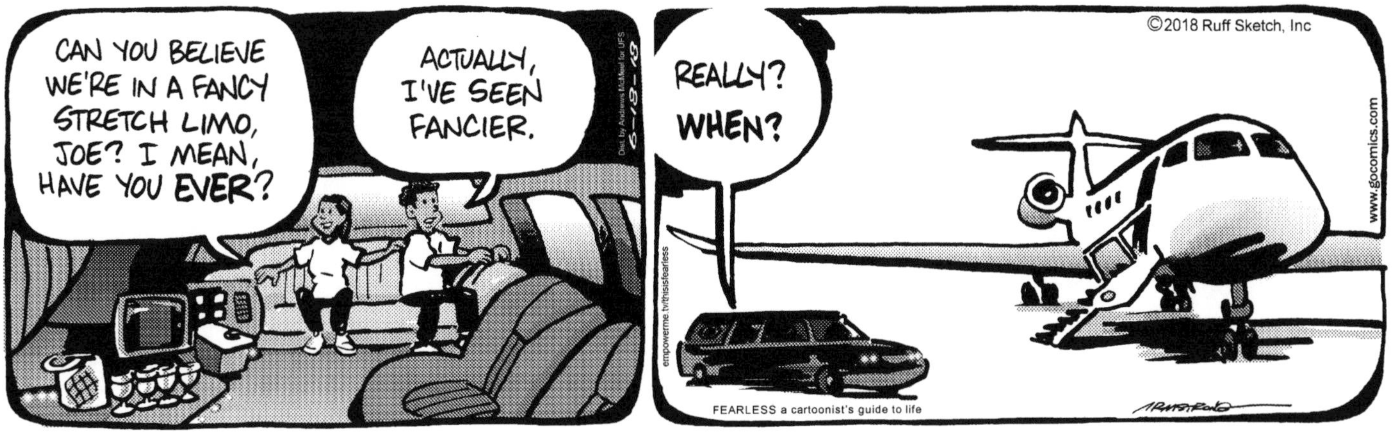
CAN YOU BELIEVE WE'RE IN A FANCY STRETCH LIMO, JOE? I MEAN, HAVE YOU EVER?
ACTUALLY, I'VE SEEN FANCIER.
REALLY? WHEN?
©2018 Ruff Sketch, Inc
www.gocomics.com
empowerme.tv/thisisfearless
FEARLESS a cartoonist's guide to life
Dist. by Andrews McMeel for UFS
6-18-18

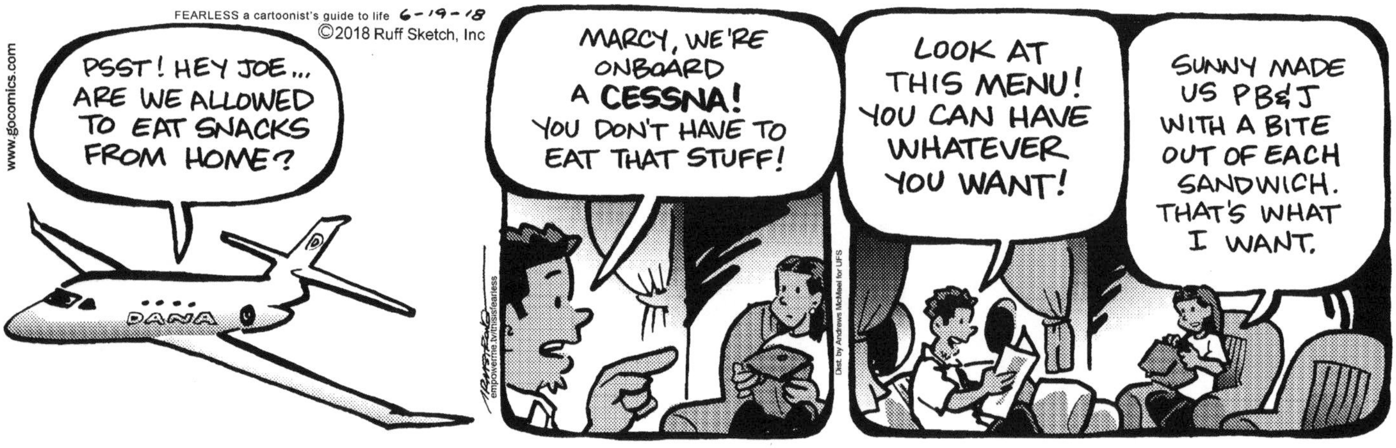
FEARLESS a cartoonist's guide to life 6-19-18
©2018 Ruff Sketch, Inc
www.gocomics.com
PSST! HEY JOE... ARE WE ALLOWED TO EAT SNACKS FROM HOME?
DANA
MARCY, WE'RE ONBOARD A CESSNA! YOU DON'T HAVE TO EAT THAT STUFF!
LOOK AT THIS MENU! YOU CAN HAVE WHATEVER YOU WANT!
SUNNY MADE US PB&J WITH A BITE OUT OF EACH SANDWICH. THAT'S WHAT I WANT.

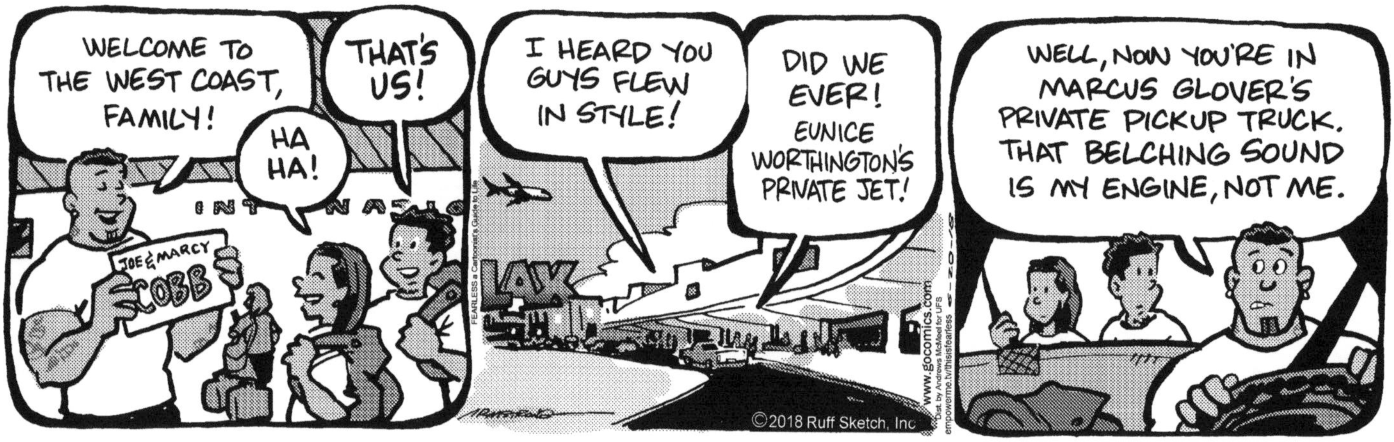
WELCOME TO THE WEST COAST, FAMILY!
HA HA!
THAT'S US!
JOE & MARCY COBB
I HEARD YOU GUYS FLEW IN STYLE!
DID WE EVER! EUNICE WORTHINGTON'S PRIVATE JET!
LAX
WELL, NOW YOU'RE IN MARCUS GLOVER'S PRIVATE PICKUP TRUCK. THAT BELCHING SOUND IS MY ENGINE, NOT ME.
©2018 Ruff Sketch, Inc
www.gocomics.com

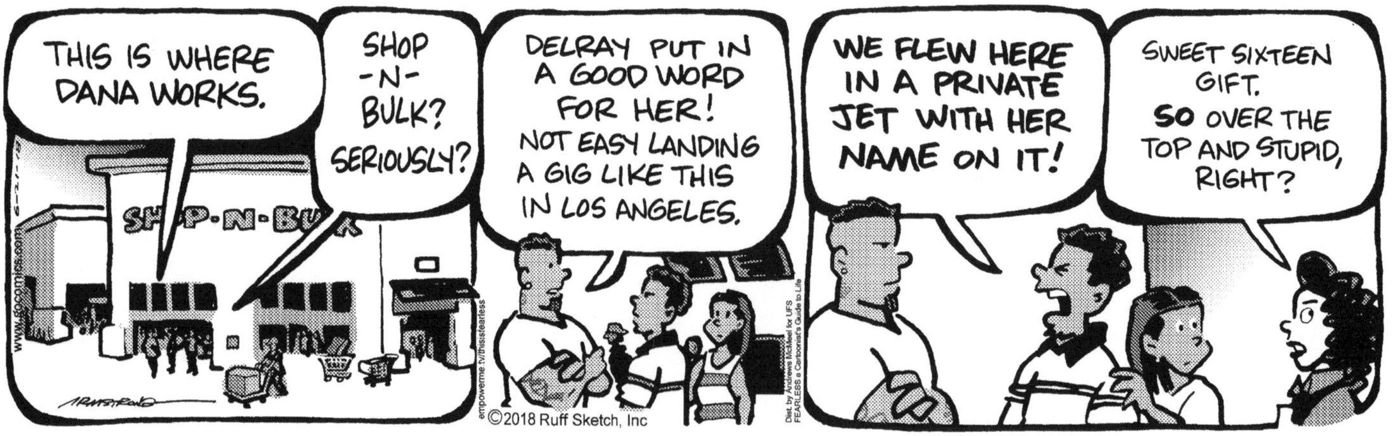
THIS IS WHERE DANA WORKS.
SHOP -N- BULK? SERIOUSLY?
DELRAY PUT IN A GOOD WORD FOR HER! NOT EASY LANDING A GIG LIKE THIS IN LOS ANGELES.
WE FLEW HERE IN A PRIVATE JET WITH HER NAME ON IT!
SWEET SIXTEEN GIFT. SO OVER THE TOP AND STUPID, RIGHT?
©2018 Ruff Sketch, Inc

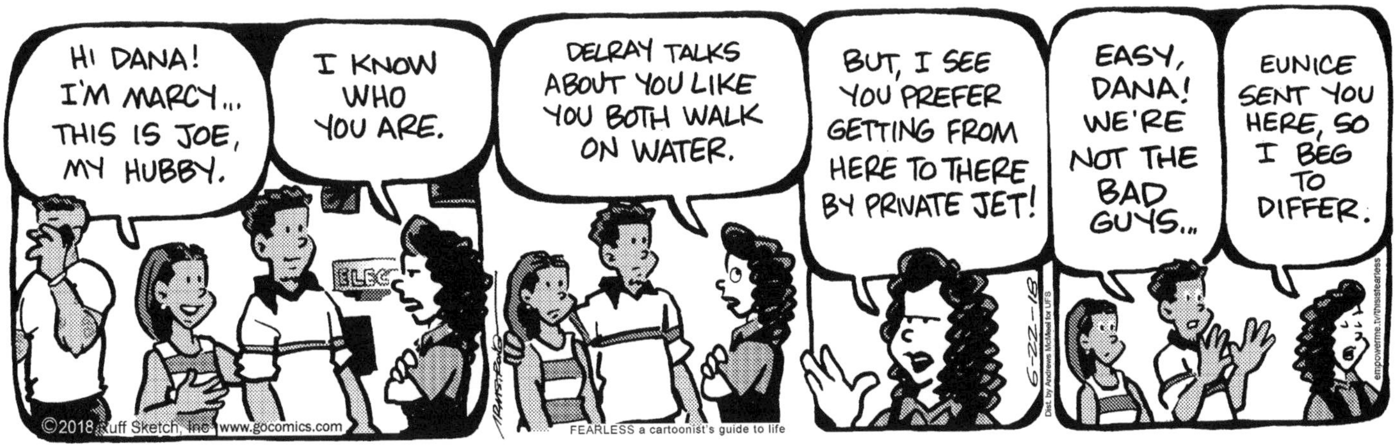
HI DANA! I'M MARCY... THIS IS JOE, MY HUBBY.
I KNOW WHO YOU ARE.
DELRAY TALKS ABOUT YOU LIKE YOU BOTH WALK ON WATER.
BUT, I SEE YOU PREFER GETTING FROM HERE TO THERE BY PRIVATE JET!
EASY, DANA! WE'RE NOT THE BAD GUYS...
EUNICE SENT YOU HERE, SO I BEG TO DIFFER.
©2018 Ruff Sketch, Inc www.gocomics.com
FEARLESS a cartoonist's guide to life
6-22-18

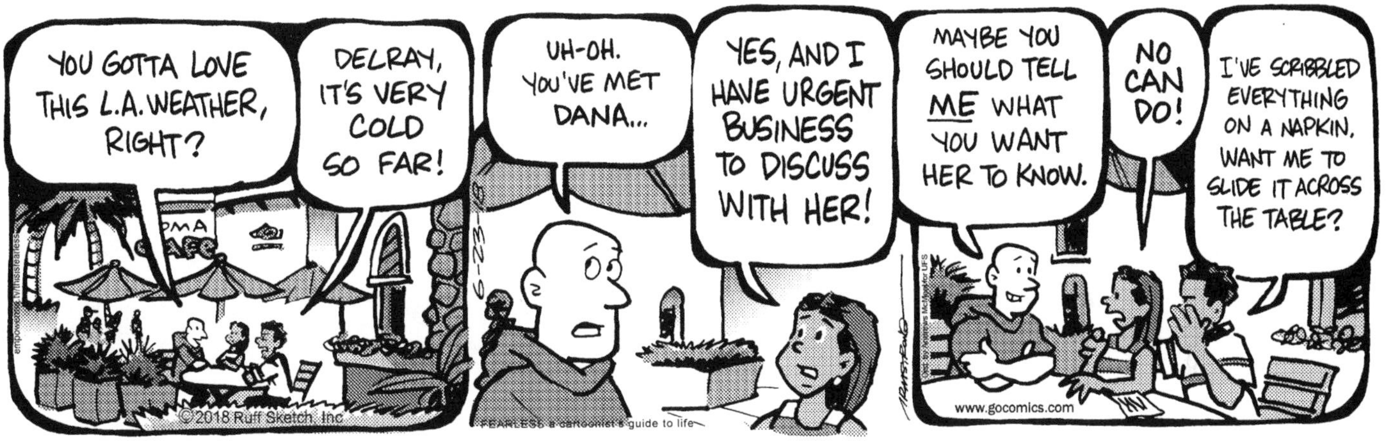
YOU GOTTA LOVE THIS L.A. WEATHER, RIGHT?
DELRAY, IT'S VERY COLD SO FAR!
UH-OH. YOU'VE MET DANA...
YES, AND I HAVE URGENT BUSINESS TO DISCUSS WITH HER!
MAYBE YOU SHOULD TELL ME WHAT YOU WANT HER TO KNOW.
NO CAN DO!
I'VE SCRIBBLED EVERYTHING ON A NAPKIN. WANT ME TO SLIDE IT ACROSS THE TABLE?
©2018 Ruff Sketch, Inc
6-23-18
FEARLESS a cartoonist's guide to life
www.gocomics.com

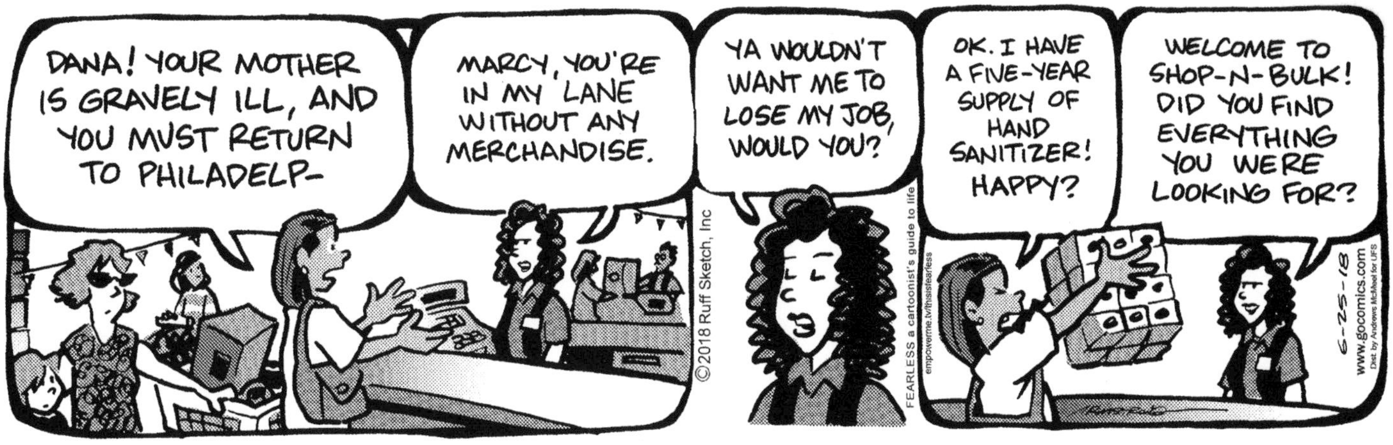
DANA! YOUR MOTHER IS GRAVELY ILL, AND YOU MUST RETURN TO PHILADELP-
MARCY, YOU'RE IN MY LANE WITHOUT ANY MERCHANDISE.
YA WOULDN'T WANT ME TO LOSE MY JOB, WOULD YOU?
OK. I HAVE A FIVE-YEAR SUPPLY OF HAND SANITIZER! HAPPY?
WELCOME TO SHOP-N-BULK! DID YOU FIND EVERYTHING YOU WERE LOOKING FOR?
©2018 Ruff Sketch, Inc
FEARLESS a cartoonist's guide to life
6-25-18
www.gocomics.com

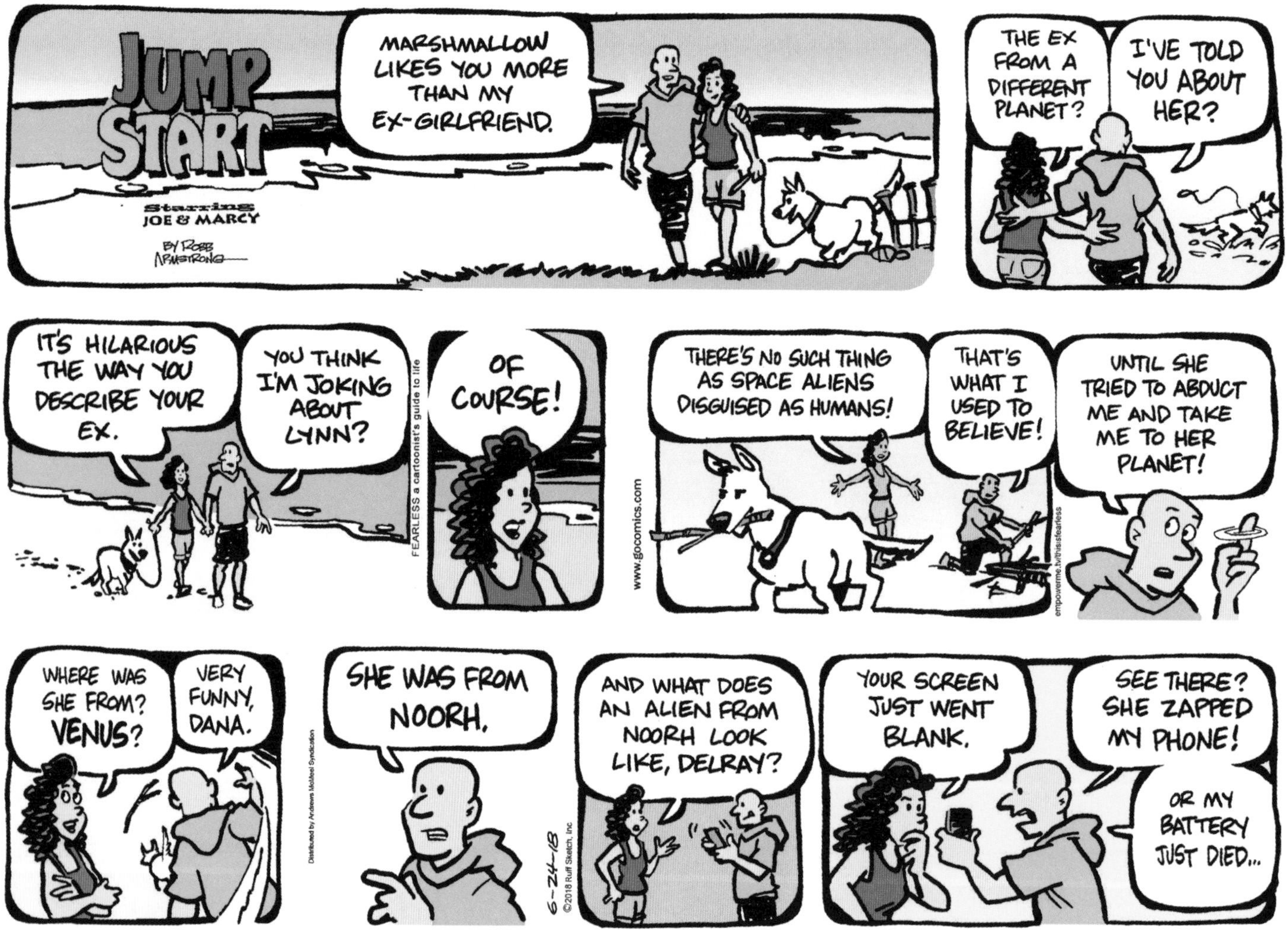

JUMP START
Starring JOE & MARCY
BY ROBB ARMSTRONG
MARSHMALLOW LIKES YOU MORE THAN MY EX-GIRLFRIEND.
THE EX FROM A DIFFERENT PLANET?
I'VE TOLD YOU ABOUT HER?
IT'S HILARIOUS THE WAY YOU DESCRIBE YOUR EX.
YOU THINK I'M JOKING ABOUT LYNN?
FEARLESS a cartoonist's guide to life
OF COURSE!
www.gocomics.com
THERE'S NO SUCH THING AS SPACE ALIENS DISGUISED AS HUMANS!
THAT'S WHAT I USED TO BELIEVE!
empowerme.tv/thisisfearless
UNTIL SHE TRIED TO ABDUCT ME AND TAKE ME TO HER PLANET!
WHERE WAS SHE FROM? VENUS?
VERY FUNNY, DANA.
Distributed by Andrews McMeel Syndication
SHE WAS FROM NOORH.
6-24-18
©2018 Ruff Sketch, Inc.
AND WHAT DOES AN ALIEN FROM NOORH LOOK LIKE, DELRAY?
YOUR SCREEN JUST WENT BLANK.
SEE THERE? SHE ZAPPED MY PHONE!
OR MY BATTERY JUST DIED...

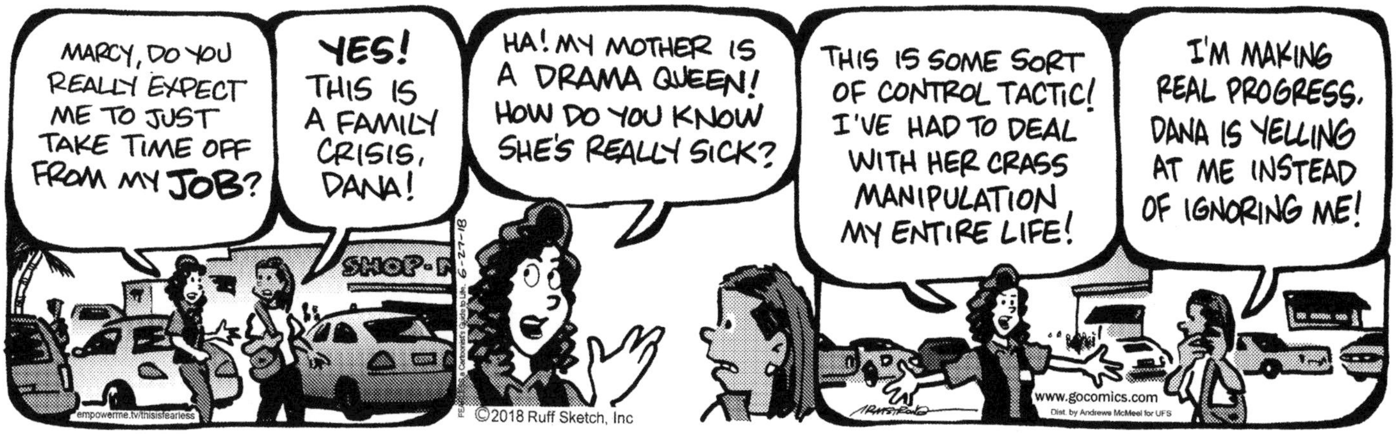
MARCY, DO YOU REALLY EXPECT ME TO JUST TAKE TIME OFF FROM MY JOB?
YES! THIS IS A FAMILY CRISIS, DANA!
HA! MY MOTHER IS A DRAMA QUEEN! HOW DO YOU KNOW SHE'S REALLY SICK?
THIS IS SOME SORT OF CONTROL TACTIC! I'VE HAD TO DEAL WITH HER CRASS MANIPULATION MY ENTIRE LIFE!
I'M MAKING REAL PROGRESS. DANA IS YELLING AT ME INSTEAD OF IGNORING ME!
6-27-18
empowerme.tv/thisisfearless
©2018 Ruff Sketch, Inc
www.gocomics.com
Dist. by Andrews McMeel for UFS

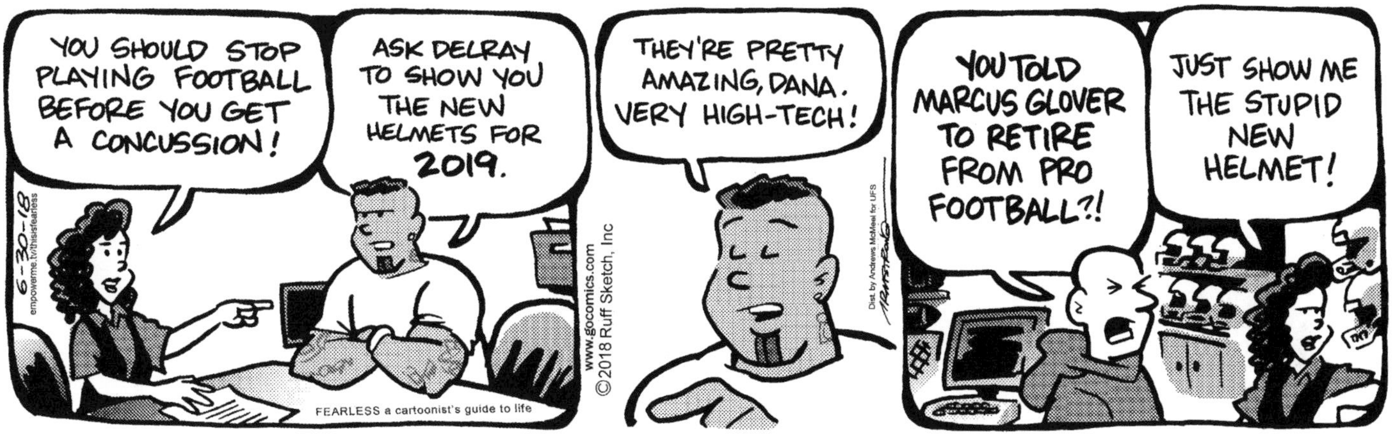
YOU SHOULD STOP PLAYING FOOTBALL BEFORE YOU GET A CONCUSSION!
ASK DELRAY TO SHOW YOU THE NEW HELMETS FOR 2019.
THEY'RE PRETTY AMAZING, DANA. VERY HIGH-TECH!
YOU TOLD MARCUS GLOVER TO RETIRE FROM PRO FOOTBALL?!
JUST SHOW ME THE STUPID NEW HELMET!
6-30-18
empowerme.tv/thisisfearless
FEARLESS a cartoonist's guide to life
www.gocomics.com
©2018 Ruff Sketch, Inc
Dist. by Andrews McMeel for UFS

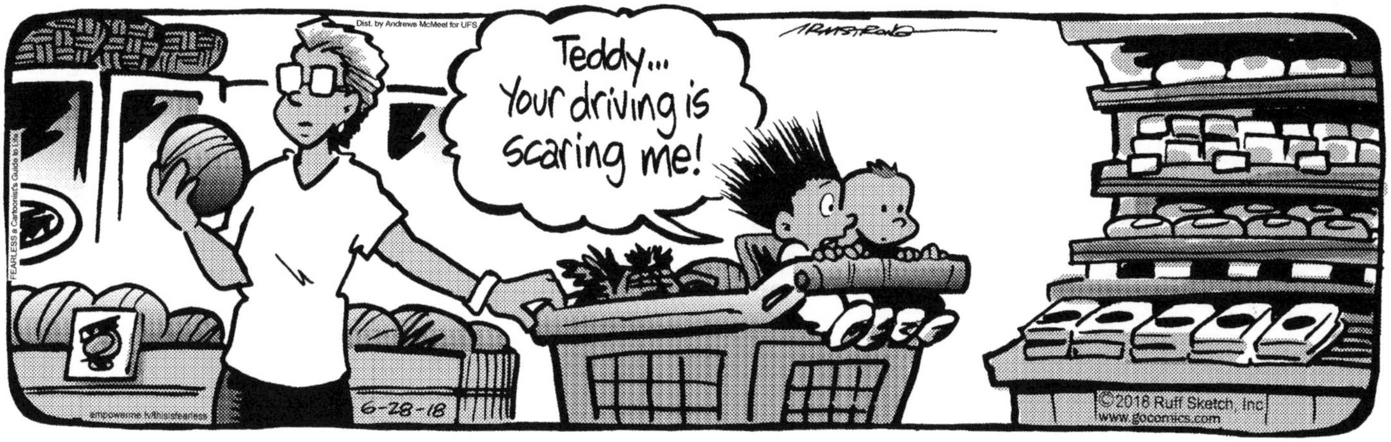
Teddy... Your driving is scaring me!
Dist. by Andrews McMeel for UFS
6-28-18
empowerme.tv/thisisfearless
©2018 Ruff Sketch, Inc
www.gocomics.com

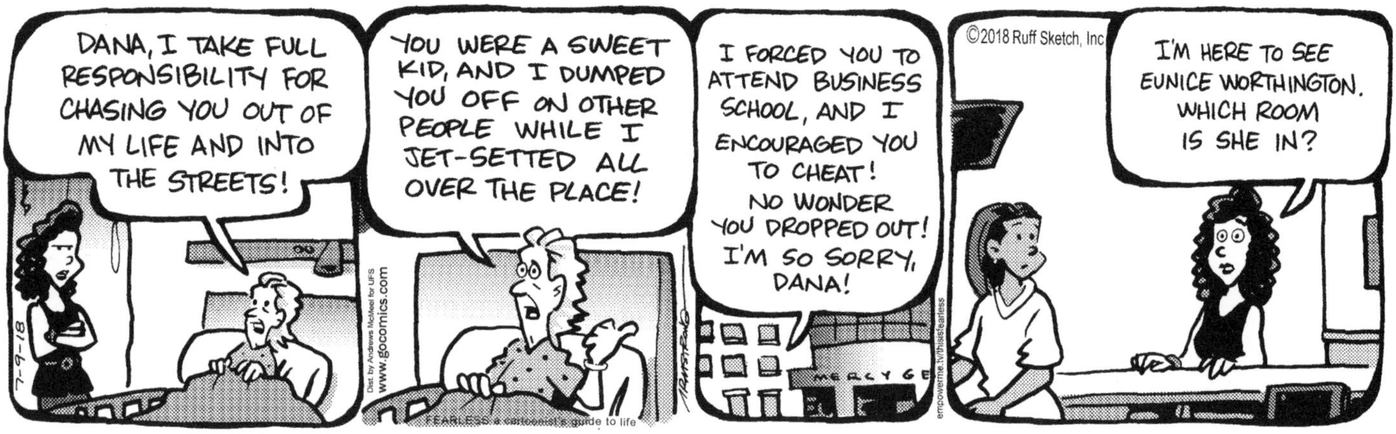
DANA, I TAKE FULL RESPONSIBILITY FOR CHASING YOU OUT OF MY LIFE AND INTO THE STREETS!
7-9-18
YOU WERE A SWEET KID, AND I DUMPED YOU OFF ON OTHER PEOPLE WHILE I JET-SETTED ALL OVER THE PLACE!
Dist. by Andrews McMeel for UFS
www.gocomics.com
I FORCED YOU TO ATTEND BUSINESS SCHOOL, AND I ENCOURAGED YOU TO CHEAT! NO WONDER YOU DROPPED OUT! I'M SO SORRY, DANA!
FEARLESS a cartoonist's guide to life
empowerme.tv/thisisfearless
©2018 Ruff Sketch, Inc
I'M HERE TO SEE EUNICE WORTHINGTON. WHICH ROOM IS SHE IN?

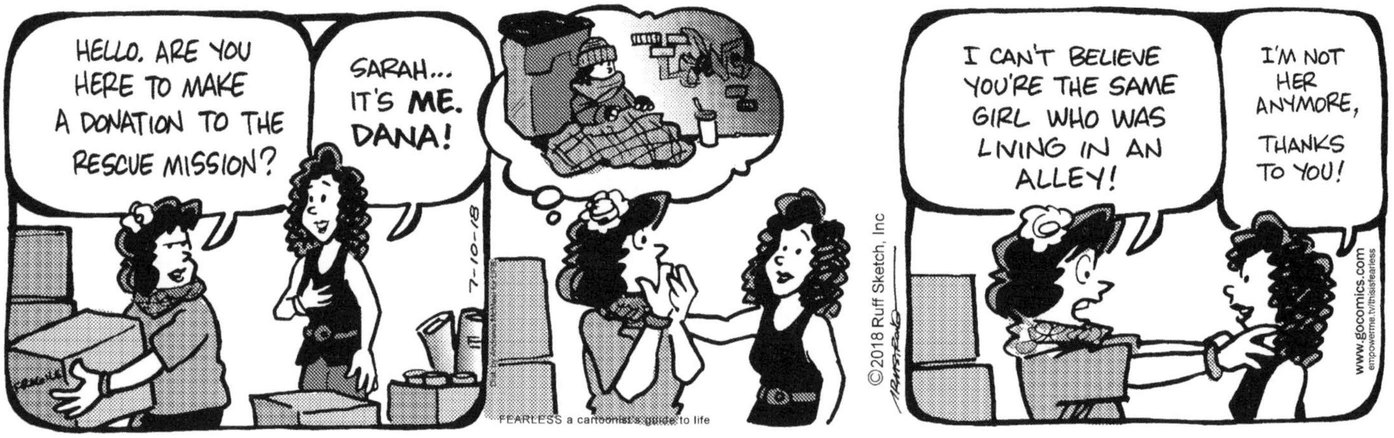
HELLO. ARE YOU HERE TO MAKE A DONATION TO THE RESCUE MISSION?
SARAH... IT'S **ME. DANA!**
7-10-18
FEARLESS a cartoonist's guide to life
©2018 Ruff Sketch, Inc
I CAN'T BELIEVE YOU'RE THE SAME GIRL WHO WAS LIVING IN AN ALLEY!
I'M NOT HER ANYMORE, THANKS TO YOU!
www.gocomics.com
empowerme.tv/thisisfearless

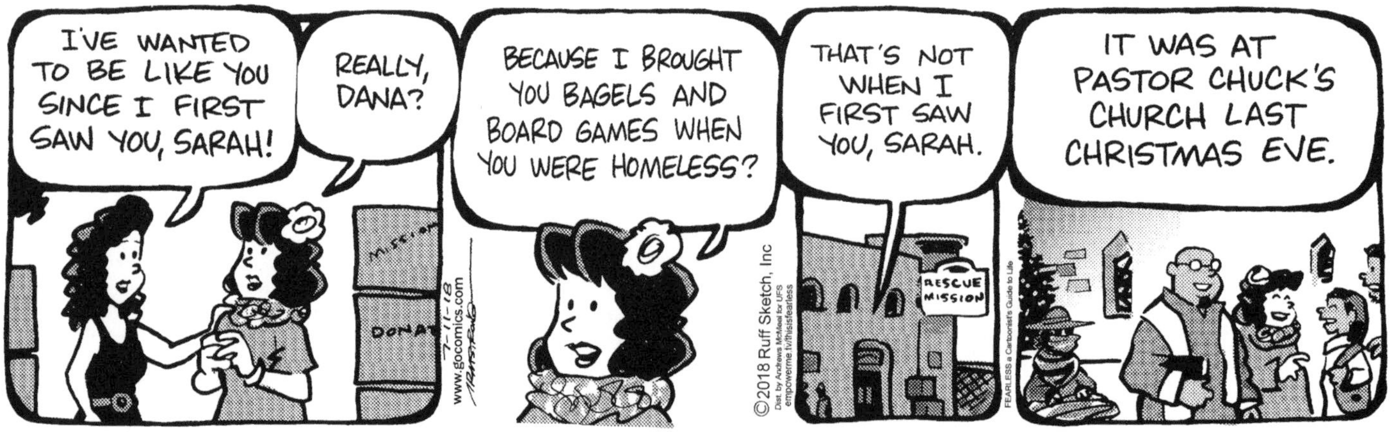
I'VE WANTED TO BE LIKE YOU SINCE I FIRST SAW YOU, SARAH!
REALLY, DANA?
7-11-18
www.gocomics.com
BECAUSE I BROUGHT YOU BAGELS AND BOARD GAMES WHEN YOU WERE HOMELESS?
©2018 Ruff Sketch, Inc
Dist. by Andrews McMeel for UFS
empowerme.tv/thisisfearless
THAT'S NOT WHEN I FIRST SAW YOU, SARAH.
RESCUE MISSION
FEARLESS a Cartoonist's Guide to Life
IT WAS AT PASTOR CHUCK'S CHURCH LAST CHRISTMAS EVE.

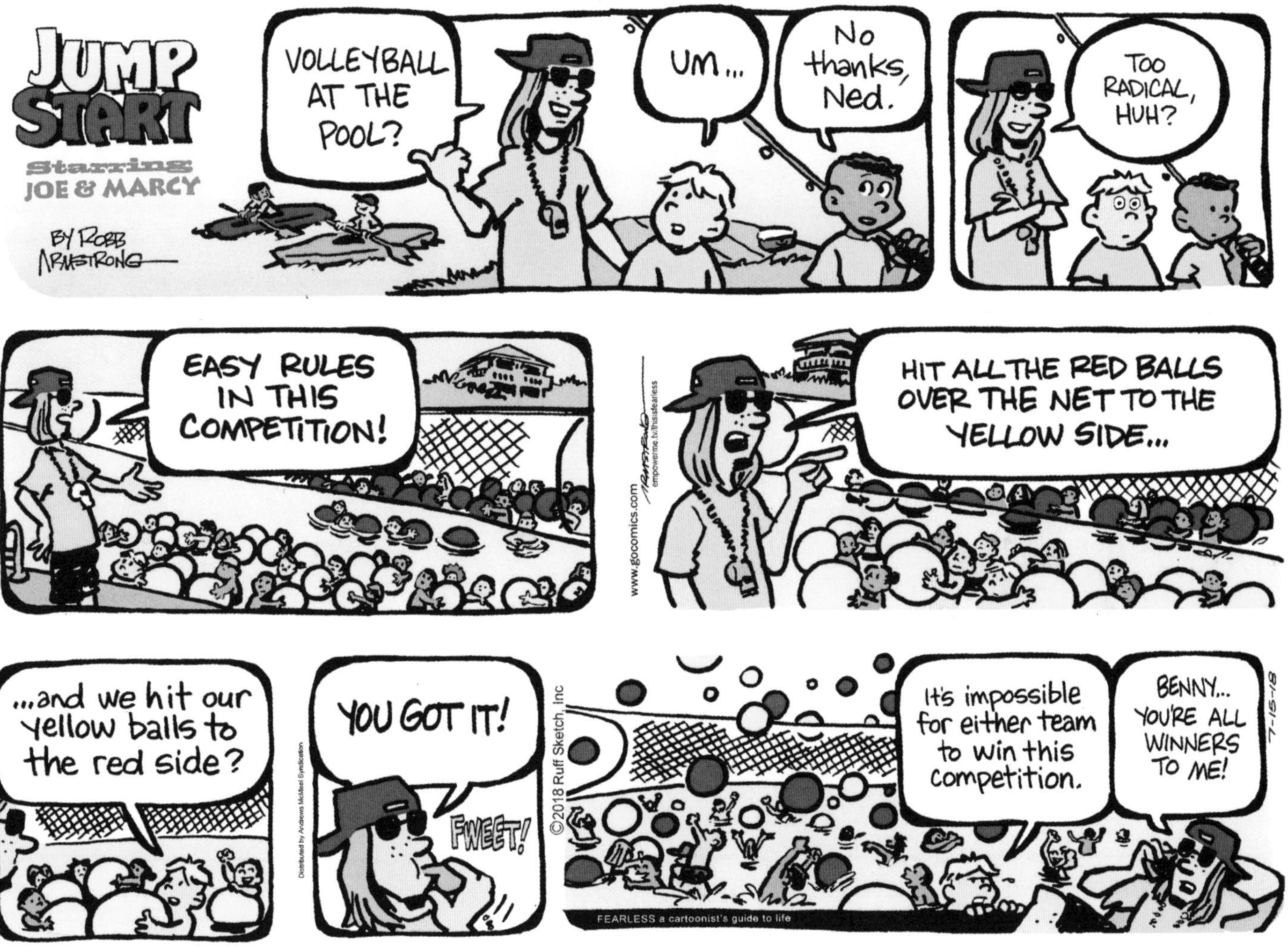
JUMP START
Starring JOE & MARCY
BY ROBB ARMSTRONG
VOLLEYBALL AT THE POOL?
UM...
No thanks, Ned.
TOO RADICAL, HUH?
EASY RULES IN THIS COMPETITION!
www.gocomics.com
empowerme.tv/thisisfearless
HIT ALL THE RED BALLS OVER THE NET TO THE YELLOW SIDE...
...and we hit our yellow balls to the red side?
Distributed by Andrews McMeel Syndication
YOU GOT IT!
FWEET!
©2018 Ruff Sketch, Inc
It's impossible for either team to win this competition.
BENNY... YOU'RE ALL WINNERS TO ME!
7-15-18
FEARLESS a cartoonist's guide to life

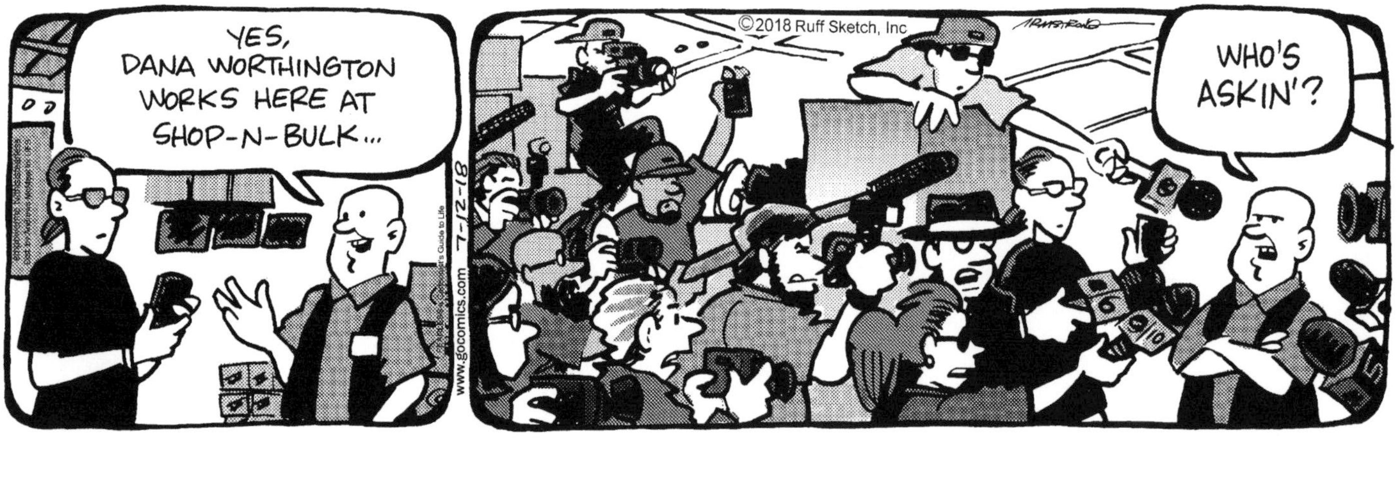
YES, DANA WORTHINGTON WORKS HERE AT SHOP-N-BULK...
7-12-18
www.gocomics.com
©2018 Ruff Sketch, Inc
WHO'S ASKIN'?

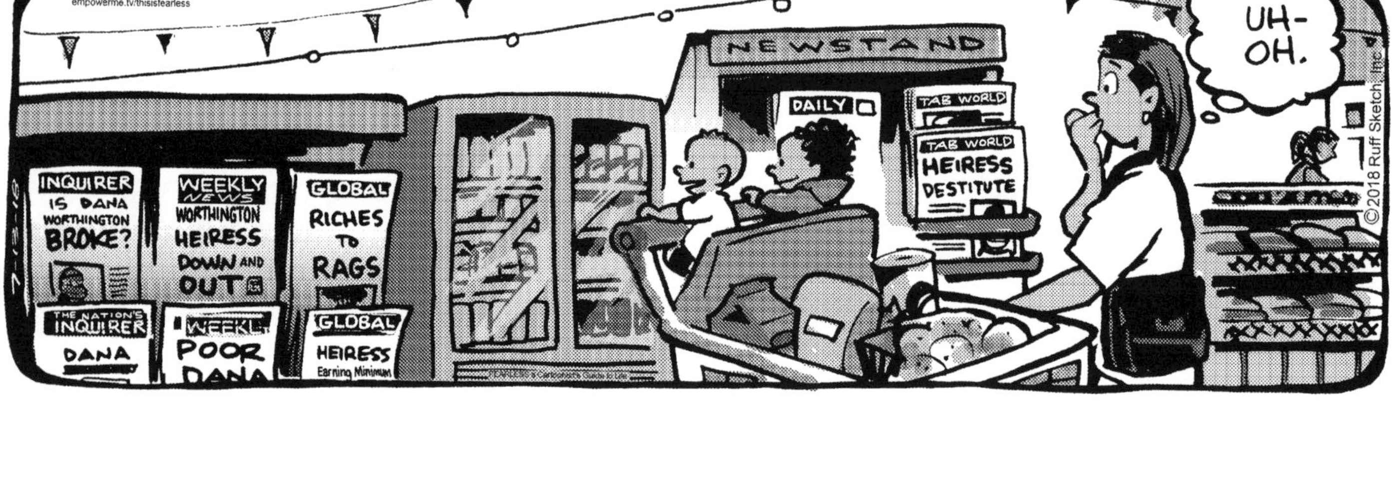
www.gocomics.com
empowerme.tv/thisisfearless
Distributed by Andrews McMeel Syndication for UFS
NEWSTAND
7-13-18
INQUIRER
IS DANA WORTHINGTON BROKE?
WEEKLY NEWS
WORTHINGTON HEIRESS DOWN AND OUT
GLOBAL
RICHES TO RAGS
THE NATION'S INQUIRER
DANA
WEEKL
POOR DANA
GLOBAL
HEIRESS Earning Minimum
DAILY
TAB WORLD
TAB WORLD
HEIRESS DESTITUTE
UH-OH.
©2018 Ruff Sketch, Inc

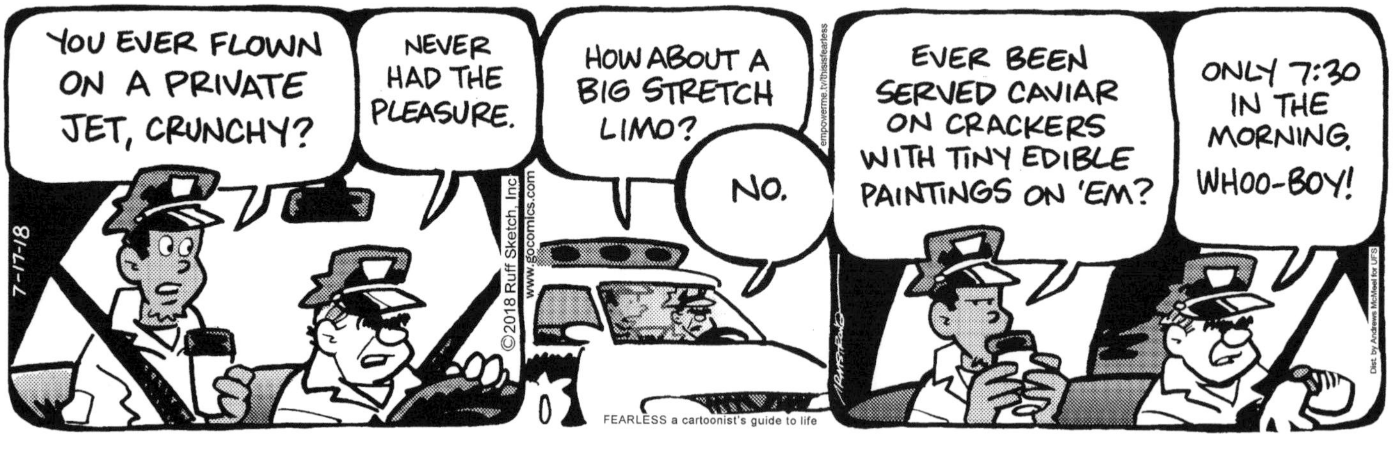
YOU EVER FLOWN ON A PRIVATE JET, CRUNCHY?
NEVER HAD THE PLEASURE.
7-17-18
©2018 Ruff Sketch, Inc
www.gocomics.com
HOW ABOUT A BIG STRETCH LIMO?
NO.
empowerme.tv/thisisfearless
EVER BEEN SERVED CAVIAR ON CRACKERS WITH TINY EDIBLE PAINTINGS ON 'EM?
ONLY 7:30 IN THE MORNING.
WHOO-BOY!
Dist. by Andrews McMeel for UFS
FEARLESS a cartoonist's guide to life

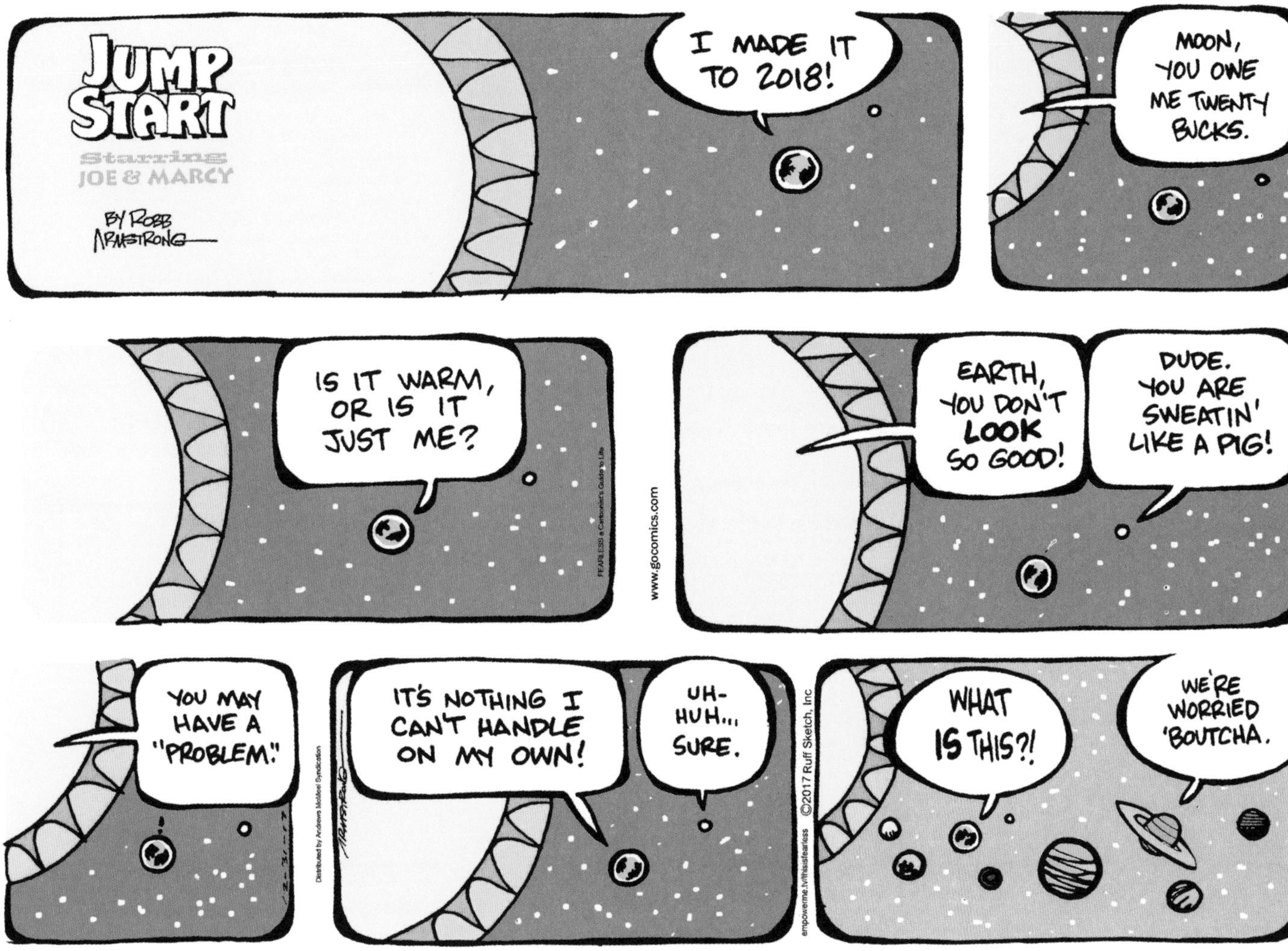
JUMP START
Starring JOE & MARCY
BY ROBB ARMSTRONG
I MADE IT TO 2018!
MOON, YOU OWE ME TWENTY BUCKS.
IS IT WARM, OR IS IT JUST ME?
FEARLESS! a Cartoonist's Guide to Life
www.gocomics.com
EARTH, YOU DON'T LOOK SO GOOD!
DUDE. YOU ARE SWEATIN' LIKE A PIG!
YOU MAY HAVE A "PROBLEM."
Distributed by Andrews McMeel Syndication
IT'S NOTHING I CAN'T HANDLE ON MY OWN!
UH-HUH... SURE.
©2017 Ruff Sketch, Inc
empowerme.tv/thisisfearless
WHAT IS THIS?!
WE'RE WORRIED 'BOUTCHA.

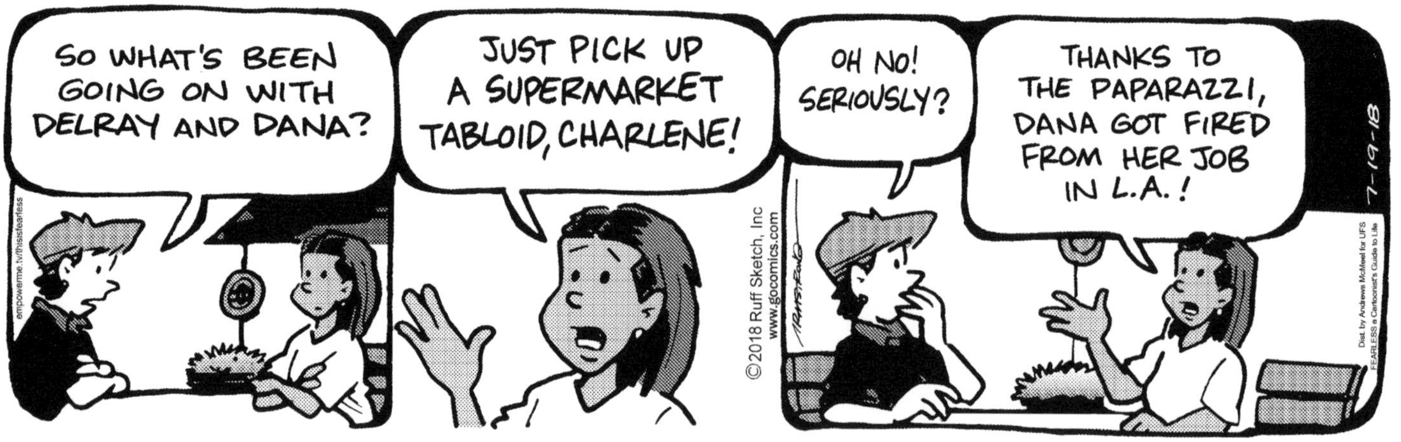
SO WHAT'S BEEN GOING ON WITH DELRAY AND DANA?
JUST PICK UP A SUPERMARKET TABLOID, CHARLENE!
OH NO! SERIOUSLY?
THANKS TO THE PAPARAZZI, DANA GOT FIRED FROM HER JOB IN L.A.!
7-19-18
©2018 Ruff Sketch, Inc
www.gocomics.com

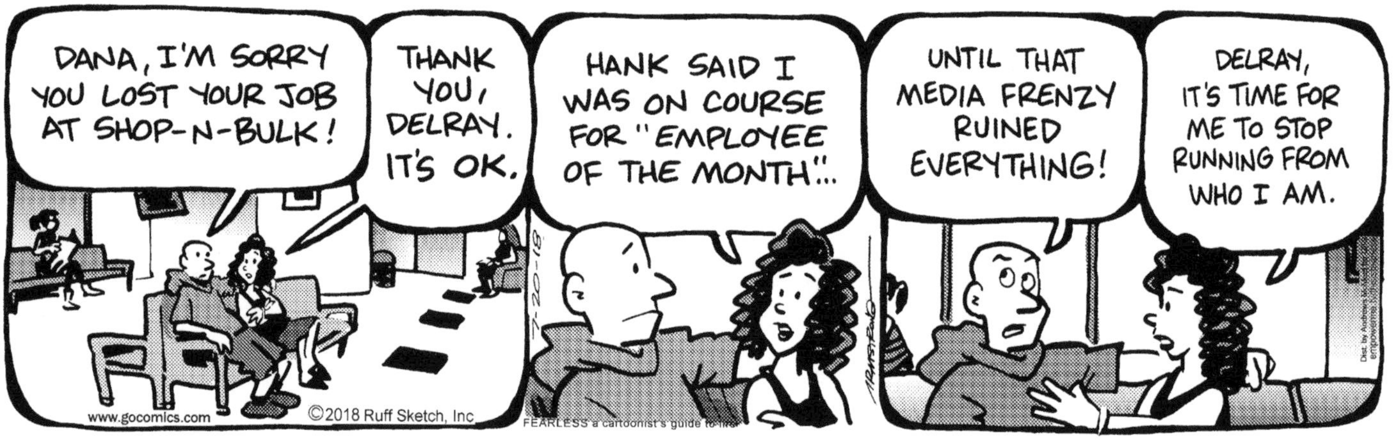
DANA, I'M SORRY YOU LOST YOUR JOB AT SHOP-N-BULK!
THANK YOU, DELRAY. IT'S OK.
HANK SAID I WAS ON COURSE FOR "EMPLOYEE OF THE MONTH"...
UNTIL THAT MEDIA FRENZY RUINED EVERYTHING!
DELRAY, IT'S TIME FOR ME TO STOP RUNNING FROM WHO I AM.
7-20-18
www.gocomics.com
©2018 Ruff Sketch, Inc
FEARLESS a cartoonist's guide to life

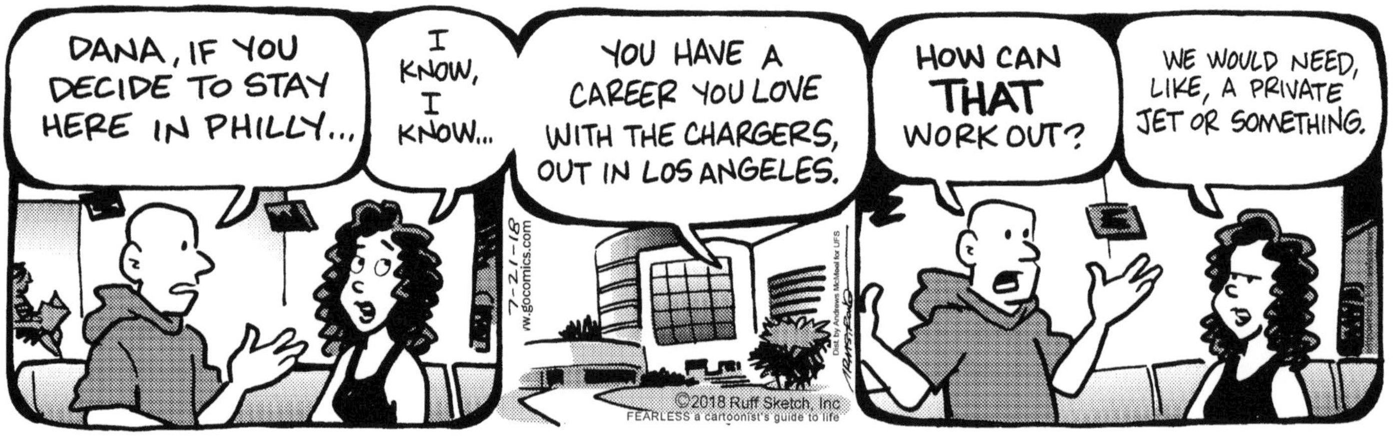
DANA, IF YOU DECIDE TO STAY HERE IN PHILLY...
I KNOW, I KNOW...
YOU HAVE A CAREER YOU LOVE WITH THE CHARGERS, OUT IN LOS ANGELES.
HOW CAN THAT WORK OUT?
WE WOULD NEED, LIKE, A PRIVATE JET OR SOMETHING.
7-21-18
©2018 Ruff Sketch, Inc
FEARLESS a cartoonist's guide to life

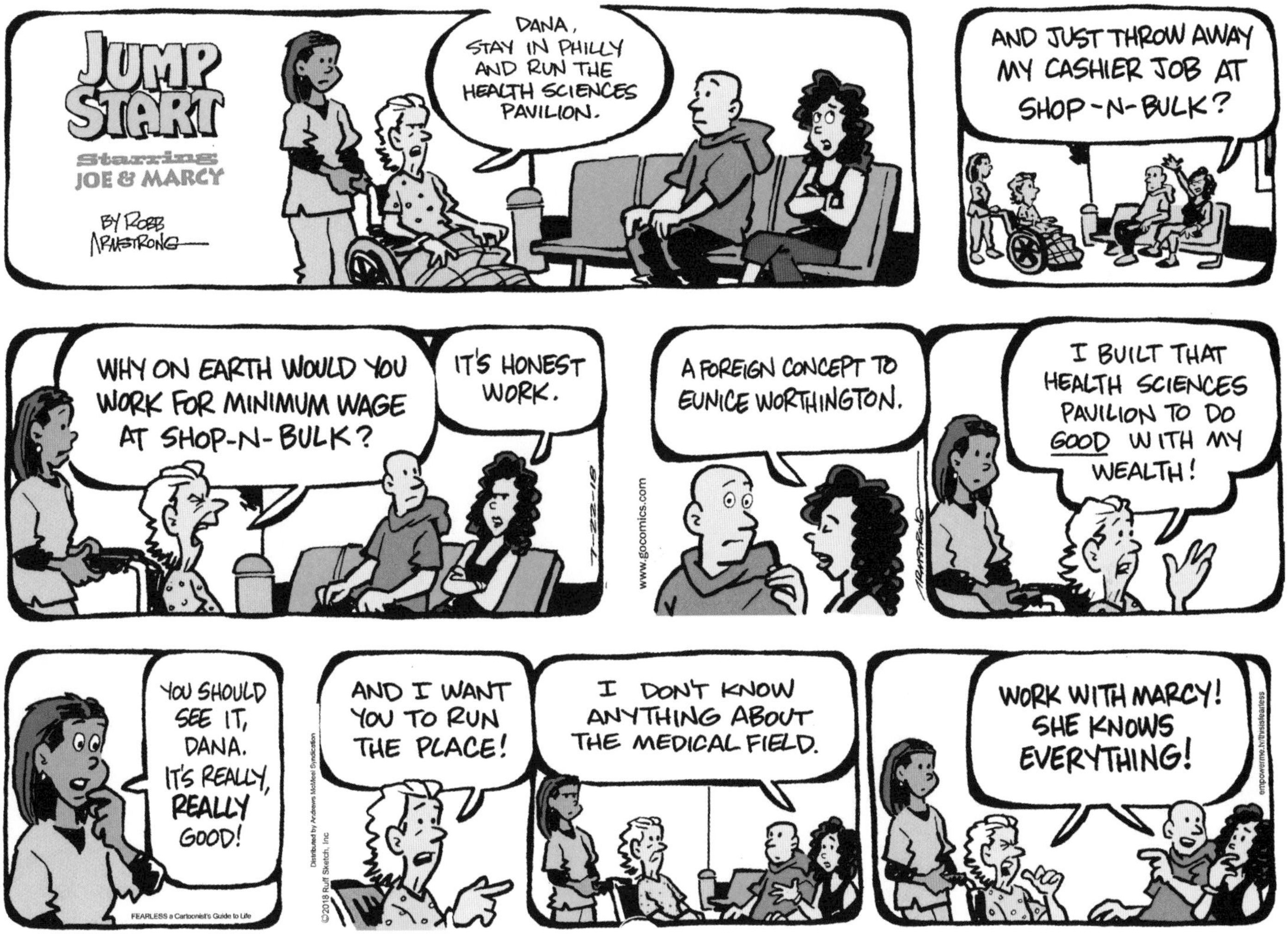
JUMP START
Starring JOE & MARCY
BY ROBB ARMSTRONG
DANA, STAY IN PHILLY AND RUN THE HEALTH SCIENCES PAVILION.
AND JUST THROW AWAY MY CASHIER JOB AT SHOP-N-BULK?
WHY ON EARTH WOULD YOU WORK FOR MINIMUM WAGE AT SHOP-N-BULK?
IT'S HONEST WORK.
7-22-18
www.gocomics.com
A FOREIGN CONCEPT TO EUNICE WORTHINGTON.
I BUILT THAT HEALTH SCIENCES PAVILION TO DO GOOD WITH MY WEALTH!
YOU SHOULD SEE IT, DANA. IT'S REALLY, REALLY GOOD!
FEARLESS a Cartoonist's Guide to Life
©2018 Ruff Sketch, Inc
Distributed by Andrews McMeel Syndication
AND I WANT YOU TO RUN THE PLACE!
I DON'T KNOW ANYTHING ABOUT THE MEDICAL FIELD.
WORK WITH MARCY! SHE KNOWS EVERYTHING!
empowerme.tv/thisisfearless

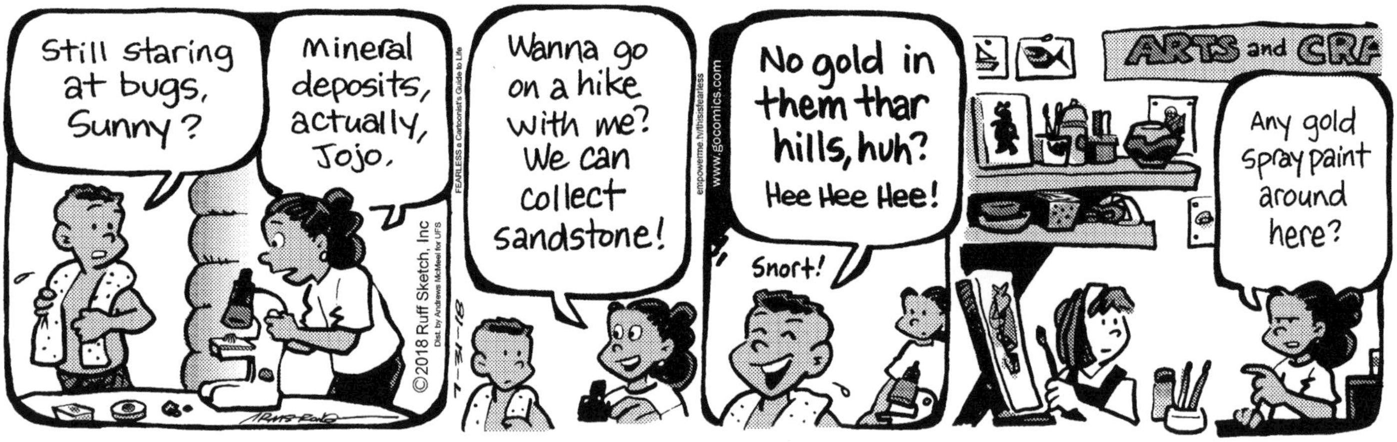
Still staring at bugs, Sunny?
Mineral deposits, actually, Jojo.
©2018 Ruff Sketch, Inc
FEARLESS a Cartoonist's Guide to Life
Wanna go on a hike with me? We can collect sandstone!
7-31-18
empowerme.tv/thisisfearless
www.gocomics.com
No gold in them thar hills, huh? Hee Hee Hee!
Snort!
ARTS and CRA
Any gold spray paint around here?

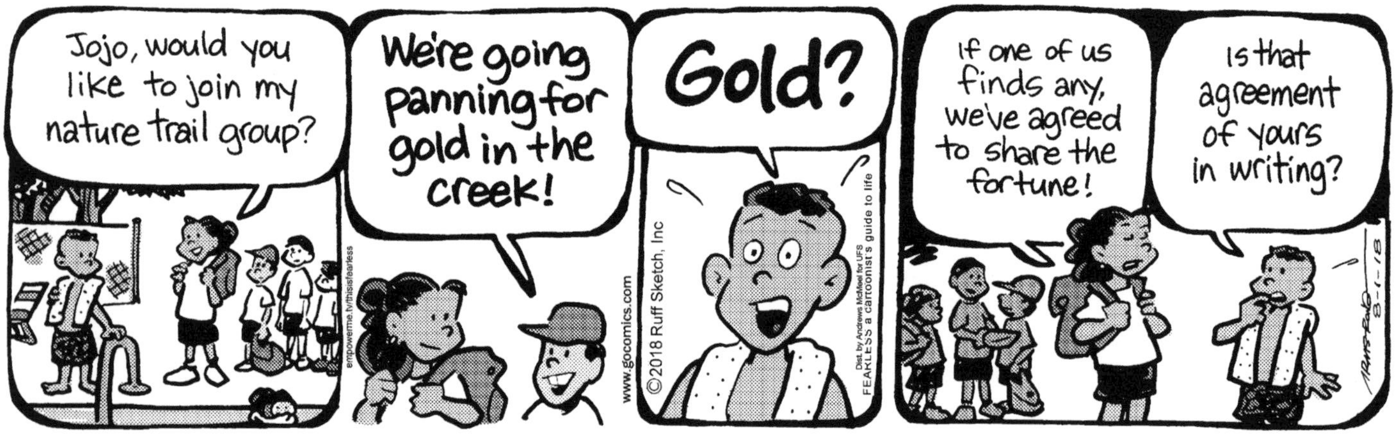
Jojo, would you like to join my nature trail group?
empowerme.tv/thisisfearless
We're going panning for gold in the creek!
www.gocomics.com
Gold?
©2018 Ruff Sketch, Inc
FEARLESS a cartoonist's guide to life
If one of us finds any, we've agreed to share the fortune!
Is that agreement of yours in writing?
8-1-18

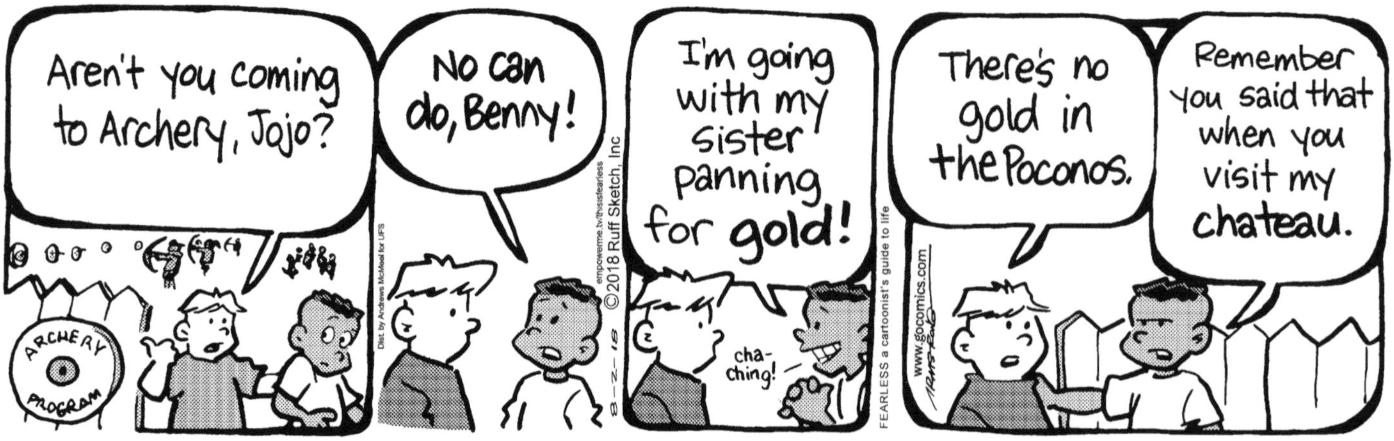
Aren't you coming to Archery, Jojo?
ARCHERY PROGRAM
No can do, Benny!
empowerme.tv/thisisfearless
©2018 Ruff Sketch, Inc
8-2-18
I'm going with my sister panning for gold!
cha-ching!
FEARLESS a cartoonist's guide to life
There's no gold in the Poconos.
www.gocomics.com
Remember you said that when you visit my chateau.

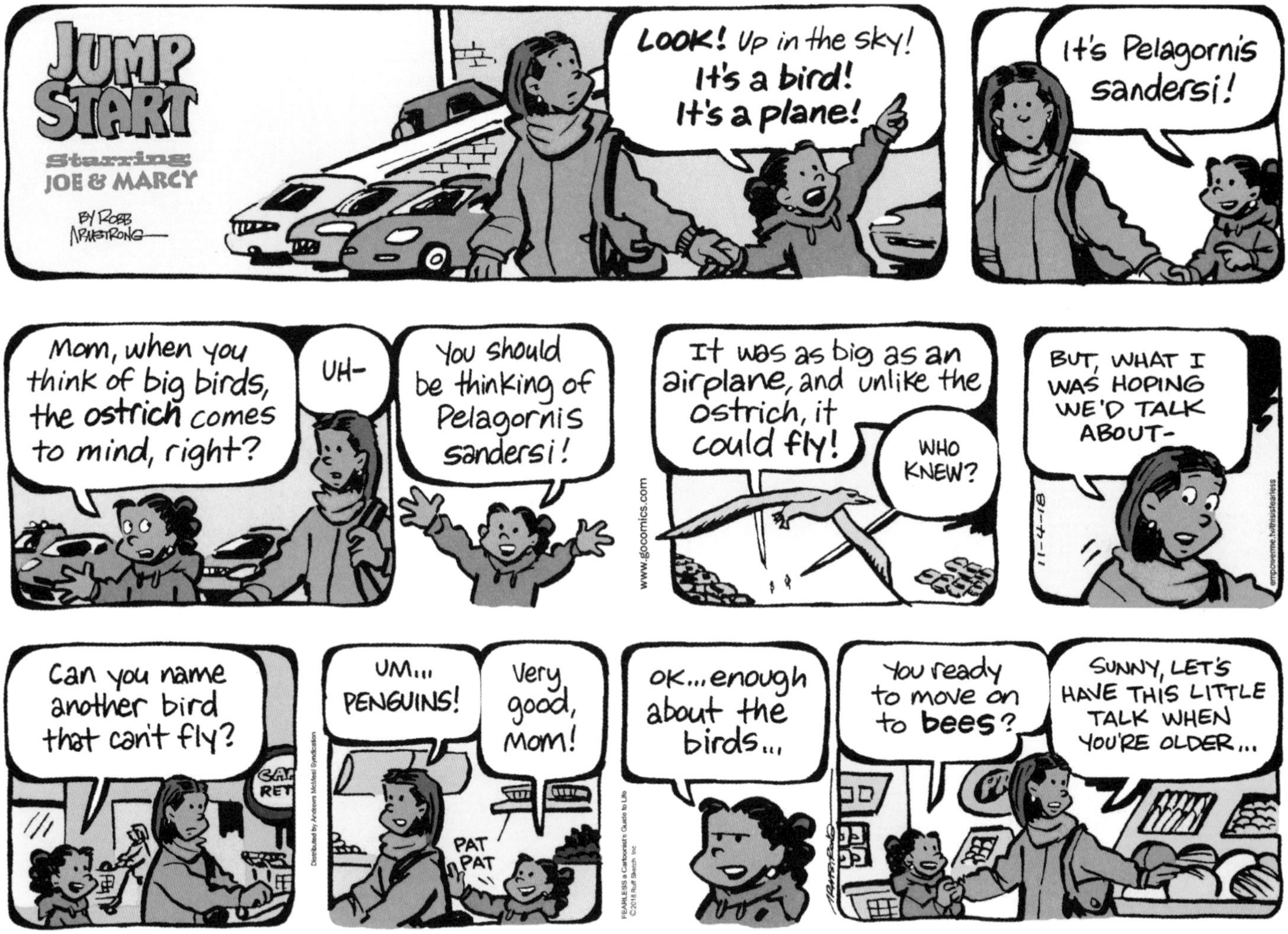
JUMP START
Starring JOE & MARCY
BY ROBB ARMSTRONG
LOOK! Up in the sky! It's a bird! It's a plane!
It's Pelagornis sandersi!
Mom, when you think of big birds, the ostrich comes to mind, right?
UH-
You should be thinking of Pelagornis sandersi!
www.gocomics.com
It was as big as an airplane, and unlike the ostrich, it could fly!
WHO KNEW?
11-4-18
BUT, WHAT I WAS HOPING WE'D TALK ABOUT-
empowerme.tv/thisisfearless
Can you name another bird that can't fly?
UM... PENGUINS!
Very good, Mom!
PAT PAT
OK...enough about the birds...
You ready to move on to bees?
SUNNY, LET'S HAVE THIS LITTLE TALK WHEN YOU'RE OLDER...

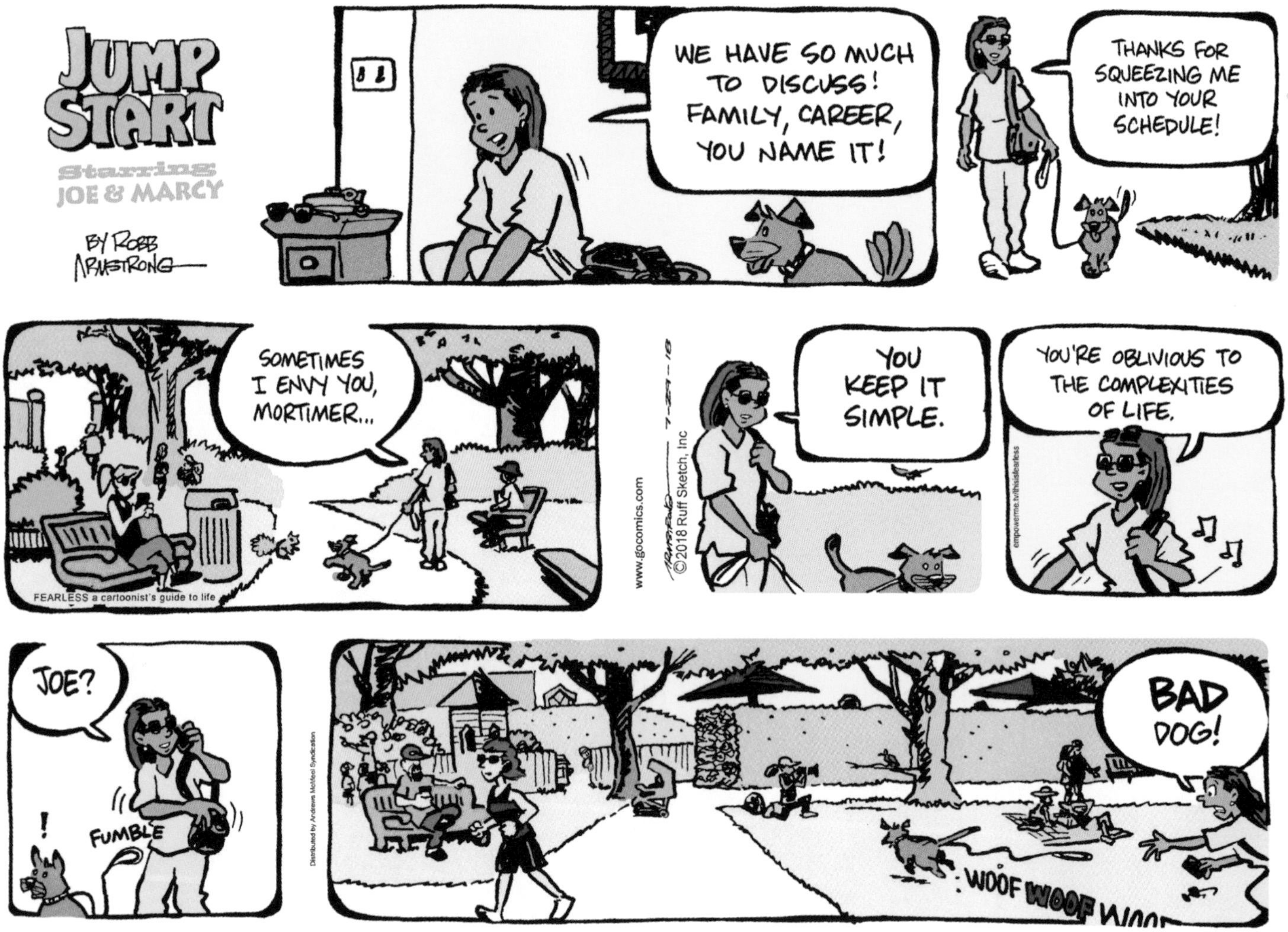
JUMP START
Starring JOE & MARCY
BY ROBB ARMSTRONG
WE HAVE SO MUCH TO DISCUSS! FAMILY, CAREER, YOU NAME IT!
THANKS FOR SQUEEZING ME INTO YOUR SCHEDULE!
SOMETIMES I ENVY YOU, MORTIMER...
FEARLESS a cartoonist's guide to life
www.gocomics.com
©2018 Ruff Sketch, Inc
YOU KEEP IT SIMPLE.
YOU'RE OBLIVIOUS TO THE COMPLEXITIES OF LIFE.
JOE?
!
FUMBLE
Distributed by Andrews McMeel Syndication
BAD DOG!
WOOF WOOF

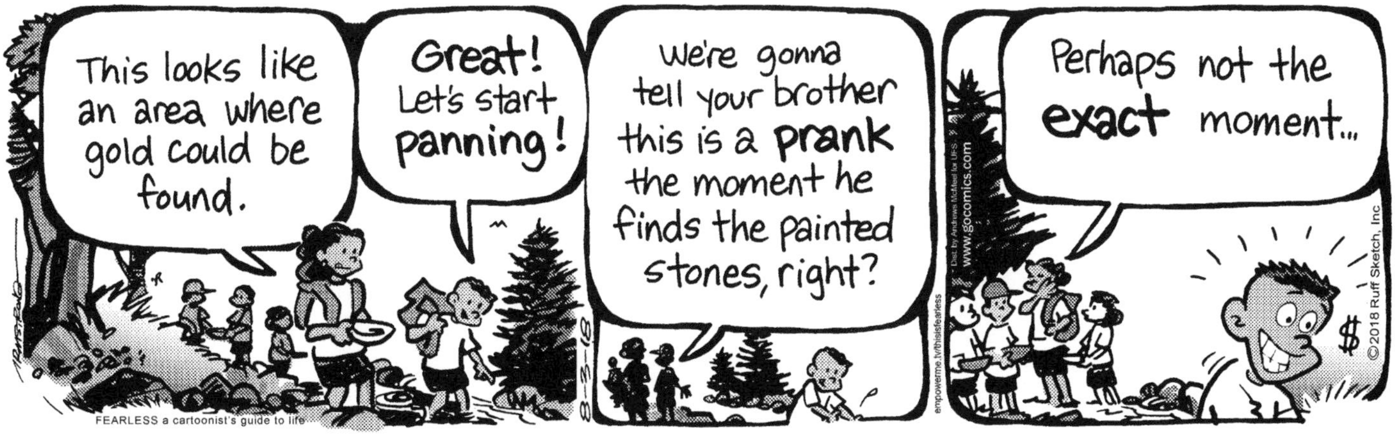

This looks like an area where gold could be found.
Great! Let's start panning!
We're gonna tell your brother this is a prank the moment he finds the painted stones, right?
Perhaps not the exact moment...
$
8-3-18
FEARLESS a cartoonist's guide to life
empowerme.tv/thisisfearless
www.gocomics.com
Dist. by Andrews McMeel for UFS
©2018 Ruff Sketch, Inc

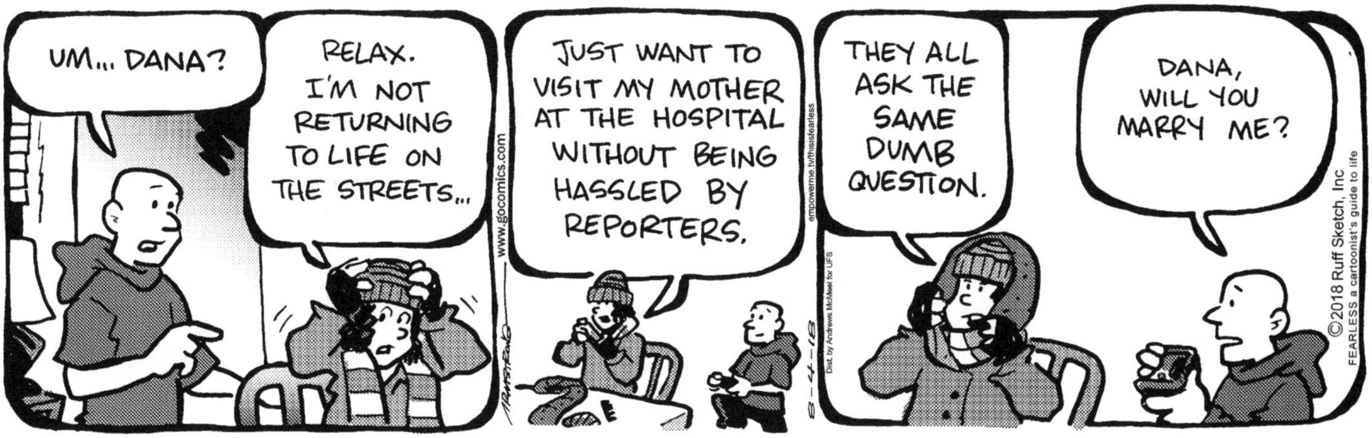

UM... DANA?
RELAX. I'M NOT RETURNING TO LIFE ON THE STREETS...
JUST WANT TO VISIT MY MOTHER AT THE HOSPITAL WITHOUT BEING HASSLED BY REPORTERS.
THEY ALL ASK THE SAME DUMB QUESTION.
DANA, WILL YOU MARRY ME?
8-4-18
www.gocomics.com
empowerme.tv/thisisfearless
Dist. by Andrews McMeel for UFS
©2018 Ruff Sketch, Inc
FEARLESS a cartoonist's guide to life

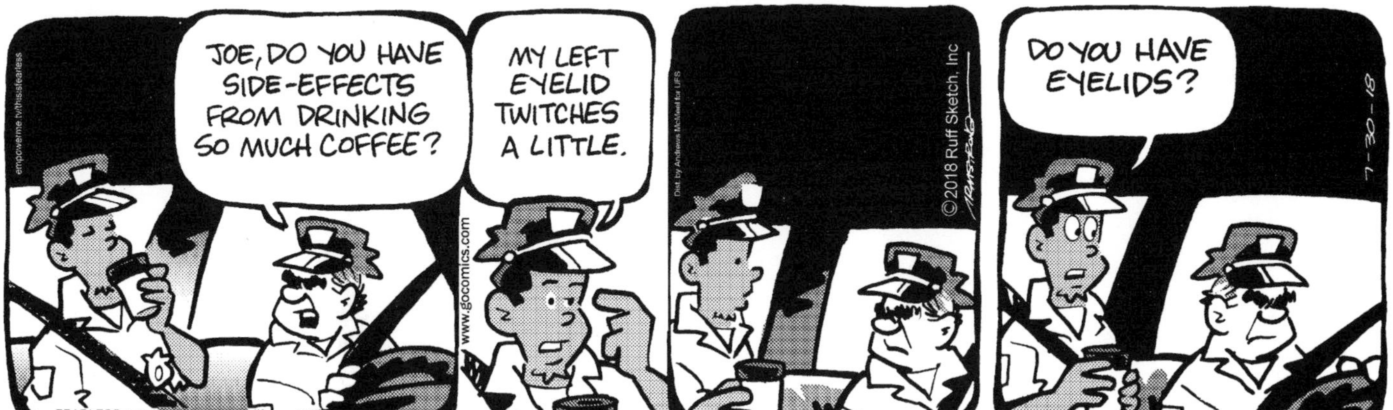

JOE, DO YOU HAVE SIDE-EFFECTS FROM DRINKING SO MUCH COFFEE?
MY LEFT EYELID TWITCHES A LITTLE.
DO YOU HAVE EYELIDS?
7-30-18
empowerme.tv/thisisfearless
www.gocomics.com
Dist. by Andrews McMeel for UFS
©2018 Ruff Sketch, Inc
FEARLESS a cartoonist's guide to life

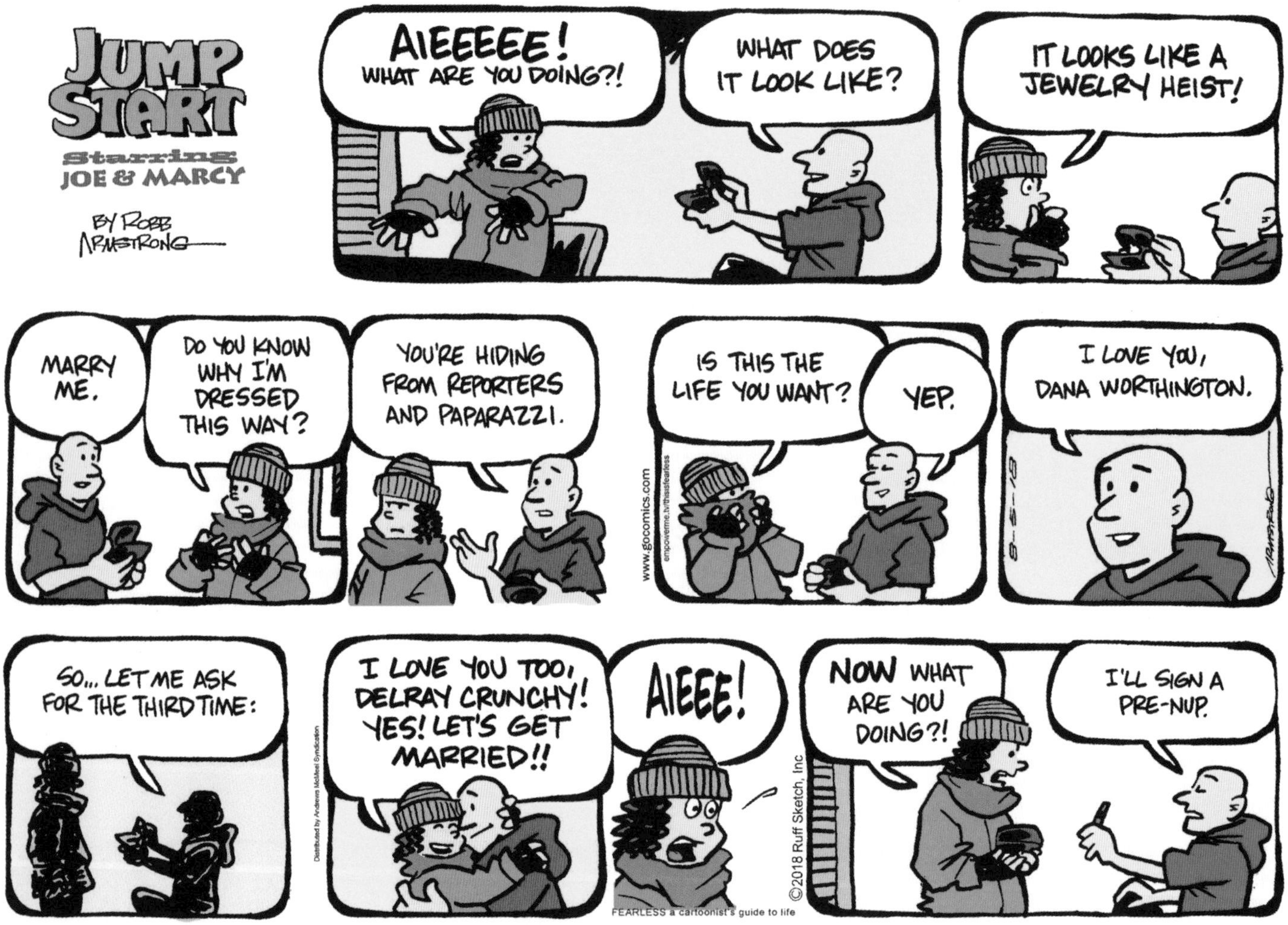
JUMP START
Starring JOE & MARCY
BY ROBB ARMSTRONG
AIEEEEE! WHAT ARE YOU DOING?!
WHAT DOES IT LOOK LIKE?
IT LOOKS LIKE A JEWELRY HEIST!
MARRY ME.
DO YOU KNOW WHY I'M DRESSED THIS WAY?
YOU'RE HIDING FROM REPORTERS AND PAPARAZZI.
IS THIS THE LIFE YOU WANT?
YEP.
I LOVE YOU, DANA WORTHINGTON.
SO... LET ME ASK FOR THE THIRD TIME:
I LOVE YOU TOO, DELRAY CRUNCHY! YES! LET'S GET MARRIED!!
AIEEE!
NOW WHAT ARE YOU DOING?!
I'LL SIGN A PRE-NUP.
www.gocomics.com
©2018 Ruff Sketch, Inc
FEARLESS a cartoonist's guide to life

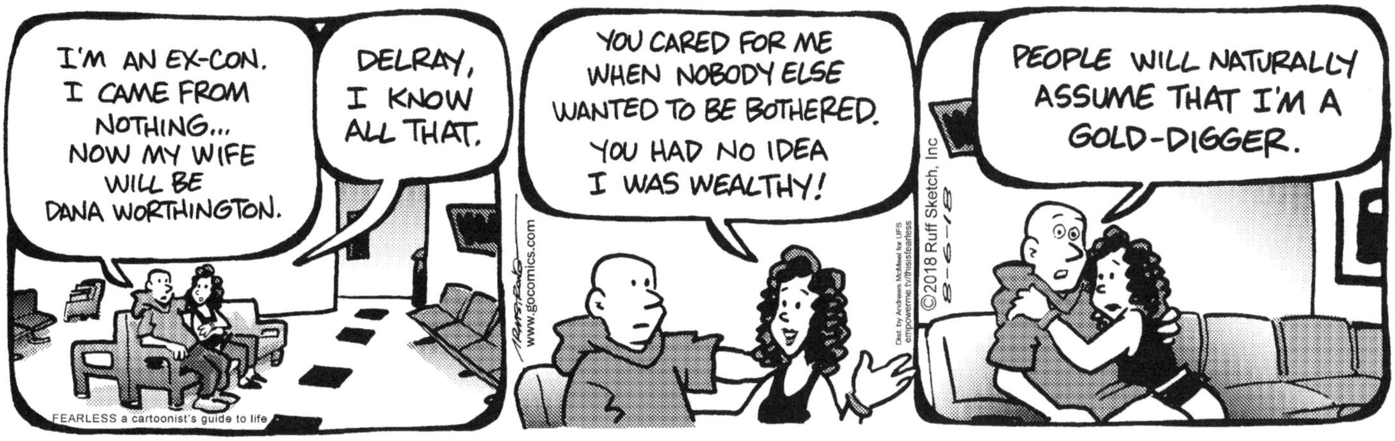
I'M AN EX-CON. I CAME FROM NOTHING... NOW MY WIFE WILL BE DANA WORTHINGTON.
DELRAY, I KNOW ALL THAT.
YOU CARED FOR ME WHEN NOBODY ELSE WANTED TO BE BOTHERED.
YOU HAD NO IDEA I WAS WEALTHY!
PEOPLE WILL NATURALLY ASSUME THAT I'M A GOLD-DIGGER.
FEARLESS a cartoonist's guide to life
www.gocomics.com
©2018 Ruff Sketch, Inc
8-6-18

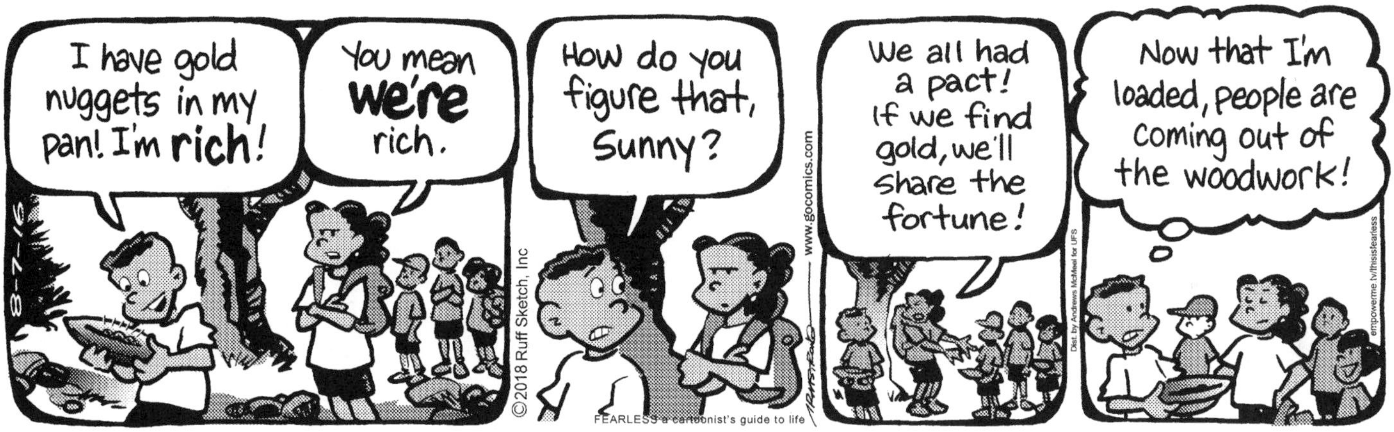
I have gold nuggets in my pan! I'm **rich**!
You mean **we're** rich.
How do you figure that, Sunny?
We all had a pact! If we find gold, we'll share the fortune!
Now that I'm loaded, people are coming out of the woodwork!
8-7-18
©2018 Ruff Sketch, Inc
FEARLESS a cartoonist's guide to life
www.gocomics.com

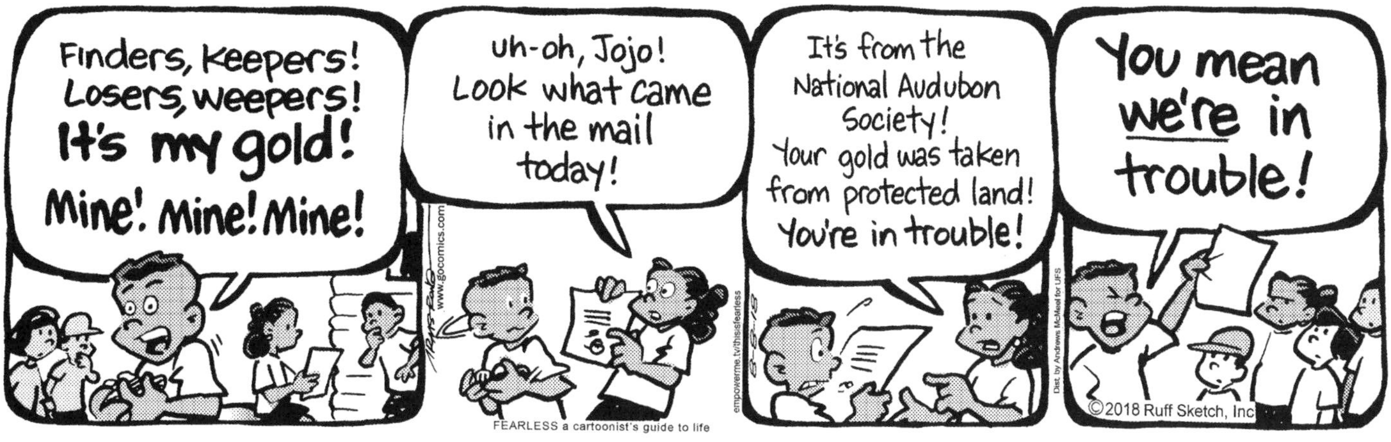
Finders, Keepers! Losers, weepers! **It's my gold! Mine! Mine! Mine!**
Uh-oh, Jojo! Look what came in the mail today!
It's from the National Audubon Society! Your gold was taken from protected land! You're in trouble!
You mean we're in trouble!
www.gocomics.com
FEARLESS a cartoonist's guide to life
8-8-18
©2018 Ruff Sketch, Inc

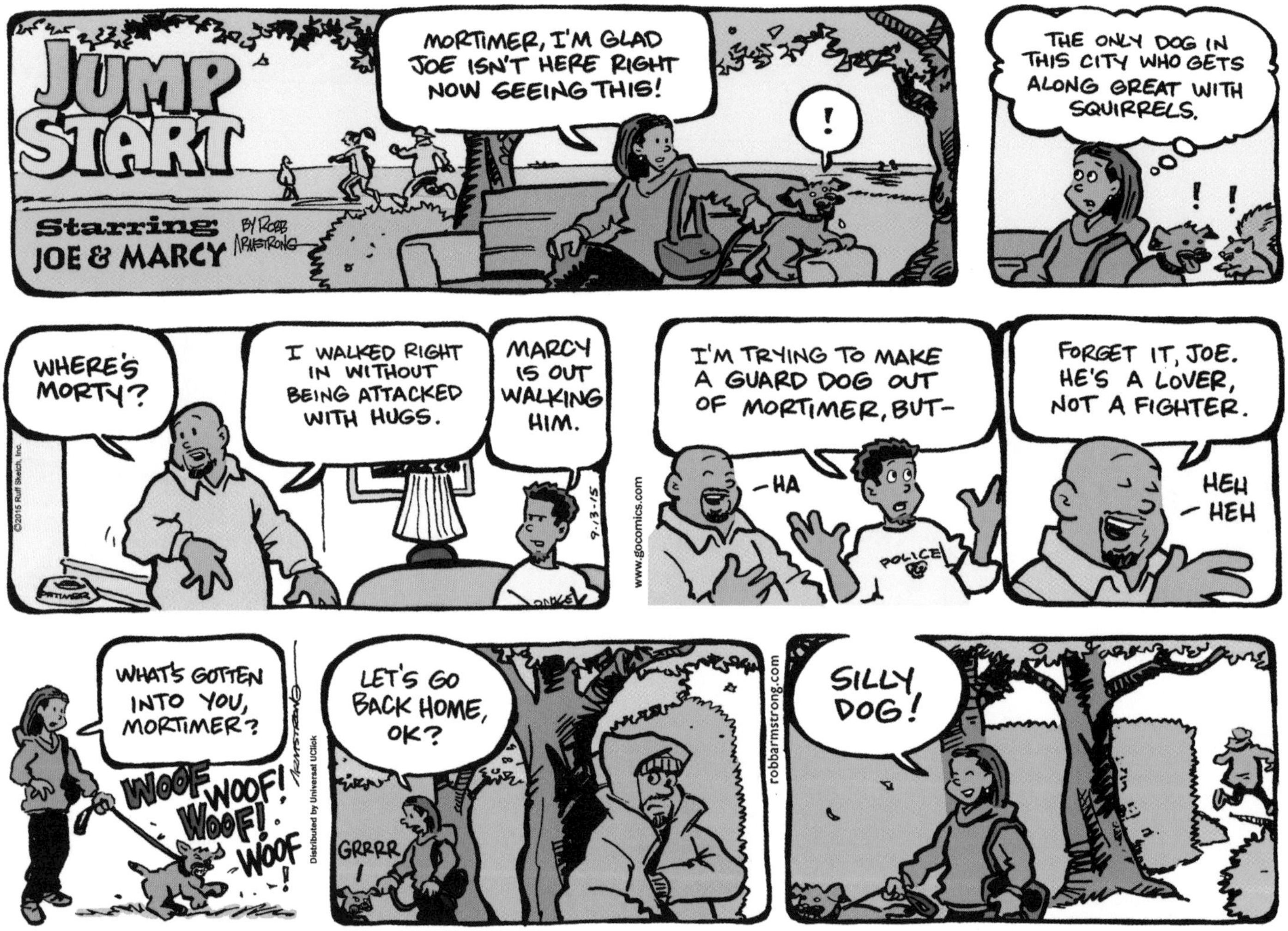
JUMP START
Starring JOE & MARCY
BY ROBB ARMSTRONG
MORTIMER, I'M GLAD JOE ISN'T HERE RIGHT NOW SEEING THIS!
!
THE ONLY DOG IN THIS CITY WHO GETS ALONG GREAT WITH SQUIRRELS.
! !
WHERE'S MORTY?
I WALKED RIGHT IN WITHOUT BEING ATTACKED WITH HUGS.
MARCY IS OUT WALKING HIM.
©2015 Ruff Sketch, Inc
9-13-15
www.gocomics.com
I'M TRYING TO MAKE A GUARD DOG OUT OF MORTIMER, BUT-
-HA
POLICE
FORGET IT, JOE. HE'S A LOVER, NOT A FIGHTER.
HEH -HEH
WHAT'S GOTTEN INTO YOU, MORTIMER?
WOOF WOOF! WOOF! WOOF!
Distributed by Universal UClick
LET'S GO BACK HOME, OK?
GRRRR !
robbarmstrong.com
SILLY DOG!

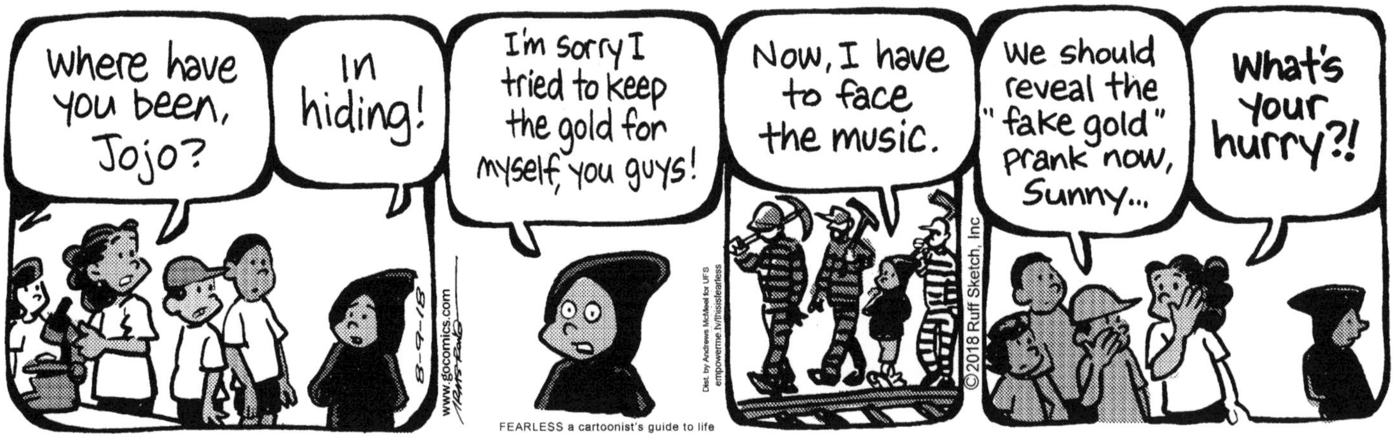
Where have you been, Jojo?
In hiding!
I'm sorry I tried to keep the gold for myself, you guys!
Now, I have to face the music.
We should reveal the "fake gold" prank now, Sunny...
What's your hurry?!
8-9-18
www.gocomics.com
Dist. by Andrews McMeel for UFS
empowerme.tv/thisisfearless
©2018 Ruff Sketch, Inc
FEARLESS a cartoonist's guide to life

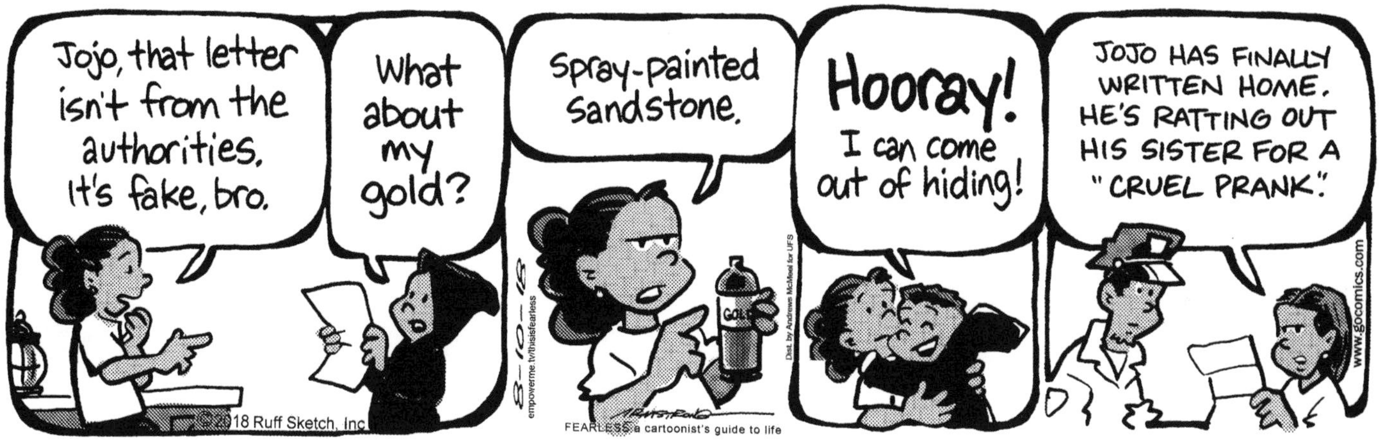
Jojo, that letter isn't from the authorities. It's fake, bro.
What about my gold?
Spray-painted sandstone.
Hooray! I can come out of hiding!
JOJO HAS FINALLY WRITTEN HOME. HE'S RATTING OUT HIS SISTER FOR A "CRUEL PRANK".
©2018 Ruff Sketch, Inc
8-10-18
empowerme.tv/thisisfearless
Dist. by Andrews McMeel for UFS
www.gocomics.com
FEARLESS a cartoonist's guide to life

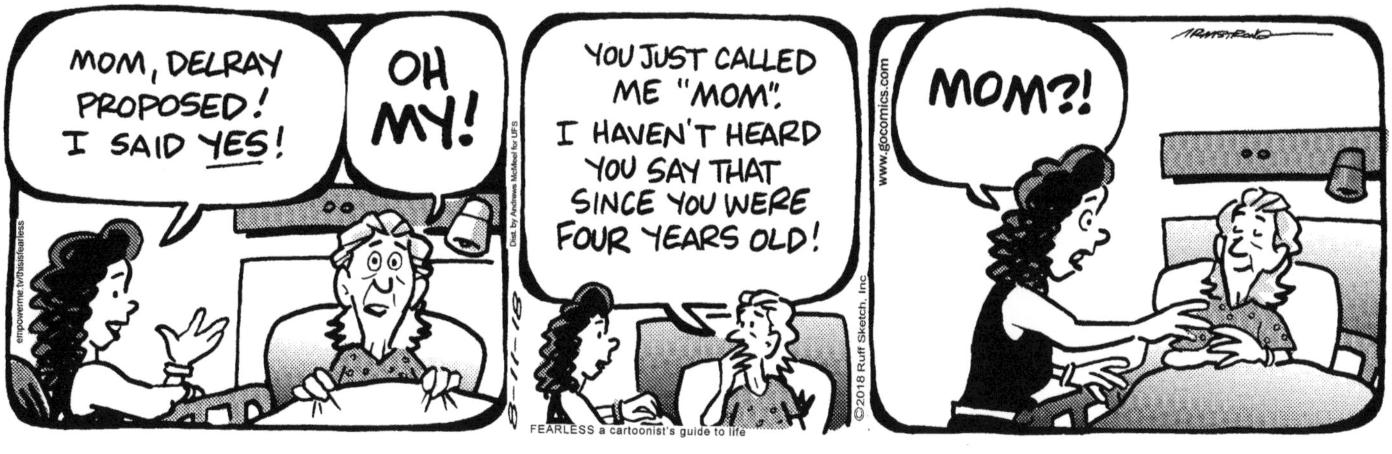
MOM, DELRAY PROPOSED! I SAID YES!
OH MY!
YOU JUST CALLED ME "MOM". I HAVEN'T HEARD YOU SAY THAT SINCE YOU WERE FOUR YEARS OLD!
MOM?!
empowerme.tv/thisisfearless
Dist. by Andrews McMeel for UFS
8-11-18
www.gocomics.com
©2018 Ruff Sketch, Inc
FEARLESS a cartoonist's guide to life

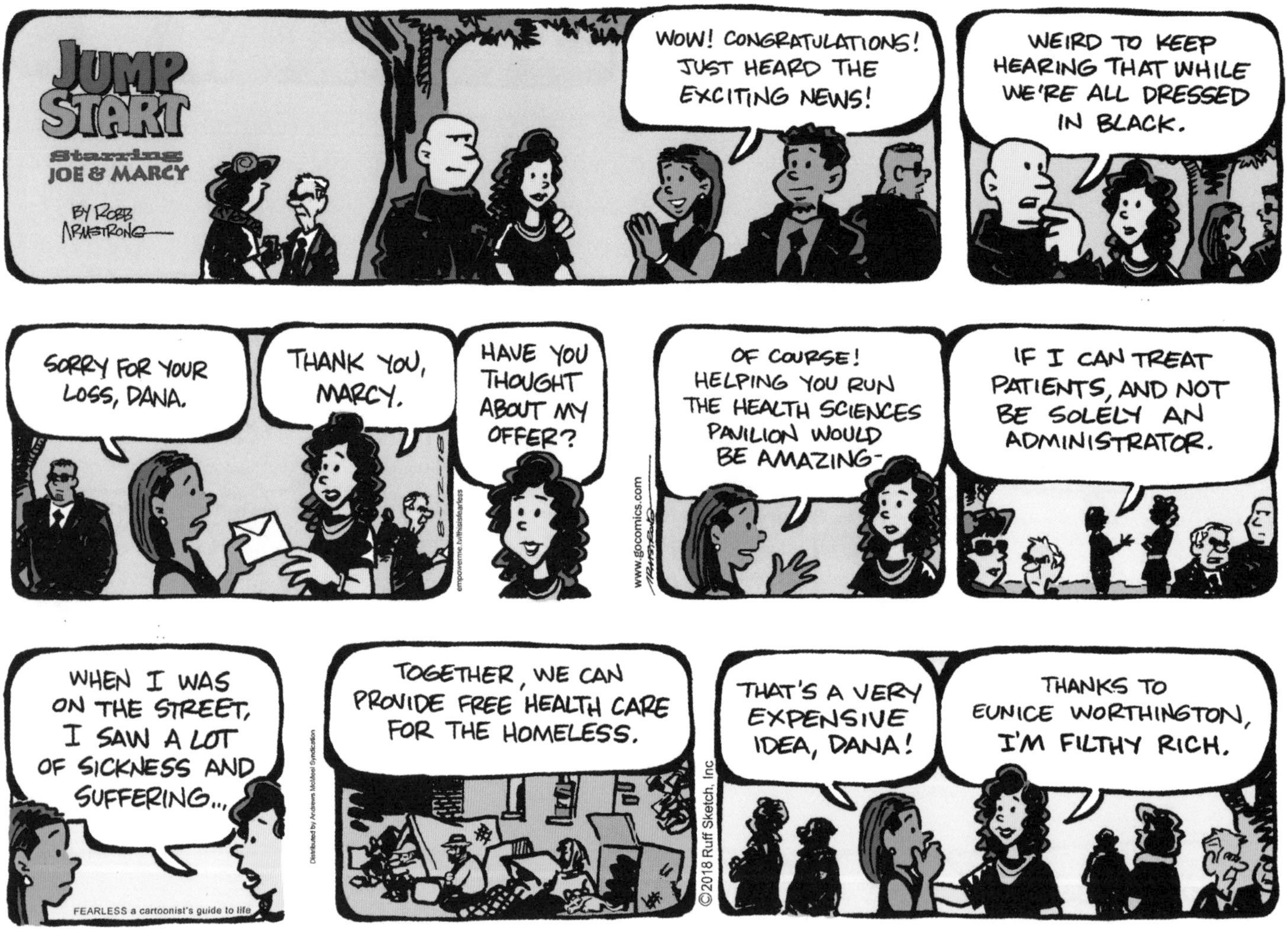
JUMP START
Starring JOE & MARCY
BY ROBB ARMSTRONG
WOW! CONGRATULATIONS! JUST HEARD THE EXCITING NEWS!
WEIRD TO KEEP HEARING THAT WHILE WE'RE ALL DRESSED IN BLACK.
SORRY FOR YOUR LOSS, DANA.
THANK YOU, MARCY.
HAVE YOU THOUGHT ABOUT MY OFFER?
OF COURSE! HELPING YOU RUN THE HEALTH SCIENCES PAVILION WOULD BE AMAZING-
IF I CAN TREAT PATIENTS, AND NOT BE SOLELY AN ADMINISTRATOR.
WHEN I WAS ON THE STREET, I SAW A LOT OF SICKNESS AND SUFFERING...
TOGETHER, WE CAN PROVIDE FREE HEALTH CARE FOR THE HOMELESS.
THAT'S A VERY EXPENSIVE IDEA, DANA!
THANKS TO EUNICE WORTHINGTON, I'M FILTHY RICH.
8-12-18
empowerme.tv/thisisfearless
www.gocomics.com
FEARLESS a cartoonist's guide to life
Distributed by Andrews McMeel Syndication
©2018 Ruff Sketch, Inc

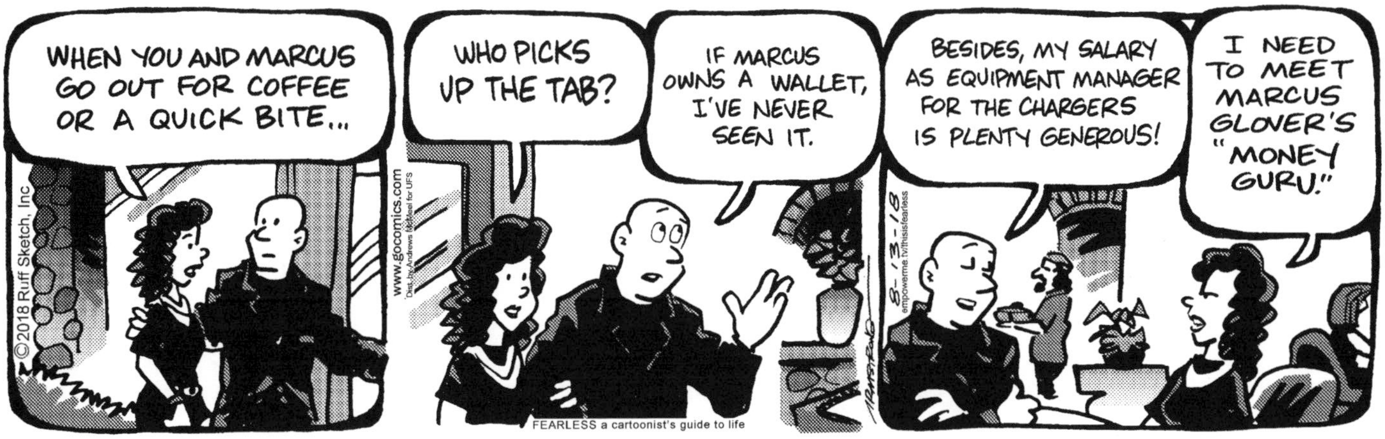
WHEN YOU AND MARCUS GO OUT FOR COFFEE OR A QUICK BITE...
WHO PICKS UP THE TAB?
IF MARCUS OWNS A WALLET, I'VE NEVER SEEN IT.
BESIDES, MY SALARY AS EQUIPMENT MANAGER FOR THE CHARGERS IS PLENTY GENEROUS!
I NEED TO MEET MARCUS GLOVER'S "MONEY GURU."
©2018 Ruff Sketch, Inc
www.gocomics.com
Dist. by Andrews McMeel for UFS
8-13-18
empowerme.tv/thisisfearless
FEARLESS a cartoonist's guide to life

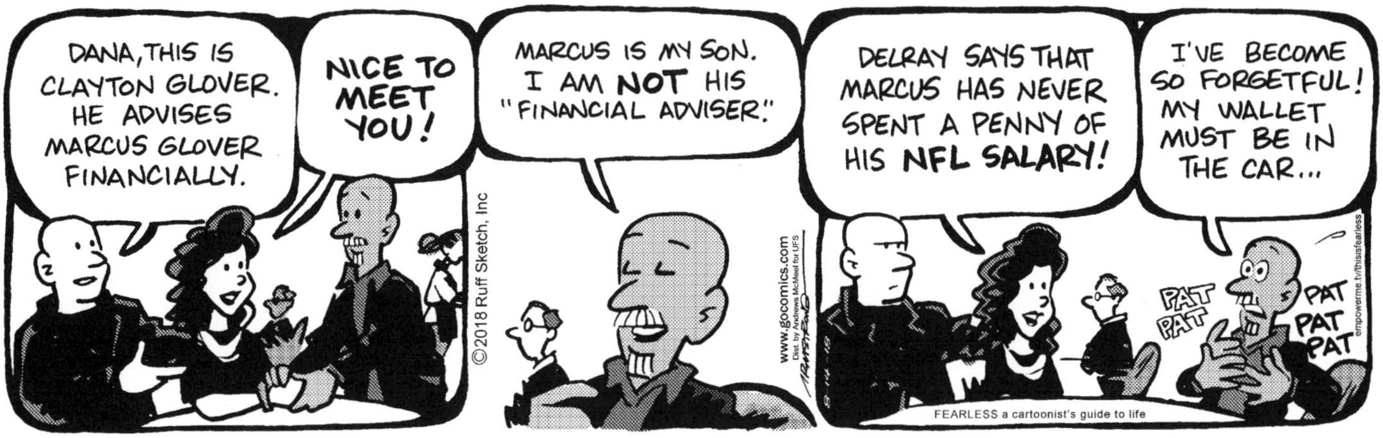
DANA, THIS IS CLAYTON GLOVER. HE ADVISES MARCUS GLOVER FINANCIALLY.
NICE TO MEET YOU!
MARCUS IS MY SON. I AM NOT HIS "FINANCIAL ADVISER."
DELRAY SAYS THAT MARCUS HAS NEVER SPENT A PENNY OF HIS NFL SALARY!
I'VE BECOME SO FORGETFUL! MY WALLET MUST BE IN THE CAR...
PAT PAT
PAT PAT PAT
©2018 Ruff Sketch, Inc
www.gocomics.com
Dist. by Andrews McMeel for UFS
empowerme.tv/thisisfearless
FEARLESS a cartoonist's guide to life

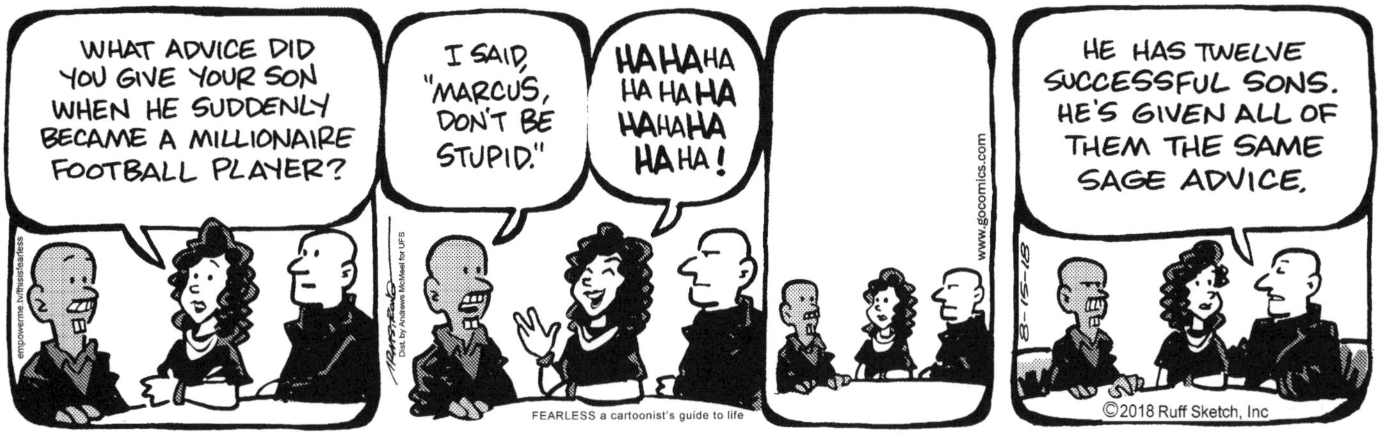
WHAT ADVICE DID YOU GIVE YOUR SON WHEN HE SUDDENLY BECAME A MILLIONAIRE FOOTBALL PLAYER?
I SAID, "MARCUS, DON'T BE STUPID."
HAHAHA HA HA HA HAHAHA HA HA!
HE HAS TWELVE SUCCESSFUL SONS. HE'S GIVEN ALL OF THEM THE SAME SAGE ADVICE.
empowerme.tv/thisisfearless
Dist. by Andrews McMeel for UFS
www.gocomics.com
8-15-18
FEARLESS a cartoonist's guide to life
©2018 Ruff Sketch, Inc

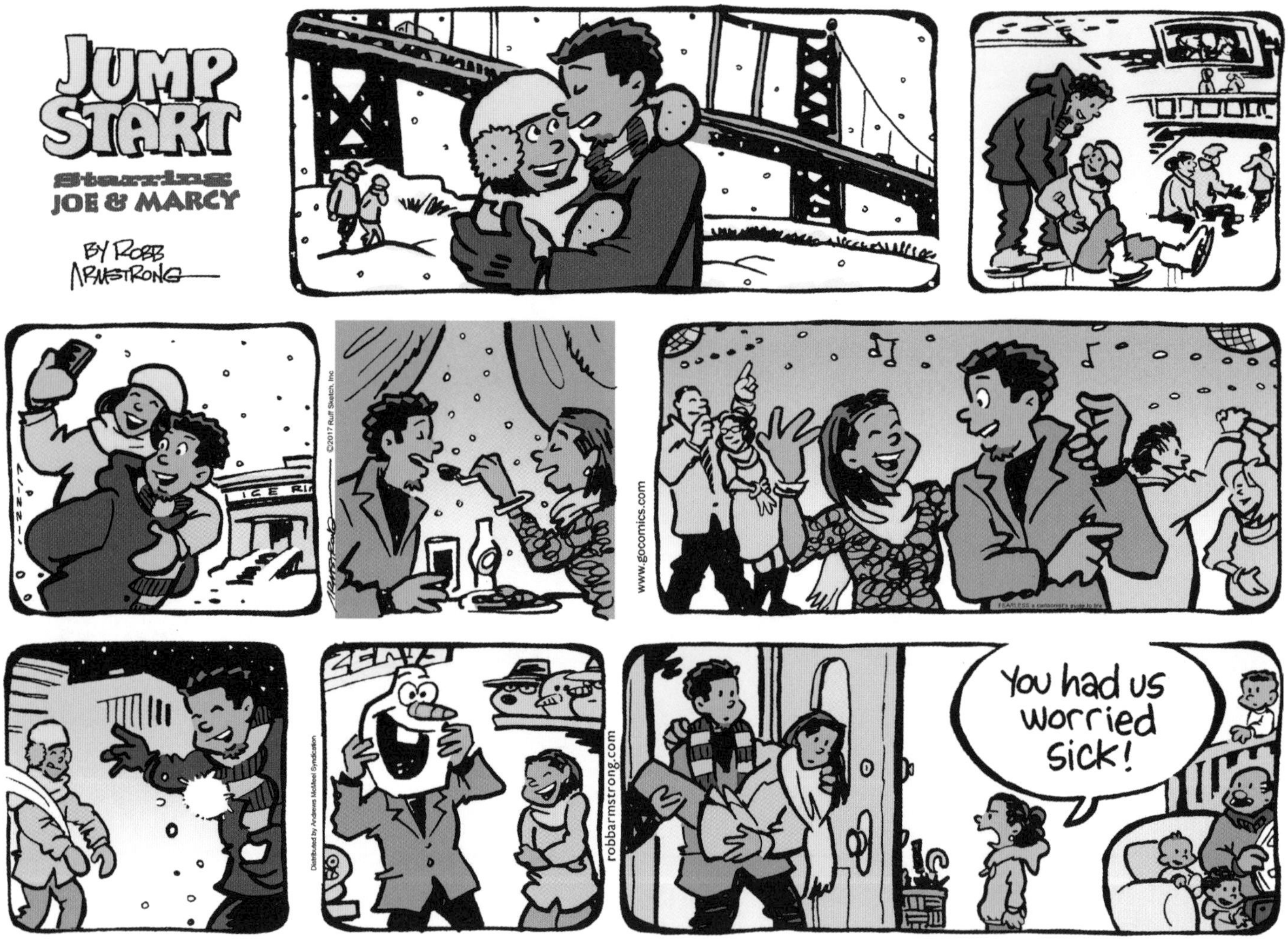
JUMP START
Starring JOE & MARCY
BY ROBB ARMSTRONG
©2017 Ruff Sketch, Inc
www.gocomics.com
Distributed by Andrews McMeel Syndication
robbarmstrong.com
You had us worried sick!

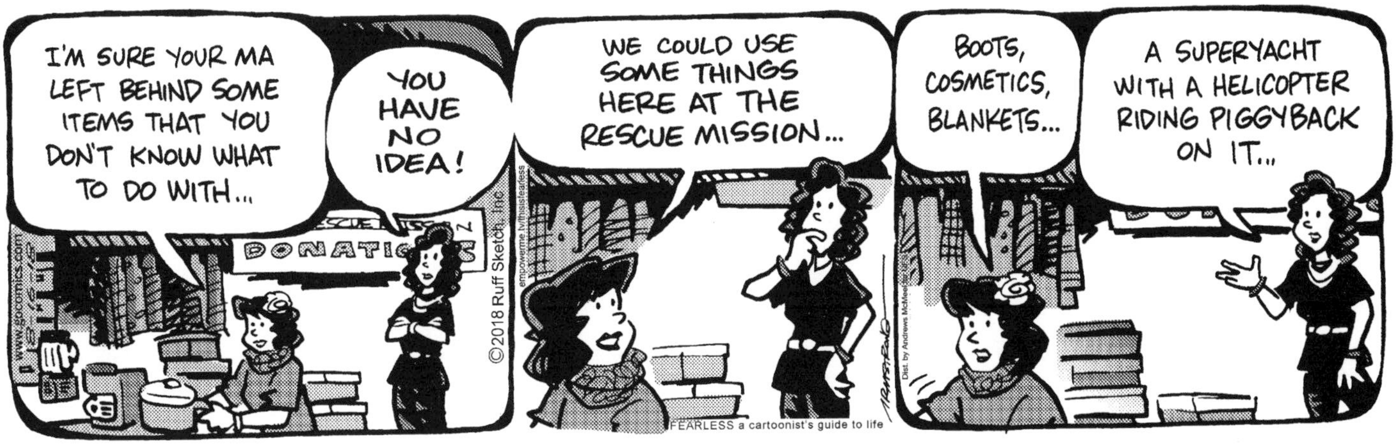
I'M SURE YOUR MA LEFT BEHIND SOME ITEMS THAT YOU DON'T KNOW WHAT TO DO WITH...
YOU HAVE NO IDEA!
DONATIO
WE COULD USE SOME THINGS HERE AT THE RESCUE MISSION...
BOOTS, COSMETICS, BLANKETS...
A SUPERYACHT WITH A HELICOPTER RIDING PIGGYBACK ON IT...
©2018 Ruff Sketch, Inc
FEARLESS a cartoonist's guide to life

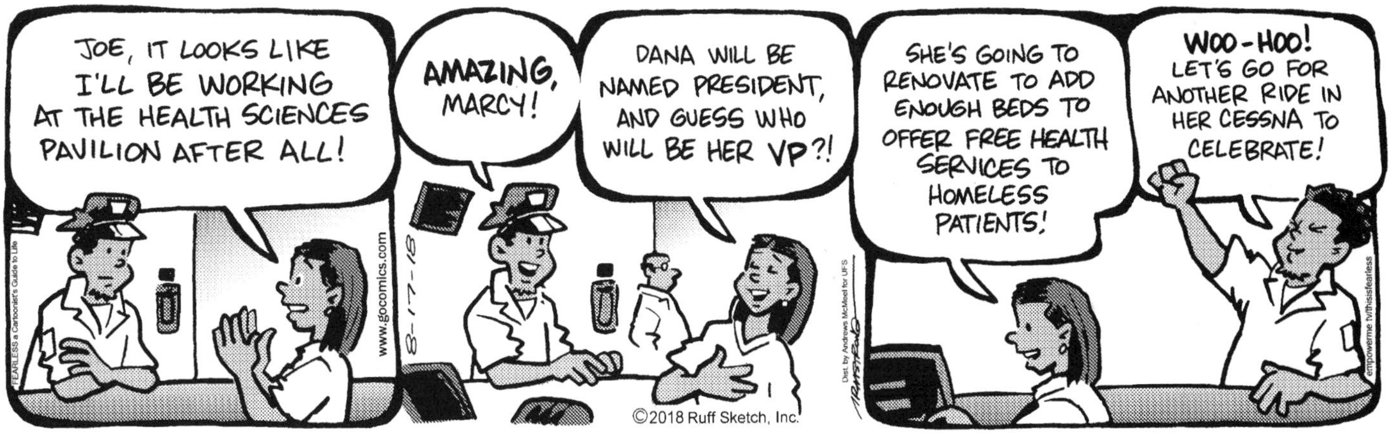
JOE, IT LOOKS LIKE I'LL BE WORKING AT THE HEALTH SCIENCES PAVILION AFTER ALL!
AMAZING, MARCY!
DANA WILL BE NAMED PRESIDENT, AND GUESS WHO WILL BE HER VP?!
SHE'S GOING TO RENOVATE TO ADD ENOUGH BEDS TO OFFER FREE HEALTH SERVICES TO HOMELESS PATIENTS!
WOO-HOO! LET'S GO FOR ANOTHER RIDE IN HER CESSNA TO CELEBRATE!
www.gocomics.com
8-17-18
©2018 Ruff Sketch, Inc.

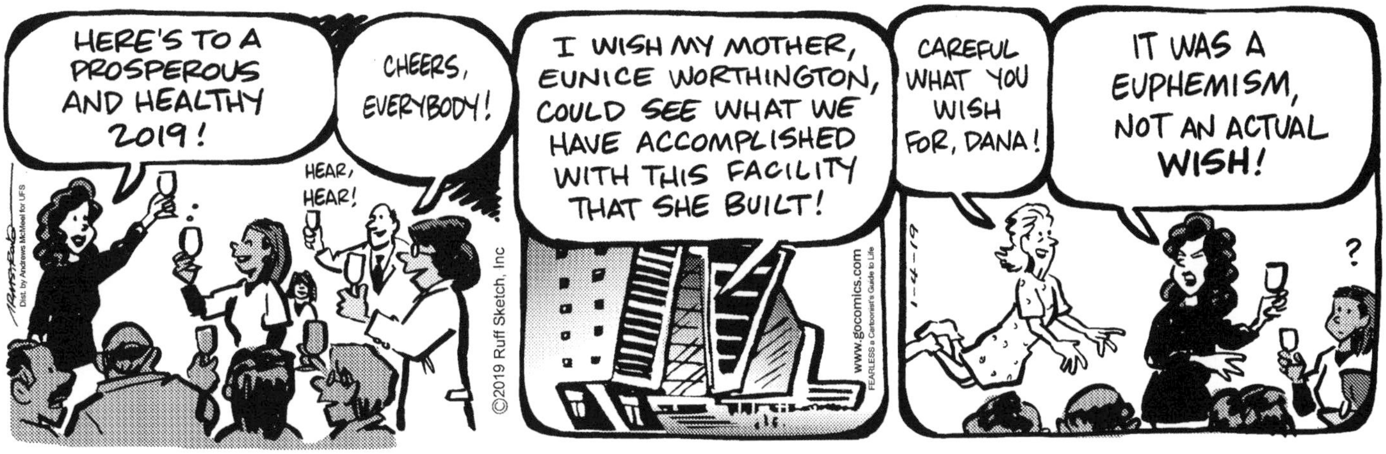
HERE'S TO A PROSPEROUS AND HEALTHY 2019!
CHEERS, EVERYBODY!
HEAR, HEAR!
I WISH MY MOTHER, EUNICE WORTHINGTON, COULD SEE WHAT WE HAVE ACCOMPLISHED WITH THIS FACILITY THAT SHE BUILT!
CAREFUL WHAT YOU WISH FOR, DANA!
IT WAS A EUPHEMISM, NOT AN ACTUAL WISH!
?
©2019 Ruff Sketch, Inc
www.gocomics.com
1-4-19

Crunchy
36"x24" mixed media on wood
by Robb Armstrong
Photographed by Johnny Dycus

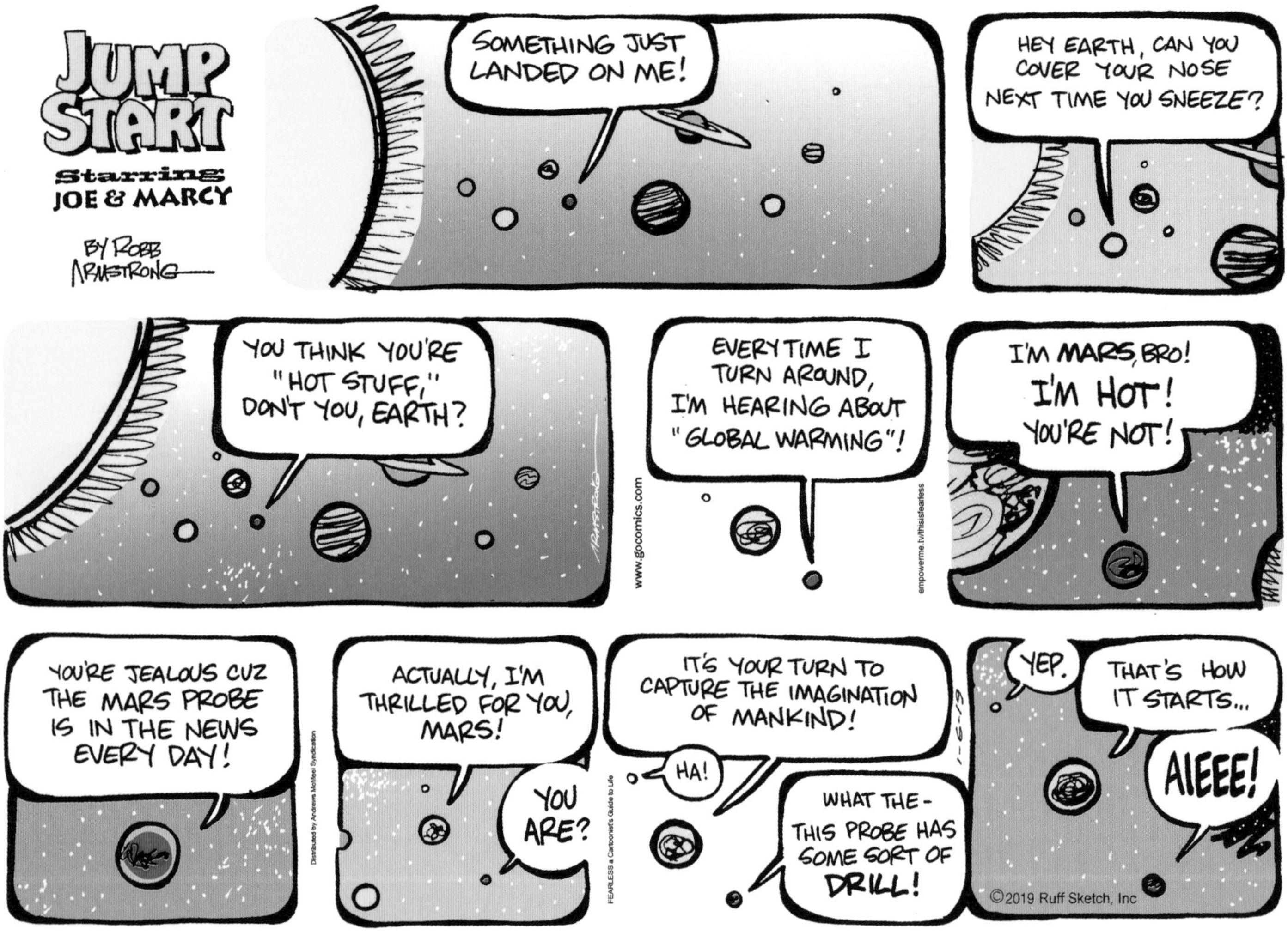
JUMP START
Starring JOE & MARCY
BY ROBB ARMSTRONG
SOMETHING JUST LANDED ON ME!
HEY EARTH, CAN YOU COVER YOUR NOSE NEXT TIME YOU SNEEZE?
YOU THINK YOU'RE "HOT STUFF," DON'T YOU, EARTH?
www.gocomics.com
EVERY TIME I TURN AROUND, I'M HEARING ABOUT "GLOBAL WARMING"!
empowerme.tv/thisisfearless
I'M MARS, BRO! I'M HOT! YOU'RE NOT!
YOU'RE JEALOUS CUZ THE MARS PROBE IS IN THE NEWS EVERY DAY!
Distributed by Andrews McMeel Syndication
ACTUALLY, I'M THRILLED FOR YOU, MARS!
YOU ARE?
FEARLESS a Cartoonist's Guide to Life
IT'S YOUR TURN TO CAPTURE THE IMAGINATION OF MANKIND!
HA!
WHAT THE - THIS PROBE HAS SOME SORT OF DRILL!
1-6-19
YEP.
THAT'S HOW IT STARTS...
AIEEE!
©2019 Ruff Sketch, Inc

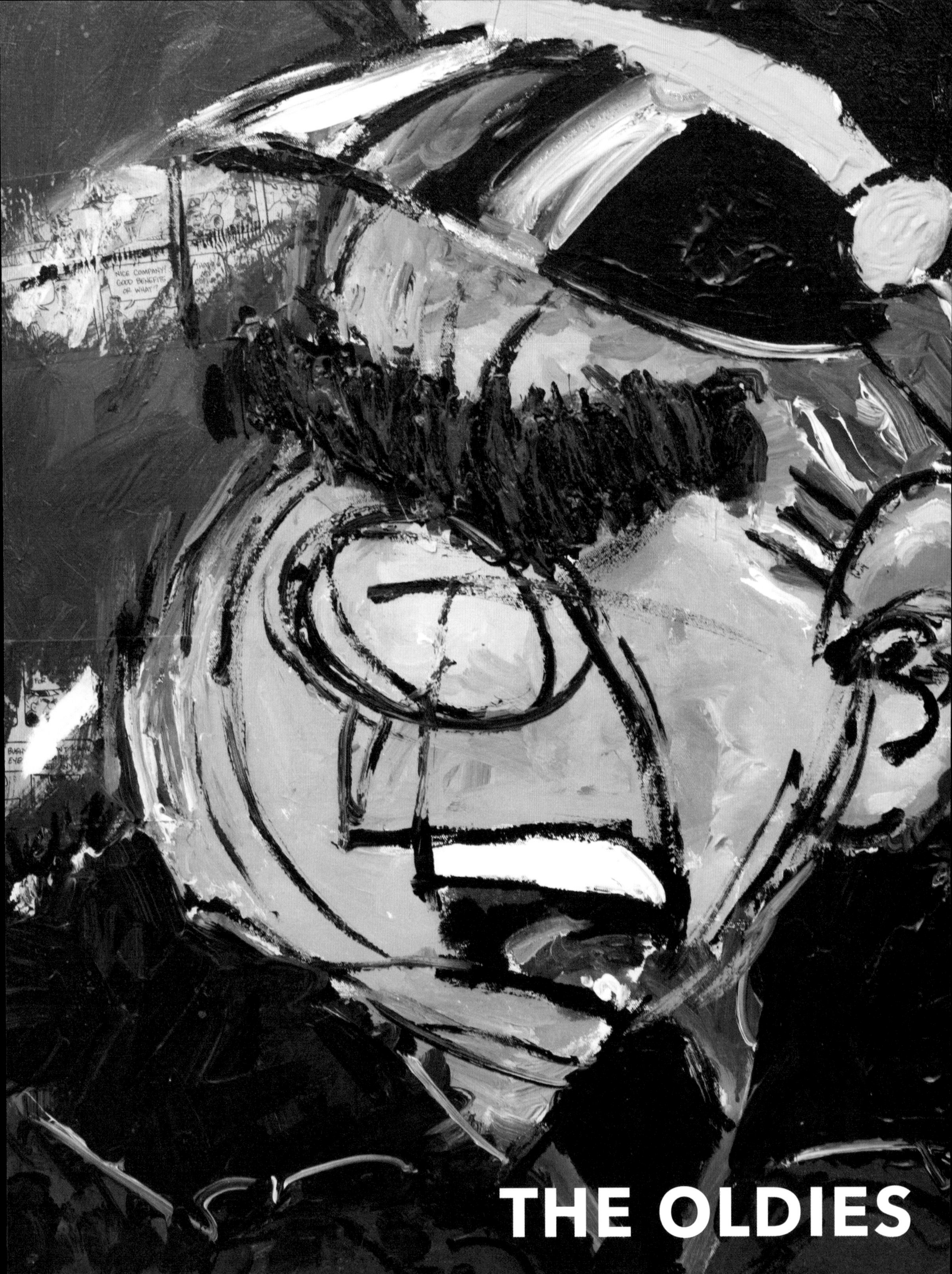
NICE COMPANY! GOOD BENEFITS OR WHAT!?

THE OLDIES

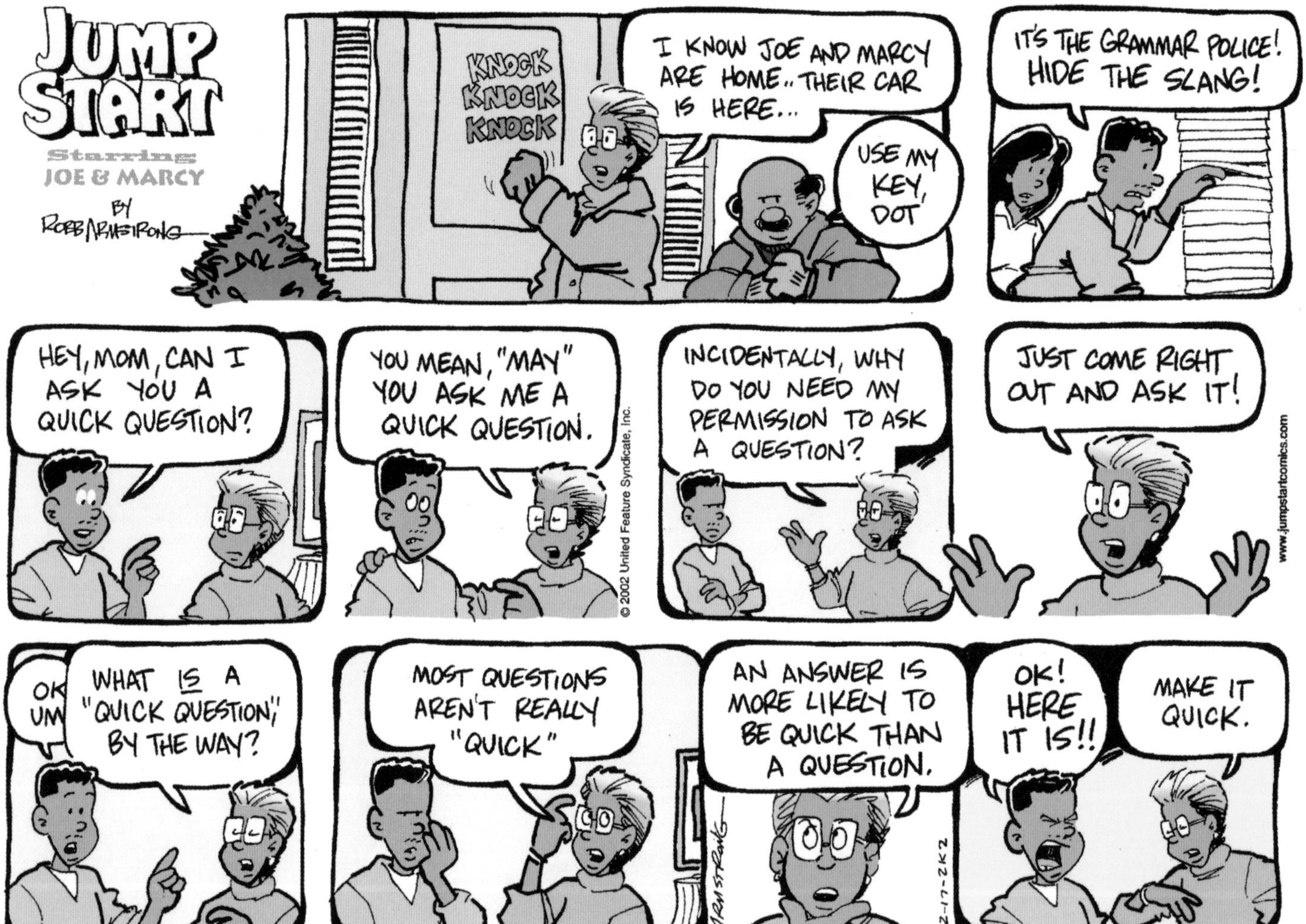
JUMP START
Starring JOE & MARCY
BY ROBB ARMSTRONG
KNOCK KNOCK KNOCK
I KNOW JOE AND MARCY ARE HOME.. THEIR CAR IS HERE...
USE MY KEY, DOT
IT'S THE GRAMMAR POLICE! HIDE THE SLANG!
HEY, MOM, CAN I ASK YOU A QUICK QUESTION?
YOU MEAN, "MAY" YOU ASK ME A QUICK QUESTION.
© 2002 United Feature Syndicate, Inc.
INCIDENTALLY, WHY DO YOU NEED MY PERMISSION TO ASK A QUESTION?
JUST COME RIGHT OUT AND ASK IT!
www.jumpstartcomics.com
WHAT IS A "QUICK QUESTION," BY THE WAY?
MOST QUESTIONS AREN'T REALLY "QUICK"
AN ANSWER IS MORE LIKELY TO BE QUICK THAN A QUESTION.
ARMSTRONG
2-17-2K2
OK! HERE IT IS!!
MAKE IT QUICK.

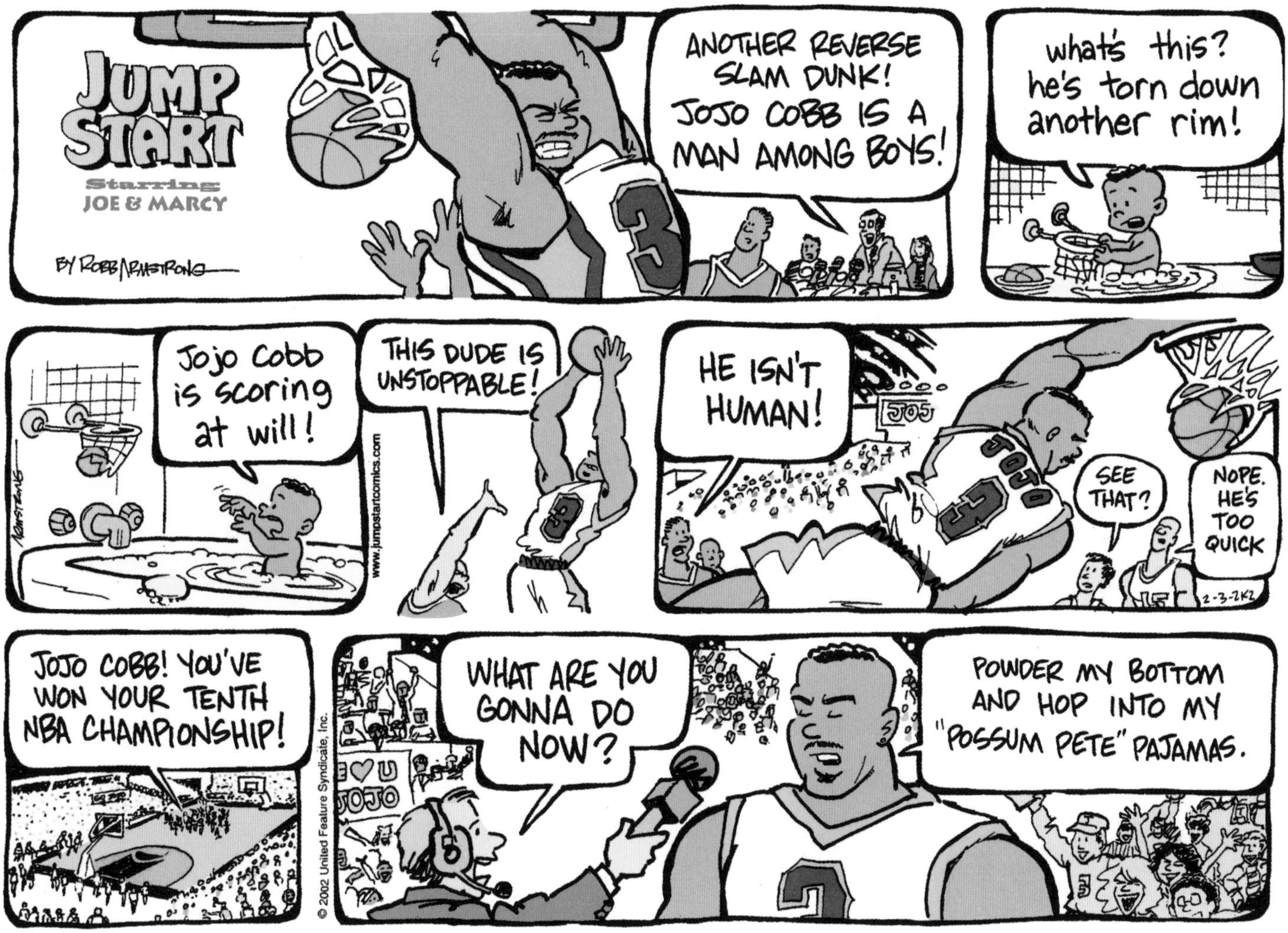
JUMP START
Starring JOE & MARCY
BY ROBB ARMSTRONG
ANOTHER REVERSE SLAM DUNK! JOJO COBB IS A MAN AMONG BOYS!
what's this? he's torn down another rim!
Jojo Cobb is scoring at will!
THIS DUDE IS UNSTOPPABLE!
www.jumpstartcomics.com
HE ISN'T HUMAN!
SEE THAT?
NOPE. HE'S TOO QUICK
2-3-2K2
JOJO COBB! YOU'VE WON YOUR TENTH NBA CHAMPIONSHIP!
© 2002 United Feature Syndicate, Inc.
WHAT ARE YOU GONNA DO NOW?
POWDER MY BOTTOM AND HOP INTO MY "POSSUM PETE" PAJAMAS.

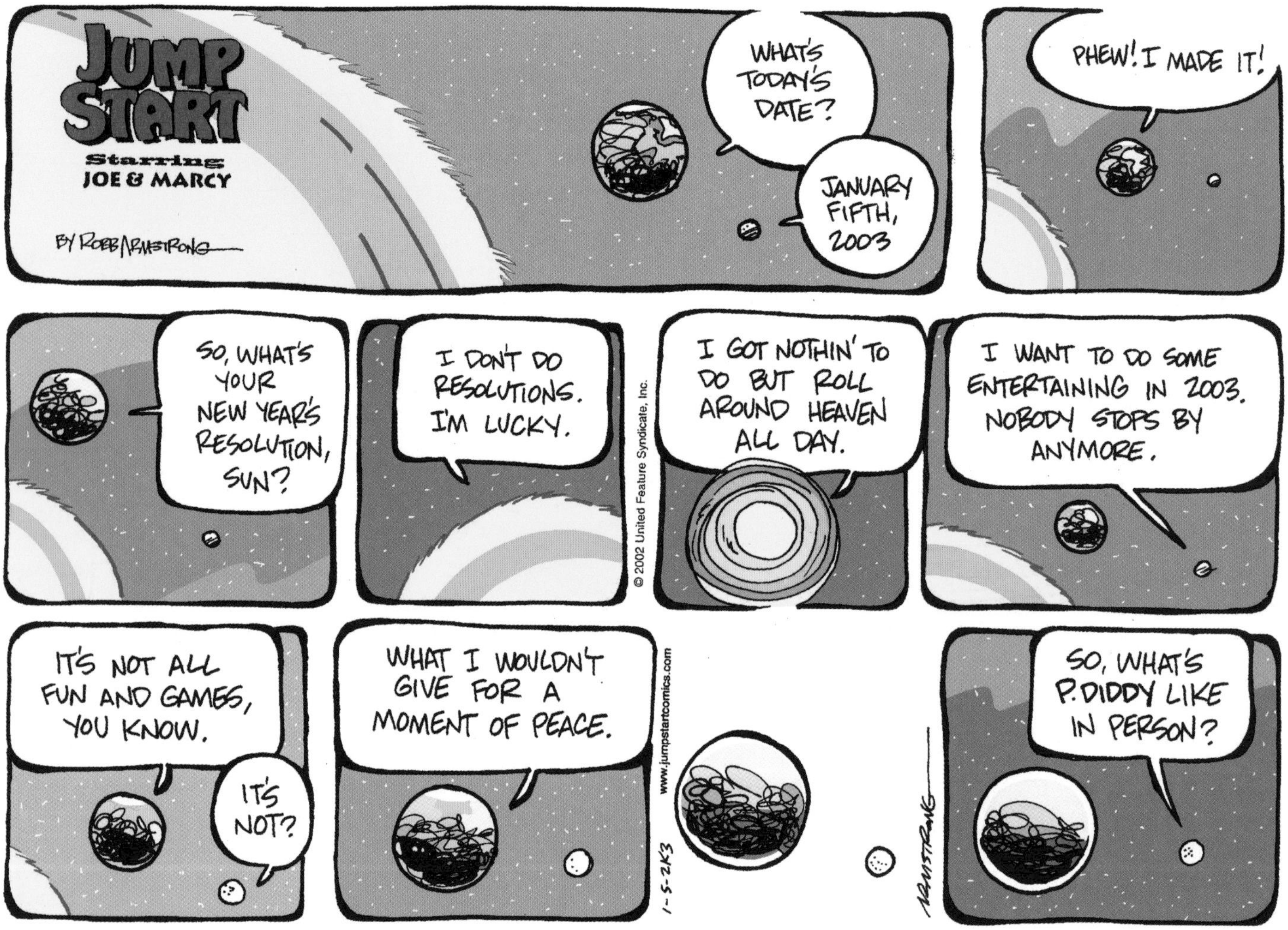
JUMP START
Starring JOE & MARCY
BY ROBB ARMSTRONG
WHAT'S TODAY'S DATE?
JANUARY FIFTH, 2003
PHEW! I MADE IT!
SO, WHAT'S YOUR NEW YEAR'S RESOLUTION, SUN?
I DON'T DO RESOLUTIONS. I'M LUCKY.
© 2002 United Feature Syndicate, Inc.
I GOT NOTHIN' TO DO BUT ROLL AROUND HEAVEN ALL DAY.
I WANT TO DO SOME ENTERTAINING IN 2003. NOBODY STOPS BY ANYMORE.
IT'S NOT ALL FUN AND GAMES, YOU KNOW.
IT'S NOT?
WHAT I WOULDN'T GIVE FOR A MOMENT OF PEACE.
www.jumpstartcomics.com
1-5-2K3
SO, WHAT'S P. DIDDY LIKE IN PERSON?

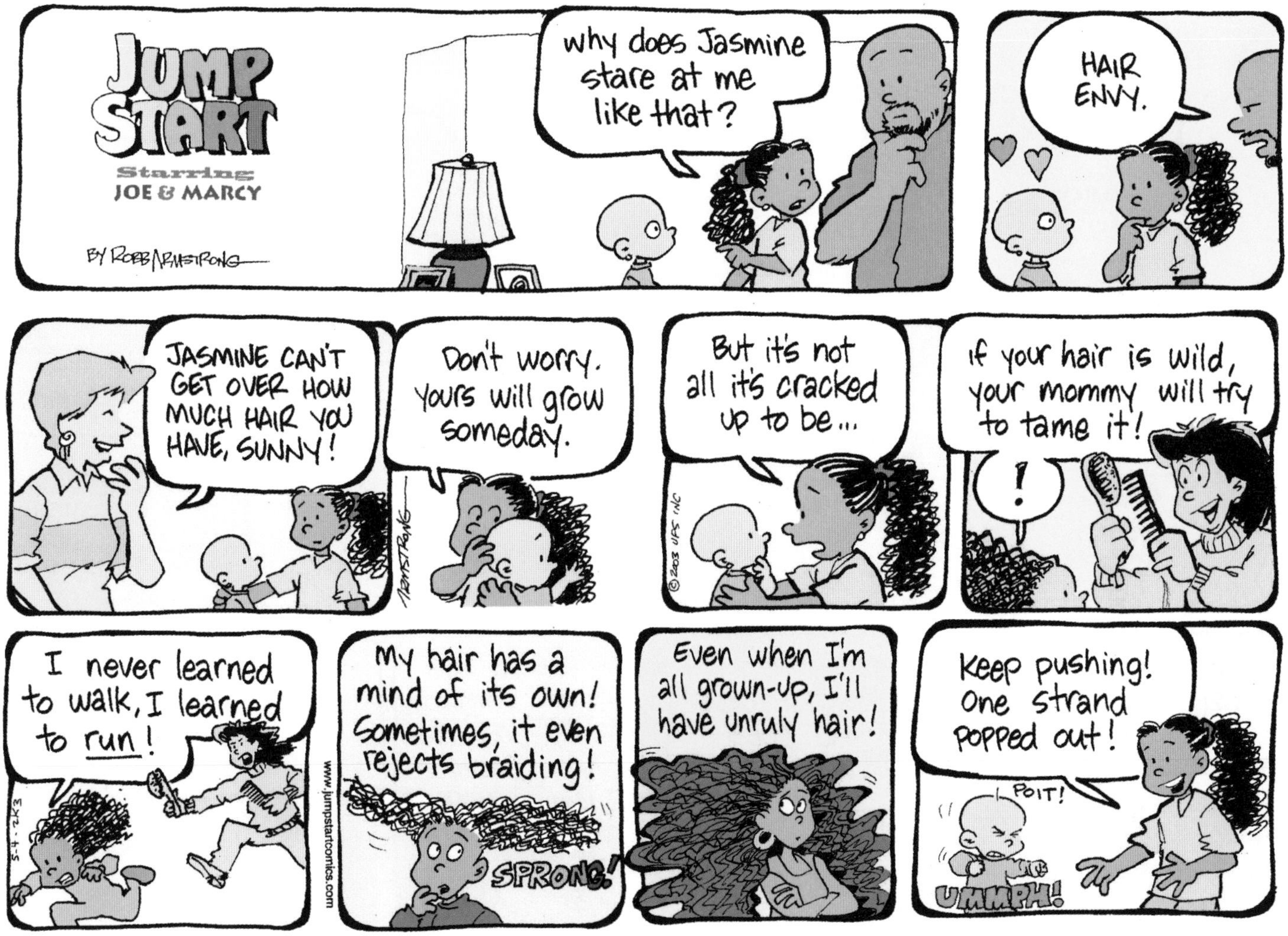
JUMP START
Starring
JOE & MARCY
BY ROBB ARMSTRONG
why does Jasmine stare at me like that?
HAIR ENVY.
JASMINE CAN'T GET OVER HOW MUCH HAIR YOU HAVE, SUNNY!
Don't worry. Yours will grow someday.
ARMSTRONG
But it's not all it's cracked up to be...
© 2003 UFS INC
If your hair is wild, your mommy will try to tame it!
!
I never learned to walk, I learned to run!
5-4-2K3
www.jumpstartcomics.com
My hair has a mind of its own! Sometimes, it even rejects braiding!
SPRONG!
Even when I'm all grown-up, I'll have unruly hair!
Keep pushing! One strand popped out!
POIT!
UMMPH!

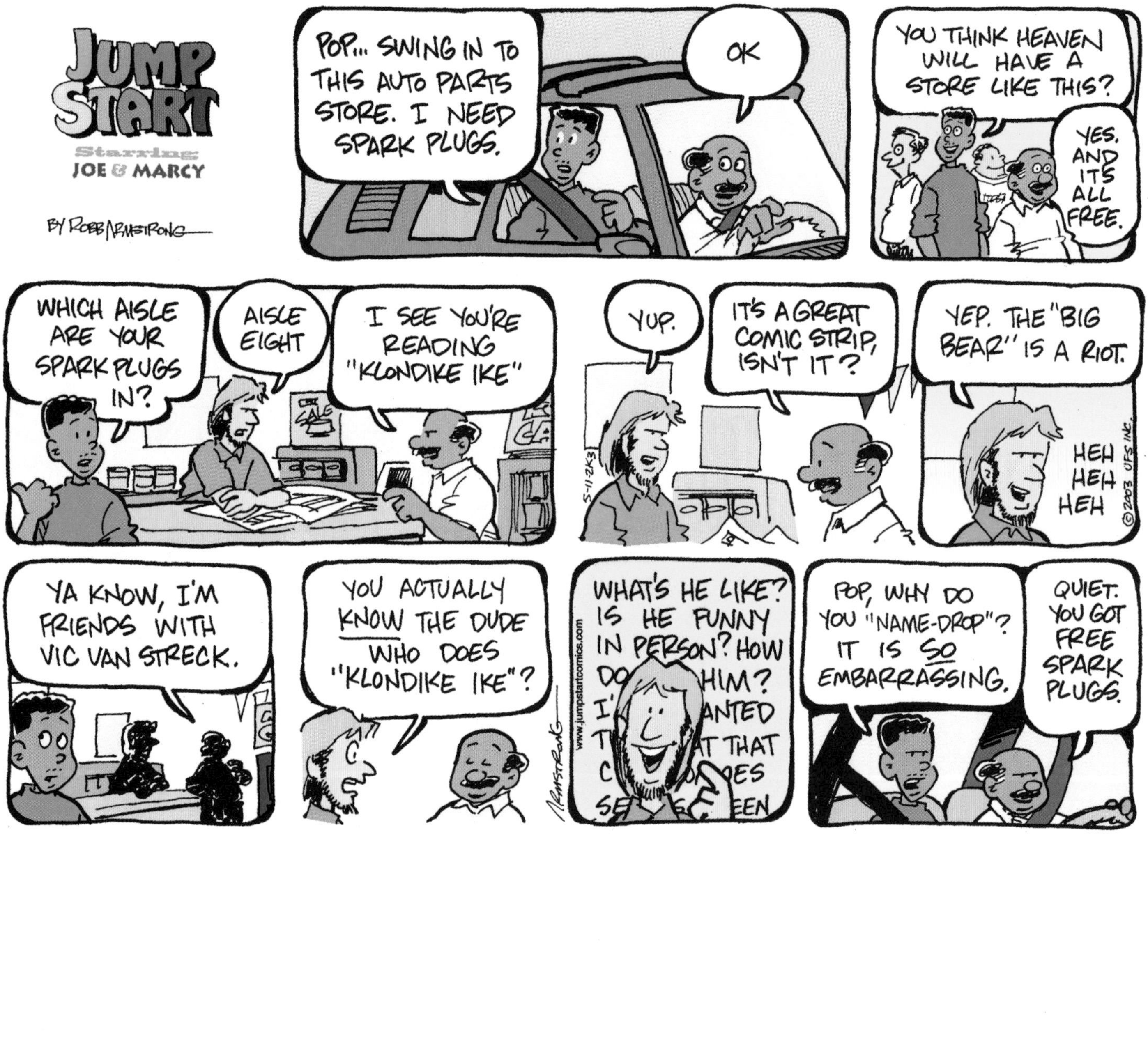

JUMP START
Starring JOE & MARCY
BY ROBB ARMSTRONG
POP... SWING IN TO THIS AUTO PARTS STORE. I NEED SPARK PLUGS.
OK
YOU THINK HEAVEN WILL HAVE A STORE LIKE THIS?
YES. AND IT'S ALL FREE.
WHICH AISLE ARE YOUR SPARK PLUGS IN?
AISLE EIGHT
I SEE YOU'RE READING "KLONDIKE IKE"
YUP.
IT'S A GREAT COMIC STRIP, ISN'T IT?
YEP. THE "BIG BEAR" IS A RIOT.
HEH HEH HEH
5-11-2K3
© 2003 UFS INC.
YA KNOW, I'M FRIENDS WITH VIC VAN STRECK.
YOU ACTUALLY KNOW THE DUDE WHO DOES "KLONDIKE IKE"?
ARMSTRONG
www.jumpstartcomics.com
WHAT'S HE LIKE? IS HE FUNNY IN PERSON? HOW
POP, WHY DO YOU "NAME-DROP"? IT IS SO EMBARRASSING.
QUIET. YOU GOT FREE SPARK PLUGS.

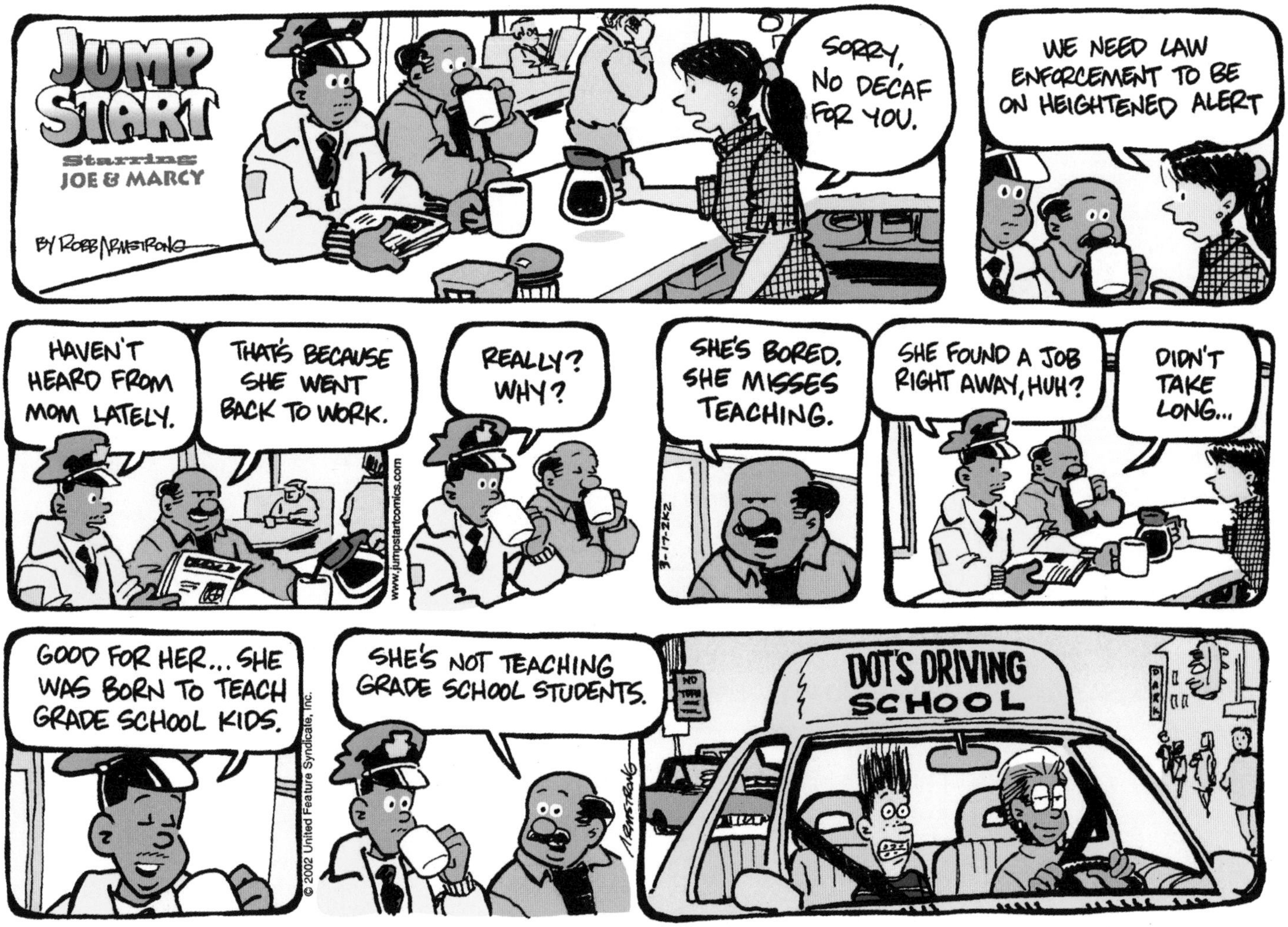
JUMP START
Starring JOE & MARCY
BY ROBB ARMSTRONG
SORRY, NO DECAF FOR YOU.
WE NEED LAW ENFORCEMENT TO BE ON HEIGHTENED ALERT
HAVEN'T HEARD FROM MOM LATELY.
THAT'S BECAUSE SHE WENT BACK TO WORK.
www.jumpstartcomics.com
REALLY? WHY?
SHE'S BORED. SHE MISSES TEACHING.
3-17-2K2
SHE FOUND A JOB RIGHT AWAY, HUH?
DIDN'T TAKE LONG...
GOOD FOR HER... SHE WAS BORN TO TEACH GRADE SCHOOL KIDS.
© 2002 United Feature Syndicate, Inc.
SHE'S NOT TEACHING GRADE SCHOOL STUDENTS.
ARMSTRONG
DOT'S DRIVING SCHOOL

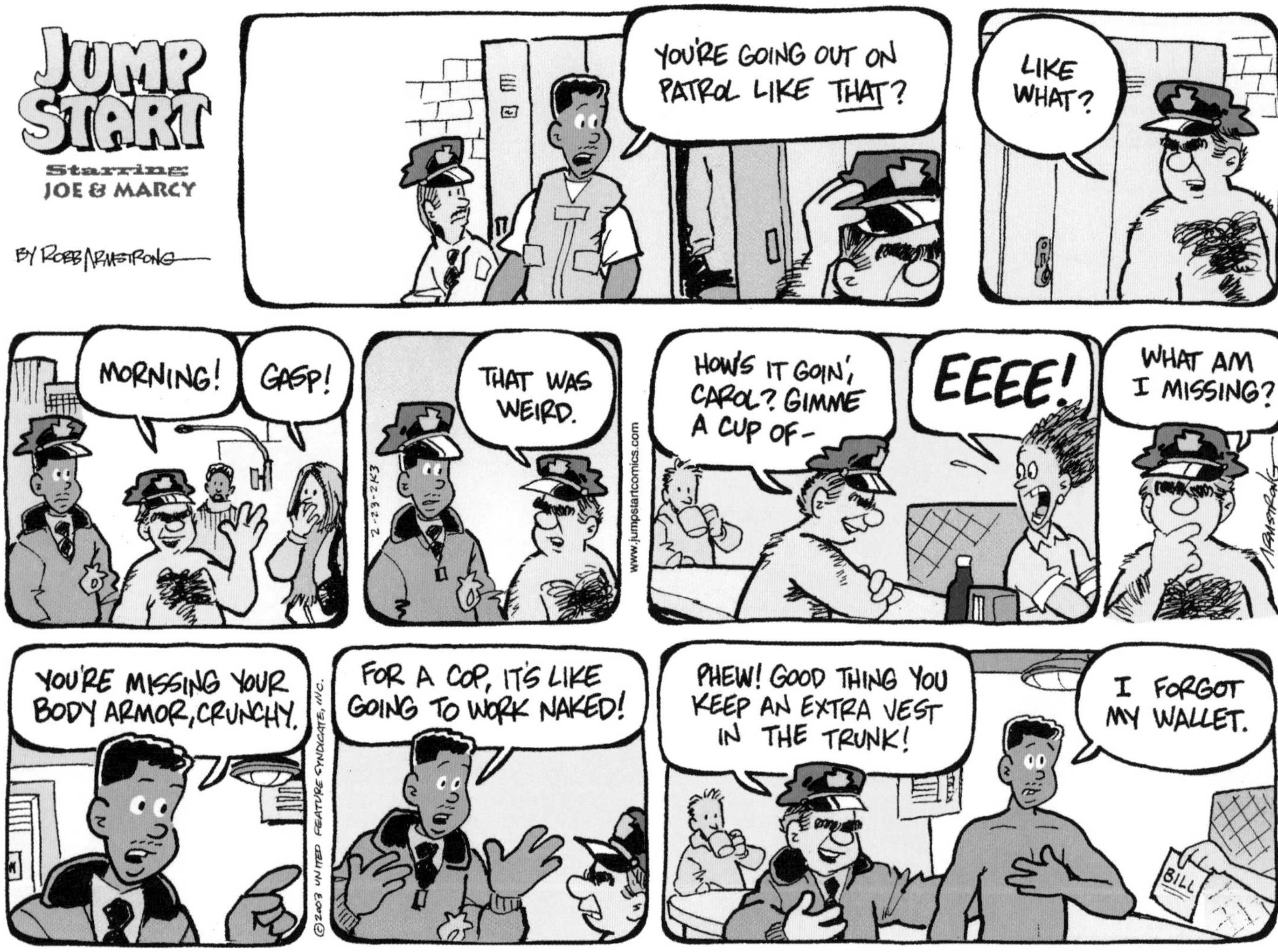
JUMP START
Starring JOE & MARCY
BY ROBB ARMSTRONG
YOU'RE GOING OUT ON PATROL LIKE THAT?
LIKE WHAT?
MORNING!
GASP!
THAT WAS WEIRD.
2-23-2K3
www.jumpstartcomics.com
HOW'S IT GOIN', CAROL? GIMME A CUP OF-
EEEE!
WHAT AM I MISSING?
ARMSTRONG
YOU'RE MISSING YOUR BODY ARMOR, CRUNCHY.
©2003 UNITED FEATURE SYNDICATE, INC.
FOR A COP, IT'S LIKE GOING TO WORK NAKED!
PHEW! GOOD THING YOU KEEP AN EXTRA VEST IN THE TRUNK!
I FORGOT MY WALLET.
BILL

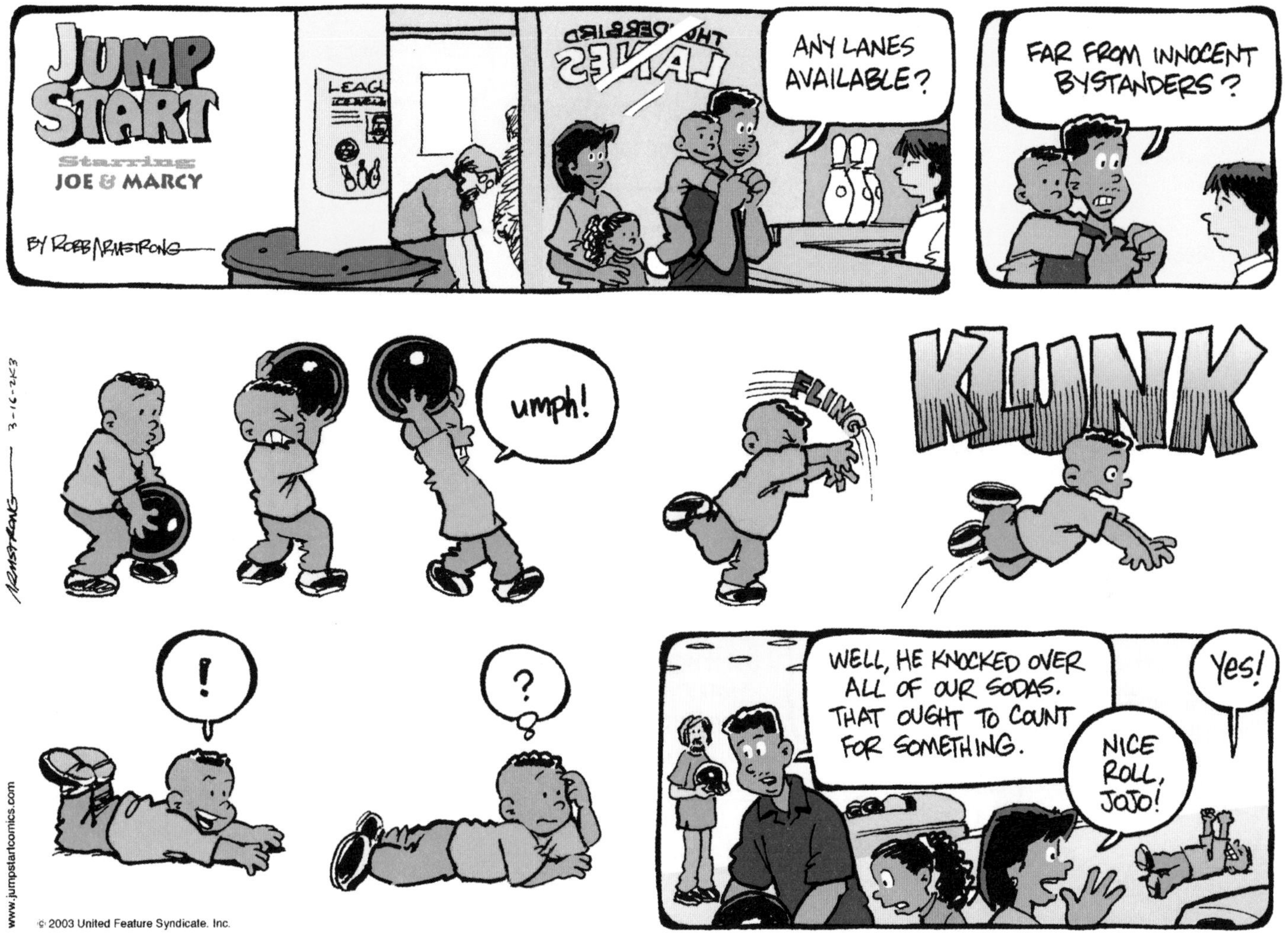
JUMP START
Starring
JOE & MARCY
BY ROBB ARMSTRONG
ANY LANES AVAILABLE?
FAR FROM INNOCENT BYSTANDERS?
umph!
FLING
KLUNK
!
?
WELL, HE KNOCKED OVER ALL OF OUR SODAS. THAT OUGHT TO COUNT FOR SOMETHING.
NICE ROLL, JOJO!
Yes!
3-16-2K3
www.jumpstartcomics.com
© 2003 United Feature Syndicate, Inc.

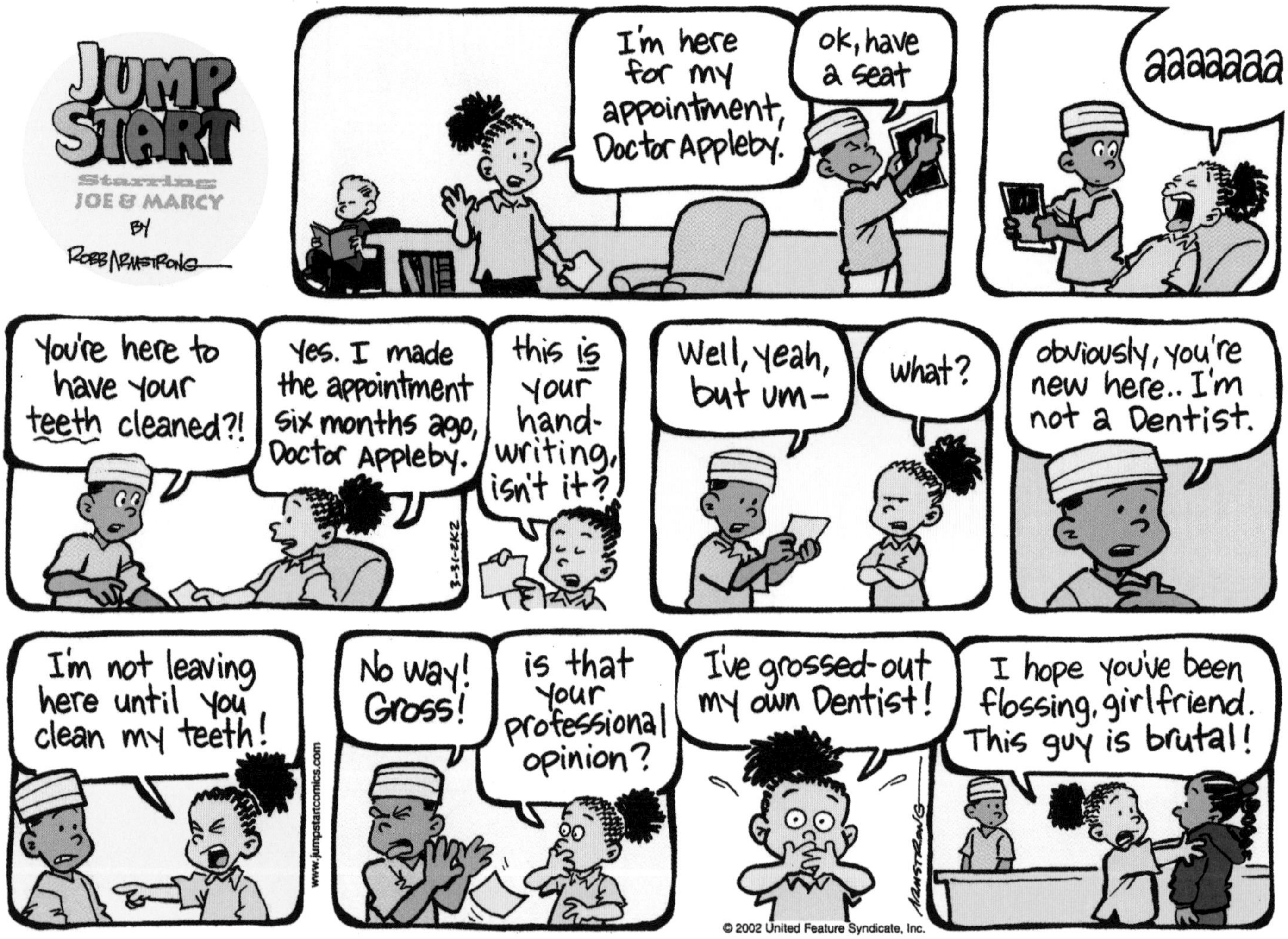
JUMP START
Starring JOE & MARCY
BY
ROBB ARMSTRONG
I'm here for my appointment, Doctor Appleby.
ok, have a seat
aaaaaaa
You're here to have your teeth cleaned?!
Yes. I made the appointment six months ago, Doctor Appleby.
this is your hand-writing, isn't it?
Well, yeah, but um–
what?
obviously, you're new here.. I'm not a Dentist.
I'm not leaving here until you clean my teeth!
www.jumpstartcomics.com
No way! Gross!
is that your professional opinion?
I've grossed-out my own Dentist!
I hope you've been flossing, girlfriend. This guy is brutal!
© 2002 United Feature Syndicate, Inc.

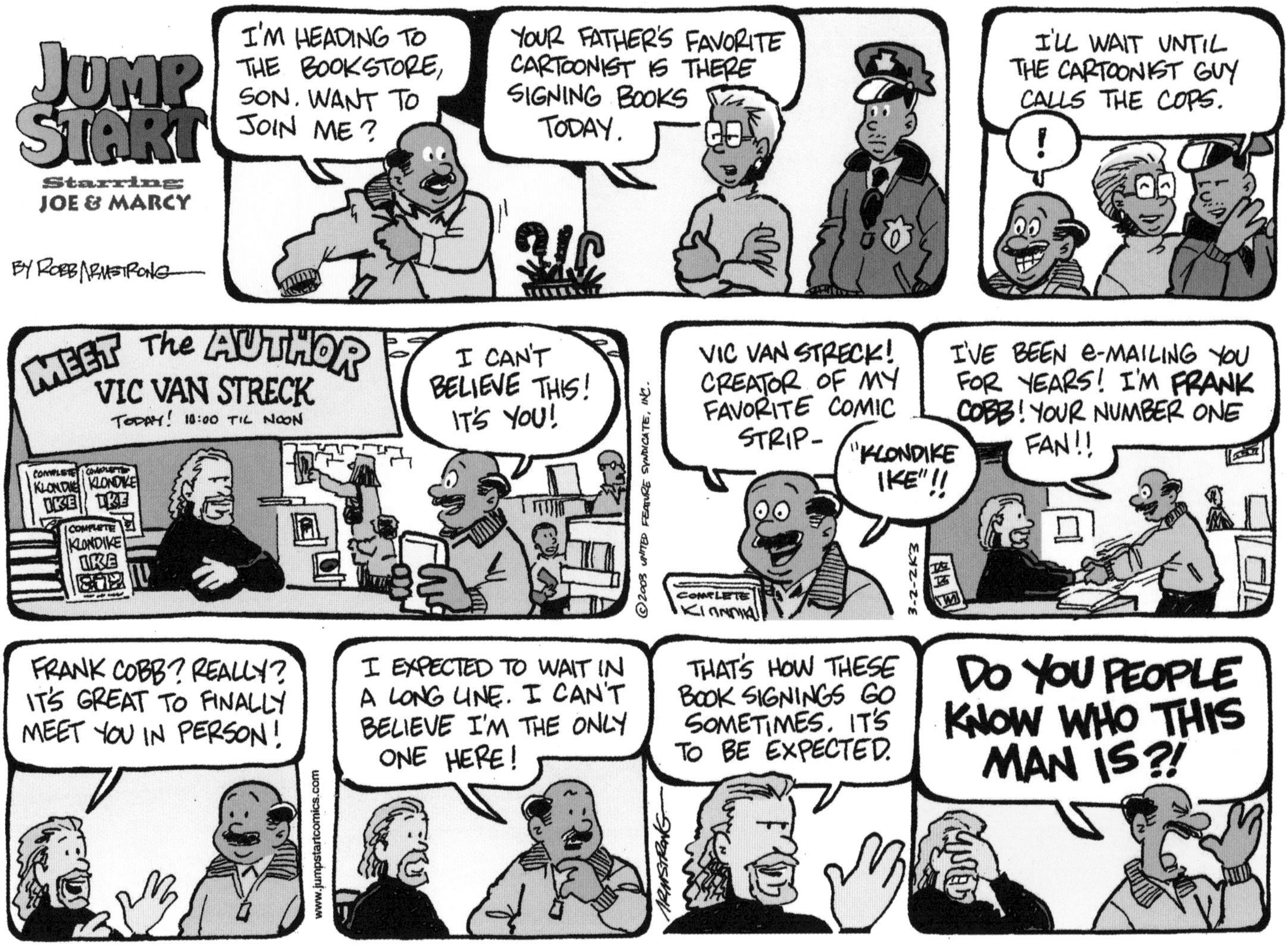
JUMP START
Starring JOE & MARCY
BY ROBB ARMSTRONG
I'M HEADING TO THE BOOKSTORE, SON. WANT TO JOIN ME?
YOUR FATHER'S FAVORITE CARTOONIST IS THERE SIGNING BOOKS TODAY.
I'LL WAIT UNTIL THE CARTOONIST GUY CALLS THE COPS.
!
MEET The AUTHOR
VIC VAN STRECK
TODAY! 10:00 TIL NOON
COMPLETE KLONDIKE IKE
I CAN'T BELIEVE THIS! IT'S YOU!
©2003 UNITED FEATURE SYNDICATE, INC.
3-2-2K3
VIC VAN STRECK! CREATOR OF MY FAVORITE COMIC STRIP-
"KLONDIKE IKE"!!
I'VE BEEN e-MAILING YOU FOR YEARS! I'M FRANK COBB! YOUR NUMBER ONE FAN!!
FRANK COBB? REALLY? IT'S GREAT TO FINALLY MEET YOU IN PERSON!
www.jumpstartcomics.com
I EXPECTED TO WAIT IN A LONG LINE. I CAN'T BELIEVE I'M THE ONLY ONE HERE!
THAT'S HOW THESE BOOK SIGNINGS GO SOMETIMES. IT'S TO BE EXPECTED.
ARMSTRONG
DO YOU PEOPLE KNOW WHO THIS MAN IS?!

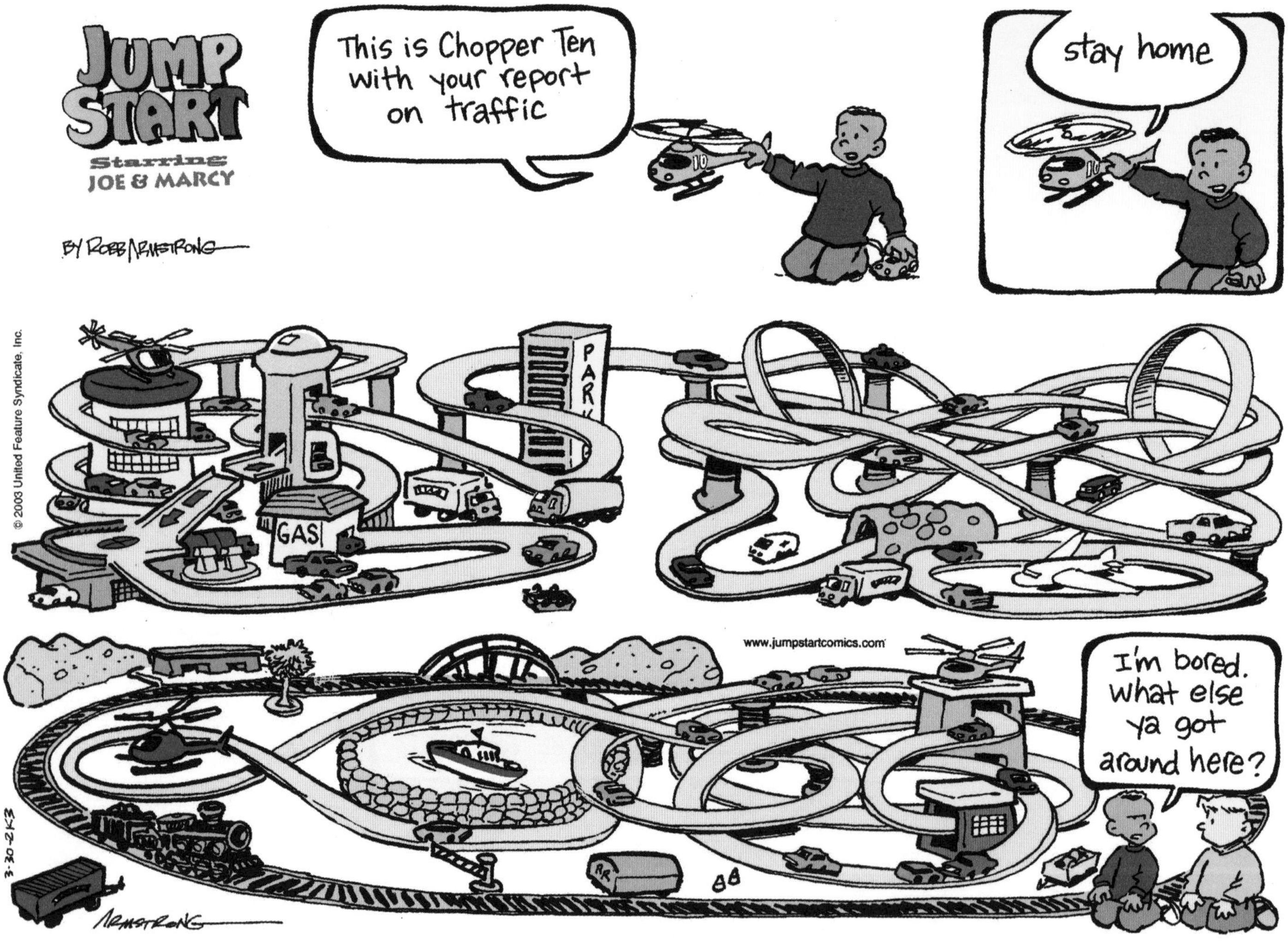
JUMP START
Starring JOE & MARCY
BY ROBB ARMSTRONG
This is Chopper Ten with your report on traffic
stay home
© 2003 United Feature Syndicate, Inc.
GAS
www.jumpstartcomics.com
I'm bored. What else ya got around here?
3-30-2K3
ARMSTRONG

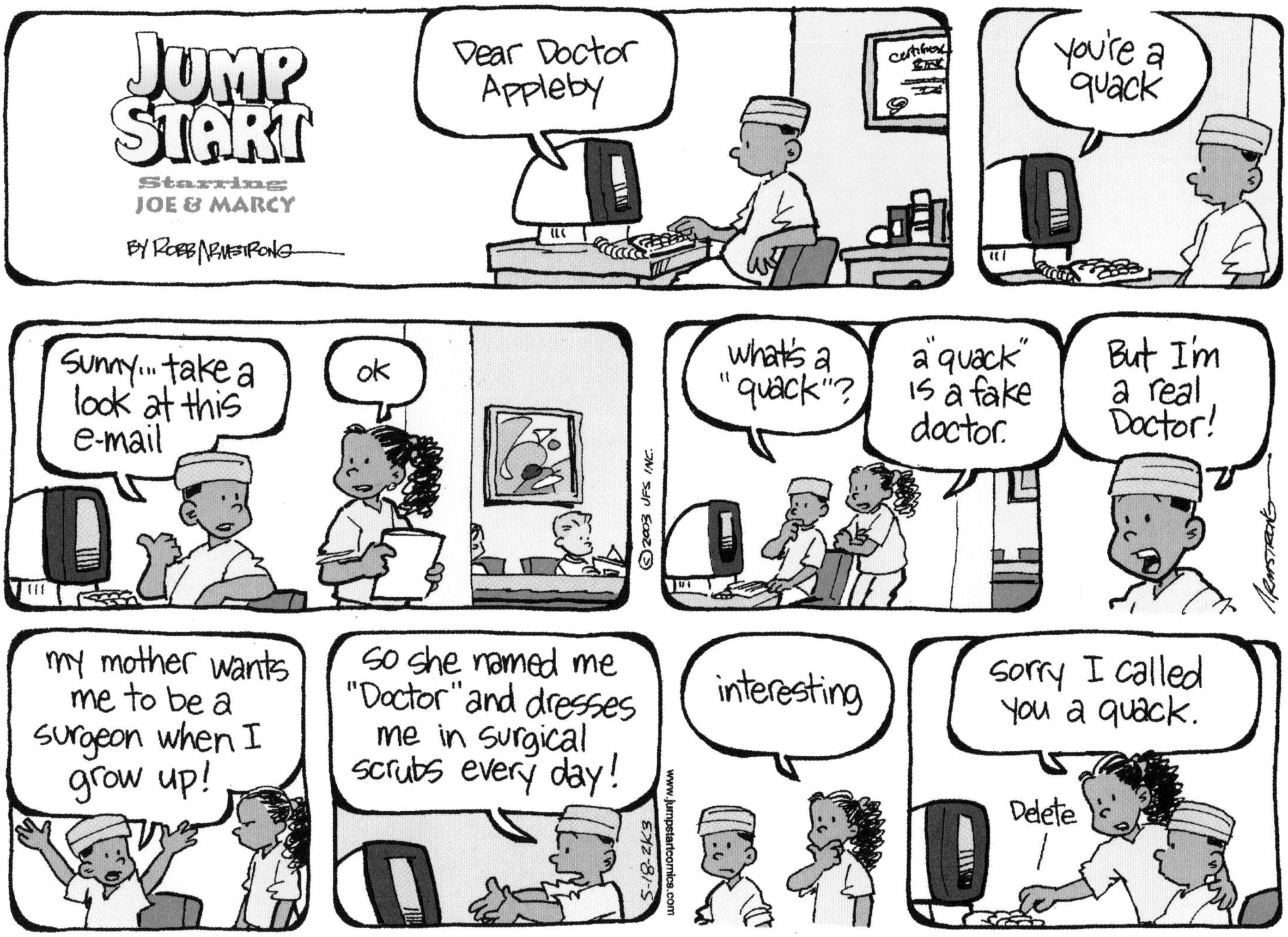
JUMP START
Starring JOE & MARCY
BY ROBB ARMSTRONG
Dear Doctor Appleby
you're a quack
Sunny... take a look at this e-mail
ok
© 2003 UFS INC.
what's a "quack"?
a "quack" is a fake doctor.
But I'm a real Doctor!
my mother wants me to be a surgeon when I grow up!
so she named me "Doctor" and dresses me in surgical scrubs every day!
5-18-2K3
www.jumpstartcomics.com
interesting
sorry I called you a quack.
Delete

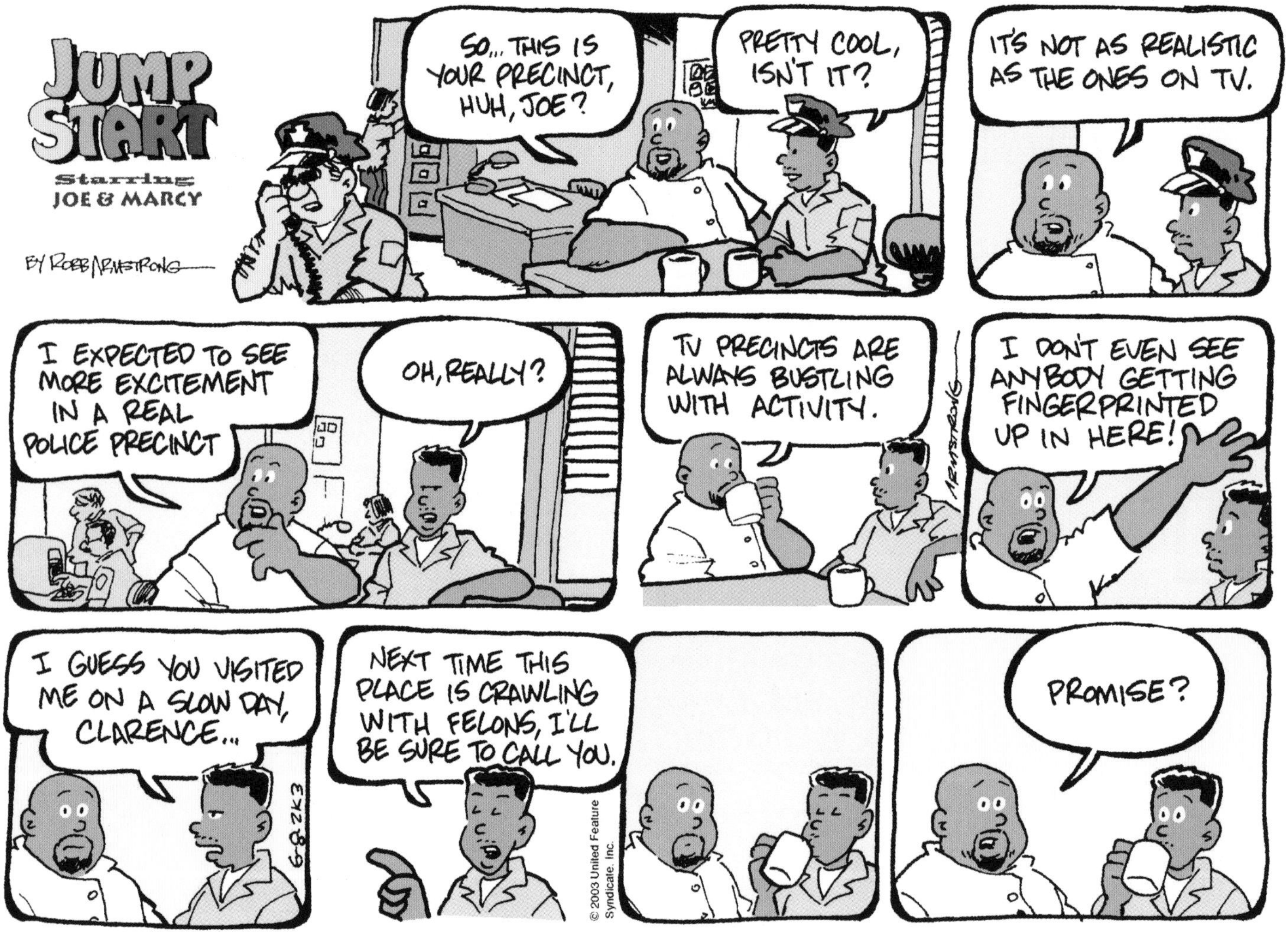
JUMP START
Starring JOE & MARCY
BY ROBB ARMSTRONG
SO... THIS IS YOUR PRECINCT, HUH, JOE?
PRETTY COOL, ISN'T IT?
IT'S NOT AS REALISTIC AS THE ONES ON TV.
I EXPECTED TO SEE MORE EXCITEMENT IN A REAL POLICE PRECINCT
OH, REALLY?
TV PRECINCTS ARE ALWAYS BUSTLING WITH ACTIVITY.
I DON'T EVEN SEE ANYBODY GETTING FINGERPRINTED UP IN HERE!
I GUESS YOU VISITED ME ON A SLOW DAY, CLARENCE...
NEXT TIME THIS PLACE IS CRAWLING WITH FELONS, I'LL BE SURE TO CALL YOU.
PROMISE?
© 2003 United Feature Syndicate, Inc.

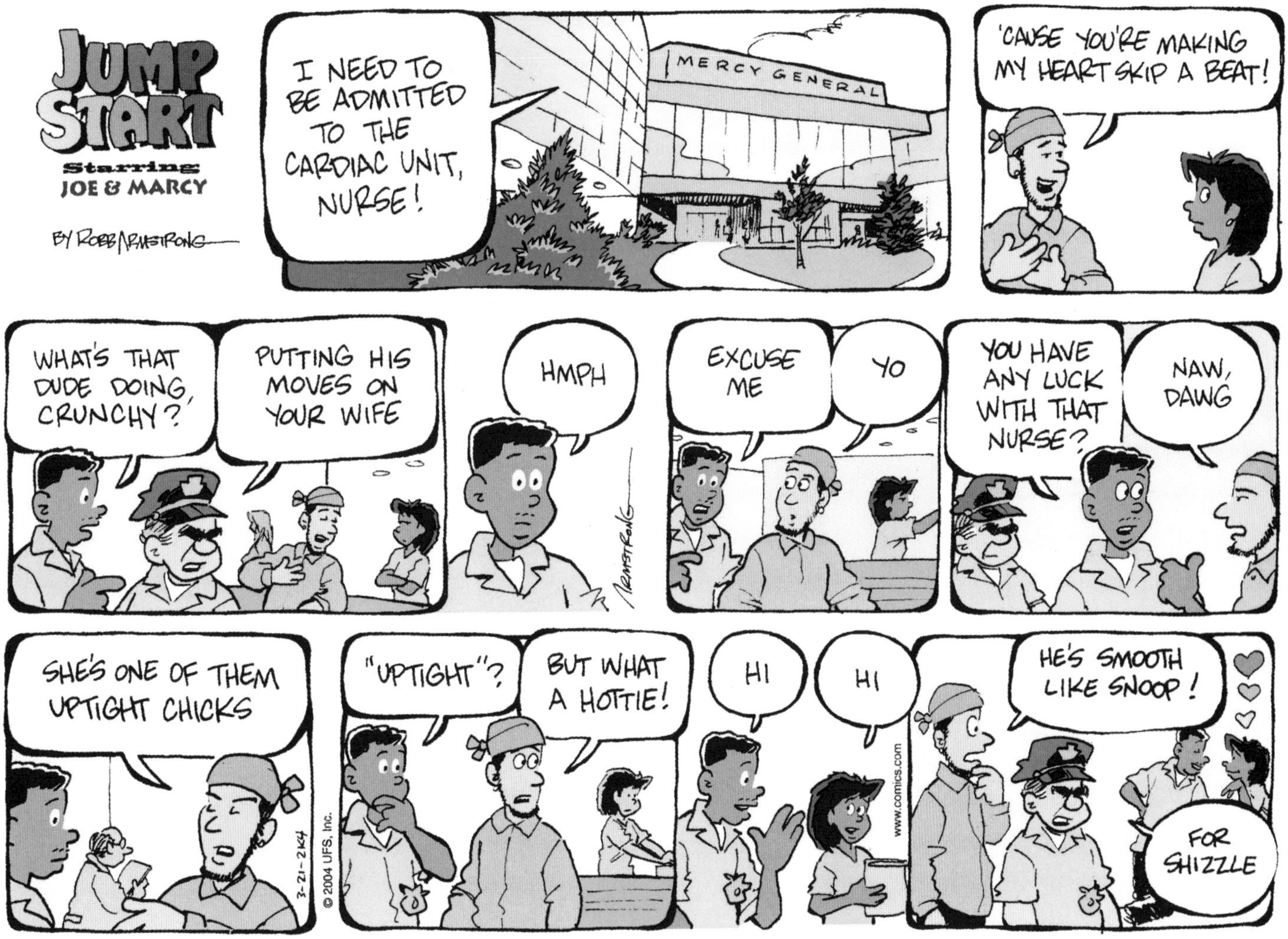
JUMP START
Starring JOE & MARCY
BY ROBB ARMSTRONG
I NEED TO BE ADMITTED TO THE CARDIAC UNIT, NURSE!
MERCY GENERAL
'CAUSE YOU'RE MAKING MY HEART SKIP A BEAT!
WHAT'S THAT DUDE DOING, CRUNCHY?
PUTTING HIS MOVES ON YOUR WIFE
HMPH
ARMSTRONG
EXCUSE ME
YO
YOU HAVE ANY LUCK WITH THAT NURSE?
NAW, DAWG
SHE'S ONE OF THEM UPTIGHT CHICKS
3-21-2K4
© 2004 UFS, Inc.
"UPTIGHT"?
BUT WHAT A HOTTIE!
HI
HI
www.comics.com
HE'S SMOOTH LIKE SNOOP!
FOR SHIZZLE

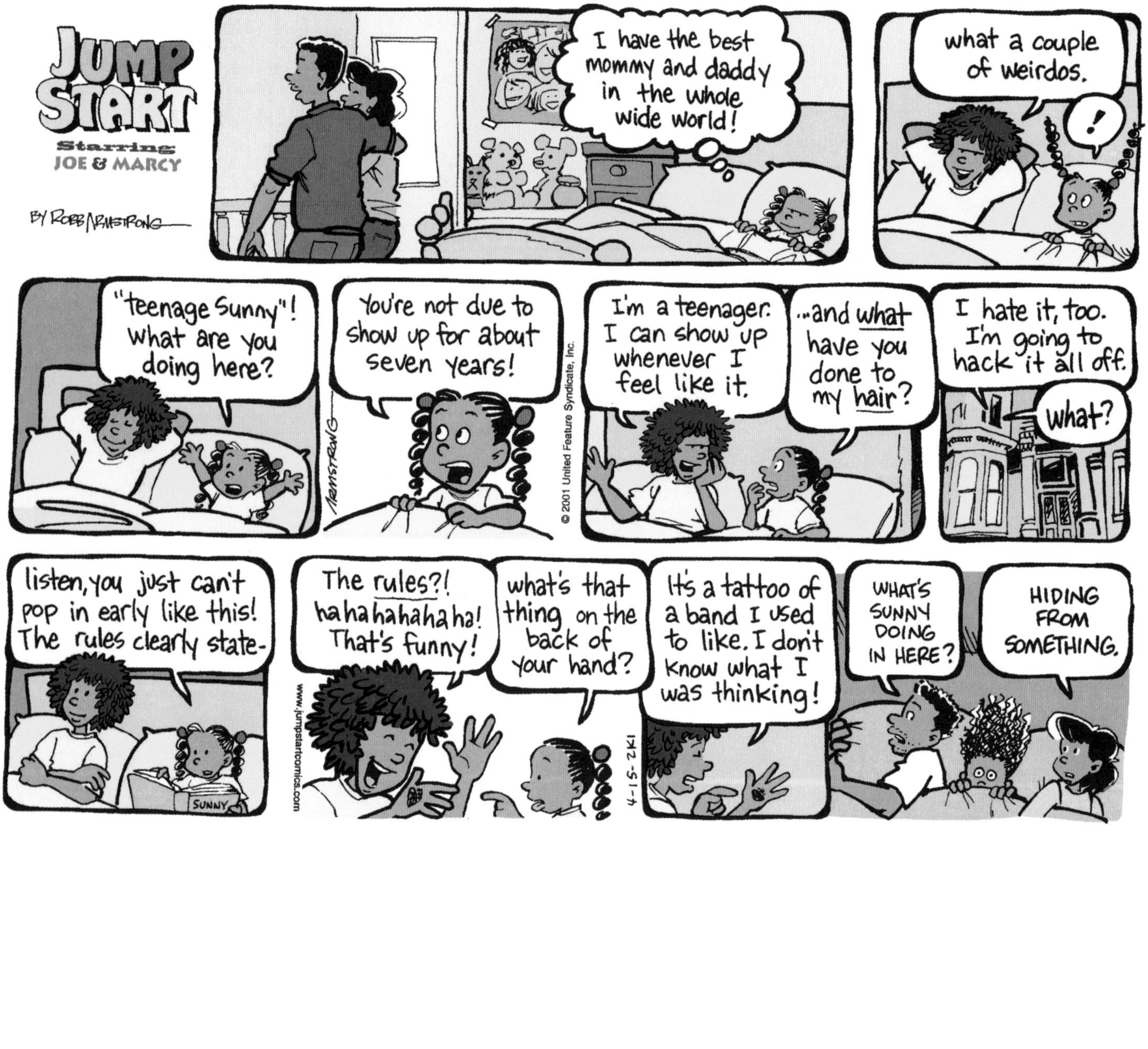
JUMP START
Starring: JOE & MARCY
BY ROBB ARMSTRONG
I have the best mommy and daddy in the whole wide world!
what a couple of weirdos.
!
"teenage Sunny"! What are you doing here?
You're not due to show up for about seven years!
© 2001 United Feature Syndicate, Inc.
I'm a teenager. I can show up whenever I feel like it.
...and what have you done to my hair?
I hate it, too. I'm going to hack it all off.
what?
listen, you just can't pop in early like this! The rules clearly state-
SUNNY
The rules?! hahahahahahaha! That's funny!
www.jumpstartcomics.com
what's that thing on the back of your hand?
It's a tattoo of a band I used to like. I don't know what I was thinking!
WHAT'S SUNNY DOING IN HERE?
HIDING FROM SOMETHING.

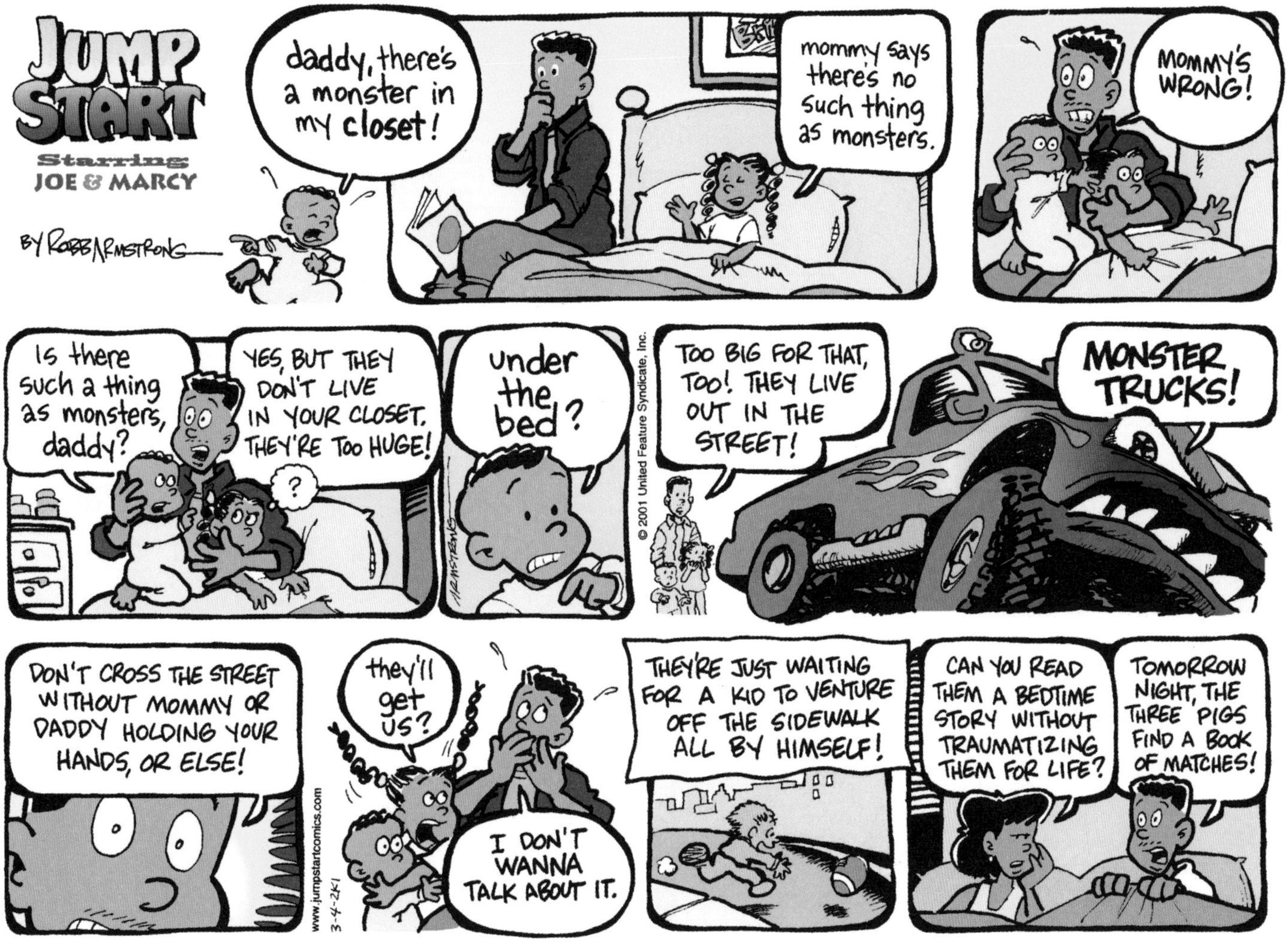
JUMP START
Starring JOE & MARCY
BY ROBB ARMSTRONG
daddy, there's a monster in my closet!
mommy says there's no such thing as monsters.
MOMMY'S WRONG!
Is there such a thing as monsters, daddy?
YES, BUT THEY DON'T LIVE IN YOUR CLOSET. THEY'RE TOO HUGE!
?
under the bed?
© 2001 United Feature Syndicate, Inc.
TOO BIG FOR THAT, TOO! THEY LIVE OUT IN THE STREET!
MONSTER TRUCKS!
DON'T CROSS THE STREET WITHOUT MOMMY OR DADDY HOLDING YOUR HANDS, OR ELSE!
www.jumpstartcomics.com
3-4-2K1
they'll get us?
I DON'T WANNA TALK ABOUT IT.
THEY'RE JUST WAITING FOR A KID TO VENTURE OFF THE SIDEWALK ALL BY HIMSELF!
CAN YOU READ THEM A BEDTIME STORY WITHOUT TRAUMATIZING THEM FOR LIFE?
TOMORROW NIGHT, THE THREE PIGS FIND A BOOK OF MATCHES!

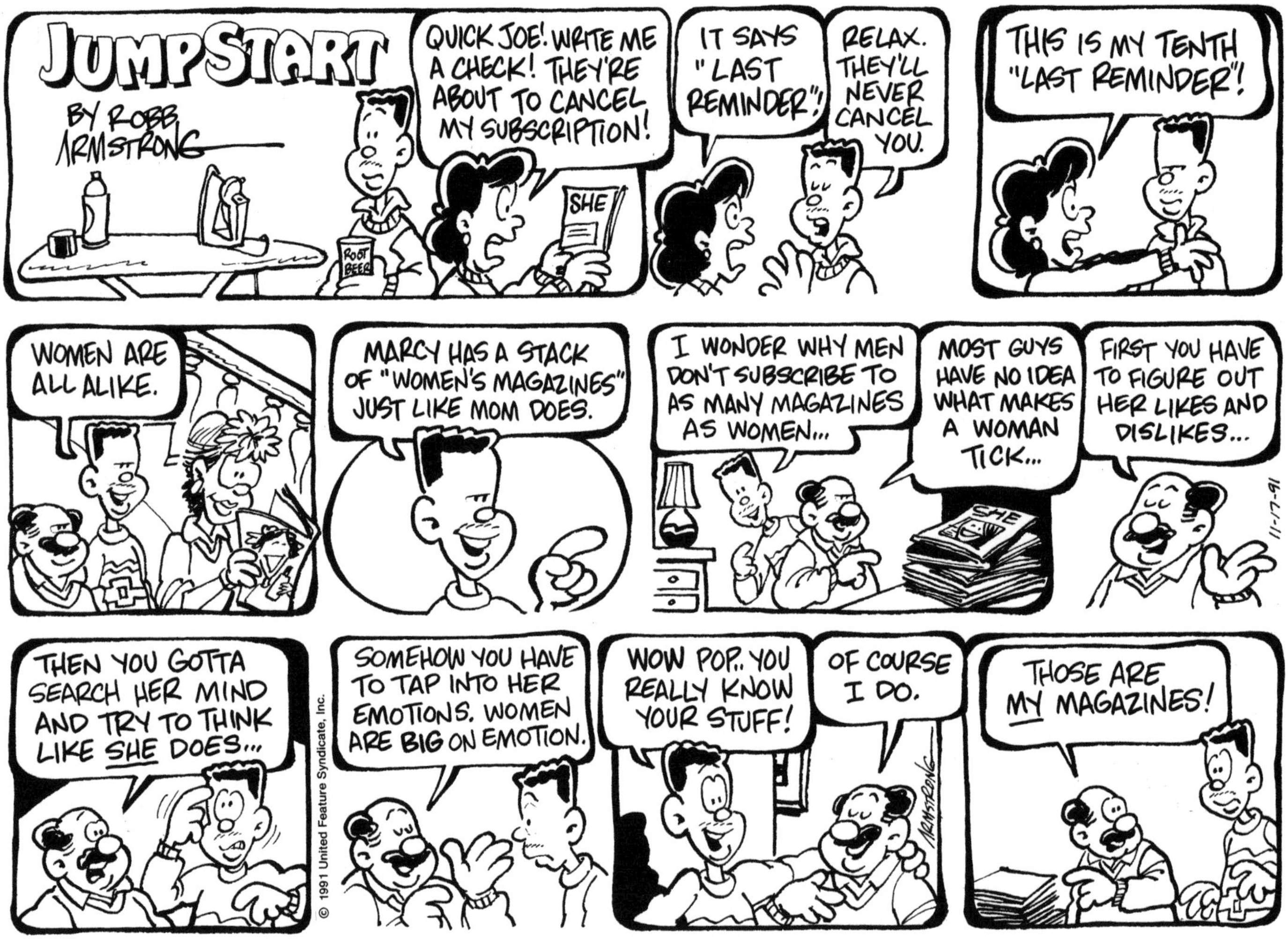
JUMPSTART
BY ROBB ARMSTRONG
QUICK JOE! WRITE ME A CHECK! THEY'RE ABOUT TO CANCEL MY SUBSCRIPTION!
SHE
ROOT BEER
IT SAYS "LAST REMINDER"!
RELAX. THEY'LL NEVER CANCEL YOU.
THIS IS MY TENTH "LAST REMINDER"!
WOMEN ARE ALL ALIKE.
MARCY HAS A STACK OF "WOMEN'S MAGAZINES" JUST LIKE MOM DOES.
I WONDER WHY MEN DON'T SUBSCRIBE TO AS MANY MAGAZINES AS WOMEN...
MOST GUYS HAVE NO IDEA WHAT MAKES A WOMAN TICK...
FIRST YOU HAVE TO FIGURE OUT HER LIKES AND DISLIKES...
SHE
11-17-91
THEN YOU GOTTA SEARCH HER MIND AND TRY TO THINK LIKE SHE DOES...
© 1991 United Feature Syndicate, Inc.
SOMEHOW YOU HAVE TO TAP INTO HER EMOTIONS. WOMEN ARE BIG ON EMOTION.
WOW POP.. YOU REALLY KNOW YOUR STUFF!
OF COURSE I DO.
ARMSTRONG
THOSE ARE MY MAGAZINES!

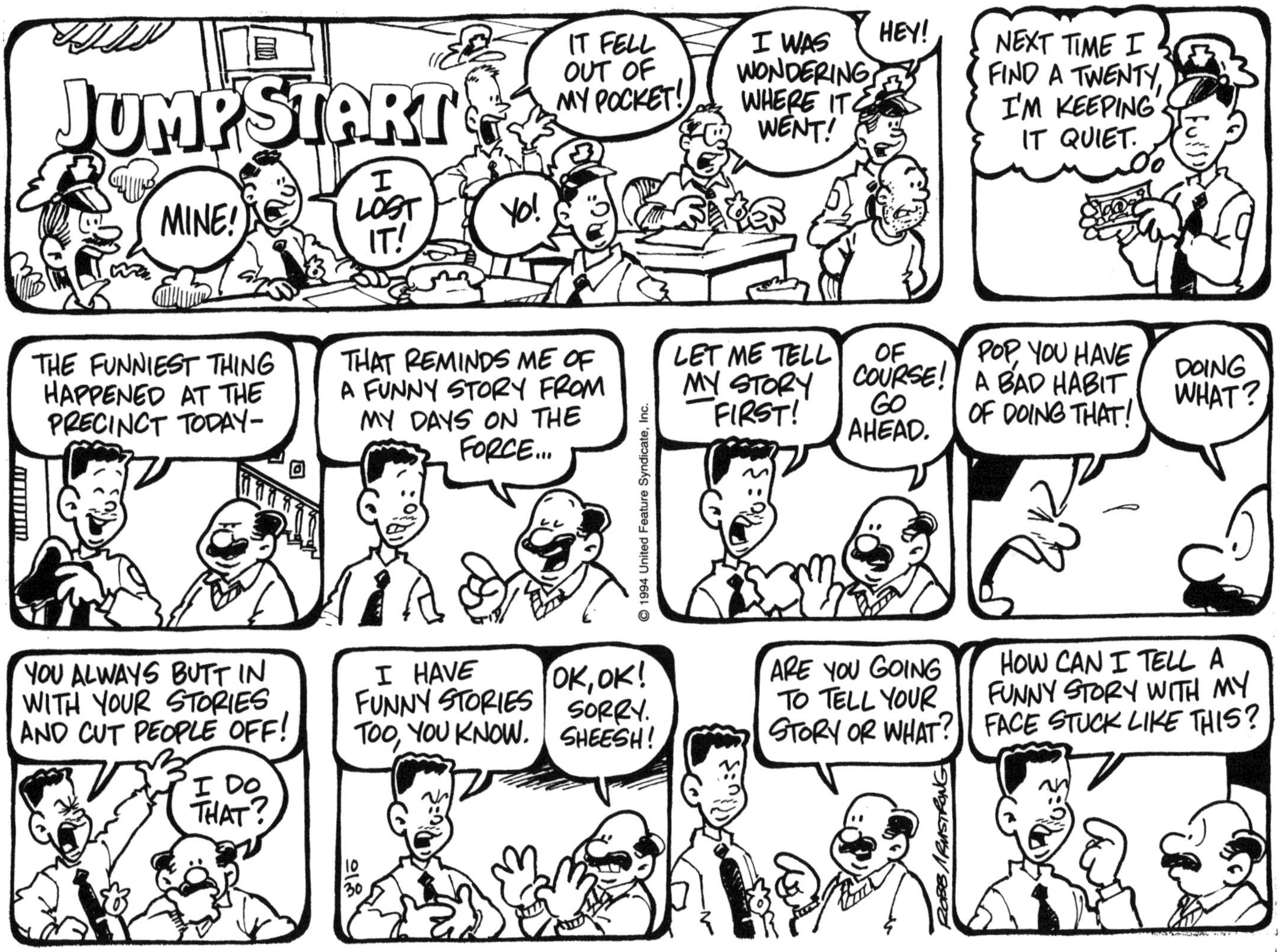
JUMPSTART
MINE!
I LOST IT!
YO!
IT FELL OUT OF MY POCKET!
I WAS WONDERING WHERE IT WENT!
HEY!
NEXT TIME I FIND A TWENTY, I'M KEEPING IT QUIET.
THE FUNNIEST THING HAPPENED AT THE PRECINCT TODAY-
THAT REMINDS ME OF A FUNNY STORY FROM MY DAYS ON THE FORCE...
LET ME TELL MY STORY FIRST!
OF COURSE! GO AHEAD.
POP, YOU HAVE A BAD HABIT OF DOING THAT!
DOING WHAT?
YOU ALWAYS BUTT IN WITH YOUR STORIES AND CUT PEOPLE OFF!
I DO THAT?
I HAVE FUNNY STORIES TOO, YOU KNOW.
OK, OK! SORRY. SHEESH!
10/30
ARE YOU GOING TO TELL YOUR STORY OR WHAT?
HOW CAN I TELL A FUNNY STORY WITH MY FACE STUCK LIKE THIS?
ROBB ARMSTRONG

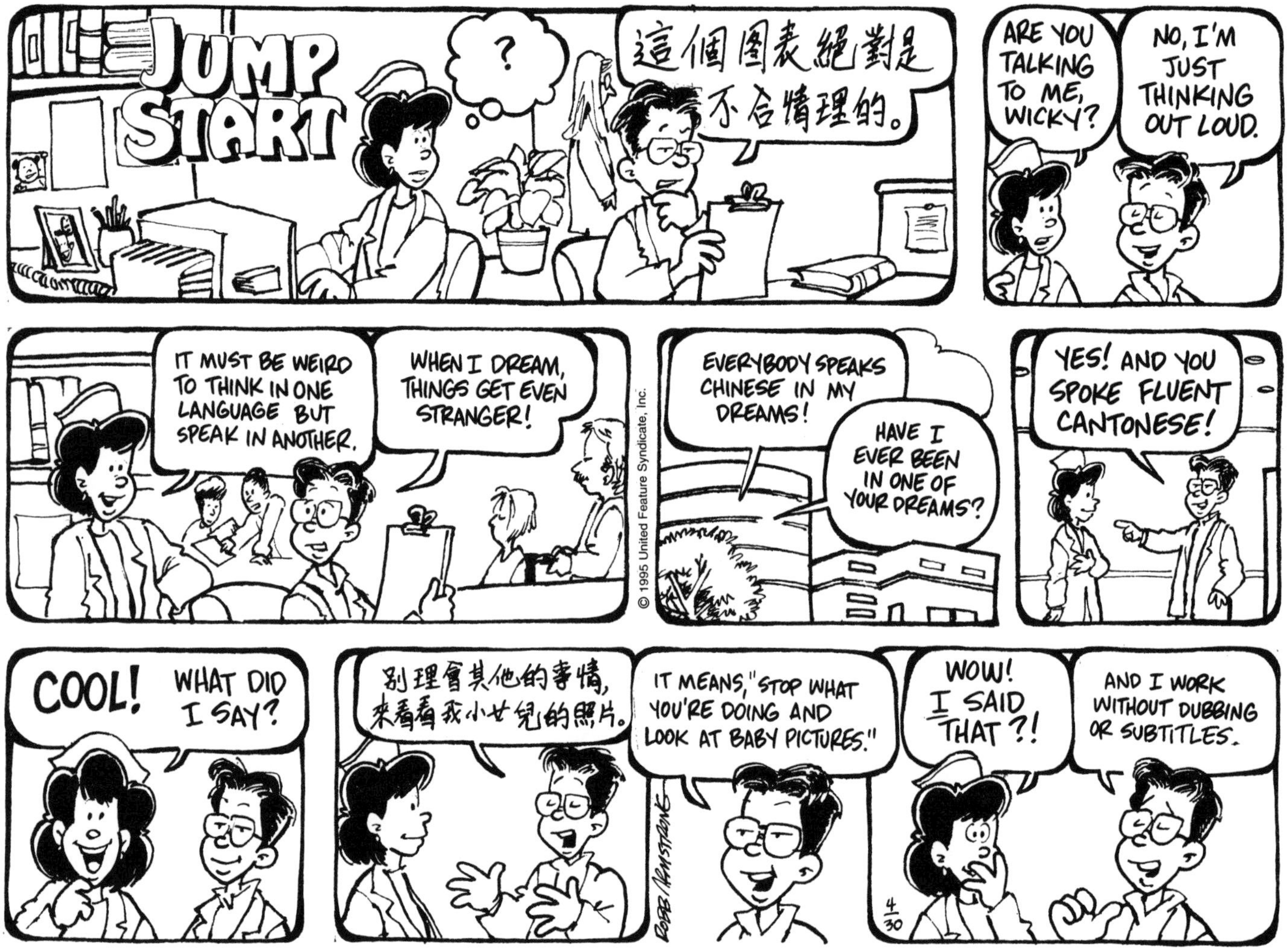
JUMP START
?
這個圖表絕對是不合情理的。
ARE YOU TALKING TO ME, WICKY?
NO, I'M JUST THINKING OUT LOUD.
IT MUST BE WEIRD TO THINK IN ONE LANGUAGE BUT SPEAK IN ANOTHER.
WHEN I DREAM, THINGS GET EVEN STRANGER!
© 1995 United Feature Syndicate, Inc.
EVERYBODY SPEAKS CHINESE IN MY DREAMS!
HAVE I EVER BEEN IN ONE OF YOUR DREAMS?
YES! AND YOU SPOKE FLUENT CANTONESE!
COOL!
WHAT DID I SAY?
别理會其他的事情，來看看我小女兒的照片。
IT MEANS, "STOP WHAT YOU'RE DOING AND LOOK AT BABY PICTURES."
WOW! I SAID THAT?!
AND I WORK WITHOUT DUBBING OR SUBTITLES.
4/30

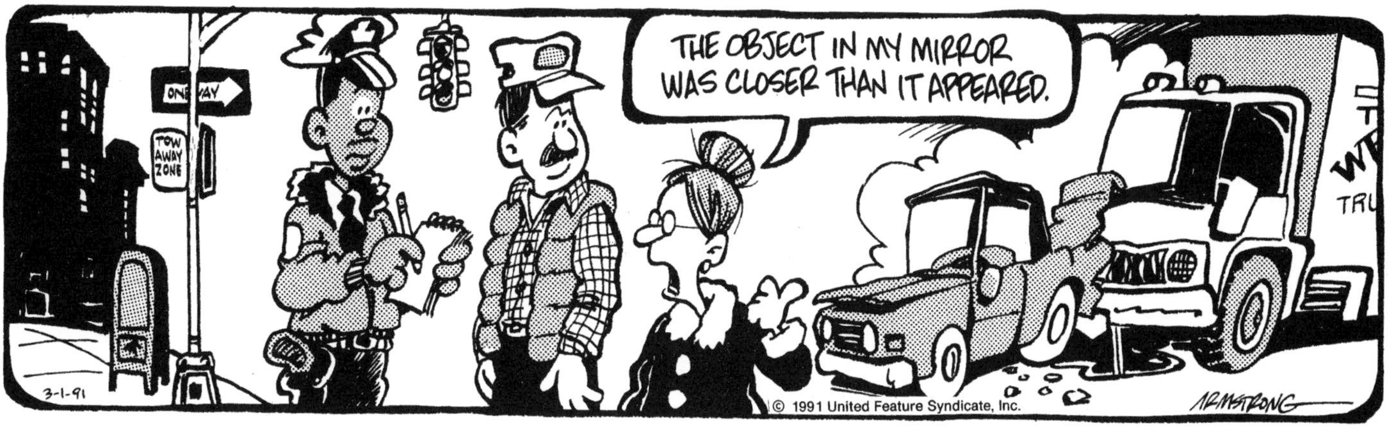
ONE WAY
TOW AWAY ZONE
THE OBJECT IN MY MIRROR WAS CLOSER THAN IT APPEARED.
3-1-91
© 1991 United Feature Syndicate, Inc.
ARMSTRONG

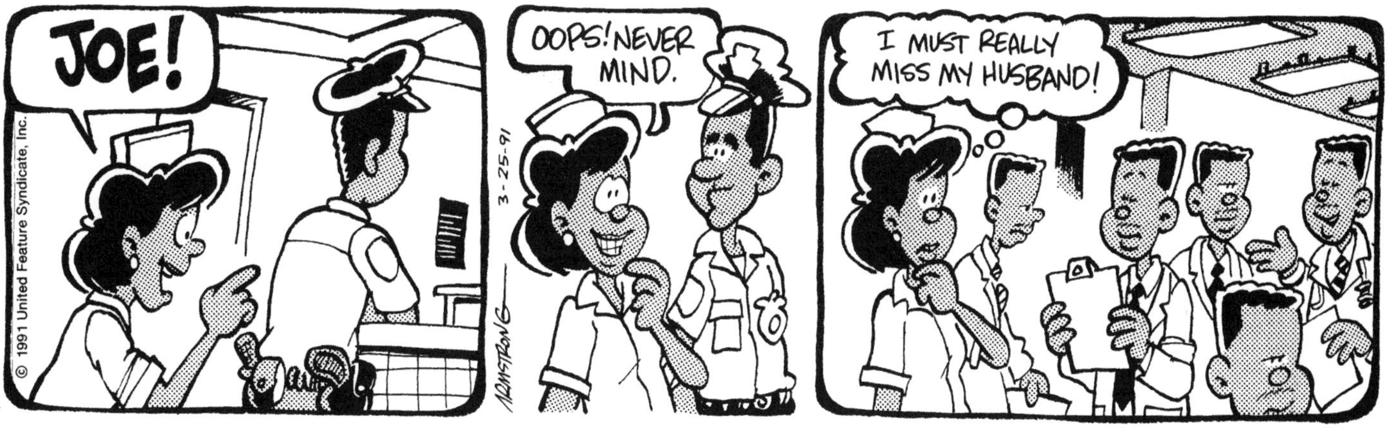
JOE!
© 1991 United Feature Syndicate, Inc.
OOPS! NEVER MIND.
3-25-91
ARMSTRONG
I MUST REALLY MISS MY HUSBAND!

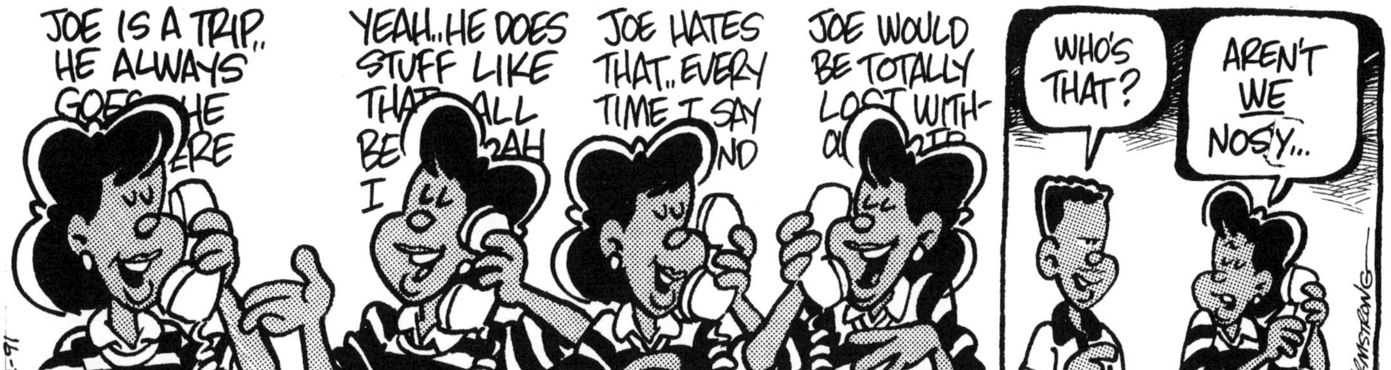
JOE IS A TRIP.. HE ALWAYS
YEAH..HE DOES STUFF LIKE
JOE HATES THAT..EVERY TIME I SAY
JOE WOULD BE TOTALLY
WHO'S THAT?
AREN'T WE NOSY..
ARMSTRONG
© 1991 United Feature Syndicate, Inc.

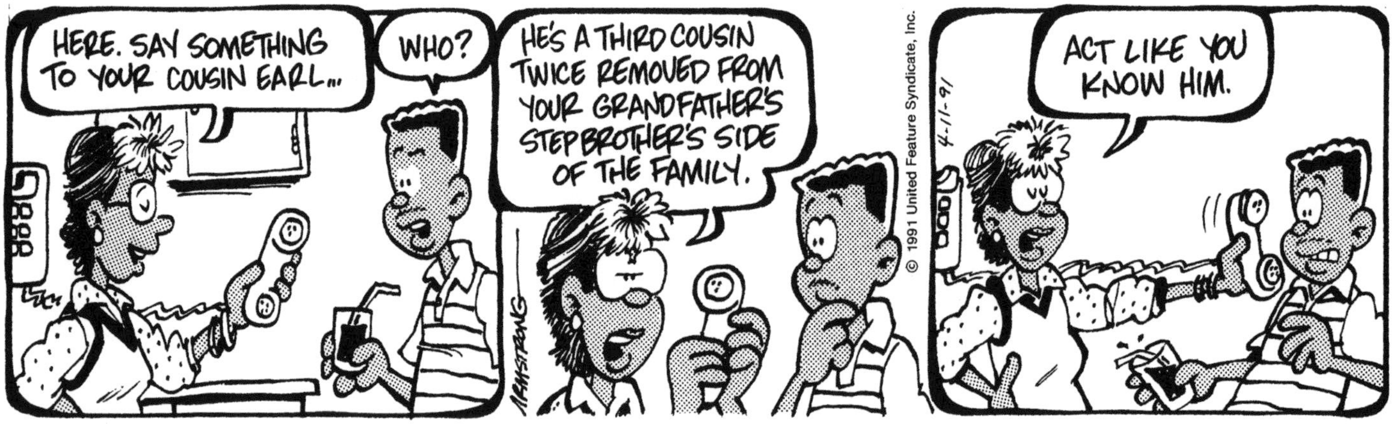
HERE. SAY SOMETHING TO YOUR COUSIN EARL...
WHO?
HE'S A THIRD COUSIN TWICE REMOVED FROM YOUR GRANDFATHER'S STEPBROTHER'S SIDE OF THE FAMILY.
ACT LIKE YOU KNOW HIM.
© 1991 United Feature Syndicate, Inc.

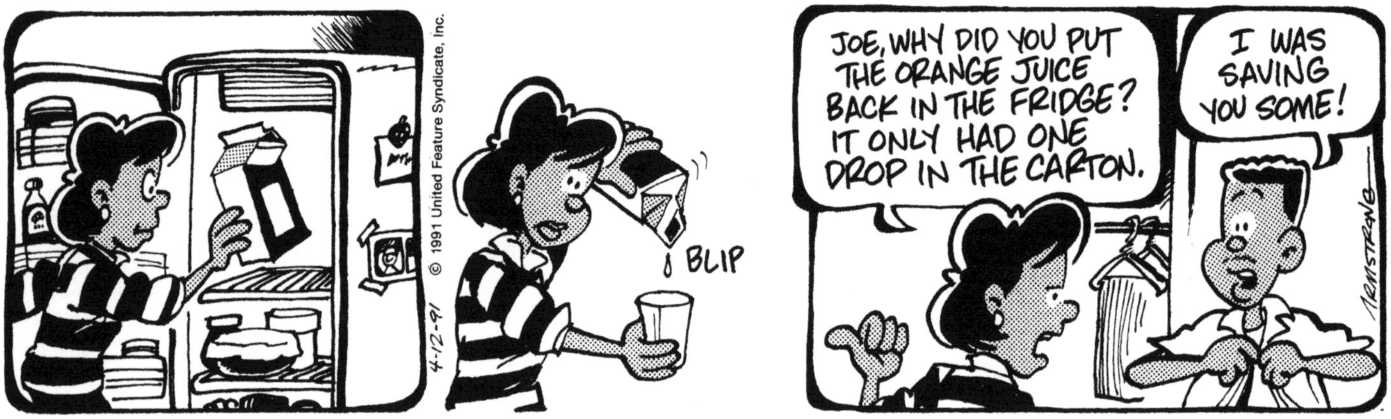
© 1991 United Feature Syndicate, Inc.
BLIP
JOE, WHY DID YOU PUT THE ORANGE JUICE BACK IN THE FRIDGE? IT ONLY HAD ONE DROP IN THE CARTON.
I WAS SAVING YOU SOME!

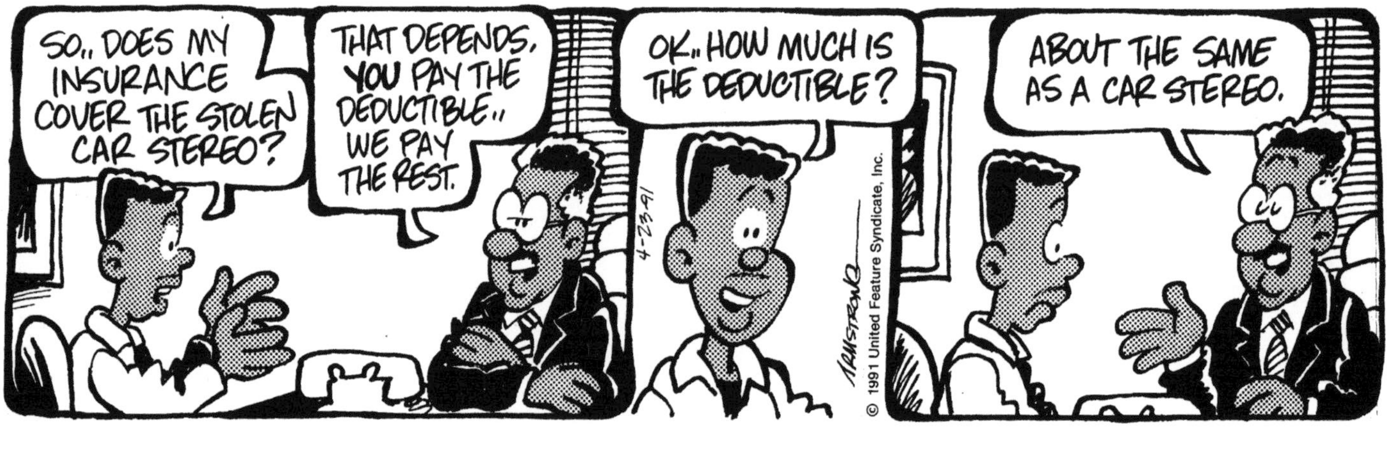
SO.. DOES MY INSURANCE COVER THE STOLEN CAR STEREO?
THAT DEPENDS. YOU PAY THE DEDUCTIBLE.. WE PAY THE REST.
OK.. HOW MUCH IS THE DEDUCTIBLE?
ABOUT THE SAME AS A CAR STEREO.
© 1991 United Feature Syndicate, Inc.

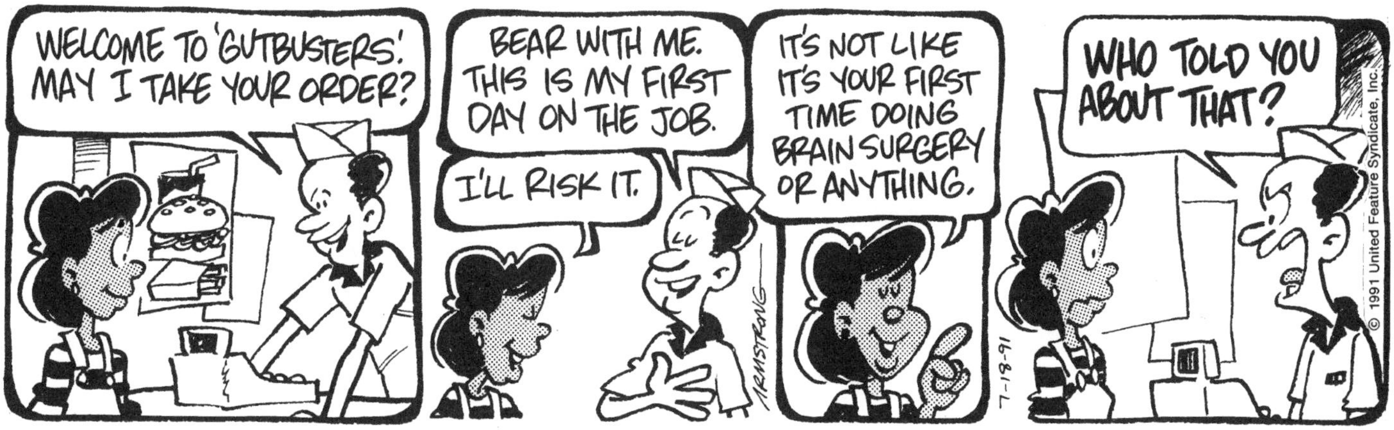
WELCOME TO 'GUTBUSTERS.' MAY I TAKE YOUR ORDER?
BEAR WITH ME. THIS IS MY FIRST DAY ON THE JOB.
I'LL RISK IT.
IT'S NOT LIKE IT'S YOUR FIRST TIME DOING BRAIN SURGERY OR ANYTHING.
WHO TOLD YOU ABOUT THAT?
ARMSTRONG
7-18-91
© 1991 United Feature Syndicate, Inc.

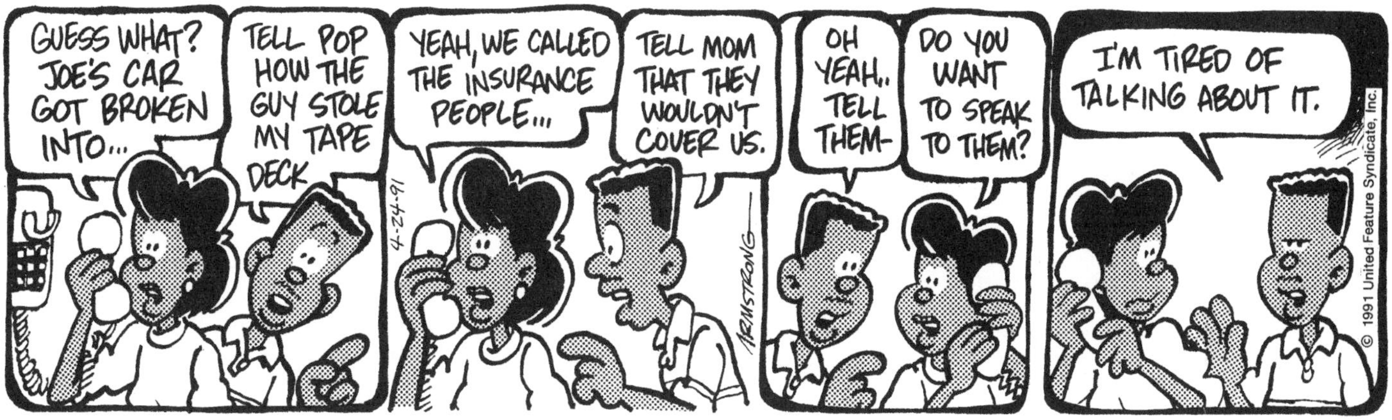
GUESS WHAT? JOE'S CAR GOT BROKEN INTO...
TELL POP HOW THE GUY STOLE MY TAPE DECK
YEAH, WE CALLED THE INSURANCE PEOPLE...
TELL MOM THAT THEY WOULDN'T COVER US.
OH YEAH.. TELL THEM-
DO YOU WANT TO SPEAK TO THEM?
I'M TIRED OF TALKING ABOUT IT.
4-24-91
ARMSTRONG
© 1991 United Feature Syndicate, Inc.

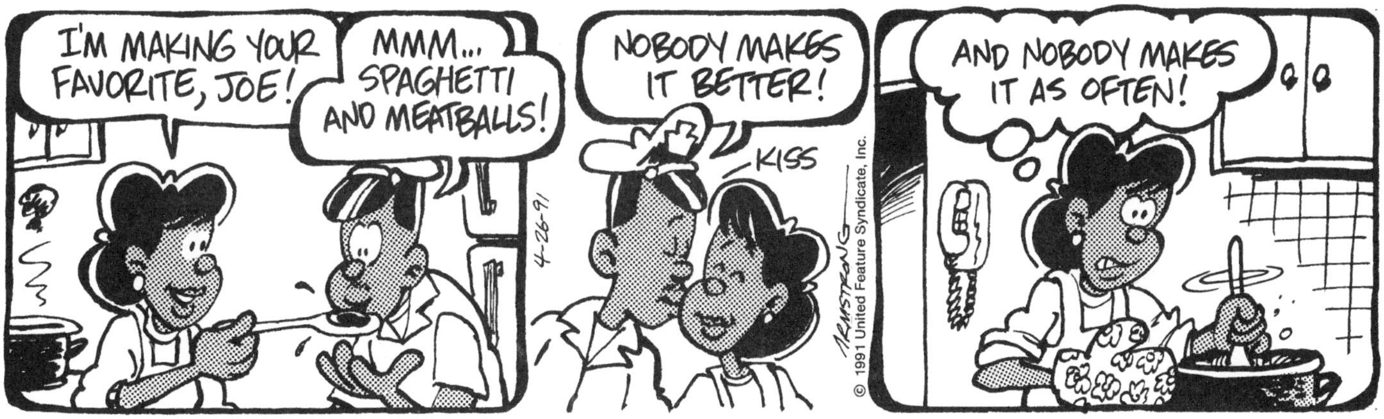
I'M MAKING YOUR FAVORITE, JOE!
MMM... SPAGHETTI AND MEATBALLS!
NOBODY MAKES IT BETTER!
KISS
AND NOBODY MAKES IT AS OFTEN!
4-26-91
ARMSTRONG
© 1991 United Feature Syndicate, Inc.

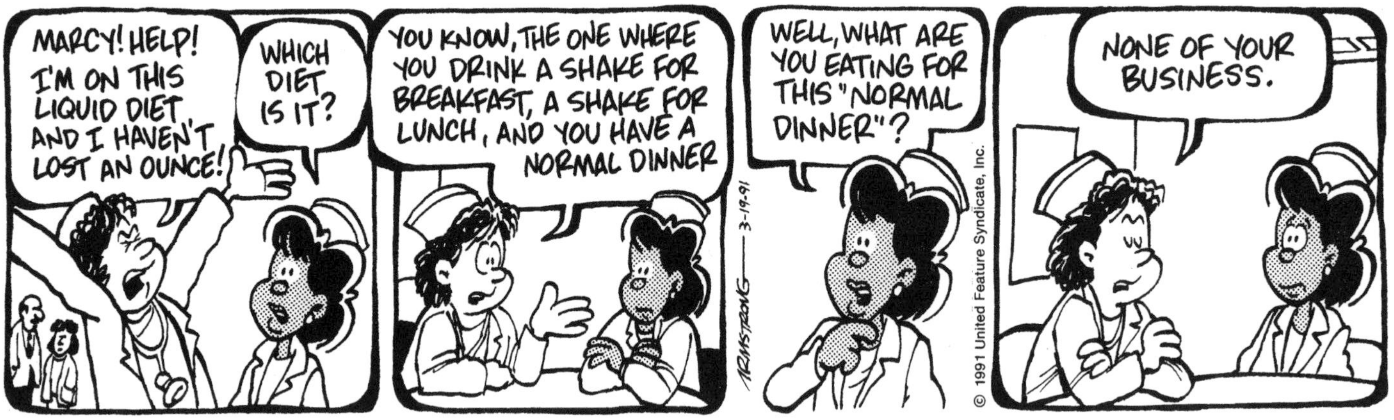

MARCY! HELP! I'M ON THIS LIQUID DIET, AND I HAVEN'T LOST AN OUNCE!
WHICH DIET IS IT?
YOU KNOW, THE ONE WHERE YOU DRINK A SHAKE FOR BREAKFAST, A SHAKE FOR LUNCH, AND YOU HAVE A NORMAL DINNER
WELL, WHAT ARE YOU EATING FOR THIS "NORMAL DINNER"?
NONE OF YOUR BUSINESS.
3-19-91
© 1991 United Feature Syndicate, Inc.

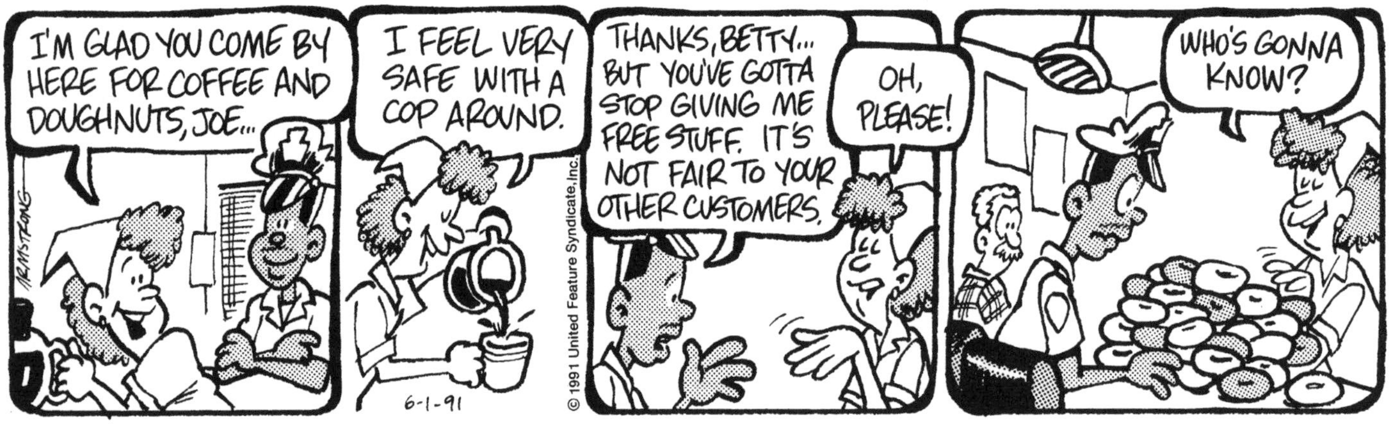

I'M GLAD YOU COME BY HERE FOR COFFEE AND DOUGHNUTS, JOE...
I FEEL VERY SAFE WITH A COP AROUND.
THANKS, BETTY... BUT YOU'VE GOTTA STOP GIVING ME FREE STUFF. IT'S NOT FAIR TO YOUR OTHER CUSTOMERS.
OH, PLEASE!
WHO'S GONNA KNOW?
6-1-91
© 1991 United Feature Syndicate, Inc.

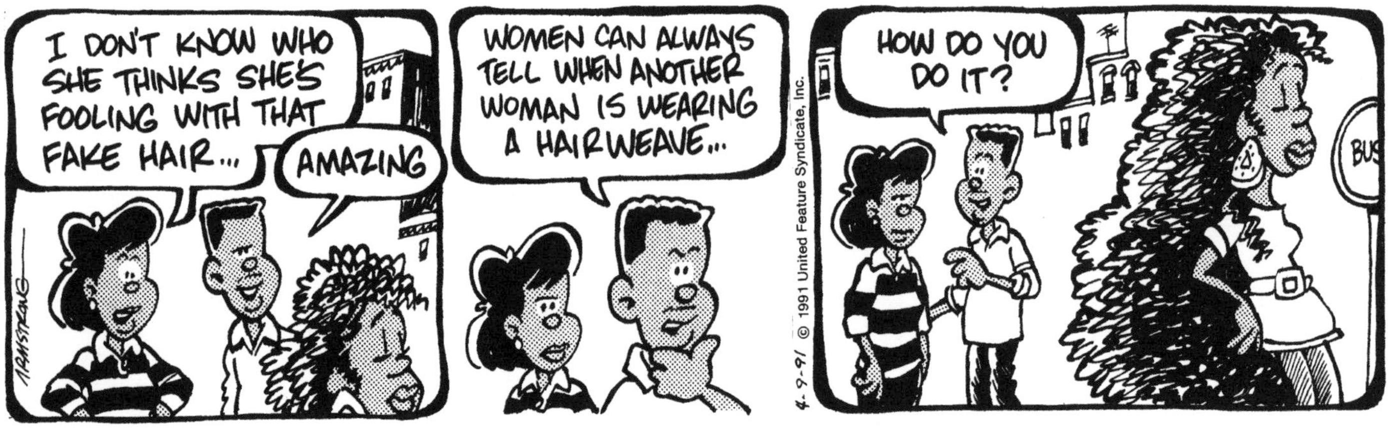

I DON'T KNOW WHO SHE THINKS SHE'S FOOLING WITH THAT FAKE HAIR...
AMAZING
WOMEN CAN ALWAYS TELL WHEN ANOTHER WOMAN IS WEARING A HAIRWEAVE...
HOW DO YOU DO IT?
4-9-91
© 1991 United Feature Syndicate, Inc.

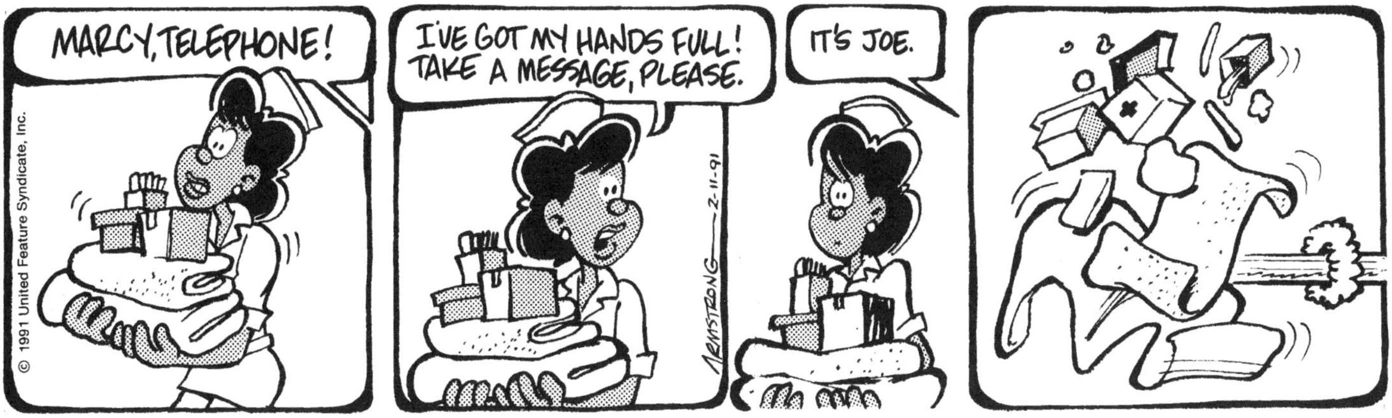
MARCY, TELEPHONE!
I'VE GOT MY HANDS FULL! TAKE A MESSAGE, PLEASE.
IT'S JOE.
© 1991 United Feature Syndicate, Inc.
2-11-91
ARMSTRONG

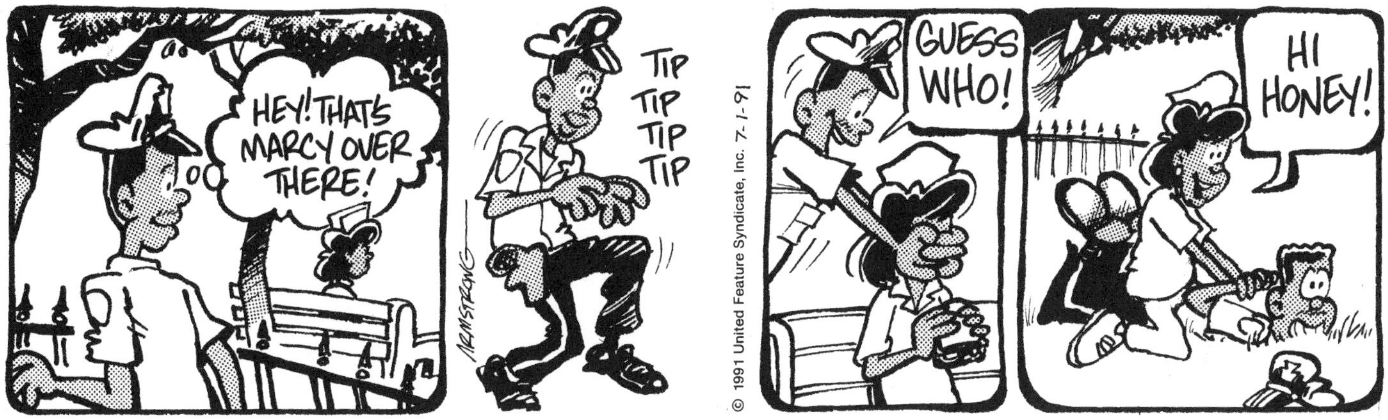
HEY! THAT'S MARCY OVER THERE!
TIP
TIP
TIP
TIP
ARMSTRONG
© 1991 United Feature Syndicate, Inc. 7-1-91
GUESS WHO!
HI HONEY!

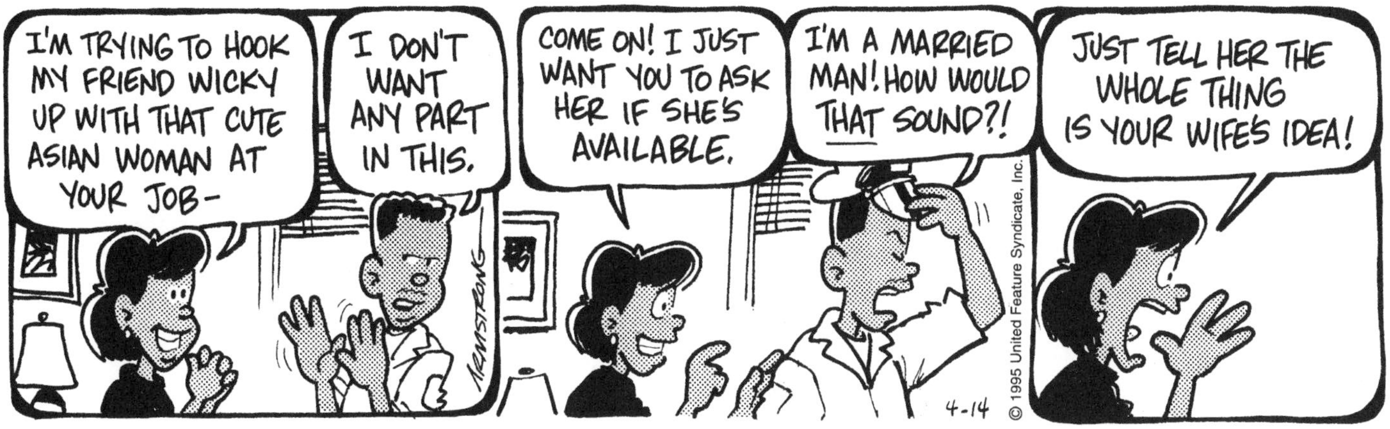
I'M TRYING TO HOOK MY FRIEND WICKY UP WITH THAT CUTE ASIAN WOMAN AT YOUR JOB-
I DON'T WANT ANY PART IN THIS.
ARMSTRONG
COME ON! I JUST WANT YOU TO ASK HER IF SHE'S AVAILABLE.
I'M A MARRIED MAN! HOW WOULD THAT SOUND?!
4-14
© 1995 United Feature Syndicate, Inc.
JUST TELL HER THE WHOLE THING IS YOUR WIFE'S IDEA!

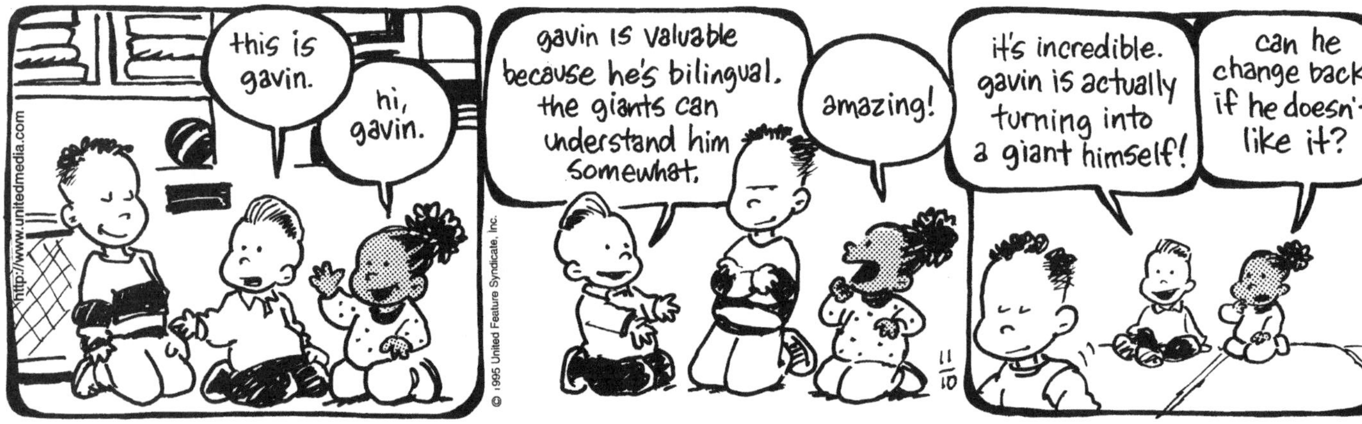
http://www.unitedmedia.com
this is gavin.
hi, gavin.
© 1995 United Feature Syndicate, Inc.
gavin is valuable because he's bilingual. the giants can understand him somewhat.
amazing!
11/10
it's incredible. gavin is actually turning into a giant himself!
can he change back if he doesn't like it?

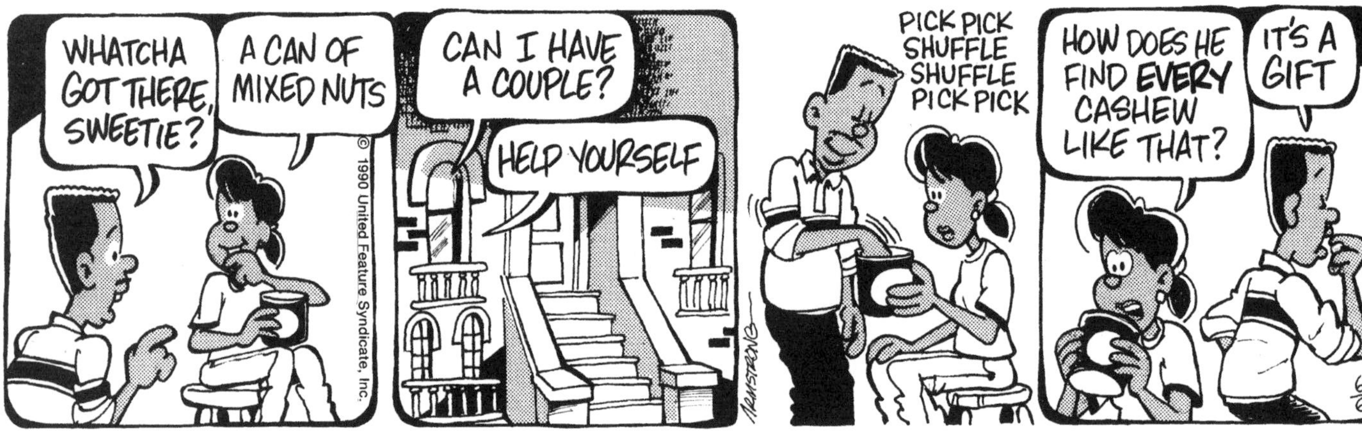
WHATCHA GOT THERE, SWEETIE?
A CAN OF MIXED NUTS
© 1990 United Feature Syndicate, Inc.
CAN I HAVE A COUPLE?
HELP YOURSELF
PICK PICK SHUFFLE SHUFFLE PICK PICK
ARMSTRONG
HOW DOES HE FIND EVERY CASHEW LIKE THAT?
IT'S A GIFT
6/6

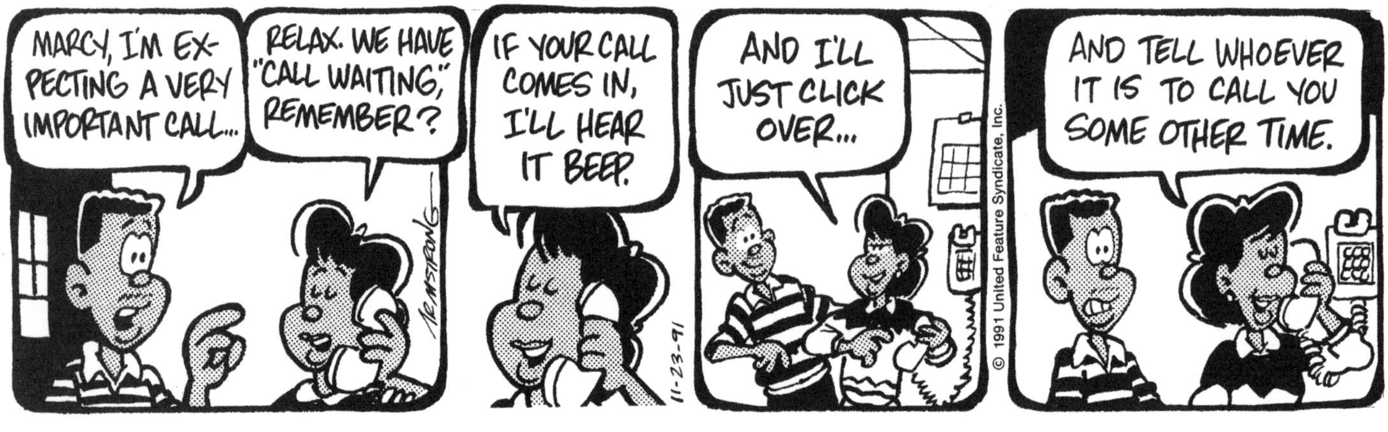
MARCY, I'M EXPECTING A VERY IMPORTANT CALL...
RELAX. WE HAVE "CALL WAITING," REMEMBER?
ARMSTRONG
IF YOUR CALL COMES IN, I'LL HEAR IT BEEP.
11-23-91
AND I'LL JUST CLICK OVER...
© 1991 United Feature Syndicate, Inc.
AND TELL WHOEVER IT IS TO CALL YOU SOME OTHER TIME.

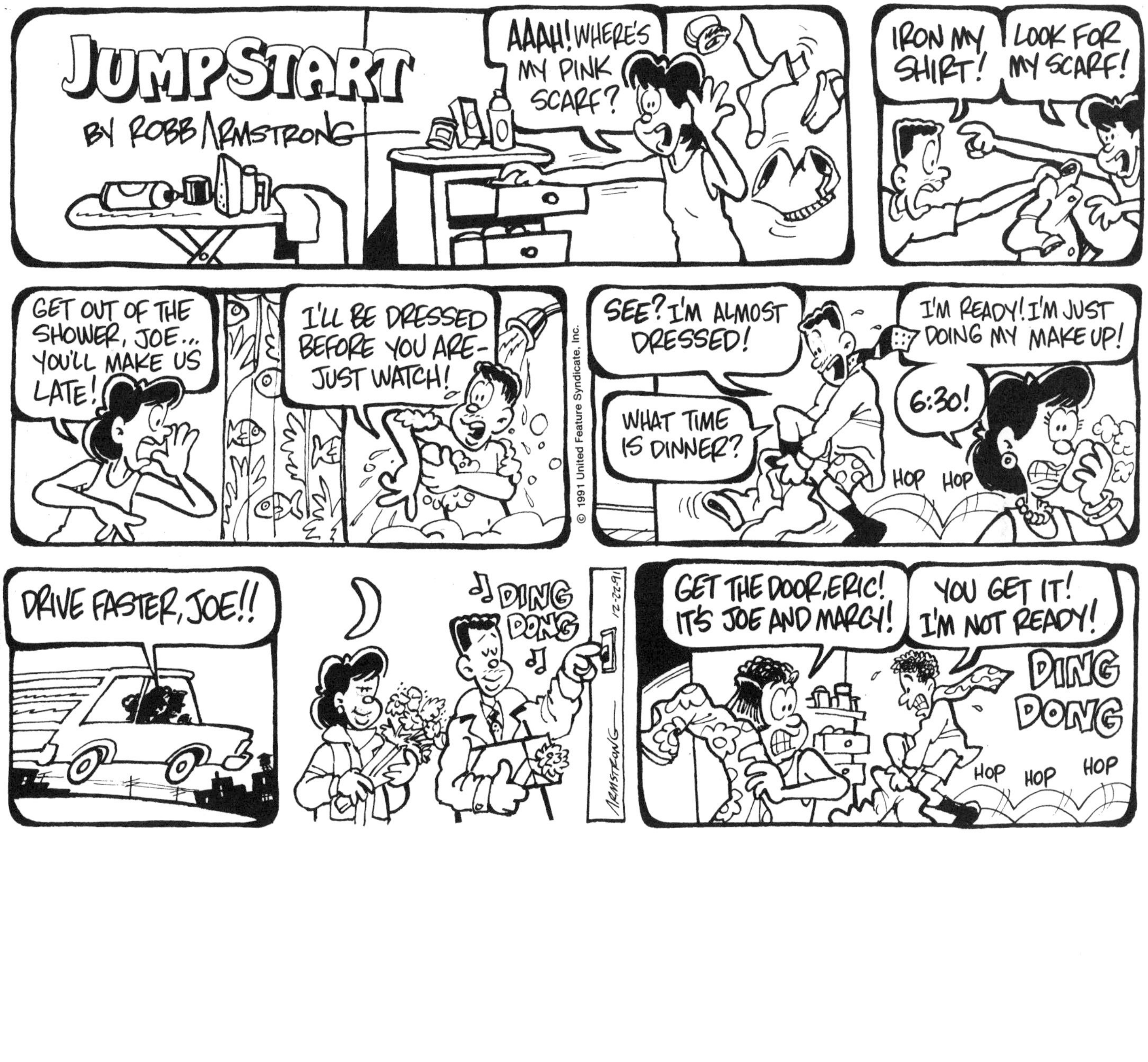
JUMPSTART
BY ROBB ARMSTRONG
AAAH! WHERE'S MY PINK SCARF?
IRON MY SHIRT!
LOOK FOR MY SCARF!
GET OUT OF THE SHOWER, JOE... YOU'LL MAKE US LATE!
I'LL BE DRESSED BEFORE YOU ARE- JUST WATCH!
© 1991 United Feature Syndicate, Inc.
SEE? I'M ALMOST DRESSED!
I'M READY! I'M JUST DOING MY MAKE UP!
WHAT TIME IS DINNER?
6:30!
HOP HOP
DRIVE FASTER, JOE!!
DING DONG
12-22-91
ARMSTRONG
GET THE DOOR, ERIC! IT'S JOE AND MARCY!
YOU GET IT! I'M NOT READY!
DING DONG
HOP HOP HOP

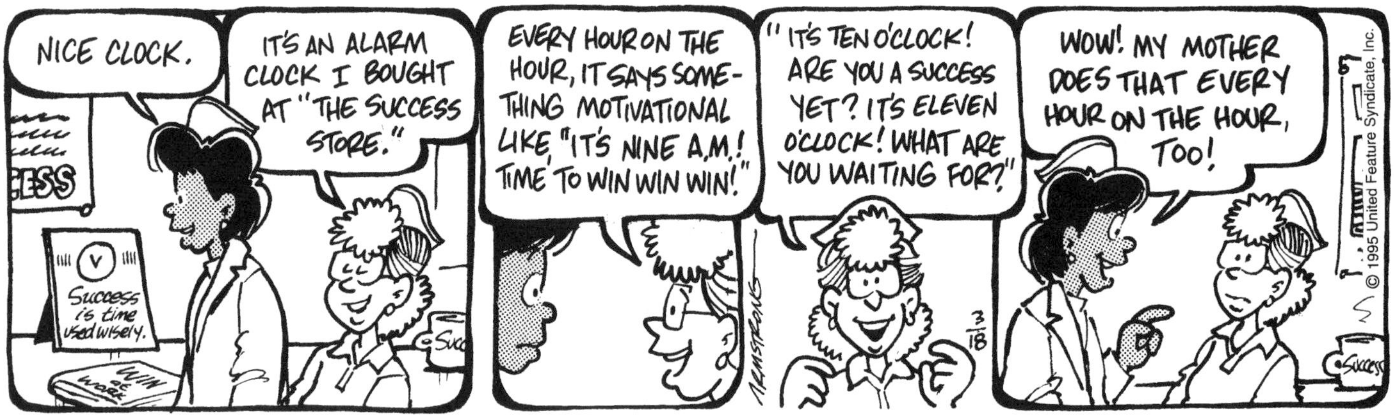
NICE CLOCK.
IT'S AN ALARM CLOCK I BOUGHT AT "THE SUCCESS STORE."
EVERY HOUR ON THE HOUR, IT SAYS SOMETHING MOTIVATIONAL LIKE, "IT'S NINE A.M.! TIME TO WIN WIN WIN!"
"IT'S TEN O'CLOCK! ARE YOU A SUCCESS YET? IT'S ELEVEN O'CLOCK! WHAT ARE YOU WAITING FOR?"
WOW! MY MOTHER DOES THAT EVERY HOUR ON THE HOUR, TOO!
Success is time used wisely.
WIN AT WORK
3/18
© 1995 United Feature Syndicate, Inc.

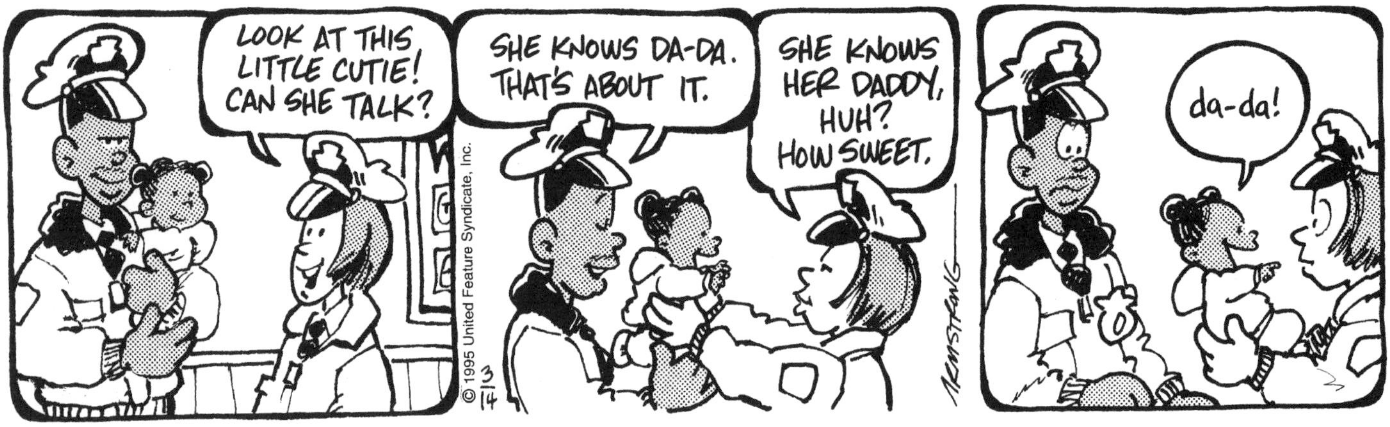
LOOK AT THIS LITTLE CUTIE! CAN SHE TALK?
SHE KNOWS DA-DA. THAT'S ABOUT IT.
SHE KNOWS HER DADDY, HUH? HOW SWEET.
da-da!
© 1995 United Feature Syndicate, Inc. 3/14

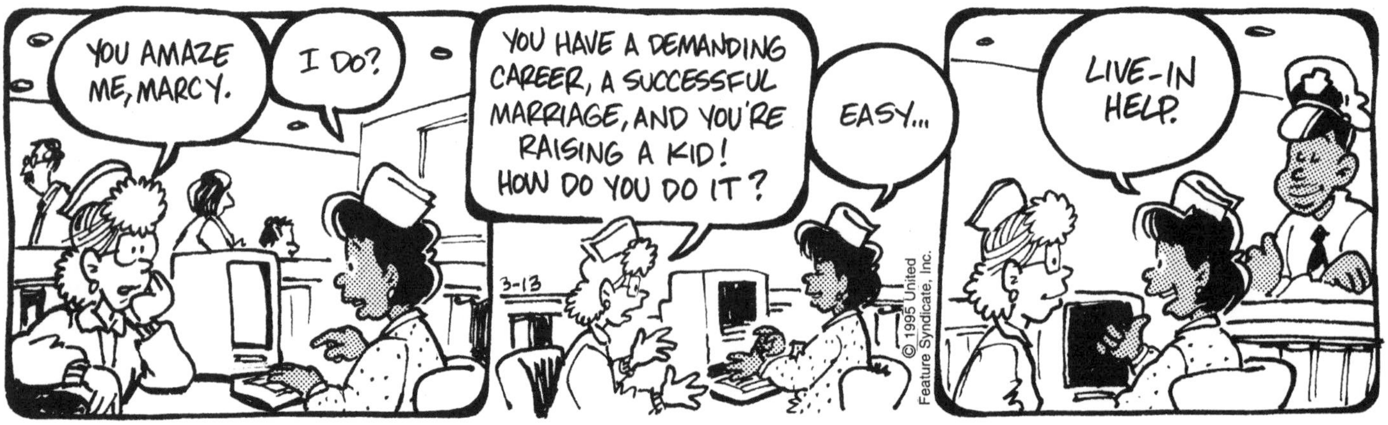
YOU AMAZE ME, MARCY.
I DO?
YOU HAVE A DEMANDING CAREER, A SUCCESSFUL MARRIAGE, AND YOU'RE RAISING A KID! HOW DO YOU DO IT?
EASY...
LIVE-IN HELP.
3-13
© 1995 United Feature Syndicate, Inc.

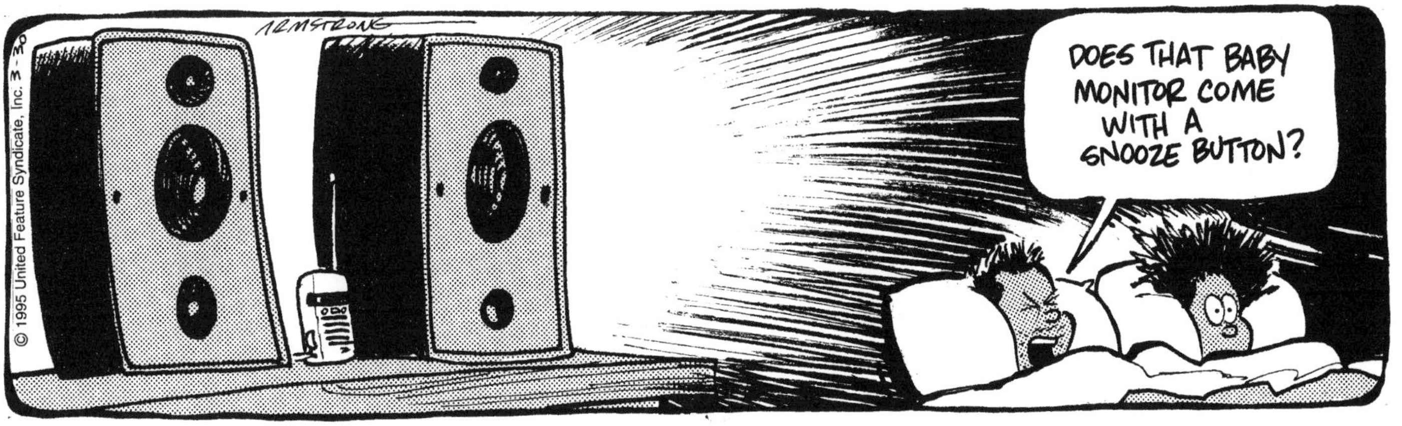
ARMSTRONG 3-30
© 1995 United Feature Syndicate, Inc.
DOES THAT BABY MONITOR COME WITH A SNOOZE BUTTON?

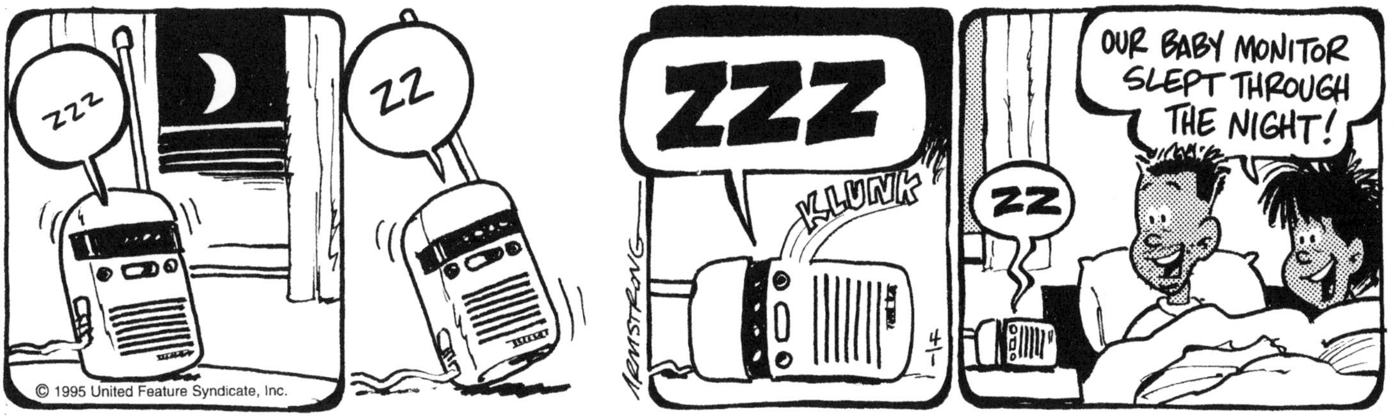
ZZZ
ZZ
© 1995 United Feature Syndicate, Inc.
ZZZ
KLUNK
ARMSTRONG 4/1
ZZ
OUR BABY MONITOR SLEPT THROUGH THE NIGHT!

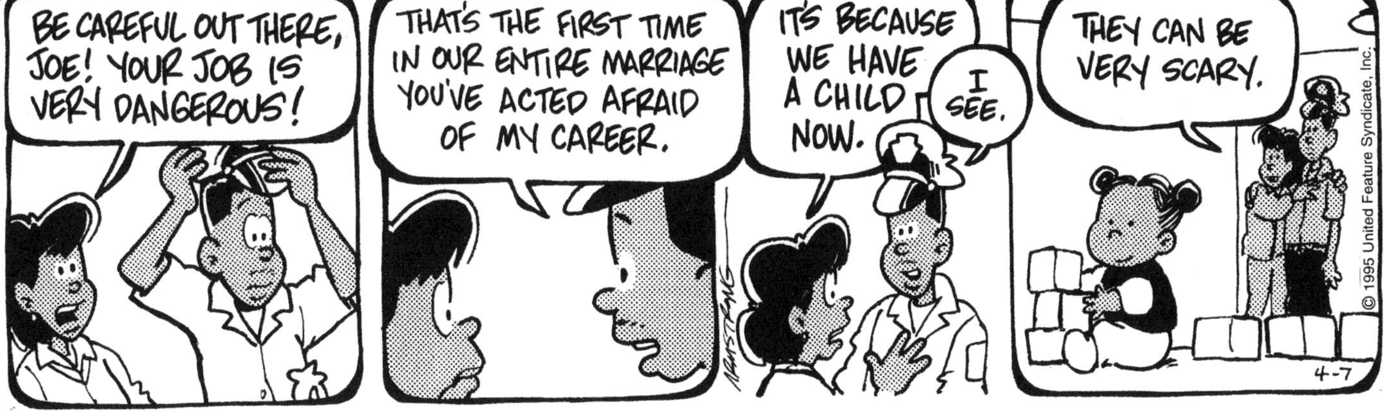
BE CAREFUL OUT THERE, JOE! YOUR JOB IS VERY DANGEROUS!
THAT'S THE FIRST TIME IN OUR ENTIRE MARRIAGE YOU'VE ACTED AFRAID OF MY CAREER.
IT'S BECAUSE WE HAVE A CHILD NOW.
I SEE.
ARMSTRONG
THEY CAN BE VERY SCARY.
© 1995 United Feature Syndicate, Inc.
4-7

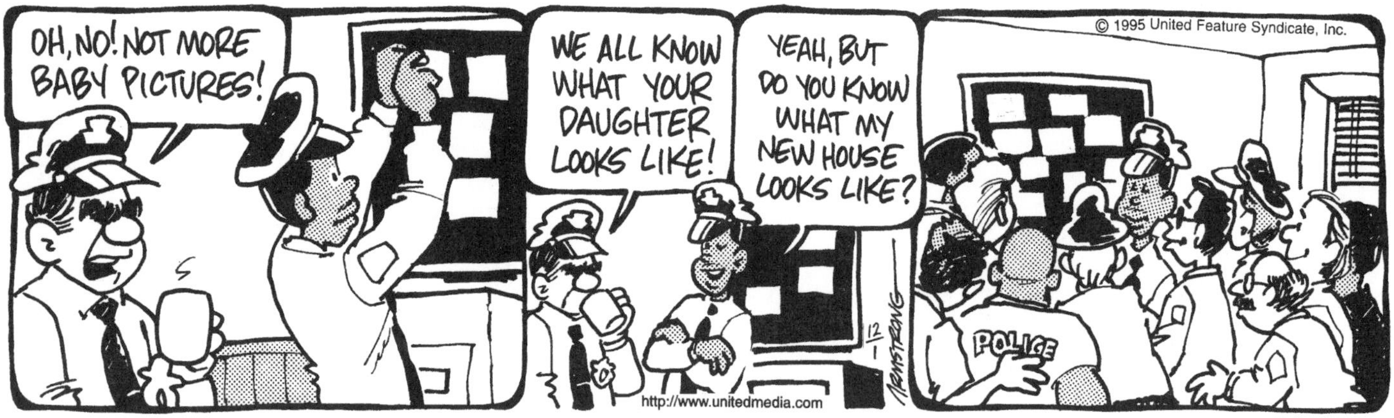
OH, NO! NOT MORE BABY PICTURES!
WE ALL KNOW WHAT YOUR DAUGHTER LOOKS LIKE!
YEAH, BUT DO YOU KNOW WHAT MY NEW HOUSE LOOKS LIKE?
POLICE
© 1995 United Feature Syndicate, Inc.
http://www.unitedmedia.com

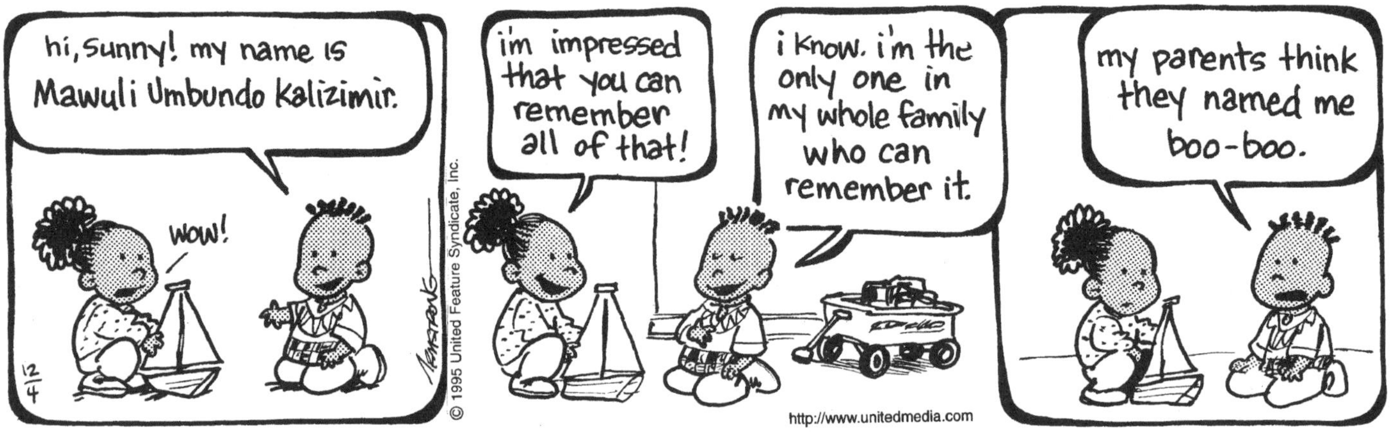
hi, sunny! my name is Mawuli Umbundo Kalizimir.
WOW!
i'm impressed that you can remember all of that!
i know. i'm the only one in my whole family who can remember it.
my parents think they named me boo-boo.
© 1995 United Feature Syndicate, Inc.
http://www.unitedmedia.com

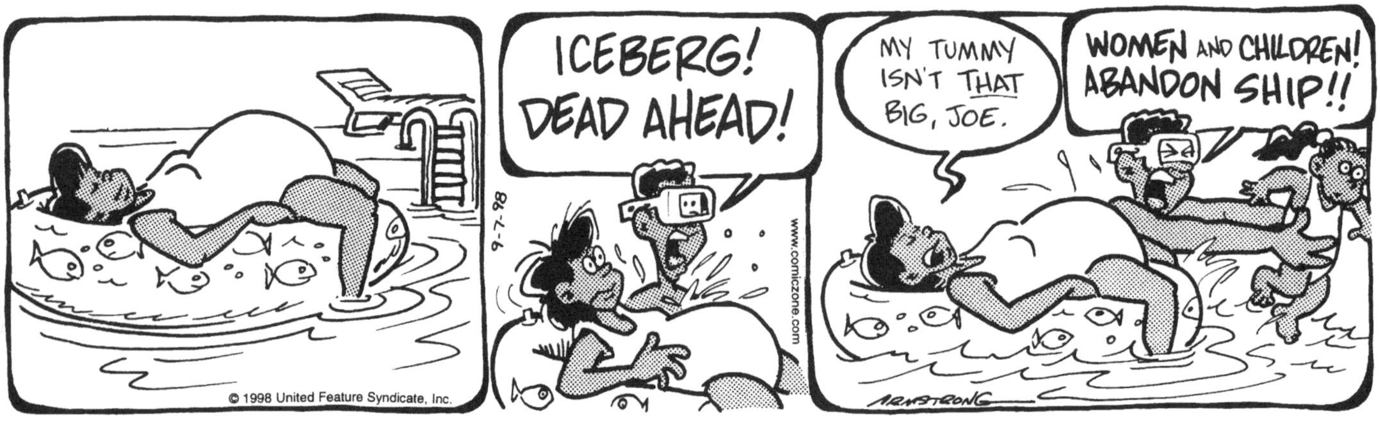
ICEBERG! DEAD AHEAD!
MY TUMMY ISN'T THAT BIG, JOE.
WOMEN AND CHILDREN! ABANDON SHIP!!
© 1998 United Feature Syndicate, Inc.
www.comiczone.com

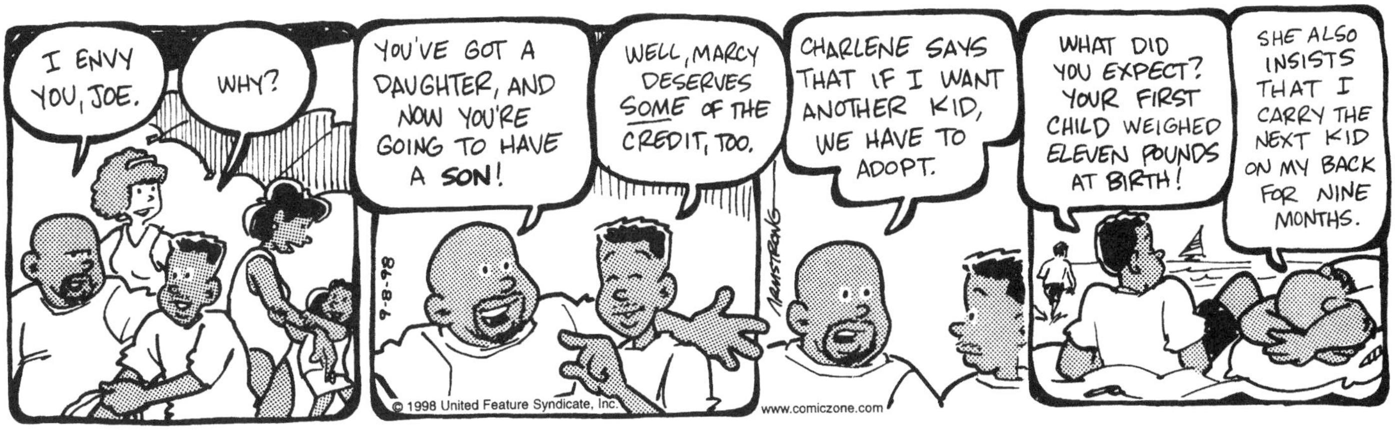
I ENVY YOU, JOE.
WHY?
YOU'VE GOT A DAUGHTER, AND NOW YOU'RE GOING TO HAVE A SON!
WELL, MARCY DESERVES SOME OF THE CREDIT, TOO.
9-8-98
ARMSTRONG
© 1998 United Feature Syndicate, Inc.
CHARLENE SAYS THAT IF I WANT ANOTHER KID, WE HAVE TO ADOPT.
www.comiczone.com
WHAT DID YOU EXPECT? YOUR FIRST CHILD WEIGHED ELEVEN POUNDS AT BIRTH!
SHE ALSO INSISTS THAT I CARRY THE NEXT KID ON MY BACK FOR NINE MONTHS.

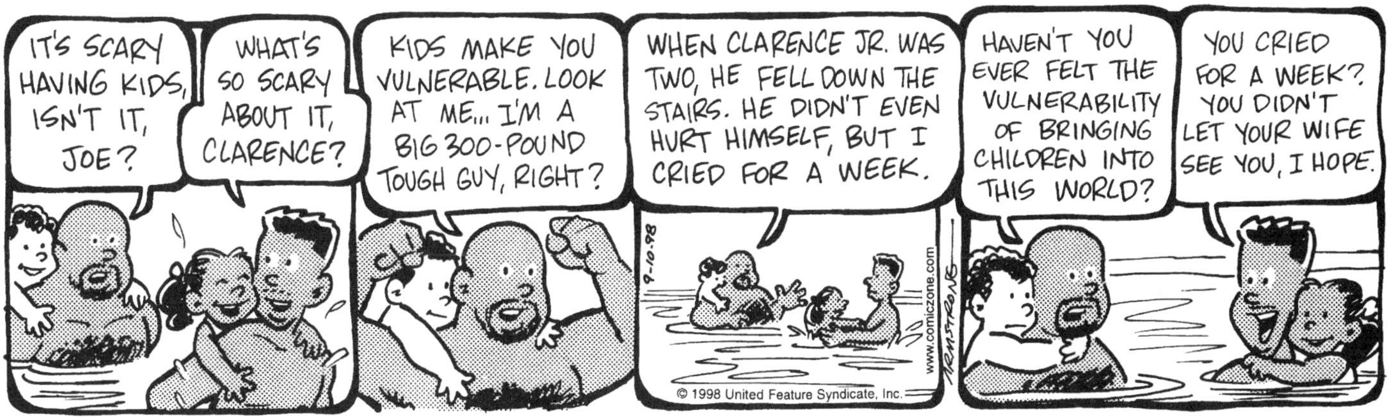
IT'S SCARY HAVING KIDS, ISN'T IT, JOE?
WHAT'S SO SCARY ABOUT IT, CLARENCE?
KIDS MAKE YOU VULNERABLE. LOOK AT ME... I'M A BIG 300-POUND TOUGH GUY, RIGHT?
WHEN CLARENCE JR. WAS TWO, HE FELL DOWN THE STAIRS. HE DIDN'T EVEN HURT HIMSELF, BUT I CRIED FOR A WEEK.
9-10-98
www.comiczone.com
ARMSTRONG
© 1998 United Feature Syndicate, Inc.
HAVEN'T YOU EVER FELT THE VULNERABILITY OF BRINGING CHILDREN INTO THIS WORLD?
YOU CRIED FOR A WEEK? YOU DIDN'T LET YOUR WIFE SEE YOU, I HOPE.

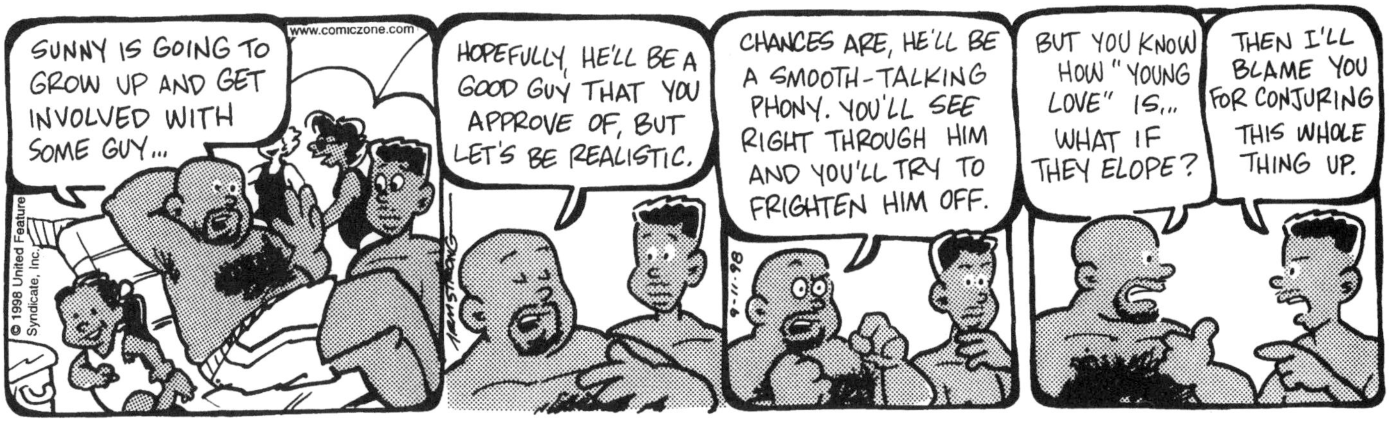
SUNNY IS GOING TO GROW UP AND GET INVOLVED WITH SOME GUY...
www.comiczone.com
© 1998 United Feature Syndicate, Inc.
ARMSTRONG
HOPEFULLY, HE'LL BE A GOOD GUY THAT YOU APPROVE OF, BUT LET'S BE REALISTIC.
CHANCES ARE, HE'LL BE A SMOOTH-TALKING PHONY. YOU'LL SEE RIGHT THROUGH HIM AND YOU'LL TRY TO FRIGHTEN HIM OFF.
9-11-98
BUT YOU KNOW HOW "YOUNG LOVE" IS... WHAT IF THEY ELOPE?
THEN I'LL BLAME YOU FOR CONJURING THIS WHOLE THING UP.

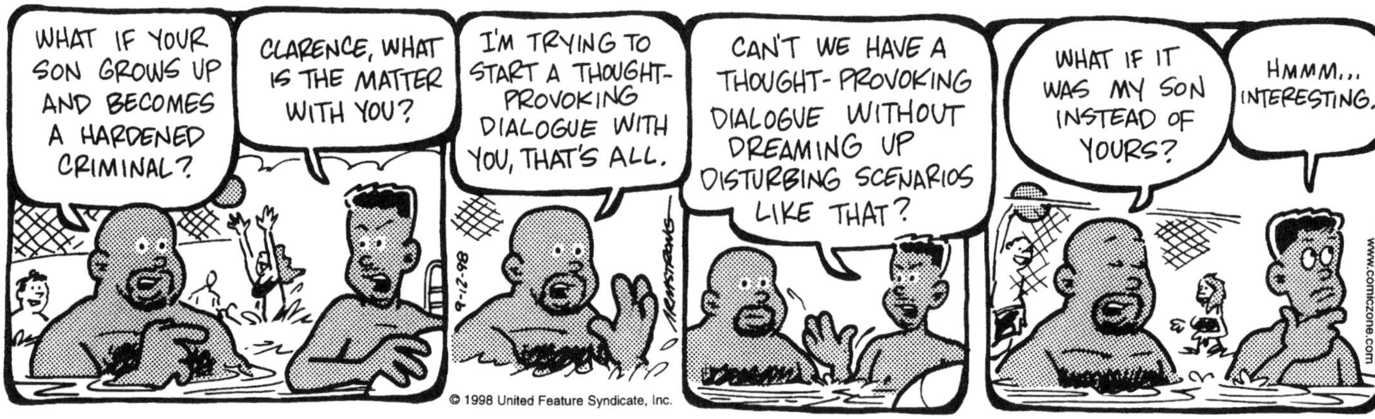
WHAT IF YOUR SON GROWS UP AND BECOMES A HARDENED CRIMINAL?
CLARENCE, WHAT IS THE MATTER WITH YOU?
I'M TRYING TO START A THOUGHT-PROVOKING DIALOGUE WITH YOU, THAT'S ALL.
9-12-98
© 1998 United Feature Syndicate, Inc.
CAN'T WE HAVE A THOUGHT-PROVOKING DIALOGUE WITHOUT DREAMING UP DISTURBING SCENARIOS LIKE THAT?
WHAT IF IT WAS MY SON INSTEAD OF YOURS?
HMMM... INTERESTING.
www.comiczone.com

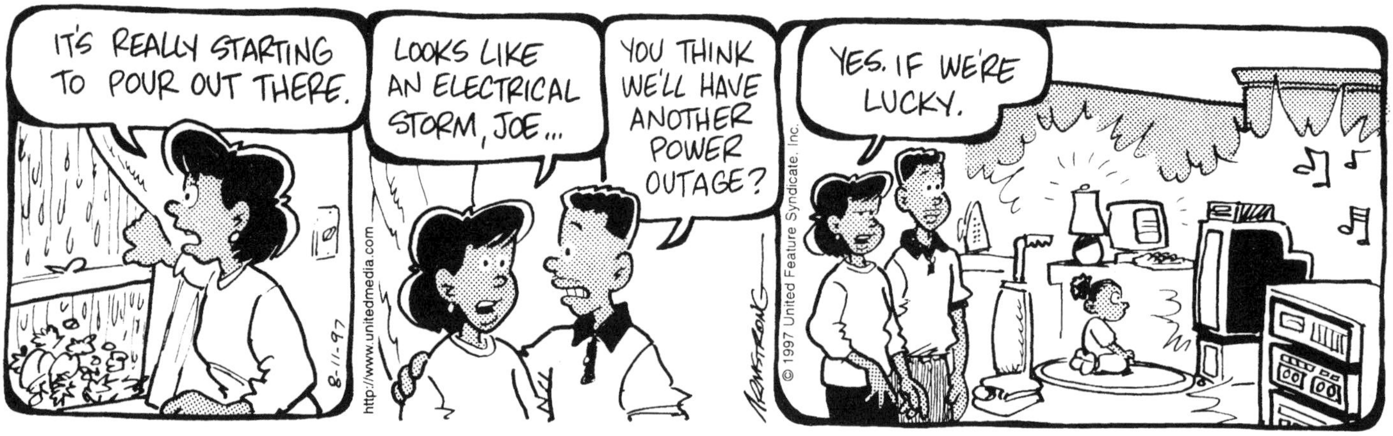
IT'S REALLY STARTING TO POUR OUT THERE.
8-11-97
http://www.unitedmedia.com
LOOKS LIKE AN ELECTRICAL STORM, JOE...
YOU THINK WE'LL HAVE ANOTHER POWER OUTAGE?
© 1997 United Feature Syndicate, Inc.
YES. IF WE'RE LUCKY.

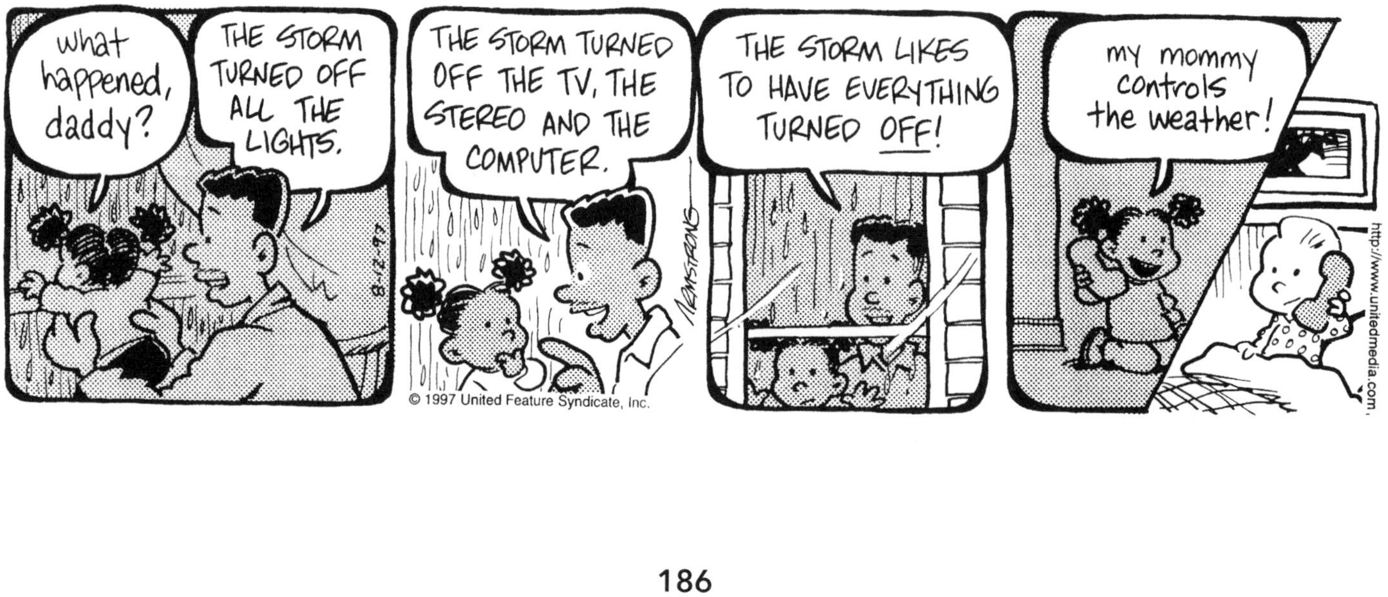
what happened, daddy?
THE STORM TURNED OFF ALL THE LIGHTS.
8-12-97
THE STORM TURNED OFF THE TV, THE STEREO AND THE COMPUTER.
© 1997 United Feature Syndicate, Inc.
THE STORM LIKES TO HAVE EVERYTHING TURNED OFF!
my mommy controls the weather!
http://www.unitedmedia.com

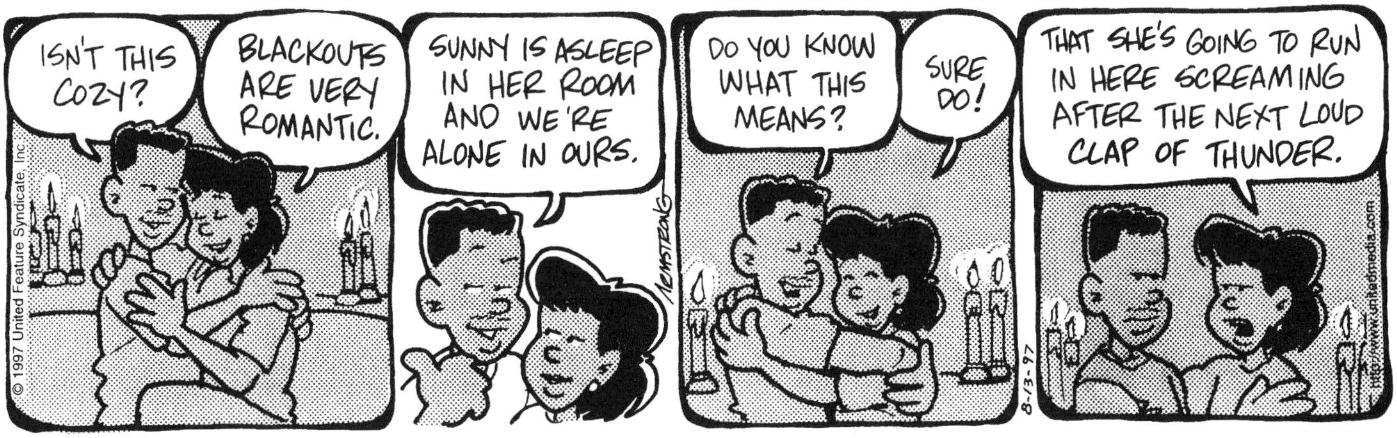
ISN'T THIS COZY?
BLACKOUTS ARE VERY ROMANTIC.
SUNNY IS ASLEEP IN HER ROOM AND WE'RE ALONE IN OURS.
DO YOU KNOW WHAT THIS MEANS?
SURE DO!
THAT SHE'S GOING TO RUN IN HERE SCREAMING AFTER THE NEXT LOUD CLAP OF THUNDER.
© 1997 United Feature Syndicate, Inc.
ARMSTRONG
8-13-97
http://www.unitedmedia.com

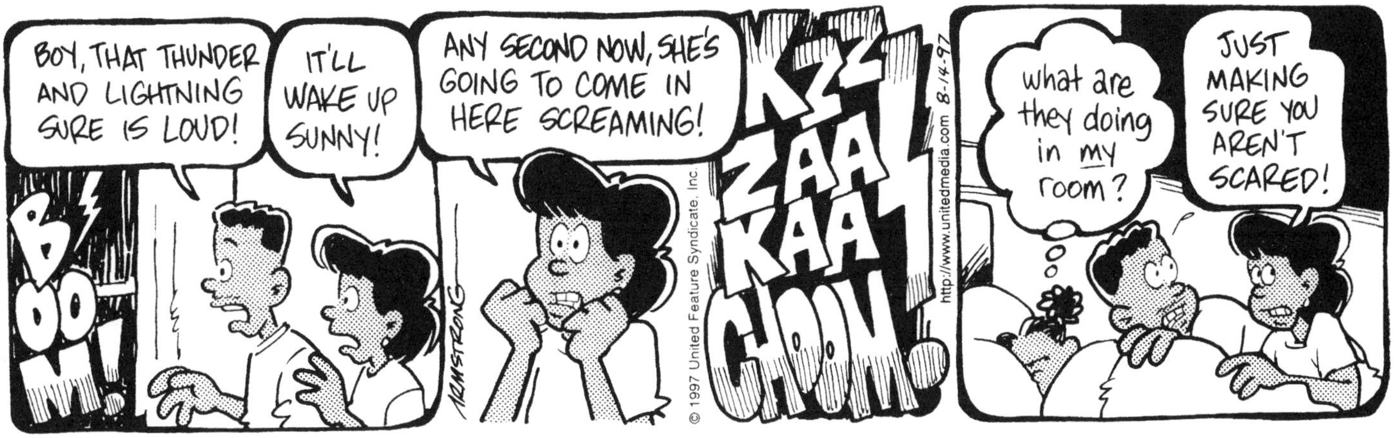
BOOM!
BOY, THAT THUNDER AND LIGHTNING SURE IS LOUD!
IT'LL WAKE UP SUNNY!
ANY SECOND NOW, SHE'S GOING TO COME IN HERE SCREAMING!
ARMSTRONG
© 1997 United Feature Syndicate, Inc.
KZZ ZAA KAA CHOOM!
http://www.unitedmedia.com
8-14-97
what are they doing in my room?
JUST MAKING SURE YOU AREN'T SCARED!

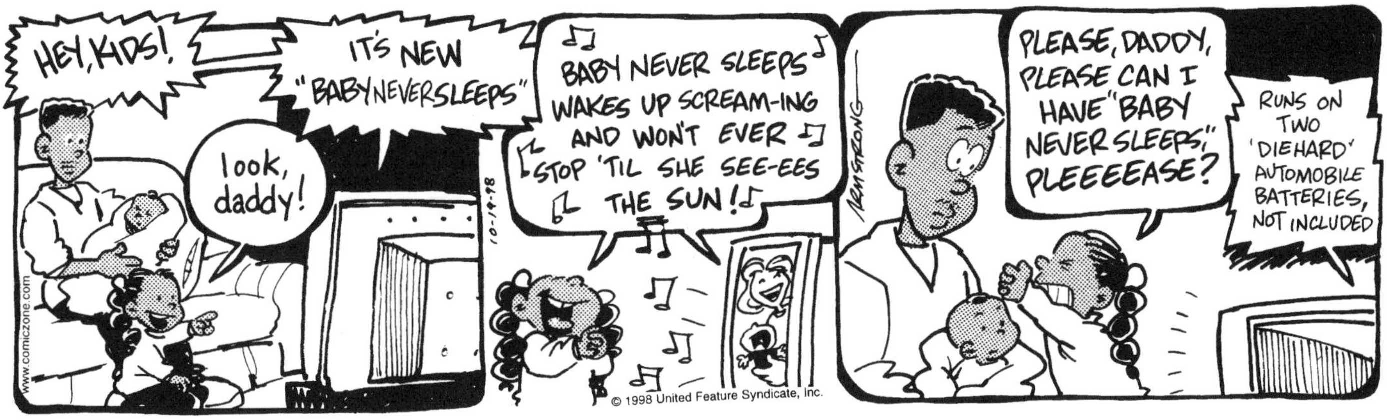
HEY, KIDS!
IT'S NEW "BABY NEVER SLEEPS"
look, daddy!
www.comiczone.com
10-19-98
BABY NEVER SLEEPS WAKES UP SCREAM-ING AND WON'T EVER STOP 'TIL SHE SEE-EES THE SUN!
© 1998 United Feature Syndicate, Inc.
ARMSTRONG
PLEASE, DADDY, PLEASE CAN I HAVE "BABY NEVER SLEEPS," PLEEEEASE?
RUNS ON TWO 'DIEHARD' AUTOMOBILE BATTERIES, NOT INCLUDED

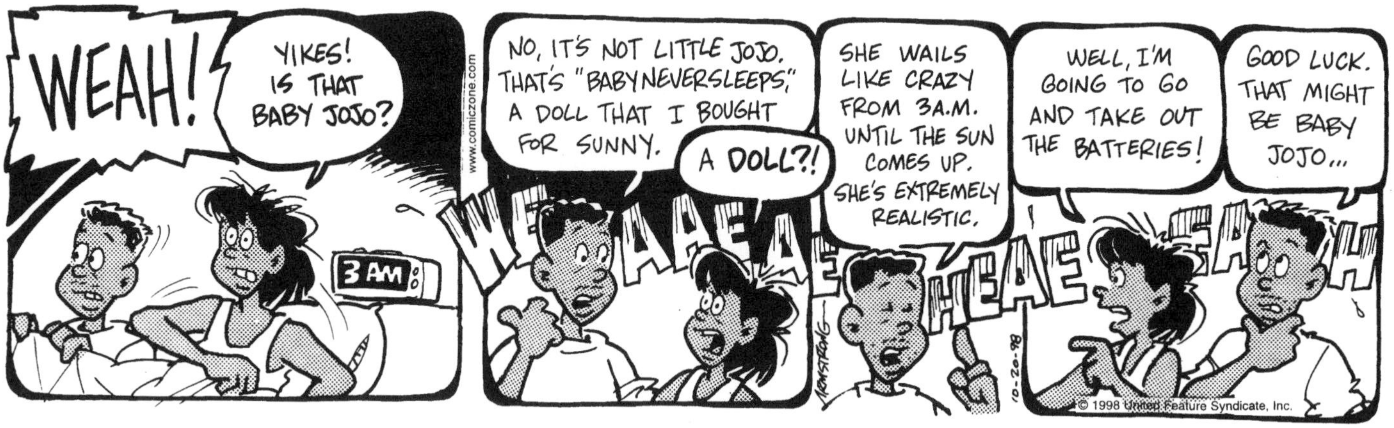
WEAH!
YIKES! IS THAT BABY JOJO?
3 AM
NO, IT'S NOT LITTLE JOJO. THAT'S "BABYNEVERSLEEPS," A DOLL THAT I BOUGHT FOR SUNNY.
A DOLL?!
SHE WAILS LIKE CRAZY FROM 3A.M. UNTIL THE SUN COMES UP. SHE'S EXTREMELY REALISTIC.
WELL, I'M GOING TO GO AND TAKE OUT THE BATTERIES!
GOOD LUCK. THAT MIGHT BE BABY JOJO...
www.comiczone.com
ARMSTRONG
10-20-98
© 1998 United Feature Syndicate, Inc.

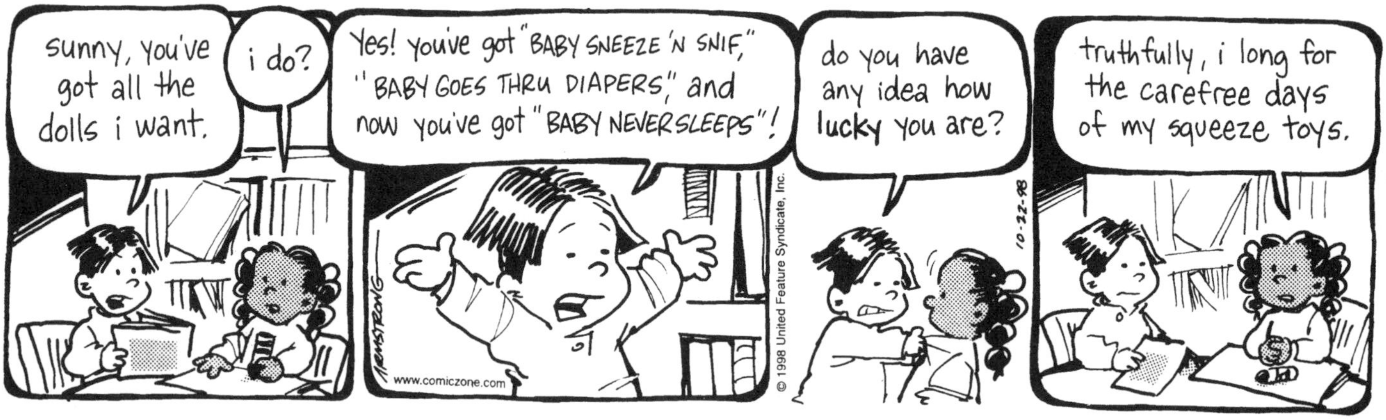
sunny, you've got all the dolls i want.
i do?
Yes! you've got "BABY SNEEZE 'N SNIF," "BABY GOES THRU DIAPERS," and now you've got "BABY NEVERSLEEPS"!
do you have any idea how lucky you are?
truthfully, i long for the carefree days of my squeeze toys.
ARMSTRONG
www.comiczone.com
© 1998 United Feature Syndicate, Inc.
10-22-98

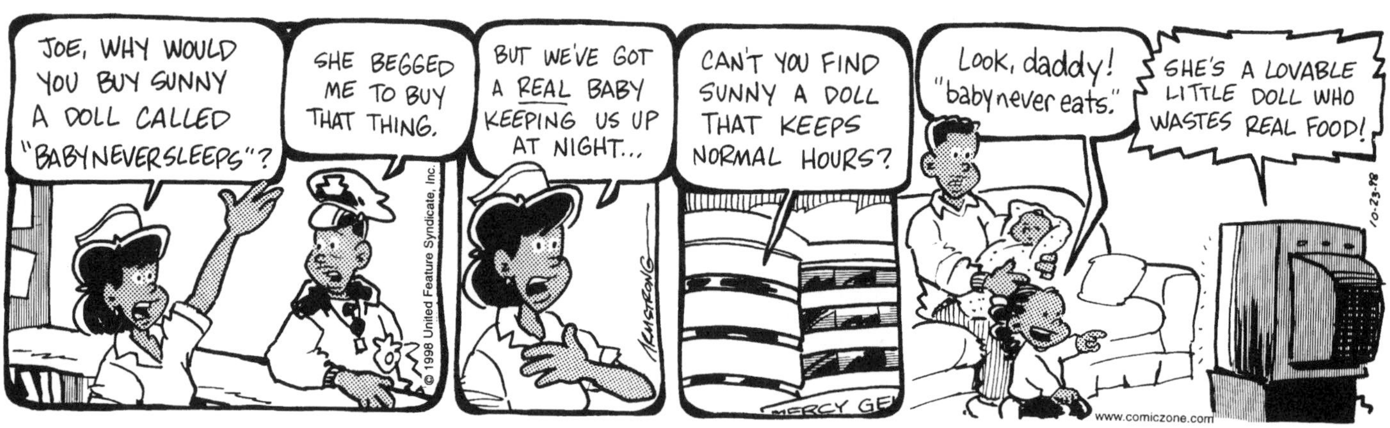
JOE, WHY WOULD YOU BUY SUNNY A DOLL CALLED "BABYNEVERSLEEPS"?
SHE BEGGED ME TO BUY THAT THING.
© 1998 United Feature Syndicate, Inc.
BUT WE'VE GOT A REAL BABY KEEPING US UP AT NIGHT...
ARMSTRONG
CAN'T YOU FIND SUNNY A DOLL THAT KEEPS NORMAL HOURS?
Look, daddy! "babynever eats."
SHE'S A LOVABLE LITTLE DOLL WHO WASTES REAL FOOD!
10-23-98
www.comiczone.com

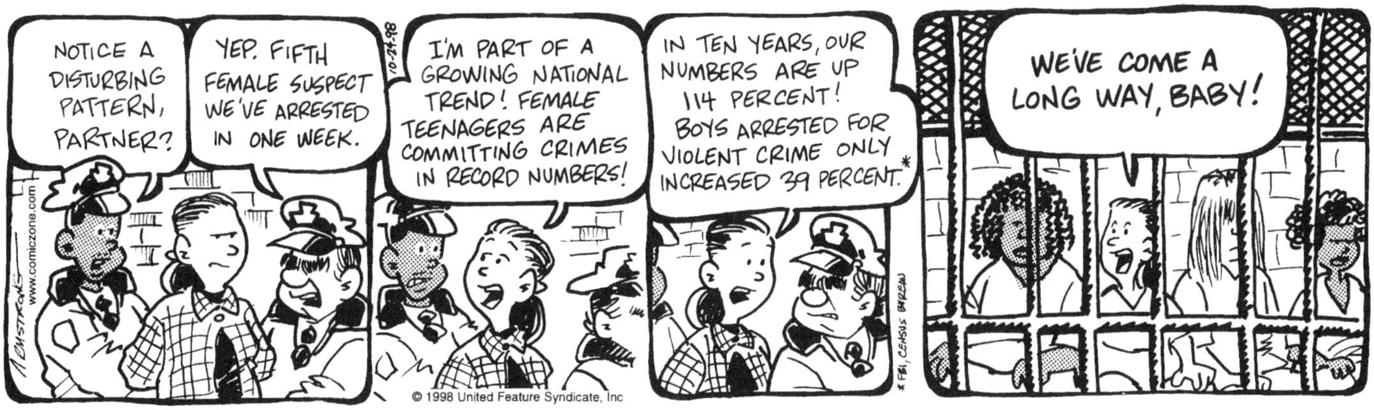
NOTICE A DISTURBING PATTERN, PARTNER?
YEP. FIFTH FEMALE SUSPECT WE'VE ARRESTED IN ONE WEEK.
I'M PART OF A GROWING NATIONAL TREND! FEMALE TEENAGERS ARE COMMITTING CRIMES IN RECORD NUMBERS!
IN TEN YEARS, OUR NUMBERS ARE UP 114 PERCENT! BOYS ARRESTED FOR VIOLENT CRIME ONLY INCREASED 39 PERCENT.*
WE'VE COME A LONG WAY, BABY!
* FBI, CENSUS BUREAU
10-24-98
ARMSTRONG
www.comiczone.com
© 1998 United Feature Syndicate, Inc

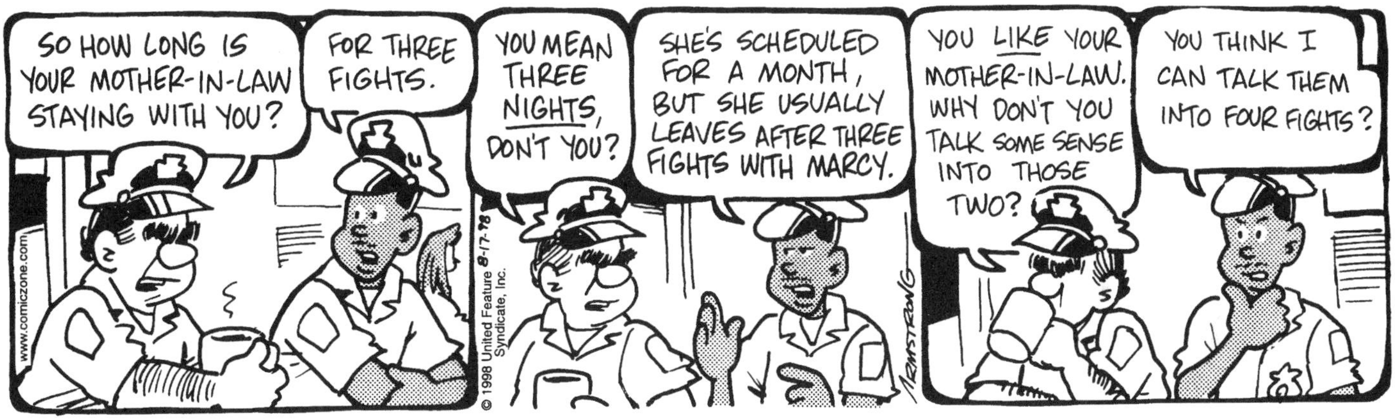
SO HOW LONG IS YOUR MOTHER-IN-LAW STAYING WITH YOU?
FOR THREE FIGHTS.
YOU MEAN THREE NIGHTS, DON'T YOU?
SHE'S SCHEDULED FOR A MONTH, BUT SHE USUALLY LEAVES AFTER THREE FIGHTS WITH MARCY.
YOU LIKE YOUR MOTHER-IN-LAW. WHY DON'T YOU TALK SOME SENSE INTO THOSE TWO?
YOU THINK I CAN TALK THEM INTO FOUR FIGHTS?
www.comiczone.com
8-17-98
© 1998 United Feature Syndicate, Inc.
ARMSTRONG

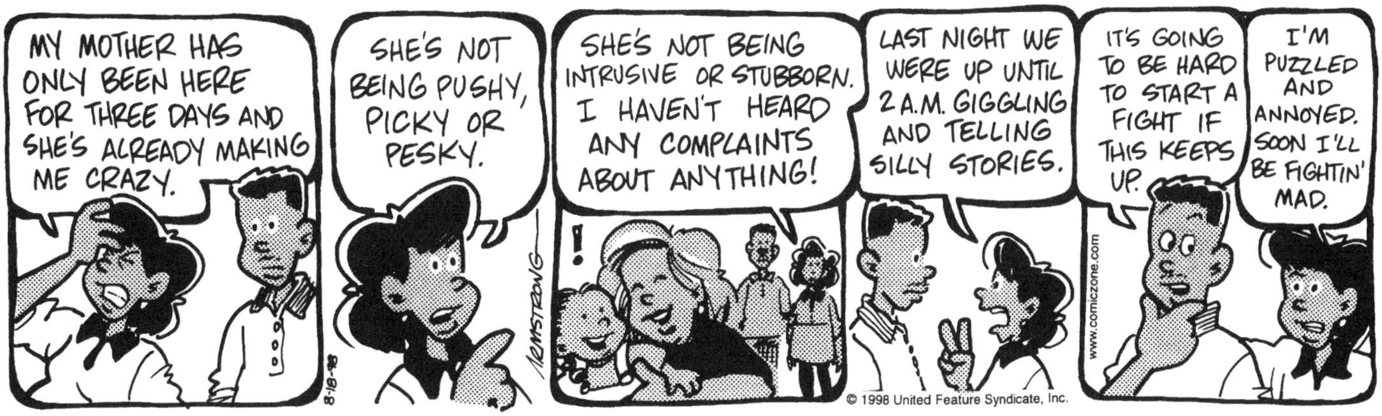
MY MOTHER HAS ONLY BEEN HERE FOR THREE DAYS AND SHE'S ALREADY MAKING ME CRAZY.
SHE'S NOT BEING PUSHY, PICKY OR PESKY.
SHE'S NOT BEING INTRUSIVE OR STUBBORN. I HAVEN'T HEARD ANY COMPLAINTS ABOUT ANYTHING!
!
LAST NIGHT WE WERE UP UNTIL 2 A.M. GIGGLING AND TELLING SILLY STORIES.
IT'S GOING TO BE HARD TO START A FIGHT IF THIS KEEPS UP.
I'M PUZZLED AND ANNOYED. SOON I'LL BE FIGHTIN' MAD.
8-18-98
ARMSTRONG
www.comiczone.com
© 1998 United Feature Syndicate, Inc.

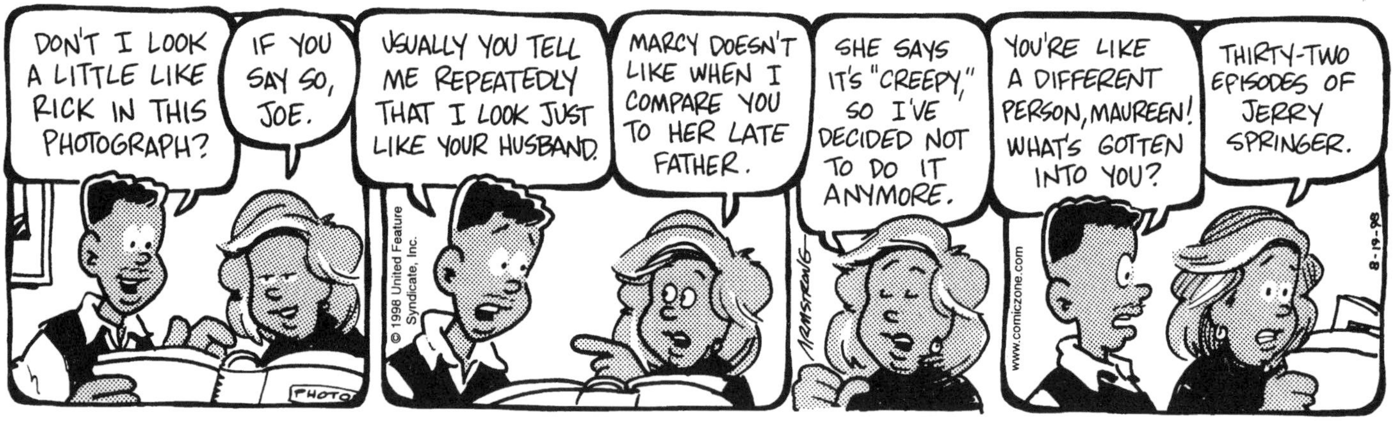
DON'T I LOOK A LITTLE LIKE RICK IN THIS PHOTOGRAPH?
IF YOU SAY SO, JOE.
PHOTO
USUALLY YOU TELL ME REPEATEDLY THAT I LOOK JUST LIKE YOUR HUSBAND.
© 1998 United Feature Syndicate, Inc.
MARCY DOESN'T LIKE WHEN I COMPARE YOU TO HER LATE FATHER.
SHE SAYS IT'S "CREEPY," SO I'VE DECIDED NOT TO DO IT ANYMORE.
ARMSTRONG
YOU'RE LIKE A DIFFERENT PERSON, MAUREEN! WHAT'S GOTTEN INTO YOU?
www.comiczone.com
THIRTY-TWO EPISODES OF JERRY SPRINGER.
8-19-98

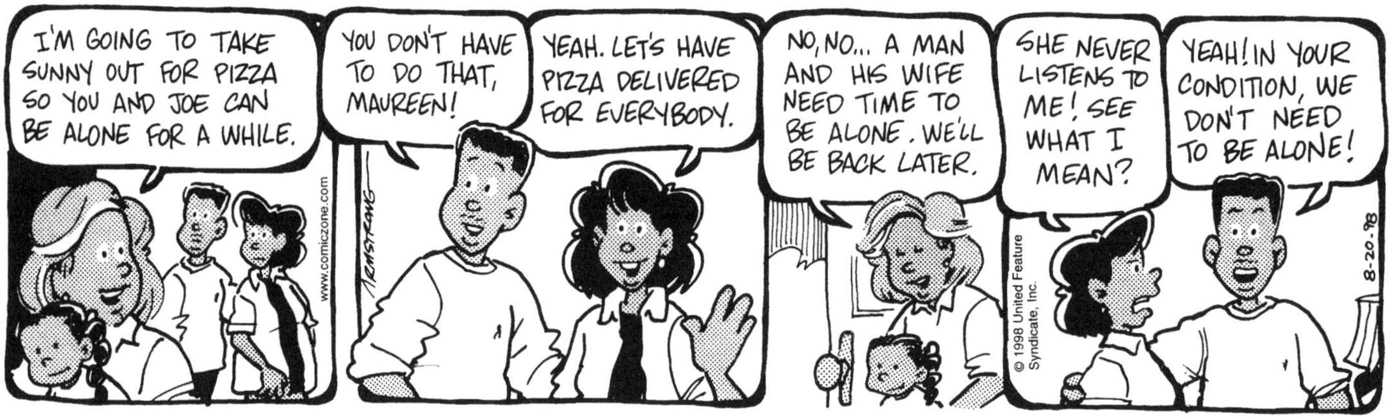
I'M GOING TO TAKE SUNNY OUT FOR PIZZA SO YOU AND JOE CAN BE ALONE FOR A WHILE.
www.comiczone.com
YOU DON'T HAVE TO DO THAT, MAUREEN!
ARMSTRONG
YEAH. LET'S HAVE PIZZA DELIVERED FOR EVERYBODY.
NO, NO... A MAN AND HIS WIFE NEED TIME TO BE ALONE. WE'LL BE BACK LATER.
SHE NEVER LISTENS TO ME! SEE WHAT I MEAN?
© 1998 United Feature Syndicate, Inc.
YEAH! IN YOUR CONDITION, WE DON'T NEED TO BE ALONE!
8-20-98

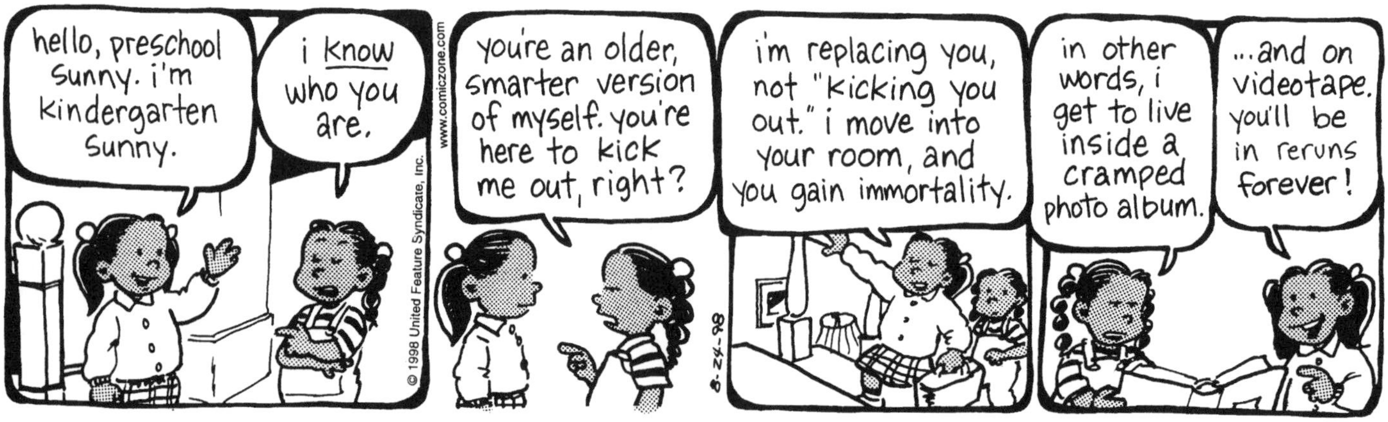
hello, preschool sunny. i'm kindergarten sunny.
i know who you are.
© 1998 United Feature Syndicate, Inc.
www.comiczone.com
you're an older, smarter version of myself. you're here to kick me out, right?
8-24-98
i'm replacing you, not "kicking you out." i move into your room, and you gain immortality.
in other words, i get to live inside a cramped photo album.
...and on videotape. you'll be in reruns forever!

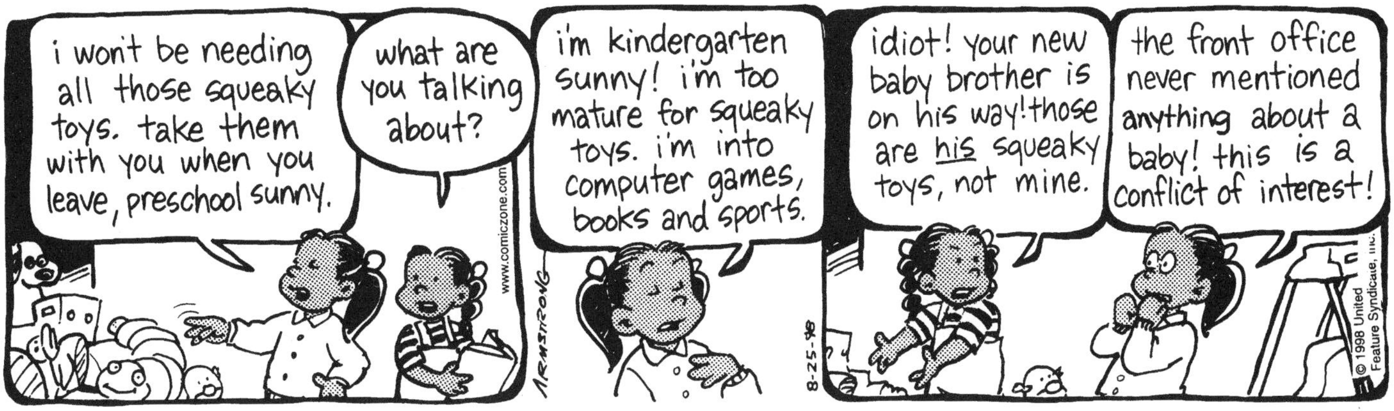
i won't be needing all those squeaky toys. take them with you when you leave, preschool sunny.
what are you talking about?
i'm kindergarten sunny! i'm too mature for squeaky toys. i'm into computer games, books and sports.
idiot! your new baby brother is on his way! those are his squeaky toys, not mine.
the front office never mentioned anything about a baby! this is a conflict of interest!
www.comiczone.com
ARMSTRONG
8-25-98
© 1998 United Feature Syndicate, Inc.

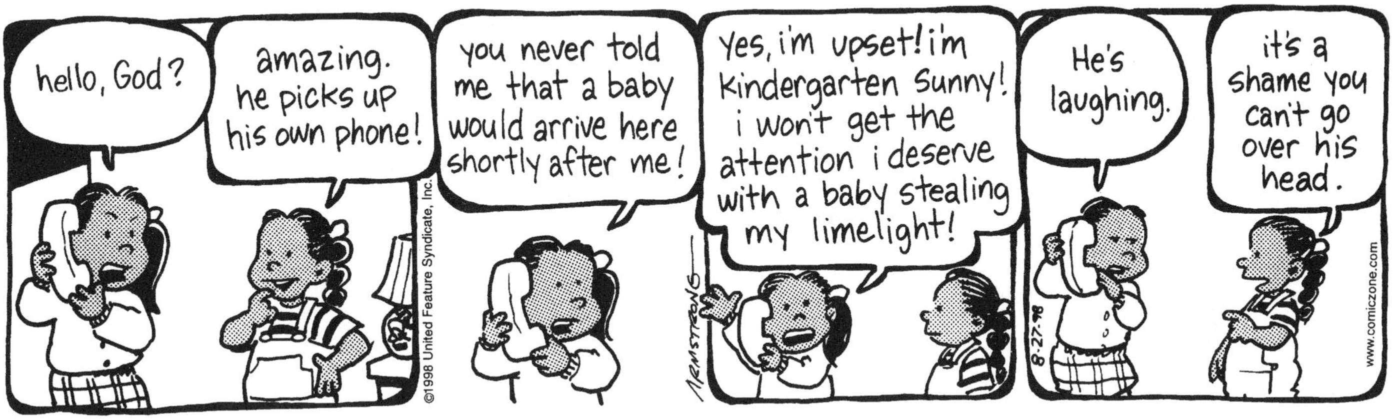
hello, God?
amazing. he picks up his own phone!
you never told me that a baby would arrive here shortly after me!
Yes, i'm upset! i'm Kindergarten Sunny! i won't get the attention i deserve with a baby stealing my limelight!
He's laughing.
it's a shame you can't go over his head.
©1998 United Feature Syndicate, Inc.
ARMSTRONG
8-27-98
www.comiczone.com

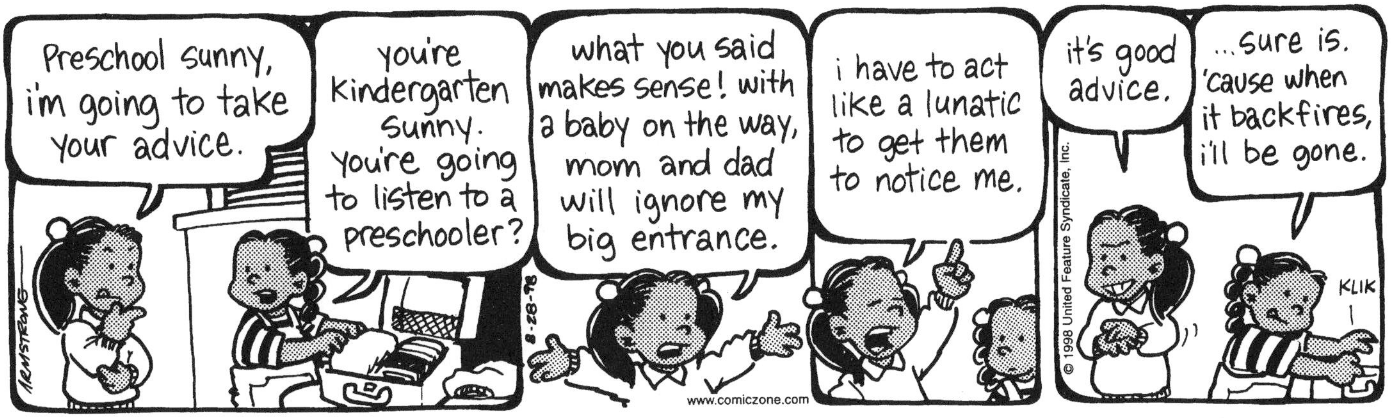
Preschool sunny, i'm going to take your advice.
you're Kindergarten Sunny. You're going to listen to a preschooler?
what you said makes sense! with a baby on the way, mom and dad will ignore my big entrance.
i have to act like a lunatic to get them to notice me.
it's good advice.
...sure is. 'cause when it backfires, i'll be gone.
KLIK
ARMSTRONG
8-28-98
www.comiczone.com
© 1998 United Feature Syndicate, Inc.

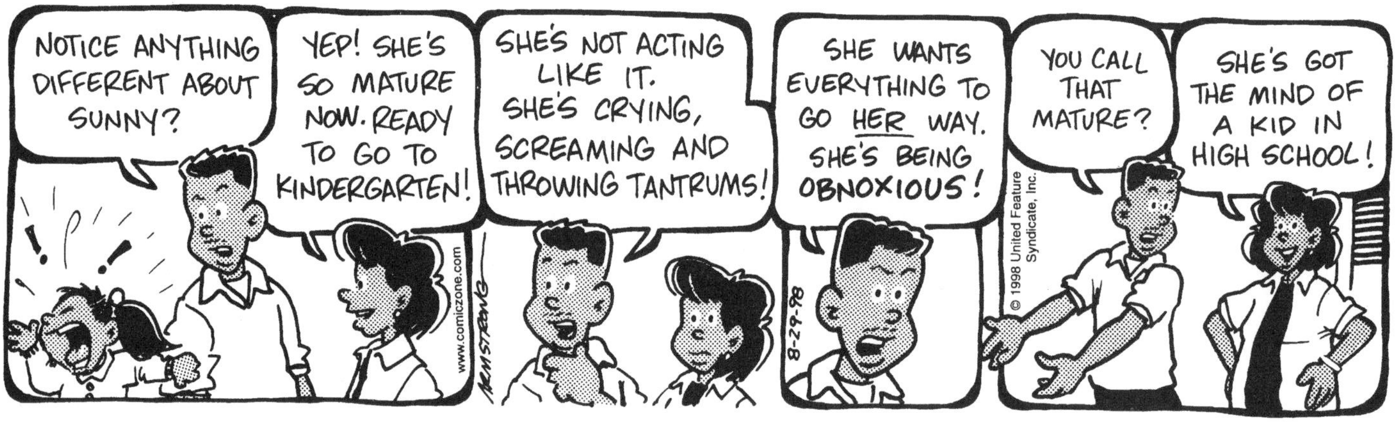
NOTICE ANYTHING DIFFERENT ABOUT SUNNY?
YEP! SHE'S SO MATURE NOW. READY TO GO TO KINDERGARTEN!
www.comiczone.com
ARMSTRONG
SHE'S NOT ACTING LIKE IT. SHE'S CRYING, SCREAMING AND THROWING TANTRUMS!
8-29-98
SHE WANTS EVERYTHING TO GO HER WAY. SHE'S BEING OBNOXIOUS!
© 1998 United Feature Syndicate, Inc.
YOU CALL THAT MATURE?
SHE'S GOT THE MIND OF A KID IN HIGH SCHOOL!

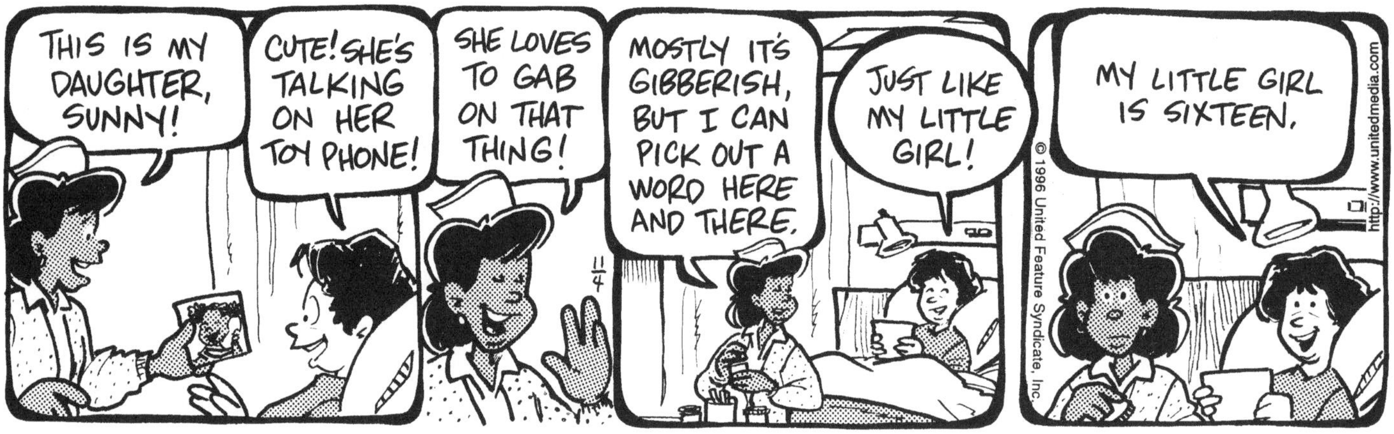
THIS IS MY DAUGHTER, SUNNY!
CUTE! SHE'S TALKING ON HER TOY PHONE!
SHE LOVES TO GAB ON THAT THING!
11/4
MOSTLY IT'S GIBBERISH, BUT I CAN PICK OUT A WORD HERE AND THERE.
JUST LIKE MY LITTLE GIRL!
© 1996 United Feature Syndicate, Inc.
MY LITTLE GIRL IS SIXTEEN.
http://www.unitedmedia.com

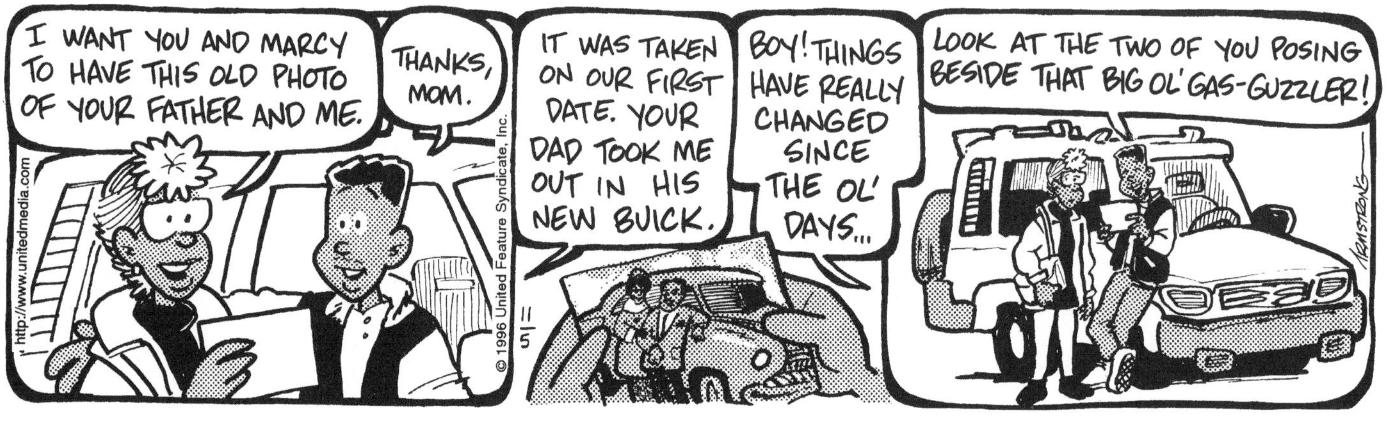
I WANT YOU AND MARCY TO HAVE THIS OLD PHOTO OF YOUR FATHER AND ME.
THANKS, MOM.
http://www.unitedmedia.com
© 1996 United Feature Syndicate, Inc.
IT WAS TAKEN ON OUR FIRST DATE. YOUR DAD TOOK ME OUT IN HIS NEW BUICK.
11/5
BOY! THINGS HAVE REALLY CHANGED SINCE THE OL' DAYS...
LOOK AT THE TWO OF YOU POSING BESIDE THAT BIG OL' GAS-GUZZLER!
ARMSTRONG

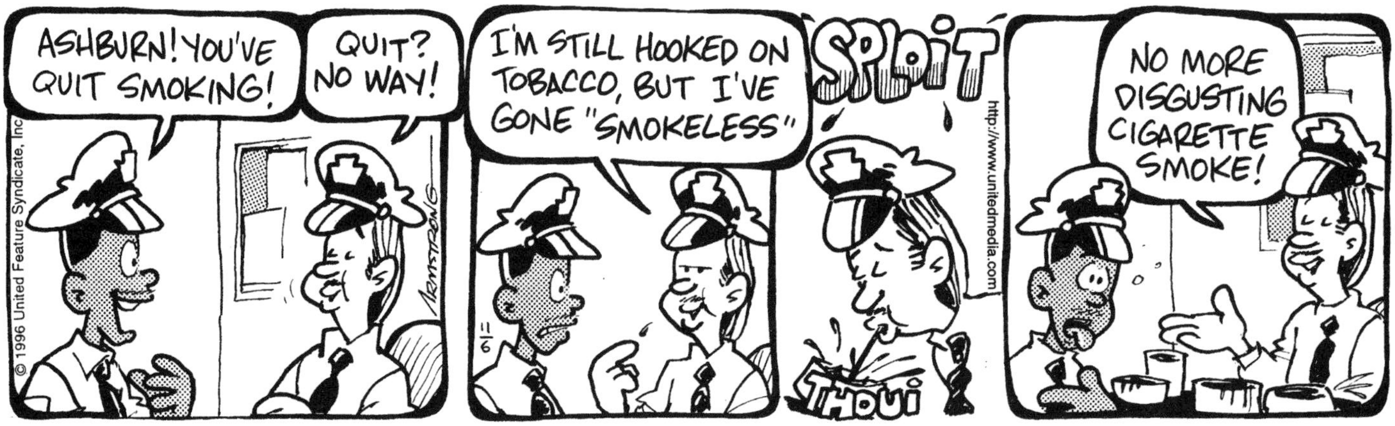
ASHBURN! YOU'VE QUIT SMOKING!
QUIT? NO WAY!
I'M STILL HOOKED ON TOBACCO, BUT I'VE GONE "SMOKELESS"
SPLOIT
THOUI
NO MORE DISGUSTING CIGARETTE SMOKE!
© 1996 United Feature Syndicate, Inc
ARMSTRONG
11/6
http://www.unitedmedia.com

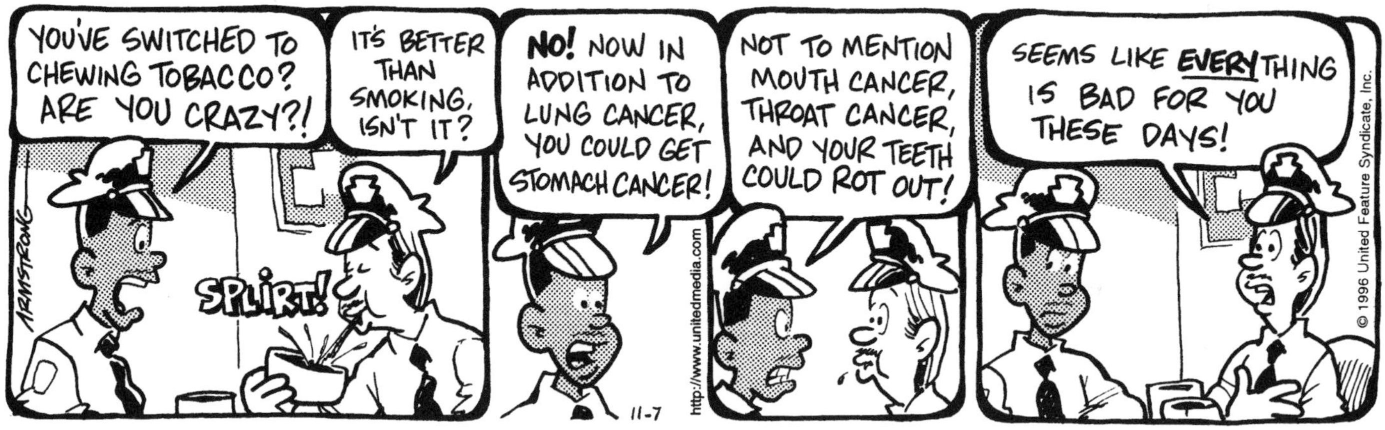
YOU'VE SWITCHED TO CHEWING TOBACCO? ARE YOU CRAZY?!
IT'S BETTER THAN SMOKING, ISN'T IT?
SPLIRT!
NO! NOW IN ADDITION TO LUNG CANCER, YOU COULD GET STOMACH CANCER!
NOT TO MENTION MOUTH CANCER, THROAT CANCER, AND YOUR TEETH COULD ROT OUT!
SEEMS LIKE EVERYTHING IS BAD FOR YOU THESE DAYS!
ARMSTRONG
11-7
http://www.unitedmedia.com
© 1996 United Feature Syndicate, Inc.

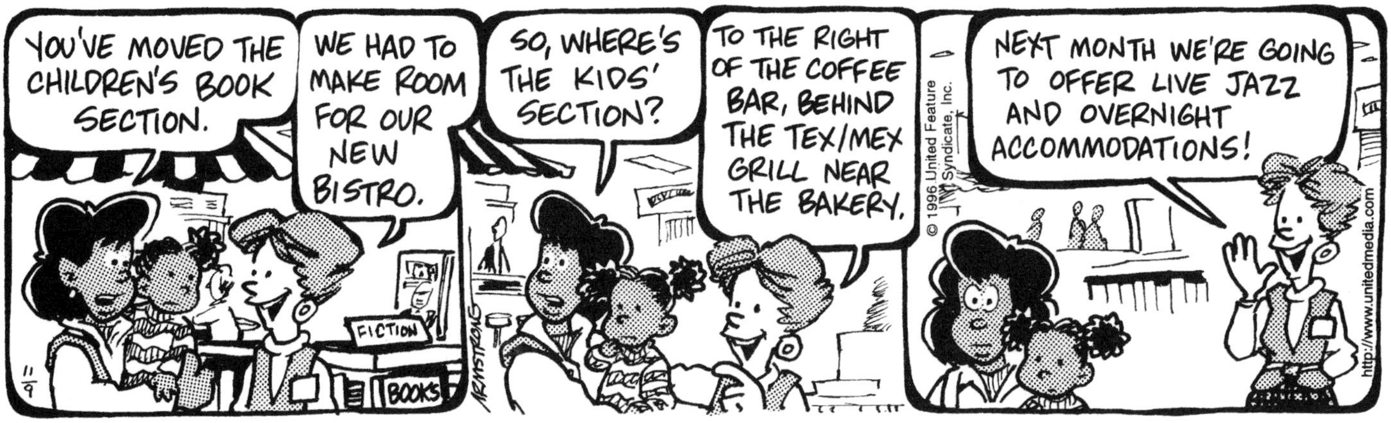
YOU'VE MOVED THE CHILDREN'S BOOK SECTION.
WE HAD TO MAKE ROOM FOR OUR NEW BISTRO.
FICTION
BOOKS
SO, WHERE'S THE KIDS' SECTION?
TO THE RIGHT OF THE COFFEE BAR, BEHIND THE TEX/MEX GRILL NEAR THE BAKERY.
NEXT MONTH WE'RE GOING TO OFFER LIVE JAZZ AND OVERNIGHT ACCOMMODATIONS!
11/9
ARMSTRONG
© 1996 United Feature Syndicate, Inc.
http://www.unitedmedia.com

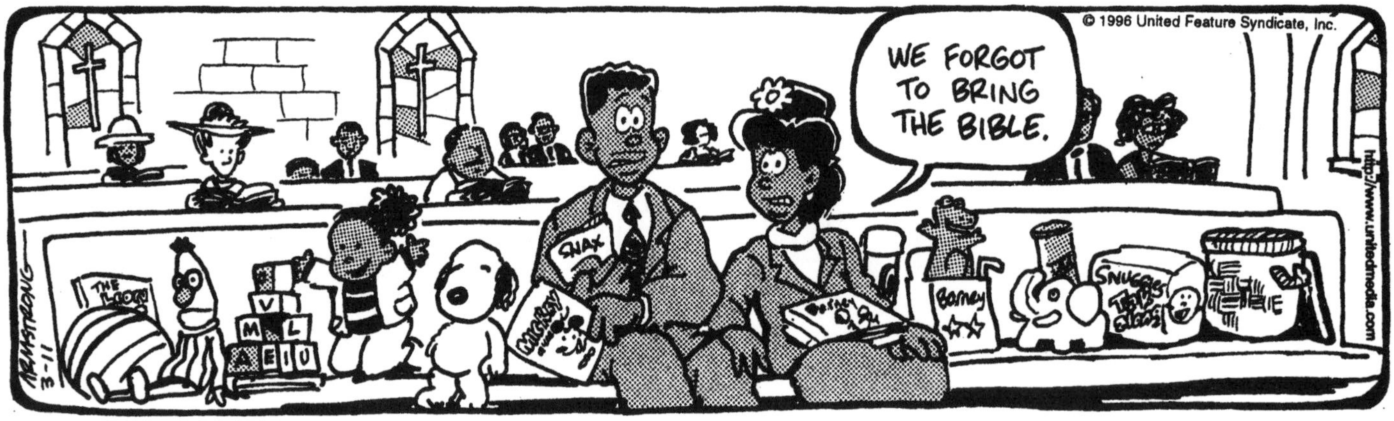
© 1996 United Feature Syndicate, Inc.
WE FORGOT TO BRING THE BIBLE.
SNAX
Barney
http://www.unitedmedia.com
ARMSTRONG 3-11

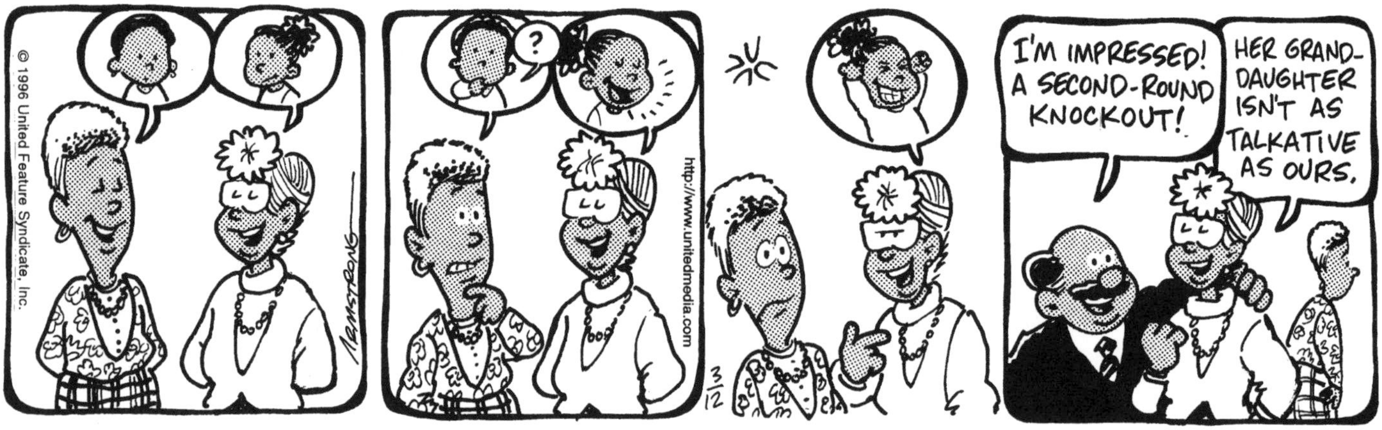
© 1996 United Feature Syndicate, Inc.
ARMSTRONG
?
http://www.unitedmedia.com
3/12
I'M IMPRESSED! A SECOND-ROUND KNOCKOUT!
HER GRAND-DAUGHTER ISN'T AS TALKATIVE AS OURS.

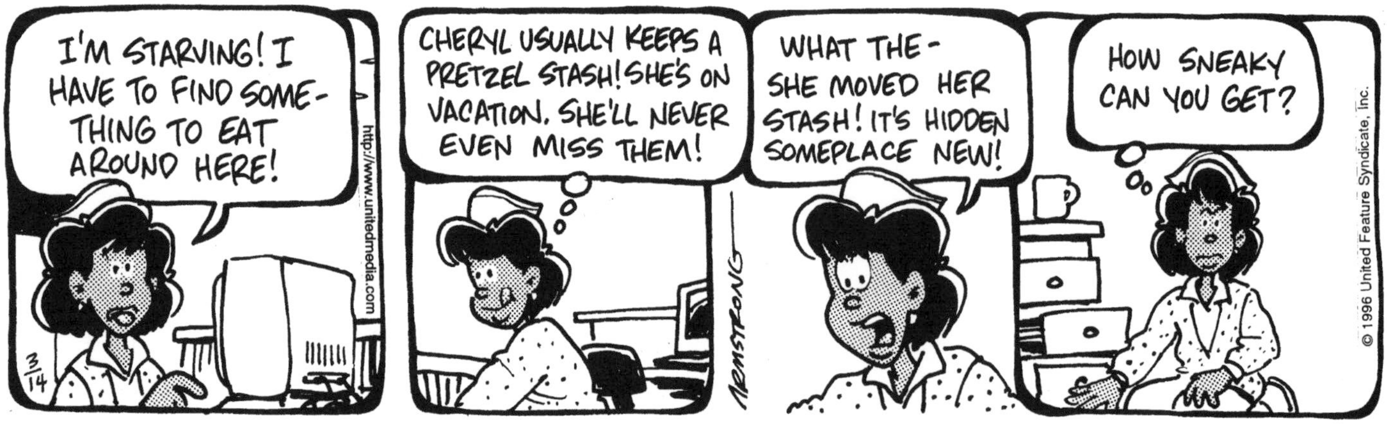
I'M STARVING! I HAVE TO FIND SOME-THING TO EAT AROUND HERE!
http://www.unitedmedia.com
3/14
CHERYL USUALLY KEEPS A PRETZEL STASH! SHE'S ON VACATION. SHE'LL NEVER EVEN MISS THEM!
ARMSTRONG
WHAT THE- SHE MOVED HER STASH! IT'S HIDDEN SOMEPLACE NEW!
HOW SNEAKY CAN YOU GET?
© 1996 United Feature Syndicate, Inc.

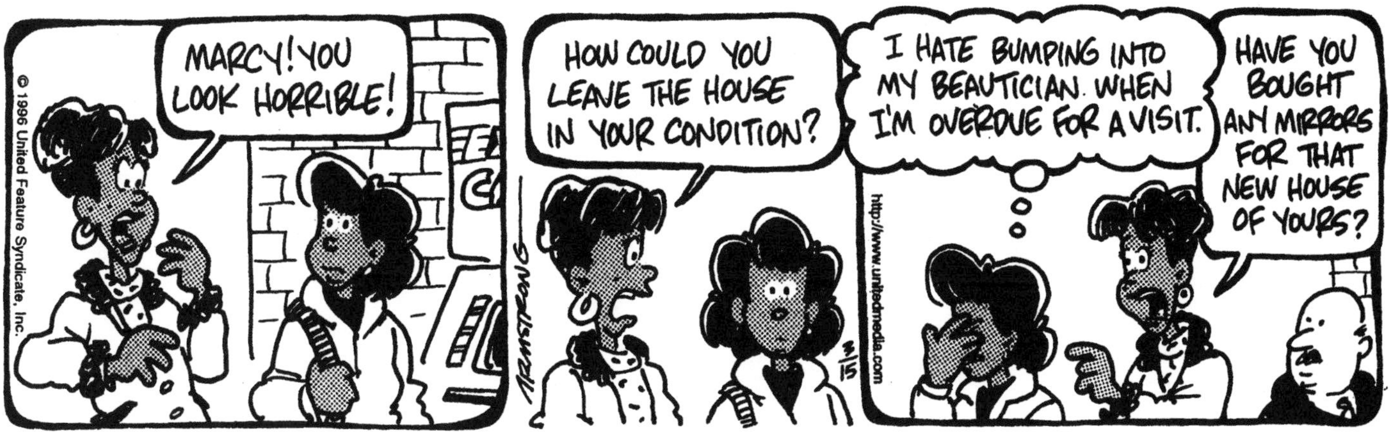
© 1996 United Feature Syndicate, Inc.
MARCY! YOU LOOK HORRIBLE!
HOW COULD YOU LEAVE THE HOUSE IN YOUR CONDITION?
ARMSTRONG
3/15
I HATE BUMPING INTO MY BEAUTICIAN. WHEN I'M OVERDUE FOR A VISIT.
http://www.unitedmedia.com
HAVE YOU BOUGHT ANY MIRRORS FOR THAT NEW HOUSE OF YOURS?

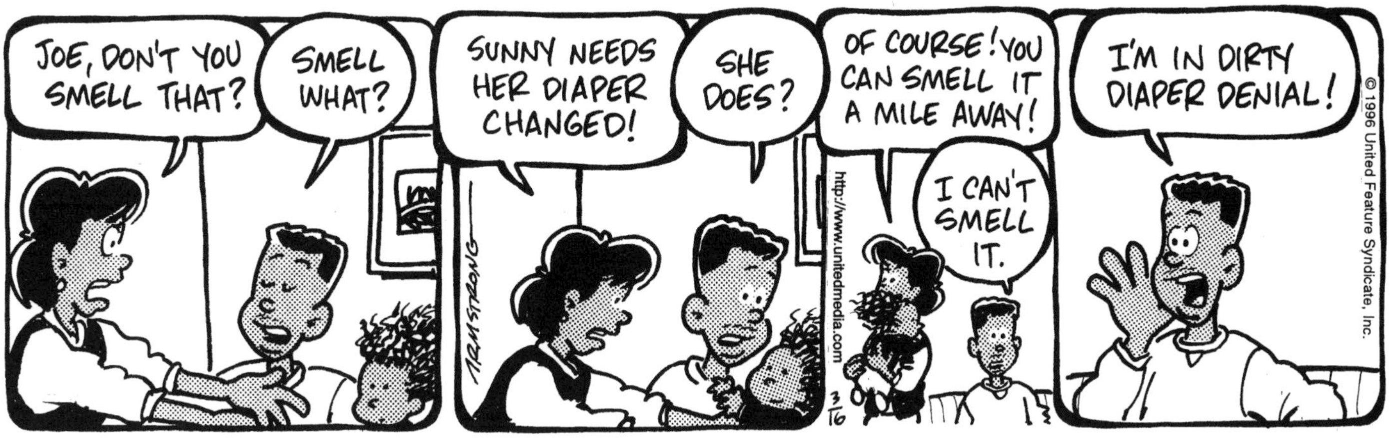
JOE, DON'T YOU SMELL THAT?
SMELL WHAT?
SUNNY NEEDS HER DIAPER CHANGED!
SHE DOES?
ARMSTRONG
OF COURSE! YOU CAN SMELL IT A MILE AWAY!
I CAN'T SMELL IT.
http://www.unitedmedia.com
3/16
I'M IN DIRTY DIAPER DENIAL!
© 1996 United Feature Syndicate, Inc.

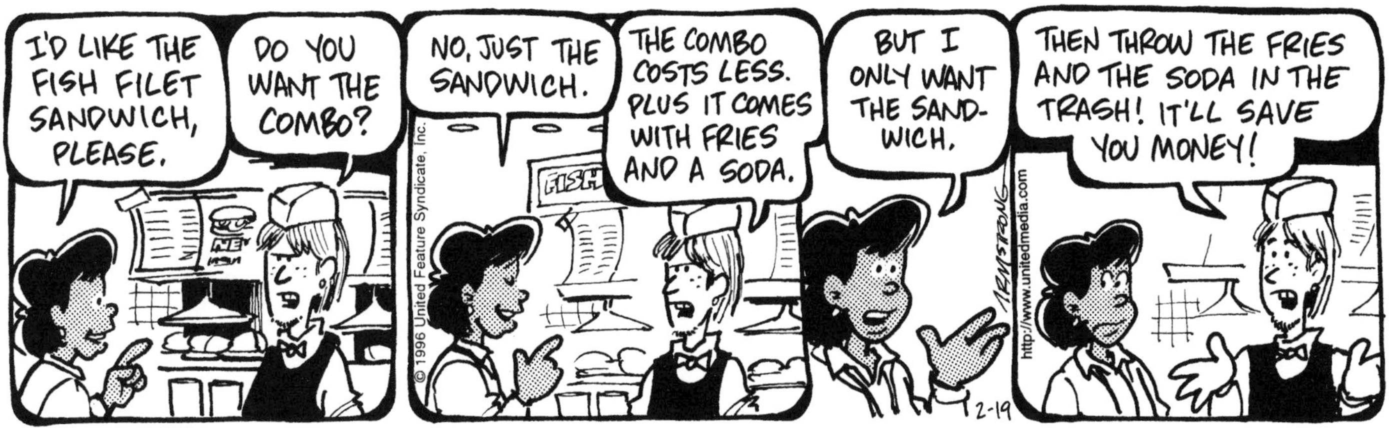
I'D LIKE THE FISH FILET SANDWICH, PLEASE.
DO YOU WANT THE COMBO?
NO, JUST THE SANDWICH.
THE COMBO COSTS LESS. PLUS IT COMES WITH FRIES AND A SODA.
© 1996 United Feature Syndicate, Inc.
BUT I ONLY WANT THE SANDWICH.
ARMSTRONG
2-19
http://www.unitedmedia.com
THEN THROW THE FRIES AND THE SODA IN THE TRASH! IT'LL SAVE YOU MONEY!

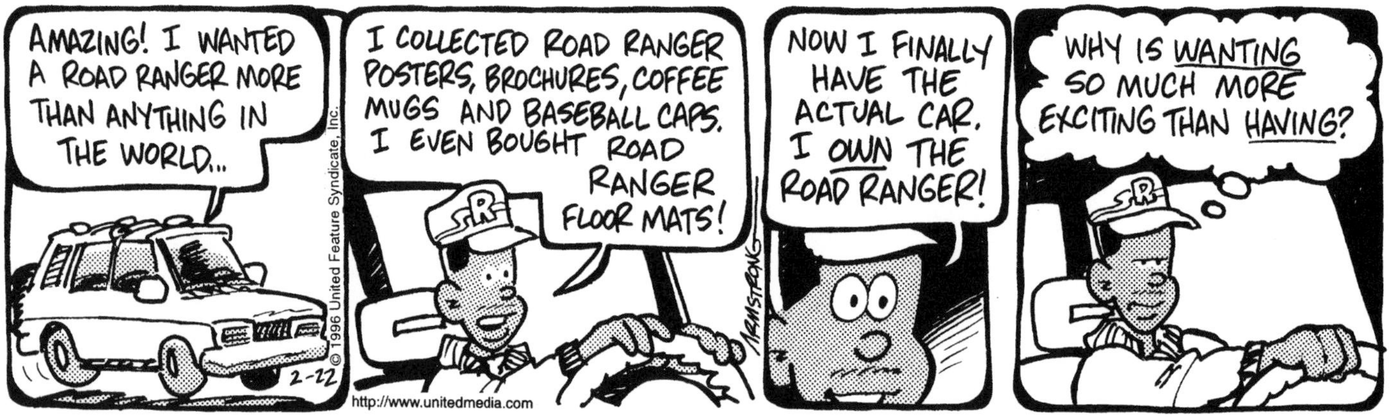
AMAZING! I WANTED A ROAD RANGER MORE THAN ANYTHING IN THE WORLD...
I COLLECTED ROAD RANGER POSTERS, BROCHURES, COFFEE MUGS AND BASEBALL CAPS. I EVEN BOUGHT ROAD RANGER FLOOR MATS!
NOW I FINALLY HAVE THE ACTUAL CAR. I OWN THE ROAD RANGER!
WHY IS WANTING SO MUCH MORE EXCITING THAN HAVING?
© 1996 United Feature Syndicate, Inc.
http://www.unitedmedia.com
2-22

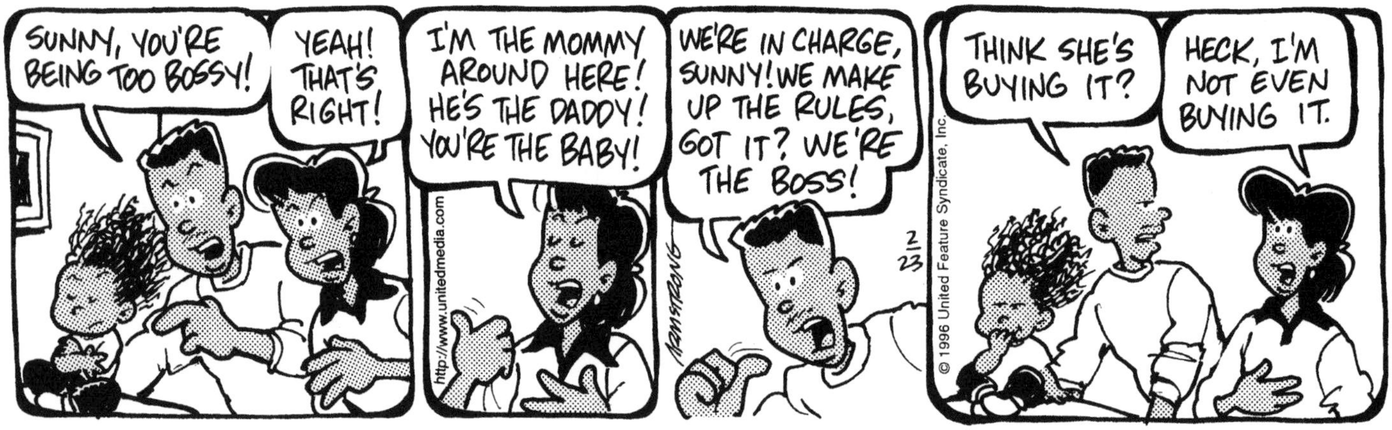
SUNNY, YOU'RE BEING TOO BOSSY!
YEAH! THAT'S RIGHT!
I'M THE MOMMY AROUND HERE! HE'S THE DADDY! YOU'RE THE BABY!
WE'RE IN CHARGE, SUNNY! WE MAKE UP THE RULES, GOT IT? WE'RE THE BOSS!
THINK SHE'S BUYING IT?
HECK, I'M NOT EVEN BUYING IT.
http://www.unitedmedia.com
© 1996 United Feature Syndicate, Inc.
2/23

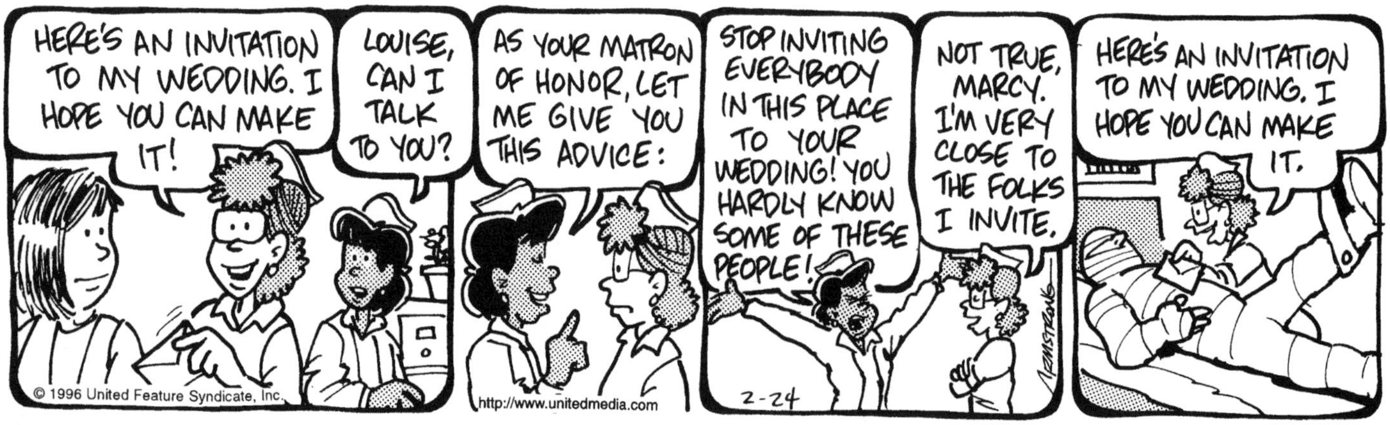
HERE'S AN INVITATION TO MY WEDDING. I HOPE YOU CAN MAKE IT!
LOUISE, CAN I TALK TO YOU?
AS YOUR MATRON OF HONOR, LET ME GIVE YOU THIS ADVICE:
STOP INVITING EVERYBODY IN THIS PLACE TO YOUR WEDDING! YOU HARDLY KNOW SOME OF THESE PEOPLE!
NOT TRUE, MARCY. I'M VERY CLOSE TO THE FOLKS I INVITE.
HERE'S AN INVITATION TO MY WEDDING. I HOPE YOU CAN MAKE IT.
© 1996 United Feature Syndicate, Inc.
http://www.unitedmedia.com
2-24

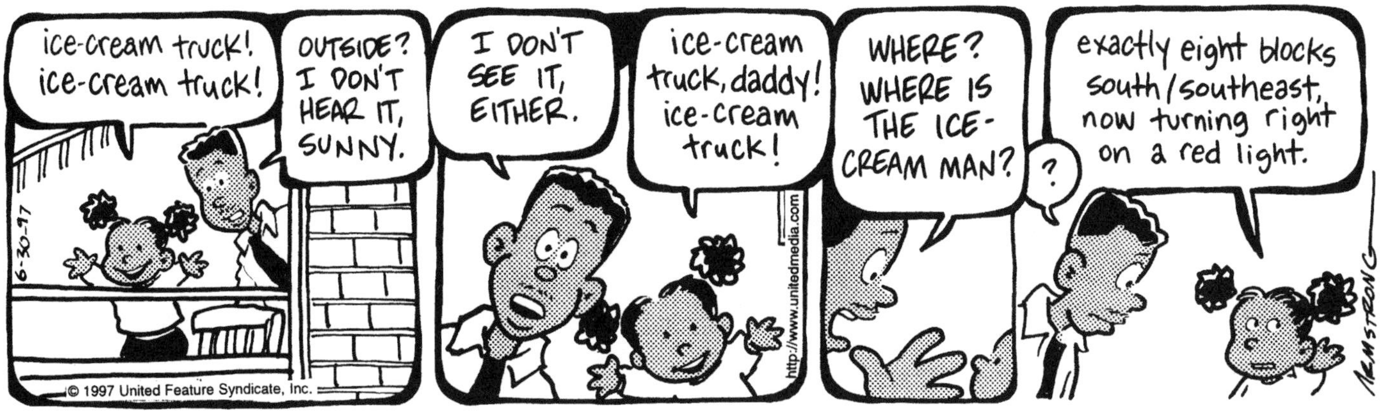
ice-cream truck! ice-cream truck!
OUTSIDE? I DON'T HEAR IT, SUNNY.
6-30-97
© 1997 United Feature Syndicate, Inc.
I DON'T SEE IT, EITHER.
ice-cream truck, daddy! ice-cream truck!
http://www.unitedmedia.com
WHERE? WHERE IS THE ICE-CREAM MAN?
?
exactly eight blocks south/southeast, now turning right on a red light.
ARMSTRONG

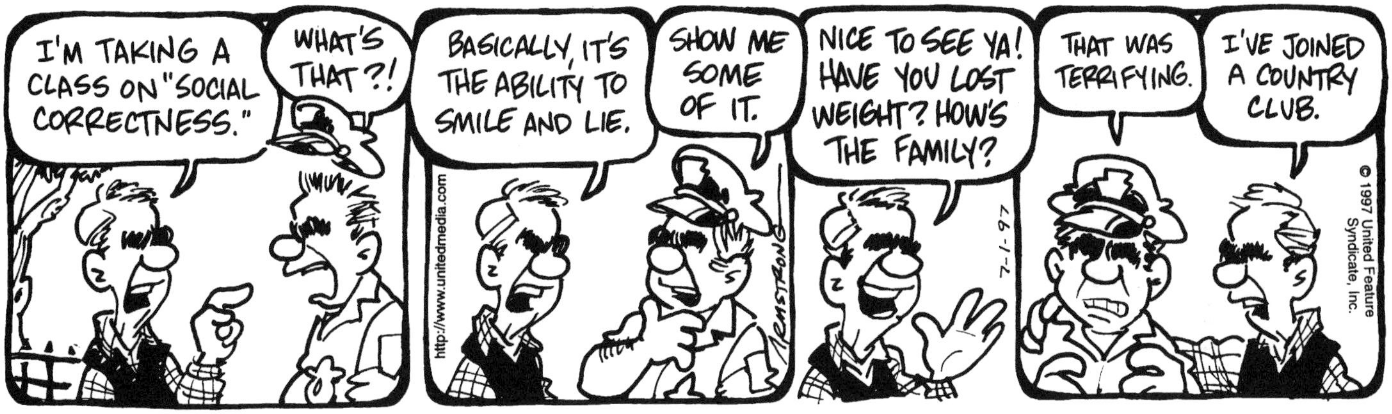
I'M TAKING A CLASS ON "SOCIAL CORRECTNESS."
WHAT'S THAT?!
BASICALLY, IT'S THE ABILITY TO SMILE AND LIE.
SHOW ME SOME OF IT.
http://www.unitedmedia.com
ARMSTRONG
NICE TO SEE YA! HAVE YOU LOST WEIGHT? HOW'S THE FAMILY?
7-1-97
THAT WAS TERRIFYING.
I'VE JOINED A COUNTRY CLUB.
© 1997 United Feature Syndicate, Inc.

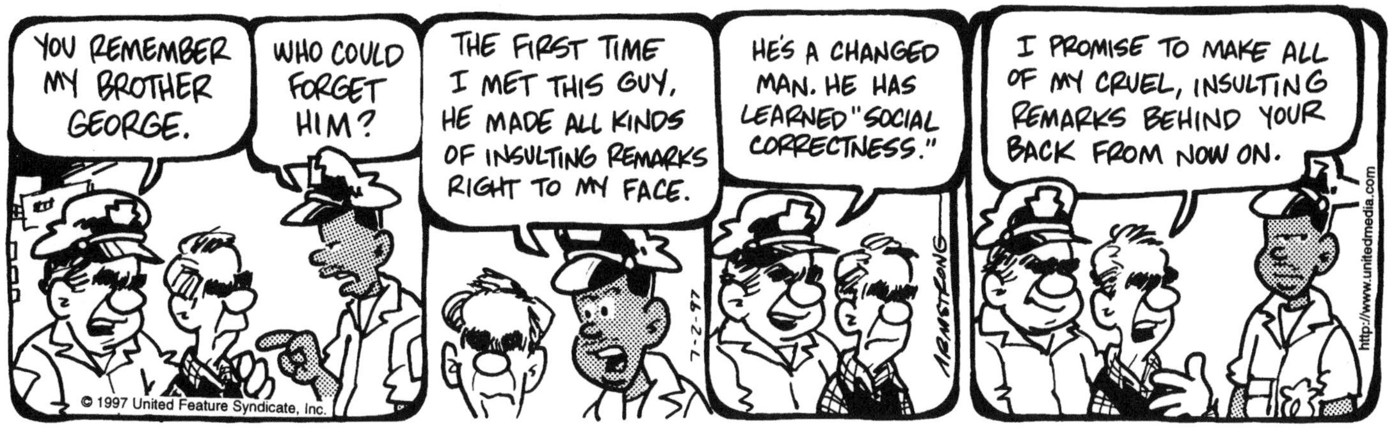
YOU REMEMBER MY BROTHER GEORGE.
WHO COULD FORGET HIM?
© 1997 United Feature Syndicate, Inc.
THE FIRST TIME I MET THIS GUY, HE MADE ALL KINDS OF INSULTING REMARKS RIGHT TO MY FACE.
7-2-97
HE'S A CHANGED MAN. HE HAS LEARNED "SOCIAL CORRECTNESS."
ARMSTRONG
I PROMISE TO MAKE ALL OF MY CRUEL, INSULTING REMARKS BEHIND YOUR BACK FROM NOW ON.
http://www.unitedmedia.com

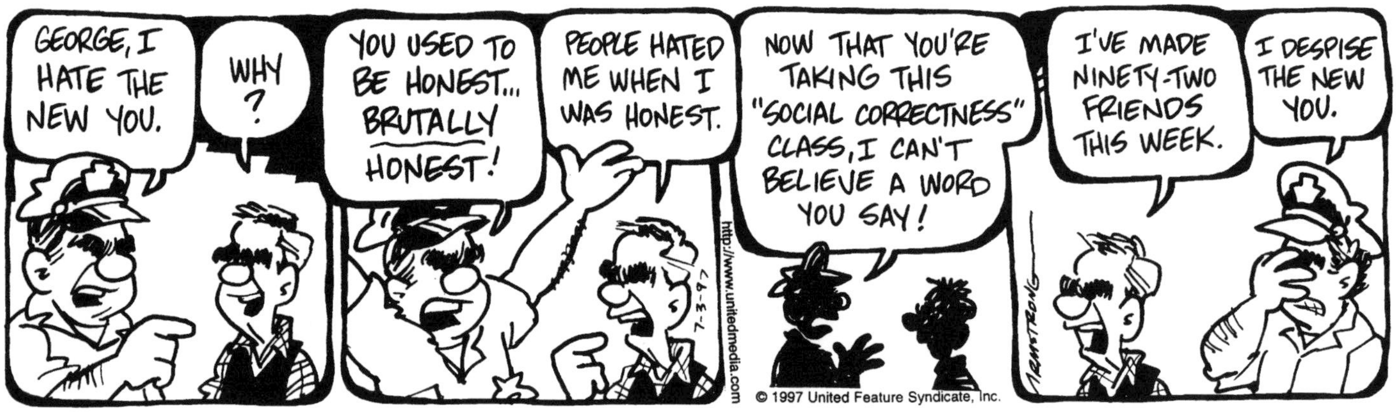
GEORGE, I HATE THE NEW YOU.
WHY?
YOU USED TO BE HONEST... BRUTALLY HONEST!
PEOPLE HATED ME WHEN I WAS HONEST.
NOW THAT YOU'RE TAKING THIS "SOCIAL CORRECTNESS" CLASS, I CAN'T BELIEVE A WORD YOU SAY!
I'VE MADE NINETY-TWO FRIENDS THIS WEEK.
I DESPISE THE NEW YOU.
7-3-97
http://www.unitedmedia.com
© 1997 United Feature Syndicate, Inc.
ARMSTRONG

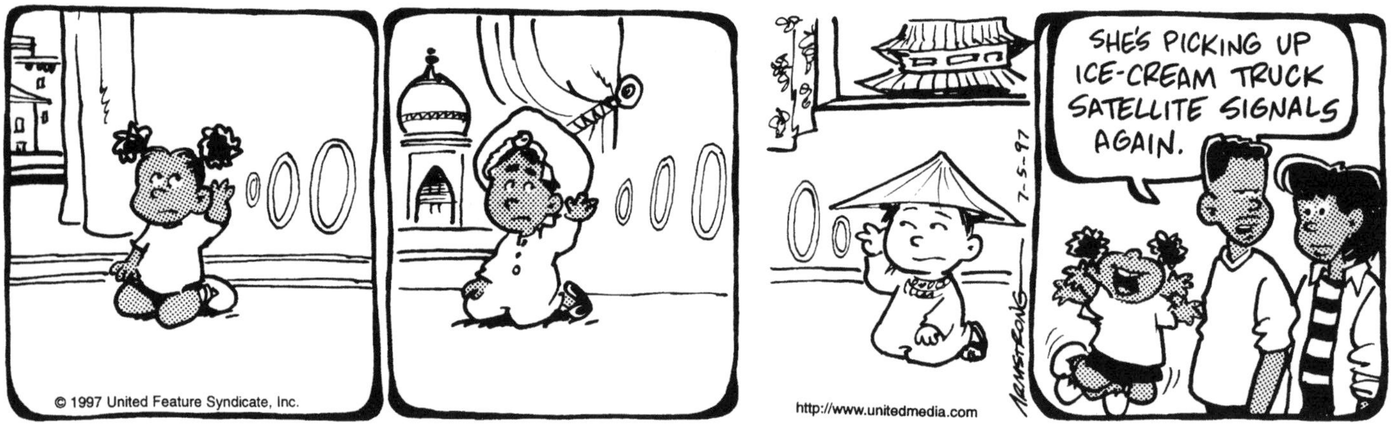
© 1997 United Feature Syndicate, Inc.
7-5-97
http://www.unitedmedia.com
ARMSTRONG
SHE'S PICKING UP ICE-CREAM TRUCK SATELLITE SIGNALS AGAIN.

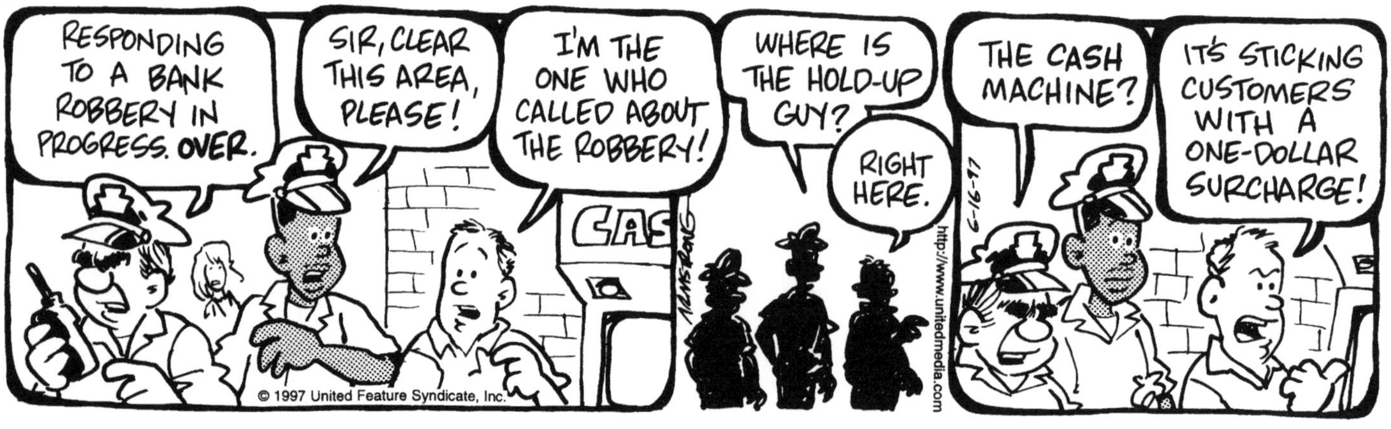
RESPONDING TO A BANK ROBBERY IN PROGRESS. OVER.
SIR, CLEAR THIS AREA, PLEASE!
I'M THE ONE WHO CALLED ABOUT THE ROBBERY!
CAS
ARMSTRONG
© 1997 United Feature Syndicate, Inc.
WHERE IS THE HOLD-UP GUY?
RIGHT HERE.
6-16-97
http://www.unitedmedia.com
THE CASH MACHINE?
IT'S STICKING CUSTOMERS WITH A ONE-DOLLAR SURCHARGE!

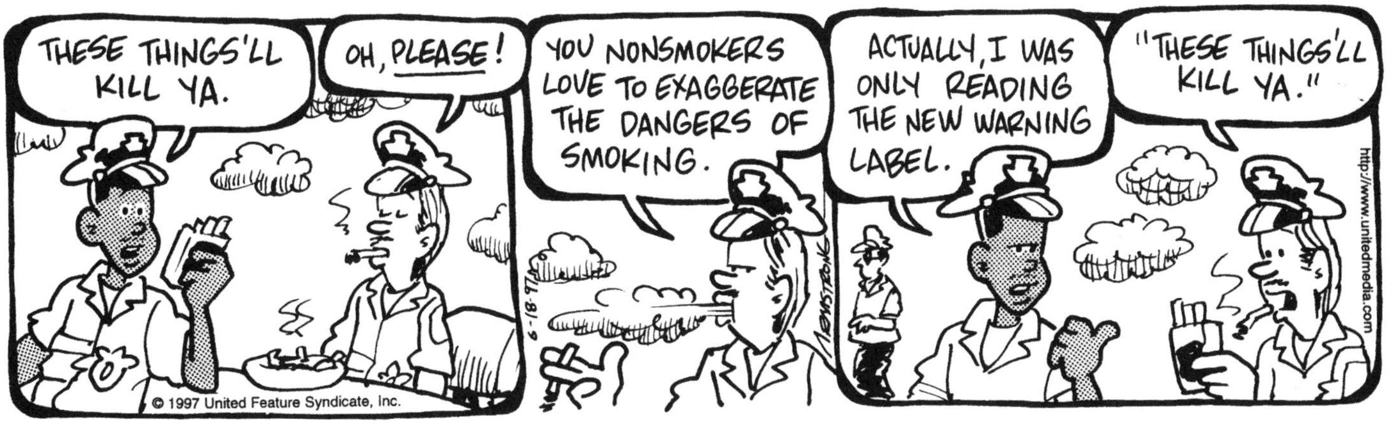
THESE THINGS'LL KILL YA.
OH, PLEASE!
YOU NONSMOKERS LOVE TO EXAGGERATE THE DANGERS OF SMOKING.
ACTUALLY, I WAS ONLY READING THE NEW WARNING LABEL.
"THESE THINGS'LL KILL YA."
6-18-97
© 1997 United Feature Syndicate, Inc.
http://www.unitedmedia.com

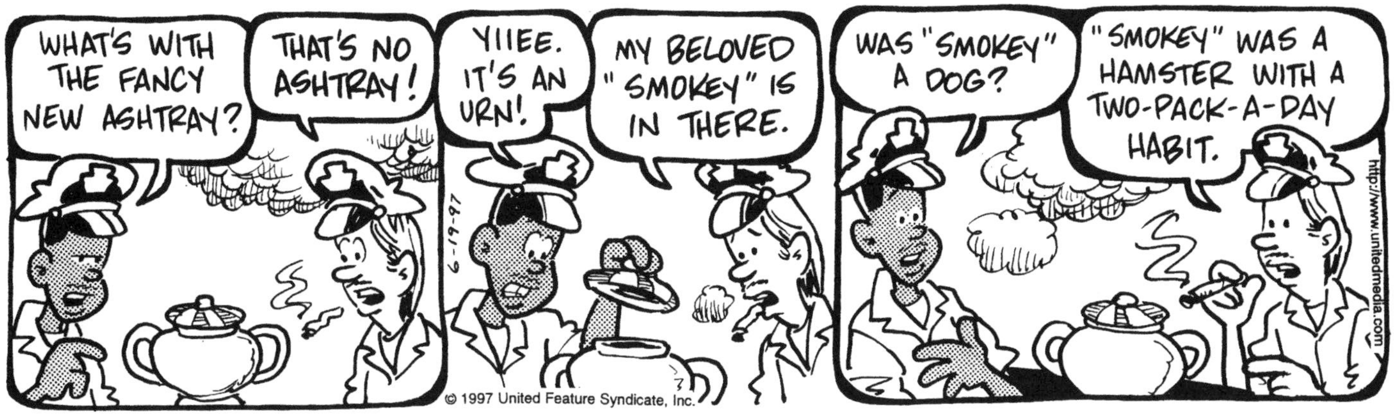
WHAT'S WITH THE FANCY NEW ASHTRAY?
THAT'S NO ASHTRAY!
YIIEE. IT'S AN URN!
MY BELOVED "SMOKEY" IS IN THERE.
WAS "SMOKEY" A DOG?
"SMOKEY" WAS A HAMSTER WITH A TWO-PACK-A-DAY HABIT.
6-19-97
© 1997 United Feature Syndicate, Inc.
http://www.unitedmedia.com

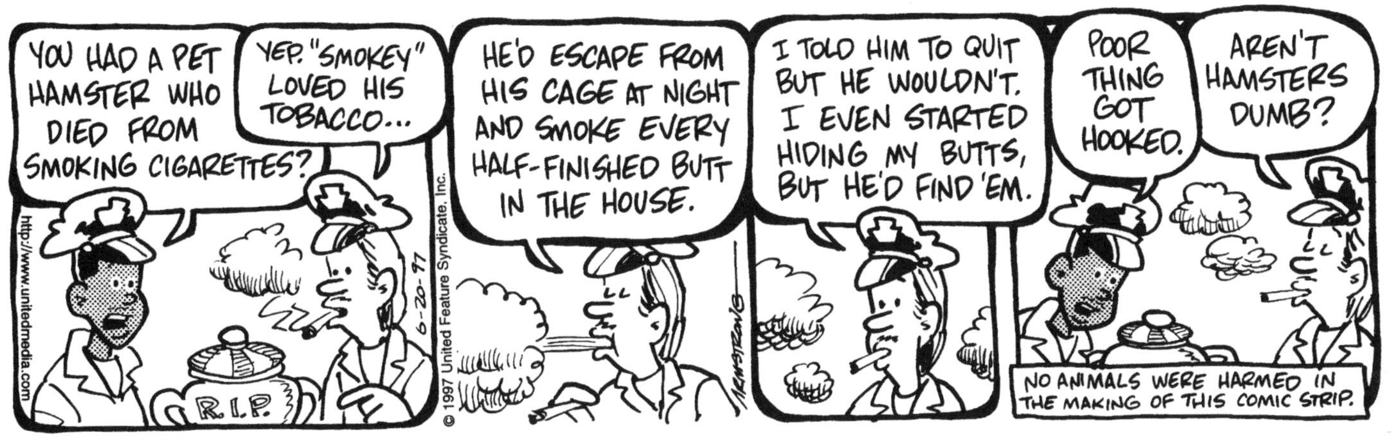
YOU HAD A PET HAMSTER WHO DIED FROM SMOKING CIGARETTES?
YEP. "SMOKEY" LOVED HIS TOBACCO...
R.I.P.
HE'D ESCAPE FROM HIS CAGE AT NIGHT AND SMOKE EVERY HALF-FINISHED BUTT IN THE HOUSE.
I TOLD HIM TO QUIT BUT HE WOULDN'T. I EVEN STARTED HIDING MY BUTTS, BUT HE'D FIND 'EM.
POOR THING GOT HOOKED.
AREN'T HAMSTERS DUMB?
NO ANIMALS WERE HARMED IN THE MAKING OF THIS COMIC STRIP.
6-20-97
© 1997 United Feature Syndicate, Inc.
http://www.unitedmedia.com

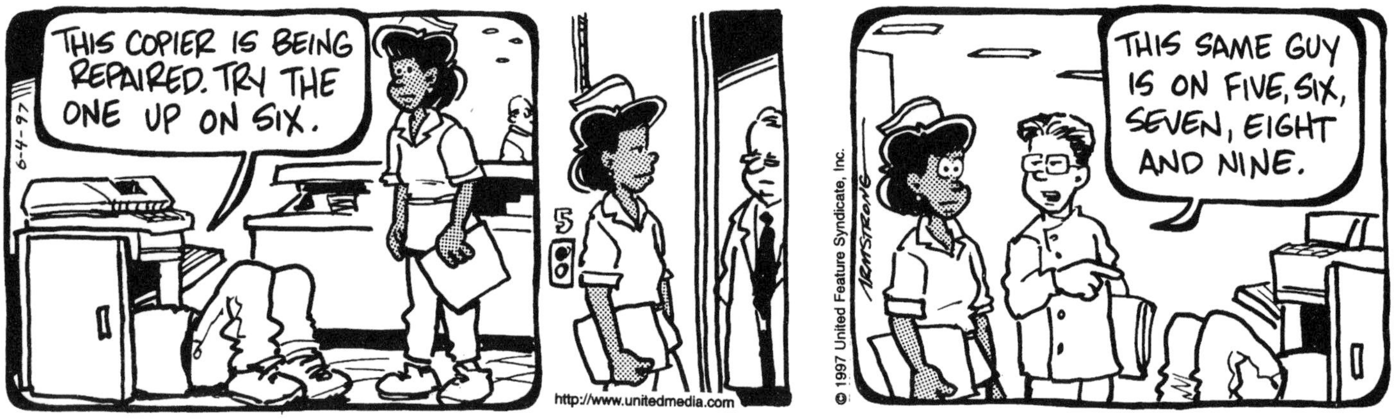

6-4-97
THIS COPIER IS BEING REPAIRED. TRY THE ONE UP ON SIX.
5
http://www.unitedmedia.com
© 1997 United Feature Syndicate, Inc.
ARMSTRONG
THIS SAME GUY IS ON FIVE, SIX, SEVEN, EIGHT AND NINE.

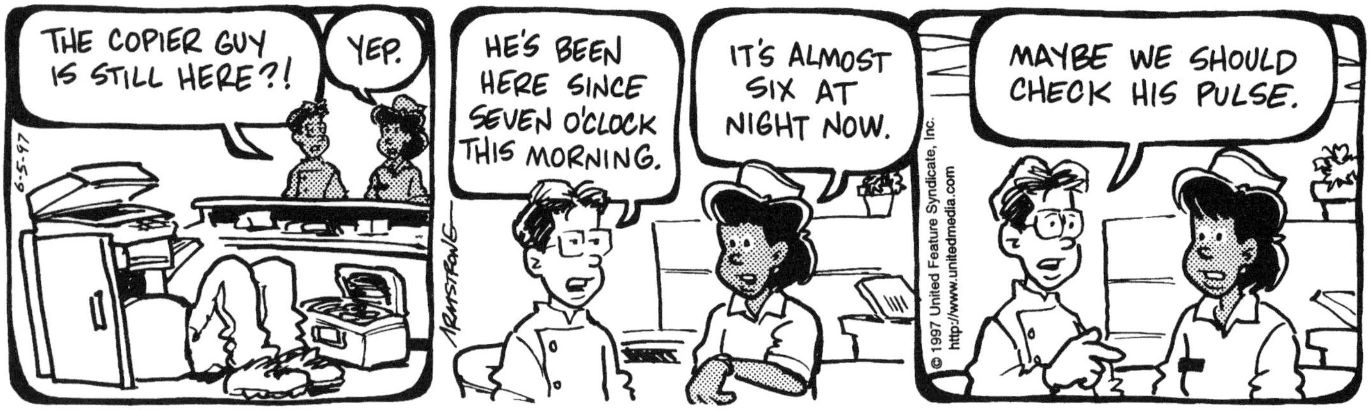

6-5-97
THE COPIER GUY IS STILL HERE?!
YEP.
ARMSTRONG
HE'S BEEN HERE SINCE SEVEN O'CLOCK THIS MORNING.
IT'S ALMOST SIX AT NIGHT NOW.
© 1997 United Feature Syndicate, Inc.
http://www.unitedmedia.com
MAYBE WE SHOULD CHECK HIS PULSE.

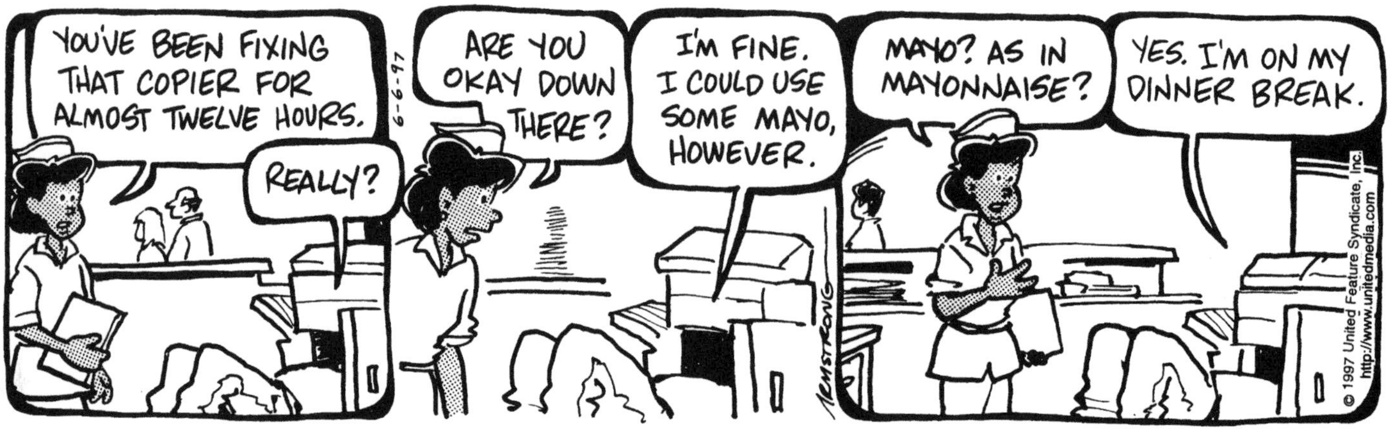

YOU'VE BEEN FIXING THAT COPIER FOR ALMOST TWELVE HOURS.
REALLY?
6-6-97
ARE YOU OKAY DOWN THERE?
I'M FINE. I COULD USE SOME MAYO, HOWEVER.
ARMSTRONG
MAYO? AS IN MAYONNAISE?
YES. I'M ON MY DINNER BREAK.
© 1997 United Feature Syndicate, Inc.
http://www.unitedmedia.com

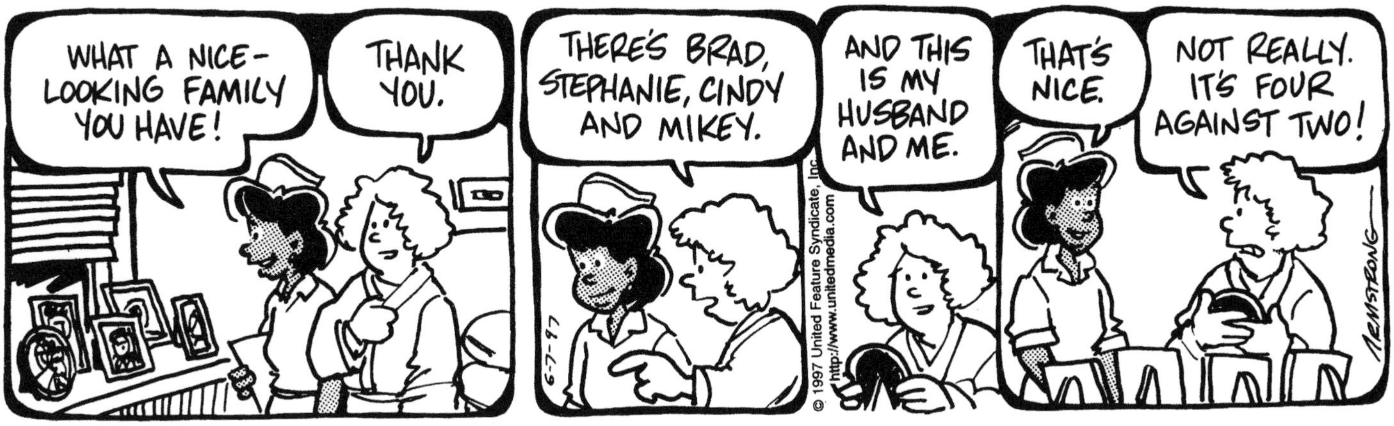
WHAT A NICE-LOOKING FAMILY YOU HAVE!
THANK YOU.
THERE'S BRAD, STEPHANIE, CINDY AND MIKEY.
6-7-97
© 1997 United Feature Syndicate, Inc.
http://www.unitedmedia.com
AND THIS IS MY HUSBAND AND ME.
THAT'S NICE.
NOT REALLY. IT'S FOUR AGAINST TWO!
ARMSTRONG

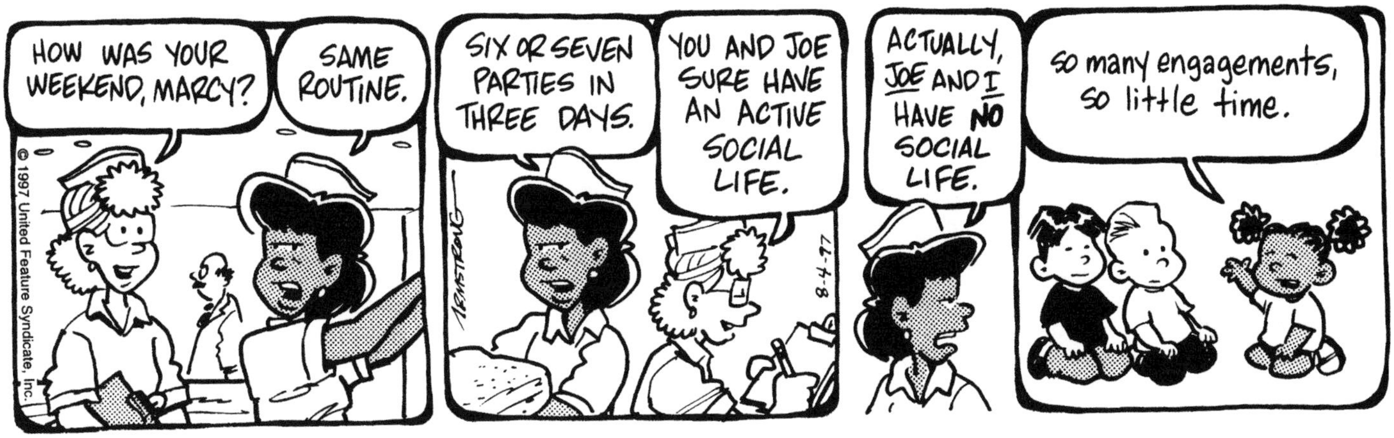
HOW WAS YOUR WEEKEND, MARCY?
SAME ROUTINE.
© 1997 United Feature Syndicate, Inc.
SIX OR SEVEN PARTIES IN THREE DAYS.
YOU AND JOE SURE HAVE AN ACTIVE SOCIAL LIFE.
ARMSTRONG
8-4-97
ACTUALLY, JOE AND I HAVE NO SOCIAL LIFE.
so many engagements, so little time.

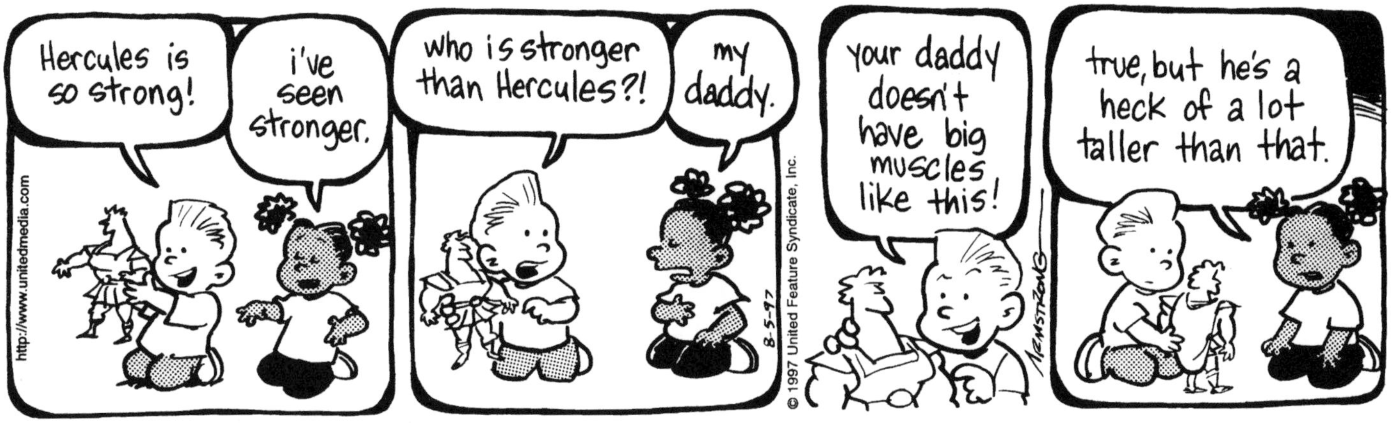
Hercules is so strong!
i've seen stronger.
http://www.unitedmedia.com
who is stronger than Hercules?!
my daddy.
8-5-97
© 1997 United Feature Syndicate, Inc.
Your daddy doesn't have big muscles like this!
ARMSTRONG
true, but he's a heck of a lot taller than that.

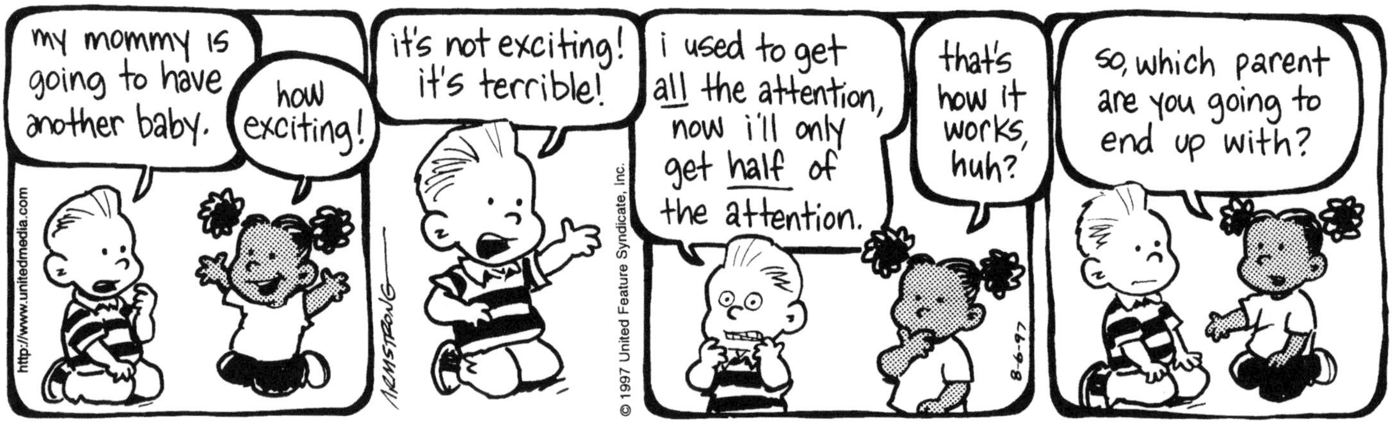

my mommy is going to have another baby.
how exciting!
it's not exciting! it's terrible!
i used to get all the attention, now i'll only get half of the attention.
that's how it works, huh?
so, which parent are you going to end up with?
http://www.unitedmedia.com
© 1997 United Feature Syndicate, Inc.
8-6-97

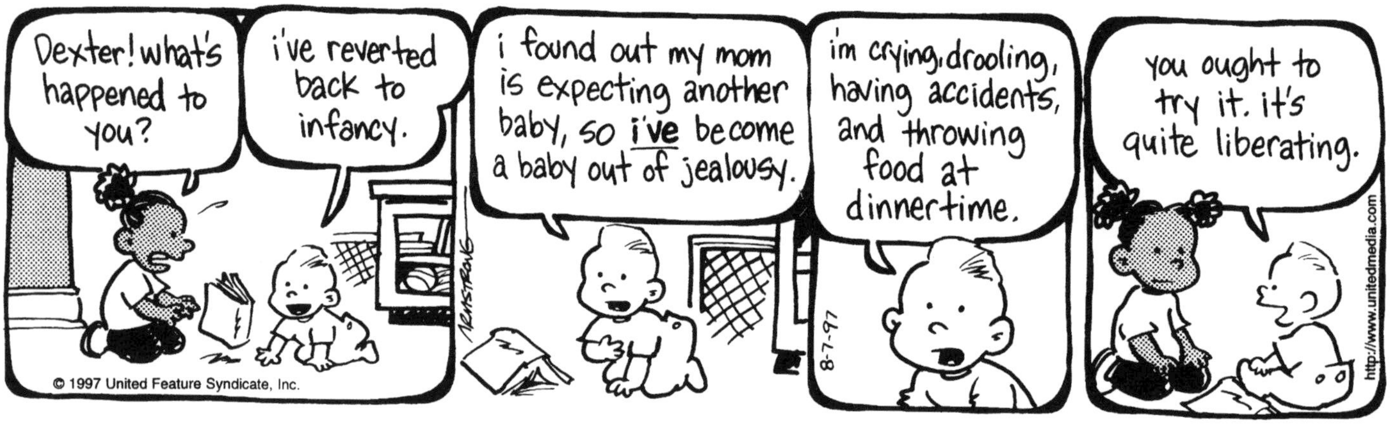

Dexter! what's happened to you?
i've reverted back to infancy.
i found out my mom is expecting another baby, so i've become a baby out of jealousy.
i'm crying, drooling, having accidents, and throwing food at dinnertime.
you ought to try it. it's quite liberating.
© 1997 United Feature Syndicate, Inc.
8-7-97
http://www.unitedmedia.com

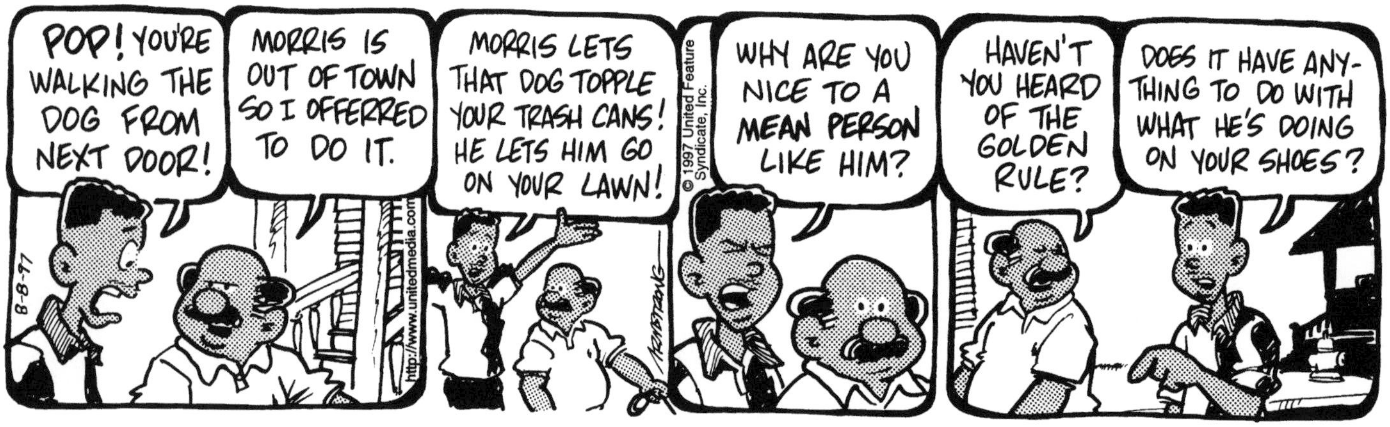

POP! YOU'RE WALKING THE DOG FROM NEXT DOOR!
MORRIS IS OUT OF TOWN SO I OFFERRED TO DO IT.
MORRIS LETS THAT DOG TOPPLE YOUR TRASH CANS! HE LETS HIM GO ON YOUR LAWN!
WHY ARE YOU NICE TO A MEAN PERSON LIKE HIM?
HAVEN'T YOU HEARD OF THE GOLDEN RULE?
DOES IT HAVE ANYTHING TO DO WITH WHAT HE'S DOING ON YOUR SHOES?
8-8-97
http://www.unitedmedia.com
© 1997 United Feature Syndicate, Inc.

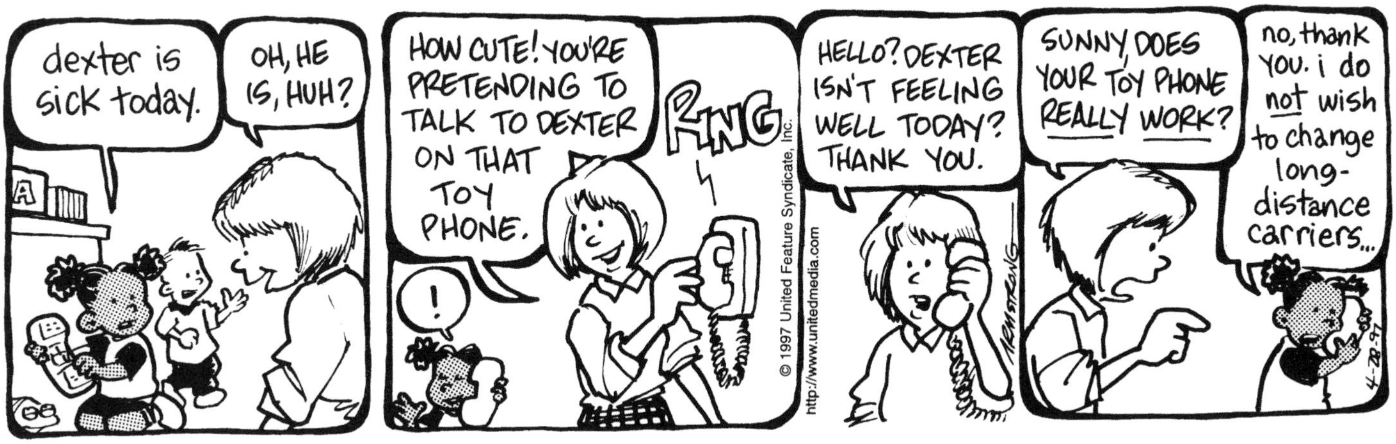
dexter is sick today.
OH, HE IS, HUH?
HOW CUTE! YOU'RE PRETENDING TO TALK TO DEXTER ON THAT TOY PHONE.
!
RING
© 1997 United Feature Syndicate, Inc.
http://www.unitedmedia.com
HELLO? DEXTER ISN'T FEELING WELL TODAY? THANK YOU.
SUNNY, DOES YOUR TOY PHONE REALLY WORK?
no, thank you. i do not wish to change long-distance carriers...
4-28-97

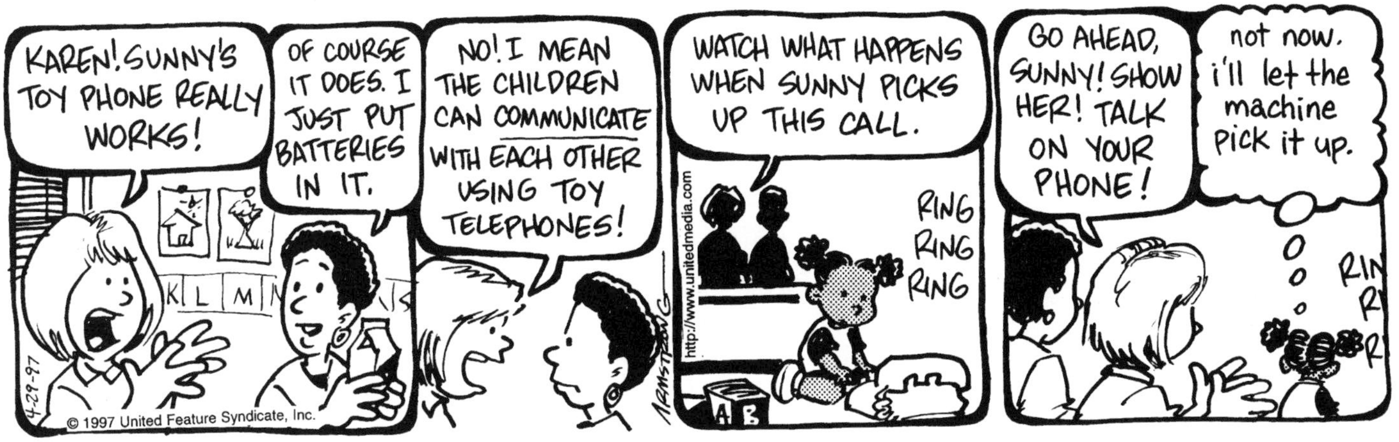
KAREN! SUNNY'S TOY PHONE REALLY WORKS!
OF COURSE IT DOES. I JUST PUT BATTERIES IN IT.
NO! I MEAN THE CHILDREN CAN COMMUNICATE WITH EACH OTHER USING TOY TELEPHONES!
4-29-97
© 1997 United Feature Syndicate, Inc.
WATCH WHAT HAPPENS WHEN SUNNY PICKS UP THIS CALL.
RING RING RING
http://www.unitedmedia.com
GO AHEAD, SUNNY! SHOW HER! TALK ON YOUR PHONE!
not now. i'll let the machine pick it up.

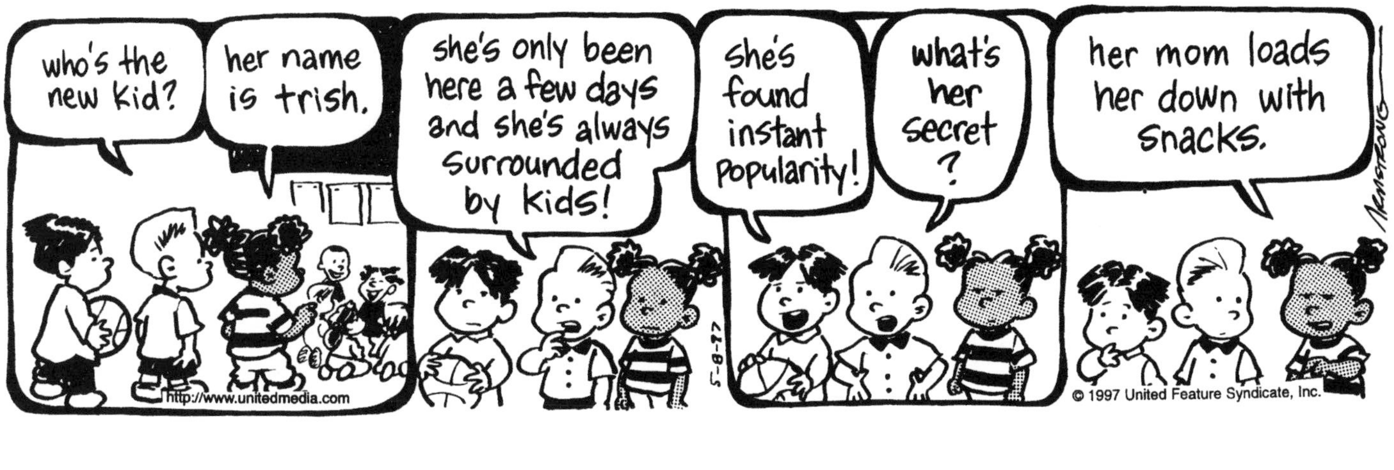
who's the new kid?
her name is trish.
http://www.unitedmedia.com
she's only been here a few days and she's always surrounded by kids!
5-8-97
she's found instant popularity!
what's her secret?
her mom loads her down with snacks.
© 1997 United Feature Syndicate, Inc.

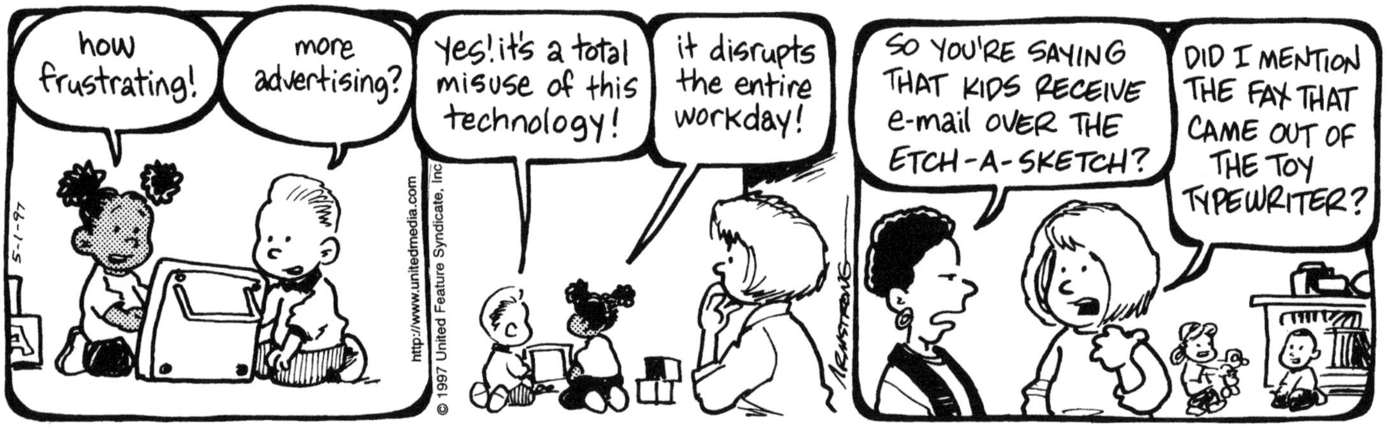
5-1-97
how frustrating!
more advertising?
http://www.unitedmedia.com
© 1997 United Feature Syndicate, Inc
Yes! it's a total misuse of this technology!
it disrupts the entire workday!
SO YOU'RE SAYING THAT KIDS RECEIVE e-mail OVER THE ETCH-A-SKETCH?
DID I MENTION THE FAX THAT CAME OUT OF THE TOY TYPEWRITER?

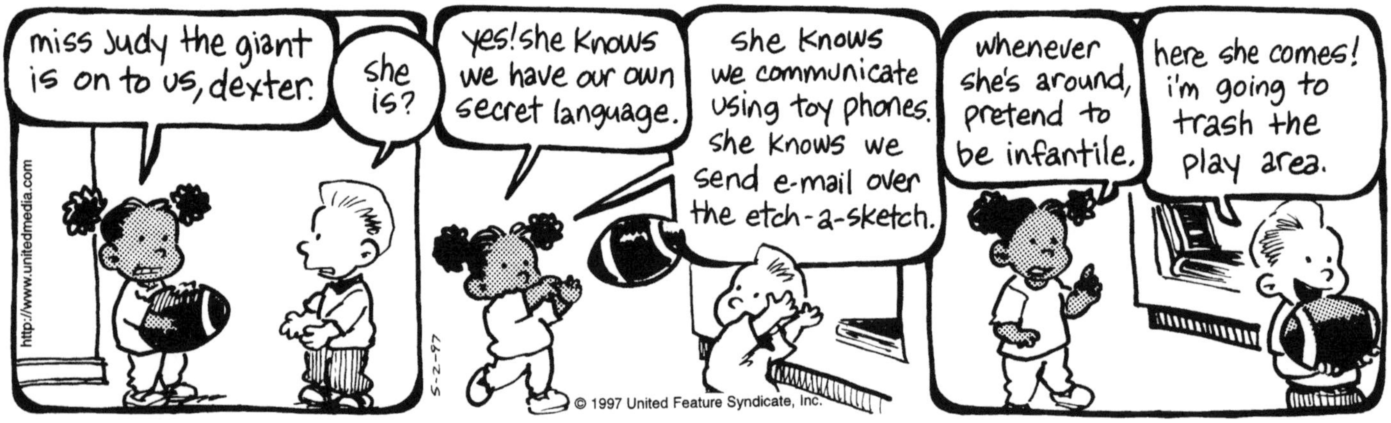
miss Judy the giant is on to us, dexter.
she is?
http://www.unitedmedia.com
5-2-97
yes! she knows we have our own secret language.
she knows we communicate using toy phones. she knows we send e-mail over the etch-a-sketch.
© 1997 United Feature Syndicate, Inc.
whenever she's around, pretend to be infantile.
here she comes! i'm going to trash the play area.

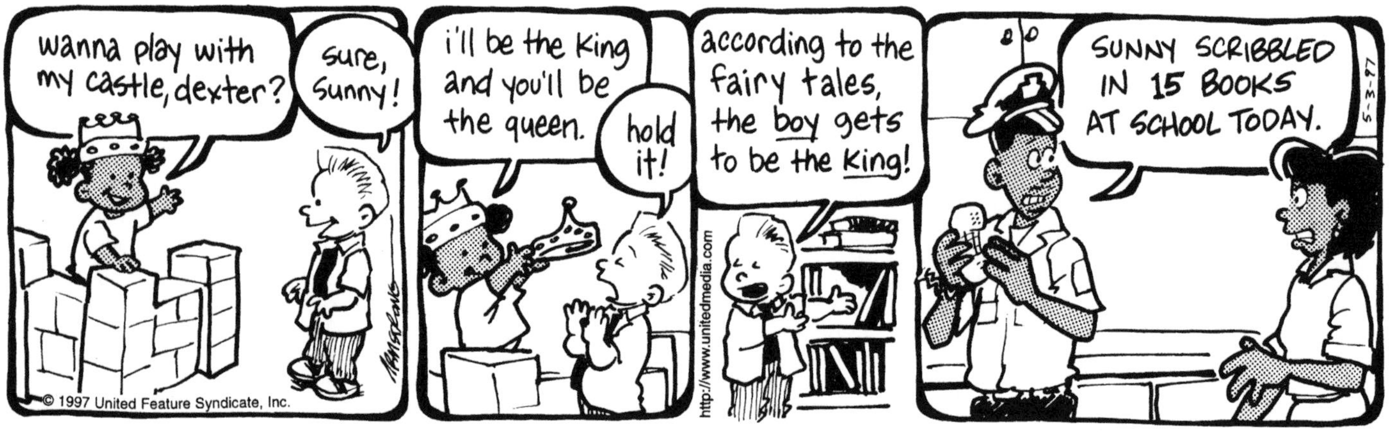
wanna play with my castle, dexter?
sure, Sunny!
© 1997 United Feature Syndicate, Inc.
i'll be the king and you'll be the queen.
hold it!
http://www.unitedmedia.com
according to the fairy tales, the boy gets to be the king!
SUNNY SCRIBBLED IN 15 BOOKS AT SCHOOL TODAY.
5-3-97

Robb Armstrong

has been called "one of the hottest cartoonists in America" by *People* magazine. His award-winning comic strip, *JumpStart*, is published every day in the *LA Times*, *The Philadelphia Inquirer*, the *New York Daily News*, *The Boston Globe*, and hundreds of other newspapers around the world. It can be read online each day at GoComics.com.

Armstrong has been featured on *Good Morning America*, MSNBC, CNN, BET, and *Good Day Philadelphia*, and he has been profiled in magazines including *Time*, *People*, *Ebony*, and *Black Enterprise*. His cartoons have also been published in *The New Yorker*.

Armstrong has spoken at the Library of Congress, the Smithsonian Institution, and Syracuse University, where he graduated in 1985 with a Bachelor of Fine Arts degree. He has also visited numerous colleges and high schools across the country, using his incredible life story to inspire others.

Peanuts creator Charles Schulz was a friend and admirer of Armstrong, and in 1994 Schulz named one of the *Peanuts* characters, Franklin Armstrong, after him. *JumpStart* characters are also on display in Orlando, Florida, as a part of the Universal Studios Islands of Adventure theme park.

In 2012, Armstrong was bestowed with an Honorary Doctorate from Holy Family University in his hometown of Philadelphia, Pennsylvania.

Following page:
Ask Doctor Appleby
36"x32"acrylic on wood
by Robb Armstrong
Photographed by Johnny Dycus

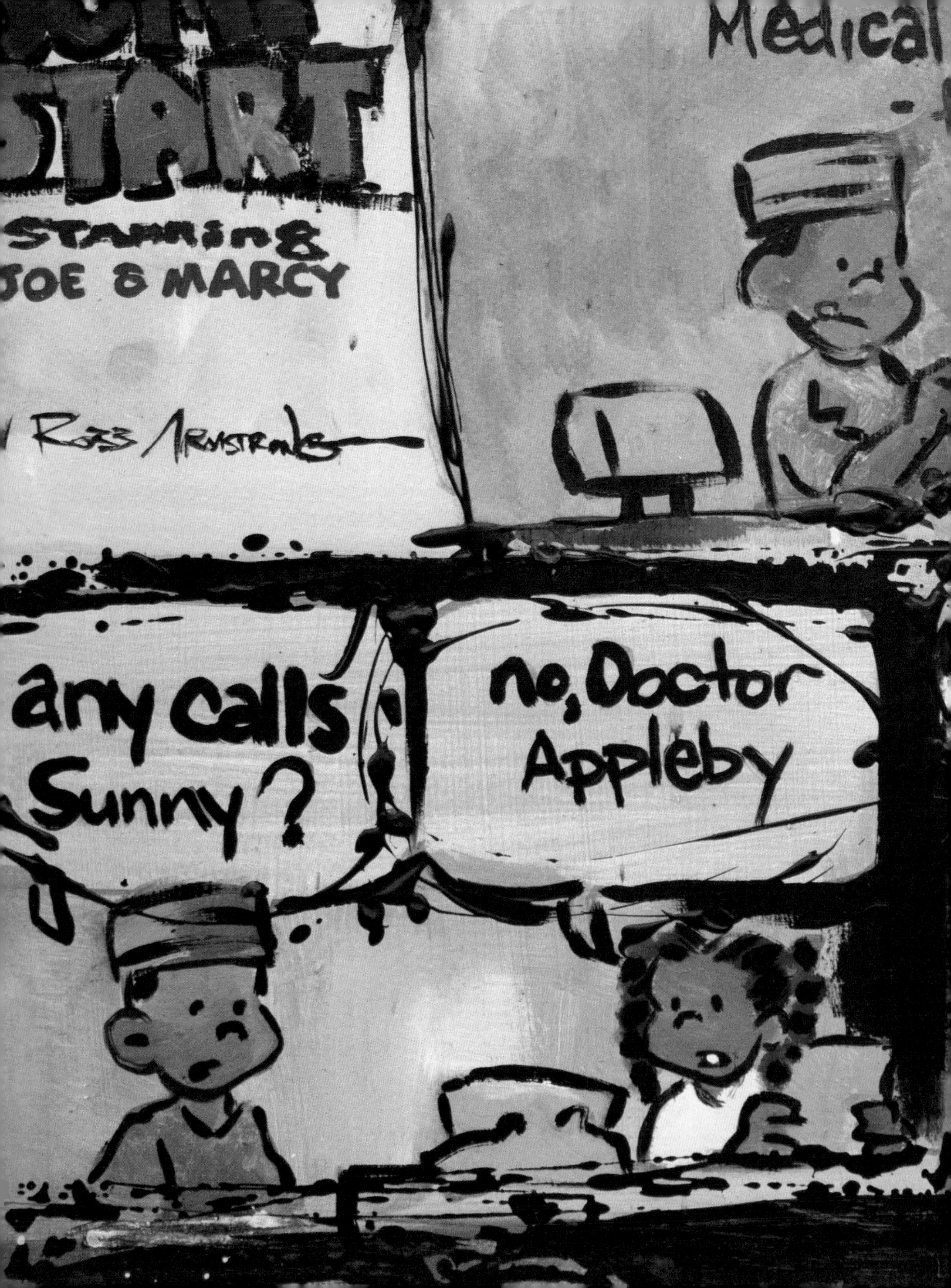
START
STARRING
JOE & MARCY
Ross Armstrong
Medical
any calls Sunny?
no, Doctor Appleby

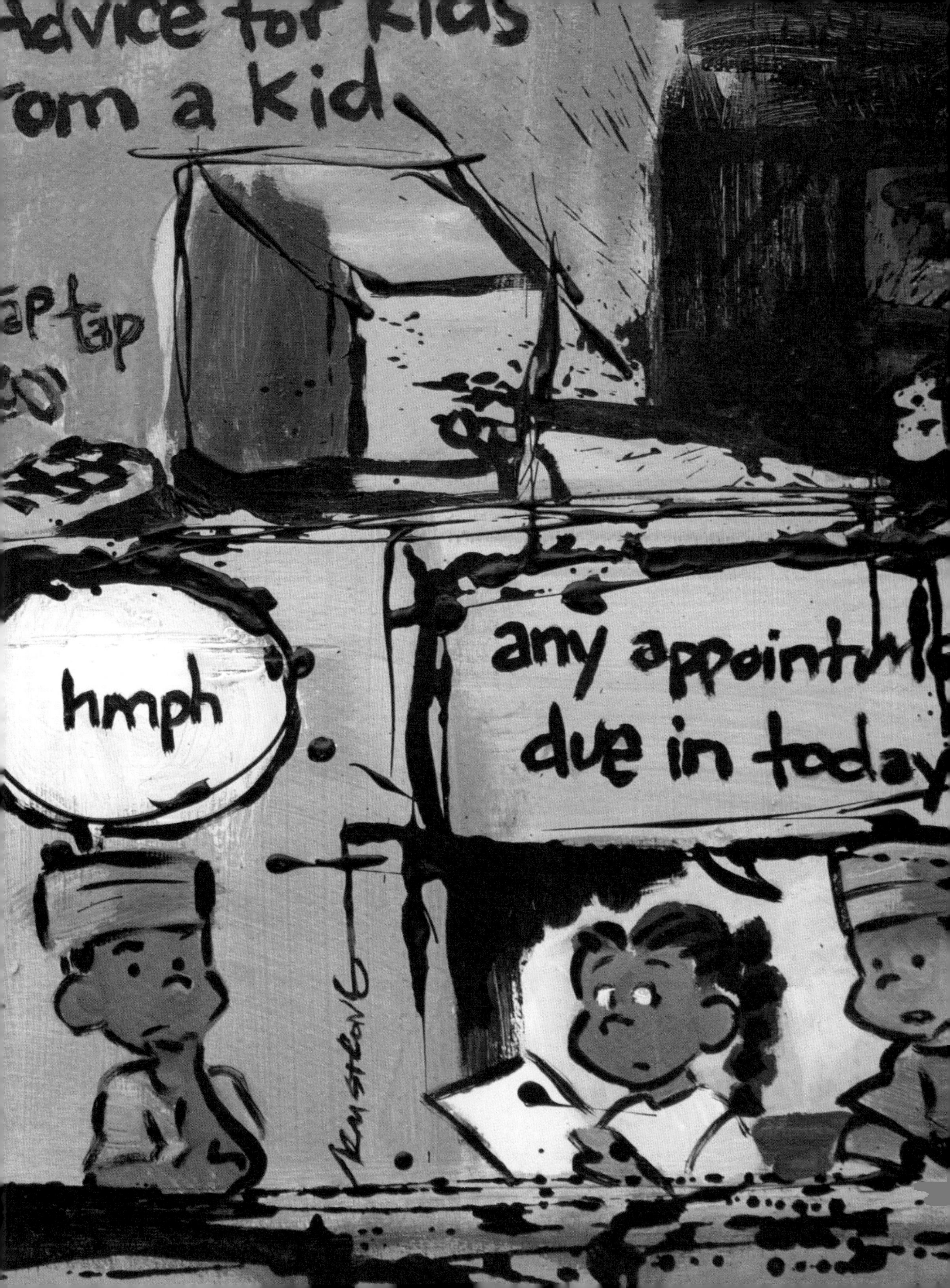

dvice for Kids
om a kid
ap tap
hmph
any appoint
due in toda